D1104218

COGNITION AND FIGURATIVE LANGUAGE

COGNITION AND
FIGURATIVE LANGUAGE

Edited by

RICHARD P. HONECK
University of Cincinnati

ROBERT R. HOFFMAN
University of Minnesota

 LAWRENCE ERLBAUM ASSOCIATES, PUBLISHERS
1980   Hillsdale, New Jersey

Lawrence Erlbaum Associates, Inc., Publishers
365 Broadway
Hillsdale, New Jersey   07642

Library of Congress Cataloging in Publication Data

Main entry under title:

Cognition and figurative language.
  Includes bibliographical references and index.
  1. Psycholinguistics.   2. Cognition.   3. Figures
of speech.   I. Honeck, Richard P.   II. Hoffman,
Robert R.
BF455.C6727   401.9   80-17225
ISBN 0-89859-047-7

Printed in the United States of America

For
Albert P. and Mary E. Honeck
and
Robert R. and Wilma J. Hoffman

Contents

PART V: PROBLEM SOLVING

Preface

This is a book about the psychology of figurative language. Of necessity, however, it is eclectic. Therefore, it should be of interest to professionals, graduate students, and advanced undergraduates in education, linguistics, philosophy, sociolinguistics, and others concerned with meaning and cognition.

The idea for this book arose in 1977 when it became clear to us that there was a pressing need to bring together the growing empirical efforts on the topic. In a sense, recognition of the theoretical importance of figurative language symbolizes the transition from the psycholinguistics of the 1960's to that of today, that is, from a linguistic semantics to a more comprehensive psychological semantics with a healthy respect for context, inference, world knowledge, and, above all, creative imagination. As befits today's mood, a number of conferences and symposia on figurative language have been held. Many of the book's contributors participated, for example, in symposia sponsored in 1977, 1978, and 1979 by the Experimental Psychology Division of the American Psychological Association. In fact, it was through various discussions at the 1977 meeting in San Francisco that our interest in this volume was finally catalyzed. The excitement and controversy generated at this symposium convinced us that experimental psychology had formally announced a lively courtship with figurative language. The Illinois conference on metaphor was convened shortly thereafter, and it rounded out the picture through its emphasis upon philosophical and linguistic inquiry. Hence, the outgrowth of this conference (Ortony, A. (Ed.) *Metaphor and Thought,* Cambridge, England: Cambridge University Press, 1979) and the present volume should complement one another.

In planning the book we had several goals. First, we wanted to provide a forum for those who have been innovators in the area in the 1970's (and some before that). Second, we wanted these authors to provide an original essay, with a summary of their past research and, more importantly, a statement of their newest empirical and theoretical efforts. Third, by virtue of the first two points, we wanted the book to be tutorial on the issues, problems, questions, procedures, theoretical directions, etc., that define the area. Looking back on the project, we are pleased to have met all these goals. And while the authors focus on a few varieties of figurative language, their underlying concern is with cognition. So issues that appear to be unique to figurative language (e.g., How is metaphor identified? What makes for a good metaphor?) turn out to have more general significance in cognition. As rhetorician I. A. Richards put it, "*Thought* is metaphoric." Mainstream semantics in the form of network theory and similar "Literalist" approaches will not be found here. Rather, these approaches are challenged, even ignored, as the authors analyze the complexities and the creativity of figurative language. The organization of the volume reflects the more basic, general concerns with cognition—from historical and philosophical background, through problems of mental representation and semantic theory, to developmental trends, and to applications in problem solving.

There are a number of people who supported this project in one way or another. In Cincinnati, Richard Honeck would like to thank his colleagues and students for having created an atmosphere conducive to intellectual fulfillment. Special thanks are due Garnett Pugh for her efficiency in handling the brunt of the secretarial activities associated with this volume. Thanks for secretarial assistance are also due Karen Wall, Olive Beard, Margo Harris, and Ann Cavan. In Minneapolis, Robert Hoffman would like to thank his sponsor, James J. Jenkins, and Winifred Strange, Kathy Casey, Gerald Siegel, Herb Pick, Jr., and all the faculty, staff, and trainees at the Center for Research in Human Learning for providing material and spiritual support, and also for providing what have been perhaps the most stimulating and exciting years of his life. Thanks are also due Elizabeth Webster and Sue Salm for helping with the typing of manuscripts and Meg Sherburne for copying manuscripts and voluminous correspondence.

Editing this volume has been hard work, though a labor of love. We hope that it stimulates others and advances our knowledge.

Richard P. Honeck
Robert R. Hoffman

I HISTORICAL AND PHILOSOPHICAL PERSPECTIVES

1

A Peacock Looks at its Legs: Cognitive Science and Figurative Language

Robert R. Hoffman
University of Minnesota

Richard P. Honeck
University of Cincinnati

INTRODUCTION

In the 1970s we have witnessed an expansion of the psychology of language to embrace new and more complex theories, new methods and new materials. There is a willingness to explore a broader range of the human potential to create, communicate, and think via the medium of language. It is fitting, therefore, that this is a book by Young Turks—Turks at least—and that their common fascination is with figurative language, since it so keenly illustrates and epitomizes the new wave of our times.

In this chapter we introduce the standard descriptions and terminology used to talk about figurative language and point out the main issues that are dealt with in the book. The chapter is organized according to some reasons why figurative language phenomena are important to theories of cognition and meaning. These reasons are discussed in an order corresponding to the major sections in the book.

.THE VARIETIES OF FIGURATIVE EXPERIENCE

Before diving into the currents and undertows of methodology and theoretics, we want to do a quick freestyle: Research on figurative language is fun. It leads one to find all sorts of intriguing phenomena. Thus, we believe we should begin with a very broad conception of the subject matter. Some figurative language forms available for study are: poetry, irony, similes, idioms, addages, intentional nonsense or anomaly, and more. There are verbal beasts like the proverbs studied by Karl Bühler and the Wurzburg group, e.g., *The most glowing colors in which the virtues shine are the inventions of those who lack them*—which seems torturous in its demand on both the concrete and the abstract levels. There are also verbal beauties like this quip by BBC commentator Ned Sherrin: *I prefer reading to sex because you can stop without losing your place.* There are "perverbs," or perverted proverbs, e.g., *Time wounds all heels.* In puns there is a phonological clang, called "paranomasia," that leads to a reconsideration of word meaning, as in *Bird cage for sale, cheep.* The homophony here involves lexical ambiguity. Groaning usually occurs as a response when the pun is "stretched." In order to forge an ambiguous meaning, some sounds are shifted to, in effect, create a new homophone: *The theoreticians disgusted the new experiment.*

Figurative Language: Forms and Structures

One of the first things one notices about figures-of-speech, as rhetoricians call them, is that there are so many of them and they all have such unusual names. Corbett (1971) lists 17 different ways of constructing figures-of-speech so as to achieve special effects. For example, *One small step for man, one giant leap for mankind,* contains "polyptoton" in that it uses two words derived from the same root, it contains "ellipsis" in that the act to which the sentence refers is only implied, it contains "asyndeton" in that the conjunction between clauses is deliberately left out, and this list goes on.

In addition to the structural-syntactical aspects, rhetoricians have also distinguished different types of figurative meaning. In "metonymy" an attribute or cause is substituted for the whole as in *The crown made an announcement.* In "synechdoche" there is an exchange of superordinates or subordinates, e.g., *The hands were at work.* Metaphor can involve "hyperbole" or overstatement as in *His eloquence could split rocks,* and it can involve "litote" or understatement as in *Frank Sinatra is not the slow-burn type.* In "oxymoron" the use of contradictory or anomalous word combinations appear, as in *sweet pain* and *thundering silence.*

The standard way of talking about the parts and structure of *metaphors* (as a distinct kind of figurative language) has evolved like slow jello into a convention. We prefer to describe it explicitly here because it is a useful scheme and because it is used throughout this volume. We start with two simple and regular, but predictably prosaic metaphors from William James (1902), the first two examples in Table 1.1.

The rhetorician I. A. Richards (1936) distinguished the thing that is being commented upon, the *topic* (he called it the *tenor*), and the thing used to talk about the topic, called the *vehicle.* The implicit relation between the topic and vehicle, the semantic basis for the metaphor, is called the *ground.* The topic and vehicle do not necessarily correspond with the subject and predicate in the sentence, as in the examples from James, but can appear as any type of word (see the third and fourth examples in Table 1.1).

TABLE 1.1
Illustrative Metaphors According to the Standard Richards-Perrine
Scheme[a]

Metaphor	Topic	Vehicle	Ground[b]
The author's writings are useful groceries.	author's writings	useful groceries	The writings contain important ideas.
The optimist has congenital anaesthesia.	optimist's attitude	congenital anaesthesia	The optimist is ignorant or unaware.
The chairman plowed through the discussion.	chairman	plowed	Committee work is hard.
He flung himself on his horse and rode madly off in all directions.	manner of riding (implicit)	madly in all directions	He was in a mental state of excited confusion.
The furious phenomenon of five o'clock.	rush hour (implicit)	furious phenomenon of five o'clock	Traffic is overwhelming and amazing.
Great weights hang on small wires.	outcomes (implicit)	minor details[c] (implicit)	Important events can depend on less important ones.

[a] The first two examples are from James (1902). Example 3 is from Black (1962), example 4 is from Leacock (1912), example 5 is from e.e. cummings (1954), and example 6 is from Smith & Heseltine (1935).

[b] These are not *the* grounds of the metaphors, but our illustrations. Topic, vehicle, and ground are abstract concepts only approximated in one person's interpretation. For example, to some, the ground of example 3 involves something like, *The chairman followed only his own opinion.*

[c] Technically, the proverb statement itself is the vehicle, while the topic is implicit in Perrine's scheme.

Another rhetorician, Lawrence Perrine (1971), refined Richards' notions. He emphasized that the explicit topic and vehicle *terms* (words and phrases) need not be the intended topic and vehicle *concepts*. The concepts or domains may also be represented implicitly, as in the fifth and sixth examples in Table 1.1. Thus, because both the topic and vehicle can be either explicit or implicit, a simple fourfold classification scheme emerges.

Aristotle and Quintillian, a Roman rhetorician of the first Century A.D., started it all going by classifying figures-of-speech. Actually, the phrase *figure-of-speech* is part of an ancient distinction between it and *figure-of-thought*. Technically, the term figure-of-thought refers to figurative meaning. The category figure-of-speech contains everything else, from paranomasia to isocolon, presumably aspects of style and sentence construction as opposed to figurative meaning. Couched in the phrase, figure-of-speech, and other distinctions in rhetoric, is the belief that nonliteral meanings are special. For instance, to the eighteenth century poet Samuel Taylor Coleridge, all figures-of-speech were a form of metaphor. In modern rhetoric some regard figurative meaning and inference as defining aspects of poetry (Perrine, 1971; Reddy, 1979). In fact, it has been the expressed goal of some rhetoricians to come to an understanding of the *cognition* of figurative language through analyses and classifications of figures (e.g., Arthos, 1965; Manns, 1977).

Historical and Philosophical Roots

The study of figurative language has intellectual roots in several disciplines as well as rhetoric. Chapter 2 by Honeck in this volume describes the trends of thought in some of these disciplines, with a focus on experimental psychology, psychodynamic psychology, linguistic theory, and philosophy. Honeck discusses certain "landmark papers" within these disciplines that appear to be relevant to the Zeitgeist in cognitive psychology in the 1970s. The personalistic aspect of history is not overlooked in Honeck's account as he ties the current preoccupation with figurative language to the backgrounds and interests of some of the researchers involved.

In Chapter 3 Johnson reviews treatments of figurative language in linguistics and philosophy and presents the major theories of metaphor in philosophy from Plato and Kant to modern times, including the logical positivists' view that metaphor possesses connotative value but not truth value. Johnson considers how metaphor is identified ("We seem to interpret an utterance metaphorically when to do so makes sense of more aspects of the total context than if the sentence is read literally") and how it works. On this latter question, Johnson extends the so-called "Interaction" view. He argues that metaphors have a "canonical" (comparative, simile) aspect but also a noncanonical (interactive) aspect. In a discussion that should be of great interest to psychologists, Johnson uses Kant's account of reflective judgment to explicate these two aspects. One consequence of this strategy is that the canonical aspect is considered to be mechanical (rule-governed) and the noncanonical aspect is considered a form of "genius," non-rule-governed and aesthetical ("a rationality without rules").

FIGURATIVE LANGUAGE AND GENERAL LANGUAGE COMPREHENSION

By the estimation of Pollio, Barlow, Fine and Pollio (1977) about four figures of speech are uttered per speaking minute on the average in free discourse. Including both novel forms and common idiomatic or frozen forms, this works out to about 21 million figures-of-speech per lifetime. Indeed, some linguists, philosophers, and psychologists have wondered whether *all* word meanings might not have metaphorical origins. As a psychological point, numerous scholars have proposed that analogic and metaphoric reasoning form the basis of all cognition (Cassirer, 1953; Edie, 1963; Jaynes, 1977; Langer, 1957; Müller, 1873; Sapir, 1977; and others). Even in traditional verbal learning tasks people spontaneously generate poetic or metaphoric mediators (Paivio, 1971, 1979). On a grander scale, idioms, metaphors and proverbs can be essential data in the anthropologist's analysis of the premises and values of an entire social group. A study can be made of the social uses of metaphor in person perception, in the expression of social mores, and in persuasion (see Bateson, 1972; Crocker, 1977).

Figurative language, we have said, is not so uncommon as it might appear at first blush. Therefore, there may not be anything psychologically special about it, in that its comprehension involves every problem in general language comprehension and semantics—e.g., encoding, implication and inference, world knowledge and contextual constraints, imagery, imagination and creativity, the problem of semantic primitives, and the problem of the relation of language and perception, and so on.

Context and World Knowledge

In what Reddy (1979) and Ortony (1979) refer to as "whole sentence metaphors," one and the same statement can be literal in one context and figurative in another: *The old rock was becoming brittle with age,* in reference to either geology or to a professor emeritus. In order to interpret such figures-of-speech, one needs knowledge and contextual information. Indeed, whether a sentence is a metaphor, a line of poetry, a literal statement, intentional nonsense, or genuine anomaly, often cannot be decided on the basis of the sentence alone.

Prior to recent experiments on context dependence (Bransford & Johnson, 1972; Jenkins, 1977) it was widely assumed that psycholinguistics in the tradition of verbal learning psychology could lead to unambiguous statements of what *the* meaning of a sentence is. Contextualism suggests a profound relativity: The reality to be captured by psycholinguistic description is not what the meaning is, but what the comprehender might experience. Indeed, linguistic constructions do not even "have" meaning: People do, and they can attribute multiple meanings to any construction. The problem then becomes one of explaining how people *constrain* the possible meanings to arrive at particular candidate interpretations. Figurative language certainly highlights this problem.

In Chapter 4, Ortony looks at the "standard definition" of metaphor, the application of language to something it does not literally denote. He finds this view and its more sophisticated linguistics version—selection restriction rule violation—inadequate for a variety of reasons. He goes on to consider the difficulties raised for this view by whole-sentence metaphors, and provides his own definition of metaphor, noting that, "it is not linguistic expressions themselves that are metaphors, but particular uses of them." Ortony's definition concentrates on the criteria of contextual anomaly, elimination of "tension" between topic and vehicle, and speaker intention, criteria he details via the work of Grice and others. Tension elimination, a part of the interpretation process, is discussed in connection with some functions performed by metaphor such as "compactness," i.e. that metaphors economically compress a great deal of information. Finally, Ortony considers the implication of his approach for psychological processing models and the distinction between metaphor and simile.

Language and Perception

As with general language comprehension, the comprehension of figurative language involves perception. This was demonstrated in a series of studies by Verbrugge and McCarrell (1977). They constructed pairs of metaphors. The metaphors in each pair had the same topic, but different vehicles—and therefore different grounds and figurative meanings. Due to the sharing of topics, however, the ground of one metaphor in a pair was true of the topic of the other metaphor. Thus, the metaphor *Billboards are warts on the landscape* could be successfully cued by the relevant ground, *Ugly protrusions on a surface*. The irrelevant ground for this metaphor was *tell you where to find businesses in the area*. Though true of the topic, the irrelevant ground did not work as a recall cue. This indicated that people were remembering the specific figurative meanings and not verbatim phrases or word meanings. The literal features appropriate for describing the word *tree* differ for *Tree trunks are straws for thirsty leaves and branches,* and *Tree trunks are pillars for a roof of leaves and branches.* In the former, a tree trunk is perceived as a hollow tube, in the latter it is perceived as a solid column. Recall, therefore, seemed due not to any fixed features of words, but to a *perceptual* act in which word meanings are restructured or a property resemblance is created.

In Chapter 5 Verbrugge refines his perception-based theory of metaphor comprehension and extends it to reconsider representation and processing notions. He reviews standard theories of metaphor comprehension from the perspective of attitudes about epistemology, such as Phenomenalism and Realism. In a new experiment reported here, Verbrugge the Realist examines and classifies people's interpretations of metaphors in order to demonstrate the operation of knowledge-based perceptual transformations. The emphasis is on how people often create fantastic or surreal images in their search for an understanding of a metaphor.

THE CANON OF COMPOSITIONALITY

The basic phenomenon is the distinction between the figurative and literal meaning of a statement, where these levels are related in nonarbitrary ways. Corresponding to it is a basic problem—how to describe, formally, the nature of this relationship. Now—most of the outstanding theories of language are built on the "canon of compositionality," that is, sentences are treated as inputs into a logical calculus, with meaning derived as a rule-based concatenation of the meanings of the component words (or morphemes). This is true for the linguistic theories of Chomsky (1965) and Fillmore (1968). Psychologists Anderson and Bower (1973) developed a theory based on binary associative relationships and pathways within a sentence. Kintsch (1974), and others following his lead, describe sentences in terms of predicate calculus and propositions. As background theories in psychology these will serve as a springboard. However, it turns out that they deal primarily, and most deal exclusively, with the literal level of meaning. This is another reason for all the recent fuss. Available theories of language structure and processing have not yet captured the relation between literal and figurative meaning. As a consequence, figurative meaning cannot be derived by these theories as a composition of the (literal) meanings of the words.

Figure 1.1 presents representations of a metaphor, *A poem is a pheasant*, according to the major theories of language. Note that in no case is figurative meaning fully explicated. The views that incorporate semantic features come close—we'll have more to say about features later.

Another good example of how figurative language violates the compositionality principle is provided by idioms. *He let the cat out of the bag* cannot be interpreted as *He started some trouble* on the basis of the literal meanings of the component words. Thus, idioms seemingly defy structural analysis. *We pulled Tom's leg* has Tom as the object of teasing in the idiom and leg as the object of pulling in the literal expression. The usual theoretical resolution of this problem is to treat idioms as complex dictionary entries akin to words (Katz & Postal, 1964; Weinreich, 1969). However, this position is challenged by Bobrow and Bell's (1973) finding that people given an "idiomatic set" (versus a "literal set") prior to seeing a potential idiom did not report "seeing the idiom first" (e.g., *John gave Mary the slip*) any more often than a control group given neither set. Moreover, Ortony, Schallert, Reynolds and Antos (1978) argue that idioms cannot involve special processing mechanisms since the nonliteral meaning cannot be derived from the words—idioms must be learned rather than figured out. This hypothesis is supported in recent studies by Swinney and Cutler (1979).

Other figurative language forms besides metaphors and idioms strain the canon of compositionality and they do so in theoretically interesting ways. Consider the proverb, *Great weights hang on small wires*; an interpretation of it, *Outcomes of important events often depend on minor details*; and an instantiation of it, *The outfielder just missed catching the fly ball when he tripped on a coke bottle. The winning run scored and they lost the game.* The proverb, interpretation, and instantiation differ in words and structures, yet they are clearly related in conceptual ways that outstrip the compositionality principle. In Chapter 6 in this volume, Honeck, Voegtle, Dorfmueller, and Hoffman argue that, in general, proverbs constrain but do not determine (i.e., compositionality does not apply) their abstract figurative meanings. Partly for this reason, proverbs constitute ideal materials for the elucidation of the abstractness of mental entities and the problem of generativity or creativity. Honeck et al. review the literature and

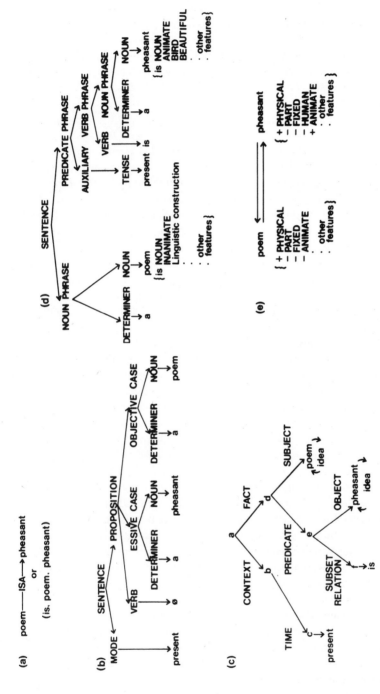

FIG. 1.1 Representations of *A poem is a pheasant* according to major theories of sentence structure. In (a) is the representation according to theories that describe meaning in terms of propositions or labeled relations (after Kintsch, 1974; Rumelhart, Lindsay & Norman, 1972; Miller & Johnson-Laird, 1976). In (b) is the representation according to Fillmore's (1968) Case grammar. The symbol, φ, indicates that this sentence, technically, has no verb. In (c) is the representation according to Anderson and Bower's (1973) associationistic theory. In (d) is something like what would be the Chomskyan deep structure, accompanied by a listing of the semantic features of the content words according to the dictionary semantics view of Katz and Fodor (1963). Finally, (e) presents the metaphor according to the conceptual dependency view of Schank (1972; Russell, 1976). The arrows in (e) indicate that the concept here is a relation proposing a state of the topic (i.e., that being a poem is a property of pheasants).

research on proverbs and compare proverbs to metaphors. This forms a foundation for their critique of what they call the "Literalist" approach to meaning, and for an elaboration of their "Conceptual Base" theory of semantics. Briefly, they assert that complete understanding of a proverb involves the creation of a microtheory that is nonlinguistic, non-imagistic, abstract, and generative, thereby allowing for the recognition and production of new instances.

ABSTRACT CONCEPTS AND MENTAL IMAGES

One source of constraints for the interpretation of figurative language often arises from imagery. A metaphor can be abstract (e.g., *A theory is a wish*) but many metaphors act as an "invitation to perceive a resemblance" (Verbrugge, 1977). The psychologists of the Wurzburg school engaged in heated debates over whether metaphors are understood in terms of images or in terms of *Gesamtvorstellung* (conceptual understanding) (see Downey, 1919). Later, the Gestalt psychologists emphasized the perceptual role of metaphors in problem-solving and creative thinking (Köhler, 1929; Werner & Kaplan, 1963). Metaphors result in the creation of a percept or image that need not be filled in with details yet has rich potential for details and symbolism. Metaphors also result in vivid images because of their emotional content and because of the bizarre or surreal character of the meaning they often suggest when taken literally. Thus, Paivio (1971, 1979) has argued that images themselves may be the medium for discovery of the figurative meaning—part and parcel of the comprehension process. These speculations, which are mirrored in discussions by linguists, poets, rhetoricians, and philosophers (e.g., Brown, 1966; Burklund, 1964; Isenberg, 1963; Shibles, 1971; Snell, 1960; Sticht, 1979) fit nicely with psychological studies of learning that show how mental imagery seems to facilitate acquistion and retention of verbal material.

The intersection of the study of imagery, verbal memory, and figurative language is mapped out in Chapter 7 by Harris, Lahey and Marsalek. Earlier experiments by Harris had shown that memory for metaphors is not necessarily less than memory for literal sentences with similar meaning. Yet, imagery is involved—people often report the experience of vivid, surreal images in reaction to metaphors. Such images sometimes fuse the topic and vehicle terms in creative ways. In some new studies presented here, Harris et al. coordinate memory data with people's verbal reports of imagery and their imagery ratings. Imagery may be reported more frequently to metaphors than literal expressions, even though metaphors are judged more difficult to imagine. Harris et al show that the results of metalinguistic tasks must be interpreted with great caution.

The use of figurative language to examine memory has been extended in a clever paradigm by Riechmann (1977). In this method, people are asked to recognize the *interpretations* of the acquisition sentences. The key is to use proverbs that, by the Richards-Perrine scheme, have implicit topics. For example, *He who spits above himself will have it all in his face,* does not refer only to spit and faces; it uses these terms to refer to underlying concepts. Thus, a literal image of the proverb differs from what most people would regard as a good interpretation, something like *Reaction against powerful people can backfire on you.* In Riechmann's original study, people who were told to concentrate on the figurative meaning of the proverbs during acquisition were better at recognizing abstractly stated interpretations of the proverbs than people told to concentrate on a mental image of what the proverbs literally described. Moreover, interpretations for high-imagery, high-comprehensibility proverbs were most difficult to recognize for both groups. In Chapter 8 Riechmann and Coste report some methodological refinements of this paradigm. They also compare some of their results with those of Harris et al. In general, Riechmann and Coste argue that there may be a trade-off between abstract understanding and imaging, and that their results define boundary conditions on the role of imagery as described by the dual-coding view.

SEMANTICS AND FEATURES

Psychologists sometimes distinguish memory for personal knowledge from memory for the meanings of the concepts and words that are used to express knowledge. This latter form, called *semantic memory,* is the aspect of cognition that is often of central concern in treatments of figurative language. There is an emphasis in linguistic theories of language (e.g., Katz, 1972) on explaining all meaning in terms of a finite set of separate, irreducible semantic units, features, or atoms, out of which all complex meanings are built. This also holds for psychological network-node theories (Anderson & Bower, 1973; Rumelhart, Lindsay & Norman, 1972). There have been extensive debates about such an approach. Some of the arguments are these:

Semantic features or primitives for words or propositions are themselves defined with words or propositions. This leads to infinite regress (Hall, 1972). As Searle (1972) put it,

> either the analysis of meaning itself contains crucial elements of the notion to be analyzed, in which case the theory fails because of circularity; or the analysis reduces the thing to be analyzed into simpler elements which lack its crucial features, in which case the theory fails because of inadequacy (p. 21).

Another argument against features is that they provide only apparent exactitude. Although semantic features are reasonably explicit and therefore amenable to test, any given listing of features can be shown to be inadequate, if only because word meanings vary from individual to individual, context to context, and time to time (Bolinger, 1965; Olson, 1970; Pollio, et al., 1977; Verbrugge & McCarrell, 1977). It is not clear, in other words, how semantic feature theories can cope with figurative "compactness" (Ortony, this volume). For figurative forms such as metaphors and proverbs, a variety of meanings can be perceived that any one feature description may fail to encompass.

A third argument against features is that it is often not clear how specific features can be justified (if at all) except in an *ad hoc* manner, nor is it clear how the features should be ordered or interrelated. It is often assumed that a linguistic description should be a model for the mental dictionary in which words are "looked up" and meanings "searched out." For example, the word "bachelor" would have as features the distinction between HUMAN and ANIMAL. Under ANIMAL would be the single sense of MALE, WITHOUT MATE. Under HUMAN would be the *two* senses of NOT MARRIED, and, HAVING LOWEST ACADEMIC DEGREE. The problem is that any given system for ordering the features can be shown to be inadequate. Again, figurative language enters as the acid test. *She welded her eyes on the bachelor,* and, *She walked right through the bachelor,* would attribute to *bachelor* features like METALLIC and NONMATERIAL. If these figurative comparisons were to be incorporated into the heirarchy, a new level of generalization would be required to define *bachelor* as both ORGANIC and METALLIC, both MATERIAL and NONMATERIAL. The thrust of this is that any fixed, static, unalterable semantic feature system may be unable to deal with metaphor, to distinguish figurative senses of words, and to show how a word can have multiple meanings in a single figure-of-speech (Bolinger, 1965; Campbell, 1975).

Those who favor the semantic feature approach reply that a set of rules can be devised to encompass figurative language. The rules would allow the semantic features to be changed, marked, altered in salience, ignored, transferred from one word to another, or in some way made flexible, fuzzy, abstract, or a matter of degree (Bickerton, 1969; Cohen, 1979; Henle, 1958; Levin, 1979; Searle, 1972; Sternberg, Tourangeau & Nigro, 1979).

Of the psychologists interested in cognition in the present century, perhaps none has paid so much attention to metaphoric meaning, in staunch defiance of the Zeitgeist, as Charles Osgood. From his earliest work on synesthesia, to the discoveries using the Semantic Differential—and the metaphorlike comparisons the instrument involves, Osgood has sought an understanding of cognition in terms of a set of basic dimensions of meaning. In Chapter 9, Osgood summarizes his work as it bears on figurative language and the mechanisms involved in metaphoric perceiving. He begins with a personal account of his past work on synesthesia. He then discusses the relationship between language and perception and postulates a "deep cognitive system" as a mediational necessity. His section on "Congruence Dynamics" presents a summary of work using the Semantic Differential and calls upon his newer "Abstract Performance Grammer" to address metaphor. Osgood presents a system for assigning algebraic signs (+,

−, and 0 or neutral) to features which interact across semantic dimensions to yield figurative meanings somewhere along the "appositeness-acceptableness-anomalousness dimension." The results of some of the "new wave" of metaphor experiments are also discussed by Osgood in terms of this approach.

Explicit semantic feature-based theories of the comprehension of metaphor were proposed independently by Johnson (1975), Ortony (1975), and Smith, Rips and Shoben (1974). Though the models differ in some subtle ways, they can be seen as special cases of Tversky's (1977) mathematicization of the axioms of the feature view. In the general theory, the perceived similarity of any two comparison stimuli—geometric shapes, pictures of faces, and, presumably, semantic-linguistic stimuli as well—is described in terms of the features that are common to the stimuli relative to the features that they do not share. An important aspect of Tversky's theory is that the order of the two stimuli in a comparison can make a difference in their perceived similarity. As one example, Tversky used the metaphorical comparison *A man is like a tree*, which has decidedly different implications than, *A tree is like a man*. In both cases, the topic makes certain features of the vehicle more salient. In the mathematics of the theory, these features are raised in weighting, leading to asymmetries in the similarity judgments.

In Chapter 10 Malgady and Johnson present a sophisticated feature-based approach. Their earlier work had revealed that the judged similarity of topic and vehicle terms is directly related to the judged ease of interpretation and judged goodness of metaphors. Moreover, judged similarity could in turn be predicted by an independent index of the number of properties shared by the topic and vehicle. Also, in metaphors as opposed to anomalies topic and vehicle were more likely to share *some* (not all, or no) properties and be rated logically false. Malgady and Johnson then showed that manipulations that increase topic-vehicle feature overlap also increase ratings of their similarity and of metaphor goodness. The next step was to refine the theoretical basis of feature theory by using Tversky's linear contrast model in conjunction with Information Theory. This scheme is used to predict asymmetry of tenor-vehicle similarity judgments, recall of metaphor, and the effects of contextual variety on comprehension and appreciation of similes. Malgady and Johnson suggest that semantic "space" models of meaning, related to modern associationism, are misguided and that scaling models of another kind are needed.

In Chapter 11, Johnson and Malgady describe a feature-system based on contextualist principles. Contextualism insists on the theoretical relevance of situational factors and on the distinction between speaker and hearer perspectives. From the contextualist view, Johnson and Malgady integrate perception concepts, such as Gibson's notion of "affordance," with notions in feature theory and Information Theory. Johnson and Malgady present a study that explores the properties people give in response to nouns, their ratings of figurativeness, and ratings of feature salience. Rated figurativeness was clearly related to potential richness of interpretation, that is, the presence of a large number of salient features made for potential. In another study, Johnson and Malgady explore people's interpretations of the abstract paintings of surrealist Rene Magritte. Here too, preference on the basis of aesthetic judgments seems related to the potential richness of interpretation. In looking over the fledgling field of the experimental analysis of figurative language, Johnson and Malgady discern an underlying attitude: Our theoretical-structuralistic descriptions (of features, encodings, or whatever) are usually abstracted from group data and, in effect, reified—that is, they are assumed to represent any one person's mental contents. A contextualist approach does not encourage such head-strong mechanistic analyses. Rather, it encourages the use of concepts in perception to describe the potential range and distribution of the properties or features people might ascribe to figurative meanings.

A vexing problem in the study of simile and metaphor, as the chapters in Section III in this volume show, is the problem of asymmetry. These forms show so clearly how apparently simple alterations in word order or meaning can make great differences in sentence meaning. The fact that asymmetry should be vexing to modern theorists can be regarded as a consequence of failure to grapple with figurative meaning at the level of syntactical theorizing. The representations in Figure 1.1 do not indicate any dramatic semantic changes that may occur if the noun phrases and verb phrases were switched in order.

Chapter 12 by Connor and Kogan deals with the asymmetry problem. Past research on their "Metaphor Triads Task" is summarized, as is the available evidence for asymmetry in semantic similarity judgments, such as Rosch's work on natural categories. In the new experiment Connor and Kogan present, people generated metaphors on the basis of sentence frames and candidate topics and vehicles (e.g., *balerina, top*). A main issue here concerns the sorts of comparisons that evoke asymmetry and the sorts that do not. As Connor and Kogan show, task constraints play a role, as do stimulus materials, whether pictorial or verbal. Aspects of reference also play a role. For instance, in comparisons involving humans, the human is usually the topic term. Connor and Kogan point out other challenges for feature theories, notably the need to incorporate features having variable salience.

DEVELOPMENTAL TRENDS

Much of the recent research on the development of figurative language understanding, which constitutes the bulk of the literature, has been reviewed elsewhere (Billow, 1977; Gardner, Winner, Bechhofer & Wolf, 1979; Pollio, et al., 1977) and we will not attempt a review here. We do want to make some general points to introduce the papers on development in this volume.

Educators have expressed mixed feelings about the use of metaphors as tutorial devices. Some assume that children take metaphors literally, thus deceiving themselves (cf., R. Miller, 1976). Since metaphor is considered a complex form of reasoning, any metaphors a child happens to create (as, *Look at those butterflies playing together,* in response to seeing snow) are presumed to reflect an impoverished vocabulary rather than a creative act (Brooke-Rose, 1965; Leondar, 1975). In "linguistic hygienics" (Rapoport, 1953), metaphors should be made explicit and their limitations pointed out. In other words, "teacher beware!" (Watts, 1944). On the other hand, some argue that metaphor and analogy are, for the child as well as the adult, a necessary aspect of conceptualizing, learning, and understanding the world (Edie, 1963; Emig, 1972; Newton, 1964; Petrie, 1979). Yet, metaphor receives little, if any, attention in language arts classes, and is relegated to the section on poetry in most language texts. The teaching of the understanding of metaphor is given little treatment in teacher education texts—however, many metaphors are *used* in school texts (see Pollio, et al., 1977). It is a euphemism to say that there is a deficiency in the way our educational system treats the understanding of metaphor. Yet, educators have claimed that reading and writing difficulties very often involve poetic or metaphorical language (Burklund, 1964; Foerster, 1974; Yandell & Zintz, 1961).

Children, it may be noted, deliberately use metaphor in their speech. Chukovsky (1968) gives the example of a child who described a bald man as having a *barefoot head.* Books by Bettelheim (1976) and Koch (1970) indicate that there is much spontaneous poetry and metaphor in children's language. One argument, probably correct, is that the "gems from babes" are delusions of the observer—because the gems are, in reality, the productions of the child's undisciplined mind. Another argument, also probably correct, is that they represent a freedom to exploit the ways in which language can express meanings. This is important, for to the extent that children understand metaphors, and to the extent that metaphor is a form of abstract reasoning, then to this extent there may be required a reworking of theories of cognitive development, such as Piaget's.

Piaget (1926) provided some now-classic examples of the interpretations of proverbs, given by children ages 9 to 11. He required the children to align interpretations with proverbs and to give their rationales for the matchings. One child matched the proverb *White dust never comes out of a coal sack* with an interpretation about wasting time—the rationale being that people who waste their time do not properly care for their children—clearly a failure to comprehend. Piaget's demonstrations of such syncretism were consistent with the notion that only older children can fully understand metaphor. Analogic "as if" sorts of reasoning are an aspect of the concrete operations and formal operations stages of intellectual development, expected only of older children and adolescents.

One may speculate whether Piaget's choice of novel, often abstract proverbs as materials and of a potentially confusing matching task, led him to this conclusion. Gentner (1977) has clearly shown that a highly simplified task involving analogies between domains that are familiar to kids (e.g., *If a mountain had a knee, where would it be?*) results in no difference between preschoolers, first graders, and adults—the kids, in short, do well at this task. So young children may be capable of some use of analogy in metaphor understanding.

As Gardner (1974) and Kogan (1975) have asserted, one must avoid confounding the child's ability to *comprehend* a metaphor with the ability to *explain* (verbally) what it is that is comprehended. Perhaps children can understand more than they can tell. The use of nonverbal tasks, for example, might "push back" the ages at which concepts or operations are attained and metaphoric reasoning is possible. Cometa and Eson (1978) tried recently to test this notion. Children of various ages were first tested on Piagetian tasks and also asked to interpret (paraphrase) metaphors such as *My thoughts are all twisted when I wake up*. The ability to paraphrase a metaphor emerged in the stage of concrete operations, but only those children who were accomplished at intersectional (cross-category) thinking could explain their paraphrases.

Stronger tests of the comprehension-explanation relationship involve getting out of the verbal domain and using picture-matching sorts of tasks. Kogan (1975) had children match pairs of pictures and then give a rationale for their matching. The pairs could represent literal comparisons (e.g., a bird and a plane can both fly) and figurative ones (e.g., an old man and a low flame are both dying). By this means, Kogan found some evidence that even 7-year-olds can understand some metaphoric comparisons. Similarly, Honeck, Sowry, and Voegtle (1978) report that 7-year-olds could understand proverbs whose meaning was displayed pictorially.

Chapter 13 by Pollio and Pickens focuses on clarification of the comprehension-explanation relationship. They begin with a summary of the area, a description of views about the epistemological status of children's metaphors, and a description of available theories of the development of metaphor comprehension. The new study they present is an extensive analysis of the performance of a large group of children, ages 8 to 17 years, on metaphor comprehension and explanation tasks. Children had to select from among candidate interpretations of metaphors (e.g., *I ate up a storm*) and, in the explanation task, they had to rationalize their interpretations of metaphors. Pollio and Pickens' analysis clearly shows the trends of figurative language understanding that occur over the years—in terms of use and in terms of preference for novel as opposed to frozen figures. Their results also implicate schooling as an inhibitor of metaphor production and so effecting an "age of literalness."

Another way to study children's figurative language is to try and coordinate the content of their productions with their perceptions of events in the world. What sort of events stimulate kids to produce metaphors, for example? This is the question addressed by Winner, McCarthy and Gardner in Chapter 14. They explore the nature of the actions or percepts that elicit metaphoric or pretend namings and word uses. First, they examine some of the metaphors spontaneously made by Adam (the child studied extensively by Brown), showing the theoretical issues that arise here in the establishment of criteria by which to judge the protocols. In contrast to the view that metaphor is mistake, children's productions do not seem to be misclassifications, but deliberate referencings (e.g., *The letter J is a cane*). In a second new study they use a game with puppets to encourage children to produce pretend names; e.g., for a small green block that the puppet made "hop." Even the preschoolers showed considerable use and understanding of metaphorical comparisons on this task. The authors liken the use of figurative language to symbolic play with perception. They describe developmental stages that begin with nonmetaphorical perception of similarity and differentiate into skills specific to metaphor and figurative language. Their study also demonstrates the possibly adverse effect that schooling may have on metaphor production, suggesting further that it is due to motivational (production) factors rather than to competence (comprehension) factors.

In conclusion, it is not yet clear how figurative understanding relates to the development of overall cognitive and linguistic skills. Nor is it clear how various tasks, such as comprehension, paraphrase, interpretation, explanation, and picture-matching, relate to one another. That the situation is so complex—as in the appearance of a stage of "literalism"—was not appreciated until the recent research was carried out. It *is* clear that kids possess remarkable capacities for figurative thought. When presented with tasks that enable them to express their full limits of cognition, those limits appear to be very wide.

FIGURATIVE LANGUAGE AND PROBLEM SOLVING

Perhaps the most extreme variety of potentially figurative language is the poetic anomaly. Example anomalous strings are: *Crackle babies furiously cellophane foreign,* and, *A legal glittering the exposed picnic knight* (from Marks & Miller, 1964). To some in philosophy, linguistics, and psychology (at least those before the 1970s), figurative language samples are merely "deviant strings" or even "meaningless' (Berggren, 1963; Carnap, 1937; Fowler, 1969; Quine, 1967). Such strings violate the rules of a theory of language, of the sort envisioned by Chomsky, for instance (1965, Chapter 5). Such a theory rests on rule-based definitions of supposed linguistic regularities representing the ideal speaker's competence for using acceptable language. It perhaps comes as little surprise that early experiments in psycholinguistics regarded anomalies as controls for the effects of syntax and semantics on information processing tasks. Most of the recall studies showed that less grammatical sentences are less well remembered (Downey & Hakes, 1968).

On the basis of the linguistic view one might also predict that people can reliably judge the grammaticality of sentences, though perhaps they are not armed with exactly the linguists' jargon. Indeed, sometimes judgments do reflect departure from grammaticality (Coleman, 1965; Danks & Glucksberg, 1973; Fillenbaum, 1970; Maclay & Sleator, 1960). This constituted early evidence for the psychological reality of the sort of grammar envisioned by Chomsky. But as some philosophers and linguists claimed (Butters, 1969; Drange, 1966), anomalies can be regarded as poetic or meaningful. The anomalous sentences Miller and Isard (1963) used were mechanically generated in a way typical to experiments that used them: The words were shuffled between sentences of similar or different structure. Yet, some meaning was creeping in: "some ingenuity is required to insure that when the words are recombined the result will be more or less anomalous" (Miller & Isard, 1963, p. 220).

Recent experiments have made the point about the meaningfulness of anomalies more forcefully. Pollio and Burns (1977) had people learn lists of anomalies taken from the classic Miller and Isard (1963) experiment, but with a twist. People who had to interpret the anomalies during acquisition remembered them about as well as were grammatical sentences by another group. We recently carried out some studies (Hoffman & Honeck, 1979; Honeck & Hoffman, 1979) that capitalized on e. e. cummings's flagrant violation of linguistic rules. Lines violating various possible combinations of linguistic rules were selected, such as, *Quarreling in a luxury of telescoped languages,* and *People move love hurry in a gently,* and, *With almost melancholy delicacy night gargles windows.* Analyses of semantic similarity judgments and of hundreds of interpretations revealed that people can reliably judge the semantic relatedness of anomalies and their interpretations—even when the interpretations themselves are metaphors, proverbs, or anomalies. The linguistic view, essentially reductionist, cannot readily countenance the interpretation of one deviant string in terms of another! If given enough semantic rope, people can conceive of a meaning for strings that are meaningless as far as some linguistics theories of truth are concerned.

In this extreme form the construal of anomaly as figurative language can be regarded as a clear case of creative discovery. In fact, the connection between figurative language and creative problem-solving is a natural one. Metaphors may be involved in solving problems which come in the form of anomalous phenomena. In Chapter 15, Pollio and Smith begin by summarizing their past work on anomaly, metaphor, and problem-solving. Extending Steinberg's (1970) work along new lines, Pollio and Smith (1979) found clear individual differences in preference for regarding anomalies as metaphorical. In a new experiment reported here, people were given a set of verbal problem-solving tasks and a set of metaphoric reasoning tasks—in an attempt to converge on the commonalities. Illustrative tasks were syllogistic reasoning, creative composition, and metaphor explanation. Using factor-analytic techniques, Pollio and Smith found that the various measures—presumably of the same mental process—appear to tap *different* processes. Pollio and Smith conclude that figurative understanding may not be a uniform set of skills, and that it cannot be equated with analogistic reasoning.

Chapter 16 by Hoffman is, in a sense, a "wrap up" and perspective on the issues raised in this volume. This conglomerative aspect is due to Hoffman's subject matter itself—the use of metaphor in scientific discovery and problem-solving, the context in which the "anomaly" that is being made sense of is the world itself (e.g., *Atoms are like solar systems; The ego is a helmsman*). Hoffman reviews some of the literature in philosophy and psychology on the status of metaphor in scientific theories—as a teaching device, and as an aspect of the psychology of science. Though there is a large literature of ideas on this subject, no one has tried to derive criteria for assessing a metaphorical theory on the basis of its metaphoricalness. It is by no means clear that metaphoricalness per se (as opposed to analogy, similarity, or imagery) is the crucial property that makes metaphorical theories either crucial (useful) or misleading. Hoffman describes the place of a metaphor in a nomological network of propositions in a theory and discusses criteria for deciding where, when, and how a metaphor will be useful to science. From the computer metaphor for mind, to the holographic model of memory and imagery, to the use of metaphors in "world views" and even in theories of metaphor itself, Hoffman's paper touches on a wide range of the uses of figurative language in the human's efforts to understand.

ON TO WHAT'S NEW

Although figurative language was a hot topic throughout much of the history of rhetoric, it certainly has been a taboo topic throughout much of the history of Western science. Beginning with Aristotle, there was a tendency to deplore it as unnecessary (albeit aesthetic) and to praise objectivity. As Anderson (1964) put it:

> As the medieval world disappeared in the face of scientific and technical advances ... so too was metaphor classified as an embellishment designed to dupe the unwary. Bacon placed metaphors among the "fantasies of the marketplace," a position followed by Hobbes, Locke, and Hume. This tradition was carried on and extended by Bentham who regarded metaphor as a ruse (p. 54).

Figurative language might have been entirely relegated to rhetoric were it not for treatments of metaphor by Freudians and by philosophers who were interested in its role in scientific theories. Much of this analytical work belongs to the present century.

This volume is organized into five sections. This one is on philosophical, historical, and psychological perspectives. The second considers issues of processing and representation. The third is on semantics and features, the fourth on developmental work, and the final section is on problem-solving. This parsing "leads" the reader through the concepts, issues, and theories involved in a nice way . . . a bit at a time. This organization also reflects the areas of concentrated experimental and theoretical work on figurative language. So . . . on to what's new.

ACKNOWLEDGMENT

Preparation of a draft of this chapter by the first author was supported by grant 1T32-HD07151 from the National Institute of Child Health and Human Development to the Center for Research in Human Learning. The authors would like to thank Mark A. Dorfmueller of the University of Cincinnati and Robert Verbrugge of the University of Connecticut for their comments on an earlier incarnation of the chapter.

REFERENCES

Anderson, C. C. The psychology of metaphor. *Journal of Genetic Psychology*, 1964, *105*, 53–73.

Anderson, J. R., & Bower, G. *Human associative memory*. Hillsdale, N.J.: Lawrence Erlbaum Associates, 1979 (Originally published 1973).

Arthos, J. Figures of speech. In A. Premminger (Ed.), *Encyclopedia of poetry*. Princeton, N.J.: Princeton University Press, 1965.

Bateson, G. *Steps to an ecology of mind*. New York: Chandler, 1972.

Berggren, D. The use and abuse of metaphor: II. *Review of Metaphysics*, 1963, *16*, 450–472.

Bettelheim, B. *The uses of enchantment: The meaning and importance of fairy tales*. New York: Knopf, 1976.

Bickerton, D. Prolegomena to a linguistic theory of metaphor. *Foundations of Language*, 1969, *5*, 34–52.

Billow, R. M. Metaphor: A review of the psychological literature. *Psychological Bulletin*, 1977, *84*, 81–92.

Black, M. *Models and metaphors: Studies in language and philosophy*. Ithaca, N.Y.: Cornell University Press, 1962.

Bobrow, S. A., & Bell, S. M. On catching on to idiomatic expressions. *Memory and Cognition*, 1973, *1*, 343–346.

Bolinger, D. The atomization of meaning. *Language*, 1965, *41*, 555–573.

Bransford, J. D., & Johnson, M. H. Contextual prerequisites for understanding: Some investigations of comprehension and recall. *Journal of Verbal Learning and Verbal Behavior*, 1972, *11*, 717–726.

Brown, S. J. M. *The world of imagery: Metaphor and kindred imagery*. New York: Russell and Russell, 1966.

Brooke-Rose, C. *A grammar of metaphor*. London: Mercury Books, 1965.

Burklund, C. E. The presentation of figurative language. *Quarterly Journal of Speech*, 1964, *41*, 383–390.

Butters, R. R. On the interpretation of "deviant utterances." *Journal of Linguistics*, 1969, *6*, 105–110.

Campbell, P. N. Metaphor and linguistic theory. *Quarterly Journal of Speech*, 1975, *61*, 1–12.

Carnap, R. *The logical syntax of language*. London: Routledge & Kegan-Paul, 1937.

Cassirer, E. *The philosophy of symbolic forms*. New Haven, Conn.: Yale University Press, 1953.

Chomsky, N. *Aspects of the theory of syntax*. Cambridge, Mass.: M.I.T. Press, 1965.

Chukovsky, K. *From two to five.* Berkeley: University of California Press, 1968.

Cohen, T. Reply to Sadock. In A. Ortony (Ed.), *Metaphor and thought.* Cambridge, England: Cambridge University Press, 1979.

Coleman, E. B. Responses to a scale of grammaticalness. *Journal of Verbal Learning and Verbal Behavior,* 1965, *4,* 521–527.

Cometa, M. S., & Eson, M. E. Logical operations and metaphor interpretation. *Child Development,* 1978, *49,* 649–659.

Corbett, E. P. J. *Classic rhetoric for the modern student.* New York: Oxford University Press, 1971.

Crocker, J. C. The social functions of rhetorical forms. In J. D. Sapir & J. C. Crocker (Eds.), *The social use of metaphor.* Pittsburgh: University of Pennsylvania Press, 1977.

cummings, e. e. *Complete Poems.* New York: Harcourt Brace, 1954.

Danks, J. H., & Glucksberg, S. Psychological scaling of linguistic properties. *Language and Speech,* 1973, *13,* 118–140.

Downey, J. E. The psychology of figures of speech. *American Journal of Psychology,* 1919, *30,* 103–115.

Downey, R. G., & Hakes, D. T. Some psychological consequences of violating linguistic rules. *Journal of Verbal Learning and Verbal Behavior,* 1968, *7,* 158–161.

Drange, T. *Type crossings.* The Hague: Mouton, 1966.

Edie, J. M. Expression and metaphor. *Philosophy and Phenomenological Research,* 1963, *23,* 538–561.

Emig, J. Children and metaphor. *Research in the teaching of English,* 1972, *6,* 163–175.

Fillenbaum, S. A note on the 'search after meaning': Sensibleness of paraphrases of well-formed and malformed expressions. *Bulletin of the Psychonomic Society,* 1970, *8,* 67–68.

Fillmore, C. J. The case for case. In E. Bach & R. Harms (Eds.), *Universals in Linguistic Theory.* New York: Holt, Rinehart, & Winston, 1968.

Foerster, L. M. Idiomagic. *Elementary English,* 1974, *51,* 125–127.

Fowler, R. On the interpretation of nonsense strings. *Journal of Linguistics,* 1969, *5,* 75–83.

Gardner, H. Metaphors and modalities: How children project polar adjectives onto diverse domains. *Child Development,* 1974, *45,* 84–91.

Gardner, H., Winner, E., Bechhofer, R., & Wolf, D. The development of figurative language. In K. Nelson (Ed.), *Children's Language.* New York: Gardner, 1979.

Gentner, D. Children's performance on a spatial analogies task. *Child Development,* 1977, *48,* 1034–1039.

Hall, R. A. Why a structural semantics is impossible. *Language Sciences,* 1972, *21,* 1–6.

Henle, P. Metaphor. In P. Henle (Ed.), *Language, thought and culture.* Ann Arbor: University of Michigan Press, 1958.

Hoffman, R. R., & Honeck, R. P. She laughed his joy and she cried his grief: Psycholinguistic theory and anomaly. *Psychological Record,* 1979, *29,* 321–328.

Honeck, R. P., & Hoffman, R. R. Synonymy and anomaly. *Bulletin of the Psychonomic Society,* 1979, *14,* 37–40.

Honeck, R. P., Sowry, B., & Voegtle, K. Proverbial understanding in a pictorial context. *Child Development,* 1978, *49,* 327–331.

Isenberg, A. On defining metaphor. *Journal of Philosophy,* 1963, *60* 609–622.

James. W. *The varieties of religious experience.* New York: Modern Library, 1902.

Jaynes, J. *The origin of consciousness in the breakdown of the bicameral mind.* Boston: Houghton Mifflin, 1977.

Jenkins, J. J. *Context conditions meaning.* Paper presented at the annual meeting of the Midwestern Psychological Association, Chicago, Illinois, May, 1977.

Johnson, M. G. Some psychological implications of language flexibility. *Behaviorism,* 1975, *3,* 87–95.

Katz, J. J. *Semantic theory.* New York: Harper and Row, 1972.

Katz, J. J., & Fodor, J. A. The structure of a semantic theory. *Language,* 1963, *39,* 170–210.

Katz, J. J., & Postal, P. *An integrated theory of linguistic descriptions.* Cambridge, Mass.: M.I.T. Press, 1964.

Kintsch, W. *The representation of meaning in memory.* Hillsdale, N.J.: Lawrence Erlbaum Associates, 1974.

Koch, K. *Wishes, lies and dreams: Teaching children to write poetry.* New York: Chelsea House, 1970.

Kogan, N. *Metaphoric thinking in children.* Paper presented at the biennial meeting of the Society for Research in Child Development, Denver, Colorado, April, 1975.

Köhler, W. *Gestalt psychology.* New York: Liveright, 1929.

Langer, S. *Philosophy in a new key.* Cambridge, Mass.: Harvard University Press, 1957.

Leacock, S. *Nonsense novels.* New York: Dover, 1971 (originally published 1912).

Leondar, B. Metaphor and infant cognition. *Poetics,* 1975, *4,* 273-287.

Levin, S. R. Reply to Searle. In A. Ortony (Ed.), *Metaphor and thought.* Cambridge, England: Cambridge University Press, 1979.

Maclay, H., & Sleator, M. D. Responses to language: Judgments of grammaticalness. *International Journal of American Linguistics,* 1960, *26,* 275-282.

Manns, J. W. Metaphor and paraphrase. *British Journal of Aesthetics,* 1977, *17,* 358-366.

Marks, L. E., & Miller, G. A. The role of semantic and syntactic constraints in the memorization of English sentences. *Journal of Verbal Learning and Verbal Behavior,* 1964, *3,* 1-5.

Miller, G. A., & Isard, S. Some perceptual consequences of violating linguistic rules. *Journal of Verbal Learning and Verbal Behavior,* 1963, *2,* 217-228.

Miller, G. A., & Johnson-Laird, P. N. *Language and perception.* Cambridge, Mass.: Harvard University Press, 1976.

Miller, R. M. The dubious case for metaphors in educational writing. *Educational Theory,* 1976, *26,* 174-181.

Müller, F. M. *Lectures on the science of language, Volume II.* London: Longmans Green, 1873, Chapter 8.

Newton, E. S. Figurative language: An Achilles heel in reading comprehension. *Journal of Reading,* 1964, *8,* 65-70.

Olson, D. R. Language and thought: Aspects of a cognitive theory of semantics. *Psychological Review,* 1970, *4,* 257-273.

Ortony, A. Why metaphors are necessary and not just nice. *Educational Theory,* 1975, *25,* 45-53.

Ortony, A. The role of similes and similarities in metaphor. In A. Ortony (Ed.), *Metaphor and thought.* Cambridge, England: Cambridge University Press, 1979.

Ortony, A., Schallert, D. L., Reynolds, R. E., & Antos, S. J. Interpreting metaphors and idioms: Some effects of context on comprehension. *Journal of Verbal Learning and Verbal Behavior,* 1978, *17,* 465-477.

Ortony, A., Reynolds, R. E., & Arter, J. A. Metaphor: Theoretical and empirical research. *Psychological Bulletin,* 1978, *85,* 919-942.

Paivio, A. *Imagery and verbal processes.* Hillsdale, N.J.: Lawrence Erlbaum Associates, 1979 (Originally published 1971).

Paivio, A. Psychological processes in the comprehension of metaphor. In A. Ortony (Ed.), *Metaphor and thought.* Cambridge, England: Cambridge University Press, 1979.

Petrie, H. G. Metaphor and learning. In A. Ortony (Ed.), *Metaphor and thought.* Cambridge, England: Cambridge University Press, 1979.

Perrine, L. Four forms of metaphor. *College English,* 1971, *33,* 125-138.

Piaget, J. *Language and thought of the child.* New York: Harcourt Brace, 1926.

Pollio, H. R., Barlow, J. M., Fine, H. J., & Pollio, M. R. *Psychology and the poetics of growth: Figurative language in psychology, psychotherapy, and education.* Hillsdale, N.J.: Lawrence Erlbaum Associates, 1977.

Pollio, H. R., & Burns, B. C. The anomaly of anomaly. *Journal of Psycholinguistic Research,* 1977, *6,* 247-260.

Pollio, H. R., & Smith, M. K. Sense and nonsense in thinking about anomaly and metaphor. *Bulletin of the Psychonomic Society,* 1979, in press.

Quine, W. V. On a suggestion of Katz. *Journal of Philosophy,* 1967, *64,* 54–62.

Rapoport, A. *Operational philosophy.* New York: Harper and Brothers, 1953.

Reddy, M. The conduit metaphor: A case of frame conflict in our language about language. In A. Ortony (Ed.), *Metaphor and thought.* Cambridge, England: Cambridge University Press, 1979.

Richards, I. A. *The philosophy of rhetoric.* New York: Oxford University Press, 1936.

Riechmann, P. F. *Does imagery facilitate memory for conceptual information?* Paper presented at the annual convention of the American Psychological Association, August, 1977.

Rumelhart, D. E., Lindsay, P. H., & Norman, D. A. A process model for long-term memory. In E. Tulving & W. Donaldson (Eds.), *Organization of memory.* New York: Academic Press, 1972.

Russell, S. W. Computer understanding of metaphorically used verbs. *American Journal of Computational Linguistics,* 1976, *44,* 1–73.

Sapir, J. D. The anatomy of metaphor. In J. D. Sapir & J. C. Crocker (Eds.), *The social use of metaphor: Essays on the anthropology of rhetoric.* Philadelphia: University of Pennsylvania Press, 1977.

Schank, R. Conceptual dependency: A theory of natural language understanding. *Cognitive Psychology,* 1972, *3,* 552–631.

Searle, J. Chomsky's revolution in psycholinguistics. *New York Times Review of Books,* June 29, 1972, pp. 16–24.

Shibles, W. A. *Metaphor: An annotated bibliography and history.* Whitewater, Wis.: The Language Press, 1971.

Smith, E. E., Rips, L. J., & Shoben, E. J. Semantic memory and psychological semantics. In G. H. Bower (Ed.), *The psychology of learning and motivation,* Volume 8. New York: Academic Press, 1974, pp. 1–45.

Smith, W. G., & Heseltine, J. E. *The Oxford dictionary of English proverbs.* Oxford: Clarendon Press, 1935.

Snell, B. *The discovery of the mind.* Translated by J. Rosenmeyer. New York: Harper and Row, 1960.

Steinberg, D. D. Analyticity, amphigory and semantic interpretation of sentences. *Journal of Verbal Learning and Verbal Behavior,* 1970, *9,* 37–51.

Sternberg, R. J., Tourangeau, R., & Nigro, G. Metaphor, induction, and social policy: The convergence of macroscopic and microscopic views. In A. Ortony (Ed.), *Metaphor and thought.* Cambridge, England: Cambridge University Press, 1979.

Sticht, T. G. Educational uses of metaphor. In A. Ortony (Ed.), *Metaphor and thought.* Cambridge, England: Cambridge University Press, 1979.

Swinney, D. A., & Cutler, A. The access and processing of idiomatic expressions. *Journal of Verbal Learning and Verbal Behavior,* 1979, *18,* 523–534.

Tversky, A. Features of similarity. *Psychological Review,* 1977, *84,* 327–352.

Verbrugge, R. R. Resemblances in language and perception. In R. Shaw & J. Bransford (Eds.), *Perceiving, acting, and knowing: Toward an ecological psychology.* Hillsdale, N.J.: Lawrence Erlbaum Associates, 1977.

Verbrugge, R. R., & McCarrell, N. S. Metaphoric comprehension: Studies in reminding and resembling. *Cognitive Psychology,* 1977, *9,* 494–533.

Watts, A. F. *The language of mental development.* Boston: S. C. Heath, 1944.

Weinreich, R. Problems in the analysis of idioms. In J. Puhvel (ed.), *Substance and structure of language.* Berkeley: University of California Press, 1969.

Werner, H., & Kaplan, B. *Symbol formation.* New York: Wiley, 1963.

Yandell, S., & Zintz, M. Some difficulties which Indian children encounter with idioms in reading. *The Reading Teacher,* 1961, *14,* 356–359.

2 Historical Notes on Figurative Language

Richard P. Honeck
University of Cincinnati

INTRODUCTION

This chapter provides a historical sketch of the intellectual background for recent psychological research on figurative language. The 1970s have seen the renaissance of figurative language. It is now a "hot" topic. Whether it will remain hot and then suffer the fate of assimilation by the ideational mainstream, as happens to most truly significant topics, is another matter. It is too early to fully assess its import. Nevertheless, figurative language phenomena do provide an important perspective on a number of issues concerning linguistic understanding. As a strong claim, they constitute a serious challenge for theories of understanding.

One dilemma in all of this concerns the nature of figurative language itself. No general, commonly accepted criteria exist by which figurative language phenomena can be distinguished from one another or from non-figurative phenomena. The historian is therefore put in the position of either accepting or rejecting an author's claim that he or she is addressing such phenomena. Most often this is an easy chore, but not always, since the boundaries of figurative language are no less fuzzy, squishy, and ill-defined than language in general. There appear to be prototypical figurative forms, such as metaphors, similes, and idioms, which most analysts have seized upon. However, there are lesser known and less well studied forms such as proverbs, metonymy, synechdoche, oxymoron, and so on. Should we also include allegory, parables, fables, and aphorisms? How about studies that *use* figurative language but do not analyze it directly? If the answers here are definitely yes, the reasons are less clear.

INTELLECTUAL ROOTS

Despite this dilemma, it is clear that current goings-on do have an intellectual history. Within this context my approach will be to describe landmark papers within psychology and allied disciplines. As such, however, this essay is less a history than a noting of streams of thought about apparently similar phenomena. Four general enterprises are traced from their late nineteenth and twentieth century "beginnings"—experimental psychology, the philosophical-rhetorical tradition, linguistics, and dynamic psychology. The chapter closes with a discussion of the 1960s and 1970s and a look into the future.

Experimental Psychology

Treatments of figurative language within the experimental framework include the post-Content psychology of Bühler; the mental testing movement, developed by Binet, Henri, and Simon, and redirected by Piaget; Gestalt psychology as interpreted by Werner and Asch; and the Neo-Behavioristic writings of Osgood and Brown.

Bühler and the Wurzburg Group. As a member of the famous Wurzburg Group, Karl Bühler was more interested in the nature of thought than in figurative language. Bühler sought to give "thought elements" the same respectability accorded sensations, images, and affects by the Content psychologists. In fact, it was Bühler more than any other Wurzburger who argued on behalf of these elements as part of the Bewusstseinslage or "imageless thoughts" made so controversial by this group. Aphorisms and proverbs were part of his methodological staples. Sometimes he used the Ausfrage method (Boring, 1950), a simple question-answer technique used previously, though more informally, by Binet in France and Woodworth in the United States (Murphy, 1929). His subjects introspected about their interpretation of a proverb, for example. He also conducted "analogy experiments" in which subjects were asked to provide a semantic match between two different series of proverbs. For example, the proverb *When the calf is stolen the farmer repairs the stall* might be linked to *One looks to the cask when the wine escapes into the cellar.* Recall of the first series, given the second, was usually excellent. Bühler concluded that the proverbs had forced subjects to think, thereby producing an effective retrieval form. This form for Bühler was unconscious, non-sensory, wholistic and at the core of meaning (cf. Blumenthal, 1970; Bühler, 1908).

Upon Wundt's death in 1920, Bühler became the leading linguistic authority in Europe, and this as a functionalist who emphasized the total field of language. Was it functionalism that sparked his interest in figurative materials? I think not. The Wurzburg milieu was critical but a more thorough answer leads us to the mental testing movement.

Mental Testing.   In the late 1880s Alfred Binet and Henri published together on memory for ideas, extending Binet's 1886 work, *The Psychology of Reasoning.* At the turn of the century and for a time thereafter Binet wrote discursively about the thought processes of his two daughters. His method too was question-answer, the results satisfying Binet that thinking need not involve imagery. As such, the Wurzburger's thesis was confirmed although Binet claimed precedence on the whole matter of imageless thought (Humphrey, 1963).

Enter Bühler, circa 1905. Bühler had read Binet, for he defers to Binet's simple term—"thought"—to describe nonsensory mental elements (Humphrey, 1963). Perhaps Bühler borrowed Binet's method and supplemented it with figurative materials. Perhaps not. What *is* clear is Binet's influence, although indirect, on Piaget.

After a brief post-doctoral stint at Bleuler's psychiatric clinic, Piaget came, around 1920, to the now famous Binet-Simon Lab in Paris. Binet having died in 1910, Simon asked Piaget to translate and standardize the Englishman Burt's Test of Reasoning. Fortunately, Piaget was diverted from psychometry owing to his fascination with the children's misunderstandings (Flavell, 1963). In his *Language and Thought of the Child* (1926), originally published in 1923, Piaget devotes an entire chapter to young children's understanding of proverbs, the same materials used in Burt's test. Later, at the Institute Rousseau, Piaget had children match two series of proverbs. The children's performance was quite poor, due to "syncretism," itself a product of egocentrism. Syncretism occurs when two propositions are fused idiosyncratically into a common schema. The result is that the two propositions, the proverbs in Piaget's studies, imply one another. Unfortunately, there has been little theoretical advance beyond Piaget's interpretation of children's *mis*understandings of complex language.

Gestalt Influences.   Figurative language seems to be an emergent and so "natural" that it could not possibly arise through associative processes. Not surprising, therefore, that Gestalt psychology represents another vector on figurative language, and this despite the fact that the original core of Gestaltists ignored language.

The broad base Gestalt influence is clear in the case of Heinz Werner. A young Werner detailed the human imitation of animal sounds in a 1919 paper. His first book, *Comparative Psychology of Mental Development* (1940) laid an incredibly eclectic groundwork for later efforts—*Expressive Language* (1955), which he edited and wrote an article for, and *Symbol Formation* (1963), written with Kaplan. Incidentally, *Comparative Psychology* contains numerous references to both Piaget's *Language and Thought of the Child* and to Bühler's early work. And *Symbol Formation* presents an entire chapter on Bühler's view of language, one of the very few airings provided Bühler in a book written in English. As we shall see, however, Werner focuses on the origins of figurative language, and simple forms at that, for he rarely considers expressive language in its full-blown, mature forms.

In *Comparative Psychology* Werner states that all forms of mature differentiated perception, including sophisticated forms of figurative language, derive from a syncretic state of the organism. This state is a primordial blending of affective, interoceptive, postural-motor, and imaginal components. Differentiation of this syncretic state has a number of products. Most important for our purposes, syncresis effects physiognomic perception whose derivatives, in turn, are multiple. For Werner (1955) physiognomic perception has four characteristics. First, it has a dynamic character as evidenced through phonetic symbolism and the young child's motor schemas. Incidentally, Werner regards phonetic symbolism as evidence for the unity of the senses, or a "sensorium commune" that allows reciprocal influence between different sensory fields. Second, it is psychophysically undifferentiated—for example, the meaning of gesture is an unanalyzable whole. Third, the total organismic character of physiognomic perception gives rise to synaesthesia in which a sensory event is interpreted in terms of a different modality—colored tone hearing (chromesthesia) is an example. The final characteristic, embeddedness in a total context of feeling and action, eventuates in the physiognomization of words. Through all of this, Werner constantly contrasts physiognomic perception with "geometrical-technical" perception, a more physical form upon which the former is dependent.

Additional evidence for physiognomic perception comes from consensual validity regarding the affective content of line drawings, from artists' self reports of their perceptions, and from children's descriptions—the dark is "like whispering," a towel hook is "cruel," and so on. Obviously, various adult descriptions as of a person's face as "sad," a building as "dreary," fit here as well. Physiognomic perception also leads to anthropomophism, personification, magical thinking, and panpsychism. If the child treats objects as if they were persons, personification occurs. When the child considers a desired object to be alive, magical thinking and panpsychism may result. Werner also claims that sympathy and empathy derive from physiognomic perception, as do some verbal expressions in certain cultures—a shamed woman in one culture may say, "My forehead is biting me"; a child asked whether his mother is good says, "No, she's sour." In general, physiognomic perception is characteristic of "primitivity"—of children, schizophrenics, preliterate peoples, and brain trauma cases. Increasing age and cultural sophistication tend to reduce the varieties of physiognomic perception.

In their book *Symbol Formation* (1963) Werner and Kaplan flesh out Werner's earlier arguments. Their basic thesis is that because physiognomic qualities can be perceived in a wide variety of events, the "symbolic vehicle" can come into being. To quote, "It is this transcendence of expressive qualities, that is, their amenability to materialization in disparate things and happenings that makes it possible for one to feel and see equations and similarities that find no place in the physical-technical construction of the world'' (p. 21). This transcendence is presumed to prompt the development of similes, metaphors, and analogies, although no details of the process are provided.

Werner and Kaplan's conception of the symbolic vehicle is interesting. Given an organism in a syncretic state there must be some mechanism that guides the state into a more specific, articulated perceptual activity. This mechanism is ''dynamic schematization,'' which allows for the establishment of semantic correspondence between symbolic vehicle (i.e., language) and referent. This correspondence is latent, however, and requires productive thought. In other words, because dissimilar events possess similar nonphysical expressive properties, and because the organism develops an intention to use one experience to denote another, a conceptual relation between symbol and referent is establishable. This idea is similar to Ogden and Richards' (1923) triangle of reference in which thought mediates symbol and referent.

There is a natural progression from Gestalt-influenced Werner's views to Solomon Asch's contributions to the study of metaphor. In a volume edited by Werner on expressive language, Asch (1955) reports that the words ''warm'' and ''cold'' were sufficient in one study to polarize impressions of an otherwise identical personality description. Asch further notes that terms used to describe experiences in every sensory modality are also used to describe psychological properties. People are experienced as ''bitter,'' ''hard,'' ''bright,'' and so on. In a later study, Asch demonstrated that certain ''double function'' terms have similar connotations in relatively unrelated languages. For example, the morpheme for ''hot'' means rage in Hebrew, enthusiasm in Chinese, sexual arousal in Thai, and energy in Hausa, a Western African language. Although the exact meaning is different there is a core meaning of sorts.

In a more theoretical 1958 paper Asch discusses the theoretical basis of metaphor, and of dual function terms in particular. Dismissing explanations appealing to intrinsic similarities between physical and psychological phenomena, or to association by contiguity, as well as generalizations from supposed commonalities, he reasons that double function terms refer to ''functional properties or modes of interaction'' (p. 93). For example, the term ''hard'' refers to something which resists change when pushed, pressed, or otherwise contacted. A hard person, then, is someone not easily swayed or influenced, and it is this imperviousness that is naively perceived.

In a seminal developmental study published in 1960, Asch and Nerlove concluded that the dual meanings of double function terms exist first as separate lexical entries, being conceptually related only in late childhood. Thus, 3–6-year-olds understood the literal physical meaning, 7–9-year-olds also applied the terms to people, but only 11-year-olds could explicitly relate the separate usages of the terms.

Little if any research on double function terms appeared for some 13 years after this study, a hiatus induced first by the predominant verbal learning psychology and, second, by syntax-oriented transformational linguistics. In any case, Asch, like Werner, saw the broader implications of figurative language, having examined its manifestations cross-culturally, developmentally, and in person perception.

Neo-Behaviorism. That brings us to the fourth experimental approach—Behaviorism. Understandably, Behaviorists have not pursued the implications of figurative language, for to do so is to credit the language user with a complex analysis of and elaboration upon the stimulus. Radical Behaviorists have taken passing shots at the topic, however. In his *Verbal Behavior* (1957) Skinner considers metaphor a matter of transferring an old reinforced response to a new stimulus that shares sensory qualities with the old stimulus. Other treatments of the topic in the early 1950s are equally lean. George Miller's 1951 book, *Language and Communication,* contains but a few lines on metaphor. Charles Osgood's 1953 tome, *Method and Theory in Experimental Psychology,* has two pages on metaphor, devoted almost exclusively to older studies of synaesthesia. And the famous 1954 psycholinguistics conference (Osgood & Sebeok, 1965) produced no reference to figurative language.

By the mid-fifties, however, Behaviorism had loosened up enough to admit mediational mechanisms. These mechanisms were used by two Neo-Behaviorists, Osgood and Roger Brown. In *The Measurement of Meaning* (1957), Osgood, Suci, and Tannenbaum report studies of lexical metaphor and of synaesthesia conducted by Osgood as a young undergraduate. Drawing on earlier collaborative work of Osgood, the authors say, "the process of metaphor in language as well as in color-music synesthesia can be described as the parallel alignment of two or more dimensions of experience, definable verbally by pairs of polar adjectives, with translations occurring between equivalent portions of continua" (p. 23). Both phenomena are subsumed under the broader principle of "mediated generalization." Accordingly, low pitch tones are represented as large, and high tones as small because large things tend to produce relatively low tones and small things high tones. Thus, a common mediation process underlies lexical metaphor as well as the synaesthete's reaction to pitch. (See Osgood, this volume, for an update and autobiography of these phenomena.)

A similar tack is taken by Roger Brown in his 1958 analysis of lexical metaphor. Brown reviews his own research showing consensual validity in the use of nonauditory words to describe opera singing. Brown explains that it is the "natural correlation of sense qualities" that provides for metaphorical extension of the names of sensory qualities. The mechanism is one of "mediated association"—someone is "cold" because their behavior is stiff and stiff things are often cold.

Brown goes beyond Osgood, however, in considering the role of context. Attention to language in isolation stimulates metaphor. One can argue just the opposite, of course, but Brown says that, "A metaphor lives in language so long as it causes a word to appear in improbable contexts, the word suggesting one reference, the context another. When the word becomes as familiar in its new context as it was in the old, the metaphor dies'' (p. 142). When the word and its context are at odds different referents are evoked that somehow enrich one another. This view is a curious mixture of mechanistic associationism, the reference theory of meaning, and a latent tribute to the creative aspect of metaphor, a tribute sparked perhaps by I. A. Richards, whom Brown cites, and to whom we now turn.

Philosophy and Rhetoric

The second and most positive, direct influence on current psychological research stems from the philosophical-rhetorical tradition. The major figures herewith are Richards and Max Black, although Ernst Cassirer (1946, 1953) would be included by some.

Richards' ideas on metaphor are detailed in his *Philosophy of Rhetoric*, published in 1936. For Richards, words do not have a fixed or correct usage. They are everywhere contextually determined by accompanying words. It follows that he rejects the Aristotelian view that metaphor is idiosyncratic, unlearnable or special. Metaphor is in Richards' words, ''the omnipresent principle of language.'' Moreover, verbal metaphor is a product of a more basic perceptual metaphorical apprehension of the world.

The key word in his analysis is ''interaction,'' which he explains in terms of the relationships between three concepts—tenor (topic), vehicle, and ground. In *A woman is a song* ''woman'' is the tenor, ''song'' the vehicle, and whatever woman and song share, the ground. But this over-simplifies Richards' view, for he considers metaphor, ''a borrowing between and intercourse of *thoughts*, a transaction between contexts. *Thought* is metaphoric, and proceeds by comparison'' (p. 94). Thus, tenor and vehicle *give us* the ideas and need not be explicitly stated in the metaphor. The sentence might be a vehicle, the vehicle and tenor may be reversible, and the ways in which we use them may be limitless. Obviously, therefore, the ground potentially shows a wide range of complexity.

Richards is quick to point out that the interaction need not work through inherent resemblances between tenor and vehicle. Disparities between them are as common. An important point, for as Richards suggests, to speak of the ''fusion'' effected by metaphor is nearly always misleading. In fact, a variety of interactions may take place between tenor and vehicle, from apparent random clash to obvious similarities to mutual selection of common features, and more recondite relationships as well.

Richards' ideas were refined by Black in the early 1960s. (Black's 1962 paper has most influenced psychologists, although he had written in 1954 on the topic.) However, Black is unhappy with the ''inconvenient fiction'' of two ideas interacting and quickly dispenses with the terms tenor and vehicle. Moreover, he chastises Richards for referring inconsistently to the vehicle as the metaphor itself, as the subsidiary subject, or even as the implication system. Similar objections are raised against the tenor concept. So he injects his own terminology—focus and frame. In *The chairman plowed through the discussion* the focus is "plowed" and the remainder of the sentence the frame.

The bulk of Black's writing distinguishes and elaborates the "substitution" and "interaction" views of metaphor. By the substitution view, all metaphorical expression is used in place of some equivalent literal expression. The metaphor remedies a gap in our vocabulary. Still, this view makes metaphor a stylistic variant, and its understanding a matter of cryptology. The language user provides not the intended meaning but some function of it so that the interpreter must apply the function's inverse to recover the intended meaning. Different functions lead to different tropes. With contradiction, irony may result; with exaggeration, hyperbole; and with metaphor, analogy or similarity. This has the effect of making metaphor condensed similarity because the metaphor can be replaced by some equivalent literal *comparison*. The comparison view, which can be traced to Aristotle, is basically a substitution view, and consists of rendering meaning through paraphrase.

Black is more comfortable with the interaction hypothesis that he summarizes in the following ways: (1) A metaphorical statement has two distinct subjects—a principle subject and a subsidiary one. (2) These subjects are often best regarded as "systems of things" rather than "things." (3) A metaphor works by applying to the principal subject a system of associated implications characteristic of the subsidiary subject. (4) These implications usually consist of "commonplaces" about the subsidiary subject but may in suitable cases consist of deviant implications established ad hoc by the writer. (5) The metaphor selects, emphasizes, suppresses, and organizes features of the principle subject by implying statements about it that normally apply to the subsidiary subject. (6) This involves shifts in meaning of words belonging to the same family or system as the metaphorical expression; and some of these shifts, though not all, may be metaphorical transfers. (7) There is in general no simple ground for the necessary shifts of meaning—no blanket reason why some metaphors work and others fail (Black, 1962, pp. 44–45).

The frame extends the meaning of the focus, although the two sets of thoughts act together. A metaphor acts like a filter. In the metaphor "man is a wolf," associations that are common to wolf are made to fit man, man thereby taking on new associations. The principal subject man is "seen through" the filter of the subsidiary subject, wolf. However, the filter can work both ways. The metaphor creates the similarity and is therefore an organizational schema for developing new meanings. In this respect, there is a close kinship between Piaget, Werner, Asch, Richards, and Black.

More recent developments within the philosophy of language have also influenced theorizing about figurative language. I refer here to the philosophy of "speech acts" (Austin, 1962; Searle, 1969, 1977) and the theory of "conversational implicature" originally enunciated by Grice in 1967 (Grice, 1975). By a standard version of the speech act view, a linguistic utterance can perform three functions—it can say something (its "locutionary force"), do something (its "illocutionary force"), and affect someone (its "perlocutionary force"). The theory focuses on the illocutionary functions performed by sentences in a context. For example, the question *You've smoked a pipe, haven't you?* may serve to inquire whether the listener has any tobacco and is willing to give some to the speaker. Here, an "indirect speech act" has been used. *Give me some tobacco,* would be a "direct" act, though less polite. In general, speech act philosophy views the primary communicative functions of language to be those of promising, warning, asserting, commanding, criticizing, and so on, and shows how these functions can be realized in quite subtle, indirect, and elegant ways.

The foregoing analysis suggests that figurative language might be treated as (indirect) speech acts since, clearly, figurative meaning is not completely specified by the literal utterance used to convey it. Thus, Steinmann (1973) argues that, "Speaking figuratively consists ... of saying (utterance meaning) what you mean (intended meaning) by not meaning what you say (sentence meaning)" (p. 224). In literal language, intended meaning and sentence meaning are consonant, as are intended meaning and utterance meaning, so that sentence meaning and utterance meaning are consonant also. In figurative language, sentence meaning and utterance meaning do not accord. Arguing in a similar fashion, Loewenberg (1975) claims that metaphors (as well-formed indicative sentences) are false and thereby fail as assertions. The listener, therefore, judges them not to be truth claims but rather speech act proposals that, "certain things be viewed or understood in a certain way" (p. 335).

The claims that figurative language can be construed within a speech act framework is not uncontroversial. The debate will likely continue for several years. Whatever the outcome, it appears that a general theory of communication should have to encompass both phenomena, as well as the phenomena captured by Grice's Cooperative Principle.

Briefly, this principle describes certain norms that appear to constrain a speaker's utterances and that the listener, in turn, implicitly assumes the speaker abides by. Four maxims compose the general principle—the Maxim of Quantity (i.e., be informative), the Maxim of Quality (i.e., be truthful), the Maxim of Relation (i.e., be relevant), and the Maxim of Manner (i.e., be perspicuous). To illustrate, suppose A and B are talking about President Jimmy Carter. If A says to B, "Oh, Carter is a chamelion," this statement, taken literally, would seem to violate the maxims of quality and relation. If B assumes that A still holds to the Cooperative Principle, then he can revise his notions about violation, rendering it only apparent, and "work out an implicature (intended by A) which is not obviously false" (Levin, 1977, p. 12). In this kind of case, A's purposive exploitation of the implicit, but strong and binding contract between conversants yields metaphor. Ortony (this volume) uses the Cooperative Principle to help pinpoint the necessary and sufficient conditions for identifying metaphor. Honeck, Voegtle, Dorfmueller, and Hoffman (this volume) use it in developing their theory of proverb comprehension.

These newer philosophical approaches to pragmatics highlight important issues in the psychology of figurative language—context, speaker-listener roles, intention, inference, etc. They underline, not linguistic competence in the form of fixed rules for producing grammatical sentences, but mastery of the entire linguistic system in the service of saying what one wants to say in a way one wants to say it.

Linguistics

Much of the current research on figurative language represents a reaction against linguistics. Our sketch of this, the third contribution to figurative language, therefore begins with Leonard Bloomfield, although it could well have begun with Wundt since Bloomfield studied with Wundt (Blumenthal, 1970). Bloomfield published a book on language in 1914 but it was his 1933 effort that influenced generations of linguists. In this book, Bloomfield sells the linguist's version of American Behaviorism. The goal of linguistics is to isolate, segment, and classify the constituents of sentences. This immediate constituent analysis must be carried out without regard to meaning. Bloomfield had not adopted Wundt's more conceptualist approach to language. The hard-nosed experimentalism was there, minus Wundt's brand of introspectionism. It is hardly surprising, therefore, that figurative language is overlooked by Bloomfield. Structuralism had begun.

By 1965, Chomsky, whose heritage can be traced through Zelig Harris to Bloomfield, approached the problems of meaning more adequately. Lexical rules in Chomsky's 1965 theory incorporate semantic features. However, these features are not free to intermingle. Special rules dictate which features are compatible. Unusual combinations of words within a sentence, such as, "misery loves company," violate such rules.

After Katz and Fodor (1963), rule violation is the context in which Chomsky (1965) deciphers metaphor:

> Sentences that break selection restriction rules can often be interpreted metaphorically or allusively in one way or another, if an appropriate context of greater or less complexity is supplied. That is, these sentences are apparently interpreted by a direct analogy to well-formed sentences that observe the selectional rules in question (p. 149).

Clearly, this is a substitution view as Black defines it.

More recent linguistics papers have amplified Chomsky's hypothesis while accepting its basic tenets. Matthews (1971), for example, asserts that violation of selectional restrictions is a necessary and sufficient condition for distinguishing metaphor from nonmetaphor. Metaphor is a matter of semantic deviance and because deviance does occur, metaphor is a performance problem—a matter of language *use*. Semantic deviance will, on occasion, be interpreted metaphorically. It is interesting in this connection that linguists, like many analysts of figurative language, restrict the tropes examined. Aside from metaphor only idioms have been examined in any detail. However, idioms are generally treated as complex dictionary entries (Weinreich, 1966). Even so, Chafe (1968) believes that idiomaticity constitutes an anomaly within the Chomskyan framework. Idioms, according to Chafe, have anomalous meanings, they exhibit transformational deficiencies of one sort or another, they are ill-formed and thus could not be generated by a base component that produces only well-formed deep structures. Idioms that are well-formed also have a higher frequency of usage than their literal counterpart.

Writing in 1972 and 1974, the psychologist, Walter Kintsch, has integrated the linguistic view of metaphor as rule violation with ideas concerning semantic memory. For Kintsch, any semantically unacceptable sentence has metaphoric potential. An unacceptable proposition is one that is not or could not be generated in semantic memory. Moreover, Kintsch appears to accept the substitution view of metaphor. The deviant sentence is interpreted, through inference, so that ''an explicit comparison is being made, involving only semantically acceptable sentences and replacing the original unacceptable sentences.'' Kintsch uses ''analogy rules'' and ''compression rules'' to help explain metaphorical usage. For stylistic reasons, the speaker decides not to express information directly but through a comparison. Analogy rules provide for an interpretation of the deviant sentence whose resultant is a non-deviant proposition. Through compression, the non-deviant proposition is ''taken into'' the original deviant proposition.

Motivation and Metaphor

Our historical sketch would not be complete without considering the motivational sources and consequences of figurative language. Psychodynamically oriented writers have most actively addressed the question of sources. First, a synopsis of Freud's analysis of dreams (Freud, 1920, 1950). The latent content or dream thoughts are transformed by the dream work, under the force of censorship, into the manifest content. The dream work accomplishes this through condensation, displacement, plastic representation, and secondary elaboration. Condensation effects information reduction through deletion, partial transmission, and blending of thoughts. Through displacement, the original thoughts are substituted for, as by allusion or transference of force. In representation, words or imagery are exchanged for the original thoughts. And in secondary elaboration, the several pieces of the dream are woven into a coherent whole. The result is a symbol system that masterfully disguises and sublimates the wish-fulfilling character of the basic dream thoughts.

These dream themes are reiterated in later psychoanalytic conceptions of metaphor (see Pollio, Barlow, Fine, & Pollio, 1977, and Rogers, 1978, for a more extended discussion of psychoanalytic ideas). Metaphor is seen to arise from repressed, unconscious, instinctual impulses that must be disguised in a cryptic symbolic form, so that partial tension reduction can take place (Brown, 1959; Isaacs, 1952; Jones, 1923; Sharpe, 1950). Evidence for this view presumably stems from the content of metaphors themselves—"Freud made a mess of things," "The Cincinnati Reds licked the New York Yankees," and so on.

In digressing a moment we might note the obvious similarities between Freud's dream theory and Chomsky's language theory. For both, basic, direct thoughts or propositions are transformed into superficial, symbolic systems that disguise their bases. The task for both theorists is to elucidate these bases by interpreting the transformational history of the disconnection. Freud's theory is less formalized, of course, but it covers more territory in the sense of the possible symbolic products of the transformational operations. These products may be night dreams, day dreams, gestures, speech style and content, and so on. For Chomsky, the only product is linguistic surface structure.

Other authors have also speculated about motivational sources. "Deep-lying impulses" says Bruner (1957), a feeling approach to experience for Kaplan (1955), and the inhibition of excitation through conditioned symbols for Luria (1960). If figurative language stems from an aroused state, then figurative expression or preference should correlate with emotionality, anxiety, drug stimulants, humor, and even certain forms of brain damage. There is some support for this claim (cf. Anderson, 1964). In general, however, empirical work on the motivational sources of figurative language is sparse.

We should also expect that certain emotional dysfunctions would interfere with the interpretation of figurative language. This hypothesis was investigated in 1944 by Benjamin, whose intellectual debt includes the mental testing movement, the time honored distinction between concrete and abstract, and a study of proverb comprehension conducted in the 1930s. Using this latter technique, he found that schizophrenics' interpretations were bizarre, incoherent, sprinkled with sex and religion, and notably literal. Benjamin argued that proverbs require "desymbolization" (p. 81) such that the intended concepts be synthesized into a general meaning and then into examples of various abstractness. The schizophrenic fails to negotiate the desymbolization process and so makes errors of all kinds. Preoccupation with the use of proverbs in testing schizophrenics has continued unabated through the years. Gorham's Proverb Test, developed in 1956, has been used alone or in conjunction with Benjamin's test in numerous studies (see Shimkunas, 1978, for a review).

Finally, remarks on the affective power of figurative language are legion. But we must be careful here. Are the tensions, imagery, aesthetic feelings and the like due to full figurative understanding of the input? The question is difficult—many effects are ineffable, and translation into words may obscure the effects. They are extremely rapid, ephemeral, and too intrinsic to the understanding itself. Hence, in a 1955 paper Kaplan rationalizes "mediation" techniques designed to bypass these problems. For example, subjects were asked to create line drawings for proverbs and then to explain their drawings. Unfortunately, codification of these drawings is difficult at best. The personality study by Asch (1958), studies on synaesthesia (Marks, 1975; Osgood, this volume), and phonetic symbolism (Taylor, 1976) are more definitive. Unfortunately, little if any research has been done on the motivational-emotional effects of phrasal or sentential tropes.

THE PSYCHOLINGUISTIC ERA

Current research on figurative language, surely the most concentrated ever, has most of its conceptual roots in the material just surveyed. Nevertheless, what has been said of psychology in general also applies here—figurative language has a long past but a short history. Little of the earlier work has had a *direct* influence upon contemporary efforts. This is not unusual in the history of figurative language, this history being more a conglomeration of discontinuities than a coherent progression toward resolution of common problems.

The Barren 60s

The 1960s were a major contribution to the discontinuity, being practically bereft of experimental analyses of figurative language. The profferings of Osgood (1958), Brown (1958), Werner (1955), and Asch and Nerlove (1960), which might have directly stimulated investigations in the 1960s, were ignored. It appears, for example, that some 13–14 years had to pass before the next round of developmental studies could be published (Billow, 1975; Gardner, 1974; Lesser & Drouin, 1975; Pollio & Pollio, 1974). Moreover, the few publications of the 60s have a distinct hit-and-run quality about them (e.g., Anderson, 1964; Koen, 1965), although Werner and Kaplan's (1963) and Wallach and Kogan's (1965) discussions of physiognomic perception are a fresh and notable exception.

Reasons for this dry period are not hard to find. The fervor that accompanied the assimilation of generative-transformational linguistics by psychology produced a bias toward the confirmation of linguistic constructs. In general, psycholinguistic researchers were concerned with the "psychological reality" of these constructs and focused on syntax, and to a lesser extent on semantics in the guise of deep structure. In general, language structure was analyzed at the expense of nonlinguistic knowledge and pragmatic context. Extensionalist aspects of semantics took second place to intensionalist aspects, such as feature theories of sense. Within this latter framework metaphors, when examined, were treated as agrammatical, part of the set of non-sentences doomed to a linguistic netherworld because they could not be generated by the base component of the theory (Chomsky, 1965) or because they were excluded by selection restriction rules (Katz & Fodor, 1963). The isolation of linguistic structure from linguistic function effectively prevented recognition of the importance of figurative language. Still, the injection of linguistic constructs (e.g., productivity) into psychology helped create an atmosphere that would initiate and support its investigation in the 1970s.

Renaissance in the 70s

Indeed, the 1970s have seen an explosion of interest in figurative language. At least two conferences on metaphor have been held, the Illinois Conference on Metaphor and Thought in 1977 and the Interdisciplinary Conference on Metaphor at the University of California, Davis, in 1978. Several symposia have been sponsored—by the Society for Research in Child Development, in 1975, by the American Psychological Association, in 1977, 1978, and 1979, and by the University of Chicago Extension, in 1978. Books on the topic have emerged from practically every relevant discipline, including Pollio et al.'s (1977) groundbreaking psychologically oriented treatise, the eclectic result of the Illinois Conference (Ortony, 1979), Levin's (1977) linguistics treatment of metaphor, Rogers' (1978) psychoanalytic treatment, and Sapir and Crocker's (1977) edited volume from the cultural anthropological perspective. Finally, enough empirical and theoretical work had emerged by the late 1970s that various reviews (see Billow, 1977; Gardner, Winner, Bechhofer, & Wolf, 1978; Ortony, Reynolds, & Arter, 1978) and a formal model of metaphoric understanding (Miller, 1979) were written. Most of the activity has centered on metaphors, although proverbs (see Honeck, Voegtle, Dorfmueller, & Hoffman, this volume), double function terms (Lesser & Drouin, 1975), and idioms (Bobrow & Bell, 1973; Swinney & Cutler, 1979) have been examined also.

Current empirical activity is distributed across a wide spectrum of categories, as even a cursory examination of this volume will reveal. Adult memory processes and developmental trends have been the favored areas, but individual differences (Pollio & Smith, this volume) and important applications such as education (Pollio, et al., 1977), and psychotherapy (Pollio, et al., 1977) have not been overlooked. Analyses of metaphor within the artificial intelligence framework have just begun (Thibadeau, 1978) as have information processing approaches based on analogy (Sternberg, Tourangeau, & Nigro, 1979). Of course, special questions are being asked about figurative language itself. Investigators want to know whether metaphor is understood by one process or more (e.g., Harris, 1976; Ortony, Schallert, Reynolds, & Antos, 1978), what makes for a good metaphor (Malgady & Johnson, this volume), how metaphor can be identified (Loewenberg, 1975; Ortony, this volume; Verbrugge & McCarrell, 1977), what the relationship is between metaphors and proverbs (Honeck et al., this volume), and whether metaphors are more complex than their presumed literal counterparts (Harris, Lahey, & Marsalek, this volume; Riechmann & Coste, this volume). These questions tap important theoretical issues about language in general.

The precise reasons for this flurry of activity are difficult to identify. Within the psycholinguistic tradition, the early 1970s saw a move toward an emphasis upon communicative performance as opposed to linguistic competence. This happened in a number of ways. The inadequacy of purely deep structural descriptions of memory for linguistic inputs became clear (Bransford & Franks, 1971) as did the role of context in fully understanding these inputs (Bransford & Johnson, 1972; Dooling, 1972). The role of semantic and pragmatic factors in language acquisition was persuasively argued by many (e.g., Bloom, 1970; Brown, 1973; Macnamara, 1972; Schlesinger, 1971). And the need to invoke complex inferential mechanisms was also recognized (Bransford, Barclay, & Franks, 1972; Kintsch & Monk, 1972). Key ideas were added to the growing dissatisfaction with merely linguistic explanations by the levels-of-processing viewpoint (Craik & Lockhart, 1972). In sum, the total language field was emphasized along with the need to incorporate great flexibility in models of linguistic understanding.

Despite these crucial changes in psycholinguistic thinking, they do not seem to directly account for the empirical thrust in the very early 1970s. That is, this thinking does not converge on figurative language. The resolution of the tension, perhaps as always, was a personal matter. This is suggested by a short survey, conducted by the author, of some of the principals involved.

One pioneer, Nathan Kogan, has had a long-term interest in figurative phenomena and specifically notes that, ''the roots of my involvement are outside of psycholinguistics.'' Instead, Kogan attributes his interest to a concern with creativity and intelligence, manifest in the 1965 book, *Modes of Thinking in Young Children,* co-authored with Wallach. The Gestalt tradition and the Werner and Kaplan influence emerge in a chapter in *Modes* on physiognomic perception. Cognitive styles, particularly their development, as ''in the shift from complementarity to similarity as a basis for grouping,'' was another major influence (see Kogan's *Cognitive Styles in Infancy and Early Childhood,* 1976). This shift prompted construction of the Metaphor Triads Task that he and his collaborators (See Connor & Kogan, this volume) have used in developmental studies (Kogan, personal communication).

Howard Gardner's involvement derived from an interest in ''the monitoring of the development of key artistic skills—for example, sensitivity to style and to form.'' In *The Arts and Human Development* (1973), written in 1970–71, he reports some research on these skills and discusses metaphor as well. His research on metaphor began with a movie on language development, made in 1971 with Kagan that included a demonstration of young children's ability to match dual-function terms with pictures. Experimental work (Gardner, 1974) followed (Gardner, personal communication).

Perhaps the most eclectic motivation appears in Howard Pollio's work. A manual for identifying figurative language forms was developed quite early (Barlow, Kerlin, & Pollio, 1971) for use in subsequent research such as that reported in Pollio et al.'s book (1977). It is interesting that this book contains no reference to landmark experiments on semantic memory such as Sachs' (1967) or Bransford and Franks (1971), or to Matthews (1971) treatment of metaphor within the Chomskyan framework. Katz and Fodor's (1963) view is represented, however. The authors borrow heavily from Gestalt and Psychoanalytic traditions and from more popular approaches to problem solving such as synectics. Individual differences and styles seem to be a theme that runs through the book (which is continued in Pollio & Smith, this volume). Pollio says that his interest stems from three factors—poetry, Koestler's book *The Act of Creation* (the parts on humor, figurative language and creativity) and personal observations of the high frequency of figures of speech in ordinary language. He became convinced that poets "weren't just talking pretty nonsense, but were talking about serious and important things in serious and important ways." His early studies were naturalistic observations (e.g., therapy) and because they were successful, fueled an interest in related issues (Pollio, personal communication).

Those who have investigated adult memory with figurative materials have, perhaps understandably, remained closer to their psycholinguistic roots. One such investigator is Robert Verbrugge who, in a series of papers dating to at least 1973 (Verbrugge & McCarrell, 1973; Verbrugge, 1975a; 1975b; 1977; Verbrugge & McCarrell, 1977) has been developing what is perhaps the most advanced, yet empirically based theory of metaphor comprehension. Of his own involvement Verbrugge says, "I have been fascinated with metaphor and analogical thought ever since adolescence—but I never expected it would become a professional preoccupation." He points to the history of physical science theories, literature, and religion ("its metaphorical and mythological qualities were especially intriguing") as formative influences. Of his reading of Chomsky's and Katz's discussions of grammar in graduate school, Verbrugge states,

I was disconcerted to see that figurative expressions were uniformly labeled as deviant, anomalous, and un-wellformed. If there was an anomaly to be caged for public show, it was on the assumption that a comprehensive theory of language does not include figurative language. Metaphor did not strike me as being extraneous to 'ordinary language' or normal cognition—no psychological or linguistic theory could be adequate without accommodating it from the outset.

Such sentiments certainly capture those of numerous students of language in the 1960s and 1970s. As his program on metaphor has broadened, Verbrugge says, "I (have) become increasingly aware of its significance for imagination, perception, recognition, language comprehension, action, and artistic expression" (Verbrugge, personal communication).

The author's interest in figurative language resulted from questions concerning the adequacy of linguistic theory and the nature of paraphrase. This interest blossomed in 1971 when I looked into the feasibility of using proverbs as research materials. (Why proverbs were chosen is unclear. Maybe it was a flier on Gorham's Proverb Test that got me to thinking about these matters.) Clearly, people's interpretations of proverbs were paraphrases but not by virtue of any linguistic transformation rule. This point was illustrated quite vividly for me in 1971. I asked several honors students in an introductory psychology class to interpret *A stitch in time saves nine.* Within two seconds, one particularly brilliant student replied, *An ounce of prevention is worth a pound of cure,* a reply since obtained several times. This reply encapsulized several views about similarity that I was discussing at the time with Paul Riechmann, Bob Hoffman, and Tony Frankfurter (now a neuroanatomist!). Clearly the student's interpretation was conceptually similar to the proverb, but not "because" of any Chomskyan transformation rules, case grammar relationships, or mental imagery. Moreover, one "deviant" sentence was used as an interpretation for another deviant sentence and this without retaining any of the major vocabulary from or using any synonyms for the words in the proverb. The class immediately recognized the similarity—it was intuitive and hard to explain. I felt that whatever was happening was incredibly abstract and beyond the reach of current linguistic and psycholinguistic theory. I still do. This led to further questions about the possible memorial result of people's attempts to understand the relationship between a proverb and its interpretation (Honeck, 1973).

Clearly, our little survey has turned up some general themes—individual differences, cognitive styles, and sensitivities form one cluster; creativity, capability, what people can do, form a related cluster; the inadequacy or even irrelevance of linguistic theory, coupled with the need to connect language with imagination, memory, perception, etc., is another; and, finally, more implicit is an interest in the phenomenology or pure experiencing of the challenge, strangeness and paradox, insight, fun, awe, etc.; in a word, the artistry and aesthetics lent by figurative language. These personal themes surely complemented the natural history of the 1960s and 1970s so as to create a sub-area of psychology that was theoretically and personally meaningful.

THE FUTURE:
BEYOND THE INFORMATION METAPHOR

Systematic research on the broad front of figurative language has just begun. Much of it is theoretically toned, although demonstrational rather than hypothesis-testing in format. Partly for this reason, it has not yet had a strong impact upon mainstream cognitive science. There is some suggestion, however, that figuration can serve as a proving ground for semantic theory. Many of the demonstrations are important because they outstrip the power of extant theory. Static network and set-theoretic models have already been challenged and found wanting (Verbrugge & McCarrell, 1977). Literalist approaches (see Honeck, et al., this volume), in general, and proposition based approaches, in particular, may bear the brunt of this newer psycholinguistics. Of such approaches Ortony, Reynolds, and Arter (1978) say,

> Propositional theories seem to be hampered by their reliance on too rigid a notion of word meaning, and this constraint is likely to lead to an overly hasty characterization of input sentences as semantically anomalous. The representation of word meanings in such models simply fails to permit the kind of flexibility that would be required to make sense of a metaphor (p. 935).

Indeed, most semantic theories have isolated lexical knowledge from the language users' other forms of knowledge, linguistic and nonlinguistic, and these latter from other means of expression. Thus, figurative language phenomena may serve to expand our conceptualizations in two additional ways. First, the total field of the figurative utterance becomes more salient. This field involves the delicate integration of word sense, syntactic form, pragmatic context, speaker-listener relationship, and goals, over time. Analysis of the field may require new techniques and assumptions, and better root metaphors, beyond the information metaphor. That leads us to the second point. Figurative language involves disengagement from or suspension of typical modes of experiencing. It has an "as if" quality. This quality places it alongside a variety of human acts, such as role playing, body language, gesture, pretending, play, pantomime, the perception of emotions and feelings, and linguistic acts such as speech acts. The information and computation metaphor seems inappropriate to these phenomena. *Perspective* is a more appealing metaphor. And figurative language would appear to be an ideal conduit for bringing these topics within the reach of a more general perspectivist theory of understanding. It is certainly worth a try. The issues here are no less than those of the representation, creation, and use of knowledge.

ACKNOWLEDGEMENTS

This chapter is a revised and expanded version of a symposium paper originally delivered at the annual meeting of the American Psychological Association, San Francisco, August, 1977. The author wishes to thank Robert Hoffman and Mark Dorfmueller for their comments on several drafts of the chapter.

REFERENCES

Anderson, C. C. The psychology of the metaphor. *The Journal of Genetic Psychology*, 1964, *105*, 53–73.

Asch, S. On the use of metaphor in the description of persons. In H. Werner (Ed.), *On expressive language*. Worcester, Mass.: Clark University Press, 1955.

Asch, S. The metaphor: a psychological inquiry. In R. Tagiuri & L. Petrullo (Eds.), *Person, perception, and interpersonal behavior*. Stanford, Calif.: Stanford University Press, 1958.

Asch, S., & Nerlove, H. The development of double function terms in children. In B. Kaplan & S. Wapner (Eds.), *Perspectives in psychological theory*. New York: International Universities Press, 1960.

Austin, J. L. *How to do things with words*. Oxford: Oxford University Press, 1962.

Barlow, J. M., Kerlin, J. R., & Pollio, H. R. *Training manual for identifying figurative language* (Technical Report #1). Metaphor Research Group, University of Tennessee, 1971.

Benjamin, J. D. A method for distinguishing and evaluating formal thinking disorders in schizophrenia. In J. S. Kasanin, (Ed.), *Language and thought in schizophrenia*. Berkeley: University of California Press, 1944.

Billow, R. M. Metaphor: A review of the psychological literature. *Psychological Bulletin,* 1977, *84,* 81-92.

Billow, R. M. A cognitive developmental study of metaphor comprehension. *Developmental Psychology,* 1975, *11,* 415-423.

Binet, A., & Henri, V. La Memoire des phrases (Memoire des idees), L'Annee Psychologigue, 1894, *1,* 24-59. Cited in chapter 12 by Brewer, W. F. in W. Weimer & D. Palermo, (Eds.), *Cognition and the symbolic processes*. Hillsdale, N.J.: Lawrence Erlbaum Associates, 1974.

Black, M. *Models and metaphors*. Ithaca, N.Y.: Cornell University Press, 1962.

Bloom, L. *Language development: Form and function in emerging grammars*. Cambridge, Mass.: M.I.T. Press, 1970.

Bloomfield, L. *Language*. New York: Holt, 1933.

Blumenthal, A. L. *Language and psychology: Historical aspects of psycholinguistics*. New York: Wiley, 1970.

Bobrow, S. A., & Bell, S. M. On catching on to idiomatic expressions. *Memory and Cognition,* 1973, *1,* 343-346.

Boring, E. G. *A history of experimental psychology*. New York: Appleton-Century-Crofts, Inc., 1950.

Bransford, J. D., & Franks, J. J. Abstraction of linguistic ideas. *Cognitive Psychology,* 1971, *2,* 331-350.

Bransford, J. D., Barclay, J. R., & Franks, J. J. Sentence memory: A constructive versus interpretive approach. *Cognitive Psychology,* 1972, *3,* 193-202.

Bransford, J. D., & Johnson, M. K. Contextual prerequisites for understanding: Some investigations of comprehension and recall. *Journal of Verbal Learning and Verbal Behavior,* 1972, *11,* 717-726.

Brown, N. O. *Life against death*. New York: Random House, 1959.

Brown, R. *A first language: The early stages*. Cambridge, Mass.: Harvard University Press, 1973.

Brown, R. *Words and things*. Glencoe, Ill.: Free Press, 1958.

Bruner, J. S. What social scientists say about having an idea. *Printer's Ink,* 1957 (July 12), *260,* 48-52.

Bühler, K. On thought connections. In Rapaport, D. (Ed.), *Organization and pathology of thought: Selected sources*. New York: Columbia University Press, 1951 (originally published in 1908).

Cassirer, E. *Language and myth*. New York: Harper, 1946.

Cassirer, E. *The philosophy of symbolic forms*. New Haven: Yale University Press, 1953.

Chafe, W. Idiomaticity as an anomaly in the Chomskyan paradigm. *Foundations of Language,* 1968, *4,* 109-127.

Chomsky, N. *Aspects of the theory of syntax*. Cambridge, Mass.: M.I.T. Press, 1965.

Craik, F. I. M., & Lockhart, R. S. Levels of processing: A framework for memory research. *Journal of Verbal Learning and Verbal Behavior,* 1972, *11,* 671-684.

Dooling, D. J. Some context effects in the speeded comprehension of sentences. *Journal of Experimental Psychology,* 1972, *93,* 56–62.

Flavell, J. H. *The developmental psychology of Jean Piaget.* Princeton, N.J.: D. van Nostrand, 1963.

Freud, S. *A general introduction to psychoanalysis.* New York: Washington Square Press, 1960 (original publication by Edward L. Bernays, 1920).

Freud, S. *The interpretation of dreams.* New York: Random House, 1950.

Gardner, H. Metaphors and modalities: How children project polar adjectives onto diverse domains. *Child Development,* 1974, *45,* 84–91.

Gardner, H. *The arts and human development.* New York: Wiley, 1973.

Gardner, H., Winner, E., Bechhofer, R., & Wolf, D. The development of figurative language. In K. Nelson (Ed.), *Children's language,* (Vol. 1). New York: Gardner Press, 1978.

Gorham, D. R. A proverb test for clinical and experimental use. *Psychological Reports,* 1956, *2,* 1–12.

Grice, H. P. Logic and conversation. In P. Cole & J. L. Morgan (Eds.), *Syntax and semantics, Vol. 3: Speech acts.* New York: Seminar Press, 1975, pp. 41–58.

Harris, R. J. Comprehension of metaphors: A test of the two-stage processing model. *Bulletin of the Psychonomic Society,* 1976, *8,* 312–314.

Honeck, R. P. Interpretive vs. structural effects on semantic memory. *Journal of Verbal Learning and Verbal Behavior,* 1973, *12,* 448–455.

Humphrey, G. *Thinking: An introduction to its experimental psychology.* New York: Wiley, 1963.

Isaacs, S. The nature and function of phantasy. In J. Riviere (Ed.), *Developments in Psycho-Analysis.* London: Hogarth, 1952.

Jones, E. *Papers in psychoanalysis.* New York: Wood, 1923.

Kaplan, B. Some psychological methods for the investigation of expressive language. In H. Werner (Ed.), *On Expressive Language.* Worcester, Mass.: Clark University Press, 1955.

Katz, J. J., & Fodor, J. A. The structure of semantic theory. *Language,* 1963, *39,* 170–210.

Kintsch, W. Notes on the semantic structure of memory. In E. Tulving & W. Donaldson (Eds.), *Organization of memory.* New York: Academic Press, 1972.

Kintsch, W. *The representation of meaning in memory.* Hillsdale, N.J.: Lawrence Erlbaum Associates, 1974.

Kintsch, W. & Monk, D. Storage of complex information in memory: Some implications of the speed with which inferences can be made. *Journal of Experimental Psychology,* 1972, *94,* 25–32.

Koen, F. An intra-verbal explication of the nature of metaphor. *Journal of Verbal Learning and Verbal Behavior,* 1965, *4,* 129–133.

Kogan, N. *Cognitive styles in infancy and early childhood.* Hillsdale, N.J.: Lawrence Erlbaum Associates, 1976.

Lesser, H., & Drouin, C. Training in the use of double-function terms. *Journal of Psycholinguistic Research,* 1975, *4,* 285–302.

Levin, S. *The semantics of metaphor.* Baltimore: Johns Hopkins University Press, 1977.

Loewenberg, I. Identifying metaphors. *Foundations of Language,* 1975, *12,* 315–338.

Luria, A. R. *The nature of human conflicts.* New York: Grove Press, 1960.

Macnamara, J. Cognitive bases of language learning in infants. *Psychological Review,* 1972, *79,* 1–13.

Marks, L. E. On colored-hearing synesthesia: Cross modal translations of sensory dimensions. *Psychological Bulletin,* 1975, *82,* 303–331.

Matthews, R. J. Concerning a linguistic theory of metaphor. *Foundations of Language,* 1971, *7,* 413–425.

Miller, G. A. Images and models, similes and metaphors. In A. Ortony (Ed.), *Metaphor and Thought.* Cambridge, England: Cambridge University Press, 1979.

Miller, G. A. *Language and Communication.* New York: McGraw-Hill, 1951.

Murphy, G. *Historical introduction to modern psychology.* New York: Harcourt, Brace, 1929.

Ogden, C. K., & Richards, I. A. *The meaning of meaning.* New York: Harcourt, Brace, 1923.

Ortony, A. (Ed.), *Metaphor and Thought.* Cambridge University Press, 1979.

Ortony, A., Schallert, D. L., Reynolds, R. E., & Antos, S. J. Interpreting metaphors and idioms: Some effects of context on comprehension. *Journal of Verbal Learning and Verbal Behavior,* 1978, *17,* 465–477.

Ortony, A., Reynolds, R. E. & Arter, J. A. Metaphor: Theoretical and empirical research. *Psychological Bulletin.* 1978, *85,* 919–943.

Osgood, C. E. *Method and theory in experimental psychology.* New York: Oxford University Press, 1953.

Osgood, C. E., & Sebeok, T. A. *Psycholinguistics: A survey of theory and research problems.* Bloomington: Indiana University Press, 1965.

Osgood, C. E., Suci, G. J., & Tannenbaum, P. H. *The measurement of meaning.* Urbana: University of Illinois Press, 1957.

Piaget, J. *The language and thought of the child.* New York: Harcourt, Brace, 1926.

Pollio, H. R., Barlow, J. M., Fine, H. J., & Pollio, M. R. *Psychology and the poetics of growth: Figurative language in psychology, psychotherapy, and education.* Hillsdale, N.J.: Lawrence Erlbaum Associates, 1977.

Pollio, M. R., & Pollio, H. R. The development of figurative language in school children. *Journal of Psycholinguistic Research,* 1974, *3,* 185–201.

Richards, I. A. *The philosophy of rhetoric.* New York: Oxford University Press, 1936.

Rogers, R. *Metaphor: A psychoanalytic view.* Berkeley: University of California Press, 1978.

Sachs, J. Recognition memory for syntactic and semantic aspects of connected discourse. *Perception and Psychophysics,* 1967, *2,* 437–442.

Sapir, J. D., & Crocker, J. C. *The social use of metaphor: Essays on the anthropology of rhetoric.* Philadelphia: University of Pennsylvania Press, 1977.

Schlesinger, I. M. Production of utterances and language acquisition. In D. I. Slobin (Ed.), *The ontogenesis of grammar.* New York: Academic Press, 1971.

Searle, J. R. *Speech acts.* Cambridge, England: Cambridge University Press, 1969.

Searle, J. R. *Speech acts: An essay on the philosophy of language.* New York: Cambridge University Press, 1977.

Sharpe, E. F. *Collected papers on psychoanalysis.* London: Hogarth, 1950.

Shimkunas, A. M. Hemispheric asymmetry and schizophrenic thought disorder. In S. Schwartz (Ed.), *Language and cognition in schizophrenia.* Hillsdale, N. J.: Lawrence Erlbaum Associates, 1978.

Skinner, B. F. *Verbal Behavior.* New York: Appleton, 1957.

Steinmann, M. Figurative language and the two-code hypothesis. In R. W. Fasold & R. W. Shuy (Eds.), *Analyzing variation in language.* Washington, D.C.: Georgetown University Press, 1973.

Sternberg, R. J., Tourangeau, R., & Nigro, G. Metaphor, induction, and social policy: The convergence of macroscopic and microscopic views. In A. Ortony (Ed.), *Metaphor and Thought.* Cambridge, England: Cambridge University Press, 1979.

Swinney, D. A., & Cutler, A. The access and processing of idiomatic expressions. *Journal of Verbal Learning and Verbal Behavior,* 1979, *18,* 523–534.

Taylor, I. *Introduction to psycholinguistics.* New York: Holt, Rinehart, & Winston, 1976.

Thibideau, R. *Design considerations for a machine to interpret metaphors* (Laboratory for Computer Science Research). Unpublished manuscript, Rutgers University, Busch Campus, 1978.

Verbrugge, R. R. Resemblances in language and perception. In R. E. Shaw & J. D. Bransford (Eds.), *Acting, perceiving, and comprehending: Toward an ecological psychology.* Hillsdale, N.J.: Lawrence Erlbaum Associates, 1977.

Verbrugge, R. R. *Perceiving invariants at the invitation of metaphor*. Paper presented at the Meeting of the American Psychological Association, Chicago, August, 1975. (a)

Verbrugge, R. R. The comprehension of analogy. Paper presented at the Meeting of the Midwestern Psychological Association, Chicago, May, 1975. (b)

Verbrugge, R. R., & McCarrell, N. S. *The role of inference in the comprehension of metaphor*. Paper presented at the Meeting of the Midwestern Psychological Association, Chicago, May, 1973.

Verbrugge, R., & McCarrell, N. S. Metaphoric comprehension: Studies in reminding and resembling. *Cognitive Psychology*, 1977, *9*, 494–533.

Wallach, M. A., & Kogan, N. *Modes of thinking in young children*. New York: Holt, Rinehart, & Winston, 1965.

Weinreich, U. Problems in the analysis of idioms. In J. Puhvel, (Ed.), *Substance and structure of language*. Berkeley: University of California Press, 1966.

Werner, H. *Comparative psychology of mental development*. New York: International Universities Press, 1940.

Werner, H. A psychological analysis of expressive language. In H. Werner (Ed.), *On expressive language*. Worcester, Mass.: Clark University Press, 1955.

Werner, H., & Kaplan, B. *Symbol Formation*. New York: Wiley, 1963.

3 A Philosophical Perspective on the Problems of Metaphor

Mark Johnson
*Southern Illinois University
at Carbondale*

INTRODUCTION: THE PREJUDICE AGAINST METAPHOR IN THE PHILOSOPHICAL TRADITION

While it is patently false that "(m)etaphor has always been one of the central problems of philosophy" (Berggren, 1962, p. 237), there is, in fact, a long and venerable tradition of philosophical interest in the topic. If there has been any predominant attitude within this tradition, it is a deeply-rooted prejudice against the use of metaphor in any cognitive discipline. This characteristic distrust can be traced at least as far back as Plato, who exhibits a curious ambivalence toward figurative language. On the one hand, Plato is justly famous for his brilliant use of metaphor, allegory, and myth to express his most profound philosophical insights. On the other hand, in the "old quarrel between philosophy and poetry" (*Republic* X, 607b), Plato defends philosophy against imitative poetry, which charms through its language while providing only copies of mere images of reality. Plato's views on metaphor are never explicitly expressed, but he seems to treat figuration as one device of rhetoric used by sophists who, caring nothing for truth, "make trifles seem important and important points trifles by the force of their language" (*Phaedrus*, 267a–b). The fault here appears to lie not so much in figurative language itself, but rather in those who would misuse its power to affect the hearer.

Aristotle takes a more consistently positive attitude toward metaphor, treating it under the art of rhetoric, as having a philosophically significant role in the skill of persuasive argument, and, under the art of poetry, as one of the poet's tools by means of which he provides knowledge through artistic imitation (*mimesis*). In fact, metaphor is the chief device by which the poet puts together previously unassociated elements "that enable us to get hold of new ideas" (*Poetics*

47

1410b). By introducing new ideas through the presentation of underlying similarities, metaphor "sets the scene before our eyes" (*Poetics* 1410b) in a striking manner, and it is because of this unique power of metaphor to induce insight that, for the poet, "the greatest thing by far is to be master of metaphor" (*Poetics* 1459a).

Although Aristotle's more favorable assessment of the cognitive import of figurative language carried over into medieval treatments of analogy, the rise of empiricism soon brought metaphor under a suspicion from which it has not yet fully emerged. When the traditional subject within which metaphor was treated, rhetoric, lost its philosophical roots and withered from a theory of persuasive argument to a taxonomy of tropes, metaphor lost its philosophical respectability. Typical of the mood and line of reasoning of empiricist condemnations of figurative language is John Locke's (1706) assertion that

> if we would speak of things as they are, we must allow that all the art of rhetoric, besides order and clearness; all the artificial and figurative application of words eloquence hath invented, are for nothing else but to insinuate wrong ideas, move the passions, and thereby mislead the judgment; and so indeed are perfect cheats: and therefore, however laudable or allowable oratory may render them in harangues and popular addresses, they are certainly, in all discourses that pretend to inform or instruct, wholly to be avoided; and where truth and knowledge are concerned, cannot but be though a great fault, either of the language or person that makes use of them (III.x.34).

This view of metaphor as unsuited for serious cognitive undertakings has dominated the thinking of philosophers writing on the subject up through the present day. Nineteenth-century romanticism produced a short-lived exaltation of the originality and creativity of metaphorical thinking, but this flourish of high praise soon toppled under the onslaught of positivism. Twentieth-century thinking about metaphor has been carried on within a context defined by the logical positivist view that sentences could be divided roughly into those that are cognitive (assertions making truth claims) and those that are merely emotive. According to this view, metaphors were classified as emotive utterances that make no truth claims, but serve only to express emotions, attitudes, and moods (cf. Ogden & Richards, 1946, p. 149). This strong empiricist posture effectively eliminated metaphor from serious consideration as a vehicle of knowledge.

THE BIRTH OF A NEW ATTITUDE TOWARD METAPHOR

It is significant that the same positivist orientation that led to the condemnation of metaphor in the first half of this century has, in the last two decades, spawned research that has led to a more favorable assessment of metaphor. Because it held up empirical science as *the* model of cognitive virtue, positivism initially banished metaphor, conceived as a poetic device, to the realm of cognitive insignificance. Within this scientific orientation, however, studies of the nature of scientific language revealed that metaphor plays a far more significant role in science than was previously acknowledged. The first stage of the dawning awareness that metaphors are not cognitively dispensable consisted in the breakdown of the verificationist project of identifying as cognitively meaningful only those sentences entailing some set of literal observation statements. It became readily apparent that individual sentences containing theoretical terms could not be reduced to (translated into) observation sentences (Hempel, 1965). Once philosophers admitted the inadequacies of this overly simplistic positivist picture of language, the way was opened to a more accurate account of the role of nonliteral language in scientific theories.

The second, and current, stage consists of studies of the nature and role of metaphor, model, and paradigm in science. Having constructed the foundation for most recent theories of metaphor, Black (1962) used his analysis of linguistic metaphor to illuminate the working of various kinds of models. Hesse (1963) extended Campbell's (1920) attack on the positivist view that models are no more than dispensable aids to theory formation. Briefly, Hesse argues that models are essential to adequate scientific explanation, which requires "metaphoric redescription of the domain of the explanandum" (p. 249), and that they make possible extensions of a theory that result in increased predictability over a wider range of phenomena. More recent treatments of metaphor and model in science (e.g., Barbour, 1974; MacCormac, 1976) have also suggested that both are essential to adequate explanation and theory construction. Although the debate over the role of metaphor in science continues, it is no longer a foregone conclusion that metaphor is dispensable. Symptomatic of the current atmosphere surrounding discussions of the cognitive significance of metaphor is the remark of so eminent an empiricist as Quine (1978) that, although metaphor "flourishes in playful prose and high poetic art, . . . it is vital also at the growing edges of science and philosophy" (p. 161).

One significant shift in recent thinking about metaphor, then, is the recognition that metaphor plays a cognitively significant role in several disciplines. It is within the context of this more positive view of figurative language that I wish to undertake the two-part task of this paper: first, to survey the chief philosophical problems of metaphor, explaining their relation to each other and summarizing the present state of philosophical discussion on each; second, having identified a fundamental problem in this field, to suggest a way of developing certain recent insights on this issue into a more detailed account of how metaphors achieve their distinctive effects.

THE PROBLEMS OF METAPHOR

The problems of metaphor that have been of interest to philosophers and linguists may be organized under three main areas: (1) What is it? That is, how may metaphor be identified and how does our apprehension of it differ from that of both literal and other non-literal speech? (2) How does it work? Under this heading fall all those questions concerning creativity in language, the distinguishing "mechanism" of metaphor, and the nature of its meaning. (3) What is its cognitive status? Included here are the important questions of its role in various cognitive disciplines and whether it is reducible to literal discourse.

How May Metaphor be Identified?

As Beardsley (1958) has noted, any adequate theory must explain how we distinguish metaphorical from other types of speech. This has seemed a reasonable starting point to many, since an answer to this question would both carve out a domain of discourse and indicate essential components of metaphoric comprehension. In addressing this issue, most linguists have suggested that there must be some syntactic or semantic deviance within a sentence that clues one to the presence of metaphor. Few linguists have held that metaphorical utterances are syntactically deviant (although there is a ground in Chomsky's theory for such a view), because metaphorical utterances may be as syntactically well formed as any other type of linguistic construction. Syntactic deviance is not a sufficient nor even a necessary criterion for identifying metaphor. The more popular approach has been to characterize metaphor "on the competence level in terms of a distinction between semantically deviant and non-deviant sentences" (Matthews, 1971, p. 424). On this account metaphor constitutes a violation of selectional restriction rules within a given context, where the fact of this violation is supposed to explain the semantic tension one experiences in comprehending any live metaphor.

   The problem with this entire approach is that it tries to elevate a condition that occasionally holds (namely, semantic deviance) into a necessary condition of metaphor. As Sanders (1973) has pointed out, it will probably be possible to provide any apparently anomalous sentence that is syntactically well formed with a context in which it is interpretable. Thus, semantic deviance (or violation of selectional restriction rules) cannot be a necessary condition of metaphor, because, as Loewenberg (1975) notes, "(a)ny sentence can be provided contexts . . . in which it can receive either literal or metaphorical interpretations" (p. 322). The allegedly deviant *She was a morsel for a monarch* might involve no anomaly, for example, in a situation where the poor woman was, in fact, a culinary treat for the cannibal king Mobu. Loewenberg correctly concludes that, because there may be no syntactic or semantic deviance at the level of the sentence, an adequate account of metaphor can only be given at the level of the *utterance* taken in its total context. The upshot of this is that "(m)etaphorical utterances are identifiable only if some knowledge possessed by speakers which is decidedly not knowledge of relationships among linguistic symbols can be taken into account" (Loewenberg, 1975, p. 331).

Although Loewenberg is correct in stressing the importance of non-linguistic and extra-sentential context, her attempt to remedy previous deficiencies falls short by assuming that metaphors are identifiable, at least in part, by their literal falsity. The inadequacy of all views resting on this assumption has been demonstrated by Binkley (1974) and Cohen (1976), who note that many metaphors *are not* literally false, so that our apprehension of them as metaphors cannot depend on this feature. The woman in Loewenberg's example may indeed have been a morsel for a voracious monarch, both literally and metaphorically. Instances of what Cohen has felicitously named "twice-true metaphors" are easy to construct, for example, *Idi Amin is an animal; He's a clown; She lives in a glass house.* Presented with such examples, we must call into question every theory that assumes that our identification and comprehension of metaphor depend upon the utterance's being literally false (Beardsley, 1958), or involving some "clash of meaning" (Henle, 1958) or contraindication (Goodman, 1968).

At present, then, no sure criteria for identifying metaphor have been found. It does seem clear that our apprehension of an utterance as metaphorical relies upon our awareness of the total speech situation in which it occurs. We seem to interpret an utterance metaphorically when to do so makes sense of more aspects of the total context than if the sentence is read literally. Consider the simple case of the sentence *All men are animals* as uttered by Professor X to an introductory biology class and as uttered later by one of his female students to her roommate upon returning from a date. In the latter instance the roommate understands the utterance as metaphorical, because to do so makes better sense of the utterance *taken in its total context.* For one thing, the non-literal reading accords with the roommate's knowledge of her friend's intentions in making such a statement.

Thus it appears that an adequate account of the identification and comprehension of metaphor must consider the role of the extra-sentential and even the extra-linguistic context of an utterance. For linguists, of course, this is a dispiriting prospect, for it destroys their project of finding some relatively small number of syntactic and semantic rules governing the interpretation of utterances in any given language. The situation may not be hopeless, however, because even though we probably cannot specify every element in the total speech situation that plays a role in one's apprehension and comprehension of an utterance as metaphorical, it may at least be possible to formalize general rules roughly governing the total speech situation. Grice (1975) has taken the initial steps in this project by trying to "represent a certain subclass of non-conventional implicatures, which I shall call *CONVERSATIONAL* implicatures, as being essentially connected with certain general features of discourse . . ." (p. 45). Whether this approach will bear fruit remains to be seen. For the present, in the absence of any set of identifying marks of metaphor, theorists continue to do what they have always done, namely, to construct their theories upon some set of alleged "clear cases" of metaphor.

How do Metaphors Work?

Although the last decade has witnessed an amazing eruption of literature on metaphor, there have never been more than a couple of basic theories variously elaborated. Basically, there are those which treat metaphor as an elliptical simile, attributing to it no significant cognitive function; and there are those which clearly distinguish simile from metaphor, claiming that the latter plays a cognitive role not open to the former. Every important theory falls under one of these headings. In what has been perhaps the single most influential article on the subject, Black (1954) identified three main theories, two of which are of the same kind.

Substitution view: A metaphor of the "A is B" form (e.g., *Man is a wolf*) is nothing but an indirect way of presenting some intended literal meaning "A is C" (e.g., *Man is fierce*).

Comparison view: A metaphor of the "A is B" form is a means of indirection by which we get at the speaker's intended literal meaning "A *is like* B, in the following respects: . . ." (e.g., *Man is like a wolf, in being . . .*). According to this view, the meaning of the metaphor is a literal set of relevant similarities picked out by the context of the utterance.

While these two standard views (both of which are types of "comparison" theory) explain the intelligibility of a metaphor and reveal part of what occurs in any metaphorical utterance, neither can account for the semantic tension between the two terms of the metaphor. Since both views see metaphor as a roundabout way for getting at the intended (literal) meaning, they tend to treat it as a cosmetic or stylistic device, and they deny that one could really mean what one says in uttering a metaphor. Thus the comparison theory (in either form) tries to circumvent the experienced semantic strain by interpreting metaphor as nothing but a way of comparing two things to see in what respects they are alike. And since any two things are similar in some respects, this kind of theory can never explain what is interesting and important about metaphor.

The other major type of view, developed by Black (1954), insists that his tensive element is fundamental to metaphor, and it sees the metaphorical direct assertion "A is B" as involving a semantic strain which issues in novel meaning and the induction of insight. While not denying the limited truth of the comparison view (namely, that the metaphor "A is B" implies its correlative simile "A is like B"), this theory goes beyond the former to claim a distinctive cognitive function (that the metaphor implies *more* than its correlative simile). To explain this "more" we must turn to this third theory.

Interaction view: In the metaphor "A is B" (e.g., *Man is a wolf*), the "system of associated commonplaces" attaching to A interacts with that which attaches to B to produce emergent metaphorical meaning. The "associated commonplaces" or "related implications" are just those things generally held to be true about the object, person, or event with which they are associated. For instance, "is a mammal," "is a predator," "travels in packs," and so on, might be associated commonplaces of "wolf." The interaction of these two systems of implications results in the selection of appropriate commonplaces of one subject that are then applied, in the same or modified sense, to the other subject-thing. The "interaction" involved here is not merely the intersection of two sets to form some new intersect set; rather, it involves a mutual influence of one *system* of commonplaces upon another.

As stated, this explanation is too vague—its crucial terms need considerable explication and definition. Although Black's theory was at one time the most detailed explanation of the creation and comprehension of metaphor, subsequent critiques of his view indicate the need for an even more detailed account of how metaphors work. Specifically, how does the filtering of one system of implications by another generate novel meaning by giving new senses to elements of each system? Several suggestions have been made as to how metaphors achieve their special effects.

One illuminating, although only partially developed, explanation of the peculiar power of metaphor for inducing insight has been inspired by Wittgenstein's (1953) notion of "seeing as" or perspectival seeing. The ability to see a given visual array first as one thing, then as another (e.g., seeing the duck-rabbit figure first as a duck, then as a rabbit) involves an imaginative activity subject to the will and not identical with an act of mere perception. I *perceive* the formal configuration on the page, but I may imaginatively notice one aspect (the duck) or another (the rabbit). Based upon this notion of visual seeing as, Aldrich (1958) suggests that aesthetic perception is best understood as a type of perspectival seeing and that the artist has a special capacity to embody certain aspects in an artwork. The poet, for instance, exploits imagistic language to reveal aspects of objects previously unnoticed.

A more thorough treatment of seeing as in relation to metaphor is Hester's (1966) explanation of the similarities and differences between visual and metaphorical aspect-seeing. "Metaphorical seeing as is a seeing as between the metaphorical subject and the metaphorical predicate, either one or both of which must be image-exciting" (p. 207). A chief difference between the visual and metaphorical processes is that the former employs images related to physical objects, while the latter "involves imagery associated with the meaning of language" (p. 208), specifically, the meanings of the subject and predicate terms of the metaphor. Another crucial difference is that with visual cases I am given one gestalt (the duck-rabbit configuration of lines) and asked to see two or more aspects, while with metaphor I must perform the reverse imaginative leap of seeing how two things share some common ground or belong together in some fundamental way. Understanding *Man is a worm* for Hester, requires an imaginative grasp of the common gestalt between men and worms, namely, the senses in which men are like worms.

This form of comparison view is too simplistic, because it reduces the act of understanding a metaphor to that of discerning similarities between two things, and it never explains how we know which similarities are relevant and in what sense they apply. Hester's view is valuable only because it draws attention to the "click of comprehension" or flash of insight induced by good metaphors. In this respect he echoes Black's claim that in understanding a metaphor we use one system of implications as a "filter" or "screen" through which we see some other system. This metaphorical screening process highlights certain associated implications, suppresses others, and redefines still others.

Such descriptions of the cognitive activity involved in processing a metaphor are notoriously superficial and seem only to identify an important phenomenon for future extensive investigation. Some philosophers have seen these accounts as indicative of what may be the primary epistemological and ontological significance of metaphor, namely, that it serves as a device for reorganizing our perceptual and/or conceptual structures. There is a ground for such a view in Black's claim that metaphor creates novel meaning by giving modified senses to various concepts. Drawing on Ryle's (1949) notion of a category mistake, Turbayne (1970) argues that metaphor is a form of "sort-crossing" in which objects ordinarily falling under one category are seen as falling under some new category. Interpreting *Man is a worm* forces us to stretch or otherwise alter our normal categorizations. Expanding Turbayne's account, Peckham (1970) describes metaphor as the creation of a novel or emergent category: "We perceive a metaphor as metaphor, therefore, when we encounter words . . . which conventionally do not belong to the same category. A metaphor, then, is an assertion that they do" (p. 405).

Goodman (1968) also sees metaphor as a "calculated category mistake" in which "a term with an extension established by habit is applied elsewhere under the influence of that habit" (p. 71). Thus metaphors involve an alteration of certain categorizations or systems of concepts. While this kind of view has tantalizing philosophical implications, no one has yet worked them out in any extended systematic way, beyond these exploratory accounts of the way metaphor can reorganize old systems of concepts or introduce new concepts.

One of the most promising developments in this direction is Haynes' (1975) extension of the interaction theory by identifying a comparative and an interactive level in the comprehension of metaphor. She explains:

> On the comparative level we are transferring characteristics of Y to X in order to say something about X. On the interactive level, placing known characteristics of Y against those of X may provide *new* insights, either about X or about a new third, Z, an irreducible synthesis by juxtaposition which it is difficult to reduce to simile or to literal language (p. 273).

I have developed an amplified and altered version of Haynes' bilevel distinction in order to penetrate more deeply into the cognitive processes involved in the comprehension of a metaphor. The following sketch of these two aspects provides the foundation for, and is considerably expanded in, the model of cognitive activity presented in the final section of this chapter.

The Canonical (Comparative) Aspect: For every metaphor there is a rule-governed, systematic procedure for spelling out the relevant respects in which *A* is similar to *B* (in the metaphor "A is B"). In other words, every metaphor implies a correlative simile that constitutes its basis in comparison (i.e., its "ground"). *Reason is is a whore* implies *Reason is like a whore*. This is what the comparison theory correctly recognizes, although it prematurely and erroneously concludes that this is *all* there is to metaphor. It is to this comparative ground that we usually refer whenever we wish to justify verbally our use of a certain metaphor. For example, one might defend the utterance *Man is the slave of his passions* by indicating the relevant respects in which the two subject-things are similar.

The Noncanonical (Interactive) Aspect: In addition to the comparative ground of every metaphor, I shall argue that all live metaphors involve a level not governed by rules. This is the level at which one experiences the insight that two entire systems of implications (attached to *A* and *B*) "belong together" in some fundamental way. The cognitive activity at this level cannot be reduced to that of the comparative level, for it consists of the alteration of certain experiential structures (e.g., categorizations, concepts), such that one discovers a formal unity between previously unassociated things. The sense in which there are no rules operative at this level is explained in the final section of this chapter.

What is the Cognitive Status of Metaphor?

Investigation of the way metaphors achieve their effects introduces a cluster of questions concerning whether a metaphor may be reduced to literal discourse without a loss of cognitive content and concerning the proper role of metaphor in various cognitive disciplines. According to the comparison theory, there is nothing unique about metaphor in making truth claims. Since a metaphor is seen as nothing more than an elliptical simile, its truth claims are thought to be none other than those of its literal paraphrase. Any distinctive achievements of metaphor will be limited to its stylistic or didactic advantages (e.g., metaphors are more striking, forceful, or pleasing).

Because they believe that metaphors are indispensable for obtaining certain insights, yet unable to identify truth claims that are not literally expressible, some philosophers have argued that the chief function of metaphorical speech is other than descriptive or cognitive. Borrowing from Austin's (1962/1975) classification of speech acts into those that are constative (i.e., make truth claims) and those several types of speech act that have performative or other nonconstative functions, Warner (1973) claims that metaphor is not primarily a vehicle for conveying information through assertions. Rather, he attributes to metaphor a unique "hortatory" or "suggestive" force, by virtue of which it encourages the reader or hearer to see one thing in terms of another. Loewenberg (1975) also thinks that metaphorical utterances are not principally assertions, and she coins the term "*proposal*$_m$" to cover the special illocutionary force of the metaphorical speech act. According to Loewenberg, one interprets an utterance as metaphorical when one judges "that the speaker was not making a truth claim about a way to view, understand, etc. those referents" (p. 335). Assertions, she thinks, may be true or false; metaphorical proposals are said to have heuristic value only.

Cohen (1975) has suggested a novel and provocative Austinian analysis of a quite different character, which does not deny metaphor a constative function. One of Cohen's main points is that seeing metaphors as analogous to instances of figurative speech acts may help to explain what is involved in our apprehension of a metaphor. This claim is grounded on Austin's (1962/1975) distinction between acts done *in* saying something (illocutions) and acts done *by* saying something (perlocutions). Uttering "I promise to pay you back," for instance, may involve the associated illocution of making a promise plus any of several possible perlocutions, e.g., your accepting my promise, making you happy, getting you off the hook, cementing our friendship, etc. Cohen argues that certain speech acts cannot be performed unless the perlocution associated with each act is possible in the given context. I cannot, for example, perform the illocutionary act of promising, if the situation of my utterance is such that I cannot make a promise. I may utter the words, "I promise to live until 1992," but since this is something I cannot promise, the normal illocution does not go through. Cohen suggests that there may be an analogue to cases of metaphor here. Our identification of an utterance as metaphorical does seem to involve some strain between the normal sense of the utterance and the total speech situation in which it occurs. Cohen summarizes this point:

> The semantic resources of the language yield novel meaning when they are made to collide, either with one another or with other parts of the speech situation. The utterance forces at our disposal yield novel acts when they are somehow askew. I have given some examples in which the force collides with meaning, but I have wished to concentrate more on collision between force and perlocutionary possibility (p. 683).

While Cohen's view is inspired by Austin, it does not, like the others mentioned above, claim that metaphors have no constative function. It is a crucial question whether metaphorical utterances can be used to make assertions, since if they cannot, their importance for cognitive disciplines is highly dubious. In place of a detailed discussion of this issue we may at least identify the four main views on this issue that still have some support:

1. Metaphor has only emotive import.
2. A metaphor does not assert truth claims but may have a heuristic value (e.g., Warner, 1973; Loewenberg, 1975).
3. A metaphorical utterance does make assertions, but its truth value is simply that of its literal paraphrase (comparison view).
4. There are metaphorical truth claims not literally expressible (e.g., Black, 1954, and Haynes, 1975, may hold this view).

At present there is no widespread agreement on this important matter, and it is not possible to mount a sustained argument for one of these views here. A full treatment of this problem would require both a study of the role of metaphor in various cognitive fields and a detailed account of the cognitive process of metaphoric comprehension.

This latter task is the central philosophical problem of metaphor today, for without a model of how we process metaphor there can be no answer to related questions about its epistemological status. In the remainder of this chapter, therefore, I should like to address this focal issue by contributing a more detailed account of the way metaphors work, drawing out the implications of this model for the cognitive status of metaphor.

According to the view I shall develop, while a literal paraphrase might give the truth claims arising from the canonical (comparative) level of metaphor, that paraphrase will never express the truth claims issuing from the interactive level. It cannot induce the insight that comes from the complex intellectual operation involved in seeing both *that* and *how* the two systems of implications can be unified in the metaphor. I shall argue that there is no mechanical (rule-governed) way for extracting a metaphor's meaning, that is, there are no syntactic or semantic rules by which to move from the literal meanings of the constituent words to the meaning of the metaphor. Yet there is a truth claim issuing at this level (namely, the metaphor itself), based upon the restructuring of certain modes of experience or organizing principles of knowledge. To explain and justify these claims, I shall draw upon Kant's account of the two types of reflective judgment as models for understanding what I have called the two levels of metaphor.

A MODEL OF METAPHORIC COMPREHENSION

Kant's Treatment of Reflective Judgment

Kant's primary philosophical commitment from about 1770 until his death in 1804 was the development of his "Critical Philosophy," in which he set out to investigate the *nature* and *limits* of human reason. The various works that constitute his major achievements in this project characteristically select one kind of mental activity, characterize the judgments (as products) produced thereby, and then investigate the mental processes that must be involved in producing the judgment in question, if it is to have the character so described. Thus, each of the major works of his critical period focuses upon one or more types of judgment, for example, propositions within science, moral precepts, judgments of natural and artistic beauty, and judgments of mere sensuous pleasure. Each step of Kant's project, therefore, contributes to a larger picture of the many ways the human subject can stand in relation to its objects.

When Kant set forth the epistemological foundations of his Critical Philosophy in the *Critique of Pure Reason* (1781), he seems to have recognized but one type of judgment, *determinate* (or logical) judgment, resulting in empirical knowledge. Briefly, a judgment is an act by which various representations are unified by (brought under) a more general representation (a concept). A concept is a rule by which the manifold or field of perceptual representations is structured in a determinate way, resulting in "empirical cognition" (knowledge of an object). The representations that are unified in an act of judgment may be elements of some perceptual field or even concepts themselves, but in either case the combination of the representations is always achieved under the guidance of some more general concept. As an instance of determinate judgment we may take, "All whales are mammals," in which the concept of being a mammal applies to the concept "whale," which, in turn, applies to various appearances that present themselves to our senses. In Kantian terms, in a determinate judgment a manifold of representations is synthesized (unified) by the faculty of imagination and brought under concepts supplied by the faculty of understanding.

By the time Kant laid out his theory of beauty in the *Critique of Judgment* (1790), he recognized a second major kind of judgment that involves imaginative reflection upon the formal structure of a manifold (or field) of representations. These "reflective" judgments do not, strictly speaking, constitute acts of knowledge, since they do not involve the determinate structuring of the manifold of representations according to a concept. Reflection is an act of reason in which my mind imaginatively "plays over" various representations in search of possible ways that they might be organized, although this process is free of the control of the understanding (= faculty that supplies concepts). What thus distinguishes a reflective from a logical judgment resulting in empirical knowledge is that, while it involves reflection on a particular in search of various universals under which it might properly fall, it does not actually produce the subsumption of a particular under some determinate concept. For example, given a particular "form of nature" (e.g., a genus or species), one may seek to bring it into a systematic whole with other such forms by reflecting upon various possible syntheses of the given manifold. To cite a specific instance, there is nothing in my knowledge of the characteristics of the species to which my dog Zobie belongs that guarantees that this species will, along with other species, unite under some genus. But by reflecting on the nature of these different species, I may be able to find an appropriate genus under which they all fall.

I want to suggest that the cognitive activity of metaphoric comprehension involves a form of this reflective process described by Kant. To relate his account to metaphor we need to examine the two types of reflective judgment, teleological and aesthetical, which he identifies. In a *teleological* reflective judgment we assume that various forms of nature (as given particulars) can be brought into a systematic heirarchy, even though there is no objective ground (that is, no properties of the object) justifying this unity. This means that in making a teleological judgment we view nature as if it were organized according to purposes, and this assumption guides our reflective attempt to organize a field of representations. But because there is nothing about an object of experience that requires that every form of nature should fit into a systematic heirarchy of empirical laws, there can be no basis in the properties of the object (hence, no objective ground) for the purposiveness of nature. The teleological judgment must, therefore, presuppose this principle that all our experience forms a system, as a "law from and to itself," and it then seeks out the requisite universal for the given particular.

Translated into scientific practice, this means that we treat nature *as art* (as the product of a rational intelligence) and, therefore, as purposive. We then search for the concepts constituting part of this presupposed systematic unity of experience. The dog example above is an instance of this type of judgment. Kant claims that these teleological judgments are cognitive, because they supply concepts that, in retrospect, are seen to help unify our experience. He insists, however, that they are not determinate judgments, since the concepts they produce are not grounded in the object, that is, are not based on properties of the objects reflected upon, but are supplied by a reflective principle of judgment.

I want to suggest that the mental activity involved at the canonical level of metaphor is strikingly similar to that involved in teleological judgment, in the following way: Based upon the assumption of a purposive unity of experience, the teleological judgment involves reflection upon a manifold in search of a concept (universal) that unifies it. Although there are no rules for discovering the desired concept, once it is found we can justify its adequacy and use it to derive further knowledge. Similarly, there are no rules for creating apt metaphors, but, once formulated, their aptness can be partially shown by spelling out the relevant likenesses between the two subject-things. This is what is meant by justifying our use of a metaphor ex post facto by referring to the canonical or comparative aspect (that is, the ground of the metaphor), even though the act of creative insight that produced the metaphor may not have depended on the recognition of these similarities at this explicit level.

This imaginative act that generates a metaphor brings us to the noncanonical level, which exhibits distinctive parallels with Kant's *aesthetical* reflective judgment. Judgments of this aesthetical kind are distinguished from those of the teleological kind, because they involve no reference to any concept but only to the judging subject's *feeling* concerning whether the act of reflection is somehow adequate to its object. Kant says (1790) that a reflective judgment is *aesthetical* when it refers some representation ''not by the understanding to the object for cognition, but by the imagination (perhaps in conjunction with the understanding) to the subject and its feeling of pleasure and pain'' (§1, p. 37). This ''pleasure'' that is the ground of an aesthetical judgment is just my consciousness that my reflective-imaginative activity somehow satisfies (is adequate to) rational standards of my understanding even though my reflective process was not guided by any rules (= concepts).

Kant divides aesthetical judgments into judgments of *sense* expressible as ''This X is agreeable or pleasant (to my senses),'' and judgments of *taste* expressed by the form ''This X is beautiful.'' Although both types of aesthetical judgment are based upon feeling, in judgments of sense some object gratifies me by producing pleasure (or pain) in affecting my senses, while in judgments of taste I experience pleasure or pain merely by reflecting on the *form* of some representation of an object. In other words, judgments of beauty are based upon the pleasure I feel as my imagination ''plays over'' the form of some representation in a *free* activity; that is, one not controlled by concepts (rules) of the understanding.

In describing the noncanonical level of metaphoric comprehension, it is judgments of taste that provide the relevant model. Kant thought that judgments of taste did not constitute knowledge, because they are not based upon subsuming a manifold under some determinate concept, that is, they do not synthesize it according to some specific rule of the understanding. Instead, the act of reflection is a free ''play'' of the imagination and understanding without the guidance of any fixed concepts applicable to the object being contemplated.

Whenever, in reflecting on the formal aspects of a perceptual field, my understanding and imagination harmonize, even though they are not forced into agreement by a rule supplied by the understanding, then I feel a pleasure in the form of the contemplated object, and I judge it to be beautiful. A similar process occurs in processing a metaphor. A metaphor asserts a formal unity between two particulars (individuals, classes, universals), yet the ground of this unity goes beyond any objective similarities between the two subject-things. Since the metaphor asserts more than that the two things are merely alike, our discovery *that* and *how* the two subject-things belong together cannot be determined from these objective likenesses alone. Rather, an act of reflection is required that results in a new way of organizing our experience. Here imagination functions in what Kant calls (1787/1968, B151, p. 164) its *productive* mode, when it spontaneously creates what is not present to sense. The use of metaphor in psychotherapy illustrates this view. If, for example, a young man in therapy can see not only that he is like his mother, but that he *is* his own mother, his entire interpretation of his experiences may be suddenly altered, as he receives a new set of categories, concepts, and experiential structures.

In terms of this analysis, it is the "free" or non-rule-governed reflective process that best characterizes the noncanonical aspect of metaphoric comprehension. That is, a metaphor may provide an organization of experience not anticipated by any set of fixed concepts one may possess. In this way an apt metaphor gives to experience a new structure not entirely explicable in terms of the similarities present at the canonical level. Since we organize our experience by means of concepts (combined into conceptual systems), the imaginative alteration of a concept or category reveals a new aspect of experience. It is this particular achievement of metaphor that has inspired the previously mentioned treatments of metaphor as a type of "seeing as." We may sum up by saying that metaphors are grounded in the likenesses between the subject-things revealed at the canonical level, and yet they establish novel relations and structures through their distinctive noncanonical activity.

Metaphoric comprehension is thus a blend of canonical and noncanonical processes having distinctive cognitive effects. Philosophers have traditionally refused to acknowledge the cognitive import of the noncanonical level, on the basis that where there are no definite concepts there can be no knowledge. They would insist that neither metaphors, nor the judgments of taste to which I am comparing them, can properly be treated as cognitively significant. I believe that this is a mistake stemming from an unrealistically narrow view of cognitive significance. To see why this might be so, we may consider metaphor in the light of Peirce's (1931–1958) description of an abductive inference, whereby we formulate a hypothesis believed to explain or unify a set of observed effects. Peirce describes the process of abduction as follows:

> The abductive suggestion comes to us like a flash. It is an act of *insight,* although of extremely fallible insight. It is true that the different elements of the hypothesis were in our minds before; but it is the idea of putting together what we had never before dreamed of putting together which flashes the new suggestion before our contemplation (Vol. 5, 180).

The imaginative interplay at the noncanonical level does, in fact, issue in a hypothesis of sorts (= the metaphor itself), which flashes before the mind. Peirce spoke of a "logic" of abduction, although he held that there could be no mechanical procedure for framing hypotheses. Yet he believed in a fundamental rationality behind the entire process, for only on this assumption could he explain his belief in the progress of science, that is, that "inquiry indefinitely prolonged" will converge on the true description of reality. Both Peirce and Kant, then, claimed a rationality for these respective cognitive acts, but neither man thought that there could be articulable rules governing them. It is this rationality without explicit rules that characterizes judgments of taste and the noncanonical aspect of metaphor and upon which the cognitive import of the latter is based.

Metaphor as a Product of Genius

To explain what is meant by a rationality (cognitivity) without rules, it is helpful to consider Kant's account of genius, for it focuses upon the act of insight tied up with the creation of a work of art, of which metaphor is an instance. Because judgments of taste directed toward artworks involve no consciously followed rules, Kant concludes that the creative act from which these works result must not be rule-governed. He thus defines genius, the talent for producing beautiful art, as "the exemplary originality of the natural gifts of a subject in the *free* employment of his cognitive faculties" (1790/1968, §49, p. 161). For our purposes the relevant point about products of genius is that, as *art,* they must conform to some rules (since the artist intends to produce some kind of object); yet beautiful art is not the result of specifiable rules, because there is no determinate concept for its ground. Thus genius generates a creative (free) imaginative activity, which can never be mechanically produced, although it somehow conforms to rational standards. Cohen (1975) has noted the relevance of Kant's account of genius to metaphor in describing metaphor as "the language's intrinsic capacity to surpass its own (putative) limits. It is the abiding device for saying something truly new—but something curiously new, for it is made out of already existing meaning" (p. 671). So understood, metaphor does seem to be what Kant called a product of genius, where genius is "the capacity to produce things which are 'original,' and hence things which cannot be made sense of by means of any rules of explication, but which nevertheless do make sense" (p. 671, n. 2).

Seeing metaphor as a product of genius, in this Kantian sense, illuminates the sense in which the noncanonical level involves a rational insight that is, at the same time, original, that is, not a mere elaboration upon concepts. It seems reasonable to hold that some sort of genius is required for the production of an apt metaphor, if we can conceive of metaphor as a miniature artwork. Aristotle may have seen this when he claimed that the creation of good metaphors "is the one thing that cannot be learnt from others; and it is a sign of genius, since a good metaphor implies an intuitive perception of the similarity in dissimilars" (*Poetics*, 1459a). In speaking of metaphor in this way, it is important not to entertain too exalted a concept of genius, such as the romantic poets held, but rather to define it more modestly as a capacity for originality.

The way Kant's account of genius and its products bears on metaphor can be seen more clearly in his definition of genius as the capacity for producing aesthetical ideas. By "aesthetical idea" he means

that representation of the imagination which occasions much thought, without however any definite thought, i.e., any *concept,* being capable of being adequate to it; it consequently cannot be completely compassed and made intelligible by language (1790, §49, p. 157).

The pregnancy of a metaphor is like the richness of an aesthetical idea, in which the creative, free interplay of the cognitive faculties involves *more* thought than can be subsumed under some concept. Indeed, we might say that in the creation of a metaphor the imagination presents "such a multiplicity of partial representations in its free employment that for it no expression marking a definite concept can be found" (1790, §49, p. 160); that is, there can be no adequate literal expressive mechanism.

Genius, according to Kant, manifests itself through spirit (*Geist*), the animating principle of the mind that calls the cognitive faculties into play in the creation of beautiful art. Spirit involves imagination in its productive capacity of "creating another nature, as it were, out of the material that actual nature gives it" (1790, §49, p. 157). Spirit is thus the principle of the mind that makes originality possible, for, as Kant says,

> to express the ineffable element in the state of mind implied by a certain representation and to make it universally communicable—whether the expression be in speech or painting or statuary—this requires a faculty of seizing the quickly passing play of imagination and unifying it in a concept (which is even on that account original and discloses a new rule that could not have been inferred from any preceding principles or examples) that can be communicated without any constraint of rules (1790, §49, p. 161).

Analogously, I have claimed that the creation of new meaning and novel insight in a metaphor cannot be mechanically generated from preceding rules or meanings, for it is a cognitive act of originality, by which we alter our way of structuring reality. Yet the metaphor *does* "make sense," in being comprehensible, in two fundamental ways. First, it manifests some underlying or latent rational structure similar to those revealed by teleological judgment. Second, the metaphor makes (that is, creates) sense by a novel projective act resulting in new significance. It is this latter semantic achievement that has led many to see metaphor as the central device for extending language and, through it, the bounds of sense.

This second way in which metaphors "make sense" is the best account I can give of Black's claim that with instances of potent metaphor "it would be more illuminating . . . to say that the metaphor *creates* the similarity than to say that it formulates some similarity antecedently existing" (Black, 1954, pp. 284–85). This is what I have meant by "rationality (cognitivity) without rules," as it applies to metaphor. This kind of rationality at the noncanonical level would have to be grounded in those subjective conditions "which we can presuppose in all men (as requisite for possible cognition in general)" (Kant, 1790, §38, p.

132). These are the conditions of the employment of judgment in general, which Kant sees as the basis of the universal communicability of the mental state in a judgment of taste. So, while this "rationality" is not that of determinate judgment, yet it is logically prior to it and is manifested in our capacity for comprehending products of genius.

Kant ties together most of the points I have been making and comes closest to relating metaphor to the presentation of aesthetical ideas in a long passage that begins,

> If now we place under a concept a representation of the imagination belonging to its presentation, but which occasions in itself more thought than can ever be comprehended in a definite concept and which consequently aesthetically enlarges the concept itself in an unbounded fashion, the imagination is here creative, and it brings the faculty of intellectual ideas (the reason) into movement; i.e., by a representation more thought (which indeed belongs to the concept of the object) is occasioned than can in it be grasped or made clear.
>
> Those forms which do not constitute the presentation of a given concept itself but only, as approximate representations of the imagination, express the consequences bound up with it and its relationship to other concepts, are called (aesthetical) *attributes* of an object whose concept as a rational idea cannot be adequately presented (1790, §49, p. 158).

By an "aesthetical attribute" Kant seems to have in mind a symbol rather than a metaphor, when he gives the example of Jupiter's eagle with lightning in its claws as an attribute of Jupiter himself. But this symbol, Jupiter's eagle, is actually a visual metaphor, described as an aesthetical attribute that supplies us with aesthetical ideas. Kant then proceeds immediately to apply this account to a poetic passage, in which a serene evening at the close of a beautiful day serves as an aesthetical attribute for the proper disposition at the end of one's life. He also cites the line, "The sun arose/ As calm from virtue springs" and claims that the intellectual concept "virtue" is here an aesthetical attribute for a sunrise. The important point is that both of these examples are alleged illustrations of the presentation of an aesthetical idea through metaphor (or simile), and in both cases Kant asserts that the aesthetical ideas generate more thought than can be brought under a determinate concept and expressed in literal language.

Kant also treats metaphor under his discussion of *hypotyposis* (literally, to bring under a type), or presentation of a concept, in its symbolical mode (1790, §59). Briefly, he argues that symbols provide an indirect presentation of a concept that has no direct (intuitive) presentation, in the following way: A symbol presents a concept indirectly on the basis of an analogical activity where the judgment (1) applies a concept to some object and (2) uses the "rules of reflection" for this first object as a means for reflecting on the nature of the symbolized object. This transference of reflection is a process similar to that described by Black (1954) as the filtering or screening process by which the primary subject of a metaphor is conceived through the secondary subject. Beyond this suggestion of the analogical basis for metaphor, Kant's discussion of hypotyposis adds little of interest to our understanding of metaphor's capacity for creating new meaning.

CONCLUSION: A SUGGESTION FOR FUTURE RESEARCH

I have drawn upon Kant's account of reflective judgment, genius, and aesthetical ideas to illuminate the distinctive nature of the intellectual operation required for the creation and comprehension of a potent metaphor. I have used Kant's descriptions of teleological and aesthetical reflective judgments as models of the canonical and noncanonical processes of metaphor. The resultant account is sketchy, but it suggests how it might be argued that some metaphors cannot be reduced to literal discourse without a loss of cognitive content. The crux of my explanation is the identification of the noncanonical level involving a rationality without rules. In other words, taken as products of genius, metaphors generate novel structurings of our experience in a way not fully anticipated by our available systems of concepts. Concepts are the rules by which we organize experience. To the extent that a metaphor alters a concept or system of concepts it is not itself governed by pre-existent rules; nevertheless, the new metaphor provides a basis for elaborating new concepts (or relations of concepts), and its adequacy may be judged at least partially by how well it "fits in with" these concepts already articulated.

The obvious objection to a view of the kind sketched here can be drawn from Kant himself, who rigorously maintains that aesthetical reflective judgments of taste are *not* cognitive and, therefore, cannot constitute knowledge. The ground of this objection is simple enough: only judgments that apply a concept to a manifold of representations can give us knowledge.

While I have no objection to preserving Kant's restriction of the term "knowledge" to the application of fixed concepts to sensuous intuition, I suggest broadening Kant's conception of cognitive significance to include reflective activity not reducible to empirical knowledge. Metaphors lead us to experience the world in novel ways. By causing a reorganization of our conceptual frameworks they institute new meaning. These foundational acts of insight are tied to truth claims because they alter the systems of fixed concepts with which we make truth claims.

So understood, metaphors may be seen as grounding the concepts that we then use to speak determinately of objects. The primary role of metaphor is thus to establish those structures we *later* articulate by means of fixed, determinate concepts (and systems of concepts). In poetry, for example, we are hardly ever tempted to try to squeeze out a set of true statements, as though that were the essence of the poem; rather, a poem makes us see the world in a new way, one not readily expressible by means of our available stock of concepts. In uses of metaphor outside poetry, too, there is more to cognitive significance than truth-functional sense, namely, there is the meaning of things prior to their objectification according to various systems of concepts.

Based upon the above survey of the central problems of metaphor, I believe that the most pressing concern in this area is to develop richer views of cognitivity coupled with a more detailed account of the way metaphor works, that is, of its "mechanism." As long as cognitivity is thought to be tied solely to determinate concepts, then metaphors will be condemned as dangerous frills wholly to be avoided, as Locke so harshly insisted, in any serious pursuit of truth. If metaphors are, on the other hand, indispensable for certain cognitive functions, this will only be acknowledged and explained as we develop a fuller understanding of human cognitive processes.

REFERENCES

Aldrich, V. Pictorial meaning, picture-thinking, and Wittgenstein's theory of aspects. *Mind*, 1958, *62*, 70–79.

Aristotle, *Poetics*. (Translated by Ingram Bywater.) Oxford:Oxford University Press, 1909.

Austin, J. L. *How to do things with words*. (2nd ed.) Cambridge, Mass.: Harvard University Press, 1975.

Barbour, I. *Myths, models, and paradigms*. New York: Harper and Row, 1974.

Beardsley, M. C. *Aesthetics: problems in the philosophy of criticism*. New York: Harcourt, Brace, 1958.

Berggren, D. The use and abuse of metaphor. *The Review of Metaphysics*, 1962–63, *16*, Nos. 2, 3, 237–258; 450–472.

Binkley, T. On the truth and probity of metaphor. *Journal of Aesthetics and Art Criticism*, 1974, *33*, 171–180.

Black, M. Metaphor. *Proceedings of the Aristotelian Society*, 1954–55, N.S. *55*, 273–294.

Black, M. *Models and metaphors*. Ithaca, N.Y.: Cornell University Press, 1962.

Campbell, N. R. *Physics, the elements*. Cambridge, England: Cambridge University Press, 1920.

Cohen, T. Figurative speech and figurative acts. *Journal of Philosophy*, 1975, *72*, 669–684.

Cohen, T. Notes on metaphor. *Journal of Aesthetics and Art Criticism*, 1976, *34*, 249–259.

Goodman, N. *Languages of art*. Indianapolis: Bobbs-Merrill. 1968.

Grice, H. P. Logic and conversation. In P. Cole & J. L. Morgan (Eds.), *Syntax and semantics* (vol. 3): *Speech acts*. New York: Academic Press, 1975.

Haynes, F. Metaphor as interactive. *Educational Theory*, 1975, *25*, 272–277.

Hempel, C. Empiricist criteria of cognitive significance: problems and changes. *Aspects of scientific explanation*. New York: Free Press, 1965, 101–119.

Henle, P. Metaphor. *Language, thought, and culture*. Ann Arbor: University of Michigan Press, 1958.

Hesse, M. B. *Models and analogies in science*. London, 1963.

Hester, M. Metaphor and Aspect Seeing. *Journal of Aesthetics and Art Criticism*, 1966, *25*, 205–212.

Kant, I. *Critique of Judgment*. (Translated by J. H. Bernard.) New York: Hafner, 1968. (Originally published, 1790).

Kant, I. *Critique of pure reason* (Translated by Norman Kemp Smith.) New York: St. Martin's, 1968. (Originally published 1781, 1st ed.; 1787, 2nd ed.)

Locke, J. *An Essay concerning human understanding.* (A. C. Fraser, Ed.) New York: Dover, 1959. (Originally published, 1706, 5th ed.)

Loewenberg, I. Identifying metaphors. *Foundations of Language*, 1975, *12*, 315–338.

MacCormac, E. *Metaphor and myth in science and religion.* Durham, N.C.: Duke University Press, 1976.

Matthews, R. Concerning a 'linguistic theory' of metaphor. *Foundations of Language*, 1971, *7*, 413–425.

Ogden, C. K. & Richards, I. A. *The meaning of meaning.* New York: Harcourt, Brace, 1946, 8th ed.

Peckham, M. Metaphor: a little plain speaking on a weary subject. *The triumph of romanticism.* Columbia, S.C.: University of South Carolina Press, 1970.

Peirce, C. S. *The collected papers of C. S. Peirce.* C. Hartshorne & P. Weiss (Eds.). 8 vols. Cambridge, Mass.: Harvard University Press, 1931–1958.

Plato. *Phaedrus.* (Translated by Hackforth.) Cambridge, England: Cambridge University Press, 1952.

Plato. *Republic,* (Translated by A. Bloom.) New York: Basic Books, 1968.

Quine, W. V. A postscript on metaphor. *Critical Inquiry,* 1978, *5*, 161–162.

Ryle, G. *The concept of mind.* London: Hutchinson's University Library, 1949.

Sanders, R. Aspects of figurative language. *Linguistics,* 1973, No. 96.

Turbayne, C. *The myth of metaphor.* Columbia, S.C.: University of South Carolina Press, 1970.

Warner, M. Black's metaphors. *British Journal of Aesthetics,* 1973, *12*, 367–372.

Wittgenstein, L. *Philosophical Investigations.* Translated by G. E. M. Anscombe. Oxford: Basil Blackwell, 1953.

4 Some Psycholinguistic Aspects of Metaphor

Andrew Ortony
University of Illinois at Urbana-Champaign

In this chapter I attempt to do three things. First, in view of the variety of implicit and explicit definitions of metaphor in the philosophical, psychological, and linguistic literature, I shall review the "standard" definition of metaphor. Second, I will attempt to furnish an alternative definition of metaphor that seems to accord better with the facts. Finally, I will discuss various issues related to the processes involved in the comprehension of metaphors. Along the way I shall make a few observations about the relationship between metaphors and meaning.

METAPHOR: THE STANDARD DEFINITION

The standard dictionary definition is that a metaphor is a word or phrase applied to an object or concept that it does not literally denote in order to suggest comparison with another object or concept. Assuming that it is possible to determine a satisfactory criterion for "literal denotation," this definition is, no doubt, adequate for the purposes of lexicographers. But, as we shall see, it is not adequate for the purposes of psychologists or theoretical linguists. The cognitive psychologist might be concerned with when and why people use metaphors, and when and how they understand them. The psychologist is concerned with the processes presumed to underlie their use and comprehension, and how, if at all, these processes differ from and are related to those involved in literal uses of language. The linguist might be concerned with the formal properties of metaphors and the semantic and pragmatic relations that they have to their literal counterparts. The linguist might also be interested in syntactic relations as they

69

pertain to certain kinds of figurative language. *None* of these interests is well served by the standard dictionary definition.

The standard dictionary definition of metaphor seems to underlie many of the discussions provided by those working in the various disciplines concerned with it. For example, to the extent that metaphor has received serious consideration in linguistics, theoreticians have tended to try to account for it in terms of selection restriction violations. A good example of such an approach can be found in Matthews (1971), who makes two claims of particular interest. One is that the presence of a selection restriction violation is "a necessary and sufficient condition for the distinguishing of metaphor from non-metaphor." The second is that the effect of such a violation is to "de-emphasize the features which figure in [it] as well as those other features most closely associated with it" (p. 424). Within the limiting machinery of selection restrictions Matthews makes a reasonable case for his conclusions. The root of the problem lies in his uncritical acceptance of a theory of semantic features and all that is implied by it. The shortcomings of the feature approach to semantics have been discussed at length both in linguistics and psychology, and Matthews himself admits that semantic features are not assumed to be either psychologically or physically real. But even if one were willing to accept feature theory and the gratuitous ad hoc features that it entails, still there would be two grave difficulties to overcome. First, one would be unable to account for a whole class of metaphors in this way. Second, one would in any case be able to say little more than that some metaphors are not literally acceptable because of some particular selection restriction violation. It should be noted that Matthews does try to deal with these problems.

The class of metaphors that I claim cannot be handled is comprised of what can be called "whole sentence" metaphors (see, Ortony, Reynolds & Arter, 1978). Whole sentence metaphors are perfectly well-formed sentences that involve no selection restriction violations. They are sentences that demand a metaphorical interpretation in some contexts, and a literal interpretation in others. Taking an example from Reddy (1969), Matthews argues that (1) is not a metaphor even though uttered about a decrepit professor emeritus.

(1)   the old rock is becoming brittle with age

He argues that underlying (1) is a "real" metaphor, (2).

(2)   the old professor emeritus is a rock.

But this seems to beg the question. Clearly, if (1) is uttered in the appropriate context it cannot be interpreted literally in any intelligible way, so there is no basis for arguing that in such a context (1) is not a metaphor. It is true that it may imply or presuppose other metaphors such as (2), but that is not a sufficient reason for denying that (1) is, or at least can be, a metaphor.

The second problem concerns some of the consequences of the view that the violation of a selection restriction is a necessary and sufficient condition for something's being a metaphor. If this is the case there would seem to be no way to distinguish metaphor from semantic anomaly or falsehood. Matthews' answer to this is to assert that it is merely a question of speaker intention—the speaker must intend to use language metaphorically. But, linguistic communication involves not only a speaker but a hearer. It normally requires that a hearer recognize the speaker's intentions, and that the speaker speaks on the basis of certain expectations about such recognition. The problem with locating certain kinds of speech acts only in the speaker's intentions to perform them is that it renders those speech acts essentially private rather than public acts. Thus, suppose that Matthews's account were accepted. Then, from the point of view of a hearer, who might assume that speakers do not normally intend to speak falsely, what is to be concluded from an utterance that is false and that violates a selection restriction? Why should the hearer not conclude that since the speaker could not have intended to speak falsely, he or she must have intended to speak metaphorically? Yet, surely it does not follow from the fact that people rarely intend to utter falsehoods that if someone does inadvertently say something that is false and that also involves a selection restriction violation, that the hearer *ipso facto* attributes to him or her the intention of speaking metaphorically. One who utters (3) is not likely to be speaking metaphorically,

(3)   Sierra Leone is the largest city in Italy

nor, as a rule, is he or she regarded as so speaking. This is not to say that (3) could not possibly be uttered or understood metaphorically, rather it is to say that the fact that it is false and involves a selection restriction violation does not license the inference that someone who uses it is speaking metaphorically. Matthews argues that the selection restriction violation must be from the speaker's point of view, but this places metaphor essentially in the mind of the speaker, and without the introduction of some kind of pragmatic analysis, there it has to stay.

I have concentrated on Matthews's treatment of metaphor not because I think it is bad—in fact, within the limitations of the theoretical framework from which he starts, I think it is probably as good as one can get—but because it seems to capture so well the essential ingredients of the standard dictionary definition approach. For Matthews, like the dictionary, metaphors operate exclusively at the lexical level, and for Matthews they involve violations of selection restrictions, which is a more technical way of saying what the dictionary says, namely that the word or phrase is applied to an object or concept it does not literally denote.

Generally speaking, psychological models of language comprehension have not concerned themselves with metaphor. Perhaps the most notable exception is Kintsch (1974), who acknowledges the importance of accounting for the comprehension of metaphor for any theory to be adequate. While sharing the general dissatisfaction with a feature theoretic account that has been mentioned above,

Kintsch nevertheless appears to substantially accept Matthews' account. Rejecting the notion of selection restriction violations, he replaces it with that of semantic anomaly, and maintains that semantic anomaly is a necessary condition for metaphor.

I have suggested that not all metaphors are semantically anomalous. Consider, for example, (4), a perfectly normal English sentence. Certainly, it is not semantically anomalous.

(4)   Regardless of the danger, the troops marched on

What determines whether (4) is a metaphor or not is the context in which it is used. In the context of an army marching to battle it is not likely to function as a metaphor, but in other contexts, such as (5), it is.

(5)   The children continued to annoy their babysitter. She told the little boys she would not tolerate any more bad behavior. Climbing all over the furniture was not allowed. She threatened to not let them watch TV if they continued to stomp, run, and scream around the room. Regardless of the danger, the troops marched on.

Here, the entire sentence, (4), is a metaphor. Contrary to the standard dictionary definition we have been reviewing, it is not really a case of a word or phrase being applied to an object it does not literally denote, because *none* of the substantive words literally denote their usual objects or concepts. Not watching TV, or the possibility of it, hardly constitutes a danger, there are no real troops, and there is no real marching. It is the whole sentence that is metaphorical, not a word or phrase within it. It is counterintuitive to insist that (4) is not a metaphor. To do so would be to base a judgment on an inadequate characterization of what a metaphor is.

One of the most well-known linguistic treatments of metaphor, and one that avoids some of the problems of the accounts discussed so far, is that due to Reddy (1969). Although he argues that metaphors occur when the normal limits of the referentiality of words are contravened, he is anxious to provide an account that does not exclude metaphorical uses of semantically well-formed sentences. However, things start to go wrong when he tries to characterize the meaning of a metaphor. He says:

> the 'meaning' of the utterance is primarily *whatever is implied by the fact that something was expressed in this curious and unconventional fashion.* The symbolic connection of precise referents is less a bearer of information than the fact that the speaker chose such and such a word in such and such a context (p. 249).

Now, whatever the meaning of a metaphorical utterance is, it cannot be what Reddy says it is. Perhaps the only thing implied by a speaker's "curious and unconventional" choice of words is that the speaker was unable to express his intentions in any other way. One would hardly suppose, however, that the *meaning* of (4) in a context like (5) was the speaker's inability to express himself otherwise. On the other hand, it does seem to suppose that a hearer's *recognition* of the curious choice of words may sometimes justify, or even trigger a nonliteral interpretation of them. Furthermore, it probably is the case that the metaphorical meaning of an utterance such as (4), is indeed related to certain implications of it, albeit not those that Reddy has in mind.

I would argue that the metaphorical meaning of a whole-sentence metaphor like (4) in a context such as (5) has to be related to those salient components of its literal meaning that do not conflict with the context, and some of these are implications of the literal meaning. For example, one of the implications of the literal meaning of (4) is that a group of people continued doing what they were already doing without concern for the consequences. Another is that the probable consequences were undesirable, another that the people were aware of this, but stubbornly unconcerned, and so on.

The utilization, in comprehension, of those salient aspects of literal meaning that do not conflict with the context, is consistent with the account of the comprehension of part-sentence metaphors that I have proposed elsewhere (Ortony, 1975; 1979a; 1979b). All metaphors give rise to what is usually called metaphorical *tension,* which is a result of the conceptual incompatibility inherent in a metaphor taken in its context. The comprehension of the metaphor requires the elimination of the tension, that is, the elimination of aspects of the meaning of words, phrases or sentences that when interpreted literally give rise to tension.

METAPHOR: AN ALTERNATIVE DEFINITION

Having found the standard account wanting, the question arises as to whether or not a superior, alternative account can be offered. What I propose to do now is to try to offer such an account. A first requirement for something to be a metaphor is that it should be pragmatically, or perhaps better, *contextually* anomalous. This means that a literal interpretation of the expression, be it a word, phrase, sentence, or an even larger unit of text, fails to fit the context. The virtue of this requirement is that it permits the classification of one and the same expression as being a metaphor in some cases and not in others. A corollary is that *it is not linguistic expressions themselves that are metaphors, but particular uses of them.* Thus, whether or not (4) is a metaphor depends upon the context in which it is used; and, as we have seen, this is as it should be. The contextual anomaly condition also permits the inclusion of sentences like (6),

(6)   The boy dived into the crowd.

since insofar as it expresses something that is literally impossible, there can be no normal context in which it will fit unless it is interpreted metaphorically. There may, however, be "abnormal" or magical contexts that will support a literal interpretation of such part-sentence metaphors, and to the extent that there are, tokens of such expressions will not be metaphors. Alice in Wonderland is full of superficially anomalous sentences that can be interpreted literally because of the bizarreness of the contexts in which they occur.

The general point that needs to be emphasized here is that *if* something is a metaphor then it will be contextually anomalous if interpreted literally (except in rare cases of ambiguous expressions wherein one reading makes sense literally and the other metaphorically, in which case the generalization is still true of the latter reading). Insofar as the violation of selection restrictions can be interpreted in terms of semantic incompatibilities at the lexical level, such violations may sometimes be the basis of the contextual anomaly. But there can be other reasons too, so that selection restriction violations, or, to use the theoretically more neutral description, lexical level semantic incompatibilities, are not the only causes of contextual anomaly. Furthermore, it seems that the distinction between the literal and the metaphorical is one of degree with there being many difficult borderline cases. If (6) is uttered in the context of a boy running into a crowd of people it seems to be more metaphorical than if it is uttered in the context of a suicidal leap from a tall building. In the latter case its status is much more difficult to determine—particularly with an arms-extended, head first leap.

While the contextual anomaly requirement appears to be necessary, it is not sufficient for the characterization of a metaphor. If taken alone it suffers from one of the shortcomings of the standard definition just criticized. It is important to exclude from the class of metaphors, genuine, unresolvable contextual anomalies. Such expressions are unresolvable in the sense that no amount of processing can eliminate the conceptual incompatibilities that exist, be they inter- or intra-sentence ones. Consequently, that part of the comprehension process concerned with the tension elimination fails. So the apparent literal anomaly inherent in metaphorically interpretable expressions, is unresolvable in genuinely anomalous ones. Again, it has to be noted that whether some particular expression is genuinely anomalous depends on the context in which it occurs.

We now have two conditions for something's being a metaphor, which, if taken conjointly seem to be necessary and sufficient. The first is the contextual anomaly condition, the second is that the metaphorical tension should in principle be eliminable. We should probably introduce a third condition, or at least, a caveat, that makes reference to the speaker's intentions and his or her expectations about their recognition. For example, one might require that the speaker intend to speak metaphorically, and that in order to do so must believe that the tension elimination condition holds, and probably also that the contextual anomaly condition holds. Presumably, the speaker must further believe, or at least expect, that the hearer will recognize these beliefs. If a speaker does not hold such beliefs, whereas one might produce a metaphor inadvertently, in the sense that a hearer might recognize that the two conditions hold, nevertheless, the hearer will wrongly attribute to the speaker certain communicative intentions that were never there, and communication may break down as a consequence. The role of intentions in language production in general is a very complex issue and one whose detailed treatment lies well beyond the scope of the present chapter. However it may well be that one has to settle for a rather weak conception of intention. An operational account of such a weak notion of intention might merely require that a speaker be willing to agree that he or she had such an intention *after the fact*, rather than postulating a specific intention as a causal component of the behavior (which would be a much stronger notion.) The intentions that speakers have as causal components of what they say are likely to be much more global than, for example, the intention to use a particular expression metaphorically. The issue of intention becomes even more complicated when it is considered in connection with the production of metaphors by very young children (see Gardner, Winner, Bechhofer & Wolf, 1978, for a discussion of this). If intention is an important component in metaphor production, as it obviously is in the use of language in general, then the attribution to very young children of the capacity to produce metaphors would suggest that children have rather more sophisticated metalinguistic skills than has generally been supposed. This would be particularly true if one relied on a strong notion of intention. Frequently-cited evidence that young children can perceive resemblances and make comparisons does not justify the conclusion that they have the ability to intentionally use language nonliterally. Comparisons themselves can be literal or nonliteral (Ortony, 1979a; 1979b); their status in this regard depends on what the speaker knows about the referents of the terms being compared, so that it is not always possible for a hearer to judge whether a comparison was or was not intended as a literal one anyway.

I now want to enlarge somewhat on the theoretical basis of my revised definition of a metaphor, namely, that a metaphor is the use of an expression that is contextually anomalous and for which the metaphoric tension is in principle eliminable. Consider first the contextual anomaly requirement. In his classic paper, "Logic and Conversation," Grice (1975) proposes that human linguistic communication is governed by what he calls the Cooperative Principle; a principle that reflects the fact that conversations normally take place against a background of speaker and hearer expectations to cooperate in communication. The Cooperative Principle comprises a number of maxims: "Make your contribution as informative as required," "Try to make your contribution one that is true," "Be relevant" and "Be perspicuous." In order to achieve adequate generalizability it appears necessary to modify and extend some of Grice's original formulations. Following the terminology of Gordon and Lakoff (1975) I shall refer to my modifications and extensions of Grice's maxims as *Conversational Postulates,* and for the purposes of illustration I will elaborate on two of them.

Gordon and Lakoff propose that there exist what they call *sincerity conditions* underlying utterances. Meanwhile, as we have seen, Grice has as one of his maxims an injunction to speak the truth. Combining these gives us the *sincerity postulate*. The problem with Grice's maxim is that it is too specific since it applies only to assertions whereas what is needed are conversational postulates that govern all speech act types rather than specific types. Grice's maxim could thus be regarded as an instantiation of the sincerity postulate. Expressed in words, the sincerity postulate would be something like "Try to mean (literally) what you say and imply." This governs not only the truth of assertions, but the felicity of promises, the genuineness of orders, and so on. The second postulate of concern to us is the *relevance postulate*, which is the same as Grice's maxim "Be relevant." Conversations would not be conversations were there to be no relevance connections between adjacent parts; in the same way, it is presumably the case that such relevance relations also distinguish a coherent text from a random collection of sentences.

One of the chief points that emerges from Grice's paper is that while conversational postulates frequently *appear* to be violated, these violations are usually only apparent, and they occur often for very good reasons. Another way of making this point is to observe that speakers very rarely opt out of the Cooperative Principle. This means that when a hearer encounters an apparent violation of a conversational postulate, rather than assuming the violation to be real, he attempts to make sense of what has been said in such a way as to render the violation only apparent. The studies reported in Clark and Lucy (1975) could be regarded as being concerned with these resolution processes as they occur in indirect requests. In the case of metaphors it seems that the contextual anomaly characteristic also arises from the apparent violation of one or more of the conversational postulates; the question is, which? Obviously not all apparent violations give rise to metaphorical interpretations. Most indirect speech acts are not metaphors. So, if the existence of contextual anomaly is a necessary condition for a metaphor, and if all apparent violations of conversational postulates give rise to contextual anomaly, then either we have to restrict the metaphor-generating sources of contextual anomaly to some specific subset of apparent violations, or, the burden of distinguishing metaphors from other cases of superficially anomalous uses will fall on the resolvability-of-metaphoric-tension condition.

It is by no means clear that a suitable subset of apparent violations can be found, although it might be worth exploring the possibility that metaphors arise as the result of the apparent violation of both the sincerity postulate and the relevance postulate together. Recall the sentence about the troops, (4), in the context of the frustrated babysitter, (5). Since reference is made to nonexistent troops, nonexistent marching, and nonexistent danger, there is an apparent violation of the sincerity postulate. Furthermore, the sudden introduction of these things, if taken literally, is clearly irrelevant, so there is an apparent violation of the relevance postulate too.[1]

If such an account were to be translated into a processing model, the comprehension of metaphors would be characterized by there first being a recognition of the violation of the two postulates followed by a process that rendered those violations only apparent, and that process, as I have already suggested, would be the process of tension elimination, to be discussed in a moment. However, I rather doubt that this model will cover even the majority of cases. First, even though whole sentence metaphors constitute particularly good candidates for it, it is probably the case that all kinds of non-metaphors violate the two postulates that I have suggested might be unique to metaphors. Second, it is not at all clear that such an analysis is appropriate for part sentence metaphors. Finally, there are good reasons for supposing that hearers often understand metaphors without any *awareness* of contextual anomaly at all. I shall have more to say on this later.

Tension elimination can be conveniently discussed in terms of three functions that metaphor can perform. These functions, which are more fully discussed in Ortony (1975), can be expressed as three theses that I shall briefly sketch now. The first is the *inexpressibility* thesis, which claims that metaphors are a means of expressing things that are literally inexpressible in the language in question. It is probably the case that many "dead" metaphors derive their origin from this fact, thereby becoming, for practical purposes, literal expressions today of what was literally inexpressible yesterday. Consider the vocabulary available in English to describe sounds. It is rather impoverished. If, in trying to describe a loud roar, one says that it was a loud roar, the range of possible noises consistent with that description may well be too great to fulfill the communicative intent. It could cover anything from the sound of a lion to that of a football crowd or airplane. However, the judicious use of metaphor or simile can serve to severely restrict that scope, as when, for example, one would say that it sounded like a railway train going through the room. Assuming that a train was not actually going through the room, such a figurative use of language would permit a descriptive "fine tuning" that is unavailable if the language is used only literally. The second thesis, the *compactness* thesis, while closely related to the inexpressibility thesis, makes a rather different point. It is not so much concerned with the fact that some metaphors have no literal equivalents as it is with the fact that in cases where there are literal equivalents such expressions are very prolix by comparison. If a woman describes her husband as a teddy bear, her intention may be to predicate far more of him than can be readily achieved using single

---

[1]Notice that we are better able to appeal to a violation of our more general sincerity postulate than we are to Grice's truth maxim, for since there are as yet no established referents for any of the substantive terms in (4), the truth value of (4) is presumably undetermined. Notice also how the question of truth is assessed relative to the context, as must be the question of sincerity in general.

discrete literal predicates. She may want to convey a host of things about him: that he is warm, cuddly, loveable, harmless, soft, etc. The compactness thesis could be regarded as capturing the "etc." aspect, and all that it entails. Finally, the third thesis is the *vividness thesis*. In essence, it suggests that there are phenomenological and psychological reasons for supposing that metaphors are more image-evoking and more vivid than even their best literal equivalents (if there are any).

The three aspects of metaphor represented by the inexpressibility thesis, the compactness thesis, and the vividness thesis all relate to the process of tension elimination. When the woman describes her husband as a teddy bear the tension arises as a result of the incompatibility of the humanness of her husband and the nonhumanness of teddy bears. Tension elimination is achieved by ignoring those salient aspects or attributes of teddy bears that are perceived as being incompatible with husbands. In this particular example the attributes are such things as "being a toy." In the general case the attributes can be much more complex and may not even be easily representable in the language. Certainly they are not restricted in the way that semantic features are (see, Ortony, 1979b). What I am proposing is that when these attributes have been eliminated the remaining salient attributes of the vehicle are attributed as a whole; that is, an entire cognitive substructure is mapped onto the topic. By predicating the nonconflicting attributes en masse, the articulation of discrete predicates is not required, nor even is a conscious recognition of them. This clearly achieves compactness. It might also achieve vividness and greater imageability since holistic representations of this kind might be closer to perceptual representations than a set of abstracted predicates articulated through the medium of language. The matter is, however, rather more complicated since the tension elimination process might be different under different circumstances.[2]

METAPHOR: SOME ISSUES CONCERNING COMPREHENSION

The psychological implications of a Gricean approach to metaphor seem clear enough. In the effort after meaning a hearer may recognize that something is contextually anomalous and that it cannot be sensibly literally interpreted in the context. The hearer then must try to construct an interpretation that resolves the apparent violations of the (sincerity and relevance) postulates. This suggests that more, and presumably deeper, processing is required that in turn should demand

---

[2]For example, suppose one distinguishes between metaphors that are based on known similarities and metaphors that require the discovery of new similarities. In the case of a metaphor based on known similarities no new knowledge will be acquired as a result of its comprehension. In such cases it may well be that comprehension is achieved not by attribute rejection but by attribute selection.

more mental effort and more processing time. But, I have suggested that there may not be very many occasions upon which such a stage model adequately describes the comprehension process. This is to say that wheras a Gricean account might be helpful in characterizing what a metaphor *is*, it does not necessarily help much in characterizing how a metaphor is *understood*. However, by providing a means for offering a more realistic notion of what a metaphor is, it may provide new prospects for investigating the comprehension of metaphors in the laboratory, an enterprise that in the past has been thwarted by the difficulty of producing interesting comparisons and adequate controls (see Ortony, Reynolds, & Arter, 1978).

For example, an experiment reported in Ortony, Schallert, Reynolds, and Antos (1978) was designed to investigate the question of whether or not metaphors (always) take longer to understand than comparable literal uses of language, as seems to be predicted by the Gricean account. Accordingly, we tried to determine whether sentences that followed a context that induced their literal interpretations would be comprehended more rapidly than those same sentences following contexts that induced metaphorical interpretations. We also wanted to determine whether the amount of context was a factor. We therefore collected reaction times to understanding sentences while varying the type and length of preceding context. In a second experiment we used a similar procedure to look at performance on idioms. It was hypothesized that with familiar idioms comprehension would be as quick as, if not quicker than, comprehension of those same expressions interpreted literally.

Results of the first experiment showed a strong main effect for length of context; targets following long contexts took much less time to understand than did targets following short contexts. Thus, for example, a sentence like (7) as it appears in a context like (8) took significantly less time to understand than if the context segment were shortened to include only the first sentence of (8).

(7) The fabric had begun to fray

(8) Lucy and Phil needed a marriage councelor. They had once been very happy but after several years of marriage they had become discontented with one another. Little habits that had at first been endearing were now irritating and caused many senseless and heated arguments. The fabric had begun to fray.

There was also a strong main effect for type of context wherein targets following contexts inducing a metaphorical interpretation [like (7) in the context of (8)] took significantly longer to understand than did targets following literal inducing contexts [like (7) in the context of (9)].

(9) The old couch needed reupholstering. After two generations of wear, the edges of the couch were tattered and soiled. Several buttons were missing and the material around the seems was beginning to unravel.

> The upholstery had become very shabby. The fabric had begun to fray.

However, there was also a significant interaction between context type and context length. The difference between literals and metaphors was greater for short contexts (4419 and 3616 msec respectively) than for long ones (2141 and 1910 msec respectively), the latter difference not itself being significant.

While these results are not capable of distinguishing decisively between alternative theoretical accounts of the underlying processes, it is worth noting that they do not seem to be consistent with a Gricean stage model. They suggest that if enough context is provided to enable the construction of a rich semantic representation of the context, then a certain amount of predictive power is provided; an interpretive framework for the target is established. This would mean that while in the short context condition, the metaphor is processed primarily in a bottom-up fashion, in the long context condition top-down processes play a larger role. The interpretation of the metaphor is already suggested by the context in the long context condition.

The data from the second experiment showed that idioms used idiomatically take significantly less time to comprehend than do those same expressions used literally. For example, a phrase like ''let her hair down'' is understood quicker if it occurs in a context that induces its idiomatic reading than if it occurs in one that induces its literal meaning. The mean reaction times for such decisions were 1383 and 1677 msec respectively. Idioms also take less time than literal translations of their idiomatic meanings (1486 msec), although not significantly less.

Our results then, particularly from the first experiment, suggest that two important variables affecting the comprehension of nonliteral uses of language in general, and of metaphors in particular, are the semantic nature of the contextual support and the amount of it. With abundant support, whole sentence metaphors appear to be (often) interpreted, as it were, directly and immediately. With little support, a Gricean stage model seems to fit the data. But, as was noted earlier, such a model does not seem appropriate for part sentence metaphors like (6). In such cases, it seems that a better approach is to think in terms of the partial application of the meaning of that part of the sentence being used metaphorically. Furthermore, since literal uses of language themselves usually capitalize on only parts of the meanings of the components, as dictated by the context, that would suggest that the process for the comprehension of nonliteral uses might, in many, if not in most cases, be fundamentally the same as that for the comprehension of literal uses. This possibility seems to be a very attractive one when worked out in greater detail (see, e.g., Rumelhart, 1979; Ortony, 1979b.)

The psychological study of metaphor is still very much in its infancy. It is not an easy area to investigate. Even if we get satisfactory answers to all the questions currently being addressed, there are many and difficult ones remaining. I shall conclude by making a few observations on just one of them, namely, the relationship between metaphors and similes.

No adequate theory of metaphor can ignore the difference between metaphor and simile. When the woman says of her husband that he is a teddy bear, she uses a metaphor; when she says of him that he is like a teddy bear, she uses a simile. Traditionally the distinction between metaphor and simile has been made in terms of the distinction between an implicit comparison (metaphor) and an explicit comparison (simile), the latter typically being marked by the presence of "like" or "as." In terms of the analysis that I have offered, it might seem that there is an important difference between metaphors and similes because the apparent violation, at least of the sincerity postulate, is immediately obvious in the case of the metaphor, but much less obvious for the simile. Thus, it is presumably false that the woman's husband is a teddy bear, but is it so obvious that he is not like one? Unless one takes "like" to mean "like in all respects" it would seem that there are respects in which he is like a teddy bear so that (10) and (11) would appear to have the same truth value.

(10)   My husband is like a teddy bear

(11)   My husband is like a teddy bear in some respects

Since, in some respects, almost everything is like almost everything else, it would seem to follow that under normal circumstances of use, (10) and (11) are true, and if they are both true they are both literal uses of language, and one might then ask why it is that similes should be discussed in the same context as metaphors at all since the corresponding metaphor, (12), is presumably false

(12)   My husband is a teddy bear.

This possibility, that similes are in fact literal uses of language, rather naturally leads to the kind of analysis Kintsch offers. One could argue that since a hearer knows that the metaphorical statement, (12), is literally false he attempts to construct a simile such as (10) from it. The answer, I think, is the one that I discuss in Ortony (1979a; 1979b), namely that the genuine similes considered literally, there are no shared salient properties.[3] If this is the case, one might then go on to argue that in fact (10) is false, and that (11) is only trivially true; that is, the respects in which the two terms are similar are trivial, irrelevant respects. This would be one reasonable way to try to reinstate the relevance of similes to metaphors. There are others.

---

[3]Actually, this claim is rather oversimplified. There may be shared properties in similes, but where there are, these properties have subtle but important differences in the different domains of the two terms.

Conclusion

I have taken the position that there is a real difference between literal and nonliteral uses of language. In terms of a general theory of meaning, this difference has been construed as partly involving a difference in (a weak notion of) speaker intentions. In the case of literal uses of language, speakers mean what they say and say what they mean. In the case of nonliteral language uses, they do not mean what they say, and, I have argued, it may be impossible for them to say what they mean within the constraints of a particular language. Implicit in my remarks has been the notion that in the general case the meaning of an utterance is related to its implications, or some of them. In the case of nonliteral uses of language, many of these are inappropriate and have to be discarded. It may well be that in terms of a theory of meaning, the distinction between literal and nonliteral uses of language is based on a difference of degree rather than anything else. That is, it may well be that some utterances are more metaphorical than others. Such a conclusion seems quite innocuous and is certainly compatible with the notion that the extreme cases might involve different kinds of cognitive processes.

ACKNOWLEDGMENTS

This chapter is based on one first presented to the Department of Psychology, University of Amsterdam, Holland, in December 1976 and subsequently at the annual meeting of the American Psychological Association in San Francisco in August 1977. The author wishes to acknowledge support from a Spencer Fellowship, awarded by the National Academy of Education, and from the National Institute of Education under grant No. HEW–NIE–G–74–0007, and Contract No. US-NIE-C-400-76-01176.

REFERENCES

Clark, H. H., & Lucy, P. Understanding what is meant from what is said: A study in conversationally conveyed requests. *Journal of Verbal Learning and Verbal Behavior*, 1975, *14*, 56–72.

Gardner, H., Winner, E., Bechhofer, R., & Wolf, D. The development of figurative language. In K. Nelson (Ed), *Children's language*. New York: Gardner Press, 1978.

Gordon, D., & Lakoff, G. Conversational postulates. In *Papers from the Seventh Regional Meeting*, Chicago Linguistic Society, 1971.

Grice, H. P. Logic and conversation. In P. Cole & J. L. Morgan (Eds.), *Syntax and semantics* (Vol. 3): *Speech acts*. New York: Academic Press, 1975.

Kintsch, W. *The representation of meaning in memory*. Hillsdale, N.J.: Lawrence Erlbaum Associates, 1974.

Matthews, R. J. Concerning a 'linguistic theory' of metaphor. *Foundations of Language*, 1971, *7*, 413–425.

Ortony, A. Why metaphors are necessary and not just nice. *Educational Theory*, 1975, *25*, 45–53.

Ortony, A. The role of similarity in similes and metaphors. In A. Ortony (Ed.), *Metaphor and thought.* Cambridge, England: Cambridge University Press, 1979. (a)

Ortony, A. Beyond literal similarity. *Psychological Review*, 1979, *86*, 161–180. (b)

Ortony, A., Reynolds, R. E., & Arter, J. A. Metaphor: Theoretical and empirical research. *Psychological Bulletin*, 1978, *85*, 919–943.

Ortony, A., Schallert, D. L., Reynolds, R. E., & Antos, S. J. Interpreting metaphors and idioms: Some effects of context on comprehension. *Journal of Verbal Learning and Verbal Behavior*, 1978, *17*, 465–477.

Reddy, M. J. A semantic approach to metaphor. In *Chicago Linguistic Society Collected Papers*, 1969.

Rumelhart, D. E. Some problems with the notion of literal meanings. In A. Ortony (Ed.), *Metaphor and thought.* Cambridge, England: Cambridge University Press, 1979.

II PROCESSING AND REPRESENTATION

5 Transformations in Knowing: A Realist View of Metaphor

Robert R. Verbrugge
University of Connecticut
and
Haskins Laboratories

Metaphor is, at root, a problem of knowing. It can serve a crucial role in the development of knowing, both for an individual (such as the reader of a novel) and for a community (such as a group of scientists). It is a powerful vehicle for recasting identity, for apprehending structure in novel ways. While metaphor can serve this role in perception and in action, its linguistic forms are especially powerful. We need to understand how the vicarious agency of language can effect a change in knowing.

EPISTEMIC COMMITMENTS

Whether we approach metaphoric language as linguists, rhetoricians, psychologists, or interpreters of literature, we inevitably make assumptions about what it means to know through language, and many of our theoretical debates are rooted in this question. Commitments on epistemological issues are unavoidable whenever we develop a theory of linguistic comprehension and production. It is important to understand the kinds of commitments one might adopt, in general, and to appreciate how they shape our thinking in the case of metaphor. Two approaches are especially important: *phenomenalism,* whose sub-types have dominated thought and debate in the Western tradition, and *realism,* which has recently attracted serious consideration and offers an important alternative to traditional views. These positions represent two answers to the question of what can be known with certainty—mental events or an environment. The two approaches can also be distinguished by the type and degree of mental mediation thought to be required for knowing; they are associated, respectively, with "indirect" and "direct" methods of knowing (cf. Shaw & Bransford, 1977).

Approaches to Knowing

Phenomenalism. The position adopted by phenomenalism may be summarized roughly as follows: There is a fundamental estrangement between an organism and its world. Gaining knowledge of that world is highly problematic. Sensory systems provide an incomplete, distorted, and ultimately arbitrary glimpse of the world; they never specify what is really there. If the organism is to succeed in knowing, it must somehow supplement the impoverished data of the senses and operate on those data so as to internally reconstruct the world that might have given rise to them. Thus, the organism must somehow acquire mental entities that stand in a *correspondence* relation with the occupants of the physical world. The reified entities possessed by the organism have been variously called concepts, ideas, models, schemata, phantasms, representations, and so on, and they are said to be acquired either through sensory experience or by some transcendental means. These constituents of mental experience ("phenomena") are all that we know with any immediacy or certainty. What we experience as a surrounding environment is no more than a hypothesis, a mental construct to which we have attributed the property of "objective reality." Knowledge in this phenomenal sphere is gained only by the interpretation of arbitrary sense symbols, and the process is mediated by reference to whatever internal representations are currently available.

Phenomenalism has supported the development of two theoretical metaphors that have become endemic. One is the classical microcosm, an ancient metaphor that views the mind as a surrogate world-within-a-world, containing objectlike ideas and a personified agent capable of viewing, retrieving, and manipulating objects in its environment. The activities of this inner *deus ex machina* mediate knowing. This ancient self-description survives in colloquial language, for we still speak of having an "idea in mind," of seeing an image before "the mind's eye," of living in "an inner world." A second and more recent manifestation of phenomenalism is found in the computer metaphor, which attributes to the mind many of the operations, representations, and anatomical components of electronic computers. Again, it is assumed that knowledge is a correspondence relation between an outer world and its internal representations, and that this correspondence can be achieved only after elaborate operations on an impoverished sensory code.

Realism. The microcosm and computer metaphors have penetrated our thought so thoroughly that alternative approaches can be difficult to conceive. One alternative deserving serious consideration is an approach to knowledge called *realism*. Its modern expression derives from the perceptual theory of Gibson

(1966, 1967, 1979) and has been elaborated by Shaw, Turvey, and others (Shaw & Bransford, 1977; Shaw, Turvey, & Mace, in press; Turvey, 1977).

Rather than a fundamental estrangement, realism proposes a synergistic relation between an animal and its environment. The fundamental unit of analysis is an animal-environment *relation*, and each component of this relation is defined only with reference to the other. Knowledge is evidenced when some invariance is preserved between them. For example, a baseball batter evidences knowledge when light, structured over time by a baseball, guides his swing. Similarly, knowledge is evidenced by a monkey recognizing what objects afford grasping, by a newborn infant taking her first breath, and by a sowbug altering its direction of movement. In none of these cases is it necessary to propose that the animal's recognition or action is mediated by an internal representation. The media of light, sound, and chemical composition are structured by environments in invariant ways, and animals can become attuned to these invariants over the course of evolution and individual development. The information available to their sensory systems is specific to environmental events, and thus is not fundamentally arbitrary or equivocal.

Realism views knowledge as an *attunement* to environmental structure, a potential for recognizing structure and guiding one's action with respect to it. The approach is a ''realism,'' because the environment has reality independent of phenomenal experience (i.e., existence is not simply a mental working hypothesis). The approach is ''direct,'' because it argues that living systems are organized to detect environmental structure without the mediation of internalized models. When we grow in knowledge, we are not acquiring novel internal objects that correspond to external objects; we are developing an attunement to structure and thereby changing our potential relationships with environments.

The property of ''attunement'' is exhibited, in primitive form, by a wide variety of physical systems. A tuning fork, for example, exhibits a selective sensitivity to particular frequencies of mechanical disturbance in its environment. From the perspective of modern physics, the fork's vibratory behavior is *not* mediated by an internal model of airborne vibration but expresses a synergy between dynamic constraints on the object (mechanical properties of the fork's prongs) and the dynamics of the surrounding medium. While reciprocities of this kind can be far more intricate in living systems, the realist faith is that the intricacies can be accommodated without postulating mediators that model the world internally. The same commitment extends to other properties that distinguish living systems from a tuning fork—for example, their plasticity to *changes* in attunement over time. Efforts are currently being made to characterize this biological plasticity in perception (Gibson, 1966, 1979) and action (Fowler & Turvey, 1978) without postulating internal mediation of the traditional kind. Realism seeks a more parsimonious account of these transformations in knowing, and an account more compatible with principles of evolution in physics and biology (cf. Shaw, Turvey, & Mace, in press).

Approaches to Knowing Through Language

Since language (especially *metaphoric* language) can be a powerful means for promoting changes in knowing, commitments on epistemic issues are as important for a theory of language as they are for theories of perception and action. These commitments shape our theoretical vocabulary for language processes and our explanations for the developmental process catalyzed by metaphor. I find realism a persuasive option for characterizing perception and action, but it is not clear how (or whether) that approach can be extended to language comprehension and imagination. While the problems in doing so have been sketched (e.g., Gibson, 1966, 1979), no extended treatment of language from a realist perspective is currently available. Yet there is strong motivation for developing such a theory. Adopting phenomenalism for human language use and realism for all other biological processes (human and otherwise) is unacceptably chimerical. It is important, therefore, to review the phenomenalist tradition in linguistic theory, and to explore whether a realist perspective might be possible.

Linguistic Phenomenalism.   Phenomenalism has seemed ideally suited as a basis for theories of language comprehension. There is an arbitrariness about the relation between linguistic structure and apprehended meaning that seems to demand interpretive activity by the listener. The structure of the *referents* of language and the acoustic or articulatory structure of *words* bear little obvious isomorphism to one another. This estrangement between signs and meanings is accepted as conventional wisdom by twentieth-century semioticians and structuralists (cf. Culler, 1975), and it defines the central puzzle for contemporary linguistic study: how signs and meanings come to be coordinated.

Much of the phenomenalist position derives from a reification of "meaning." In keeping with the metaphor of mind-as-microcosm, meanings are typically objectified as internal idea-objects that come to be associated with word-objects (or sensations). With meanings thus reified, it is possible to become fixated on the problem of structural correspondence between words and ideas (or corresponding real objects). The failure to find simple first order isomorphisms between these objects, or to find *any* nonequivocal relations, has had a major consequence for theories of comprehension; specifically, it has fostered the view that substantial interpretive mediation is necessary. In contemporary psychological theories, comprehension is typically mediated by (among other things) an internal dictionary that permits translation from the arbitrary word-images into meaningful idea-images that correspond to referents in the environment. This perspective on language has many historical antecedents, and it has often served, by analogy, to inspire phenomenalist theories of perception. Plato, for example, spoke of the senses as scribes, writing descriptions of the world for an internal psyche to interpret (Bundy, 1927). Berkeley drew an even more explicit analogy between words and sensations, noting that each is arbitrary with respect to its referent, and he described how a mental dictionary for interpreting arbitrary sensations is developed through experience and divine benevolence (Berkeley, 1709/1964). Since both comprehension and perception are viewed as interpretive activities, in which meanings are attributed to arbitrary and equivocal signs, neither language nor the senses can be a source of certain knowledge about the environment. All that can be known with certainty are the ''internal'' phenomena of one's own interpretation.

Reification of meaning has also created the unsolvable conundra of where meaning is *located,* and whether it is supplied entirely by the mind or is carried (at least in part) by words themselves. As with theories of perception, the various subtypes of linguistic phenomenalism differ in the extent of the contribution they attribute to the listener's mental activity. At one extreme, there is minimal emphasis on the listener's contribution and a focus on the meaning ''contained'' in the words themselves. In colloquial thought, words are treated as carriers of meaning; people put meaning into words and their listeners unpack it. Reddy (1979) has pointed out how pervasive this notion is in ordinary language and has dubbed the underlying metaphor the ''conduit metaphor.'' It is an elaboration of the microcosm metaphor into a theory of communication. Ideas are conducted from one inner world to another, transported in small compartments by the train of speech. The listener's obligation is to extract the ideas from the words, thereby acquiring internal entities that correspond to the internal entities in the speaker. The comprehension process tacitly presupposed by the conduit metaphor has the magical immediacy of the ancient eidola theories of perception, which held that physical images of objects enter the senses and become mental contents. As one weakens in magical or positivist resolve, heavier emphasis comes to be placed on an interpretive contribution by the listener. This may be necessitated by a noisy ''channel,'' deliberately or unconsciously evasive diction on the part of the speaker, or formal ambiguities in word and sentence meaning. From an extreme constructivist perspective, one might argue that a sentence or text itself woefully underspecifies the meaning; the linguistic signs are only partially, as well as equivocally and arbitrarily related to meaning. As a result, the signs must be heavily supplemented by the listener's prior knowledge of linguistic and literary conventions, the speaker's biography and intent, the culture of the time, and the context of utterance. As with all representationalist theories, this knowledge about the environment is thought to be embodied in corresponding internal models (constructed from our prior experience or supplied by genetic endowment).

Linguistic Realism: Comprehension Without Representation.   Realism has been developed largely in the domain of perceptual theory, and to some extent in the domains of coordinated action (Turvey, Shaw, & Mace, 1978) and memory (Turvey & Shaw, 1979). It is a considerable challenge to understand how a theory of language might be developed from this perspective. A useful starting point is to adopt Berkeley's strategy of seeking a deeper identity between perception and language. However, rather than viewing perception as a linguistic process, we need to view language comprehension as a species of perception.[1]

Fundamental to a realist theory of perception is the belief that meaning inheres in relationships between an animal and its environment. Meaning is not an a priori attribute of *environments,* to be ingested by empty animals, nor is it an a priori attribute of *animals,* used to supplement and order a meaningless chaos of sensations. If we view language from the realist perspective, a similar conclusion follows immediately: Linguistic meaning inheres in the *relationship* between a listener and speech, between a reader and a text, and ultimately between language users and their social environments. Meaning is not a reified entity contained either in words or in people's minds. It is not a formal property of sentences (as isolated objects), but a *psychological relation.* It is only by habitual acts of synecdoche that we characterize sentences themselves as meaningful, synonymous, and so on. These are *psychological* predicates; to attribute them to words or sentences only creates confusion. For example, it can lead us to vastly overestimate the equivocality of communicated meaning, when in its full ecological context (considering both sentential and organismic constraints), a sentence can be the occasion for a highly determinate experience. Similarly, it is strictly inappropriate to ask whether a particular sentence is or is not metaphoric, or whether it is a good or a poor metaphor. As the formalists keep being reminded, answers to these questions only approach determinacy when the language user and context of use are specified.

The major puzzle for a realist perspective on language is to define the type of psychological relation exhibited during comprehension and production. One may accept the premise that an optic array is richly structured and that an animal can be directly attuned to that structure, but it is not clear that the acoustics of speech or the optics of print specify events with the same directness. For example, it is not clear that a baseball player's relation to the printed words "looming baseball" is strictly analogous to that player's relation to a real baseball hurtling in from the pitcher's mound. The player's experiences in the two cases may be similar but the words and the event share no obvious invariant. How then can the words be the occasion for experiencing the event? Phenomenalism took the arbitrariness of this relation between physical and psychological entities as pervasive to cognition. Realism acknowledges the absence of word-referent isomorphisms, but it does not accept the view that words are *representations* (substitutes) for objects or events. Thus, the nature of their structural corre-

---

[1] While this paper focuses on *comprehension* (following an unfortunate tradition), *production* is assumed to be complementary. For simplicity of diction, the paper often refers to *listeners* only; however, its arguments are also meant to apply to *speakers, writers,* and *readers* with equal force. Comments about the nonequivocality of linguistic specification may apply with less force to the printed medium, due to its peculiar status as a frozen metaphor for speech.

spondences is secondary to their psychological function, and the apparent arbitrariness of such relations should not be taken as exemplary of the animal-environment relation in general. As an alternative, realism seeks to accommodate language function in a broader theory of cognition based on the perception of *nonarbitrary* invariance. In particular, a resolution to the puzzle of language will most likely come when we have a better understanding, within the realist framework, of such psychological functions as imagination and recollection. It is worth sketching briefly what the relations between these functions and language might be, although the sketch will necessarily be tentative.

We know that language leads us to experience events, to view them from fixed and moving points of observation, to move about in social and geographic environments. These imaginal experiences are similar in quality to experiences we have in nonimaginal contexts. This mode of experience will be called *virtual perception (action)*, on rough analogy to the virtual images of optics; in each case, the relation between the experiencer and the event is largely preserved as one moves from the real to the virtual. It is commonplace historically to note the similarity of imagination to perception, but it has also been commonplace to describe both processes in terms of the microcosm metaphor. Thus, imagination has been identified as the manipulation of image-objects before a mind's eye in an inner space. While the pervasiveness of this metaphoric self-description merits attention and explanation, it does not lend reified images any necessary utility as mediators in cognition (cf. Pylyshyn, 1973). It should be possible to acknowledge the reality and value of virtual experience without accepting its conventional metaphoric description. How such a biological process arises and how its ongoing functioning is constrained are questions that go beyond the scope of this chapter. However, two related issues are especially relevant here and merit further comment: the structural similarities of imagination to perception, and the constraining influence of language on the imaginal process.

Traditional accounts of imagination have treated imagery as static, picturelike, and concrete; images are inner objects. But if the identities of objects and events are defined pre-eminently by abstract and dynamic invariants (e.g., Gibson, 1966, 1979; Turvey, 1977), it is inappropriate to define imaginal experiences of them in terms of picturelike qualities. The realist view suggests a different account of the structural similarities between imagination and perception: imagining is *dynamic*, borrowing on the rhythm, flow, and juncture of direct perception and action. It is not a succession of static, two-dimensional snapshots, any more than perception is. Experiences of "concreteness" or "vividness" are possible symptoms of imagining, but they are not necessary or defining properties, because the identities of objects and events are relationally defined (cf. Bransford & McCarrell, 1974). Thus, it may not be surprising that imageability is such a fickle correlate of metaphoric recall and other measures (cf. Harris, Lahey, & Marsalek, 1978, and this volume; Riechmann & Coste, 1978, and this volume).

As noted above, it is clear that language can evoke and guide virtual experience. It activates and constrains an attunement to structure, a structure that may be very different from that specified by the immediate physical environment. In a sense, the imagination is an autonomous animation system, whose content and flow are constrained from several directions—by language, by the immediate social and geographic context, and by the persisting influence of earlier contexts. Language can activate roughhewn events, modulate the identities of participating objects, and constrain their dynamic relationships. But the modulatory power of words depends crucially on the developmental experience a person has had with language. A realist theory will need to explain how early experience in a social environment potentiates the later impact that words have on a person's imagination. In this context, it is important to note that children do not experience sentences in a vacuum, as isolated symbol strings, nor do they experience sentences as merely parallel accompaniments of events. Sentences are embedded in richly structured social and physical events, and in fact are essential *constituents* of many events. As a result, specific word and sentence forms are experienced as recurrent covariates of specific types of events—that is, in the child's social environment, they occur consistently and uniquely as constituents of these events. Thus, they come to be as *specific* to (and potentially informative of) those events as physical information that *necessarily* specifies the events.

It has been commonly noted that a covariate can come to induce a state of attunement to the event with which it covaries. Phenomena of this kind have been a central focus of many learning theories (cf. Bolles, 1975; Pavlov, 1955), and of theories of recollection in the associationist tradition (e.g., Hamilton, 1859; Hollingworth, 1926; Russell, 1921). In the memory literature, the phenomenon has often been called *redintegration*, a process by which re-experiencing a constituent induces reminding of a previously experienced whole. If we view words as covariant constituents of events, we can consider the following possibility: The symbolic function of language operates through redintegration. During an individual's development, linguistic structures acquire an intricate control over the activation of virtual experience. Their covariant appearance in earlier events of a certain abstract structure enables them to redintegrate comparable *virtual* events at a later time. From this perspective, language comprehension can be classified as a species of imagination; it is a process of apprehending virtual events, where the identities of these events are modulated by spoken or printed speech. Since this process operates through redintegration of direct experience, the semantics of linguistic comprehension is necessarily rooted in the semantics of perception and action.

If we treat comprehension as a species of imagination, and treat imagination and perception as biological processes unmediated by internal representations, then an unusual conclusion follows: Language comprehension is unmediated by internal representations. I will call this process *comprehension without repre-*

sentation (since it is somewhat revolutionary). For example, we can assert that a person "comprehends" without supposing that this achievement is mediated by processes that unpack, supplement, and disambiguate meanings carried by word strings, or that it is mediated by accessing representations in internal dictionaries, or that it is mediated by the construction of internal representations that correspond to objects in some hypothetical outer world. Belief in the need for representational mediation of this kind has been fostered by the microcosm metaphor, by the structural ambiguities found when sentences are analyzed in isolation of communication settings, and by the observation that sentences themselves do not exhaust meaning. The realist position agrees that the listener is a crucial participant in placing closure on meaning, but emphasizes the richness of information available in natural communication settings to a listener who is appropriately attuned through cultural and linguistic experience.

This position does not deny that linguistic experience has persisting effects on a language user (the phenomena of learning and memory), nor that the experience prompted by a linguistic event can extend beyond the structure of that event itself (the phenomena of inference and generativity). Indeed, the redintegration hypothesis relies on persisting effects of experience and predicts a resultant attunement to more than the covariate currently present. However, the realist position parts company with its phenomenalist cousins on several grounds: It sees in the social environment a firm basis for certainty (validity) in communication; it denies the explanatory utility of the microcosm metaphor (with its attendant representations, homunculi, and computational costs); and it redefines meaning as a property of the person-environment relation (rather than a property solely of words, of concepts, or of referents). For the realist, words in themselves do not have meaning; they are the occasion for an attunement that is meaningful.

Metaphor as a Catalyst for Knowing

When we explore a linguistic phenomenon, such as metaphoric language, we need to view the person-language relation from two perspectives. From the vantage point of listeners, we need to understand what styles of virtual experience are available and how these may be guided by encounters with language. From the vantage point of linguistic forms, we need to understand what styles of thought they may potentially catalyze, how they influence the current attunement, and what kinds of events the forms are typically embedded in. This section explores some of the characteristics that distinguish metaphor as a style of experience.

Metaphoric processes are not solely dependent on language as a source of activation or medium of expression. Perceptual experiences can be metaphoric—for example, recognizing a familiar object in the guise of a cloud, or recognizing a familiar ocean-wave undulation in a field of grain. Metaphoric processes can also be manifested in coordinated movement—for example, when someone imitates the gait and grimaces of a chimpanzee, or when an athlete doing a hitch-kick jump imagines he is walking up stairs.

Metaphoric processes are also evident in thought (both verbal and nonverbal). As a style of thought, metaphor has received considerable attention as a component of primary process thinking and dream-work (Freud, 1900/1950), as a symptom of psychopathology (cf. Anderson, 1964; Arieti, 1974), and as a component of insight in psychotherapy (cf. Pollio, Barlow, Fine, & Pollio, 1977). Most analyses of metaphoric thought are found in the clinical literature; these accounts have emphasized the affective facets of metaphor, but they have also tended to treat it as a symptom of pathology. The *affective* aspect is certainly compatible with the realist approach to cognition. The meaning of events (virtual or otherwise) depends on what they afford us; emotionality is integral to our perception of whatever threat or opportunity is specified. This suggests that affect should be more integral to semantic description than is typically the case. Characterizations of meaning have tended to focus on the properties of "external" events, overlooking the affective, person-dependent facet of meaning. This is the result of a habitual process of synecdoche, addressing the whole by speaking only of the part. The *complete* event under study is a relation between person and environment, between listener and language, and the structure of this event is laced with motive.

In contrast, the clinical emphasis on *pathology* has been unfortunate. It has only served to advance the view that metaphoric processes are deviant, irrational, and primitive, playing only an ancillary role in mature thought. This reflects a general attitude of hostility toward fantasy, an attitude that treats fantasy as antithetical to rational living. An alternative is to view fantasy as an integral component of productive thought. This viewpoint has its proponents in the clinical literature (e.g., Arieti, 1976; Kris, 1952; Rogers, 1978), and it will also be promoted here. Metaphor is a style of thought in which fantasy is always mingled to some degree, but it is not simply a flighty precursor to productive thinking, nor is it an ornamental afterthought. Metaphor is *integral* to the development of knowledge, and fancy plays a crucial role in the process.

As a starting point toward a definition, metaphor may be described as a catalyst for a change in understanding. More specifically, metaphoric processes are a transitional phase in which there is a partial transformation of a topic's identity by a second identity. In this activated complex of dual identities, an unusual structural organization of the topic stands out in high relief. If attunement to this structure in the topic survives, there is a change in knowing. In other cases, the fanciful complex may dissipate with no lasting impact on understanding.

An excellent example of this process has recently been recounted by Schön (1979). He tells the story of a group of researchers who were trying to design synthetic-bristle paint brushes that would spread paint as smoothly as brushes made of natural bristles. Their efforts had shown little success until, one fine day, one of the researchers noticed something: "You know, a paintbrush is a kind of pump." This was somewhat confusing at first, since they had been viewing the brush as a flat surface that spreads paint. The simile requested that they reattune themselves to see the brush as a hollow medium through which fluid is forced under pressure. This proved to be productive in their design work, and they ultimately came to define a new class of systems, called "pumpoids," of which pumps, brushes, mops, and dishcloths were all examples. The story illustrates one direction in which an unstable dual identity can be resolved: The metaphoric structuring becomes a conventional one. The brush was not totally re-identified as a pump, nor did it slip back to its former identity as a spreading surface. The relations thrown into relief by the metaphor lasted as a permanent possibility of perception, and left the brush with a new identity.

The transitional role of metaphor in knowing is evidenced repeatedly in the physical sciences, as well as in problem-solving. the reading of literature, personal growth, and many other domains. In the early phases of its life cycle, metaphor transports us with new insights, while in its later phases it can freeze us in new convention. This is the ironic fate of many successful metaphors: The topic becomes essentially *identified* with the vehicle, and our perception of its identity becomes frozen by the new constraints. It is an inherent risk in the metaphoric enterprise, and it is a gamble that psychologists have taken repeatedly when treating organisms as hydraulic machines, as measuring instruments, as stimulus-response connectors, as charged particles, as containers of miniature inner worlds, and as computing devices ("the brain is a computer"). When the phenomenon under study is closely identified with the metaphoric vehicle, distinctions tend to be lost and the metaphor becomes dogma, rather than a catalyst for changes in understanding.

METAPHORIC COMPREHENSION

Traditional Views of Metaphoric Structure and Process

Traditional views of metaphor have focused on the *sentences* that occasion metaphoric thought. Analyses are typically directed at determining the formal properties by which a metaphoric sentence may be identified, and explaining how the meaning of the sentence is related to its form. These analyses inevitably make assumptions about psychological processes in metaphor users, though these assumptions are not always explicit. Indeed, the analyses are often presented as *independent* of users, as if a characterization of meaning can gain closure by treating a sentence as a formal "object." Whether one accepts this formalist claim or not, it is clear that the proposed relation between sentence form and sentence meaning has direct implications for a psychological model.

For example, the linguistic phenomenalist might argue that sentence meaning (or intended meaning) is arbitrarily and ambiguously related to sentence form, and that comprehension must therefore be mediated by processes that correct, supplement, or disambiguate the problematic form.

Black (1962) has offered a useful classification of approaches to metaphoric structure and process. His analysis illustrates the close coupling between formal descriptions and comprehension processes, and it provides an important backdrop to the approach being developed here. (It will also prove useful for structuring the findings of an experiment to be described in the final section of this chapter.) Black distinguishes three approaches: the substitution view, the comparison view, and the interaction view.

1. *Substitution View.*   The most influential tradition in rhetorical theory has treated metaphor as a kind of error in diction and logic. Metaphoric terms are viewed as intruders in a sentence because they make it literally unintelligible. For example, the sentence *Highways are snakes* could be viewed as an error in denotation, wrongly classifying highways as snakes. The sentence cannot mean what it says directly, because that is anomalous from the standpoint of normative logic. Thus, metaphoric sentences are said to communicate *indirectly,* because they mean something different from what they "really" say. The approach is called a *substitution* view because, in the production of a metaphor, an intruding term is thought to substitute for the literal term that constitutes the true underlying intent. To comprehend this underlying intent, a listener must invert the substitution, replacing the intruder by a literal term (or concept) compatible with the rest of the sentence. In comprehending *Highways are snakes,* one might (with luck) obtain something like *Highways are long and thin,* or *Highways are curvey.*

The substitution view clearly manifests the general perspective of linguistic phenomenalism in treating metaphoric sentences as equivocal specifiers of meaning that demand special cognitive supplementation. Rhetoricians supporting this view offer two kinds of reasons for these mischievous uses of language (Black, 1962): metaphoric terms are useful where no literal terms are available, and they are useful for ornamental effects. Other rhetoricians do not dispute these two functions, but argue that they seriously understate the range of communicative functions served by metaphor. The substitution view has also had some proponents in the psycholinguistic literature—in particular, psychologists of associationist persuasions (Brown, 1958; Brown, Leiter, & Hildum, 1957; Koen, 1965; Osgood, Suci, & Tannenbaum, 1957). These psychologists have treated the intruding word as a low-probability associate of the surrounding context. The anomaly is corrected during comprehension if the word or context elicits the appropriate high-probability associate, thereby substituting it for the intruder. Unfortunately, there is no guarantee in this system that intruders will have any similarity to what they are replacing (e.g., they could be associates by contiguity rather than similarity). This places metaphor on a continuum with word salad, indistinguishable from anomaly and other sure signs of irrationality. Again, this approach underrates both the power of metaphor and the degree of constraint on its content.

The substitution view seems most applicable when the properties asserted by a metaphor are already known to be true of the topic (i.e., when they are "high-frequency associates"), and when the metaphoric term is only a passing means for directing attention to those properties. However, it does not prove very helpful when a novel interpretation of the topic is intended, when both the topic and vehicle are of continuing interest, and when the sentence effects a nonliteral (fanciful) experience. In addition, it treats metaphor as an equivocal and aberrant linguistic form—not an integral form capable of semantic precision. This creates the need for a special comprehension process to decipher the user's intent, which violates the canons both of parsimony and of realism.

2. *Comparison View.* Rather than focusing on component words in a sentence, the comparison view treats entire sentences as aberrant. On the surface, the sentences falsely assert or presuppose some relation of identity or class membership; at a hidden level, they state a well-formed comparison. Specifically, the underlying form asserts that two domains of knowledge, the topic and vehicle domains, are *similar* in some respects, in spite of their manifest differences. In production, a speaker may say *Highways are snakes* instead of the intended comparison *Highways are like snakes*. To comprehend this utterance, a listener must invert the substitution, replacing the anomalous metaphor with an unprovocative assertion of similarity. The sentence *Highways are snakes* would be interpreted to have a meaning of the following form: *Highways are similar to snakes in that both have property X*. Thus, the meaning of a metaphor is held to be equivalent to that of the corresponding simile, which is equivalent, in turn, to a literal assertion of common properties.

As Black (1962) notes, the comparison view is a special case of the substitution view, focusing on the equivocality of sentence form (rather than word form) in the specification of meaning, and emphasizing that both domains (not just the topic) must be included in the underlying sentence meaning. Like any substitution view, it necessitates the postulation of special comprehension processes to cope with the ambiguity, and it also requires procedures for ferreting out similarities in the representations of each domain. A wide variety of psychological and linguistic models have been inspired by the comparison view, varying in part with the structural predispositions of their authors. Featural models propose mechanisms for detecting common features between pairs of terms or concepts (e.g., Leech, 1969; Malgady & Johnson, 1976, and this volume; Matthews, 1971). Information processing models propose comprehension operations that include a test for matching properties in the two domains (e.g., Sternberg, 1977). Models inspired by propositional calculi treat metaphor as a condensed assertion of similarity; the resulting burden for comprehension is to reconstruct the under-lying proposition that was truncated on the way to surface structure (e.g., Kintsch, 1974; Mack, 1975; Miller, 1979).

All of these versions of the comparison view stress the intuition that metaphor deals in *resemblances,* and they seem most applicable to metaphors that draw our attention to similarities between two domains as they are currently understood. The comparison approach fails to account for metaphors that lead a comprehen-der to understand a topic in a novel fashion. No list of pre-existing similarities can substitute as an equivalent for the transforming effect that the vehicle of such a metaphor exerts on the topic's identity. As Black (1962, p. 37) puts it, "it would be more illuminating in some of these cases to say that the metaphor creates the similarity than to say that it formulates some similarity antecedently existing." For this reason, Black is unwilling to accept the view that similes or metaphors have equivalent underlying semantic forms. With regard to highways and snakes, for example, he might argue that *comparing* a highway and a snake is very different from *viewing* a highway *as* a snake (cf. his footnote, p. 37). While Black does not elaborate on this difference, it is important to note that the process of *seeing-as* implies a fanciful mode of perceiving, and it implies an apprehension of two identities in a single structure. (The significance of these points will be elaborated below.)

The comparison view is also problematic in assuming that an enumeration of *similarities* exhausts the semantic content of a metaphor. Yet the differences that forestall a total *identification* of topic and vehicle are surely of equal importance. For example, a highway and a snake can be very similar in shape, but they differ in composition, intentionality, source of motion, anatomy, and many other fac-tors, and these all resist transformation in varying degrees. The points of resis-tance are familiar and obvious in this example, but when metaphor is used productively, they are not at all obvious at the outset. When a metaphor is being used to explore a phenomenon in the laboratory, to explore a personality in therapy, or to explore an emotion in poetry, the points of resistance are as informative as the points of success. In short, the comparison view fails to formalize the *dialectic process* by which distinct identities are mutually ac-commodated.

A final problem concerns the symmetry of the underlying representation for the metaphor's meaning. Implicit in the comparison view is a belief that the topic and vehicle are interchangeable in the underlying form. For example, the metaphor *A is B* is held to have the following underlying proposition: *A and B are similar in that both have property X.* But this is equivalent to *B and A are similar in that both have property X.* One concludes that the metaphor *A is B* and the reverse metaphor *B is A* will have the same meaning. However, at least two symmetry conditions must be met for this conclusion to follow: The sentences must have no asymmetry in thematic focus, and similarity relations must be symmetric.

The first condition of symmetry is usually not met: Metaphors, in practice, have a thematic focus, the *topic* or "principal subject" (Black, 1962). The topic is viewed from the perspective of a vehicle or "subsidiary subject." This difference in semantic function is evident when people attempt to recall metaphoric sentences (Verbrugge & McCarrell, 1977). For example, the ordering of the topic and vehicle is rarely reversed in recall; to the extent that recall is not verbatim, this observation alone suggests the nonarbitrariness of word order. In addition, the grounds that successfully prompt recall are usually more closely related to the vehicle than the topic; this asymmetry in prompting reflects the predominant role of the vehicle in guiding the interpretation of the topic. An asymmetry in roles is also evident when people rate the similarity between the terms of a metaphor or simile (Harwood & Verbrugge, 1977); for example, the rated similarity of *children* to *rabbits* can differ markedly following exposure to *Children skipping rope are like rabbits,* compared to *Rabbits are like children skipping rope.*

The second premise of symmetry (that similarity relations are symmetric) is also invalid as a psychological claim. For example, in the study just mentioned, Harwood and Verbrugge (1977) found that the rated similarity of *children* to *rabbits* can differ significantly from the rated similarity of *rabbits* to *children,* even when the preceding linguistic context is held constant. More broadly, Tversky (1977) has summarized findings from a wide variety of perceptual tasks, and presents a convincing case that similarity relations are asymmetric when psychologically conceived. He proposes that similarity be modeled by a weighted matching function that assesses featural differences as well as similarities, but with one domain receiving a disproportionate weighting. While his model successfully predicts that asymmetries in similarity will accompany changes in metaphoric word order, it remains a sophisticated form of comparison model, since it operates on stable representations of pre-existing features. As a result, it fails to model the changes in similarity that accompany a radical reattunement to the topic (as in the case of the paintbrush viewed as a pump).

3. *Interaction View.* Black (1962) ultimately argues for an interaction theory of metaphor and seeks to make its tenets more explicit than earlier proponents have done (e.g., Richards, 1936). His goal is to incorporate several properties and processes that are not successfully handled by either a substitution or comparison theory: the reorganization of the topic domain, the distinct roles played by the topic and vehicle, and the (possibly permanent) alterations in word meaning that accompany interpretation.

Black argues that the topic and vehicle have systems of "associated implications," including commonplace cultural beliefs and personal attitudes, and unusual connotations established by prior discourse. In a metaphor, some of the implications associated with the vehicle are applied to the topic, altering the topic's system of implications. In the process, "the metaphor selects, emphasizes, suppresses, and organizes features of the principal subject by implying statements about it that normally apply to the subsidiary subject'' (Black, 1962, pp. 44–45). Thus, in seeing the topic *as* the vehicle, one experiences it as having properties that are alien to its typical identity. This is different from what one experiences during a comparison, where the two domains are assumed to have independent and conventional identities.

Black characterizes the process as a "filtering" of the topic by the vehicle. In the case of *Highways are snakes,* for example, highways are viewed through a snake filter. Snakelike properties of highways loom into prominence (indeed, they may be created for the first time by imposition of the filter), and other properties are suppressed. The process is interactive, because the filter alters the identity of the topic, and the topic, in turn, influences the nature of the filter. For example, if we say *Highways in a rainstorm are snakes* or *Alpine highways are snakes,* the kinds of snakelike properties that define the filter vary with the topic. We experience the identity of the snakes as more slippery, more sinuous, etc., depending on context. The interaction is not symmetric, however, since the vehicle is usually the dominant transformer of identities. (It is also important to note that neither domain is completely malleable under the other's influence. The highway is not likely to acquire a head and a tail because it is basically unending. And the snake is not likely to draw attention to the patching of potholes, because it is difficult to transform snakes in a comparable fashion. Explaining these reciprocal *constraints* is one of the greatest challenges facing a theory of metaphor. No proposal, including Black's, has successfully met this challenge.)

The interaction view has not inspired as much experimental or theoretical work as the other views, although findings compatible with an interactional approach have been reported by Honeck, Voegtle, and Sowry (1978), Tourangeau and Sternberg (1978), and Werner and Kaplan (1963). Strong evidence for an approach of that kind has also been reported by Verbrugge and McCarrell (1977) and Verbrugge (1974, 1977). These studies explored the recall of topics that were originally encountered in metaphoric sentences and later were prompted by phrases, sentences, or drawings that specified the related metaphoric grounds (resemblances). For example, listeners encountered the topic *tree trunks* either in the sentence *Tree trunks are straws for thirsty leaves and branches,* or the sentence *Tree trunks are pillars for a roof of leaves and branches.* The metaphors led listeners to organize tree trunks in two unusual (though very different) ways. When the phrase *are tubes that conduct water to where it's needed* was provided as a prompt during recall, people who had heard the *related* sentence (tree trunks-straws) showed very high correct recall, those who had heard only the topic (tree trunks) showed low levels of recall, and those who had heard the *unrelated* sentence (tree trunks-pillars) showed very poor recall. These results suggest that the vehicle has a powerful influence in reorganizing the identity of the topic; only prompts that specify a compatible organization can effectively reactivate the original experience. In a further study using randomly coupled "arbitrary metaphors" (Exp. 3, Verbrugge & McCarrell, 1977), the effectiveness of grounds in prompting the recall of "principled metaphors" was shown to be more than the additive sum of prompting their topics and vehicles as independent entities. This suggested that there was a strong interaction during the comprehension of the principled metaphors, possibly a process in which the topic and vehicle became fused by a common organization. The appearance of isolated topic and vehicle fragments in the recall of arbitrary metaphors (but not of principled metaphors) was a further indication that successful comprehension entails an interaction or partial fusion of identities.

Critique of the Interaction View

There are two aspects of Black's interaction view that I find especially congenial. The first is his tacit recognition of the element of fantasy in metaphoric interpretation; as noted above, fantasy is implicit in the process of *seeing-as*, because it entails an experience that has no literal or conventional equivalent. Definitions of *fantasy* are many and sundry; consistent with the general approach being developed here, I would offer the following as a starting point: In fantasy, the unconventional or impossible is experienced to be continuous with what is real. Fantasy has many genres, from puppetry and poetry to jokes and story-telling, and metaphor is one of its favored devices. Metaphors assert or presuppose that one identity (A) is also another (B), that A has been *transformed* into B by some alchemical process. Rather than evading this unconventional possibility and substituting a conventional paraphrase, the listener may accommodate to its request and experience a transformation of A into B. This venture into fantasy may not only be "healthy" and productive (as argued above), but it may also be the *conventional* response.

Levin's (1977, 1979) recent discussions of semantic interpretation are relevant here. Levin distinguishes two possible types of interpretation, *linguistic construal* and *phenomenalistic construal*.[2] Linguistic construal alters the metaphor to fit conventional reality. The metaphor is viewed as an illogical and deviant assertion; interpretation rectifies the problem by normalizing the de-

---

[2]Levin's use of the term "phenomenalistic" is unfortunately confusing in the context of this chapter. In the sense defined in an earlier section, both of Levin's modes of construal are examples of "linguistic phenomenalism"; each mode assumes that language is equivocal, that it demands interpretive mediation, that its construal is mediated by internal representations, and that all one can know with certainty is one's interpretation. His use of the term "phenomenalistic" relates more directly to the *content* of these representations; the term labels a lack of adherence to the concepts currently held to represent objective reality. Less confusing terms, for purposes of this chapter, might be "unconventional" and "fanciful." Another possible source of confusion must be noted. Levin speaks of the content of the phenomenalistic construal as an *imagined* world sharply distinct from the *actual* world. In contrast, the approach developed here sees fanciful processes as *continuous* with conventional modes of perceiving; fantasy exploits and transforms our current attunements to what is real.

viancy. As we have seen, most accounts of metaphor have taken this perspective; the substitution and comparison views, for example, seek to substitute a realistic term or assertion for the threatening anomaly. As an alternative, Levin proposes that the meaning effected by a metaphor can be the result of a qualitatively different kind of interpretive process, phenomenalistic construal, in which one imagines an unconventional reality to fit the metaphor. The comprehender experiences an unconventional structuring of identities, imagining that A has, in fact, *become* B—that highways have become snakes, skyscrapers have become giraffes, raccoons have become human. This fanciful, exploratory quality of metaphoric comprehension is not acknowledged by most psychological models, yet it can be of tremendous significance when metaphor appears in psychotherapy, dreaming, scientific thought, coaching, play, and many other activities. Levin needlessly restricts this kind of process to poetry; even so, his views on poetic construal provide an important parallel to Black's interaction view and to the approach being developed here.

The second congenial element of Black's view is the proposed directionality of influence between the topic and vehicle, and the corresponding difference in their roles. Rather than a symmetric juxtaposition of two domains, metaphor is viewed as an asymmetric filtering or transformation of the topic by the vehicle. Evidence for a directional interaction has been summarized above. Such a process seems to be demanded, for example, by the kinds of asymmetries in meaning that derive from a reversal of word order (Harwood & Verbrugge, 1977; Tversky, 1977).

While I am sympathetic to most of Black's account of the interaction process, there are a few important points of emphasis and perspective on which I differ. The first is an issue of semantic representation. While Black is open to treating metaphoric meaning as a pragmatic phenomenon, his interpretation process seems to occur in a self-contained medium of terms and meaning representations, largely abstracted from psychological processes. In general, I would prefer to avoid speaking of linguistic meaning as if it were independent of potential language users and their experiences. Thus, I find it more congenial to speak of "interaction" as a descriptive property of a style of *thought* (virtual experience) that is guided by a sentence. It may be heuristic to imagine that concepts participate in events in a medium of formal notations, but the ever-present risk is that these events will become reified as operations on "mental representations" that mediate comprehension. At this point, my preference for viewing comprehension as an event in a medium of virtual experience, rather than of verbal or propositional notation systems, is motivated mainly by theoretical principle. Questions of this kind are notoriously difficult to put to empirical test (cf. Anderson, 1978). However, a series of prompted recall findings reported elsewhere (Verbrugge, 1974, 1975, 1977) provide at least a prima facie case that the medium of metaphoric comprehension is closely related to direct experience. In those studies, listeners were able to recall metaphoric sentences in response to verbal descriptions, cartoon drawings, and even piano passages, when these prompts specified the perceptual invariants that constituted the grounds of the original sentences. One parsimonious account of these data (an account compatible with realism) is that the grounds of the linguistic metaphors were apprehended in a virtual perceptual medium. As a result, when the relations were later re-experienced in optical or acoustic media, recall was directly afforded (without the need for translation of the events into a non-figural medium).

These considerations suggest that semantic descriptions should be cast in terms of the invariants that structure perception and action, rather than forcing all of them into a single mathematical mold, such as a calculus of propositions, that simply *represents* a world. As in Black's analysis, identity is often characterized as a set of predicates that are local, adjectival, independent, and heterogeneous in contextual origin. In contrast, those of a realist bent (e.g., Gibson, 1966; Jenkins, 1974; Shaw & Pittenger, 1977; Verbrugge, 1977) prefer to view identity as a system of relationships that are globally defined, structural (geometric), interdependent, and context-contingent. Since metaphor traffics in similar and transformed *identities,* the assumptions one makes in defining "identity" are crucial to a theory of metaphoric structure and process. Realism suggests that a linguistic semantics rooted in perception and action is the most appropriate basis for explaining the comprehension process and the experienced identities of topic and vehicle.

Another concern I have about Black's view is that "interaction" connotes an interplay of two separate identities. Black is rightly wary of the extreme views that see metaphor as a total fusion, identification, or mystical union of disparates. On the other hand, the process of *seeing-as* (a brush as a pump, a highway as a snake) is, in practice, a process oriented toward a single entity. The experience is peculiarly dual at the same time, because two types of identity are perceived to coexist in a single structure, identities that one might not previously have thought capable of coexisting. Total separation and total fusion are not the only theoretical options available; indeed, they are only the endpoints on a continuum of possibilities. The transitional dual identity can show varying degrees of fusion, incongruity, stability, and permanency. This partial fusion of the topic and vehicle is often more obvious in the case of metaphoric *production.* The linguistic *expression* of a metaphoric experience can be viewed as a movement from a largely *undifferentiated* state to an action in which the topic and vehicle are differentiated as separate elements (cf. Werner & Kaplan, 1963). For example, one could perceive ocean waves in a wind-blown field of wheat and announce *The field is an ocean!* Given the historical preoccupation of psychologists with *comprehension*, it is not surprising that the metaphoric domains are assumed to be *discrete* and *contiguous* as theoretical and psychological entities, replicating the properties they manifest in the linguistic forms that initiated comprehension.

Transformation View:
The Specification of Dual Identity

For the reasons just described, I would like to christen a fourth view of metaphor: the *transformation view*. This approach has been developed in the preceding discussions of interaction and of metaphor as a catalyst for knowing, and it may be summarized as follows. To comprehend a metaphor is to perceive familiar structures or transformations in an unusual context. The metaphor leads us to recognize these relations in a curious way: by inviting us to *transform* the topic into the vehicle. If we are receptive, the metaphor will specify a virtual experience in which the vehicle modulates the identity of the topic, thereby mingling two identities in a single event. If this attempted transformation of the topic's identity proves productive, the process will leave in its wake a permanent possibility for perception, the capacity to recognize those invariants in the topic domain on later occasions. The transformation of the topic is *partial,* because the topic is not reidentified completely as the vehicle. The transformation is *directional,* since the vehicle is typically the dominant source of constraints on the new identity and the topic is comparatively plastic under its influence. The transformation is *imaginal,* a type of virtual experience; in the case of linguistic metaphor, comprehension is a species of recollection guided by language. The transformation is *psychological,* because it is an aspect of a psychological relation or process, rather than a property of relationships holding over linguistic forms. Finally, the transformation is *fanciful,* in the sense that the experience is unconventional and unusual, not that it is necessarily "untrue" or "impossible." An ocean-wave event may well be specified in the light structured by a field of wheat. The invariants of pumping may genuinely be present in the interactions of brush, paint, and surface. As the brush example illustrates, the virtual experiences specified by metaphor may *seem* fantastical on our first encounter, but they often become "literal" as the new modes of perceiving and acting gain familiarity.

Special Devices, or Special Consequences?

It is usually accepted that any word class, sentence form, or narrative structure can serve as the occasion for metaphor. For any specific type of linguistic form, one may ask how it activates and guides a specifically metaphoric thought process. Such a process could be treated as a *special* procedure that is engaged only when certain types of deviant forms are detected (as is suggested by the substitution and comparison views). It is also possible that a class of linguistic forms will engage the *same* kind of process, whether operating "literally" or "metaphorically." The label "metaphoric" would then denote a degree of unconventionality in the experience that is specified, rather than denoting a property of the linguistic form itself or denoting a special comprehension strategy *discontinuous* with "normal" comprehension. Several studies have assessed the question of whether metaphor invokes a special processor that demands more time for its labors or that operates subsequent to a failure of literal construal. A recent experiment by Ortony, Schallert, Reynolds, and Antos (1978) provides suggestive evidence for the contrary view—that metaphoric and literal interpretations result from a common process. These researchers found no difference in the time required to understand a sentence in an extended context where its role was metaphoric, compared to an extended context where its role was literal. Arguments against dichotomous interpretive processes for literal and figurative language have also been advanced on theoretical grounds (e.g., Pratt, 1977; Verbrugge, 1977).

This chapter focuses on a particular sentence form, *A is B,* that links two nominal expressions. An underlying assumption has been that nominal expressions redintegrate constraints on *structural* identity and on *transformations* in which the structures can participate. According to the transformation view, the sentence form *A is B* specifies that invariants of B apply to A; the impact of the linguistic expression "B" is to modulate the identity of A by structural and transformational invariants of B. The way that A's identity has already been established and modified (by the expression "A," prior narrative context, environmental setting, etc.) will necessarily constrain the modulatory influence of B. We need to consider the possibility that the modulatory processes activated by the *A is B* form are similar across many kinds of uses now seen as different: assertions of class membership (or adjectival properties), assertions of presumed or altered identity, metaphors, definitions, and so on. This would obviate the need to postulate special processes that determine which of several uses is intended (disambiguation), and special processes for construing each type of use.

Much of what is attributed to special processors may simply be differing types of resolutions to a common request: that two identities be accommodated in a single structure or event. Consider, for example, the following sentences: *Highways are snakes, That boat is a freighter, Skyscrapers are buildings, My uncle is a plumber, My father is a son, Elizabeth Taylor is the princess, The barn is a restaurant.* The resolutions to these multiple identities are determined in part by whether and how the identities can coexist, and in their full communication settings these sentences are not ambiguous. Metaphoric resolutions appear when the identity of the predicate cannot be wrought fully over the topic, and when conventional constraints on the identity of the topic are partially overridden. The *degree* of transformation will depend not only on these conventional constraints, but on individual "cognitive style"; people vary tremendously in their resistance or willingness to flow with fancy (cf. Feirstein, 1967; Klein, Gardner, & Schlesinger, 1962; Pollio, 1977). Thus, it is pointless to focus on a sentence and to ask whether it is or is not metaphoric. The sentence's success in occasioning a metaphoric transformation is not solely under the sentence's control.

AN ILLUSTRATIVE EXPERIMENT

The transformation view treats meaning as a psychological relation between a listener and language; during comprehension, the listener experiences a kind of creative recollection guided by linguistic structure. This process is open to experimental investigation from many angles, focusing on various facets of the psychological relation and exploiting a variety of methodologies. In the case of metaphoric language, two important topics for study are the styles of imaginal experience that metaphors occasion, and the role of sentence structure as a constraint on these experiences. Deborah Davidson, Richard Santucci, and I have recently conducted a study of these two questions; this section will be devoted to a summary of our results. Although simple in design and open-ended in task, the study has proven to be remarkably informative about imaginal processes, the role of sentence form, and the variation of both as a function of individuals and materials.

With our focus on the people reading a metaphoric sentence, we were interested in whether their experiences tended to be fanciful or realistic. More specifically, we wanted to determine whether there was any qualitative evidence in readers' reported experiences for the various ''views'' of metaphor: *substitution* (responses exhibiting a realistic focus on one domain), *comparison* (a realistic focus on similarities in two domains), *interaction* (a somewhat fanciful focus on one domain, showing a marked influence on its identity by the second), or *transformation* (a fanciful, directional, partial fusion of two domains).

With our focus on sentence structure, we were interested in the effects of two structural factors. The first was the *order* of the two noun phrases in a sentence of the form *A is B*. As noted above, a simple comparison view suggests that order should have little or no influence, while the interaction and transformation views both propose directional processes and therefore predict a strong influence of word order. For example, if people report experiencing *transformations* of identity, the *direction* of the transformations should be consistently controlled by word order; specifically, the topic (defined here by sentence position) should be transformed by the predicate.

The second structural factor of interest was sentence *form*, simile (*A is like B*) or metaphor (*A is B*). These sentence forms differ only by the presence or absence of the word *like*. According to the comparison view, this formal difference in surface structure is of no semantic consequence; the two forms are held to have the same underlying deep structure or propositional representation. Yet metaphor seems to make a more dramatic request of the comprehender, since it asserts an identity, while the simile hedges by asserting only a similarity. Is this merely a ''stylistic'' difference, influencing the degree of reader surprise and pleasure, but not otherwise influencing the communicated experience? Neither the interaction view nor the transformation view can accept that this formal difference is ''merely stylistic.'' The metaphor form seems more likely to evoke an imaginal experience in which the topic's identity is transformed, while the simile is more likely to evoke a process of comparison in which the roles of the two terms are relatively equivalent. If so, the frequency of experiencing fanciful transformations should be greater in response to metaphors than to similes.

Design of the Study

The experiment was designed to allow a comparatively direct measure of the kinds of experiences people have when reading a metaphoric sentence. Rather than being subtle about it, we simply asked people to write out a description of the images or thoughts that came to mind when they read a sentence. They were given one sentence at a time, written at the top of a sheet of paper. They were allowed four minutes to write a verbal description of what came to mind, and they were invited to draw a sketch as well. Each person received a total of 10 sentences.

A sample set of materials is presented in Table 5.1 for the word pair *skyscrapers* and *giraffes*. There were four conditions of sentence type, defined by crossing two word orders (AB and BA) with two sentence forms (simile and metaphor). (Order AB is also labeled "Preferred," because it is the word order chosen by more than 50% of readers, in a separate study, when asked which of the two sentences they preferred.) All 10 sentences received by any one person were of the same sentence type (same order and same form). Twenty-five young adults participated in each of the four sentence-type conditions.

There are risks that accompany the benefits of this design. Given the length of the four-minute period, the descriptions were bound to contain more than the reader's immediate experiences. On the other hand, the longer protocols were more likely to show evidence of the analogical elaborations that characterize extended metaphoric thought. Presenting the sentences in isolation would be a problem if one were interested in how discourse context constrains a reader's experience. But our primary concern in this experiment was with sentence structure and how it constrains interpretation. We were willing to let the remainder of constraints on interpretation be supplied by the readers themselves, which produced considerable variability in the specifics of the reported experiences. In

TABLE 5.1
Sample Materials

	Simile Form	Metaphor Form
Order AB (Preferred)	Skyscrapers are like giraffes. (A is like B)	Skyscrapers are giraffes. (A is B)
Order BA (Non-preferred)	Giraffes are like skyscrapers. (B is like A)	Giraffes are skyscrapers. (B is A)

natural communication settings the extrinsic constraints would normally be much tighter. Fortunately, the range of types of responses was sufficiently small to make classification manageable and the study of sentence structure profitable. Finally, as with any set of introspective protocols or dream reports, our readers' descriptions could communicate only a partial account of their experiences and this made classification an interpretive act in its own right. To minimize errors or biases, the descriptions and sketches were classified by three judges, working independently, and the judgments were pooled. The response protocols were randomized before classification, and judges were not aware of which sentence form or word order had been presented.

Classification of Descriptions

The first major distinction was between *condensed* and *uncondensed* descriptions. Borrowing on Freud's use of the term in discussing dream content (Freud, 1900/1950), we defined *condensation* as the combination, in a single imagined event, of elements from two or more domains—in this case, the topic and vehicle domains. Most of the condensed responses were *transformations;* for example, a skyscraper might be visualized with a giraffe's head, nibbling planes out of the sky, or a giraffe might appear with an elevator up its neck and an observation deck on its head. The transformational responses were subclassified as *A becomes B,* if A's identity had been transformed by B's, or as *B becomes A,* if the reverse was true. The following response is an example of an *A becomes B* transformation:

I saw large, tall, windowed buildings which became very skinny and developed spots. (Response to *Skyscrapers are giraffes.*)

The following two responses exemplify the *B becomes A* direction:

I see a giraffe with a body like a building, running through the jungle telling how he's earthquake proof. (*Giraffes are skyscrapers.*)

Tall towering above all else in its environment. The giraffe is tallest of the animals in the jungle—seeming to touch the sky. Little men running up stairs towards the top look through the eyes of the giraffe. When he gets there, he sees the sky. (*Giraffes are skyscrapers.*)

When a description included both directions of transformation, it was scored as *Both.*

Some of the condensed descriptions combined elements of the two domains *without* transforming one domain into the other. These responses were classified as *metonymic*, because they tended simply to juxtapose elements of the two domains in a single event.[3] An (unduly optimistic) example is the following:

Not so much an image, but the basic contrast between the natural and manmade. I guess I see a plain in Africa with giraffes grazing on tippy-top branches, and way in the hazy distance is a modern African city complete with skyscrapers. It's O.K. because there won't have to be a showdown, and the two worlds of one continent can continue to coexist. (*Skyscrapers are like giraffes.*)

To summarize thus far, condensed responses were classified either as *transformational* or *metonymic*, depending on the type of blending of the two domains. The transformational responses were further classified into *A becomes B, B becomes A,* or *Both*, depending on the direction of transformation.

The second broad category, *uncondensed* descriptions, contained responses that did *not* combine elements of the two domains in a single event. If part or all of a description focused predominantly on one domain, it was classified as *focus on A* or *focus on B*. Where both domains became the focus of discussion at some point (typically in successive sentences, separate paragraphs, or separate drawings), the response was scored as *focus on both A and B*. This type of *symmetric* response is illustrated by the following two examples:

New York. The sky is only seen in strips. You look all the way up to see the top of a tall silver-gray-slim-majestic skyscraper.
  Giraffes—eating leaves from the branches of a tree. (*Skyscrapers are like giraffes.*)

Giraffes are tall and huge and tower over basically everything in their environment, every animal in comparison to a giraffe seems miniature in size. The same goes for skyscrapers, they are tall and bigger than mostly all the others around them in the city. (*Skyscrapers are giraffes.*)

The focused responses were also classified by the type of description given to the domain of focus. The description was judged to be a *transformational focus*, if the domain of focus was markedly influenced by properties or peculiarities of the other domain. For example, in response to the sentence *Highways are*

---

[3]This type of condensation is called "metonymic" in honor of *metonymy*, a figure of speech that traffics in relations of contiguity. Some prefer to restrict metonymy to part-part relations, and leave part-whole relations to a figure of speech called *synecdoche;* thus, some condensed responses might more appropriately (though even less pronounceably) be called *synecdochic.* A distinction between metaphoric and metonymic processes has many historical antecedents. In theories of associationism, a distinction was frequently made between association by similarity and association by contiguity, with a tendency to view contiguity relations as fundamental. More recently, Jakobson and Halle (1971) have distinguished between metaphoric and metonymic "poles" in linguistic and narrative structure.

snakes, some readers reported experiencing a highway that actively twisted its way through the hills and valleys. Similarly, in response to *Giraffes are skyscrapers*, some readers visualized an extremely tall giraffe, looming high above the surrounding jungle. Like the change in the highway, this hyperbolic magnification of the giraffe demonstrated the other domain's influence, yet there was no explicit evidence in the description for condensation. This type of response raises a troublesome question for the classification of uncondensed and condensed transformations. The responses contained alterations of identity that were fanciful and interactional, but contained no *explicit* evidence of partial fusion or dual identity, and therefore were classified as uncondensed. However, given the abstractness of the invariants that characterize identity, it may be inappropriate to demand that specific *elements* (such as fangs or windows) must accompany the description of a transformed topic. Condensation need not be a surrealism of *concrete elements*. By a broader definition, evidence for the modulatory influence of an abstract transformational invariant (writhing) or structural invariant (great relative height) could be sufficient for identifying condensation. In light of these considerations, it is clear that the criteria for condensed descriptions (as described above) were conservative; if anything, they led to underestimates of the frequency of fusional transformations.

An uncondensed description that focused on A or B, but for which *no* strong influence of one domain on the other was apparent, was classified as a *neutral focus*. For example, a reader might simply describe a giraffe of conventional anatomy and setting, or the New York City skyline, or both in succession (as in the symmetric responses presented above).

Where an uncondensed description failed to focus on either domain, it was classified as *grounds* or as *other*. Responses that described similarities (sometimes differences) between the two domains were classified in the *grounds* category. These responses tended to be more abstract and generalized than the focused responses, and sometimes contained no verbal or pictorial elements that clearly specified either domain. For example:

> Stately, dignified, a graceful form against a blue, blue sky. (*Giraffes are skyscrapers.*)

The *other* category took the uncondensed leftovers.

To summarize, the uncondensed responses were subdivided into those containing a *transformational focus* on one domain (A or B), a *neutral focus* on one domain (A or B), a summary of *grounds,* or anything else (*other*). In many cases the focused responses dealt successively with each domain; these were labeled *focus on both A and B*. However, since the focus on each domain could be either neutral or transformational, four combinations of *both* responses were possible; for simplicity, these are pooled in the following analysis.

General Findings

The results of the classification are presented in detailed form in Tables 5.2 and 5.3 for the condensed and uncondensed responses, respectively. The tables present the percentage of responses falling in each category for each of the four sentence conditions. The data are pooled over the three judges, the ten word pairs, and the readers (25 per sentence condition). (By several measures, interjudge reliability was found to be very high.) The results are presented in more compact form in Table 5.4, where they have been pooled over the two conditions of word order.

1. *Fanciful Transformations.* Of most general interest were the *types* of experiences people reported in response to the sentences. The bottom row of Table 5.4 summarizes the overall distribution of response types, pooled across the four sentence conditions. The most striking finding was the high proportion of transformational responses: 49% of all responses exhibited transformational condensation and another 22% showed a transformational influence without condensation.

At the outset, these results support the claim that *fanciful* experiences are common when comprehending metaphor. The condensed responses are necessarily fanciful, and many of the uncondensed transformations were fanciful as well. Thus, formalizations of meaning that reduce sentence content to conventional realism miss an essential quality of the comprehension experience: magic. The evidence for this was overwhelming, appearing for every word pair and sentence type. Among the readers, there was certainly variation in their readiness for fanciful experience, but it was striking how strong that readiness tended to be on average, even in a setting that was not particularly solicitous of creativity. In this context, it may be more appropriate to say that the fanciful experiences were responses conventionally solicited by the *sentences,* not responses for which the *readers* maintained an unusual readiness.

Another important facet of this general finding was the pervasiveness of a particular type of fanciful experience—namely, transformations of one domain by another. For most of the transformational responses (whether condensed or uncondensed), the relation between the two domains showed a strong directionality. One of the two domains was clearly the underlying identity and the starting point for a process of transformation. (In unusual cases, including some of the most powerful metaphoric fusions, the directionality was ambiguous or dual; these responses were included in the *Both* category.) These results provide strong evidence for *interactional* processes in comprehension, since a large proportion of responses (condensed and uncondensed) demonstrated a directional modulation of one domain's identity by the other. More specifically, they provide evidence for *transformational* processes, since nearly half of all responses clearly exhibited a partial fusion of the two identities.

There was little support in the response protocols for a *comparison* view of meaning. The typical experience was not an egalitarian comparison that left the two identities unaltered. Nor was it an asymmetric comparison of the kind suggested by Tversky (1977), where one domain dominates a comparison process but again leaves the topic's identity unaltered. For example, the responses classified as *grounds* accounted for only 15% of all responses (see Table 5.4). While some of these responses did display the qualities of an essay of comparison and contrast (as various versions of the comparison view might predict), many were simply abstract. The more abstract responses could be reports about the invariants by which two events have become partially fused, rather than manifestations of a process of comparison.

Responses suggesting a *substitutional* process are even more difficult to identify. Some of the uncondensed descriptions that focused on only one of the two domains might be interpreted as substitutional, but only where the characterization of the topic was conventional and realistically possible. However, as noted above, the alteration of the topic's identity in these focused responses often took a fanciful turn, and this argues for a more interactional approach. Some of the metonymic responses might also be considered substitutional—specifically, the responses we have called *mistaken identity* solutions. In these cases, an identification (perceived or expected) is abandoned as erroneous, and another identity is substituted in its place. For example, several readers responded to the sentence *Strawwrappers are snakeskins* with a story about a practical joke at a fast-food place: someone tears off the end of a strawwrapper and, instead of a straw, a little green snake jumps out! Although this is a condensed description, it is really a type of conventional construal; it neatly resolves the stated identity by juxtaposing a real snake and a real strawwrapper, and not altering or reinterpreting either one.

Our thousand protocols contained a wealth of evidence that metaphor can catalyze an identity-transforming process, in which familiar structural or transformational constraints are applied in a new domain. This process often extended well beyond the immediate assertions of the sentences themselves. For example, in response to the metaphor *Leaves are fingers*, one person wrote the following:

> I see a tree with thousands of fingers growing as leaves. The wind blows them and they move and wave. Birds fly into the tree and the fingers grab them and hang on to them. But they soon let them go. At night the fingers curl up into fists. Sometimes they "cup" together to hold bird nests.

Another person, working the transformation in the opposite direction, wrote the following:

> If we all had leaves as fingers we couldn't do very much. We wouldn't be able to pick very many things up and in the fall our "fingers" would fall off! They would be pretty colors though.

A third reader not only transformed the fingers, but the person's body and context:

I imagine a large person planted in the soil. He has many fingerlike leaves that are blowing in the wind.

Each of these descriptions exemplifies the process of analogical extension: The metaphor serves as the starting point for a *series of metamorphoses* in the topic domain, each of which brings new insight or fanciful pleasure.

The descriptions also showed a variety of efforts to accommodate the two identities to one another. For example, the third reader above graciously planted the person in the soil so that his compatibility with a leafy tree would be enhanced. Other readers particularized the leaves as pine needles or as five-lobed structures, again enhancing the degree of shared identity. In all of these cases, we see a *reciprocal* action between the topic and vehicle, constraining each other's identity where there is freedom to do so (i.e., where linguistic and environmental context do not fully constrain them).

2. *Effect of Word Order.* The order of the two noun phrases in the sentences presented to readers had a strong effect on the directionality of the experienced transformations. In general, the *first* term of a sentence more frequently specified the domain that was transformed. For example, 44% of the people who read *Skyscrapers are giraffes* experienced a condensed transformation of skyscrapers into giraffes (A becomes B), while only 12% experienced the opposite direction of transformation (B becomes A). Similarly, of those reading *Giraffes are skyscrapers*, 35% experienced giraffes turning into skyscrapers (B becomes A) and 28% experienced the opposite direction. This pattern of ordinal differences was also found for the corresponding similes. Pooled results for all ten word pairs are presented in Table 5.2. A strong interaction between word order (AB, BA) and direction of transformation (A becomes B, B becomes A) was observed both for similes ($t = 5.07$, $p < .001$) and for metaphors ($t = 6.34$, $p < .001$); response frequencies were concentrated in cells where the first term in the sentence was the domain transformed.[4] A similar interaction between word order and focus of transformation appeared in the distribution of uncondensed transformations (Table 5.3); the interactions were significant both for similes ($t = 4.82$, $p < .001$) and metaphors ($t = 7.00$, $p < .001$).

These results provide a further demonstration that the sentence form A *is (like)* B is not psychologically symmetric. The grammatical subject of the sentence is more likely to specify the *psychological* subject or focus, and this distinguishes

---

[4]The t-statistics assess the following question: Given a condensed transformational response, what are the odds that it will be in the A *becomes* B direction, and do these odds differ for the two sentence orders?

TABLE 5.2
Condensed Responses (as Percentages of Total Responses)

Sentence Condition	Transformational			Metonymic	Total Condensed
	A becomes B	B becomes A	Both		
Simile					
Order AB	25.6	13.6	2.4	4.7	46.3
Order BA	15.5	19.9	3.1	8.5	46.9
Metaphor					
Order AB	37.6	16.4	4.3	1.9	60.1
Order BA	24.9	27.7	4.3	2.4	59.3

its role from that of the predicate noun phrase. Thus, contrary to the traditional comparison view, a metaphoric sentence is not a symmetric equation or equivalence relation. The sentence directs attention differentially to the topic. This is compatible with the more general finding (or rediscovery) that the sentence subject typically establishes what is "given," and the predicate proffers what is "new" (cf. Clark & Haviland, 1977).

One must hasten to add, however, that word order is only one of several factors that can exert an influence on a metaphor's directionality. A second influential factor is a directional bias that can favor one member of a particular pair of noun phrases, independent of their order in a sentence. For both similes and metaphors, the directionality of condensed transformations was more sharply defined for Order AB than for Order BA (see Table 5.2); the distribution of these responses suggests a bias toward the *A becomes B* transformation. It is important to recall that particular sentence orders were labeled as Order AB because they were the sentences people had rated as *Preferred* in an earlier study. It is likely that these preferences for one of the two word orders (A is B) expressed a bias toward taking one of the domains (A) as the focus for attention and modification. One clear example of this was the word pair *schools-prisons*. The *Schools are (like) prisons* word order was preferred in the rating task, and the corresponding transformation (schools becoming prisons) was much more frequent than the reverse direction in readers' descriptions, even when the readers encountered *Prisons are (like) schools*. Of the condensed transformations for this word pair, 83% showed the schools-become-prisons direction (pooling over all sentence conditions). Another good example was the word pair *highways-snakes*. The *Highways are (like) snakes* order was preferred, and this was reflected in a bias toward highways-become-snakes transformations. It seemed relatively easy for people to imagine highways as snakelike: Highways can be long and thin, they can wind sinuously through the hills, they can have slippery "backs" with stripes down the middle, and so on. Turning snakes into highways does not seem to be

TABLE 5.3
Uncondensed Responses (as Percentages of Total Responses)

Sentence Condition	Transformational Focus		Neutral Focus		Focus on Both A and B	Grounds	Other	Total Uncondensed[a]
	A	B	A	B				
Simile								
Order AB	18.1	6.9	12.7	11.1	15.5	18.8	1.6	53.7
Order BA	12.7	13.7	12.0	12.0	16.7	18.0	1.3	53.1
Metaphor								
Order AB	17.9	7.9	6.8	5.1	9.6	10.7	1.2	39.9
Order BA	8.1	16.8	6.3	4.7	8.8	12.4	1.2	40.7

[a] Sum of each row, less percentage of responses focusing on both A and B.

as easy or productive. One person visualized a group of snakes forming freeway-like cloverleafs. Another visionary saw ants marching in columns along a snake's back. In general, however, transformations of this type were relatively infrequent. This seems to be due, in part, to a greater difficulty in applying idiosyncrasies of highways to snakes than vice versa.

These results suggest that the directionality of the metaphoric process can be influenced as much by intrinsic differences in subject matter as by changes in sentence structure. Explaining the preferences associated with particular topic-vehicle pairs is an especially strong challenge for any proposed theory of metaphor. Some preferences may derive from conventional (even clichéd) directions of comparison, as in the *schools-prisons* example. Personal relevance or familiarity may also affect what is taken as the preferred focus of attention (or *topic*). On the other hand, greater familiarity with relationships in one of the two domains could also lead that domain to play the role of *vehicle*, as could its relative proto-typicality of some shared relationship. Preferences may also be based on the ease with which constraints on one identity can be applied to another, as in the *high-way-snake* example. Explaining these preferences is important for understanding judgments of literary quality, the acceptance of scientific models, the content of mythologies, the progress of psychotherapy, and many other phenomena beyond the normal confines of psycholinguistics. It will also prove important for under-standing why such processes as personification, animism, anthropomorphism, reification, and materialism are so prevalent in human cognition.

3. *Effect of Sentence Form (Simile or Metaphor).*   While the difference in surface structure between the similes and metaphors was slight, it had a signifi-cant impact on readers' experiences. The most striking difference between the two sentence forms appeared in the frequencies of condensed transformation: 58% of all responses to metaphors contained clear evidence of condensed trans-formation, while this was true of only 40% of the responses to similes (see Table 5.4); the difference was strongly significant across all word pairs, $F(1,9) = 52.9$, $p < .001$.[5] This demonstrates that, ceteris paribus, the metaphor form is more likely to evoke a fanciful, directional transformation in which two identities are partially fused. Evidence for an effect of sentence form was also found for the other subtype of condensation: Similes evoked a greater number of metonymic condensations than metaphors. For example, for the *skyscraper-giraffe* word pair, 14% of the responses to similes were metonymic condensations; these were cases in which the two domains were juxtaposed, but retained their separate

----

[5]The F-statistics are based on analyses of variance for designs crossing sentence form and sentence order; the 10 word pairs served as a repeated measure. Scores were the number of readers (out of 25) who produced a response of the designated type. The several tests are not strictly independent. Categorical data analyses completed to date verify the significant differences reported here.

TABLE 5.4
Percent Responses by Category (Pooled over Orders AB and BA)

Sentence Form	Condensed		Uncondensed				
	Transformational	Metonymic	Transformational	Neutral	Both A and B	Grounds	Other
Simile	40.0	6.6	22.1	11.3	16.1	18.4	1.5
Metaphor	57.6	2.1	22.7	5.3	9.2	11.5	1.2
Overall	48.8	4.4	22.2	8.3	12.6	15.0	1.3

identities (giraffes observing cities from afar, giraffes walking around the city streets, and so on). In marked contrast, *none* of the responses to the corresponding metaphors were of this type. Across the ten word pairs, metonymic responses were significantly more frequent for similes (7% on average) than for metaphors (2%), $F(1,9) = 10.5$, $p < .01$.

Differences between the sentence forms were also found for some of the uncondensed response categories. Neutrally focused descriptions of the topic and vehicle occurred more frequently in response to similes (11%) than to metaphors (5%). This difference was strongly significant, $F(1,9) = 33.4$, $p < .001$. Differences were also present in response categories that manifest a symmetric (nondirectional) perspective on two domains. Grounds responses tended to be more frequent to similes (18%) than to metaphors (12%), $F(1,9) = 29.1$, $p < .001$. A similar difference was found for the uncondensed responses that focused on *both* domains (e.g., in successive paragraphs or separate drawings). It is interesting to note that these evenhanded descriptions appeared more frequently in response to similes (16%) than to metaphors (9%), $F(1,9) = 28.6$, $p < .001$.

While these differences are not strictly independent of one another, the categories in which they appear show a consistent pattern. Similes are more frequently associated with responses in which elements of the two domains retain their separate identities, and in which the two domains are treated symmetrically (by juxtaposition, back-and-forth comparison, or a focus on resemblances). Metaphors are more frequently associated with responses in which elements of one or both domains are transformed in identity, and in which the two domains show an asymmetric division of roles as transformer and transformed. The differences between the simile and metaphor forms are not categorical, but more a matter of degree; as constraints on the course of thought, they are gently firm, not rigid. Of the two forms, metaphor makes the stronger request for a transformation of identity. While the request may not always be honored, a writer's use of the metaphor form (rather than a simile) is at least more likely to catalyze a reader's thought in a transformational direction. Thus, the choice between the two forms is a genuine degree-of-freedom available to the writer for guiding the reader's thought. Evoking a transformational process could be considered desirable for its dramatic force, playfulness, and impact on understanding, while in other circumstances it might be a nuisance, warping the topic in ways that only distract the reader. If the two forms were truly equivalent in semantic force, there would be no systematic basis for the writer's choice.

The goal of semantic description is presumably to characterize distinctions of meaning made by users of a language. While we can gain some economy by attributing *identical* forms to semantically *similar* expressions, it is all too easy to obliterate important distinctions in the process. It is also all too easy to slip into the habitual synecdoche of treating semantic representations as properties of the linguistic forms themselves. Semantics should be conceived more broadly as the analysis of a psychological relation, a relation between linguistic forms and language users. From this perspective, and with data in hand, it is reasonable to argue that the metaphor form does have a distinct semantic function. Its function goes well beyond the induction of surprise and pleasure, for it can catalyze a process that transforms understanding. It may not be possible for a writer to achieve this function as effectively, or at all, by other linguistic means.

SUMMARY AND PROSPECTS

This chapter has had three objectives: to outline the framework of a theory of metaphor compatible with nonrepresentational realism, to distinguish the new approach from some traditional views of metaphor, and to describe a study of the processes catalyzed by metaphoric sentences. The first section discussed the epistemological bases of a realist approach to language. In contrast to phenomenalism, realism rejects the need for internal representations that correspond, by hypothesis, to an unknowable world beyond. The relation of person to environment is not one of problematic correspondence, but of necessary synergy. Applied to language, this logic argues the surprising conclusions that validity in communication is the norm, and that comprehension and production are unmediated by representations. Metaphoric language poses a special challenge, because it has traditionally been thought to epitomize equivocality of meaning and a need for representational mediation. The approach to metaphor developed here seeks to avoid these problems by viewing the person-language relation as an irreducible, dynamic synergy, by taking an individual's attunement to invariants as the generative base for the experiences prompted by language, and by interpreting the multiple effects of a single sentence form as context-dependent resolutions to an invariant "request."

In the second section, the *transformation* view of metaphor was contrasted with several traditional approaches. In the spirit of linguistic phenomenalism, the *substitution* and *comparison* views treat metaphor as an arbitrary or ambiguous substitute for a hidden meaning; each view postulates special mechanisms for reconstructing the underlying conventional meaning. In contrast, the transformation view treats meaning as a property of a psychological relation, not of linguistic forms (whether surface or deep), and it argues that this relation can be specific and precise when the full context of ecological support is considered. The transformation view is similar to the *interaction* view, in treating metaphor as a directional and fanciful alteration of a topic's identity, but the two views differ on issues of semantic representation, topic-vehicle differentiation, and underlying epistemology. According to the transformation view, metaphor may lead to (or flow from) a partial fusion of two identities. The transformation is *catalyzed* by (not *represented* by) linguistic forms, which both initiate and constrain the redintegrative process. Once initiated, the process can develop autonomously into a series of metamorphoses that alter one's attunement to structure in both domains.

These properties of metaphoric understanding were illustrated in the third section of the chapter, which summarized a study of the experiences people report after reading a metaphoric sentence. Transformational experiences were reported with high frequency, while a minority of responses showed a neutral focus on one domain, both domains, or on resemblances in general. The study demonstrated a strong effect of word order on the directionality of transformation, although this effect was overridden to some extent by a preference for taking one of the two domains as the focus of transformation. The study also demonstrated consistent differences in the experiences evoked by simile and metaphor sentence forms. The metaphor form produced significantly more fanciful and asymmetric transformational responses, while the simile form more frequently produced neutral and symmetric responses. The effects of word order and sentence form exemplify the redintegrative constraints that are "conventionally" exerted by sentence structure. The idiosyncratic constraints exerted by the readers were not systematically controlled, but the variability in readers' responses attested to their powerful role.

This chapter has provided only the starting point for a realist theory of metaphor. The agenda for future theory and research is long. Progress in our understanding of metaphor depends on solutions to a much broader range of problems than those within the immediate scope of linguistic metaphor itself. From the perspective of *process,* general solutions to the nature of recollection and imagination are needed, with special attention to how these are guided (or "tuned") by language. In the case of metaphoric language, we need to develop more explicit analyses of the process of transformation, viewed as a dynamic biological process in a social environment. Such an account must be able to identify the conditions (both autonomous and environmental) that catalyze the process, to predict the time course of its development, and to explain its directionality and relative permanence. In addition, an effective theory must explain how fantasy derives from perception and action, and how it subserves their reattunement; in short, it must explain how fantasy can find a natural home in realism.

From the perspective of *content*, a realist theory of metaphor depends on a broader understanding of perceptual invariants and their role in linguistic semantics. If these invariants supply the "content" of virtual experiences (including those prompted by metaphor), they should offer a more appropriate medium for defining identity than any single structural grid that might be forcibly applied to all experience. The challenge, therefore, is to demonstrate that perceptual invariants provide the natural medium for our representations (as theoreticians, not minds) of metaphoric meaning. A successful analysis will allow us to define the structural factors that constrain fusion, to predict the direction and extent of transformation for specific combinations of terms, and ultimately to explain why certain metaphors strike us as fresh, exciting, or profound.

The payoff from a realist theory of metaphoric processes can be enormous. If we can explain how a linguistic metaphor catalyzes a change in knowing, our understanding should extend to a broad range of developmental processes, both linguistic and nonlinguistic, individual and social. If we can identify what governs the separation and fusion of identities in metaphor, our understanding should extend to all phenomena of multiple identity, including play and imitation, recollection and reverie, dissociation and age regression, transparency and figure-ground separation, and coarticulated movement. Many would argue that, without the microcosm as our favored self-description, these goals are unattainable. On the contrary, they may be realistic only if we are.

ACKNOWLEDGMENTS

Preparation of this chapter was supported by a fellowship to the author from the University of Michigan Society of Fellows, a grant from the University of Connecticut Research Foundation, grants from the University of Connecticut Computer Center, and a grant to Haskins Laboratories from the National Institute of Child Health and Human Development (HD-01994). Support from all of these sources is gratefully acknowledged.

Portions of this chapter derive from a paper presented at the Conference on Metaphor sponsored by the Department of Rhetoric, University of California at Davis, April 28-29, 1978 ("Metaphor: The virtual perception of multiple identity"); and from a paper presented at the symposium, *Metaphor and image: Recent psycholinguistic research* (R. Hoffman, Chair), at the meeting of the American Psychological Association, Toronto, August 29, 1978 ("Metaphor and the recognition of identity"). Special thanks are due to the entire staff of the Department of Rhetoric at Davis, and to Robert Hoffman, for their organizational skills, enthusiasm, and constructive criticism. I have also profited greatly from the suggestions of Richard Honeck, Robert Katz, Kathleen McCormick, and Brad Rakerd, who were as mystified as I by earlier drafts—and were able to tell me where and why. The chapter is dedicated to Chicory (who thrives on foodscraps and fantasy).

Correspondence may be addressed to Robert R. Verbrugge, Department of Psychology, University of Connecticut, Storrs, CT 06268.

REFERENCES

Anderson, C. D. The psychology of the metaphor. *Journal of Genetic Psychology,* 1964, *105,* 53–73.

Anderson, J. R. Arguments concerning representations for mental imagery. *Psychological Review,* 1978, *85,* 249–277.

Arieti, S. *Interpretation of schizophrenia* (2nd Ed.). New York: Basic Books, 1974.

Arieti, S. *Creativity: The magic synthesis.* New York: Basic Books, 1976.

Berkeley, G. An essay toward a new theory of vision. In A. A. Luce & T. E. Jessup (Eds.), *The works of George Berkeley.* London: Thomas Nelson and Sons, 1964. (Originally published, 1709.)

Black, M. *Models and metaphors.* Ithaca, N.Y.: Cornell University Press, 1962.

Bolles, R. C. *Learning theory.* New York: Holt, Rinehart & Winston, 1975.

Bransford, J. D., & McCarrell, N. S. A sketch of a cognitive approach to comprehension. In W. Weimer & D. Palermo (Eds.), *Cognition and the symbolic processes.* Hillsdale, N.J.: Lawrence Erlbaum Associates, 1974.

Brown, R. W. *Words and things.* New York: Free Press, 1958.

Brown, R. W., Leiter, R. A., & Hildum, D. C. Metaphors from music criticism. *Journal of Abnormal and Social Psychology,* 1957, *54,* 347–352.

Bundy, M. W. The theory of imagination in classical and medieval thought. *University of Illinois Studies in Language and Literature,* 1927, *12* (2–3), 1–471.

Clark, H. H., & Haviland, S. E. Comprehension and the given-new contract. In R. O. Freedle (Ed.), *Discourse production and comprehension.* Norwood, N.J.: Ablex Publishing Corporation, 1977.

Culler, J. *Structuralist poetics.* Ithaca, N.Y.: Cornell University Press, 1975.

Feirstein, A. Personality correlates of tolerance for unrealistic experiences. *Journal of Consulting Psychology,* 1967, *31,* 387–395.

Fowler, C. A., & Turvey, M. T. Skill acquisition: An event approach with special reference to searching for the optimum of a function of several variables. In G. Stelmach (Ed.), *Information processing in motor control and learning.* New York: Academic Press, 1978.

Freud, S. [*The interpretation of dreams*] (A. A. Brill, Trans.). New York: Modern Library, 1950. (Originally published, 1900.)

Gibson, J. J. *The senses considered as perceptual systems.* Boston: Houghton Mifflin, 1966.

Gibson, J. J. New reasons for realism. *Synthese,* 1967, *17,* 162–172.

Gibson, J. J. *The ecological approach to visual perception.* Boston: Houghton Mifflin, 1979.

Hamilton, W. *Lectures on metaphysics and logic* (4 Vols.). Edinburgh: W. Blackwood and Sons, 1859.

Harris, R. J., Lahey, M. A., & Marsalek, F. E. Imagery and memory for metaphors. In R. Hoffman (Chair), *Metaphor and image: Recent psycholinguistic research.* Symposium presented at the meeting of the American Psychological Association, Toronto, August 1978.

Harwood, D., & Verbrugge, R. R. Metaphor and the asymmetry of similarity. In W. Kintsch (Chair), *Recent psycholinguistic research with metaphors.* Symposium presented at the meeting of the American Psychological Association, San Francisco, August 1977.

Hollingworth, H. L. *The psychology of thought.* New York: Appleton, 1926.

Honeck, R. P., Voegtle, K., & Sowry, B. Proverbial understanding in a pictorial context. *Child Development,* 1978, *49,* 327–331.

Jakobson, R., & Halle, M. *Fundamentals of language.* The Hague: Mouton, 1971.

Jenkins, J. J. Remember that old theory of memory? Well, forget it! *American Psychologist*, 1974, *29*, 785-795.

Kintsch, W. *The representation of meaning in memory*. Hillsdale, N.J.: Lawrence Erlbaum Associates, 1974.

Klein, G. S., Gardner, R. W., & Schlesinger, H. J. Tolerance for unrealistic experiences: A study of the generality of a cognitive control. *British Journal of Psychology*, 1962, *53*, 41-55.

Koen, F. An intraverbal explication of the nature of metaphor. *Journal of Verbal Learning and Verbal Behavior*, 1965, *4*, 129-133.

Kris, E. *Psychoanalytic explorations in art*. New York: International Universities Press, 1952.

Leech, G. N. *A linguistic guide to English poetry*. London: Longman, 1969.

Levin, S. R. *The semantics of metaphor*. Baltimore: Johns Hopkins University Press, 1977.

Levin, S. R. Standard approaches to metaphor and a proposal for literary metaphor. In A. Ortony (Ed.), *Metaphor and thought*. Cambridge, England: Cambridge University Press, 1979.

Mack, D. Metaphoring as speech act: Some happiness conditions for implicit similes and metaphors. *Poetics*, 1975, *4*, 221-256.

Malgady, R. G., & Johnson, M. G. Modifiers in metaphors: Effects of constituent phrase similarity on the interpretation of figurative sentences. *Journal of Psycholinguistic Research*, 1976, *5*, 43-52.

Matthews, R. J. Concerning a 'linguistic theory' of metaphor. *Foundations of Language*, 1971, *7*, 413-425.

Miller, G. A. Images and models, similes and metaphors. In A. Ortony (Ed.), *Metaphor and thought*. Cambridge, England: Cambridge University Press, 1979.

Ortony, A., Schallert, D. L., Reynolds, R. E., & Antos, S. J. Interpreting metaphors and idioms: Some effects of context on comprehension. *Journal of Verbal Learning and Verbal Behavior*, 1978, *17*, 465-477.

Osgood, C. E., Suci, G., & Tannenbaum, P. *The measurement of meaning*. Urbana: University of Illinois Press, 1957.

Pavlov, I. P. [*Lectures on conditioned reflexes*] (S. Belsky, Trans.). Moscow: Foreign Language Publishing House, 1955.

Pollio, H. Metaphoric style: Personal cognition and figurative language. In W. Kintsch (Chair), *Recent psycholinguistic research with metaphors*. Symposium presented at the meeting of the American Psychological Association, San Francisco, August 1977.

Pollio, H. R., Barlow, J. M., Fine, H. J., & Pollio, M. R. *Psychology and the poetics of growth*. Hillsdale, N.J.: Lawrence Erlbaum Associates, 1977.

Pratt, M. L. *Toward a speech act theory of literary discourse*. Bloomington: Indiana University Press, 1977.

Pylyshyn, Z. W. What the mind's eye tells the mind's brain: A critique of mental imagery. *Psychological Bulletin*, 1973, *80*, 1-24.

Reddy, M. The conduit metaphor—A case of frame conflict in our language about language. In A. Ortony (Ed.), *Metaphor and thought*. Cambridge, England: Cambridge University Press, 1979.

Richards, I. A. *The philosophy of rhetoric*. Oxford: Oxford University Press, 1936.

Riechmann, P. F., & Coste, E. L. Role of imagery in comprehending and remembering metaphor. In R. Hoffman (Chair), *Metaphor and image: Recent psycholinguistic research*. Symposium presented at the meeting of the American Psychological Association, Toronto, August 1978.

Rogers, R. *Metaphor: A psychoanalytic view*. Berkeley: University of California Press, 1978.

Russell, B. *The analysis of mind*. London: Allen & Unwin, 1921.

Schön, D. A. Generative metaphor: A perspective on problem-setting in social policy. In A. Ortony (Ed.), *Metaphor and thought*. Cambridge, England: Cambridge University Press, 1979.

Shaw, R. E., & Bransford, J. D. Introduction: Psychological approaches to the problems of knowledge. In R. E. Shaw & J. D. Bransford (Eds.), *Perceiving, acting and knowing: Toward an ecological psychology*. Hillsdale, N.J.: Lawrence Erlbaum Associates, 1977.

Shaw, R. E., & Pittenger, J. Perceiving the face of change in changing faces: Implications for a theory of object perception. In R. E. Shaw & J. D. Bransford (Eds.), *Perceiving, acting, and knowing: Toward an ecological psychology.* Hillsdale, N.J.: Lawrence Erlbaum Associates, 1977.

Shaw, R. E., Turvey, M. T., & Mace, W. Ecological psychology: The consequence of a commitment to realism. In W. Weimer & D. Palermo (Eds.), *Cognition and the symbolic processes II.* Hillsdale, N.J.: Lawrence Erlbaum Associates, in press.

Sternberg, R. J. *Intelligence, information processing, and analogical reasoning.* Hillsdale, N.J.: Lawrence Erlbaum Associates, 1977.

Tourangeau, R., & Sternberg, R. J. *Aptness in metaphor* (ONR Tech. Rep. No. 13). New Haven: Department of Psychology, Yale University, 1978.

Turvey, M. T. Contrasting orientations to the theory of visual information processing. *Psychological Review,* 1977, *84,* 67-88.

Turvey, M. T., & Shaw, R. E. The primacy of perceiving: An ecological reformulation of perception as a point of departure for understanding memory. In L-G. Nilsson (Ed.), *Perspectives on memory research: Essays in honor of Uppsala University's 500th anniversary.* Hillsdale, N.J.: Lawrence Erlbaum Associates, 1979.

Turvey, M. T., Shaw, R. E., & Mace, W. Issues in the theory of action: Degrees of freedom, coordinative structures, and coalitions. In J. Requin (Ed.), *Attention and performance* (Vol. 7). Hillsdale, N.J.: Lawrence Erlbaum Associates, 1978.

Tversky, A. Features of similarity. *Psychological Review,* 1977, *84,* 327-352.

Verbrugge, R. R. *The comprehension of analogy.* Unpublished doctoral dissertation, University of Minnesota, 1974.

Verbrugge, R. R. *Perceiving invariants at the invitation of metaphor.* Paper presented at the meeting of the American Psychological Association, Chicago, August 1975.

Verbrugge, R. R. Resemblances in language and perception. In R. E. Shaw & J. D. Bransford (Eds.), *Perceiving, acting, and knowing: Toward an ecological psychology.* Hillsdale, N.J.: Lawrence Erlbaum Associates, 1977.

Verbrugge, R. R., & McCarrell, N. S. Metaphoric comprehension: Studies in reminding and resembling. *Cognitive Psychology,* 1977, *9,* 494-533.

Werner, H., & Kaplan, B. *Symbol formation: An organismic-developmental approach to language and the expression of thought.* New York: Wiley, 1963.

6 Proverbs, Meaning, and Group Structure

Richard P. Honeck
University of Cincinnati

Katherine Voegtle
State University College at Oswego

Mark A. Dorfmueller
University of Cincinnati

Robert R. Hoffman
University of Minnesota

OVERVIEW

This chapter describes the "state of the art" of the psychology of proverbs. Our interest is less in the nature of proverbs, however, than in the light they shed on two interrelated problems—the nature of abstract mental entities and the generativity of behavioral acts. We approach these problems of knowledge from a "Phenomenalist" as opposed to a "Realist" perspective (see Verbrugge, this volume). That is, we claim that language understanding involves the elaboration and integration of "information" that, by itself, is insufficient to specify either abstract mental entities or their result, the recognition and production of novel instances.

In general, the lessons to be gleaned from in-depth inquiry into proverbial understanding constitute a serious challenge for and constraint upon semantic theory. The chapter builds on this claim by first describing the "common view" of proverbs, one that we reject but that our experience suggests is held by many investigators, and that, together with the Literalist approach (see the following), either naively ignores proverbs (and metaphors, etc.) or rejects them as idle anomalies bereft of theoretical import. We then lay out the basic psychological properties of proverbs, the implications of which take us far beyond the common view and begin to mark the Literalist approach as inadequate and incomplete. We

127

conclude with a fairly exhaustive review of the literature on proverbs, and a prologue to a theory of proverbial understanding featuring a comparison of metaphors and proverbs as a means of developing the theory.

THE COMMON VIEW OF PROVERBS

Proverbs are part of the language medium of every culture, certainly of every literate culture. As adults in an English speaking culture, we are familiar with and can recognize hundreds of proverbs, although there are thousands more that are unfamiliar to us. Proverbs typically comment on social activities—religion, sex, commerce, law, medicine, education, and so on. Parents, teachers, judges, and the clergy, as purveyors of social consciousness, have been, through the millenia, reliable repositories of witty, edifying sayings. Indeed, the flavor and much of the content of the world's religions was encapsulated in proverbial form by the Hebrew prophets, Christ, and the Buddha. Nevertheless, the contemporary influence and prestige of proverbs is minimal compared, say, with the Elizabethan age, which was "soaked in proverbs" (Smith & Heseltine, 1935).

Today, proverbs tend to elicit reactions of both a pure associative and a rational-emotive sort. Benjamin Franklin's Poor Richard's Almanac, Confucious, Mao Tse Tung, Aesop's Fables, and TV commercials are popular associations to proverbs. The many rational-emotive reactions to proverbs decompose into considerations of time, truth, esthetics, paradox, humor, and quaintness—a completely intuitive factoring of such reactions that, unfortunately, we cannot pursue here.

Reactions to proverbs as experimental materials are often negative because, their detractors say, proverbs are familiar and reflect only rote memory processes—not more important reconstructive remembering; they are rare and restrictive in use—by implication, have no ecological validity; they have undesirable surface characteristics—that cannot easily be corrected and act as confounds; they were constructed by sages rather than by the common folk—by implication, special and incapable of being constructed anew; and, they are even contradictory at times—the height of nonsense!

The common view leads to the conclusion that proverbs should be consigned to study by rhetoricians, philologists, and cultural anthropologists (e.g., Seitel, 1977). In fact, such interests as in the origin, history, collection, translation, etc. of proverbs are served by many paroemiologists (see Mieder, 1975). The journal *Proverbium* also serves these interests as do various journals of folklore.

THE LITERALIST APPROACH

Within psychology the common view is aided, abetted, and generally complemented by what can be called the Literalist approach. This approach is epitomized in various degrees by network (Collins & Quillian, 1969), feature (Rips, Shoben, & Smith, 1973; Smith, Shoben, & Rips, 1974), set-theoretic (Meyer, 1970) and propositional (network) approaches (Anderson & Bower, 1973; Kintsch, 1974; Norman & Rumelhart, 1975) to semantic processing. Although these models were developed for slightly different purposes and have used somewhat different tasks and materials, they share certain basic assumptions or claims. In our view, these claims preclude their adequately handling, or, more fundamentally, even recognizing the existence of, figurative language phenomena.

In general, whether explicitly or implicitly, Literalist approaches involve the following core claims (whose precise nature varies with the particular model): Primitive elements (e.g., features, concepts, propositions) are said to exist in memory—the element postulate. Words are representable in memory as a static collection (i.e., a dictionary) of elements—the dictionary postulate. The elements are related in terms of links or paths bearing labels describing the nature of the relationship (e.g., case relation, part-whole) and varying in their directionality—the link postulate. Words that are semantically similar are "closer together" in memory than are disjoint words, that is, distance is a direct function of element overlap—the distance postulate. The labels or descriptions on the paths place restrictions upon possible element combinations—the restriction postulate. Elements combine in a compositional, non-Gestalt manner—the compositionality postulate. Remembering constitutes an attempt to match input elements or element structures with those already stored; stored elements are usually content-addressable, and matching is a matter of compatibility of input element structure with memory element structure—the matching postulate. Outputs (recall, true-false judgments, etc.) reflect knowledge as a verification process—the verification postulate. (The ultimate form of the verification view is procedural semantics which replaces the proposition as the basic element or sense of a linguistic unit, with mental procedures for deciding when the unit applies to an event. See Miller & Johnson-Laird, 1976.)

THE PSYCHOLINGUISTIC PROPERTIES OF PROVERBS

Our view of the nature of proverbs is quite the opposite of the common view. As we shall see, the naive psychological assertions that form this view are false. Moreover, proverbs have a number of interesting properties that not only make them ideal experimental materials but that, by their implication, severely strain the adequacy of Literalist claims.

The basic property of proverbs is that they can be understood on both a literal and a figurative level. All other properties depend upon this fact. To use the statement *Bees have honey in their mouths and stingers in their tails* as a proverb is to say something about some X such that X has both positive and negative properties; for example, that people can be kind one moment and cruel the next. The proverb, *qua proverb*, contains no specific information about real bees, honey, mouths, stingers, or tails. The proverb is a whole, an emergent. Moreover, there may be more than one figurative interpretation for a proverb and they may not be on the same "level." Literalist approaches have no mechanisms for handling these phenomena—that is, the literal-figurative distinction, noncompositionality, and figurative levels. What proverbs "say" (as a literal statement) does not match what they are about or refer to. Therefore, they must be treated by the "matching postulate" as merely false or anomalous. The figurative level contains information not totally specifiable by the literal level, hence the "compositionality postulate" is also violated. In short, Literalist models can not recognize the distinction between truth-falsity, anomaly, and figurative communication.

A second property is that the relationship between the literal and figurative levels is constrained. That is, the figurative level embeds and is directed by information at the literal level. This is true despite the large "distance" that may obtain between the levels. Clearly, this second property forces us to examine both levels more closely, especially the literal level. Literalist approaches take this level for granted as a "given" that is frequently reconstructed as a propositional structure. Unfortunately, such propositions often turn out to be unanalyzed (and uninterpreted) concepts. Thus, the application of these approaches to figuratively related linguistic constructions, which often do not share major vocabulary, is difficult at best. If propositions do not share "arguments," how can they be related?

To say, for example, that *Great weights hang on small wires* comes to mean *The outcome of important events may depend on seemingly minor details,* because the latter is an inference from the former, may only confuse matters if inference is used as a special, stop-gap mechanism. Too often, Literalist approaches, among others, invoke inference as an ad hoc explanation when the distance between element configurations does not lend itself to a match (i.e., when pattern recognition fails). A related problem is that a dictionary view cannot countenance the context-dependent creation of ever fresh, potentially unlimited elements. Stated more abstractly, the general problem is that whereas B is not A, A constrains (but does not determine) B by interacting with the total language context to effect novel transformations on the old elements. As William James remarked, "A permanently existing idea which makes its appearance before the footlights of consciousness, is a mythological an entity as the Jack of Spades."

The first two properties suggest a useful rapprochement with the depth of processing (Craik & Lockhart, 1972) framework. Indeed, Baddeley (1978) argues that advancement of this framework has been frustrated by failures in attempts to distinguish levels within the semantic level. Proverbs "stop the world" (as Castenada's sorcerer would have it) for the would-be interpreter—

overcoming the literal barrier can be problematical. Thus, we can examine the memorial consequences of processing on a literal or figurative level. In addition, we might ask how imagery is related to these two levels. Is imagery, aroused by the literal level, incompatible with figurative understanding? (What do images of the literal level of the "great weights" proverb have to do with its figurative meaning?) Or can it assume figurative potential in the same way as the verbal statement itself?

We should also note in connection with the constraint property that there are a number of kindred linguistic forms such as precepts, adages, apothegms, truisms, maxims, bywords, aphorisms, paradoxes, morals, fables, Wellerisms, and so forth. No theoretical distinctions motivate the use of these different labels. However, proverbs are typically less constrained in their figurativeness than these other forms, with respect to both the interpretation itself and to the range of its illustration or "representative potential" (McKane, 1970). Maxims, for example, (e.g., *Haste makes waste*) are generalizations about a single domain of experience, while a proverb typically extends to a large number of different domains.

A third property of proverbs is that the figurative level need not be, although it often is, signaled by the syntax or the semantics of the statement itself. Their figurativeness can be disguised in a simple literal statement. This property makes many proverbs seem quite innocent and innocuous. An important consequence, however, is that a proverb need not be altered or mutilated in *any* way to observe the effects of context. Compare this with part-sentence metaphor and simile where the existence of anomaly *within* a linguistic construction can invite a figurative interpretation, irrespective of context. Thus, proverbs provide an interface, par excellence, for examining the relationship between semantics and pragmatic context.

Without context, the interpreter is on his/her own. To a child, the statement *Bees give honey from their mouths and stings from their tails* may mean just that and no more. The child may naively accept the statement as a true description of a very concrete reality. Perhaps the trueness and the imagery prevent the child from getting over the literal "hump." In the absence of a metalinguistic perspective, the child needs context. Figurative meaning may only be recognized in the context of a real life situation—e.g., someone roasting a wiener has their clothing catch on fire. In sum, the interplay between semantics and pragmatics highlights a number of issues—how context and sentence meaning are integrated; how nonliteral modes of processing develop and can be facilitated; what kinds of constructive processes (entailment, presupposition, implication, etc.) are drawn upon to facilitate figurative processing; what is a proverb, and can any utterance assume proverbial status in some context; what does a figurative interpretation accomplish; when is it appropriate, etc.

This line of reasoning prompts consideration of a fourth property. *Proverbs potentially relate a large number of instances that can themselves be literally and referentially unrelated.* A ''good'' interpretation potentially allows a large number of instantiations, and it is of some interest to determine how an interpretation modulates the number and range of its instantiations. On a literal level, the instantiations may have nothing in common, their resemblance being mediated only through their relationship with the interpretation. As McKane (1970) puts it, ''The proverb may initially present a barrier to understanding, but when it is intuited it throws a brilliant light on the situations it fits'' (p. 23). The instantiations can be familiar, personally meaningful episodes or novel or hypothetical ones. The extensional meaning of a proverb, therefore, consists not simply of already encountered instances, but of many possible instances, as these are coded by the interpretation.

Take the ''great weights'' proverb, for example. It could be applied to athletics (e.g., We see a winning run score as the ball just eludes the shortstop's glove), to war (e.g., A gun accidentally fires and the battle begins), to medicine (e.g., The surgeon's hand slips and an artery is cut), and so on. A proverb, qua proverb, is clearly generative by way of allowing the recognition and production of instances, new and old, as part of the same system (group). This kind of featureless family resemblance is anathema to Literalist approaches.

The fifth property of proverbs concerns their truth value: *Uttered in context, a proverb as a figurative statement is neither necessarily true nor necessarily false.* A proverb, as a literal statement, is simply inappropriate and irrelevant and (apparently) violates the Gricean (1975) principle of cooperation. The violation is indeed only apparent, however, for the figurative level is usually intended to be *appropriate* to the context being described. Across instances, however, proverbs are rarely, if ever, either true or false. In fact, this is unlikely even in the case of single instances.

Are proverbs best considered as probabilistically true then? Perhaps not. A verification mode may not be the most fruitful one for considering the function of proverbs. Proverbs provide a *perspective,* a ''seeing as'' or way of construing. And truth value, in its strict logical sense, may be only one aspect of the perspective. Furthermore, proverbs, like metaphors, are not ''hedges'' or ''fuzzy'' concepts that are merely deviant from more formal logical statements. Rather, they provide a means of focusing on salient aspects of complex events. To treat a proverb as a proposition, therefore, is to misrepresent its basic function, since propositions, or rather the assertions they make, are traditionally considered to be either true or false.

Aside from their basic properties, proverbs may possess additional characteristics. First, proverbs often incorporate other kinds of figurative language. For example, figurative understanding of *At the foot of the candle it is dark* requires recognition of the symbolic nature of lightness and darkness and of the idiomatic usage of the word foot. The metaphor must be understood in *Hard work is fortune's right hand and stinginess her left* before it can be used proverbially.

Second, proverbs often express or invite contrasts. Great weights are compared with small wires in *Great weights hang on small wires*. The contrast is only a little less obvious in *A peacock should frequently look at its legs*. Quite often the contrast is subtly implied. In *A stitch in time saves nine* there is the implication that if something in need of stitching is not stitched, more stitches will be required.

While the properties and characteristics reviewed above are important in their own right, they converge on a more fundamental fact, namely, that they are derivatives of an interpretive process. There can be no figurative level without interpretation. Phenomena such as the transformation of literally unrelated instances into a coherent system, the figurative rendering of a semantically nondeviant form, a figurative meaning constrained but not determined by the literal level, and perspective, collectively bespeak the need to invoke interpretation. We believe such interpretations are tacit, abstract, and generative—more on this point later.

To summarize so far, our view is inconsistent with the common view of proverbs and with its more sophisticated complement, the Literalist approach. Figurative meaning is not literal meaning, nor is it necessarily representable in verbal, imagistic or propositional formats, verifiable in terms of a two-valued logic, or reducible to preexisting, attributive concepts.

The next section reviews the empirical work on proverbs. This work was conducted in the absence of a well developed conception of proverbs. Nevertheless, it is generally consistent with our views as expressed above.

EMPIRICAL RESEARCH

The experimental psychological study of proverbs began with Karl Bühler (1908) who used proverbs and aphorisms to study thought. This tack was abandoned after Bühler, although proverbs began to be used to assess intelligence and psychopathology. For example, norms established through the Stanford-Binet test indicate that almost all children less than 11 years old and a majority of adults have difficulty interpreting even some familiar proverbs (McNemar, 1942). Some developmental research, which we review later on, supports this conclusion. For the average adult, performance on the proverbs subtest of the Stanford-Binet correlates about .75 with full scale performance (Terman & Merrill, 1973). Schizophrenic individuals give notoriously literal interpretations of proverbs if they give any at all (Benjamin, 1944). Clearly, the ability to interpret proverbs in a fully figurative way is dependent upon healthy, advanced cognitive mechanisms.

In-depth analyses of these mechanisms did not begin until the early-to-mid 1970s. There are several reasons for the hiatus. Surely the sway of Behaviorism over American psychology for 50 years is one. And the press of Chomsky's syntax-based linguistic theory upon the psycholinguistics of the 1960s is partially responsible, although the contrary could be argued from a Kuhnian standpoint. Of course, the Literalist approach of the 1960s and 1970s helped suppress interest in figurative understanding. A final reason for the hiatus, which pertains more to our emotions than to our intellectual history, reflects the common view of proverbs. It might be glossed as, ''Thou shalt not proverb.''

Despite this attitude, perhaps because of it, ''proverb studies'' have been done. A fairly exhaustive survey of these studies is provided in four categories—individual differences, experimental studies of adult processing, developmental trends, and processing considerations.

Individual Differences

We have already alluded to the use of proverbs in testing intelligence. Their use in evaluating schizophrenia has been only slightly more enlightening (see Honeck, this volume). Benjamin describes his technique in a classic 1944 paper. Schizophrenic individuals were read proverbs of varying complexity and familiarity (e.g., *When the cat's away, the mice will play; He travels swiftest who travels alone*) and asked to interpret them. The interpretations, Benjamin reports, were overwhelmingly literal and, if not literal, then neologistic, incoherent, or reflective of personal preoccupations.

Benjamin's view of proverb interpretation is interesting and generally consonant with our own. He states, ''The classic proverb . . . is built up of one or more substantive symbols, usually objects of nature of everyday life . . . combined with predicates which have varying degrees of figurative or literal value'' (p. 80). For a true interpretation, ''the symbols must be translated into the respective figures, categories, and actions they represent, a process which we have called . . . desymbolization. Following desymbolization, the meaning of the proverb can be expressed in various ways, from the most specific and concrete examples through the general to the abstract'' (p. 81). While this view can be reconstructed as a four phase process—literal meaning, desymbolization, general meaning, illustration—Benjamin argues that the proverb's meaning is wholistically grasped. Yet, he classifies disturbances of interpretation in terms of the component phases.

In an attempt to standardize scoring methods, develop parallel test forms, and provide normative data for more meaningful interpretation of abnormal populations' responses to proverbs, Gorham (1956) developed a test that included multiple choice items in addition to the usual free response technique. Gorham's Proverbs Test consists of three different forms of 12 proverbs each. This test has been used extensively with schizophrenic individuals both in clinical and experimental settings. Experimental studies have investigated possible bases of responses to the test. Is it primarily verbal intelligence or psychopathology (Shimkunas, Gynther, & Smith, 1967)? Can the test measure overinclusiveness in delusional schizophrenics (Goldstein & Salzman, 1965)? Shimkunas (1970) argues that autistic responses decrease and abstract responses increase as psychopathology lessens and that this supports the hypothesis that the locus of cognitive deficit in schizophrenia is the loss of abstraction (see also Shimkunas, 1972; 1978). Unfortunately, these several studies are plagued by inadequate definitions and potential confounds intrinsic to the study of schizophrenia.

Adult Processing

The studies reported in the following were done by different investigators at different times with different purposes in mind. Nevertheless, they strike variously at the postulates that comprise the Literalist approach. And they make some interesting and novel contributions to method and theory along the way.

In general, the methodology employed in these studies amounts to a *PX–PY* strategy. That is, the effect of relating a proverb (*P*) with some *X* (e.g., an interpretation or instantiation) is compared with that of relating *P* with some *Y* (e.g., a poorer interpretation). Studies of subjects' operations on *P* such as interpretation, imagery, and so on also conform to this *PX* vs. *PY* paradigm.

What's Remembered? We begin with Bühler (1908) who, as a member of the Wurzburg Group, became embroiled in the famous imageless thought controversy (see Honeck, this volume). Bühler used both question-answer and recall techniques to grapple with this controversy. For example, his subjects were asked: "Do you understand, 'The most glowing colors in which the virtues shine are the inventions of those who lack them'?" The subject reported his introspections while attempting to understand. Using prompted recall techniques, pairs of proverbs might be presented, one proverb subsequently being used to cue the other. Recall was good, as it was in his "analogy experiments." In the latter, the subjects first read a series of proverbs, then a second series, including foils, and were asked whether any of the second were remindful of the first. For example, *When the calf is stolen, the farmer repairs the stall* served to cue, *One looks to the cask when the wine escapes into the cellar.* In other experiments, single words from the proverbs were prompts.

The recall studies, especially, convinced Bühler that thoughts can be nonsensorial. Indeed, sentence understanding is an apperceptive process wherein knowledge meets the sentence half-way. Moreover, people remember their thoughts, the thoughts are wholistic (emergent) and *the* basic agent of recall (Humphrey, 1963). Tied to these conclusions was Bühler's caveat that language materials be used that force people to think.

Using similar materials and technique, Honeck (1973a) reached much the same conclusion 65 years later. He demonstrated that a proverb is remembered better if it is interpreted than if its deep structure is repeated. Also, no interaction between acquisition conditions and proverb imagery level was evident. Honeck concluded that the interpretations provided an appropriate, elaborative context that facilitated the encoding of a "conceptual base"–an abstract, nonlinguistic, imagery free mental representation.

In a follow-up study, Honeck, Riechmann, and Hoffman (1975) substantiated the conceptual base hypothesis. Experiment 1 demonstrated that proverbs presented in acquisition along with either a conceptually related or an unrelated interpretation are better prompted in recall by the former. In Experiment 2, stories proved to be as effective recall prompts as nouns from the proverbs. The stories illustrated an intended figurative meaning of the proverbs. For example, the proverb *In due time the fox is brought to the furrier* was cued by a three sentence story about a successful jewel thief who was eventually caught by a detective.

Actually, the argument for this hypothesis rested on more than the mere fact that the proverbs shared only conceptual relationships with the interpretations and the stories. Like the experimenter-provided interpretations in Experiment 1, the subjects' interpretations (written during acquisition) were typically stated in abstract, general, nonstorylike terms. The interpretations were not instantiations—e.g., *Everything comes home* was an interpretation for the "fox" proverb. Furthermore, interpretation quality and recall performance were directly related, the more so for low-imagery proverbs. In short, the better the subjects could explain a proverb to themselves, the better they were able to recognize novel, concrete instances of it. Theoretically, any of a large number of stories having the same figurative meaning could have served equally well as prompts. Moreover, it is highly unlikely that the interpretations per se mediated recall. Their very abstractness precluded their being remembered. More plausibly, a conceptual representation of each interpretation effected recognition of the figurative meaning of the stories and facilitated reconstruction of the literal proverb form. Thus, the facilitative effect of abstract explanatory context, and the suggestion of generativity and of nonverbal form, constrained our inferences toward the conceptual base viewpoint. Potter, Valian, and Faulconer (1977) make a similar claim based on their work with words and drawings.

Brewer and Bock's (1976) investigation also supports this viewpoint. During acquisition, the subjects were read proverbs and, in the normal comprehension condition, asked to remember the proverbs. In the deep comprehension condition they were told to select that one of two sentences which illustrated the proverb. Deep comprehension better allowed recognition of a new figuratively related proverb (versus a new unrelated proverb) than normal comprehension. Bühler's result once again!

Imagery and Level of Understanding. Thus far we have dwelled upon the abstract, conceptual (nonlinguistic) nature of memory representation. We have also claimed that a conceptual base is imagery free. It is intuitively clear that imagery evoked by the literal proverb level *must* be quite different from that which could possibly constitute an interpretation. We assume here that imagery follows upon understanding and that it is somehow palpable and probably conscious. The evidence reported below accords with this perspective on imagery-language-thought relationships.

In Honeck's (1973a) study, proverb imagery level (high vs. low) did not interact with the acquisition conditions. In both experiments reported by Honeck, et al. (1975), however, proverb imagery level interacted with another treatment factor. This suggests, though it does not require, that a conceptual base contains imagery. All three experiments solicited recall. Does imagery affect primarily recall? Are other properties of the proverbs involved?

Riechmann's (1974) study clarified some of the methodological and theoretical issues. He argued, after Bower (1970), that interaction effects involving imagery do tend to occur in recall but not recognition tasks. During acquisition, Riechmann's subjects were instructed to either interpret or to image proverbs that varied orthogonally on imageability (high vs. low) and comprehensibility (high vs. low) dimensions. They were then given a modified recognition test in which interpretations of the proverbs were presented as target items, along with foil items. The subjects made a yes-no judgment and indicated their degree of confidence. The results showed better recognition by the interpretation group, although the imagery group was above chance. High-interpretability items (i.e., interpretations for high-interpretability proverbs) were recognized better than high-imagery items, especially those in the low-imagery, high interpretability category. Moreover, the imagery group showed chance recognition of interpretations for high-imagery, high-interpretability proverbs. This result implied a "representational rivalry" between literally based imagery and figurative interpretation. It is analogous to Brooks' (1968) findings that perceptual and imaginal activities within the same modality can conflict. Riechmann and Coste (this volume) report some recent complications in, as well as some replication of, these general findings.

In general, the entire pattern of results, including the rivalry notion, favor the conceptual base hypothesis rather than the dual-coding hypothesis (Paivio, 1971), which predicts better performance under conditions favoring imagery formation. More broadly, the results are consonant with a model that treats imagery as a product of level of processing. Accordingly, the same image could, as a token, represent many depths. In cases of deep processing, literal imagery may be incompatible with figurative understanding. This thesis is in fact stronger than our claim that a conceptual base is imagery free, since it suggests that a conceptual base, which is formed through deep level processing, *cannot* be (or is inconsistent with being) imagistic. An image that is an instantiation of a conceptual base retains its deeper meaning via the base. Similarly, an image representing a literal level of processing can, through interpretation, acquire a nonliteral meaning. Note, in this regard, that, overall, the subjects in Riechmann's imagery group successfully recognized most target interpretations. Here the images, if the images were indeed responsible, could be said to have figurative symbolic value.

The model of imagery just presented is reminiscent of Selz's extension of the work of the Wurzburg Group. A staunch anti-associationist, he viewed *relations* as imageless. Asked to provide a synonym for "parson," someone might respond "chaplain." For Selz, words and their relationship function as a wholistic "organic complex" (Humphrey, 1963). A conceptual base is such a complex, abstract, imageless thought relation. Pylyshyn (1973) defends a similar position. Franks (1974) explains the notion this way:

> images are consciously experienced aspects of particular derivations generated from tacit knowledge—the structure of an image is determined by tacit knowledge structures. Particular meanings are generated from tacit knowledge and sometimes these derivations are manifested in imagery. But all images have underlying tacit meanings. Images are not units of storage—they are products. In process terms, images are outputs of underlying tacit structures (p. 238).

Our position is that under certain conditions, such as those requiring elaborative processing, imagery is better conceived in this radical way (see Anderson, 1978, and Kosslyn & Pomerantz, 1978, for a different view).

Synonymy Without Features. Synonymy between experimental materials was often only assumed in the above studies of memory. The investigators constructed the materials using their own intuitions. The success of most of the experimental manipulations is testimony to the commonality of subjects' and experimenters' thought processes. Nevertheless, more empirical if not principled techniques are needed for constructing materials of this sort.

Development of synonymous constructions is difficult enough even when they are related transformationally (Anisfeld & Klenbort, 1973). Creation of synonymy through lexical substitution is more risky (Honeck, 1971). However, it is still possible to "paraphrase" a sentence without using its major vocabulary or propositional structure (Honeck, 1973b). In fact, the materials used in the above memory studies were related in this "parasyntactic" way.

Suppose all the interpretations of a base are parasyntactic. Will bidirectionality hold between base and interpretation? Hoffman and Honeck (1976) tested the "judgmental parity hypothesis," the psychological counterpart of bidirectionality. This hypothesis states that the relationship between two linguistic constructions, C-1 and C-2, is reciprocal, in that if C-1 is judged as being highly similar in meaning to C-2, the reverse should also hold.

A two phase procedure was used. In phase 1, the subjects ranked a set of interpretations in terms of their conceptual similarity to their base proverbs. The rankings were highly consensual during this phase. In phase 2, different subjects ranked a set of proverbs, including the base, in terms of their conceptual similarity to a given interpretation (see Table 6.1). Typically, the original proverbs were judged as more closely related to the interpretations than were the foil proverbs.

The phase 1-phase 2 relationship, plotting the similarity of interpretations to proverbs against the similarity of proverbs to interpretation, was also deciphered. Analyses revealed an r of 0.57 and only a linear trend. Thus, as the goodness of a phase 1 interpretation increased, the base proverb was judged as conceptually closer to that interpretation in phase 2. Additionally, as interpretation goodness decreased, variability in choice of the base proverb increased.

These results are of some theoretical import. Not only could people agree on the conceptual similarity between sentences sharing *no* propositional overlap, but they also selected the source sentence with increasing accuracy as this consensually defined similarity increased. However, this selection did not occur in a perfectly ordered (one-to-one) way. A one-to-one relationship would have produced a slope = 0.50, whereas the actual slope was 0.35, suggesting a compromise between perfect ordering and a step function in which the source sentence is always chosen and then drops to near neutrality.

The results support the conception of synonymy as a "two-way street." In fact, the strong form of the judgmental parity hypothesis—that the relationship is linear—was upheld. This is not to claim that synonymy is always symmetrical for it need not be. In fact, synonymy may have both symmetrical and asymmetrical components, depending upon the total context of judgment (although synonymy, at the *precise moment of its conception,* must be symmetrical). This is consonant with Hoffman and Honeck's observation that as synonymy diverges, there is increasing uncertainty concerning the identity of the source (base). That is, symmetry can be construed as inversely related to semantic distance. The slope of the function, since it indicated that unit conception of similarity in phase 1 was not matched by unit conception of similarity in phase 2, also implied asymmetry. Essentially all of these conclusions, as well as Hoffman and Honeck's, were replicated by Hoffman (1976) who used parasyntactically related interpretations of anomalous poetry lines (from e.e. cummings), in conjunction with the bidirectionality paradigm.

It is tempting to speculate that any two linguistic constructions can be made synonymous by virtue of some context or "possible world." That is why theories of synonymy, and of meaning, therefore, must come to grips with what Hoffman

TABLE 6.1
Sample Family Used by Hoffman and Honeck (1976)

Proverb: Great weights hang on small wires.
Good interpretation: The outcome of important events often depends on seemingly minor details.
Mediocre interpretation: An event is often more important than it seems.
Poor interpretation: Important problems will come to those who don't care much.
Unrelated interpretation: People naturally spend more time thinking about important events.
Foil: It is the open eye that weeps.
Foil: The best fruit falls to the pig.
Foil: When the enemy retreats, build him a golden bridge.

and Honeck term "semantic infinity," the language user's ability to, "understand and generate an infinite number of semantic relationships within a language" (p. 82). Thus, *A stitch in time saves nine* can, with a little mental work, be made to mean *The moon is made of green cheese*.[1] The perception and production of synonymy is rarely dependent on such mental overelaboration, however. Our inferences are normally more restricted, the relationship between input and output more easily understood, therefore. Following this line of thought, Hoffman and Honeck postulate that synonymy can be conceived as "shared limits of inference." This implies that there are no permanently existing cases of synonymy but only statements containing information that in some delineable context temporarily enjoy the relationship of conceptual similarity.

Family Dynamics. Clearly, the above view of synonymy is a feature-less or, more basically, a "primitive-less" one. There were no pre-existing elements in the materials employed in those several studies. Common elements could have been constructed ad hoc, but this pinpoints the vacuity of the features hypothesis. A general theory of synonymy would do better to begin with time- and context-bound interdependencies between members of groups or families, somewhat in the sense of Wittgenstein (1953). Features could then be considered to arise in the special case of members locally related within highly cohesive (well known, highly differentiated) families. The existence of features indicates an advanced form of knowledge (whether derived genetically or through extensive learning). To construe knowledge as verification (of propositions) may require, a priori, a well articulated, differentiated, system onto which the proposition can be mapped. That is, the verification mode of knowledge can be applied appropriately only to those domains whose features and feature relationships are easily identified. An analogy may be helpful here. The history of geometry shows a progression from Euclidean (dealing with lines, angles, coordinates, etc.) to projective (dealing with perspective), to topology (dealing with open-closedness, near-far, inside-outside, etc.). As Piaget (1953) points out, however, the child's developing conception of geometry is quite the reverse. Topological relationships must be learned before Euclidean and projective conceptions can be understood. Now—the Literalist approach is basically Euclidean in the sense that a three or *n*-dimensional space is populated with pre-existing, distinctive elements that interact in various ways. Proverbs are more topological or at least projective in character and thereby invite the invention of new features. It is interesting in

---

[1]To illustrate, suppose there are two astronauts on the moon. Volcanoes begin to erupt all around them, endangering their lives as well as their spacecraft. With a wry smile on his face, one astronaut says, *A stitch in time saves nine* and the other, only slightly amused, says, *The moon 'is' made of green cheese*. Both utterances pragmatically imply essentially the same idea, namely, to get out of there as fast as possible. In general, our view of semantic infinity emphasizes the nonlinguistic basis of creativity as opposed, say, to one (e.g., Chomsky, 1965) that would appeal to the projective use of a small number of exclusively linguistic rules.

this connection that when asked to interpret unfamiliar proverbs without supportive context, that mature, intelligent adults can appear more childlike in their
attempt to "get around" the literal proverb level.

The "dynamic family" approach to synonymy and figurative translation was
pushed to a limit by Honeck, Voegtle, and Sowry (in press). They asked college
students to match a picture of the literal content of a proverb with either a
one-sentence target (correct) scenario instantiating an interpretation of the proverb, or a foil scenario designed to be a poorer instance. For example, the picture
for the proverb, *The cow gives good milk but kicks over the pail,* was paired with
The boy gave his father a watch for Christmas but wore it every day thereafter,
the target scenario, and with, *The boy gave his mother a bouquet of flowers but
then asked if he could watch the late movie.* The results indicated that the subjects
were successful despite the wide discrepancy in literal meaning between the
pictures and scenarios. Apparently, the subjects, guided by an analogic
framework, constructed abstract ideas that served to relate the materials figuratively. It is as if, to use one example, the subjects had tacitly constructed and
solved the four-term analogy—The cow gives good milk: The boy gave his father
a watch for Christmas:: The cow kicks the pail: The boy wore the watch every
day thereafter.

While nonlinguistic inputs would appear to offer precious insights into figurative understanding, they have been used infrequently (but see Johnson & Malgady, this volume). Werner and Kaplan (1963) examined numerous studies of
the relationships between line drawings and either single words or connected
discourse. Kaplan (1955) had adults produce and then explain their line drawings
of the meaning of proverbs. Kaplan discussed the drawings in terms of their
physiognomic, motoric, and psychophysically undifferentiated (fusion of symbol
and meaning) character. More recently, Verbrugge (1977) has used pictures to
elucidate the abstract relations specified by metaphorical sentences (see also
Verbrugge, this volume).

We conclude this section with a study by Honeck and Dorfmueller (1978) who
combined direct and indirect methods to further examine the conceptual base
hypothesis. They did so in the context of an intriguing analysis of the relationship
between family resemblance and generativity.

Two studies were conducted. In Study 1, college students rated the semantic
similarity between all possible pairs of the four sentence-members of each of
eight families. They also answered questions about the members. Each family
consisted of a proverb (e.g., *He who spits above himself will have it all in his
face*), an interpretation of the proverb (*It is unwise to be hostile to someone who
is more powerful than yourself*), and two instantiations (*The boy picked a fight
with the town bully and went home with a black eye; The storekeeper who pulled
a gun on the mobster was fatally shot the next day*).

The ratings suggested that the interpretation was at the hub of an inference
chain with the proverb and scenarios (instantiations) far apart on the periphery.

The interpretations were most ''central''—they were chosen as most representative of family meaning, closest in meaning to other members, and the best potential mnemonic (redintegrative cue). Although second most central, the proverb was judged hardest to interpret and most variable in meaning.

In Study 2, different subjects studied the sentence families (minus one scenario) and then received one family member, specified in acquisition, to prompt recall of the other members. A fourth group received a new scenario as a recall cue. Recall of content words showed the interpretation prompt group best (60%), the proverb and old scenario groups intermediate (about 40%), and the new scenario group worst (23%). (An imagery-based explanation of this result was made implausible by pilot work that produced no group differences when subjects were *un*informed as to which item would serve as a recall cue.) No relationship obtained between either the order of recall of family members, or their recall level, and proximity to other members. However, the closer a member was to others, the better it cued recall of the others. Finally, the interpretation itself was the worst recalled and most often the last recalled (or, at least, the last reported).

In conclusion, within a family of conceptually related sentences, the most central item, an abstractly stated interpretation, was most generative because, as Honeck and Dorfmueller assert, it was closer to the conceptual base for each family. However, the interpretations were not complex sentences embedding other family members as propositions, as in Bransford and Franks (1971). And whereas Rosch and Mervis (1975) cogently point out that prototypicality (a form of centrality) is not dependent upon all-or-none possession of criterial attributes, they do emphasize that a prototype has the *most* attributes in common with other family members. If there were *any* attributes or features shared by family members in the Honeck and Dorfmueller (1978) study it is not clear what these could be! We prefer, therefore, to treat centrality (and prototypicality) in terms of dynamic family interdependency, even if we do not yet fully understand how families are created.

Developmental Trends

The original, fascinating exploration of children's understanding of proverbs was carried out by Piaget (1926). Children aged 9-11 years were given a series of proverbs like *Drunken once will get drunk again* and then a set of sentences, some of which expressed the ideas suggested by the proverbs. Thus, *It is difficult to break old habits* corresponded to the ''drunken'' proverb. The children read the proverbs and the sentences and selected the matching sentence.

Piaget reports that the children rarely understood the proverbs although they thought that they did. He invokes the notion of syncretism to explain these misunderstandings—the children apprehend and apply the whole before appreciating the analytic significance of its parts. The child's literal understanding of a proverb and of a phrase creates wholistic schemas that mutually warp and distort. The result is a very general schema that unites the two propositions and creates implications without a logical, analytic base. The propositions become fused in an idiosyncratic way.

In his 1944 text, Watts reports his study on the ability of over 1000 children aged 11–14 years to interpret proverbs. They were given 50 common proverbs and four interpretations for each. The mean number of correct choices ranged from 16.1 to 27.1. This rarely cited study seems to appear out of the blue, historically speaking, in a chapter on metaphor and analogy.

To our knowledge, Richardson and Church (1959) published the next relevant investigation. They asked children aged 8–12 years to interpret common proverbs. Ratings of the interpretations indicated a trend toward increased figurative understanding and of syncretism, mixed with figurative understanding. Children aged 11–12 gave figurative interpretations only about one-fourth of the time. The authors concluded that consistent figurative understanding waits upon an analytic task attitude and a metalinguistic perspective.

As part of a larger study, Billow (1975) asked 5–13 year-olds to interpret proverbs. Only 13-year-olds showed any sign of understanding—40% correct interpretations. A test of combinatorial reasoning presumed to tap Piagetian formal operations did not correlate with proverb comprehension. Cometa (1978) reports somewhat more success. He read both rare and common proverbs to children in grades 1, 3, 4, and 8, and asked them to interpret them. Cometa argued that proverbs draw upon combinatorial reasoning, a formal operational skill, since, in his view, proverbial understanding requires the "redefinition" of the words within the proverb both with respect to one another and to context. The results were mixed. Only those children who had demonstrated combinatorial logic (by passing the "combination-of-chemicals" task) gave an adequate paraphrase of at least 5 of the 7 proverbs used. However, 7 of the 15 "Late Concrete" children (who had not passed the chemicals test), adequately paraphrased at least one proverb. Cometa concludes, somewhat surprisingly, that if formal logic is defined by the chemicals task, "then formal operational reasoning is *not* the cognitive ability which underlies children's comprehension of proverbs" (p. 7).

We might conclude, based on the preceding four studies, that the ability to understand proverbs does not appear until age 11 or so. This may be true if understanding is measured through active interpretation or explication. Interpretation is a production task, however, and such tasks notoriously underestimate abilities relative to comprehension tasks. Aside from the production factor itself, such tasks typically introduce debilitating information processing loads, frustration, confusion, and so on. Piaget's method did not require production as such but undoubtedly constituted an ideal means of inducing syncretic phenomena.

Honeck, Sowry, and Voegtle (1978) attempted to assess understanding with a comprehension task. They had children aged 7, 8, and 9 years compare an orally presented proverb (e.g., *Bees give honey from their mouths and stings from their tails*) with two thematic pictures—a nonliteral correct interpretation of the proverb and a foil. The child simply pointed to the "correct" picture. Thus, the proverb about bees was compared to a picture of a girl whose pantleg catches fire while roasting a wiener, and that of a girl about to be hit in the head by a baseball while opening a present. In the wiener roast, the positive and negative consequences stem from the same source whereas this is not the case in the present-opening scenario. The children at all ages performed above chance. Honeck, et al. argued that the pictures served as an easily understood, ecologically valid contextual framework for organizing the common figurative meaning of proverb and picture.

More recently, Chambers (1977) has replicated this finding with 10-year-old children. He also demonstrated that they could successfully match a verbal scenario (e.g., *The wind made the sailboat move fast, but blew down the houses nearby*) with the correct picture (e.g., wiener roast vs. present-opening) and with the correct proverb.

In conclusion, little is known regarding children's understanding of proverbs beyond the simple fact that receptive comprehension precedes interpretation and explication, and the latter increase with age. Of course, the experimental literature is small. Nonetheless, progress undoubtedly waits upon a more refined conception of the proverb and, consequently, of the skills and operations needed to understand it.

One Stage or More?

The studies using proverbs have implicitly assumed that literal understanding precedes figurative understanding. This hypothesis of two stages receives indirect support from many of these studies. Of course, the fact that figurative understanding has taken place does not necessarily imply that comprehension occurred in two stages. More convincing evidence is provided by Brewer, Harris, and Brewer (1974). Having assumed that the two-stage hypothesis is true, they argued that it should take longer to understand a proverb presented after a figurative interpretation than before it, whereas no difference due to order should arise when a literal interpretation is used. Both levels should be computed when the proverb is presented first. Thus, a figurative level could be quickly matched to a figurative interpretation. When presented second, the extra step needed should add to the time to match the figurative interpretation. This is essentially what happened. Finally, using more mundane materials, Clark and Lucy (1975) concluded that literal meaning is computed before conveyed meaning.

Contrary results are reported by Harris (1976), Glucksberg, Hartman and Stack (1977), Ortony, Schallert, Reynolds, & Antos (1978), and by Tanhauser (1978) who used metaphors, and by Kemper (1978). Kemper claims that figurative understanding need not proceed according to the scheme of inferentially based models, which assert that indirect meaning is only computed if the direct meaning does not fit the total informational context. She prefers the position, based on Gricean conversational implicature, that there need be no delay in understanding. She observed that the latency to read and correctly decide that a proverb was appropriate to a preceding paragraph designed to effect a nonliteral meaning, was no longer than that effected by a "literal paragraph."

Research on the two-stage issue has just begun. No hard conclusions are possible. A basic problem, perhaps the fundamental one in the entire area, concerns the nature of the "literal level." Is there more than one? Does it include the results of presupposition, entailment, and of implication in general? If so, where do only literal implications leave off and figurative ones begin? Perhaps, as in certain cases of ambiguity, the potential for figurative understanding develops along with what will eventuate in literal understanding. Context certainly plays a large role. Under zero or typical context conditions, more normative and therefore literal meanings develop. Under less ordinary conditions of use, a figurative interpretation may not only be appropriate but the "natural" priority meaning. However, clarification of those issues clearly waits on an adequate combination of theory and of more subtle, sensitive paradigms and measures of processing.

THEORETICAL CONSIDERATIONS

Our purpose in this section is to suggest directions for a theory of proverb understanding. Toward this end, and to highlight the issues involved, proverbs will be compared with metaphors. Writing on figurative language has focused on metaphors, to the exclusion of other figurative forms. This circumstance will tend to limit our knowledge of figurative understanding.

A Comparison of Metaphors and Proverbs

The comparison of metaphors and proverbs breaks down into two not unrelated problems—how they are identified and how they are understood. Their identification can conveniently be discussed in terms of their form, content, contexts of use, and function.

Both metaphors and proverbs are expressed through a large variety of structures. Many proverbs conform to phrase structure "formulas" that rely on the systematic positioning of key words—*Don't count your chickens before they're hatched, Don't cry over spilt milk*, etc.; *Young saint, old devil, Young angel, old devil*, etc. More abstract phrase patterns are also used such as, "X (a noun)... (a verb)X"—*Like cures like, Money begets money*, etc. Metaphors also often rely upon such formulas. The "isa" construction is perhaps the most frequent—*Man is a wolf; Baseball is a poem*, etc. Another format is X is the Y of the X'—*This is the foot of the mountain, Andre' Weil is the Bobby Fischer of mathematics*, etc. (Miller, 1977).

While these and other frames for proverbs and for metaphors do appear to be somewhat productive, they hardly serve to distinguish the two. No surface characteristic alone is likely to accomplish this, most obviously because meaning is involved. Moreover, literal statements often assume the frames mentioned. Conversely, proverbs and metaphors can assume practically any literal format when used as literal statements. In the absence of illustrative context, some proverbs and perhaps all whole-sentence metaphors are indistinguishable from literal statements. For example, the statement *Regardless of the danger the troops marched on* (after Ortony, this volume) is metaphorical in the context of young children who continue to cause mayhem despite their father's warning that they might receive no dessert for dinner. Thus, the classification of metaphor as verbal, nominal, prepositional and so on, when these labels reflect syntactic criteria, fails to mark a statement as metaphor. The status of a statement as proverbial or metaphorical has nothing in particular to do with lexical or syntactical (phrase structural) formats.

Other formats have been adduced to honor the distinction, however. Perrine (1971) classifies metaphor in terms of the four categories created by combining explicit or implicit tenor with explicit or implicit vehicle. Clear cases of metaphor tend to fit the explicit tenor, explicit vehicle category. Proverbs fall in the implicit tenor, explicit vehicle category. Since, in metaphor, the vehicle is traditionally something that is compared to the tenor, Perrine claims that the literal (tenor) term must be inferred. He gives as an illustration Shakespeare's *Night's candles are burnt out,* which is Romeo's description of the night sky to Juliet.

Miller's (1977) taxonomy of metaphor includes ''sentential metaphors,'' which ''use an otherwise unobjectionable sentence in an incongruous context'' (p. 49). Miller's example is *John has lost his marbles,* uttered in a context otherwise having nothing to do with marbles. Like Perrine, Miller argues that the referent (Miller's term for topic or tenor) is not always preserved by the metaphor and that it must therefore be inferred.

At least some proverbs, like whole-sentence metaphors, are pragmatically deviant without being semantically deviant. Moreover, if one assumes that proverbs require a referent to be identified, then proverbs deflate to whole-sentence metaphors. We can ignore the assumption for the time being, since Miller implies that maxims or proverblike statements (Miller does not discuss proverbs per se) such as *Haste makes waste* are not metaphors because they do not seem to express any resemblance or analogy. The resemblance criterion is crucial to Miller's analysis of metaphor. However, it is difficult to see how *John has lost his marbles* expresses a resemblance (in a marble-less context) and maxims (or proverbs) do not. Miller states that *Haste makes waste* expresses a causation or identity relation. But this relation is clearly internal to the sentence. The similarity relation in *John has lost his marbles* is clearly external; that is, it is a relationship between the sentence vehicle as a whole (the relatum for Miller) and some to-be-inferred referent.

For now, consider the claim that a proverb is a topic-less metaphor. Since this claim, which is basically an instantiation view of understanding, has serious theoretical implications, we will consider it in some detail. In general, our criticisms of it condense to the necessity of postulating an abstract interpretive process, a process that the instantiation view of meaning tends to ignore.

We must first ask what constitutes a topic (referent). For Miller (1977), a referent is "the concept that is being talked about" (ms. p. 25). For Perrine (1971) it is some literally illustrative context for the proverb. By either definition, a topic is some specific, particular "event" which bears a similarity relationship to the proverb and, presumably, serves to disambiguate it.

But we only know that a presumed topic context actually disambiguates if the topic-proverb relationship is *first* interpreted. Indeed, in the absence of an adequate interpretation, proverbs, metaphors, and other statements have *no* topic or referent. Linguistic understanding is not automatic upon the provision of context. In conclusion, the proverb as topic-less metaphor hypothesis is both vague and presumptive of an interpretive process.

Let us pursue this. It is simply not the case that people have stockpiled in memory a set of topics (or propositions) that are associated with and serve to interpret a given proverb. Several lines of evidence support our argument. First, it is an inefficient, uneconomical memorial strategy. Second, as previously noted, even adults have difficulty interpreting some common proverbs. Thus, recognition of a familiar proverb does not guarantee quick, effortless understanding. Third, novel, unfamiliar proverbs, for which no pre-existing specially earmarked topics could possibly exist, can be understood (see our second section). A related observation is that statements do not become proverbs until used as such. New proverbs are thereby continually coming into use. There can be no stored topics for as yet nonexistent proverbs. Finally, when interpreted, a proverb specifies an *indefinitely large number* of "topics" that would otherwise have been conceptually unrelated to one another. Most of these topics must be constructed and could not possibly pre-exist as convenient tags on each proverb. This last point carries the implication that the interpretive process must be generative (see Honeck & Dorfmueller, 1978). In conclusion, the understanding of proverbs cannot require the a priori existence of topics. There are no memorial "givens" either as topics or as proverbs. Topics do not necessarily bring proverbs to life, they simply prevent them from dying.

If format neither identifies nor distinguishes proverbs and metaphors, perhaps an analysis of content will be more revealing. Both proverbs and metaphors tend to focus on certain broad domains of knowledge. Unfortunately for our purposes, these domains overlap for the two forms. Nor does the concreteness of the statements expressing either form serve to distinguish the two. Metaphors are typically concrete but they need not be—e.g., *A proverb is a theory*. Nor does concreteness guarantee their comprehension. Similarly, as literal statements, proverbs can be quite concrete, though this very concreteness can make them paradoxically opaque. For example, *Great weights hang on small wires,* though easy to image as a particularized literal form, is correspondingly difficult to interpret figuratively. The literalizing effect of imagery may be partly responsible for this.

It has sometimes been suggested (e.g., Benjamin, 1944) that proverbs make use of symbols. If we mean by symbols, equivalences such as light with knowledge, dove with peace, etc., then this statement is only trivially true. The vast majority of proverbs contain no such symbols. Nor do metaphors, although metaphors can accommodate symbols.

Perhaps we should follow the lead of authors who identify metaphors as semantically deviant utterances (Chomsky, 1965; Kintsch, 1974; Levin, 1977; Matthews, 1971). If only part-sentence metaphors are considered, our analysis would be simple, since they must be deviant to be identified as metaphors. Only some proverbs are semantically deviant. A figurative mode is easily triggered by proverbs such as *Laws catch flies but let hornets go free,* since laws can do no such thing. Even the pragmatically deviant *Policemen catch flies but let hornets go free* signals a figurative interpretation since it is simply strange, not impossible (false!) that policemen act this way. But a statement such as *A net with a hole in it won't catch any fish* is perfectly acceptable and literal in the context of the end of a day spent fishing that has seen no luck owing to a defective net. It is proverbial in the context of an attempt to explain figurative language phenomena with Behaviorist concepts.

In conclusion, it is clear that criteria relating to deviance, whether semantic or pragmatic, are not sufficient to distinguish metaphors from proverbs. Both part-sentence metaphors and some proverbs are semantically deviant. All whole-sentence metaphors, and proverbs in context, are pragmatically deviant. And both can be semantically deviant as well, in that same context.

Ortony (this volume) adds to the criterion of contextual deviance that the tension attendant upon the deviance be resolvable—that is, the metaphor must be interpretable. This criterion is invoked to preclude as metaphors apparently uninterpretable deviance, as in *The angry molecule golfed the car cigarette.* This same criterion could well be applied to proverbs used in an illustrative context.

As both metaphors and proverbs can be semantically well-formed literal statements, perhaps we should more closely consider their contexts of use. Metaphors are rarely encountered outside of text or conversation. And whereas the same applies to proverbs, the relationship each form bears to larger context is quite different. Metaphors, especially part-sentence metaphors, have a spontaneous quality. They flow with and are integrated into the context. Nonetheless, they are specific to the context, their meaning is particularized by it. The user of metaphor, moreover, often does not intend that it be extended beyond the specific context. The upshot of these considerations is that all metaphor is parasitic upon context inasmuch as it is identifiable only by means of it, and understandable primarily in relation to it. Metaphor is "context-driven."

Proverbs are used in different ways and for different purposes than metaphors. Proverbs typically comment on a context in order to make a point of general significance about it. For this reason, they are hardly spontaneous and may rely more (than is the case for metaphor) upon their user's conscious intention. Their successful interpretation in a single context in fact *signals the creation of a group* of instances. Significantly, in the absence of illustrative context, a proverb is more likely to be interpreted (a fortiori identified) in a figurative way than is a whole-sentence metaphor. These several observations strongly suggest that proverbs are not nearly so context-driven as metaphors. Proverbs function "at a distance" from context. They are, in this sense, more "knowledge driven."

Let us return to our observation that (whole-sentence) metaphors are less likely than proverbs to be identified and interpreted as such under zero-context conditions. Given our characterization of metaphor as context-driven, the basis of this claim becomes clear. Contextualized statements are bound to the temporal parameters of their context. Examination of whole-sentence metaphors reveals that they are almost inevitably stated in the past or, less frequently, the future tense. This is because the context, of which metaphors are an integral part, establishes a deictic temporal reference point for utterances (hence, the past progressive tense in Ortony's example, *Regardless of the danger, the troops marched on*). A metaphor can, therefore, be tentatively defined as a (pragmatically deviant, tension resolvable) contextualized statement that is temporally restricted in use and form.

By contrast, proverbs stated in English inevitably use the simple present (non-past) tense. Utterances that are comments or reports almost inevitably use the simple present-tense to "locate" an event in the present (Lyons, 1977, p. 678). However, a present tense statement need not be contemporaneous with its referent (e.g., *She reads psycholinguistics*). In fact, the present tense is as temporally neutral as English can become. Neutrality, in turn, allows "omnitemporal potential"—multiple events anywhere on the "time line" from past through future can be referred to. (By contrast, the change, for example, from *Great weights hang on small wires* to *Great weights hung (were hanging, will hang, will be hanging) on small wires*, presupposes application to a particular event at a specific time relative to the time of the statement's expression.) When there is a clear referent for such a statement (or, as we have suggested, even when there is not) and the statement is also pragmatically deviant, the interpreter, under the press of the cooperative principle, may attempt to reconcile the statement with the referent. In this case, the statement is likely to be figuratively construed. The larger context will determine whether it should be distinguishable as an abstract comment or as a speech act. Thus, the statement *A shoe is part of a soccer player's equipment* may be proverbial if uttered by someone who has watched a soccer team with fancy shoes lose, but a request if uttered before the game by a shoeless player to a team aide.

It is not present tense and its implication of temporally unrestricted application that guarantees generality, however. It is the principled discrepancy between the statement and its context that serves this purpose by cuing the interpreter that an abstract interpretation is needed. The concrete character of most proverbs is ideally suited to this purpose. The clash of the concreteness of the statement and of the context initiates a search for a compromise. (This is the paradoxical effect of concreteness.) The compromise is necessarily abstract and generative. Other cues, such as the frequent presence of the definite article when there is no definite referent, support the need for an abstract interpretation.

The above considerations suggest that a proverb can be defined as *a pragmatically deviant, relatively concrete, present-tensed statement used to create a theoretical perspective for grouping referentially and literally distinguishable events.*

The different functions served by metaphors and proverbs should be elucidated. Both can perform a variety of speech acts, though metaphors are more likely to be used to evoke, say, irony or hyperbole, and proverbs to express promises, warnings, postdictions, and the like. However, speech act functions are secondary in that they rely upon more basic functions. In the case of metaphors, this function is one of expressing, in a compact way, what might otherwise be hard to express (Ortony, this volume). A metaphor economically chunks several pieces of information that, if expressed literally, would be prolix and lose the original insight lent by the metaphor. For discovery metaphors (Ortony, this volume) the vehicle may well serve as a new, "possible world" for an old, familiar topic, which thereby assumes new meanings.

These several "functions" are also served by proverbs. However, they are dependent upon the proverb's primary function, which is to promote the development of an interpretation in the form of an abstract, generative theoretical model. This model not only reconceptualizes the nature of the topics or situations that fall within its scope, but in so doing, places them within a larger system. Thus, the context-driven character of metaphors localizes their functions within the context, while the knowledge-driven character of proverbs extends theirs to as yet unknown contexts. In this sense, the possibilities inherent in a proverb are much greater. A metaphor is used perhaps once and thrown away. A proverb is intended to be used for eternity. That is why there are no dictionaries of metaphors, though there are of proverbs.

TOWARD A CONCEPTUAL BASE THEORY

Preliminary Comments

This final section provides a sketch of a theory of proverb understanding. The theory specifies four phases—a preparatory or *problem recognition phase,* a *literal transformation phase,* a figurative or *theory formation phase,* and an *instantiation phase*. By the theory, complete understanding requires that a literal statement be recognized as incongruent in some context, that the statement and the context be transformed, such that a miniature theory arise that resolves the incongruity, and which can be used for recognizing and producing novel instances. Postulation of the four phases is generally consistent with the research reviewed above. However, each phase involves a number of sub-processes whose nature and organization is less clear. We wish to emphasize that someone who fully understands a proverb has solved a large problem as well as a number of smaller ones. In general, we see linguistic understanding as requiring the acquisition and use of problem solving skills.

The Problem Recognition Phase

Certain conditions precede problem solution. We call these conditions "The Paradigmatic Situation." In general, in The Paradigmatic Situation the interpreter is confronted with a relatively concrete, present-tensed statement that is pragmatically deviant, that is the statement does not appear to fit the context. The context can be irrelevant to the statement ("irrelevant-context-situation") in the sense that the interpreter is pressed (asked, believes it to be appropriate, etc.) to interpret the statement when there is no "given" or "old" information in the immediate total perceptual or memorial context relevant to the statement. For example, you are asked "out of the blue" to interpret *The best pears fall into the pigs mouth.* (You might also be told that it is a proverb, or that it means more than it says, that it doesn't have anything in particular to do with pigs or pears, etc.) In the "relevant-context-situation" the statement is uttered when the perceptually or memorially given information is potentially relevant to the statement. In both the relevant and irrelevant context situations, however, the interpreter must believe at least that the source of the statement adheres to Grice's Cooperative Principle—that is, it must be believed that the statement is serious and is about something. Given this belief, the interpreter has a problem, albeit an "ill-defined" problem. In the irrelevant-context-situation, the interpreter realizes that there is a goal to be met for which the statement, taken literally, is irrelevant, but which only apparently violates maxims regarding relevance and sincereness. The interpreter also realizes that the literal statement can be used, somehow, to meet the (undefined) goal. Thus, in this situation, the adoption of a metalinguistic perspective, one that sees language as an object to be used, would appear to be greatly facilitative of, if not prerequisite to, further problem solving. (Partly for this reason, of course, children have difficulty interpreting, let alone explicating their interpretations of proverbs.) Because the context is irrelevant to what the statement is about, there will be large individual differences in the problem solving strategies employed and in their results.

In the relevant-context-situation, problem solving is guided by the context. Assuming the interpreter recognizes the problem, then the task becomes one of reconciling the statement with the context. Clearly, however, the context may be more or less convergent upon the statement. The interpreter may know *merely* that the context is relevant. This represents an extremely interesting case because the literal statement serves to organize the context, to "shed light" upon it—the statement helps to parse reality and to create properties compatible with transformations upon the literal statement. Here the context presents no topic. The topic must be discovered. Call this Case 1. In Case 2 the topic is already known and the statement serves to *emphasize* it. In Case 3, the topic is already salient and the statement serves as further emphasis. The statement as proverb is redundant here, but there is still a problem to be solved. Depending upon which case obtains, problem solution will be more or less guided and smooth.

Regardless of whether the literal statement is interpreted in a relevant- or irrelevant-context-situation, there is an incongruity or discrepancy between the initial state (the statement) and a desired state. This incongruity creates a tension that "sets the stage" for the Literal Transformation Phase.

Literal Transformation Phase

Having recognized the problem, the interpreter uses the information "specified" by the literal statement and by the context (depending upon the Case) to transform both. The theoretical difficulty arises, however, as to how literal statement information should be conceptualized in the theory. We claim that because the interpreter has realized that (a) the statement cannot be construed literally and that (b) it can be construed as providing a novel perspective, that the statement has no single, a priori representation in memory. The statement has no representation apart from its function within a paradigmatic situation. This is not to argue that statements cannot have normative meanings, only that such meanings constitute a *limiting case* in terms of possible contexts of use—here, "zero context," which can be considered a "best bet" that captures prior contexts of use. Propositional notations typically represent zero-context situations and, hence, are inadequate for our purposes. However, Kintsch and Van Dijk (1978) and others have been developing a theory of text comprehension in which the interpretations of text "micropropositions" are modulated by text "macrostructure."

In any event, the interpreter reorganizes and elaborates upon the statement. A variety of recodings may occur in the irrelevant-context-situation, including imagery (sometimes quite elaborate), lexical decomposition, association, etc. Understandably, strategies are more constrained, less variable in the relevant-context-situation. The upshot of these elaborations and inferences (logical and pragmatic) is that a *contrast* emerges between two "lines" or "ideas." The contrast, in turn, usually leads to further inferences. The lines, and therefore the contrast, are obvious in some cases. For example, "great weights" contrast with "small wires" in *Great weights hang on small wires*. Falling from the window contrasts with falling from the roof in *It is better to fall from the window than the roof*. The implications of the contrasts are immediate—the weights can fall, the wires may break, the wires are critical; a fall from the roof will be more damaging, so fall from the window. In short, most proverbs promote an "internal tension" or incompatibility with probable consequences. A "but" is usually elicited at some point in processing. The "buts" may be more rapidly evoked in relevant-context-situations, particularly when the topic is known. Here, the incompatibility helps "suggest" a similar incompatibility within the *field* of the literal statement. The field of the literal statement may function similarly in Case 1 situations. (Literal-statement-field refers to initial information gleaned from the literal statement and recodings of this information. Context-field refers to initial information gleaned from the context and recodings of this information.)

The literal-statement-field and the context-field do not constitute figurative meanings. They add literal information to the literal information already constructed. Presumably, recoding and elaboration stop at a point that maximizes the possibility of a comparison between the new information (statement or context) and the "given" information (context or statement). That is, a "law of conceptual comparisons" seems to operate—events are compared on whatever level and in whatever way they *can* be compared. (This law might be added as a corollary to Hoffman and Honeck's (1976) "semantic infinity hypothesis.") Thus, the last process to develop during the second phase involves the *selection of format*. The format serves to relate the statement-field with the context-field. A variety of formats might be selected. Because two contrastive lines usually develop, however, analogies, particularly 4-term analogies (i.e., A:B::C:D), are commonly used, where these two lines serve as either A and B or C and D terms. (Note that we *reconstruct* what the interpreter does as the formation of a format. He or she does not consciously recognize that "this is an analogy problem," for example.) The format does not by itself solve the problem—if an analogy has been formed, it must be solved.

The Figurative Phase

The problem recognized by the interpreter in The Paradigmatic Phase, and put in a format in the Literal Transformation Phase, is solved during the Figurative Phase. Its solution yields a theory that is nonverbal and non-imagistic, yet abstract, general, and generative. The structure of the theory is unclear, but the following considerations are relevant to the issue.

The "paradox of concreteness" was alluded to earlier. The interpreter must reconcile a relatively concrete statement with a more-or-less well known (i.e., concrete) context. Since these two fields cannot be pattern-matched on the basis of perceptual or imagistic features, they can only be related in an abstract medium. Thus, it would be misleading to suppose that the two fields are ''trans-formed,'' one into the other, or ''fused,'' especially if these terms are meant to imply imagistic operations of a surrealistic sort. The literal-statement-field, espe-cially in a particularized form, cannot be made to fit the context-field. This is an important point, for it is frequently asserted that understanding proceeds through instantiation (e.g., Anderson, Pichert, Goetz, Schallert, Stevens, & Trollip, 1976; Anderson & Ortony, 1975) and, specifically, that instantiation *is the basis of* understanding. Anderson, et al., for example, found that ''actress'' was a better recall prompt than ''woman'' for the acquisition sentence, *The woman was outstanding in the theater*. Clearly, however, it is only because an interpretation arousing a ''show business'' schema occurs, and is a likely one at that (for subjects *and* experimenters), that ''actress'' was effective. Moreover, because people can recognize a relationship between a cue and an item in memory, it does not necessarily follow that the cue (or its referent) was inferred during acquisi-tion. Thus, the use of highly understandable and therefore easily imaged (scenes for) sentences may make it appear as if sentence *meaning* is stored in the form of instantiations. However, Marschark and Paivio (1977) found that more abstract sentences (e.g., *Quotations are illegal*) could also be cued by inferentially re-lated cues (e.g., ''plagiarism'') though, as usual, concrete sentences were better recalled. These results suggest that people must use an abstract interpretive process in order to make such cues effective. We do not dispute the fact of instantiation, but to claim that a verbal input is understood *in terms of* an instance only begs the question. How does instantiation take place?

Particularization may, during the Literal Transformation Phase, facilitate formation of the literal-statement-field. For example, a frequent strategy, espe-cially in the irrelevant-context situation, is to develop an elaborate image which incorporates lavish, vivid, detailed, particular information. For *A net with a hole in it won't catch any fish* one might imagine a fishing vessel at sea, men pulling in a net, the fish escaping from the net, exasperation on the men's faces, etc. Such imagery is used in the service of the abstract, however. The interpreter realizes that particularization is inappropriate (i.e., it is not what the proverb means), but uses it to help generate clues to a more general understanding.

In relevant-context-situations, such imagistic elaboration is probably less frequent—both fields ''rise to the abstract'' more quickly and effortlessly. This is because the statement and context cannot easily be fused in any perceptual-cognitive sense. For example, suppose the statement, *The cow gives good milk but kicks over the pail,* is uttered in a context (e.g., a boy gives his father a watch for Christmas but wears it every day thereafter). First, it is not clear what elements should be fused—the boy with the cow, the watch with the milk, perhaps. But how? The boy does not become cowlike or a watch more milklike. Second, the actual scenes to be fused would have to be much more complex than this (e.g., a cow being milked, with a boy giving his father a watch at Christmas), and seems quite improbable therefore. Third, crucial elements would be left out of even complex images—the interpreter's evaluation of the two happenings, the inference that the boy's wearing the watch effectively took it away from his father, etc. In short, nonimageable conceptual elements would be missing from the images. In general, the problem is not solved by arranging the statement-field and context-field into an "imagery analogy." That is not to say that analogy is not used as a heuristic, only that solutions to the analogy do not depend upon imagistic (or any obviously perceptual) fusion of its terms. In conclusion, while instantiation, especially in the form of imagery, may be useful during the Literal Transformation Phase, it is neither necessary nor sufficient as a means of figurative interpretation.

In essence, the interpreter has no choice—the two fields *must* be related in an abstract medium. A basic problem, as Bever (1975) points out, is that there must be an "executive" that generates "knowledge of which features of the representation of the stimulus in each faculty to extract so that the translation would be the same bidirectionally" (p. 79). Bever argues that this problem dissipates if one holds to a "federated faculties" model (as opposed to a "common core" or "lingua mentis" model). In this model a linguistic representation would be unidirectionally mapped by one kind of code into, say, a visual representation. The reverse would be accomplished by a different code. The deeper commonality here is a set of common operations or "building blocks." Clearly, active problem solving mechanisms are called for, however. Individuals do construct theories that overlook differences at less elaborate levels of processing. In our "cow" - "boy" example above, a common interpretation, verbally stated, is "People often undo the good they have done." Under these circumstances, we claim that the interpreter has constructed the following common abstraction—W enables X at time 1 and this is evaluated positively, W cancels $(W{\rightarrow}X)^+_{t_1}$, and this is evaluated negatively. That is, the two fields have been reconciled in an abstract medium of functions involving contextually determined evaluations of cause-effect relationships.

In general, the interpretations of proverbs take the form of such abstract structures (conceptual bases). These structures function as theories. The theories become independent of their original fields yet integrate them by explaining their common significance. In effect, the interpreter creates a "possible world" in which two fields condense to one. The primary value of the theory is that it allows the production and recognition of novel instances—it "predicts" old and new events as instances of its domain (see Bransford & Franks', 1976, discussion of the value of "decontextualization" and resulting abstractness). The theory is generative. People often sense this power by realizing that their newly constructed interpretation of a proverb extends beyond the immediate context, backward and forward on the "time line." Moreover, they sense this without foreknowledge of any particular instances. Their intuition precedes instantiation.

(This appears to happen regardless of how well a proverb appears to specify a domain—e.g., *Laws catch flies but let hornets go free* vs. *Great weights hang on small wires.*)

Instantiation Phase

In the instantiation phase, the theory is extended to new events. These new events become instantiations of the theory—that is, instantiations are events captured by a theory. At this point the original proverb becomes but a symbol or name for the theory. Because the proverb is not arbitrarily related to the theory, however, the proverb as symbol can be used to reconstruct the theory anew (as with familiar proverbs). The "Cycle of Meaning" (Honeck, 1977) is complete.

Extension of a theory to new instances means, of course, that it is generative. Hypothetically, there is no limit to the number of instances a theory can generate. Some of the instances can be "old" events whose significance is changed or perhaps realized for the first time. Some instances will be new events never encountered or imagined previously. In short, the major consequence of the theory is that a *group* will form in which the instances will be more or less related to the theory, and to one another, through the theory. Let's pursue this.

The creation of a theory by a person constitutes a psychological "big bang." The formation of a group through a theory, spawns a number of phenomena whose very existence is group-dependent. Prototypicality is a good example. In general, prototypes are instances that best illustrate the theory of their group. (That never presented instances can be judged most prototypical attests to the operation of a theory.) The assumption that a group is created by a theory has several implications for prototypes: (a) There may be better prototypes than those actually encountered. This is because the instances are inexhaustible and a new one might be more "ideal." (b) Their relationship with other instances will be asymmetrical. A prototype will be judged less similar to a poorer prototype than the poorer prototype to the prototype. This is because the prototype is "closer" to the theory, and directional judgments of similarity ask people, in effect, to judge the distance from the "referent" term to the theory.[2] (c) Prototypes should generate valid new instances better than should poorer prototypes. (d) Prototypes should be better retrieval cues, in a redintegrative sense, than poorer prototypes, for old instances. (e) Prototypes should lose potential as new events because their

---

[2]Actually, both instances are compared in terms of the theory. Given this assumption, however, various models could predict the result being discussed. For example, the similarity of Red China to North Korea would be less than the reverse on the one model because to make Red China equivalent to North Korea would require a greater extension of the "theory" of these countries than would making North Korea equivalent to Red China. On another model, the difference between the "distance" from the theory (T) to the good (G) prototype versus the theory to the poor (P) prototype carries a negative algebraic sign compared to the reverse comparison—i.e., TG-TP < TP-TG. The first comparison is likely to yield contrast effects and the second, assimilation effects.

identity is more closely tied to the theory. Prototypes are more functionally fixated. (f) Prototypes need not share any features with other instances in the group. This is because similarity is a function of the theory not of the instances (see the following).

The notion of a group has important consequences for theories of similarity and imagery. Consider similarity. The instances within a group are similar only to the extent that they are subsumed by the theory. Since these instances can be similar in the absence of any common features (see the "Synonymy Without Features" section) it is clear that groups need not be organized or cohere on the basis of primitives shared in toto, or in part, by group members. Indeed, one of the advantages of treating similarity as an outgrowth of theory is that no primitives need be postulated (The primitives are in the theory if they are anywhere.). Similarity becomes a mediated relationship between two or more instances in a group. Similarity is rarely in the stimuli. In fact, "stimulus features" most often come about through extensive problem solving and learning: that is, learning produces, among other things, *distinctions,* which we tend to then reify as "features." Groups may in fact incorporate "local" instances related by virtue of such features. For example, an interpretation of *Policemen catch flies but let hornets go free* can be created that generates instances having to do with local matters relating to law as well as to broader, more global domains of knowledge. In sum, events are similar only because someone creates a theory that can relate the events and only rarely because the events have pre-existing features in common.

We have already discussed imagery. In terms of group theory, images (of instances) are derivative. We usually image what is important and what we understand. Consequently, the significance of images can be quite abstract. An adult's image of an event can be much more significant than a child's. At the same time, therefore, one and the same image can face in two directions—toward the literal and toward the figurative. An image of a proverb-as-symbol is another example. In any case, images do not define a group, nor does a "general image" constitute the basic representation of a group, though it might a prototype. This latter, prototype-as-general-image, hypothesis emerges primarily when a group appears to be composed through feature combination, i.e., when the instances are either well known or simple or both. As applied to a group formed through proverb interpretation, this hypothesis seems quite incredible. A proverb is a play—the cast changes, the characters remain the same. Images are of casts.

Concluding Remarks on the Theory

The four phases, although interdependent, are strictly sequential, at least for initial attempts at solving a proverb. The solution may automatize and become more parallel as experience with a particular proverb (and proverbs in general) grows, and with relevant context.

The view that language interpretation is problem solving tends to suggest that interpretation is a conscious process. This is rarely the case. Children apparently acquire language through some very complicated problem solving. We rarely attribute intention or consciousness to their efforts. That, as adults, we usually understand language quickly and effortlessly tends to mask the enormous set of skills which underlie this understanding. We have discussed proverbs because they "stop the world" and make us more aware of what these skills are and how they are used.[3]

REFERENCES

Anderson, J. R. Arguments concerning representations for mental imagery. *Psychological Review,* 1978, *85,* 249–277.
Anderson, J. R., & Bower, G. H. *Human associative memory.* Hillsdale, N.J.: Lawrence Erlbaum Associates, 1979 (originally published 1973).
Anderson, R. C., Pichert, J. W., Goetz, E. T., Shallert, D. L., Stevens, K. V., & Trollip, S. R. Instantiation of general terms. *Journal of Verbal Learning and Verbal Behavior*, 1976, *15*, 667–679.
Anderson, R., & Ortony, A. On putting apples into bottles: A problem of polysemy. *Cognitive Psychology,* 1975, *7,* 167–180.
Anisfeld, M., & Klenbort, I. On the functions of structural paraphrase: The view from the passive voice. *Psychological Bulletin,* 1973, *79,* 117–126.
Baddeley, A. The trouble with levels: A re-examination of Craik and Lockhart's framework for memory research. *Psychological Review,* 1978, *85,* 139–152.
Benjamin, J. D. A method for distinguishing and evaluating formal thinking disorders in schizophrenia. In Kasanin, J. D. (Ed.), *Language and thought in schizophrenia.* Berkeley: University of California Press, 1944.
Bever, T. Some theoretical and empirical issues that arise if we insist on distinguishing language and thought. In D. Aaronson & R. W. Rieber (Eds.), *Developmental psycholinguistics and communication disorders.* N.Y.: New York Academy of Sciences, 1975.
Billow, R. M. A cognitive developmental study of metaphor comprehension. *Developmental Psychology,* 1975, *11,* 415–423.
Bower, G. H. Imagery as a relational organizer in associative learning. *Journal of Verbal Learning and Verbal Behavior,* 1970, *9,* 529–533.
Bransford, J. D., & Franks, J. J. Toward a framework for understanding learning. In G. Bower (Ed.), *The psychology of learning and motivation,* Vol. 10. New York: Academic Press, 1976.
Bransford, J. D. & Franks, J. J. The abstraction of linguistic ideas. *Cognitive Psychology,* 1971, *2,* 331–350.
Brewer, W. F. & Bock, J. K. *Comprehension and memory of the literal and figurative meaning of proverbs.* Unpublished manuscript, University of Illinois, 1976.
Brewer, W. F., Harris, R. J., & Brewer, E. F. *Comprehension of literal and figurative meaning.* Unpublished manuscript, University of Illinois, 1974.
Brooks, L. R. Spatial and verbal components in the act of recall. *Canadian Journal of Psychology,* 1968, *22,* 349–368.

---

[3]We have focused on the relevant-context-situation in our discussion. Clearly, however, people *can* interpret proverbs when in the irrelevant-context-situation, although their theory is likely to be less generative and precise.

Bühler, K. On thought connections. In Rapaport, D. (Ed.), *Organization and pathology of thought: Selected sources*. New York: Columbia University Press, 1951. (Originally published, 1908.)

Chambers, J. *Proverb comprehension in children*. Doctoral dissertation, University of Cincinnati, 1977.

Chomsky, N. *Aspects of the theory of syntax*. Cambridge, Mass.: M.I.T. Press, 1965.

Clark, H. H., & Lucy, P. Understanding what is said from what is meant: A study in conversationally conveyed requests. *Journal of Verbal Learning and Verbal Behavior*, 1975, *14*, 56–72.

Collins, A. M., & Quillian, M. R. Retrieval time from semantic memory. *Journal of Verbal Learning and Verbal Behavior*, 1969, *8*, 240–247.

Cometa, M. *The child's understanding of proverbs: A cognitive developmental analysis*. Paper presented at the Fourth Annual Interdisciplinary Conference on Linguistics, University of Louisville, April, 1978.

Craik, F. I. M., & Lockhart, R. S. Levels of processing: A framework for memory research. *Journal of Verbal Learning and Verbal Behavior*, 1972, *11*, 671–684.

Franks, J. J. Toward understanding understanding. In W. B. Weimer & D. S. Palermo (Eds.), *Cognition and the symbolic processes*. Hillsdale, N.J.: Lawrence Erlbaum Associates, 1974.

Glucksberg, S., Hartman, D. E., & Stack, R. *Metaphor comprehension is an automatic and parallel process*. Paper presented at the 1977 meetings of the Psychonomic Society, Washington, D.C.

Goldstein, R. H., & Salzman, L. F. Proverb word counts as a measure of overinclusiveness in delusional schizophrenics. *Journal of Abnormal Psychology*, 1965, *70*, 244–245.

Gorham, D. R. A proverb test for clinical and experimental use. *Psychological Reports*, 1956, *2*, 1–12.

Grice, H. P. Logic and conversation. In P. Cole & J. L. Morgan (Eds.), *Syntax and Semantics* (Vol. 3): *Speech Acts*. New York: Academic Press, 1975.

Harris, R. J. Comprehension of metaphors: A test of the two-stage processing model. *Bulletin of The Psychonomic Society*, 1976, *8*, 312–314.

Hoffman, R. R. *Conceptual similarity among the interpretations of anomalous sentences*. Doctoral dissertation, University of Cincinnati, 1976.

Hoffman, R. R., & Honeck, R. P. The bidirectionality of judgments of synonymy. *Journal of Psycholinguistic Research*, 1976, *5*, 173–183.

Honeck, R. P. Figurative language: History and prospect. In W. Kintsch (Chair), *Recent psycholinguistic research with metaphors*. Symposium paper presented at the meetings of the American Psychological Association, San Francisco, August, 1977.

Honeck, R. P. Interpretive versus structural effects on semantic memory. *Journal of Verbal Learning and Verbal Behavior*, 1973, *12*, 448–455. (a)

Honeck, R. P. Semantic similarity between sentences. *Journal of Psycholinguistic Research*, 1973, *2*, 137–151. (b)

Honeck, R. P. A study of paraphrases. *Journal of Verbal Learning and Verbal Behavior*, 1971, *10*, 367–381.

Honeck, R. P., Sowry, B., & Voegtle, K. Proverbial understanding in a pictorial context. *Child Development*, 1978, *49*, 327–331.

Honeck, R. P., & Dorfmueller, M. *Sentence prototypes can be generative*. Paper presented at Annual Meeting of the Southern Society for Philosophy and Psychology, Orlando, Florida, March, 1978.

Honeck, R. P., Voegtle, K., & Sowry, B. Figurative understanding of pictures and sentences. *Journal of Psycholinguistic Research*, in press.

Honeck, R. P., Riechmann, P., & Hoffman, R. Semantic memory for metaphor: The conceptual base hypothesis. *Memory and Cognition*, 1975, *3*, 409–415.

Humphrey, G. *Thinking: An introduction to its experimental psychology*. New York: Wiley, 1963.

Kaplan, B. Some psychological methods for the investigation of expressive language. In H. Werner, (Ed.), *On Expressive Language*. Worcester, Mass.: Clark University Press, 1955.

Kemper, S. *On the role of conversational implication in proverb comprehension.* Paper presented at the Fourth Annual Interdisciplinary Conference on Linguistics. University of Louisville, April, 1978.

Kintsch, W. *The representation of meaning in memory.* Hillsdale, N.J.: Lawrence Erlbaum Associates, 1974.

Kintsch, W., & Van Dijk, T. A. Toward a model of text comprehension and production. *Psychological Review,* 1978, *85,* 363-394.

Kosslyn, S. M., & Pomerantz, J. R. Imagery, propositions, and the form of internal representations. *Cognitive Psychology,* 1977, *9,* 52-76.

Levin, S. *The semantics of metaphor.* Baltimore: Johns Hopkins University Press, 1977.

Lyons, J. *Semantics* (Vol. 2). New York: Cambridge University Press, 1977.

Marschark, M., & Paivio, A. Integrative processing of concrete and abstract sentences. *Journal of Verbal Learning and Verbal Behavior,* 1977, *16,* 217-231.

Matthews, R. J. Concerning a linguistic theory of metaphor. *Foundations of Language,* 1971, *7,* 413-425.

McKane, W. *Proverbs: A new approach.* Philadelphia: The Westminster Press, 1970.

McNemar, Q. *The revision of the Stanford-Binet Scale.* Boston: Houghton Mifflin, 1942.

Meyer, D. E. On the representation and retrieval of stored semantic information. *Cognitive Psychology,* 1970, *1,* 242-300.

Mieder, W. *Selected writings on proverbs by Archer Taylor.* Helsinki: Academia Scientarium Fennica, 1975.

Miller, G. A. *Images and models, similes and metaphors.* Paper presented at the Illinois Conference on Metaphor and Thought, University of Illinois, Champaign, September, 1977.

Miller, G. A., & Johnson-Laird, P. N. *Language and perception.* Cambridge, Mass.: Belknap Press (Harvard University Press), 1976.

Norman, D. A., & Rumelhart, D. E. *Explorations in Cognition.* San Francisco: Freeman, 1975.

Ortony, A., Schallert, D. L., Reynolds, R. E., & Antos, S. J. Interpreting metaphors and idioms: Some effects of context on comprehension. *Journal of Verbal Learning and Verbal Behavior,* 1978, *17,* 465-477.

Paivio, A. Imagery and language. In S. J. Segal (Ed.), *Imagery: Current cognitive approaches.* New York: Academic Press, 1971.

Perrine, L. Four forms of metaphor. *College English,* 1971, *33,* 125-138.

Piaget, J. How children form mathematical concepts. *Scientific American,* 1953, November, 202-206.

Piaget, J. *The language and thought of the child.* New York: Harcourt, Brace, 1926.

Potter, M. C., Valian, V. V., & Faulconer, B. A. Representation of a sentence and its pragmatic implications: Verbal, imagistic, or abstract? *Journal of Verbal Learning and Verbal Behavior,* 1977, *16,* 1-12.

Pylyshyn, W. W. What the mind's eye tells the mind's brain: A critique of mental imagery. *Psychological Bulletin,* 1973, *80,* 1-24.

Richardson, C., & Church, J. A developmental analysis of proverb interpretations. *Journal of Genetic Psychology,* 1959, *94,* 169-179.

Riechmann, P. F. *Does imagery facilitate memory for conceptual information?* Unpublished doctoral dissertation, University of Cincinnati, 1974.

Rips, L. J., Shoben, E. J., & Smith, E. E. Semantic distance and the verification of semantic relations. *Journal of Verbal Learning and Verbal Behavior,* 1973, *12,* 1-20.

Rosch, E., & Mervis, C. B. Family resemblances: Studies in the internal structure of categories. *Cognitive Psychology,* 1975, *7,* 573-605.

Seitel, P. Saying Haya sayings: Two categories of proverb use. In J. D. Sapir & J. C. Crocker (Eds.), *The social use of metaphor: Essays on the anthropology of rhetoric.* University of Pennsylvania Press, 1977.

Shimkunas, A. M. Hemispheric asymmetry and schizophrenic thought disorder. In S. Schwartz (Ed.), *Language and cognition in schizophrenia.* Hillsdale, N.J.: Lawrence Erlbaum Associates, 1978.

Shimkunas, A. M. Conceptual deficit in schizophrenia: A reappraisal. *British Journal of Medical Psychology,* 1972, *45,* 149–157.

Shimkunas, A. M. Reciprocal shifts in schizophrenic thought processes. *Journal of Abnormal Psychology,* 1970, *76,* 423–426.

Shimkunas, A. M., Gynther, M. D., & Smith, K. Schizophrenic responses to the proverbs test: Abstract, concrete, or autistic? *Journal of Abnormal Psychology,* 1967, *22,* 128–133.

Smith, E. E., Shoben, E. J., & Rips, L. J. Structure and process in semantic memory: A featural model for semantic decision. *Psychological Review,* 1974, *81,* 214–241.

Smith, W. G., & Heseltine, J. E. *The Oxford Dictionary of English Proverbs.* Oxford: Clarendon Press, 1935.

Tanhauser, S. L. *Levels of interpretation: A study of metaphor-literal differences.* Paper presented at the Fiftieth Annual Meeting of the Midwestern Psychological Association, Chicago, May, 1978.

Terman, L. M., & Merrill, M. A. *Stanford-Binet Intelligence Scale: Manual for the third revision form L-M.* Boston: Houghton Mifflin, 1973.

Verbrugge, R. R. Resemblances in language and perception. In R. E. Shaw & J. D. Bransford (Eds.), *Perceiving, acting, and knowing: Toward an ecological psychology.* Hillsdale, N.J.: Lawrence Erlbaum Associates, 1977.

Watts, A. F. *The language and mental development of children.* London: Harrap, 1944.

Werner, H., & Kaplan, B. *Symbol Formation.* New York: Wiley, 1963.

Wittgenstein, L. *Philosophical Investigations.* New York: Macmillan, 1953.

7 Metaphors and Images: Rating, Reporting, and Remembering

Richard J. Harris

Mary Anne Lahey

Faith Marsalek
Kansas State University

INTRODUCTION

In casually thinking about metaphor, many people view it as an obscure, esoteric, poetic kind of language quite unlike the way most of us talk. Although such a view is questionable in light of the frequent use of metaphor in colloquial speaking, a reasonable corollary of such a "naive theory" is that metaphor is cognitively more demanding, e.g., harder to understand and less likely to be remembered, than literal language. Reaction-time studies (Harris, 1976; Tanhauser, 1978) have already shown that some metaphors take no longer to read, understand, or paraphrase than nonmetaphorical equivalents. The present series of studies focused on memory for metaphors, especially examining the use of imagery in encoding metaphors, in comparison to nonmetaphors.

Unlike most literal language, metaphors necessarily involve two separate domains of meaning. One of these (the topic or tenor) is the basic subject of the utterance, while the other (the vehicle) is the mode of speaking about that subject. For example, in *her eyes were pearls,* the topic is *eyes* and the vehicle is *pearls.* Each has connections to a body of stored knowledge that would not typically be related to the other. What the metaphor does is to call the hearer's attention to some resemblance (the ground) of the two domains of knowledge, for example, the fact that both pearls and eyes are round and capable of sparkling. Computing such a resemblance is a basic task in metaphor comprehension. The semantic domains of the topic and vehicle can interact in dynamic and creative ways during this comprehension process. In the process of discovering the similarities of the topic and vehicle, our perception and understanding of both may be altered, as the domain of the vehicle is used as a template for understand-

163

ing or reinterpreting the domain of the topic (Tourangeau & Sternberg, 1978). For example, in the popular computer metaphor of information processing, one views information processing as processes of input, output, subroutines, closed loops, etc. This altering of one's thinking about the topic is what Levin (1977) has called "phenomenalistic construal."

Developing experimental materials to study metaphor memory is a difficult process, especially in regard to finding a suitable type of control stimulus. Some researchers have chosen to keep critical target stimuli constant and vary only the context, which determines whether the target is literal or metaphorical (Ortony, Reynolds, & Arter, 1978; Ortony, Schallert, Reynolds, & Antos, 1978; Tanhauser, 1978): This has the advantage of limiting the materials to ambiguous sentences made metaphorical only by a context. Other studies (Harris, 1976, 1979a) have used literary metaphors of proven artistic value but strikingly different from contemporary ordinary language. Still others (Verbrugge, this volume) have compared metaphors with similes but in so doing necessarily limit themselves to simile-like metaphors. The approach used in the present work and by Harris (1979b) employed sets of three sentences expressing as close to the same abstract idea as possible, but one sentence used a novel metaphor, one a dead metaphor, and one a nonmetaphorical phrase (e.g., *the ivy cuddled up to the window, the ivy crept up to the window, the ivy grew up to the window*). While in principle it is of course impossible to build such sentence sets where all members express *exactly* the same meaning, such stimuli provided at least some control that would not be possible with totally different items for metaphors and nonmetaphors.

Memory for Metaphors

In a series of studies using both cued recall and forced-choice recognition of sentences from such sets as *The wind tickled the wheat, The wind rocked the wheat,* and *The wind blew through the wheat,* Harris (1979b) found no difference in memory for metaphors and nonmetaphors. Errors in recall tended to be less metaphorical than the stimulus sentence, rather than more metaphorical. On the level of individual sentences, there was no correlation of how metaphorical a sentence was and how likely it was to be recalled correctly. Thus, there was no support for the naive prediction that metaphors are necessarily more difficult than nonmetaphorical language.

The above studies used everyday-English sentences as materials. However, in a series of studies using archaic literary metaphors, Harris (1979a) found that metaphorical target sentences (quotations from Shakespeare) were correctly recognized on a subsequent forced-choice recognition test more often than semantically similar nonmetaphorical targets. This finding occurred both when stimulus sentences were presented as an isolated list of materials and when they were presented in the meaningful context of the play. The results could not be attributed to comprehensibility, since metaphors and nonmetaphors were independently rated as equally comprehensible, nor were they due to a response bias of subjects choosing the most apparently Shakespearean items, since the results were replicated in a condition where subjects were told that some of the stimulus sentences were in fact adaptations of Shakespeare written by the experimenter.

Thus it appears that metaphors are no more difficult to remember than nonmetaphors and are sometimes even easier. Just how the metaphors are encoded and how such a process might differ from that used to encode nonmetaphorical sentences has not been carefully examined, however.

Imagery Encoding

It seems intuitively appealing and has been suggested (e.g., Billow, 1977; Honeck, 1976; Verbrugge, 1977) that imagery is a useful mnemonic for comprehending and remembering metaphors. Exactly how imagery is involved is less clear, however. It may be that the memory representations of metaphors are closer to perceptual representations than are most language-initiated representations. Still, since a metaphor involves two disparate semantic domains and is typically a literally anomalous expression, any image constructed would likely be nonveridical, that is, what it pictures could not literally occur in objective reality. For example, cancer could not actually grow around the U.S. Presidency, and the Kansas City Royals could not literally cream the Yankees. Such images are *surrealistic*. Webster's New Collegiate Dictionary defines *surrealism* as ''the principles, ideals, or practice of producing fantastic or incongruous imagery or effects in art, literature, or theater by means of unnatural juxtapositions and combinations.'' Surrealism is perhaps most graphically exemplified by Salvador Dali's imagery of melting timepieces and clouds that are simultaneously a lamp or human face. Besides fine arts, surrealistic imagery is also widely used in children's cartoons and political cartoons. It may also be very important in the construction of memory representations for metaphorical language.

Studies of the use of imagery to remember metaphors are difficult for several reasons. Since images are not directly controllable or observable, it is difficult to determine when someone is using an imagery mnemonic and still harder to determine if such an image is surrealistic. The technique used in the present research was to ask subjects to indicate during the response task which items they had encoded with imagery. While this is admittedly not a totally valid measure, it seemed preferable to some more obtrusive measure taken during encoding. In addition, some instructional manipulations were used. It is widely known that instructions to use imagery can have sizable effects on memory. Similarly, an incidental versus intentional learning set, which may be induced by instructions, is often a powerful manipulation of processing depth.

Experiment 1 examined the effect of instructions to use imagery on memory for metaphorical and nonmetaphorical sentences. Experiment 2 also used recognition memory but in an incidental-learning paradigm with a task designed to induce a very shallow level of processing. Finally, Experiment 3 was an exploratory study to probe the precise nature of surrealistic imagery used to encode metaphors.

EXPERIMENT 1

This recognition memory study assessed the relative frequency of image use in encoding metaphors, dead metaphors, and nonmetaphors by asking subjects to indicate during recognition if they had used an image to encode that particular sentence. A second variable examined was the effect of specific instructions designed to encourage imagery encoding. Studies of paired-associate learning (e.g., Bower & Winzenz, 1970; Collyer, Jonides, & Bevan, 1972) have shown that imagery instructions can lead to better recall than repetition instructions, natural-language-mediation instructions, or sentence-generation instructions.

Method

Subjects. The subjects were 78 native English-speaking undergraduate psychology students at Kansas State University. They received course credit for participation and were tested in small groups.

Materials and Design. Forty-eight sentence sets were constructed. Each sentence set contained three simple sentences, as close as possible to each other in meaning, except that one contained a novel metaphor, one a dead metaphor, and one a nonmetaphorical expression. The dead metaphors were technically metaphorical but have long since come into common usage; they were thus considered an intermediate type between metaphors and nonmetaphors. In most cases the actual metaphor occurred in the verb, although occasionally it was in the predicate complement. An independent rating study (Harris, 1979b) obtained mean ratings of metaphoricity, that is, how metaphorical each sentence was, on a five-point scale from 1 (very nonmetaphorical) to 5 (highly metaphorical), of 3.74, 2.91, and 1.67 for the novel metaphors, dead metaphors, and nonmetaphors, respectively. Four sample sentence sets appear in Table 7.1. Three lists of 48 sentences each were constructed. In each list there were 16 novel metaphors, 16 dead metaphors, and 16 nonmetaphors, in random order. Twenty-six subjects heard each of the three lists. Each member of a given sentence set always appeared in the same position in each list for all subjects, with one third of the subjects hearing the novel metaphor sentence from any given sentence set, one third the dead metaphor, and one third the nonmetaphor. Every subject heard exactly one of the three sentences from each sentence set, with sentence set completely counterbalanced across lists and subjects.

TABLE 7.1
Sample Stimulus Sentence Sets

---

1. Metaphor: The ivy cuddled up to the window.
   Dead metaphor: The ivy crept up to the window.
   Nonmetaphor: The ivy grew up to the window.

2. Metaphor: The gentle wind tickled the wheat.
   Dead metaphor: The gentle wind rocked the wheat.
   Nonmetaphor: The gentle wind blew through the wheat.

3. Metaphor: The maple tree branches flirted with the telephone wires.
   Dead metaphor: The maple tree branches nudged the telephone wires.
   Nonmetaphor: The maple tree branches touched the telephone wires.

4. Metaphor: The junior-high gang members were a school of piranhas.
   Dead metaphor: The junior-high gang members were a bunch of devils.
   Nonmetaphor: The junior-high gang members were very mean.

Procedure.   The subjects heard one of the three tape-recorded continuous lists of 48 sentences each, read in normal intonation and speed with a 3-sec interval between sentences. At the end of the list of sentences each subject received an answer sheet containing 48 sets of three sentences each, the metaphor, dead metaphor, and nonmetaphor of each set. The sentence sets appeared in the response task in the same order in which one of their members had occurred in the acquisition list. The order of the three sentences within any given set was random but constant for all subjects. The subject was to check which of the three sentences in each set had been played on the tape recorder. They were also asked to place a *p* (for "picture") beside any recognized sentence for which they recalled using an image to encode. Subjects worked at the task at their own speed.

At the beginning of the experiment, half of the subjects had heard Regular instructions and half heard Imagery instructions. The Regular instructions were:

> This is an experiment studying your memory for sentences. You will hear a long list of sentences on the tape recorder. Listen carefully to these sentences and try to remember as much about them as possible.

Subjects in the Imagery-instruction group heard the Regular instructions plus the following:

> In order to help remember them better, try to make a mental picture, called an image, of each sentence as you hear it. For example, if one sentence was *The turtle smoked a cigar,* you might picture a cartoon turtle sitting in an easy chair puffing on a cigar.

No subjects were given any specific information on what kind of memory test would follow the presentation of the list.

Ratings. In order to obtain independent measures of imageability and informativeness of the stimulus sentences, three sets of auxiliary ratings were collected.

An independent group of 45 new subjects from the same pool as used in the memory experiment was given a written version of one of the three lists of 48 sentences (15 subjects per list). They were asked to "think of a mental picture (image) that you think would help you understand and remember that sentence" and then to rate each sentence on an imageability scale from 1 (very hard to image) to 5 (very easy to image). The same three lists were given to 31 new subjects from the same pool (10 on lists 1 and 3, 11 on list 2) to rate for informativeness:

> For each sentence below, try to think of a situation in which it might be used. After you do this, rate the sentence on the basis of how much you would learn from it. Choose a number from 1 (less informative) to 5 (more informative) to indicate the amount of information the sentence contains.

In order to obtain relative informativeness ratings for a whole sentence set by the same subjects, a third group of 50 new subjects from the same pool was given a list of the 48 sentence-sets of three sentences each, in random order within each set, and asked to rank the sentences in each set from 1 (most informative) to 3 (least informative). As with the other rating tasks, there was no time limit.

Results and Discussion

Recognition Memory. The data were analyzed by a multivariate analysis of variance, using nine dependent variables: the number of metaphors, dead metaphors, and nonmetaphors recognized correctly; the number of metaphors, dead metaphors, and nonmetaphors for which the use of an image was reported; and three difference variables, one for each sentence input type, which consisted of the number of times that sentence was falsely recognized as the *more* metaphorical of the two distractors minus the number of times it was recognized as the *less* metaphorical distractor. This last set of variables was included to probe for trends of errors moving in a *more* or *less* metaphorical direction from the input sentence, i.e., reconstructing a remembered idea in a more or less metaphorical surface structure than its input form.

The mean numbers of responses in each category appear in Table 7.2. Analyses, using Hotelling's T^2 test, of the number of sentences recognized correctly indicate that there was no significant effect of instruction type at the .05 level. This finding was supported by the low correlations of the metaphoricity

TABLE 7.2
Mean Number of Choices (out of 16) in Each Response Category
Recognition Sentence Type

Input Sentence Type and Instruction Type	Metaphor	Dead Metaphor	Nonmetaphor	Correlation with Imageability
Regular Instructions (Expt. 1)				
Metaphor	11.49	2.72	1.80	.028
Dead Metaphor	1.97	11.54	2.49	.094
Nonmetaphor	2.11	3.43	10.46	−.150
Imagery Instructions (Expt. 1)				
Metaphor	11.77	2.43	1.81	.023
Dead Metaphor	1.62	12.21	2.18	−.003
Nonmetaphor	1.59	3.55	10.87	−.066
Counting Instructions (Expt. 2)				
Metaphor	10.27	3.31	2.42	−.066
Dead Metaphor	2.13	11.09	2.78	−.130
Nonmetaphor	2.15	4.58	9.27	−.100

ratings (how metaphorical each sentence was on a 1–5 scale) for each sentence (Harris, 1979b) and the probability of that sentence being correctly recognized in Experiment 1 ($r = .22$ and .13 for Regular and Imagery instructions groups, respectively). Neither was there a main effect of input sentence type, a finding that replicated several earlier studies (Harris, 1979b). There was only a slight, nonsignificant trend in both instructions groups for nonmetaphors to be correctly recognized slightly less often than the two metaphorical types.

The analysis of the difference variables for the false recognition responses showed no differences in the pattern of errors as a function of instruction type. Given incorrect recognition, metaphors were more often falsely recognized as dead metaphors than as nonmetaphors, dead metaphors more often recognized as nonmetaphors than as metaphors, and nonmetaphors more often recognized as dead metaphors than as metaphors, with only the last difference significant at the .05 level, through construction of confidence intervals.

As can be seen in Table 7.3, more reports of imagery occurred for all three sentence types under Imagery instructions than Regular instructions, although the difference between the two types of instruction was significant only for the dead metaphors, $F(1,76) = 6.22$, $MS_e = 10.98$, $p < .015$. The difference approached significance for the metaphors, $F(1,76) = 3.04$, $MS_e = 15.18$, $p < .085$, but not for the nonmetaphors. Collapsed across instruction type, the number of reported images did not differ between the metaphors and dead metaphors, but was significantly less for the nonmetaphors at the .05 level, as determined through construction of confidence intervals. Thus, it may be concluded that subjects used imagery somewhat more often when specifically told to, but a better predictor of imagery use was the input sentence type, with images

TABLE 7.3
Mean Number of Imagery-use Reports[a,b]

Instruction Type	Input Sentence Type		
	Metaphor	Dead Metaphor	Nonmetaphor
Regular (Expt. 1)	6.21	5.00	3.79
	(−.02)	(.16)	(.38)
	[.24]	[.24]	[.26]
Imagery (Expt. 1)	7.74	6.87	4.21
	(−.02)	(.10)	(.13)
	[.18]	[.29]	[.43]
Counting (Expt. 2)	4.73	3.62	2.35
	(−.05)	(.05)	(−.15)
	[.31]	[.25]	[.03]

[a] Correlations with imageability ratings in parentheses.
[b] Correlations with metaphoricity ratings in brackets.

reported to be used more often in encoding metaphorical than nonmetaphorical sentences.

The mean number of imagery reports for each sentence in each instructional condition was correlated with the metaphoricity ratings from Harris (1979b). These correlations, which appear in Table 7.3, are only very modest.

The fact that images were reported more often with metaphorical than non-metaphorical sentences suggests that imagery may be a more frequently used mnemonic with metaphors than with more literal language, even though it is not necessarily all that effective. Just why images tend to be used with metaphors is a psychologically important question.

Although *The ivy cuddled up to the window* cannot be imaged in the photographic sense that *The ivy grew up to the window* can be, it is on the *cuddled* sentence, whose imagery code must necessarily be less "realistic" and thus more constructed and creative, that subjects more often report using imagery. This suggests that such imagery need not be a "mental picture" that could be reproducible in a photograph. However, there is no reason that the construct of imagery must be interpreted so concretely (Kosslyn & Pomerantz, 1977; Shepard, 1978). Apparently such constructed and interpreted imagery, possibly incorporating the resemblance of the topic and the vehicle (i.e., the ground), as pointed out by Verbrugge and McCarrell (1977), happens very naturally and easily. The fact that the present study and Harris (1979b) have shown no metaphor-nonmetaphor differences in the number of sentences remembered correctly argues against a naive theory that metaphors are inherently more difficult to understand or remember and for that reason require a more complex constructed imagery mnemonic.

Images encoding metaphors do have an advantage over those encoding nonmetaphors, in that there are two literal semantic domains, that is, from the topic and the vehicle, from which to draw material to construct the image. In the example above, one may draw on the semantics of horticulture (*ivy*) and/or interpersonal affection (*cuddled*). In fact the images most typically used probably involve some dynamic nonliteral ("anomalous") combination of the two domains in a sort of surrealistic fusion or "plastic reshaping" (Verbrugge & McCarrell, 1977), for example, some ivy growing on a human arm or ivy partially in the form of an arm abutting the top of a window frame that has the contour of a human shoulder line. The nature of such imagery is more carefully examined in Experiment 3.

Imageability Ratings.   The mean imageability ratings across all sentence sets were 3.21, 3.63, and 3.73 for metaphors, dead metaphors, and nonmetaphors, respectively. These differed significantly, $F(2,88) = 13.54$, $p < .001$, with post hoc Scheffé tests showing that metaphors differed from dead metaphors and nonmetaphors, which did not differ from each other. Thus, the metaphors were actually the hardest sentence type to develop an image for, in spite of images being most often reported used as a mnemonic!

The correlations of the imageability ratings and the metaphoricity ratings (from Harris, 1979b) were −.18, −.05, and −.02 for metaphors, dead metaphors, and nonmetaphors, respectively.

A mean imageability value for each stimulus sentence was obtained from the ratings. In order to test for a possible relationship of imageability and memorability, correlations of imageability and the probability of correct recognition for each sentence type × instruction type cell were computed and appear in Table 7.2. Imageability is clearly not a good predictor of memorability, the two measures being essentially uncorrelated.

Similarly, correlations of imageability and the number of reported images were obtained for each stimulus sentence type and appear in Table 7.3. Imageability clearly does not predict the probability of an imagery report either.

Informativeness Ratings.   The mean informativeness ratings from the separate-list informativeness ratings were 3.15, 3.14, and 3.10 for metaphors, dead metaphors, and nonmetaphors, respectively. These did not differ significantly and thus did not offer any support for a hypothesis that metaphorical sentences are more informative than nonmetaphorical ones.

However, for the rank-order informativeness ratings, the mean rankings were 2.30, 1.75, and 1.95 for metaphors, dead metaphors, and nonmetaphors, respectively, ranging from 1 (most informative) to 3 (least informative), with a chance ranking of 2. Sign tests were performed on each of the three possible pairs of sentences from each stimulus sentence set and showed that metaphors were rated significantly less informative than the other two types, which did not differ from each other.

The apparent inconsistency of the results of the two informativeness judgments reveals a curious fact about metaphor. In the condition where a given subject sees only one of the three sentences in each sentence set, there is no difference in perceived informativeness, thus arguing against any explanation of metaphors being seen as carrying less information than nonmetaphors. However, in the rank-order informativeness rating, where subjects concurrently see all three sentences in each sentence set, the metaphors are consistently rated less informative. The discrepancy between the two ratings may reflect the common perceptions of the metaphor as difficult and obscure language. Although the first informativeness rating and the memory results, as well as other research, suggest metaphors are no more difficult or less informative than nonmetaphors, people still have the intuitive idea that they are. Thus when they see all three sentences in a set together, as in the rank-order informativeness rating, the metaphor artifactually appears to carry less information, but this is only a contrast effect to the more "familiar" nonmetaphor and dead metaphor. Thus the separate-list informativeness ratings are probably the more accurate.

To further explore the dimension of informativeness, the separate-list informativeness mean ratings were correlated with the mean ratings of imageability and metaphoricity (Harris, 1979b). The informativeness-imageability correlations were .17, −.12, and .18 for metaphors, dead metaphors, and nonmetaphors, respectively. The informativeness-metaphoricity correlations were −.15, −.15, and .17 for metaphors, dead metaphors, and nonmetaphors, respectively.

The striking lack of correlation among these variables certainly does not suggest that imageability, informativeness, memorability, and metaphoricity are measuring the same dimensions. Thus there are a number of reasonable hypotheses that simply find no support here—more imageable sentences are remembered better, more informative sentences are more imageable, more metaphorical sentences are more informative.

The fact that the metaphors were judged as less imageable than nonmetaphors makes even more puzzling the finding that metaphors were more likely to evoke retrospective reports of imagery encoding. One possible explanation for this apparent contradiction may stem from the task itself. The ratings are metalinguistic tasks and thus not really a case of natural processing. In these tasks subjects were asked to concentrate on one particular aspect of the sentence (imageability, informativeness, metaphoricity) and not necessarily to process it as a whole unit, as in natural discourse comprehension, which requires consideration of a variety of dimensions.

Although these sorts of rating tasks may be very useful, caution should be used in drawing firm conclusions from them. The type of materials being rated, as well as the nature of the rating dimension, may interact to alter the task. Support for this position has come from an unpublished study (King & Lahey, 1978) in which the same imageability and informativeness rating tasks were given using advertisements containing either metaphorical or nonmetaphorical wording. Results showed that the metaphorical advertisements were rated significantly more imageable than were otherwise comparable nonmetaphorical ads, in contrast to the single-sentence ratings of the present study. The informativeness ratings, on the other hand, showed no significant difference between metaphorical ads and nonmetaphorical ads, which corroborated the present results in the single-sentence ratings. All of this casts some doubt on the equivalency of the tasks with different materials and suggests an interaction of rating dimension and stimulus material, thus implying caution in generalizing the results of rating tasks.

EXPERIMENT 2

Although there was no metaphor-nonmetaphor difference in the number of correctly recognized sentences in Experiment 1, it is possible that this occurred because there was sufficient time and cognitive capacity available to adequately process all three types of sentences. Experiment 2 was designed to use the same task as in Experiment 1 but in an incidental-learning paradigm with an obtrusive intersentence interval task (counting the number of words in that sentence) intended to induce a shallow level of processing. If metaphor comprehension really involves a deeper level of processing or an otherwise greater amount of conscious cognitive activity than is required for understanding nonmetaphors, it is possible that under these adverse conditions subjects will not be able to process the metaphors adequately enough to recognize them at the level at which they can recognize the nonmetaphors. No imagery instructions were used in Experiment 2; however, subjects were still asked on the recognition task to report instances of images used. Although it would be surprising to find that images were used as often as in the intentional-learning task of Experiment 1, the same effect of sentence type on the number of reported images under incidental learning would indicate at least a deep enough level of processing of the metaphors to construct an image, even without anticipation of using it later.

Method

The materials were the same three lists of sentences used in Experiment 1, and the subjects were 45 undergraduate psychology students from Kansas State University. Fifteen subjects heard each of the three acquisition lists, preceded by the instructions:

> This is an experiment studying how efficiently you can process meaningful information in sentences presented relatively rapidly. You will hear a list of sentences on

the tape recorder. After each sentence there will be a brief pause in which you are to write down the number of words in the sentence you just heard. Do so as quickly as possible. For example, if the sentence was *The boy hit the girl*, you would write down 5; if it was *George Washington was the commander of the Continental army*, you would write down 9. Once a sentence has been played, it will not be played again, nor will the tape be stopped at any time before the entire list has been played. Any questions?

Subjects were given a sheet of paper with 48 blanks to write down the number of words in each sentence as the tape played. No mention was made of any memory task to follow. At the end of the list, the same forced-choice recognition answer sheets used in Experiment 1 were handed out, and subjects filled them in at their own speed.

Results and Discussion

Memory Data.   The mean numbers of responses of each sentence type appear at the bottom of Table 7.2. The correct responses were analyzed by a one-way analysis of variance. Unlike what was found in Experiment 1, there was a significant difference (.05 level) in the number of correct recognitions across the three sentence types, $F(2,88) = 9.93$, $MS_e = 3.87$, with nonmetaphors being the most difficult. Tukey's HSD test showed that only the dead metaphor and nonmetaphor means differed significantly, however. The mean numbers correct for each sentence type were slightly below those obtained in Experiment 1, though still quite high, even under the distracting condition of counting words and the surprise of an incidental memory test. There was only a negligible correlation ($r = .15$) of the probability of a correct recognition and the metaphoricity ratings from Harris (1979b).

Like Experiment 1, the number of images reported for the three sentence types differed significantly, $F(2,88) = 19.33$, $MS_e = 3.29$, $p < .001$, although, as expected, the overall mean numbers of imagery reports was lower than in Experiment 1. Tukey's HSD test subsequently revealed each of the three means to be significantly different from the other two at the .05 level. These means appear at the bottom of Table 7.3, along with correlations with imageability and metaphoricity. Thus, even under the difficult conditions of this experiment, subjects still often reported using images and were more likely to do so with metaphorical input sentences. It seems clear from Experiment 2 that metaphors and nonmetaphors were both processed reasonably well under heavy attentional and motivational disadvantages. In fact, the memory decrement in Experiment 2 compared to Experiment 1 occurred primarily in the nonmetaphors, suggesting that, if anything, they and not the metaphors are the most difficult sentence type! At any rate, there is certainly no support for the naive hypothesis that metaphors are more difficult to code or process, even under adverse conditions. This is consistent with Harris (1976), who found in a reaction-time study that difficult literary metaphors took no longer to correctly paraphrase than nonmetaphors.

Counting Data. The mean number of errors in counting, out of a possible 16, across all three lists was 9.0, 7.8, and 7.4 for metaphors, dead metaphors, and nonmetaphors, respectively. These differed significantly, $F(2,88) = 8.08$, $p < .001$, with post hoc Scheffé tests showing that metaphors differed from both dead metaphors and nonmetaphors, which did not differ from each other. Thus it was apparently more difficult to correctly count the number of words in a metaphorical than a nonmetaphorical sentence.

The number of counting errors was correlated with the number of recognition errors on each sentence. Additionally, correlations between the number of counting errors and the number of reported images were computed. This set of correlations was done both for the total number of reported images for input sentences and for the number of reported images only for those sentences correctly recognized. With the exception of the correlation of counting errors and recognition errors for nonmetaphors, which was .35, none of the correlation coefficients exceeded .16. Counting errors are not, therefore, a good predictor of either recognition errors or the number of images reported to be used on this task.

The greater number of counting errors for metaphors may be attributed to differential saliency of the input sentences. The metaphors were novel, while the dead metaphors and nonmetaphors were commonplace. The metaphors were vivid and striking, while the other types were ordinary and unexciting. Hearing the metaphors was thus more distracting than hearing the other sentences and interfered with the low-level processing required in the word-counting task.

EXPERIMENT 3: A PILOT STUDY
OF THE NATURE OF METAPHOR IMAGERY

Although Experiments 1 and 2 suggest that imagery may be frequently used in coding metaphors, they do not say much about the exact nature of these constructed images. Experiment 3 was designed to probe the nature of the image evoked by a metaphorical sentence. Specifically, it was of interest whether such an image would include only the semantic domain of the topic of the metaphor or also the semantic domain of the vehicle. If only the topic domain were used in the image, it would not discriminate among the three sentences in a sentence set, but an image creatively synthesizing the topic and vehicle of the metaphor could so discriminate. Because of the difficulty of reporting images completely and still adequately controlling time intervals, Experiment 3 did not involve memory but simply asked subjects to describe, in either pictures or words, the images they constructed for different sentences. These protocols were then examined for the type of information they contained.

Method

The 36 subjects were undergraduate psychology students from Kansas State University. To prevent the task from becoming too tedious, only the first 24 sentence sets from Experiments 1 and 2 were used. Each of three groups of 12 subjects each received a booklet with the first 24 sentences from one of the three lists from the earlier experiments. They were told this was an experiment studying what kinds of images people use. They were told to:

> Read each sentence, think about it, and make a mental picture of what that sentence talks about. Then in the space in the box beneath the sentence, either describe in words what your image is or draw a little picture of your image. You may either write or draw, whichever is easier for you, but be sure to make your writing legible and the objects in your drawing clearly identifiable.

Subjects worked individually and at their own speed. Every subject formed and reported images for eight metaphorical sentences, eight dead metaphors, and eight nonmetaphors, in random order, with each sentence in each set being imaged by 12 subjects.

Results

The subjects' reported images were scored independently by two of the experimenters (Harris and Marsalek). There was agreement on all but 12% of the responses. The score for these responses was determined by mutual discussion between the scorers. The scoring categories were (a) topic semantic domain only, with no mention of the vehicle domain (e.g., a picture of the sun over mountains for *The rising sun kissed the mountains*). (b) Both topic and vehicle semantic domains (e.g., a sun with a face on it and lips actually kissing the mountains). (c) imported metaphor. Responses in this third category were metaphorical but not in the intended sense above. These responses were either general personification of some inanimate object (e.g., a smiling face on the sun but no kissing) or the metaphorical use of a second semantic domain but not the one suggested by the

TABLE 7.4
Mean Number (out of 8) of Each Type of Reported Image
(Experiment 3)

	Sentence Type		
Image Type	*Metaphor*	*Dead Metaphor*	*Nonmetaphor*
Topic Only	5.22	5.36	6.64
Topic + Vehicle	2.19	1.92	—
Imported Metaphor	.39	.33	.97
Other	.25	.28	.44

vehicle (e.g., a personified sun with arms caressing the mountains). Many of the reaponses in this category were some type of metaphorical response to non-metaphorical sentences, a possible task artifact arising from the presence of so many metaphors and dead metaphors in the list. (d) The fourth category included omissions, misinterpretations, and other unclassifiable responses. The obtained classification of subjects' images appears in Table 7.4. The correlation of imageability and the number of topic + vehicle images evoked by each sentence were .20 and .13 for metaphors and dead metaphors, respectively.

Discussion

The first conclusion from Experiment 3 is that subjects often used some type of image involving the vehicle domain. For the metaphors and dead metaphors, which did not differ from each other, 30.2% of the total responses involved either the topic + vehicle or some less appropriate but also metaphorical response, that is, imported metaphors. Even for the nonmetaphorical sentences, 12.1% of the responses involved metaphors, although this may have been in part a task artifact of being included with other obviously metaphorical sentences in the within-subjects design.

In looking over the topic + vehicle images reported, one cannot help but be struck by their creativity and complexity. For example, one subject pictured the sentence *The two reporters torpedoed difficult questions at the President* by showing two stick figures with ''Press'' labels on their hats standing at some distance from the President at a podium giving a speech. Coming out of the two reporters' open mouths were small torpedoes with question marks on them flying toward the President. Not only are both the topic and vehicle semantic domains present, but they are intertwined in some complex ways, as in questions on the torpedoes and torpedoes coming out of the men's mouths. Another example pictured *The strip miners tortured West Virginia* by having an outline of the state of West Virginia strung up on two poles with a man wearing a miner's cap lashing a whip at the strung-up map. Such dynamic interactions of two semantic domains as are present in these and many other examples also involve metonymy, a type of figurative language where a part of the whole or a symbol for it is used to stand for the whole (e.g., an outline map for West Virginia, question marks for spoken questions). Not a single topic + vehicle response merely pictured the two semantic domains *juxtaposed* but rather had them intricately *fused,* in the sense of Verbrugge (1977).

GENERAL DISCUSSION

These studies have demonstrated that subjects report using images more frequently to encode metaphorical than nonmetaphorical sentences, even though in a purely metalinguistic task they rate the same metaphorical sentences as being more difficult to image. While such images may sometimes be simply literal icons representing particular objects or events, they are frequently highly creative, constructed, literally anomalous "surrealistic" images involving both the topic and the vehicle fused in dynamic interaction. One has only to look at the protocols in Experiment 3 to be impressed with the creativity, complexity, and surrealism of many of the images constructed. As complex and creative as they are, they are still apparently easily and quickly constructed, since images were reported used even under the adverse conditions of counting words in Experiment 2. The fact that people can construct interpretations for novel metaphors so easily is further evidence for the creativity of language, in a manner even more abstract and impressive than that discussed by Chomsky (1968), in that we can all easily understand and create metaphors fusing two disparate semantic domains perhaps never before unified conceptually.

Although the effect is clearly not a strong one, there is some indication, especially from Experiment 2, that metaphors are remembered more easily than nonmetaphors. Past studies from this laboratory (Harris, 1979a; Harris, 1979b) have shown either no metaphor-nonmetaphor difference in memory or, in the case of literary materials (quotations from Shakespeare), a consistent superiority of metaphors. Using the approach of having subjects read concrete sentences preceded either by a context giving the target sentence a literal meaning or one giving it a metaphorical meaning, Tanhauser (1978) similarly found no differences between literal and metaphorical items in either reading time, verification time, or correct recognitions shortly thereafter. However, her metaphorical-context targets were recognized better than the literal-context targets on a yes-no recognition test 24 hours later. Clearly it is not necessarily the case that metaphors are more difficult to remember, even if they are more difficult for linguists and psychologists to analyze and theorize about.

Why might metaphors be easier to remember than nonmetaphors? In part it may be due to a relatively greater salience of metaphors, as shown by the distractability effect on counting errors in Experiment 2. Also important, however, is the greater number of encoding possibilities for metaphors, due to the presence of two semantic domains from which to construct associations to stored knowledge and interpretations of the input for storage in memory. This richer matrix of meaning may provide a more helpful retrieval aid upon recall or recognition than is possible with the typical nonmetaphorical materials. If an especially dynamic and creative image was constructed, that would also be a helpful mnemonic.

The question arises as to whether any usefulness of imagery in encoding metaphors was due to the interaction of the two semantic domains or to the bizarreness and novelty of such creative and nonphotographic images. Since the two are typically confounded, as they are in the present studies, just which is the critical factor would not be obvious. However, a series of studies have examined the issue of bizarreness in imagery in paired-associate memory tasks (Collyer,

Jonides, & Bevan, 1972; Hauck, Walsh, & Kroll, 1976; Nappe & Wollen, 1973; Senter & Hoffman, 1976; Wollen, Weber, & Lowry, 1972). Subjects were instructed to remember two words by forming an image that was interacting or noninteracting and bizarre or commonplace. It was consistently found that interactiveness of the images improved memory but that bizarreness had a detrimental effect or no effect on memory. Also, the bizarre images took longer to form than the common ones. Although these studies have not examined sentence materials, the findings suggest that the interaction of the two semantic domains in metaphors is a more important determinant of memory than the frequent bizarreness of the resulting image.

Further study of the surrealistic imagery used to encode metaphors should be helpful in constructing more global theories of imagery (cf. Kieras, 1978). In the theories and research on imagery reviewed by Kieras, there is seldom any serious consideration of surrealistic imagery, but rather a focus on concrete, realistic imagery. The fact that surrealistic images are constructed so readily suggests that imagery may be less perceptual and more flexible than has been generally assumed. In fact, surrealistic imagery is much more widely used than merely in encoding metaphors (e.g., fantasy thinking, preoperational thought, dreaming, pathological thought, creative problem solving). It will surely have to be included in any successful general theory of imagery.

The results of the rating tasks, especially the inconsistency of results from the two informativeness ratings and the low imageability ratings for metaphorical sentences, suggest a real caution in interpreting data from metalinguistic tasks involving metaphors. People's intuitions about metaphors are often highly inaccurate, especially in the direction of thinking them to be more difficult, less informative, and less imageable than they truly are. In a natural language processing situation or even the list-learning paradigm of Experiments 1 and 2, metaphors can be understood and remembered at least as easily, if not more easily, than nonmetaphors, but most people's intuitions about their difficulty is the opposite. This argues that ratings, while useful, must be recognized as metalinguistic; their unidimensional focus likely involves different processes than those involved in normal comprehension.

Although not its major purpose, the present studies offer some converging evidence on the issue of metaphor comprehension. The fact that memory was so good under the highly adverse conditions of Experiment 2, with nonmetaphors significantly the hardest sentence type to remember, argues against metaphors being harder, taking longer to comprehend, or involving extra stages. This is consistent with the results of Harris (1976), who found no metaphor-nonmetaphor difference in the latency to initiate a paraphrase, and an earlier unpublished study by Harris that found no recognition-memory difference for metaphors and nonmetaphors as a function of whether there had been five seconds or one second between each sentence in the stimulus list. However, these results for metaphors are not consistent with evidence found for a two-stage process in the comprehension of proverbs (Brewer, Harris, & Brewer, 1974) and conversationally conveyed requests (Clark & Lucy, 1975). With these two types of sentences there was evidence for an initial stage of interpreting the sentence literally, followed by a second stage (if necessary) of constructing a nonliteral interpretation. It should be noted, though, that both proverbs and indirect speech acts involve two distinct levels of meaning for the whole sentence, whereas metaphors are typically anomalous at the literal level. Also, metaphors are far more widespread and a more integral part of natural language than are proverbs or indirect speech acts.

Obviously, many questions remain to be answered about metaphor, perhaps more than there were when our research began. Reaction-time methodology may offer a useful means of further investigating the metaphor comprehension process and how imagery may be involved in it. It may both be overly optimistic and naive, however, to expect this methodology to clearly identify a sequence of stages in a serial process of comprehension. Another very promising approach may be the work of Robert Sternberg and his colleagues (e.g., Tourangeau & Sternberg, 1978) using multidimensional scaling techniques to study both comprehension and appreciation of metaphors. Sternberg has been able to generate some empirically testable predictions about both metaphor comprehensibility and aesthetic pleasingness, the latter an obviously important but as yet operationally undefined and largely unexplained dimension. In any case, it is certain that the work on metaphors will continue and probably will improve in the quality of both the theory and the methodology. At last metaphor is generally recognized as the common and pervasive linguistic phenomenon that it has always been. As such, it must and will be taken seriously by any theory of language processing or memory that claims to have any generality at all.

ACKNOWLEDGMENT

This work was supported by grant MH 28493-01 from NIMH and a faculty research grant to the first author from Kansas State University. Appreciation is expressed to Cathy Haverfield for data collection, Ron Crosier for statistical analysis, and Richard Honeck, Robert Hoffman, Tony Dubitsky, Kris Bruno, and Greg Monaco for helpful comments on various stages of the manuscript. Some of this work was presented at the APA Symposium on Metaphor, Toronto, August 1978.

REFERENCES

Billow, R. M. Metaphor: A review of the psychological literature. *Psychological Bulletin,* 1977, *84,* 81–92.
Bower, G. H., & Winzenz, D. Comparison of associative learning strategies. *Psychonomic Science,* 1970, *20,* 119–120.

Brewer, W. F., Harris, R. J., & Brewer, E. F. *Comprehension of literal and figurative meaning.* Unpublished paper, University of Illinois, 1974.

Chomsky, N. *Language and mind.* New York: Harcourt, Brace and World, 1968.

Clark, H. H., & Lucy, P. Understanding what is meant from what is said: A study in conversationally conveyed requests. *Journal of Verbal Learning and Verbal Behavior,* 1975, *14,* 56–72.

Collyer, S. C., Jonides, J., & Bevan, W. Images as memory aids: Is bizarreness useful? *American Journal of Psychology,* 1972, *85,* 31–38.

Harris, R. J. Comprehension of metaphors: A test of the two-stage processing model. *Bulletin of the Psychonomic Society,* 1976, *8,* 312–314.

Harris, R. J. Memory for literary metaphors. *Bulletin of the Psychonomic Society,* 1979, *13,* 246–249. (a)

Harris, R. J. Memory for metaphors. *Journal of Psycholinguistic Research,* 1979, *8,* 61–71. (b)

Hauck, P. D., Walsh, C. C., & Kroll, N. E. A. Visual imagery mnemonics: Common v. bizzare mental images. *Bulletin of the Psychonomic Society,* 1976, *7,* 160–162.

Honeck, R. P. Cinq questions sur la semantique. *Bulletin de Psychologie,* 1976, No. Spécial (La mémoire semantique), 116–124.

Kieras, D. Beyond pictures and words: Alternative information-processing models for imagery effects in verbal memory. *Psychological Bulletin,* 1978, *85,* 532–554.

King, L. M., & Lahey, M. A. *The effects of metaphorical language on the perception of advertisements.* Unpublished manuscript, Kansas State University, 1978.

Kosslyn, S. M., & Pomerantz, J. R. Imagery, propositions, and the form of internal propositions. *Cognitive Psychology,* 1977, *9,* 52–96.

Levin, S. R. *The semantics of metaphor.* Baltimore: Johns Hopkins University Press, 1977.

Nappe, G. W., & Wollen, K. A. Effects of instructions to form common and bizarre mental images on retention. *Journal of Experimental Psychology,* 1973, *100,* 6–8.

Ortony,A., Reynolds, R. E., & Arter, J. A. Metaphor: Theoretical and empirical research. *Psychological Bulletin,* 1978, *85,* 919–943.

Ortony, A., Schallert, D. L., Reynolds, R. E., & Antos, S. J. Interpreting metaphors and idioms: Some effects of context on comprehension. *Journal of Verbal Learning and Verbal Behavior,* 1978, *17,* 465–477.

Shepard, R. N. The mental image. *American Psychologist,* 1978, *33,* 125–137.

Senter, R. J., & Hoffman, R. R. Bizarreness as a nonessential variable in mnemonic imagery: A confirmation. *Bulletin of the Psychonomic Society,* 1976, *7,* 163–164.

Tanhauser, S. L. *Levels of interpretation: A study of metaphor-literal differences.* Paper presented at the Midwestern Psychological Association, Chicago, May 1978.

Tourangeau, R., & Sternberg, R. J. *Understanding and appreciating metaphors.* Technical Report No. 11, Department of Psychology, Yale University, June 1978.

Verbrugge, R. R. Resemblances in language and perception. In R. Shaw & J. Bransford (Eds.), *Perceiving, acting, and knowing.* Hillsdale, N.J.: Lawrence Erlbaum Associates, 1977.

Verbrugge, R. R., & McCarrell, N. S. Metaphoric comprehension: Studies in reminding and resembling. *Cognitive Psychology,* 1977, *9,* 494–533.

Wollen, K. A., Weber, A., & Lowry, D. H. Bizarreness versus interaction of mental images as determinants of learning: *Cognitive Psychology,* 1972, *3,* 518–523.

MENTAL IMAGERY AND THE COMPREHENSION OF FIGURATIVE LANGUAGE: IS THERE A RELATIONSHIP?

8

Paul F. Riechmann
Westfield State College

Ellen L. Coste
Mount Holyoke College

INTRODUCTION

Mental imagery is frequently associated with metaphor. Upon hearing *My doctor is an elephant,* a listener may imagine a woman with an elephantine body wearing a white lab coat. *She pried her husband away from the antique store* might elicit a scene in which a woman is physically struggling to remove her stationary spouse—perhaps using a lever in the process. Most people would probably report an image of a boy sucking the food right off his plate like a vacuum cleaner for *The boy inhaled his dinner.*

Imagery Theories of Metaphor Comprehension

It has been suggested that these images may be more than intriguing; images may play a large role in the comprehension of metaphor. Verbrugge (1977) has argued that imagery is a means by which the two or more semantic domains in metaphor can be "fused." For instance, the domains of people and elephants in *My doctor is an elephant* are bridged by an image that incorporates both. In the absence of an image of an elephant, the assertion that someone *is* such a beast could be absurd or, at least, confusing; a creature cannot belong to two species at once. Yet if the listener attempts to imagine such a thing, the perceptual constraints on how the particular person will "fit" the image (she doesn't have a trunk, four legs, a tail, large ears, or gray skin) might very well lead to a likely interpretation for the sentence (she is *big* like an elephant).

Miller (1979) has argued that a listener is willing to go through these imagistic distortions in order to discover the truth presumably present in every utterance.

Rather than discount as pure fabrication the statement that someone has inhaled a dinner (clearly, lungs cannot digest food), a person instead may generate images, trying to discover the speaker's meaning.

Problems with Imagery Theories

The difficulty in all this is that we can have abstract metaphors that are comprehensible but are nearly impossible to imagine in a perceptual manner—for example, *Love is a theory* or *Dreams are the judicial system of the unconscious.* Therefore, if some metaphors are imaginable while others are not, it will be difficult to present a strong argument for imagery as being more important to the comprehension of metaphor than to the comprehension of any other kind of language. Perhaps imagery is important in the comprehension of perceptually concrete metaphors just as it may be in the comprehension of perceptually concrete nonmetaphorical sentences. Nevertheless, we are left with the task of explaining nonimaginable sentences in both the metaphorical and nonmetaphorical cases. In other words, any special qualities of metaphor may have little to do with imagery.

The arguments presented to this point allow for the possibility that even if imagery plays a role in the comprehension process only for easily imagined sentences, this role may be very important in those cases. Moreover, since easily imagined sentences probably are more frequent than those not so easily imagined, an imagery-based analysis of metaphor (as well as nonmetaphor) comprehension is not surprising.

However, any viable imagery-based analysis has to take into consideration the current debate over imagery's role in cognitive processing. This extensive debate has been summarized elsewhere (Anderson, 1978; Kieras, 1978; Kosslyn & Pomerantz, 1977). Essentially, it is not clear whether imagery is a deep-level or shallow-level process (Craik & Lockhart, 1972)—i.e., whether imagery is an important part of the semantic-interpretation process or is better described as a peripheral-process phenomenon. It is also not clear whether image representations are stored in memory or are transient components of the comprehension process.

Basic Arguments

If imagery is a shallow-level process, it may bias comprehension toward the literal—as opposed to the intended figurative—meaning of a metaphor, so that the image has a distracting effect (Franks, 1974; Riechmann & Van Wyk, 1977; Verbrugge, 1977). Someone might interpret *The boy inhaled his dinner,* for example, to mean that the boy literally inhaled—and choked on—his dinner. On the other hand, the notion of a deep-level image can be confusing. What does it mean to say that someone has a semantically accurate image of a metaphor?

Paivio (1971) points out that discussions of imagery in relation to metaphor most often refer to "images with general rather than specific meaning" (p. 472). Yet can an image be anything *but* specific? Paivio's comment could imply two qualitatively different categories of imagery, although, as indicated by Park and Arbuckle (1977), distinguishing between types of imagery might weaken the argument for an imagistic representation. Anderson (1978) argues further that imagery is specific, shallow-level, and, particularly in the case of metaphor and other figurative language, potentially distracting.

It is more difficult to take a stand on the issue of whether images are stored or whether they are transient representations with the stored representations being abstract propositions. Kosslyn & Pomerantz (1977) and Anderson (1978) argue that it may be impossible to resolve this issue on the basis of behavioral data. We feel that we too may inevitably be compelled to adopt this noncommittal position. We presently believe that images are *not* stored. However, the data to be reported here are also consistent with a model in which shallow-level images may be stored *along with* a more abstract, conceptual base (Honeck, Riechmann, & Hoffman, 1975).

MEMORY FOR PROVERBS

General Methodology

The first set of studies to be described here used sentence proverbs as materials rather than metaphors or some other kind of figurative language. Metaphors differ from proverbs in that the latter tend to be more abstract and difficult (Billow, 1977). Nevertheless, the proverb results probably can be, with caution, generalized to metaphor. In any event, we later report a study using metaphorical sentences as materials.

The purpose of the initial proverb studies was not to study the comprehension of figurative language *per se*, but to define any limitations of imagery's well known mnemonic effect with verbal materials. It was hypothesized that if imagery was a shallow-level process, the usual experimental manipulations of imagery ratings and instructions would fail to improve memory performance when both a shallow (literal) and a deep (figurative) level of interpretation were possible *and* when the memory cue was related to the deep level interpretation but *not* to the shallow level one. Proverbs were used because they seemed to provide the clearest difference between levels of interpretation. For example, the proverb *That which will not be butter must be made into cheese* can be interpreted in a shallow manner—cheese is made from the curd and so forth—or it can be interpreted to mean "If something does not lend itself to one approach, try another approach." In like manner, *He who spits above himself will have it all in his face* can be interpreted from the literal perspective of gravity and fluid dynamics or from a more abstract perspective: "It is unwise to insult someone who is more powerful than yourself."

The memory cues for the proverbs in these studies were actually *interpretations* like those given in quotations for the two proverbs above. The interpretations were related to the proverbs conceptually but shared no content words, overall phrase structure, or basic propositional structure with them. Thus, if subjects' images only involved the shallow aspects of a proverb (e.g., butter and cheese), the images should have been of little or no aid in recognizing the interpretations or remembering the proverbs.

Evidence that Imagery Interferes with Comprehension

Riechmann (1975), who devised and implemented the novel methodology described above, reported results suggesting that imagery did not facilitate the processing of sentence proverbs and that it may even have had an interfering effect. Two groups of 17 subjects each listened to a list of 20 proverbs, each read twice and separated by a 5-sec pause and followed by a 10-sec interval before the next proverb. One group was instructed to "form a mental image of each of the proverbs," and the other to "try to comprehend the meaning of each proverb as accurately as possible." Both groups were instructed to "try to remember as much as you can about everything" but were given no other warning about a memory test. In an immediate recognition and confidence rating task, subjects listened to 50 sentences—20 interpretations of the acquisition list proverbs and 30 filler interpretations of other proverbs. As described earlier, the interpretations were related to their corresponding proverbs in only a semantic manner. As another example, if the proverb was *A friendly denial is better than an unwilling compliance,* the interpretation was *State your feelings honestly or you will get into something you did not want to.* Half of the proverbs had previously been rated by a separate group of 22 subjects as high in ease of imagining and half as low. Also, half had been rated as high in ease of comprehension and half as low, completing a factorial *Instructions × Imagery × Comprehensibility* design. For instance, the "friendly denial" proverb was in the low-imagery, high-comprehensibility category. A high-imagery, low-comprehensibility proverb was *Crows bewail the dead sheep then eat them,* with the interpretation *Some people take delight in the misfortune of others even though they feign an expression of sorrow.*

A 10-point recognition scale was constructed by combining the yes-no responses with the 5-point confidence ratings. An analysis of variance computed for the resulting scores showed a strong, significant discrimination between the target and filler interpretations, supporting the notion of an abstract, conceptual representation in memory and vindicating the use of unorthodox memory cues. It would be difficult to account for this result based on the storage of a verbal code or an imaginal code, since neither would be sufficiently similar to the target interpretation. However, most likely Anderson (1978), and certainly Paivio (1971), would argue that the storage of both codes together could account for the result.

The results for target interpretations alone (see Table 8.1) showed a consistent and significant advantage for the group instructed to comprehend relative to the group instructed to image, regardless of the imagery-comprehensibility category. Just the opposite would have been expected if imagery facilitated semantic processing. Nevertheless, it is possible, since both groups were told to "remember . . . everything," that the group instructed to comprehend also formed images as a mnemonic strategy. If so, the implication could be that imagery did facilitate recognition of a semantically related target when imagery was combined with a more abstract, perhaps verbal, representation of the proverb. This sort of analysis would suggest a dual-coding explanation (Paivio, 1971). However, such an explanation would not adequately account for the *consistent* advantage shown by the comprehend group over the image group in all proverb categories— particularly in the low-imagery ones. This advantage should have disappeared with low-imagery sentences according to a dual-coding analysis, because an image code would probably not have been available to pair up with the other code. A better explanation of these results is that instructions to comprehend yielded a memorial representation that was semantically general enough to be accessed by the target interpretation and was more general than a representation yielded by instructions to concentrate on an image. This explanation is more easily accommodated by a conceptual-base approach (Chase & Clark, 1972; Honeck, Riechmann, & Hoffman, 1975; Pylyshyn, 1973) than by a dual-coding one. Nevertheless, a dual-coding approach cannot be totally discounted; dual representations in conjunction with the appropriate *process* might have yielded behavioral data identical to that resulting from a conceptual-base model (Anderson, 1978).

Another result that was inconsistent with the notion that imagery facilitates semantic memory was that interpretations of low-imagery proverbs were recognized significantly better overall than those of high-imagery proverbs. Furthermore, the low-imagery, high-comprehensibility category yielded the best peformance, while the high-imagery, high-comprehensibility category yielded the worst. Apparently, ease of comprehension aided recognition of semantically related sentences, but ease of imaging did not. However, at least one other conclusion is possible—the target interpretations may not all have been equally synonymous with the subjects' own interpretations of the proverbs, so that the interpretations for the low-imagery, high-comprehensibility proverbs (which yielded the best recognition scores) may have been better than those in the other categories.

Riechmann and van Wyk (1977) controlled for this possibility by holding constant the degree of semantic variability in the subjects' own interpretations of each proverb. Sixteen subjects were asked to "describe what you think the

TABLE 8.1
Mean Recognition Scores for Proverb Interpretations

	Low I		High I		
Instructions	Low C	High C	Low C	High C	Fillers
Comprehend	6.62	7.97	6.12	5.84	4.23
	(6.76)	(7.77)	(7.58)	(7.03)	(3.77)
Image	6.00	7.34	5.60	5.01	4.33
	(5.56)	(6.46)	(6.51)	(5.70)	(3.20)

Note: "I" refers to imagery, "C" to comprehensibility. The scores in parentheses are from Riechmann and van Wyk (1977); the others are from Riechmann (1975).

proverb means'' for 69 proverbs. Afterwards, two judges composed a modal interpretation for each proverb that represented the majority of the 16 interpretations. For 27 proverbs the variability of the 16 interpretations was too high to allow a modal interpretation. For the remaining 42 proverbs, three judges used a 7-point scale to rate the *semantic agreement* of each subject's interpretation with the modal version, yielding a mean and standard deviation for each proverb. Twenty proverbs and their modal interpretations were selected, with semantic agreement held relatively constant around a high value of 5.3 and the standard deviation held below 2.0.

Next, the procedure employed by Riechmann (1975) was repeated. The recognition of interpretations was again significantly better for the comprehend group than for the image group. Also, again, there was no interaction between instructions and the imagery-comprehensibility category of proverbs, reinforcing the conclusion that imagery in this task was not serving as a mnemonic for conceptual information. Holding semantic agreement constant across proverb categories, however, did change the pattern of findings: Unlike Riechmann's earlier results, there were *no* significant effects due to imagery or comprehensibility. See Table 8.1.

These null effects did not substantially weaken the conclusion of Riechmann's (1975) study. Small imagery and comprehensibility effects were anticipated, because the control of semantic agreement allowed only small, albeit significant, scale differences between the low and high values: The imagery means were 5.15 (low) and 5.93 (high), and for comprehensibility, the means were 5.06 and 5.59. The relation of the semantic agreement, imagery, and comprehensibility ratings is of interest in itself and deserves further research. Some initial investigation by Sacks and Eysenck (1977) suggested that the essence of a high-imagery sentence may be that it is likely to have a single dominant interpretation, whereas a low-imagery sentence incorporates several potential ones. They divided their subjects into two categories of thinking styles, convergers and divergers, and found that concrete sentences were recognized better than abstract ones only for the convergers—implying that the mnemonic effect of imagery is due to convergence on a single interpretation and only aids people who think that way. Thus by controlling semantic agreement and using proverbs that tended to have single interpretations, Riechmann and van Wyk may have eliminated most of the variation in the imagery ratings. A close relation between semantic agreement and comprehensibility is also plausible: A sentence for which subjects cannot agree on an interpretation should probably be low in comprehensibility. Consequently, the semantic agreement control may have destroyed the sought-after manipulation of imagery and comprehensibility.

In spite of the just described lack of variability in imagery and comprehensibility, Riechmann and van Wyk did find an interesting interaction effect between the two variables. The experimenters asked the subjects, after completing the recognition task, to go back and attempt to recall the proverb corresponding to each interpretation they had claimed to recognize. This was requested in order to validate the recognition measure—that is, to ensure that subjects were really remembering the correct proverb when saying they recognized an interpretation. A binary measure was used—a response was scored as correct if it suggested that the subject remembered the proverb and did not merely paraphrase the target interpretation. Recall was significantly lower for the high-imagery, high-comprehensibility category (31%) than for the other three categories (approximately 43%), which did not differ among themselves.

This latter result presents problems for a dual-coding model. If two codes are being stored, the low recall for high-imagery, high-comprehensibility proverbs suggests some kind of "representational rivalry" occurring between the two codes. Allowing this possibility forces a revision of the dual-coding model: *Two codes yield better memory than one code only if they are conceptually consonant with each other.* Yet this revision, by suggesting a dimension on which the two codes can be compared, implies an underlying, abstract representation, that is, a conceptual-base model that can accommodate the proposition that two relatively shallow representations can rival each other during encoding and lead to an impoverished representation.

Accessing Stored Images

The major finding of the studies reported so far is that neither imagery instructions nor high-imagery ratings help subjects much in recognizing the interpretations of proverbs. A more speculative implication is that imagery *impedes* performance on this task. Nevertheless, imagery may play a very important role in the comprehension process, yielding a deep-level memorial code but failing to aid memory if the cue-to-remember does not access the stored representation. That is, *encoding specificity* (Tulving & Thompson, 1973) may have to be taken into account in the present task. If care is taken to increase the probability of the cue accessing a stored imaginal code, any possible facilitation of memory for conceptual information due to images should be more evident.

One approach to testing this hypothesis is to manipulate the degree of propositional relationship between memory cues (interpretations of proverbs) and subjects' reported images of the proverbs. A dual-coding argument predicts that conditions conducive to imagery should improve memory when this relationship is high. When it is low, the prediction would be that the target interpretation should not be as likely to access any image code that may have been stored. A nonsignificant interaction between the propositional relationship and imagery conditions would be evidence in favor of a conceptual-base position and against a dual-coding one.

Riechmann and O'Mara (1977) conducted such an experiment. For the first part of their study, they obtained 42 proverbs, using a high semantic-agreement rating from Riechmann and van Wyk (1977) as a criterion for selection. Fifteen subjects were interviewed and asked to describe their mental image for each of the 42 proverbs. They were encouraged to be candid and the interviewer sometimes asked for clarification but tried not to ask suggestive questions or direct the subject's description. Three judges rated the propositional overlap between each tape-recorded image description and the proverb's target interpretation. The experimenters had previously broken each target into three major propositions, so the judges' task consisted of reaching a consensus on the number of these propositions present in the subject's image description. For example, the proverb *The monkey takes the chestnuts out of the fire with the dog's paw* had the target interpretation *Those who are clever use others to accomplish their goals for them,* which was broken into the propositions *some (people) are clever, (people) can use others,* and *(people) have goals.* A relationship score was obtained for each proverb by averaging the judges' ratings across 15 subjects.

TABLE 8.2
Examples of Proverbs/Interpretations from Riechmann and O'Mara
(1977)

Low imagery, low relationship:
Reputation is often measured by the acre. / Sometimes people are judged by their material possessions rather than by their personal attributes.

Low imagery, high relationship:
All of the keys do not hang on one man's belt. / No individual has the answers to every question or the abilities to do everything.

High imagery, low relationship:
It takes many shovelsful of earth to bury the truth. / Trying to conceal what is right can be difficult.

High imagery, high relationship:
He who spits above himself will have it all in his face. / You must realize the consequences of your actions, for they may backfire on you.

TABLE 8.3
Mean Recognition Scores in Riechmann and O'Mara (1977)

Instructions	Low I		High I		
	Low R	High R	Low R	High R	Fillers
Comprehend	8.25	6.83	7.29	7.79	3.69
Image	7.79	5.52	6.71	6.83	4.07

Note: "R" refers to relationship.

For the second part of the study, 16 proverbs were selected (see Table 8.2 for examples) so that four were in each cell of a 2 × 2 factorial design (low and high imagery and low and high relationship) and so that comprehensibility and semantic agreement were relatively constant across conditions. The means for the low (5.13) and high (6.11) categories of imagery were better differentiated than in the Riechmann and van Wyk (1977) study. On the 3-point relationship scale, the low and high means were 1.03 and 1.80, respectively and, as with the imagery means, were significantly different. Again using a procedure similar to that used by Riechmann (1975), 26 subjects listened to the list of proverbs. Half were instructed to interpret each proverb, and half were instructed to form an image of each. A list of interpretations was presented immediately after the acquisition stage; half of them were targets.

As in the earlier studies, the subjects had little trouble differentiating target and filler interpretations in the recognition task. The advantage of the comprehend group over the image group was also clearly evident (see Table 8.3), although this effect failed to reach significance statistically. The recognition scores also failed to show a significant difference between low and high imagery, a finding consistent with both Riechmann (1975) and Riechmann and van Wyk (1977). The main effect for relationship was significant, but in the direction opposite to that predicted by the dual-coding argument—recognition of interpretations was better when relationship was low than when it was high, whereas the dual-coding argument would seem to be that recognition should increase when the cue is related to a stored image and can access it.

The interaction between imagery and relationship was not significant for the recognition scores, but for subjects' *recall* of proverbs this interaction was statistically significant. See Figure 8.1. Subjects were asked to write the proverbs for those interpretations they claimed to recognize. With low-relationship conditions, a Newman-Keuls analysis showed that recall significantly decreased as imagery increased. With high-relationship, recall significantly increased as imagery increased. Proverbs in the high-imagery category were recalled at statistically similar levels regardless of relationship, although recall was slightly higher in the high-relationship category. Consequently, if an image was being stored, its saliency apparently allowed it to be accessed even by an interpretation cue not strongly related to the image. However, if the semantic overlap (relationship) between an interpretation cue and a stored image of the proverb was high but the image was given a low-imagery rating, accessing the image was evidently less successful.

It may be useful to briefly examine this somewhat paradoxical notion of a low-imagery, high-relationship proverb. Why should an interpretation be highly related to an image if the subject reported difficulty forming the image for that particular proverb? Indeed, if a low-imagery rating is interpreted to mean that the subject was unable to form *any kind* of mental image, it is paradoxical to say that this "nothingness" was related to something else. The paradox disappears if low-imagery is interpreted to mean that the subject was unable to form an image that accurately expressed the *figurative meaning* of the proverb but may have been able to form some other image. More specifically, assume that the subject formed an image for which the imagery rating was low but for which the description was related propositionally to the interpretation of the proverb. One low-imagery, high-relationship proverb was *Iron may be rubbed so long that it becomes heated.* At first, this proverb seems to belong to the high-imagery category. It is easy to form an image of a piece of iron being rubbed and, for emphasis, turning red. It probably received its low-imagery rating, though, because of the difficulty of incorporating in an image the proposition of "so long"—that is, the proposition that state X does not occur until act Y is carried out *persistently* and *provocatively*. But when describing the image, a subject might incorporate the proposition by saying something like, "The person *persistently* rubbing the iron has a *provocative* look in his eye and the iron is turning

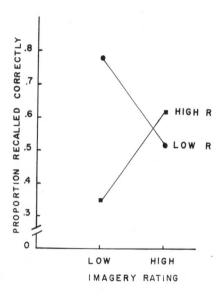

FIG. 8.1. Mean correct-recall proportions as a function of proverb imagery rating and image-interpretation relationship, from Riechmann and O'Mara (1977).

red hot." Such a description would receive a high-relationship rating from the judges, but the subject might rate the proverb low-imagery, because the idea of provocation is not literally represented in the image; the subject reports more verbally than is present perceptually. Of course, this analysis is only speculation, since the subjects rating imagery were not explicitly instructed to incorporate the *figurative* meaning of the proverbs in their images but only to "rate how easy or difficult it was for the proverb to evoke a mental image" (Riechmann & van Wyk, 1977). We have no way of knowing if subjects actually assigned low-imagery ratings when important parts of a proverb's figurative meaning were absent from their mental images.

Returning to Riechmann and O'Mara's results, their relationship × imagery interaction apparently is compatible with either a dual-coding or a conceptual-base position. If dual codes are stored, the interaction effect implies that the image code facilitates memory only when it is easy to form an image but that this facilitation occurs even when the conceptual relationship between the image and interpretation cue is relatively low. (This last point is inconsistent with the encoding-specificity prediction, however, since high-imagery proverbs perhaps should not have been accessed quite so well when in the low-relationship category.)

On the other hand, the dual-coding position has little to say that would predict the superior recall for the low-imagery, low-relationship proverbs, although it can *accept* such a finding—a single, verbal code *can* give memory performance superior to that with dual codes. A conceptual-base approach can account for this effect more comfortably, however, by treating images not as representations containing deep-level information but as temporary particulars providing a "working surface" for the comprehension process and creation of a conceptual base. High-imagery conditions provide more potential "tools" for comprehending the proverbs, but when these images are inappropriate to the figurative meaning of the proverb, they can interfere with the comprehension. Thus, inappropriate (low-relationship) images disrupt comprehension little when they are "absent" (low-imagery), but *do* disrupt comprehension (and the subsequent development of a sound conceptual base) when they are "present" (high-imagery). Appropriate images (high-relationship) are helpful when "present" (high-imagery).

The conceptual-base position also can account for the poor recall of the low-imagery, high-relationship proverbs by saying that these are proverbs for which the figurative meaning is similar enough to the literal meaning that their image descriptions are rated high-relationship, but the images do not adequately express some of the nuances of figurative meaning necessary to be an aid to comprehension. In addition to the earlier example of *Iron may be rubbed so long that it becomes heated*, the low-imagery, high-relationship proverb *All of the keys do not hang on one man's belt* also demonstrates the difficulty of expressing nuance in an image; it is easy to imagine a man with a bunch of keys, but not quite so easy to imagine *absent* keys. Consequently, this image could possibly interfere with comprehension rather than aid it. Of course, it should be added that the dual-coding position can account for the low-imagery, high-relationship result simply by assuming that only one (verbal) code was stored. The weakness of dual-coding is evident in this case only when trying to account for the large discrepancy in performance between this mean and the low-imagery, low-relationship mean—something we have shown the conceptual-base approach is able to handle with greater facility.

Implications of Proverb Studies

Whether imagery can be a memorial code or only a transient stage of comprehension, the studies above suggest that imagery can inhibit the processing of language in a figurative manner and that imagery's commonly reported mnemonic effect with concrete sentences can be eliminated when the sentence's meaning is stated implicitly rather than explicitly. On one hand, an implication is that imagery can increase the depth of processing in a semantic task (Craik & Lockhart, 1972), but only when certain conditions (concreteness, explicitness) are met. On the other hand, conceptual-base theorists take these limitations of imagery to imply that imagery is merely a shallow-level representation or description of a deeper-level base.

It is interesting to note that these conclusions may generalize to *visual* processing as well. Peterson and Graham (1974) reported findings in a visual-detection task that reinforced the notion that imagery by itself, probably because of its shallow-level character, has at least as much potential for interfering with, as for facilitating, mental processing when a semantic representation must be held in memory. The experimenters had their subjects identify a visual stimulus after saying in which of two noise-filled screens it had been presented. Sometimes the subjects were told beforehand the name of the stimulus to be presented, but with the understanding that the cue may be incorrect. Subjects who were instructed to form images of the cues showed poorer performance when the cues were incorrect than when no cues were presented. Control subjects showed no significant performance differences between the incorrect-cue and no-cue conditions. Both groups showed the same improvement in performance when the cues were correct. These data suggest that the improvement in detection may have been due to a similarity between visual imagery and visual perception. As we have been arguing, imaginal representations probably tend to be specific and tend to inhibit the semantic flexibility required in many mental tasks.

A STUDY OF IMAGERY AND METAPHOR

Earlier, we reviewed Verbrugge's (1977) argument for a perceptual basis to the comprehension of metaphor. The argument that a mental image fuses the semantic domains in a metaphor is intuitively persuasive. However, the studies reported here suggest a more complicated relationship. Riechmann and his colleagues were working with proverbs, which, as we warned earlier, tend to be more abstract than metaphors, so imagery could play a more important role in metaphor comprehension than was suggested by their studies.

Riechmann and Coste (1978) investigated this possibility by having subjects recall metaphorical sentences. We reasoned that if images do fuse the semantic domains during metaphor comprehension, images should be more important to the comprehension of metaphorical, than nonmetaphorical, sentences; the disparate semantic domains of a metaphor may *require* imagery for comprehension to occur, whereas a semantically consistent, literal sentence may be comprehended without using imagery. Of course, imagery could be a *post*-comprehension process regardless of sentence metaphoricity, but an image that was part of the comprehension process would presumably have a stronger effect on a memory code than would an image occurring later in time. If so, high-imagery materials and instructions to form images should improve the recall of metaphors more than they improve the recall of nonmetaphors. Other differences that might affect recall could exist between metaphor and nonmetaphor, but we were uncertain as to what controls should be—and could be—implemented in this initial study.

Subjects in Riechmann and Coste's experiment listened to a list of 24 sentences with a 5-second interval following each. The sentences had previously been rated for metaphoricity on a 5-point scale by a group of subjects (Harris, 1976) and were selected so that eight were in each of three categories: *high, medium,* and *low metaphoricity* (Harris, from whom the sentences were obtained, referred to the categories as metaphors, dead metaphors, and nonmetaphors, respectively). An example of a high-metaphoricity sentence was *The blissful honeymoon crash landed in a divorce.* Examples of medium- and low-metaphoricity sentences were, respectively, *The jogger puffed around the corner* and *The bulldozers dug up the cornfield.* In obtaining the metaphoricity ratings for these sentences, Harris (1976) instructed his subjects that a highly metaphorical sentence was meaningless if taken completely literally but that it could be interpreted. He also pointed out, with examples, that some metaphors have become commonplace through frequent usage. These instructions probably increased the subjects' sensitivity to metaphoricity in the sentences and may have yielded greater variability in the ratings than would have occurred otherwise. As it was, the mean ratings for our high, medium, and low metaphoricity categories were 3.79, 2.52, and 1.64 respectively. Across these same three categories, the mean Imagery ratings, which we obtained in an earlier study, were fairly well equated (3.91, 4.03, and 4.43 respectively) even though no great effort was made to balance them.

There were 22 subjects in each of four groups, which differed in their instructions. Group *M* was instructed to memorize the sentences. Group *MI* was instructed to memorize and to form mental images. Group *MIR* was to memorize, form images, and—for purposes to be explained later—rate the ease with which each image was formed. Group *IR* was similar to *MIR* except that they were told the experiment was a study of imagery and were not instructed to memorize. All groups had a 5-sec interval following the presentation of each sentence in which to carry out the instructed processing. In an immediate memory task, subjects were cued for written recall with the subject-noun of each of the 24 sentences. Two recall measures were used: the proportion of major content words recalled correctly (verbatim recall) and the proportion of propositions recalled correctly (propositional recall).

It was expected that recall performance would be higher for the image groups (*MI, MIR*, and *IR*) than for Group *M* and that this advantage would be greater for high-metaphoricity than for medium- or low-metaphoricity sentences, yielding a metaphoricity × instructions interaction. The verbatim-recall results failed to show the predicted main effect for instructions or the metaphoricity × instructions effect. There was a significant metaphoricity main effect, and the high-metaphoricity sentences were recalled more accurately (mean = .45) than were medium- (mean = .37) or low-metaphoricity ones (mean = .40). It should be noted, however, that metaphoricity did not correlate significantly with verbatim recall. Because there was no significant interaction, the recall superiority of high-metaphoricity could not be conclusively attributed to imagery. Moreover, none of the correlations between imagery and verbatim recall (overall or by instruction group) were significant. A simpler explanation would be that something about metaphorical sentences made them more salient; perhaps this something—elicited regardless of instructions—was imagery, perhaps not.

Whatever attribute of the high-metaphoricity sentences was responsible for the improved verbatim recall, that attribute had no observable effect on how well subjects recalled the *ideas* expressed in the sentences. The propositional recall scores showed no significant metaphoricity main effect and, as with verbatim recall, no metaphoricity × instructions interaction. However, there was a significant main effect for instructions which, according to a Newman-Keuls analysis, was caused by the difference between the *MIR* and *M* groups and that difference only.

Returning to the main question: Does imagery facilitate the comprehension of metaphor? Let us suppose that it does. The higher verbatim-recall scores for metaphorical sentences could be credited to the formation—and possible storage—of images. The lack of a metaphoricity × instructions effect could be due to the *automatic* elicitation of imagery by metaphor; if the comprehension of metaphor requires imagery, the probability of imagery occurring might already be high without instructions to encourage it. If so, correlations between imagery and metaphoricity might be expected, although not necessarily, since sentences rated lower in metaphoricity could have been rated high-imagery, lowering the correlation but not implying any weakness in the metaphor-imagery relationship. In a preliminary study to the one just described, we had subjects rate imagery for 48 of Harris' sentences. The correlation between these mean ratings and metaphoricity was only −.28. We reasoned, however, that if subjects were forced to rate imagery quickly and frequently had to do so for metaphorical sentences, *and* if imagery was a more essential process for the comprehension of high-metaphoricity than low-metaphoricity sentences, imagery might be rated highly only in those cases where it was essential. However, the correlation between this new imagery rating obtained from the *MIR* and *IR* subjects in the recall experiment and the metaphoricity ratings was −.23, which was similar to the original correlation of −.28 and not larger as predicted. (Although these two correlations were similar, it is interesting to note that the correlation between ratings of imagery obtained in the preliminary, nonpaced task and of imagery obtained from the *MIR* and *IR* groups was only −.15. Evidently, those two ratings were tapping different processes. It is not clear whether the difference was of the nature suggested above.)

In our search for some empirical relationship between imagery and metaphor, we computed correlations between the imagery ratings and various recall measures. None of these correlations were significant. The only noticeable trend was for the correlations computed for the individual instruction groups between imagery (from the nonpaced study) and propositional recall to increase as the groups' recall performance *decreased*. The *MIR* group, which had the best recall, yielded an $r = .01$. For group *IR*, $r = .03$. For Group *MI*, $r = .46$, a shade short of significance at the .05 level. For the subjects in Group *M*, who were not instructed to use imagery, r declined to −.23.

The low correlations with imagery may have been due, in part, to the low variability of the imagery ratings, which were biased toward higher values. We presently are in the process of generating a set of sentences that are highly variable on *both* the metaphoricity and imagery scales. Any relations between imagery and metaphor comprehension should stand out under these circumstances.

COMPARISONS WITH
FINDINGS OF HARRIS ET AL.

Harris, Lahey, and Marsalek (this volume) also reported low correlations with imagery using the same materials from which Riechmann and Coste (1978) drew their sample of sentences. Harris et al., in addition, reported evidence in Experiment 1 of better memory for medium-metaphorical (dead-metaphorical) than low-metaphorical (nonmetaphorical) sentences, although there was no significant difference between high-metaphorical and low-metaphorical performance. It is not clear how this finding should be interpreted relative to our findings of better verbatim recall for high-metaphorical sentences. We employed a recall task with a one-word cue, whereas Harris et al. employed a forced-choice recognition task in which the two incorrect alternatives were lexically and semantically similar to the correct alternative, except for changes in metaphoricity. Consequently, their task reduced, in most cases, to one of recognizing the correct verb, a task in which subjects could plausibly succeed without having retained the meaning of the sentence. Their results might have been stronger, and perhaps more consistent with our verbatim recall results, if subjects had been asked to perform a more difficult memorial task such as recognizing sentences presented individually during the test phase.

Regardless of metaphoricity's effect on memory, we cannot concur with Harris et al. that the effect is due to imagery. The data from our laboratory offer no firm support for such a conclusion. Also, the evidence on which they base their conclusion is of questionable validity. During the forced-choice recognition test, their subjects were asked "to place a p (for 'picture') beside any recognized sentence for which they recalled using an image to encode." Although it is not very difficult for us to accept the validity of a subject's report of a *presently-existing* image, the assumption is more debatable that subjects can discriminate between their memory of forming an image and their *inference* that they must have done so. Furthermore, the subjects certainly felt an implicit demand to place p's by a few of the sentences regardless of what they remembered about forming images, and the most probable candidates for such randomly-placed p's would be the one sentence in each triplet that was most different from the other two—in other words, the most metaphorical one. If this did indeed happen, the only empirical evidence presented by Harris et al. for the involvement of imagery in metaphor comprehension would be suspect. Their finding in Experiment 3 that subjects can form images, often surrealistic, of metaphorical sentences is interesting but does not necessarily implicate imagery in the actual process of comprehension.

CONCLUSION

We have made some progress in trying to define the cognitive processing relationship between imagery and metaphor. As suggested by our introductory comments, the idea of no relationship whatsoever is difficult to accept. It would also be especially difficult to disregard Verbrugge's (1977) argument for imagery's role in the fusion of metaphor's disparate semantic domains. Experiment 3 by Harris et al. (this volume) is one demonstration of imagery's powerful ability to fuse ideas.

We are arguing, however, for *boundaries* to imagery's role in the comprehension and remembering of metaphor. "Semantic fusion" frequently occurs with abstract sentences containing disparate domains even though we are unaware of any metaphoricity. In other words, comprehension of metaphorlike sentences can occur without the formation of concrete, perceptual representations. Extending this logic, we speculate that the unique attribute of metaphor is not disparate domains of meaning that have to be fused—perhaps the fusion of ideas is common to all language comprehension—but merely the presence of slightly more peculiar combinations of semantic domains. The comprehension process may be identical to, and as image-free as, that for low-metaphoricity language.

Once the point above is appreciated, it is no longer clear why imagery should be essential to comprehending metaphor. Instead, imagery becomes a tangential phenomenon or, at best, a process essential only at a shallow level of processing. A deeper-level conceptual base is required to interpret and ''approve'' any fusions of images. This conceptual base is also dominant in any memorial representation. Theories that give dominance to imagery, on the other hand, predict experimental effects that have proven to be elusive. Until we find reliable evidence of these effects, a non-imaginal explanation of comprehension will remain the more viable conclusion.

REFERENCES

Anderson, J. R. Arguments concerning representations for mental imagery. *Psychological Review,* 1978, *85,* 249–277.

Billow, R. M. Metaphor: A review of the psychological literature. *Psychological Bulletin,* 1977, *84,* 81–92.

Chase, W. G., & Clark, H. H. Mental operations in the comparison of sentences and pictures. In L. W. Gregg (Ed.), *Cognition in learning and memory.* New York: Wiley, 1972.

Craik, F. I., & Lockhart, R. S. Levels of processing: A framework for memory research. *Journal of Verbal Learning and Verbal Behavior,* 1972, *11,* 671–684.

Franks, J. J. Toward understanding understanding. In W. B. Weimer & D. S. Palermo (Eds.), *Cognition and the symbolic processes.* Hillsdale, N.J.: Lawrence Erlbaum Associates, 1974.

Harris, R. J. *Metaphorical sentences as stimulus materials* (KSU-HIPI Report #76-11). Manhattan, Kansas: Human Information Processing Institute, 1976.

Honeck, R. P., Riechmann, P. F., & Hoffman, R. R. Semantic memory for metaphor: The conceptual base hypothesis. *Memory & Cognition,* 1975, *3,* 409–415.

Kieras, D. Beyond pictures and words: Alternative information-processing models for imagery effects in verbal memory. *Psychological Bulletin,* 1978, *85,* 532–554.

Kosslyn, S. M., & Pomerantz, J. R. Imagery, propositions, and the form of internal representations. *Cognitive Psychology,* 1977, *9,* 52–76.

Miller, G. A. Images and models, similes and metaphors. In A. Ortony (Ed.), *Metaphor and thought.* Cambridge, England: Cambridge University Press, 1979.

Paivio, A. *Imagery and verbal processes.* Hillsdale, N.J.: Lawrence Erlbaum Associates, 1979, (originally published 1971).

Park, S., & Arbuckle, T. Y. Ideograms versus alphabets: Effects of script on memory in ''biscriptual'' Korean subjects. *Journal of Experimental Psychology: Human Learning & Memory,* 1977, *3,* 631–642.

Peterson, M. J., & Graham, S. E. Visual detection and visual imagery. *Journal of Experimental Psychology,* 1974, *103,* 509–514.

Pylyshyn, Z. W. What the mind's eye tells the mind's brain: A critique of mental imagery. *Psychological Bulletin,* 1973, *80,* 1–24.

Riechmann, P. F. *Does imagery facilitate memory for conceptual information?* Paper presented at the meeting of the Eastern Psychological Association, New York, April, 1975.

Riechmann, P. F., & Coste, E. L. The role of imagery in comprehending and remembering metaphor. In R. Hoffman (Chair), *Metaphor and image*. Symposium presented at the meeting of the American Psychological Association, Toronto, August 1978.

Riechmann, P. F., & O'Mara, J. A. *Memory for proverbs as a function of the propositional overlap between imagery and the retrieval cue*. Unpublished manuscript, 1977.

Riechmann, P. F., & van Wyk, P. *The role of imagery in semantic memory: Approaching a definition*. Paper presented at the meeting of the American Psychological Association, San Francisco, August 1977.

Sacks, H. V., & Eysenck, M. W. Convergence-divergence and the learning of concrete and abstract sentences. *British Journal of Psychology*, 1977, *68*, 215–221.

Tulving, E., & Thompson, D. M. Encoding specificity and retrieval processes in episodic memory. *Psychological Review*, 1973, *80*, 352–373.

Verbrugge, R. R. Resemblances in language and perception. In R. Shaw & J. Bransford (Eds.), *Perceiving, Acting, and Knowing: Toward an Ecological Psychology*. Hillsdale, N.J.: Lawrence Erlbaum Associates, 1977.

III FOUNDATIONS IN SEMANTIC THEORY

9 The Cognitive Dynamics of Synesthesia and Metaphor

Charles E. Osgood
Institute of Communications Research
University of Illinois

I arrived at Darmouth College in the fall of 1935, firmly convinced that I was destined to write The Great American Novel, but after introductory psychology and then a course in experimental with the late Professor Theodore Karwoski (affectionately known as "The Count") I forgot all about writing novels. Karwoski and a young associate, Henry Odbert, were busily working on—of all things—*color music synesthesia,* and by my junior year I was busily working along with them, much more as a colleague in research than as an undergraduate assistant. Looking back at those years, I realize now that the pattern for my whole professional life was being set—moving from color-music synesthesia into metaphor and via metaphor into the origins of the Semantic Differential Technique and what was to be a major concern with universals in human cognizing and sentencing.

Rather than viewing color-music synesthesia as a phenomenon in a few freak individuals whose "sensory wires are crossed," Karwoski and Odbert viewed it as a fundamental characteristic of human cognizing—more vivid in some (who regularly indulge as a means of enriching their enjoyment of music) but shared by many others who display the same "rules" for relating sights to sounds. Karwoski, Odbert and Osgood (1942) conducted research in which three conditions were used: In one, practiced synesthetes were asked to draw their "responses" to simple melodic forms played on a single instrument—e.g., a tone that simply gets *louder* and then *softer,* where typical drawings were forms that get *thicker* and then *thinner* again, bands of color that get *richer* and then *paler* again, and explicitly meaningful ones such as a little car that comes *closer* and then goes *further* away. In a second, subjects who had never even thought of "seeing things" when they heard music, were told that they had to draw *something* for each auditory stimulus—and they produced exactly the same types of "synesthetic" translations. In the third, 100 unselected sophomores were given a purely verbal "metaphor" test, in which the auditory-mood and visual-spatial relations observed in complex synesthetes were simply translated into pairs of polar adjectives (e.g., LOUD-soft; SMALL-LARGE), with instruction to circle that term in the second pair which "goes best" with the capitalized term in the first. Once again the relations displayed by "real" synesthetes were chosen, here, 96% linking LOUD with LARGE. Karwoski, Odbert and Osgood summarized this research with the statement that the cognitive processes in both color-music synesthesia and in metaphorical use of language can be described as the parallel alignment of two or more dimensions of experience, definable verbally by pairs of polar adjectives and with "translations" occurring between equivalent regions of the continua.

After graduation and marriage in the summer of 1939, I decided to stay on for an extra year at Dartmouth, working as everything from mimeograph operator and lab assistant to co-researcher and co-author. I also got to work with Ross Stagner, who had just arrived. Stagner and Osgood (in research resulting in a 1946 published paper) adapted the notion of "parallel polarities" to the measurement of social attitudes and stereotypes, by using sets of 7-step scales defined by pairs of opposites (e.g., rating PACIFIST against scales like *fair-unfair, valuable-worthless,* and *strong-weak*). Of course, later at Illinois (in the early 1950's, after I had immersed myself in Hullian Behaviorism at Yale), this became the Semantic Differential Technique. Much later, this SD technique was to be extended cross-linguistically across (now) 30 language-culture communities, and the results clearly demonstrated the universality of three affective features of meaning, Evaluation (E), Potency (P) and Activity (A). Interestingly (to me, at least!) my undergraduate thesis at Dartmouth, jointly in Anthropology and Psychology, was a study of synesthetic and metaphorical relations in field reports on five widely separated primitive cultures—Aztec and Pueblo Indian, Australian Bushman, Siberian Aborigine, Negro (Uganda Protectorate), and Malayan. The generality of certain parallisms was quite striking, e.g., *good* places and things being *up* and *light* but *bad* being *down* and *dark* (members of a privileged clan called themselves "white bones" as against all others who were "black bones"!).

This chapter is organized under three major topics, each with certain major subdivisions. The first is titled simply *Synesthesia,* and it falls easily into *cross-modality,* purely perceptual synesthesias, and *perceptuolinguistic synesthesias;* the second is titled *Congruence Dynamics,* and it divides naturally into *gross affective* vs. *fine denotative* cognitive interactions, both leading into the "rules" involved here; and the third is titled simply *Metaphor,* where a useful distinction is between metaphoricity *in phrasing* and *in sentencing.* Each of these sections will be introduced with a more detailed statement.

SYNESTHESIA

Synesthesias appear in a wide variety of forms, but .all involve *meanings* in nonlinguistic perceptual cognizing—which surely was much earlier in the human species than linguistic cognizing. The evidence falls rather naturally into two types: (1) *Cross-modality perceptual synesthesias*, with which much of the earlier research was concerned. Here, meaningful translations are made between one sensory domain and another (e.g., auditory/visual modalities). A transition via *phonetic symbolism* leads naturally into (2) *perceptuolinguistic synesthesias*, with which much of the most recent research has been concerned. Here, meaningful parallelisms are drawn between perceptions in one sensory modality (usually vision) and words in language (usually polar adjectives).

Cross-Modality Perceptual Synesthesia

The earlier research was often designed, and interpreted, in terms of the "freak individuals" who have neural "cross-circuiting' of the sensory fibers" for two modalities (much of this literature is reviewed in a 1938 monograph by Karwoski and Odbert, titled simply "Color-music"). For examples: Langfeld in 1914 reported the case of a girl who associated certain specific colors with different notes on the musical scale, with very high consistency over an interval of over seven years; Dallenbach in 1926 tells of a subject who associated colors with the notes of bird calls. But then there was a man who consistently "saw" #1 as yellow, #2 as blue, #3 as red . . . and, of course, #8 as black—and anyone who has played pool will recognize these as the colors of the balls having these numbers! On the other hand, there was a little girl who recalled her friends as *pink*-faced and her enemies as *purple*-faced—where "true" synesthesia could well be involved.

In his *Words and Things* (1958, Ch. 4) Roger Brown provides an extended review of the literature relevant to *phonetic symbolism*. As early as 1929 Edward Sapir reported a study relating syllabic speech sounds to meanings (e.g., given *mal* and *mil*, both said to refer to "table," subjects were to decide which one would refer to a *large* and which to a *small* table), and he found impressively consistent agreement on the relative "sizes" of vowels. In 1933 Stanley Newman extended the Sapir type of research, demonstrating quite convincingly that larger magnitudes are associated with vowels having the production characteristics of large oral cavity, low vocalic resonance, and tongue articulation toward the back of the mouth. In 1954 Wissemann reported research on the *creation* of onomatopoeic words in response to a wide variety of (often very unusual) sounds. Most subjects used different (a la Newman) vowels to express the pitch (*high-to-low*) and tone-color (*bright-to-dark*) of the sounds they heard, and these two dimensions were in almost perfect correlations (*high* with *bright* and *low* with *dark*). In my own informal experimentation with male students in my psycholinguistics seminar, I ask them which of three girls they'd like to date and then, with gestures, to describe their probable body builds; they definitely would prefer *Miss Lavelle* (described like an *8*) to either *Miss Pim* (more like a *1*) or *Miss Bowloav* (definitely a big fat 0)!

Returning now to Dartmouth it will be recalled that, in the first condition of the Karwoski, Odbert and Osgood (1942) study, synesthetic visualizers related simple tone-patterns (e.g., *loudness* varied in the auditory modality) to variables like *thickness, richness* (saturation) and *nearness* in the photisms they drew (visual modality)—thus "pure" perceptual (nonlinguistic) synesthesia. In another study, run more or less in parallel, Odbert, Karwoski and Eckerson (1942) first had ordinary subjects indicate the dominant *moods* of short classical excerpts on the Hevner "Mood Circle" and then had them, on a second run-through, say what *colors* seemed appropriate for each excerpt. There was rather remarkable consistency in the colors chosen—for example, the color *green* for Delius' *On Hearing the First Cuckoo in Spring* and *red* for Wagner's *Rienzi Overture*. Again anticipating verbal metaphor, when subjects were merely given the mood adjectives—going around the Hevner "circle" from *vigorous* through *gay* and *leisurely* to *sad* and *solemn*—and asked to give the appropriate colors, even *more* consistent relations appeared.

Murray Miron's doctoral thesis at Illinois (published version, Miron, 1961) was a cross-language (American English/Japanese) demonstration of lawful affective connotations in phonetic symbolism. When CVC syllables that were nonsense in *both* languages were rated on appropriate Semantic Differential (SD) scales, American and Japanese subjects displayed correlations with each other of .57 and .91 for vowels and consonants respectively on the Potency factor—low frequency sounds being associated with felt *power* and *size*. On the Evaluative factor, front consonants were rated more *pleasant* than back, again for both languages. Our West German cross-cultural research colleague Suitbert Ertel (1969) reversed the usual SD techniques—having *meaningful* (translation-equivalent) concepts rated by Czech and German subjects against *meaningless* phonetic syllable pairs. Relying for interpretation on a few meaningful E, P and A scales, Ertel was able to show great similarity of E and P loadings across the languages. Brown, Black and Horowitz in 1955 (see Brown, 1958) selected 21 antonymic word-pairs of about equal length (e.g., *warm-cool*) and these were translated into Chinese, Czech and Hindi by native speakers of these languages, who also recorded their pronunciations of the word-pairs. Eighty-five Harvard and Radcliffe students guessed which of the paired English words corresponded to each of the foreign words *as spoken*. Not only was there significantly higher than chance agreement in choice among the subjects, but their guesses were correct *twice* as often as incorrect—where "correct" means choosing the appropriate English translation.

Question: Are such cross-modality perceptual synesthesias *innate* or *ac-*

quired? Although one may grant an innate predisposition toward synesthetic relations, just *what* color, sound, smell, taste, etc. "translations" develop would seem to depend on *learning*, and in Neobehaviorism of the post-Hullian variety what is called *mediated generalization* would seem to be responsible. Take the case of auditory pitch and visual size: It is characteristic of the physical world that large-sized resonators produce low frequency tones and small-sized ones high frequency tones (think of series of organ pipes, bells, drums, or even hollow logs, and of the "voices" of men vs. boys, big dogs vs. little ones, or even of lions vs. mice). This means that any meaningful (*mediating*) process that comes to be associated with the perceptual signs in one modality (e.g., the danger significance of threatening big dogs vs. the safety significance of playful little dogs) will tend to spread (*generalization*) to the correlated perceptual signs in the other modality. At a later point—after we have considered perceptuolinguistic synesthesias—I will detail the affective (grosser) and denotative (finer) cognitive dynamics involved.

Perceptuolinguistic Synesthesia

As was noted earlier in connection with the Karwoski et al. research, when one of the "sensory" dimensions of perceptual parallelisms was represented by words—thus a shift away from synesthesia toward metaphor—the lawfulness of the process became even more apparent and stable across individuals (e.g., LOUD going with verbal *near* rather than *far*, TREBLE being *up* and BASS being *down*, MAJOR chords being *light* and MINOR being *dark*, and so forth). Very similar notions have been expressed by some gestalt psychologists. To the book *On Expressive Language*, edited by Heinz Werner (1955), Kaden, Wapner and Werner (1955) have contributed a delightful experiment in which subjects were to adjust luminant words projected in front of them in an otherwise totally dark room "to subjective eye-level" by raising or lowering the projected words with a hand dial; the striking finding was that words like *rising* and *climbing* had to be *lowered* relative to the pre-experimental determination of "eye-level," while words like *plunging* and *falling* had to be raised—i.e., the upward-meaning words *seemed* visually higher and the downward-meaning words *seemed* lower to the subjects!

In the late 1950's—while in the Southwest in connection with psycholinguistic field work being sponsored by the Social Science Research Council—I turned back to my interests in synesthesia and metaphor (Osgood, 1960). Four language-culture groups (Mexican Spanish, collected by Sol Saporta; Navajo, collected by Susan Ervin; American English, collected by C.E.O.; and Japanese, by Hiroshi Azuma) were used. The subjects were to "rate" the set of 28 verbal concepts listed in Table 9.1 (mainly oppositional terms, not given as pairs but rather in the numbered order shown on the table) against the pairs of visual "opposites" displayed here as Fig. 9.1 (without the verbal labels, of course).

TABLE 9.1
Verbal Concepts Used in Synesthesia Experiment

1. HEAVY	10. QUIET	20. NOISY
2. GOOD	11. BLUE	21. GREY
3. FAST	12. BAD	22. SLOW
4. HAPPY	13. LIGHT	23. WHITE
5. UP	14. DOWN	24. CALM
6. ENERGETIC	15. BLACK	25. MAN
7. LOOSE	16. WOMAN	26. YELLOW
8. STRONG	17. LAZY	27. WEAK
9. EXCITEMENT	18. TIGHT	28. SAD
	19. GREEN	

Each graphic pair was presented on one of the cards in a deck that was randomized in order across subjects (see pp. 210–211).

Rotated factor loadings for the verbal Concept Matrices (as rated against the visual alternatives) yielded clear evidence for a "universal" Evaluative Factor I; for all cultures, particularly *good, happy,* and *white* were ⁺E and *bad, sad* and *black* were ⁻E. Also there was a "universal" Potency Factor II: *strong, heavy* and *man* were ⁺P and *weak, light, yellow* and *woman* were ⁻P. However, Activity seemed to spread across Factors III and IV: *energetic, excitement* and *noisy* were ⁺A and *lazy, calm,* and *quiet,* along with *slow,* were ⁻A in III, but *light, tight* and *white,* along with *fast,* were ⁺A and *heavy, excitement* and *woman* were ⁻A in IV.

Perhaps not surprisingly, the rotated factor loadings for the Visual-alternative Matrices seemed to be a blend of purely perceptual and mainly affective meaning variables: Factor I appeared to be a sort of Flatness perceptual factor, with *rounded, horizontal, homogeneous, straight* and *blunt* best characterizing it. On the other hand, even for the visual domain Factor II does seem rather Evaluative in nature, being characterized by *colorful, light, thin, up,* and *large* at one pole and *colorless, dark, thick, down* and *small* at the other. Factor III was at least suggestive of a Figure vs. Ground Factor (with *clear, straight, homogeneous* and *up* at one pole and *hazy, crooked, rounded, heterogeneous* and *down* at the other).

Some of the consistent visual characterizations of oppositional verbal concepts are interesting in their own right, and they certainly tie in with the earlier Karwoski et al. findings: *Happy* is UP, COLORFUL, LIGHT, and CLEAR, but *sad* is DOWN, COLORLESS, DARK and HAZY; *heavy* is DOWN, THICK, DARK, and LARGE, but *light* (*weight* having been specified) is UP, THIN, LIGHT and (except for Anglos) SMALL; *excitement* is VERTICAL, COLORFUL, CROOKED and SHARP, but *calm* is HORIZONTAL, COLORLESS, STRAIGHT and BLUNT; *woman* is COLORFUL, THIN (except for Mexicans), LIGHT, BLUNT and ROUNDED (except for Navajos), but *man* is

VERTICAL (*woman* tending to be HORIZONTAL), COLORLESS, THICK, DARK, SHARP and ANGULAR. These trends for four cultures suggest "universal" tendencies.

As regards the "synesthetic" application of terms based on sensory continua to human *personality characteristics,* an early study by Asch (1955) examined adjectives of this type in a number of historically unrelated languages—Biblical Hebrew, Homeric Greek, Chinese, Thai and several others. Just like English, all of these languages describe many personality traits with words or phrases that have obvious sensory bases. For just one example, in English the word *straight* when applied to persons implies honesty and trustworthiness, whereas its opposite, *crooked* implies dishonesty and untrustworthiness—and exactly the *same* synesthetic (or is it metaphoric?) parallelism was found by Asch in all of the languages he analysed. Brown, Leiter and Hildum (1957) asked students to describe *operatic voices* by selecting (a) from a list of ten antonymous adjective-pairs and (b) from a set of 20 music-critic-derived adjectives (e.g., *cold, pinched, gravelly, dulcet, voluptuous*) those best describing each voice. Generally, for example, baritones tended to be *dull, heavy* and *thick* as compared to *bright, light,* and *thin* tenors; when adjective clustering was examined by factor analysis, the strongest natural grouping contained oppositional pairs like *warm-cold, lusterous-dull,* and *expansive-pinched,* going along with obviously Evaluative *like-dislike.*

Given the evidence both for universality of pervasive and primitive E, P and A affective features of meaning (cf., Osgood, May & Miron, 1975) and for the dominant role of such features in perceptuolinguistic as well as cross-modal synesthesias (as presented here), the prospect for creating a nonlinguistic *graphic differential* seemed bright (!) indeed. At our Center for Comparative Psycholinguistics, in 1967, Leon Jakobovits initiated research on the development of such an instrument: A large number (64) of contrastive pairs of visual patterns (see Figure 7:2 in Osgood, May & Miron, 1975) were selected for cross-cultural investigation with American English (Jakobovits), Delhi Hindi (K. G. Agrawal), Finnish (Perti Oünap), German (Suitbert Ertel), and Japanese (Yasumasa Tanaka). Native-speaking subjects rated subsets of 50 randomly selected, translation-equivalent, concepts (e.g., *love, tongue, sleep*), drawn from our 600+-concept *Atlas of Affective Meanings,* on 7-step scales defined by the oppositional pictograms—as well as on 12-scale pancultural SDs of the usual verbal sort. To summarize the results succinctly: (1) although pancultural factor analysis yielded clear evidence for a "universal" E factor, there was minimal evidence for "universal" P or A factors; (2) there was evidence for what might be called "denotative contamination"—e.g., ANGULAR vs. ROUNDED pictograms separating concepts like *chair, triangle* and *house* from *cloud, smoke* and *snake.* We concluded that most of the pictograms were too complex, lending themselves to caricatures of real objects—in contrast to the simpler, more abstract visual polarities used in my 1960 four-culture study.

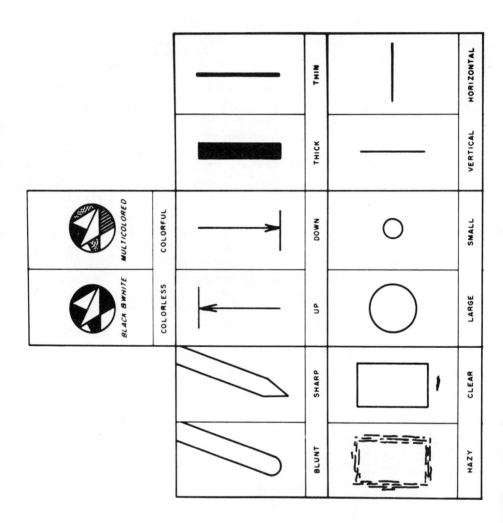

THIN · THICK · COLORFUL · COLORLESS · DOWN · UP · SHARP · BLUNT

MULTICOLORED · BLACK & WHITE

HORIZONTAL · VERTICAL · SMALL · LARGE · CLEAR · HAZY

210

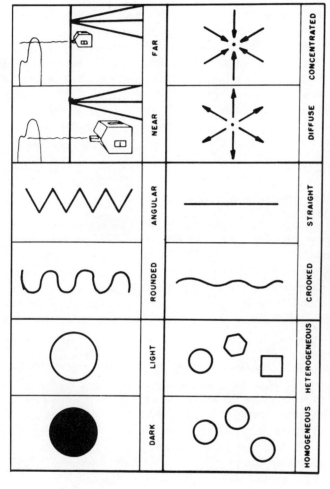

FIG. 9.1. Visual alternative-pairs used in Synesthesia Experiment.

Nevertheless, the verbal nature of the usual Semantic Differential makes it inapplicable to many subject populations—members of nonliterature cultures, brain-damaged aphasics, thought-disordered schizophrenics, and children younger than about six years—and the need for a nonverbal graphic differential persisted. A few years later, Patrice French, then a graduate research assistant in our Center, picked up this problem: First she demonstrated (using sub-sets of scales drawn from the Jakobovits' work) that *abstract* concepts, which could not have visual similarities to the oppositional pictograms, yielded *higher* within-factor scale correlations than picturable *concrete* concepts. Then she developed and tested a series of possible short-form GDs (graphic differentials), using the correlations for E, P and A scores obtained with the usual short-form SD with those obtained with each succeeding GD as a criterion. The final graphic differential in this series yielded satisfactory results (see French, 1977, for details, and also for the pictograms used)—the GD/SD correlations being .88 for E, .46 for P, and .49 for A—and there was little evidence of "denotative contamination."

The Intimate Parallelism of Processing
in Perceptual and Linguistic Channels

In this section we will first consider two very general principles of Neobehaviorism—an "Emic" Principle and an "Ambiguity" Principle, both of which will be shown to operate in linguistic as well as perceptual channels—and then review evidence, both casual and experimental, for interaction *between* and parallel processing *across* perceptual and linguistic channels. (For details see Osgood, 1979b, 1979c.).

An "Emic" Principle.   In perceiving and comprehending we usually have situations where *percepts are variable but their significances are constant.* By virtue of the fact that both things and organisms are mobile with respect to each other, the *percepts* produced by the distal signs of things will be variable through many stimulus dimensions. Thus, for example, the *retinal size* of the image (hence percept) produced by APPLE object must *vary* with distance, yet, given the *stable* visual features (roundness, redness, stemness, etc.) of the percept plus the (often) terminal reinforcement of eating the APPLE, the meaningful *significance* of these varying percepts will be *constant.* It follows that these will be differences that do *not* make a difference in meaning. This constant significance is *the constancy phenomenon,* long familiar to psychologists—the "thingness," "thatness," and "whoness" in perception.

In behaving and expressing we usually have situations where *intentions are constant but the program for action must be variable.* Thus, although the percepts of APPLE object (visual image sizes) will vary with distance, the child will learn to vary his behaviors to the common apple-getting *intention* appropriately—APPLE-on-table (some distance away) eliciting locomotor approach, APPLE a bit beyond reach yielding reaching-and-grasping, APPLE at crooked-arm's distance perhaps producing "inspection for bugginess," and only very big APPLE image a few inches from the face eliciting biting movements. This dual function of constancy-classes of perceptual signs—having a common significance and yielding a common intention, but being associated with variable behaviors—is the basis for *control and decision* in Neobehaviorism.

Why do I call this the "Emic" Principle? Just as the classes of physically different *phones* (as received) "converge" upon a common *phoneme* (differences in sound that make a difference in meaning) and these "diverge" into contextually determined phones (as produced)—and similarly for *morphs/ morphemes* and *semes/sememes*—so do classes of signs "converge" upon common meanings (in comprehending) and these "diverge" into contextually determined behaviors (in expressing). But even more than this: One can claim that there is a *syntax of behaving* just as there is a syntax of talking—and, of course, the former is prior in development. For a child to make biting, then grasping, then reaching movements in that order—all in thin air—as he approaches the desired APPLE would be just as "ungrammatical" as it would have been for Caesar to have announced, "Vici, vidi, veni!"

An "Ambiguity" Principle. In perceiving and comprehending, signs (linguistic or perceptual) are often *ambiguously* related to more than one significance-intention mediation process—in contrast to the "Emic" Principle, where signs were *unambiguously* related to a single dominant mediation process. Just as many words in a language are to some degree polysemous (including Homonomy)—witness as familiar examples, *he went to the BANK, it was a LIGHT one, the SHOOTING of the hunter was terrible*—so are many perceptual signs, not only classic ambiguous figures like the Necker Cube, but everyday cases like the significance of the facial expressions of men on a picket-line as seen on TV (sullen anger or grim determination?) or of the combination of a tight-lipped smile with shaking of a fisted hand (intent to threaten or to display pride at completion of some effortful task?). On the behaving/expressing side, although the *intention* of the actor/speaker is always unambiguous *to him* at the moment, he will often use the *same* outputs to express quite different intentions—the smiles of pleasure, of confidence, of derision, and so forth.

Given the ubiquity of ambiguity for signs in both perceptual and linguistic channels, why aren't we hopelessly ambiguated much of the time? The answer is that, in most cases, *convergent contextual signs serve to disambiguate.* In language, *he ROWED to the bank, it was a light PLAY,* and *the shooting of the hunters BY THE NATIVES was terrible;* in perception, the tight-lipped-smile plus shaking-of-a-fisted-hand BY A BOXER will be interpreted as "threatening" just BEFORE the fight but as "prideful satisfaction" just AFTER his winning it. When my friend exclaims "duck!" while we're touring a barnyard, I'm likely to

look around for that bird, but, when passing by a busy sandlot baseball field, I'm
likely to "duck" my head!

Evidence for Interaction Between Linguistic and Perceptual Channels.
First, *some casual* (but still very convincing) *observations*. Gestural pointings,
lookings, head-bobbings/shakings, and the like normally accompany conversations. Gestures often substitute for phrases (e.g., "I could/SLITTING MO-
TION ACROSS SPEAKER'S THROAT/the bastard!") or even whole clauses
("They've got our car back in the shop again, so . . . PRAYERFUL POSTURE
OF HANDS PLUS HEAVENWARD-LOOKING EYES!). It is also most
significant that emphatic gestures typically parallel linguistic stress ("I will/
$\frac{\text{nót}}{\text{FISTED-HAND-DOWN-SHARPLY}}$/wear that ridiculous tie!") and appear
utterly ludicrous when displayed from stress points ("I will nót wear that
ridiculous/$\frac{\text{tie}}{\text{SAME GESTURE}}$/").

Second, *some evidence for parallel processing across channels*. The or-
dinariest of human communicative competences—and those most often used in
research with young children—are Simply Describing and Simply Acting Out. In
the former, meanings of *perceived* states and events must be encoded "up" into
the "deep" semantic system (comprehension) and then these cognitions must be
decoded "down" into appropriate *verbal* expressions (production); in the latter,
the meanings of *words and sentences* must be encoded "up" into the same
semantic system (comprehension) and then these cognitions must be decoded
"down" into *nonlinguistic behavioral operations* on appropriate entities in the
immediate environment (production). My favorite example here is this: two
coeds, walking along a campus path, see a third girl approaching with a *mini-
miniskirt* on; after she has passed, one coed says to the other, "She also dyes her
hair!" Note that the use of anaphoric *she* implies an immediately prior cognition
(which could only be perception-based) and that the *álso* identifies it as something like [THAT GAL / IS WEARING / A REALLY SHORT SKIRT].

And finally, some *extraordinary* parallel processing in psycholinguistic experiments. Early research reported by Osgood, Suci and Tannenbaum (1957, pp.
275–284) had demonstrated that the affective E-P-A meanings of phrasal
adjective-noun combinations (like *shy secretary, treacherous nurse, breezy husband*) were quite predictable from the measured affective meanings of their
single-word components via the Osgood/Tannenbaum "congruity formula."
Hastorf, Osgood and Ono (1966) found that the affective meanings of different
posed facial expressions (by CEO, sans little mustache!), fused in a stereoscope,
could also be predicted this way, and Ono, Hastorf and Osgood (1966) showed that
the more *incongruent* the facial expressions presented stereoscopically, the
greater the likelihood of the viewer expeiencing *binocular rivalry* (e.g.,
COMPLACENCY/RAGE yielding more rivalry than DISMAY/REPUGNANCE).
Rumjahn Hoosain (1977) has demonstrated that conjoining outline "faces" (e.g.,

pairing of a SMILING, DOWN-TURNED EYEBROWS, WIDE-OPEN EYES "face" with either congruent *I passed the exam* or incongruent *I flunked the exam*) is much faster for congruent than for incongruent pairings.

The evidence—both casual and experimental—would appear to support the following inescapable conclusions: (1) *that the "deep" cognitive system is essentially semantic in nature;* (2) *that this same cognitive system is shared by both perceptual and linguistic information-processing channels;* (3) *that there is continuous interaction between these channels in ordinary human communication.* Yet, with only a few exceptions (my own research and theorizing being one of them), in linguistics and even psycholinguistics there has been relatively little concern with the *semantics* of nonlinguistic, perceptual cognizing.

CONGRUENCE DYNAMICS

Now we must look into the role of cognitive congruence dynamics in human perceiving, thinking and talking.[1] In the present context, such dynamics fall quite naturally under two sub-headings: (1) *gross affective dynamics,* on which we have amassed a great deal of information over the past 20 years at our Center for Comparative Psycholinguistics; (2) *fine denotative dynamics,* where we have less research evidence, but which leads naturally into metaphor in the final major section of this chapter.

Gross Affective Dynamics

On the Whys and Wherefores of E, P, and A. There seems to be no doubt that E, P and A as affective dimensions of meaning are, indeed, *human universals* (see Osgood, May & Miron, 1975, Ch. 4). In the SD technique, sets of teenage subjects in each of (now) 30 communities rated the 620 *concepts* in our *Atlas* (concrete ones like FLOWER, CHEESE, SNAKE, LIPS, and TABLE; abstract ones like ADOLESCENCE, ENVY, ZERO, INFINITY, and SEX) against short-form 12-scale differentials (the 4 scales for each factor in their language having the highest loadings on a monsterous pancultural factor analysis), each 7-step scale being defined by bipolar adjectives like *nice-awful* (E), *big-little* (P), and *fast-slow* (A).

Now, since subjects are required to rate *all* items—to produce "sentences" like *SNAKE* (is) *quite fast* and *ADOLESCENCE* (is) *slightly little*—it follows

---

[1]For already published anticipations the reader is referred to Osgood and Richards (1973), a paper in *Language* titled "From Yang and Yin to *And* or *But,"* and to Osgood (1979a), a paper in *The International Journal of Psychology* titled the same, but with "in Cross-cultural Perspective" added, which reports remarkably consistent data across 12 language-culture communities.

that in many cases our native speakers will be forced to produce "sentences" that would be semantically anomalous. Literally speaking, a TORNADO cannot be either *fair* or *unfair* (only humans can have such attributes), so subjects should check the middle of the scale (defined as *neither* qualifier applying or *both equally*). In fact, most subjects check the -3 position, thus creating a "sentence" that says *TORNADO* (is) *very unfair!* This is obviously *metaphorical usage* of the scale—by virtue of the shared affect, both TORNADO and *unfair* being $^-$E. In other words, often the SD technique literally forces the metaphorical usage of scales, and the lawfulness of such usage (reflected in the massiveness of E-P-A factors) clearly testifies to the importance of these gross affective features of meaning. The price paid, of course, is that the many finer (denotative) features "get lost" in the SD "shuffle."

Componential Analysis of the Color Category.   In our analyses of each of the 50 or so conceptual domains (categories) tapped in our *Atlas of Affective Meanings* we always include a componential analysis—where we intuit the possible *denotative* features that might be determining affect attribution. The small (8 concept) Color Category will serve as an example: Here we "intuited" the obvious physical dimensions and selected appropriate concept-pairs for testing—thus, for Brightness (WHITE/BLACK, WHITE/GREY and GREY/ BLACK), for Hue (RED/BLUE and YELLOW/GREEN), for Saturation (RED/ YELLOW and BLUE/GREEN) and for a Color component (COLOR/GREY, COLOR/WHITE and COLOR/BLACK).

When we checked for what we call Universals (biases toward one or the other orientation across our 30 language-culture communities that are significant at the .01 level or better), we found the following: Brightness (WHITE) is universally GOOD ($^+$E), Active ($^+$A) and Familiar ($^+$FAM) as compared with Darkness (BLACK), but Darkness is more Potent ($^+$P) and Conflictual ($^+$CI); since humans are primates and depend most on vision, this pattern of Universals seems entirely reasonable. As to Hue, it will be recalled that Odbert, Karwoski and Eckerson (1942) found the red end of the spectrum to connote more Activity than the blue end, and our cross-linguistic data strongly confirm this, RED and YELLOW being universally more Active ($^+$A) than BLUE and GREEN, but BLUE being universally the more Good ($^+$E); for primitive man, sun and fire meant warmth and liveliness (RED is also high in Potency), but the BLUEs and GREENs were probably associated with life-giving water and the fertility of growing things. Saturated RED and BLUE tend to be universally more Potent ($^+$P) than Unsaturated YELLOW and GREEN—and this universal may well have a physiologically-based affect determination. Finally, as to the Color/Noncolor component, we find that COLOR is universally more Good ($^+$E), more Active ($^+$A) and less Conflictual ($^-$CI) than the Noncolor concepts (GREY, WHITE and BLACK)—which certainly fits the metaphorical uses of terms like *colorful* (attractive, lively, healthy, etc.) vs. *white* and *black* (pale and sickly or gloomy and threatening).

Cross-Category Affective Congruence-Based Metaphorical Relations.   As part of a larger study on affective relations among our Colors, Emotions, and Days of the Week categories, our Yugoslav colleague, Vid Pečjak (1970) had subjects in seven of our communities—American English, Belgian Flemish, Netherlands Dutch, German, Italian, Yugoslav Slovenian, and Japanese—pair the terms in each category with those in each other. The correlations between Color and Emotion concepts were quite high across these communities (⁺.63), but those between Colors and Days of the Week were lower (⁺.30). However, there were definite clusters between the Colors and Days. GREY goes with MONDAY for six of the seven communities but never with SATURDAY, GREEN and BLUE tend to go with WEDNESDAY (5 communities) but never with SATURDAY, YELLOW and GREEN go with THURSDAY (5 communities) but again never with SATURDAY—but RED *does* go with SATURDAY (6 of the 7 communities), yet *never* goes with MONDAY or SUNDAY! White, as might be expected (at least for Christian-Western communities), goes with SUNDAY for five of the seven communities (but not for either Yugoslavians or, perhaps surprisingly, for Americans, who related SUNDAY to GREEN).

The Primitiveness and Pervasiveness of E, P and A.   In a 1969 paper, I tried to account for the *pervasiveness* of these affective dimensions of meaning. First I noted the marked similarity of the E-P-A factors to the dimensions of feeling and emotion, which was first pointed out to me by M. Brewster Smith: Wundt's Pleasantness/Unpleasantness, Tension/Relief and Excitement/Quiet; Schlosberg's Pleasantness/Unpleasantness, Rejection/Attention (P?) and Activation/Sleep; and my own "naming" (Osgood, 1966, a study of the semantics of communication via facial expressions) Pleasant/Unpleasant, Controlled/Uncontrolled, and Activated/Unactivated. Then I suggested that it is the *primitiveness* and innateness of this emotional reaction system of the human animal that underlies the universality of the affective E-P-A components of meaning.

Testimony to this primitiveness of the affective meaning system is the fact that visual-verbal synesthesia does not appear to be lost even in severely impaired anomic aphasics. In this connection, it is most relevant that Sylvia Scheinkopf (1970), using mainly the visual graphic-pairs developed in my 1960 study of the cross-cultural generality of visual/verbal synesthesia, clearly demonstrated that anomic aphasics perform very much like normals on this task. They could point *appropriately* to visual alternatives for the verbal concepts presented to them, despite their manifest difficulties in naming and word-finding, or even describing the graphic pairs verbally. In other words, these more primitive affective aspects of meaning survive the effects of even severe brain damage. Yet further testimony to the primitiveness of the affective meaning system and its cross-modality pervasiveness is to be found in studies of non-verbal (gestural, postural, facial) communication among humans. In one study (of many that could be offered) Gitin (1970) had subjects rate 36 photographs of just *hands* in various posturings against 40 SD scales; her first three factors were clearly A (*active, interesting, exciting*, etc.), E (*pleasant, good, friendly*, etc.), and P (*dominant, strong, certain*, etc.), and in this ordering of magnitude.

Fine Denotative Dynamics

We must begin with a brief sketch of some relevant aspects of my *Abstract Performance Grammar* (APG).[2] This will lead to statement of the crucial *rules for fine semantic interactions* in the processing of sentential cognitions—here restricted to *simplex* (single-clause) *sentences* as opposed to complex (multiple-clause) ones. Then we will see how such interactions function to shift the meanings of words (*within* constituents) and of phrases (*between* constituents). And finally some of the most relevant experimental literature will be summarized.

A Bit of APG$_O$.   The subscript O, of course, simply indicates that this is an Osgoodian APG conception. At the most central Representational (meaningful) Level, four structural mechanisms are proposed—a LEXICON, an OPERATOR, a BUFFER, and a long-term MEMORY—of which only LEX and OPR will concern us here. It is LEX that—given the acquisition of meanings via sign- and feature-learning principles in the theory—performs the feats of transducing meaning-*less* (in themselves) sensory percepts into meaning-*full* code-strips of semantic features in *comprehending* and of transducing meaning-*full* semantic code-strips into meaning-*less* (in themselves) motor programs for behavior *in expressing*.

Whereas LEX functions on a "*wordlike*" *unit basis* (cf., Osgood & Hoosain, 1974), OPR functions on a "*whole-constituent*" *unit basis* (subject and object noun phrases and the verb phrases relating them). Thus, in comprehending, the "upcoming" code-strips for word forms from LEX are assigned by OPR to its postulated three constituents for simplexes, utilizing language-specific cues for constituent boundaries, and the semantic information *within* constituents is necessarily fused. In expressing, this process must be reversed, with the "down-coming" whole-constituent semantic information from OPR being analyzed by LEX into sets of code-strips for word units and these being ordered by LEX according to the within-constituent rules of its language for talking via motor-skill programs.

---

[2]I refer the reader to *Lectures on Language Performance* (Osgood, 1979b) for an overview of this general performance theory.

At the grossest level of analysis, simplexes are assumed to be *tripartite* in structure. With the M's representing the *meanings* of whole constituents, [M_1 (SNP) / —(M)→(VP) / M_2 (ONP)] is postulated to be the natural ordering determined by prelinguistic perceptual cognizing of events and states in the environment.[3] For simplex sentences expressing *stative* relations we would have [the ball (FIGURE) / is on (STATE) / the table (GROUND)] and for those expressing *action* relations [the little boy (SOURCE) / picked up (ACTION) / the poodle puppy (RECIPIENT)].

At the finest level of analysis, the semantic *features* elicited by Signs ($f_1 \ldots f_k \ldots f_n$) are those mediator *components* ($m_1 \ldots m_k \ldots m_n$) at the Representational Level that, in APG_0, are assumed to derive from the *overt behaviors* made to Significates (things signified). Therefore these m_n semantic components (features) will: (1) be *bipolar and reciprocally antagonistic* in nature (behaviorally speaking, it is just as impossible to have a simultaneously $\pm m_k$ as it would be to simultaneously open and clench one's hand) and (2) be *nonarbitrarily Positive vs. Negative* in the signing ($+/-$) of their antagonistic poles (nonarbitrarily in principle, at least). This characteristic is related to the Unmarked (positive) vs. Marked (negative) distinction in linguistic parlance, of course, but also, as it turns out (cf., Boucher & Osgood, 1969), to affective Positiveness (E^+) vs. Negativeness (E^-). The reader should note that, once meanings are transduced "upwards" via the LEXICON, everything that transpires in APG_0 information processing is entirely semantic in nature.

Rules for Fine Semantic Interactions Within and Between Constituents. Given the reciprocally antagonistic nature of mediator components (semantic features), it must follow that, functionally, *within* any constituent of a simplex cognition *each component* (semantic feature) *can have only one sign and one value at any one moment*. Given this basic theoretical constraint, *the rules for semantic fusions*, both within and between constituents, will be the following:

1. that *same sign* polarity fusions ($+/+$ or $-/-$) of unequal intensities will yield intensification of meaning (e.g., in combinations such as *violent anger* or *plead with humbly*);
2. that fusions of *signed with unsigned* (zero) *codings* ($+/0$ or $-/0$) will yield *modification of meaning,* the whole constituent assuming the polarity and intensity of the signed term (thus *lively hope* making the hopefulness $^+$Active and *plead with sincerely* making the pleading $^+$Moral);
3. that fusions of *opposed signs* on the same feature ($+/-$) will yield cancellation of meaning or anomalies (e.g., *casual excitement; plead with tolerantly*).

---

[3]It might be noted that for 60% of world languages (see Greenberg, 1963), including English, SVO is the basic order within simplexes; 30% are SOV and only 10% are VSO, hence displaying less correspondence to the assumed prelinguistic ordering.

With regard to rule (3), it should be noted that opposed signs yield cancellations of intensity *toward* zero if they are nonpolar and/or imbalanced (e.g., a +1 fusing with a −2) and that the "true" sense of anomaly should only occur if they are both polar and balanced (+3 and −3).[4] Even here there is the question of whether OPR will reject such combinations as "uncognizable" *or* may allow the features in question to simply reduce *to* zero; we often use such anomalies effectively, as in *he's sure a youthful old duffer!*

Within-Constituent Congruence Dynamics. With the Semantic Interaction Technique (see Osgood, 1970, for details), the appositeness/acceptability/anomalousness of words brought into syntactic confrontation within noun phrases or verb phrases can be investigated, using the judgments of carefully instructed ordinary speakers. The above rules of fine semantic fusion have been tested with judgments of interpersonal verb/adverb and emotional adjective/noun confrontations. Clearly supportive results have been obtained: for examples (with the modal judgments in parentheses), in verb/adverb sets, *attack suddenly* (apposite), *attack deliberately* (acceptable), *attack casually* (anomalous); in adjective/noun sets, *sudden surprise* (apposite), *sudden interest* (acceptable), *sudden contemplation* (anomalous).

In our interpersonal verb/adverb analyses, beyond affective E, P and A features, we were able to identify features we characterized as Associative/Dissociative, Initiating/Reacting, Ego-/Alter-oriented, Supra-/Sub-ordinate, Future-/Past-oriented, Terminal/Interminal, and Deliberate/Impulsive. In our emotion adjective/noun analyses, again beyond pervasive E, P and A, we could identify what we call Extrinsic/Intrinsic, Cognitive/Gut, Onto-Ego/Out-of-Ego, and Social/Asocial features, along with the same Future-/Past-orientation, Supra-/Sub-ordinate and Terminal/Interminal features also found in the verb/adverb interactions.

Between-Constituent Congruence Dynamics in Processing Simplex Cognitions. Again, given the reciprocally inhibitory nature of semantic features, it must follow in theory that simplex cognitions as wholes will be *perfectly congruent* only when, for each feature, the *algebraic product* of the signs of the codings across the three components (M_1, − (M) →, M_2 above) is *positive* (i.e., +++, +−−, −+−, or −−+) and the *absolute values* (intensities) of the codings are *the same* (e.g., all three components 2 on the feature or all 1). This *implies,* of course, that given the signs and intensities of any two components of a simplex cognition on a given feature, the *congruent* sign and intensity of any third component is predicted (see Osgood & Richards, 1973, for details; also, Abelson & Rosenberg's notion of "symbolic psychologic," 1958). For example,

---

[4]For coding the polarities and intensities of semantic features, I use the 7-step "scale" ($^+3$ through 0 to $^-3$) familiar in Semantic Differential reserach.

given that *Henry Kissenger* is coded -2 by someone and that, in ordinary English, *favors* is coded $+2$, that someone—who hasn't the foggiest idea of what *retaliative economic strikes* means—when he reads that *Henry Kissenger / favors / retaliative economic strikes* must congruently code the M_2 as a -2 (quite bad)!

Of course, in ordinary cognizing of simplex sentences *perfect* congruence—particularly for the M_1 and M_2 constituents—rarely is the case. *This* implies that there will usually be semantic interactions *across* the constituents, these resulting in meaning shifts *within* them, the magnitudes of shift being functions of the degrees of incongruity. Our research indicates that fusions are typically "leftward"—from "commentative" M_2 into "topical" M_1. Thus, hearing that *Tom / is / a lively guy*, the "liveliness" (^+A) is likely to be carried into the Meatning of *Tom*, but given a negative Relation, *is not*, it may be "dullness" (^-A) that carries into *Tom*. It is here, of course, that the dynamics of *metaphors* and *similes* will be handled in APG_O. However, if (as in the Kissenger example above) the M_2 has near-zero loading on a feature, then the shift may be "rightward" from M_1 to M_2.

Some Relevant Literature.   A general theory of semantic feature interactions and fusions in determining similarity judgments and meaning shifts in a wide variety of perceptual and linguistic materials has recently been presented by Amos Tversky in a paper titled "Features of Similarity" (1977). It is related to the notions I have offered above. Just one of many experiments he reports will have to suffice here.

The two sets of schematic faces displayed in Fig. 9.2 were both shown to two groups of subjects. For Group A the four faces in each set were presented in a randomly ordered row (*not* as shown here), and the subjects were instructed simply to *partition* the set into two subset *pairs* of faces on the basis of overall similarity. The most frequent partition of Set 1 was c/p (smiling faces) vs. a/b (nonsmiling faces) and of Set 2 was a/c (nonfrowning faces) vs. b/q (frowning faces), the substitution of q (Set 2) for p (Set 1) thus changing the grouping of faces. All this is mute testimony to the dominance of affective Evaluation. For Group B the faces in each set were presented as shown in Fig. 9.2, and the subjects were instructed simply to select that one of the three faces below most similar to the "target" face on top. As is evident in the percentages below the three faces in the "choice" set, b was chosen most frequently in Set 1 (but rarely in Set 2) while c was chosen overwhelmingly in Set 2, confirming what Tversky calls his *diagnosticity principle*—and also being consistent with the dominance of the Pleasantness/Unpleasantness (E) affective factor in facial communication (cf., Osgood, 1966; Cüceloğlu, 1970). The diagnosticity principle refers to "the classificatory significance of features, that is, the importance or prevalence of the classifications that are based on these features" (p. 342).

A series of papers by Richard C. Anderson and various associates in the

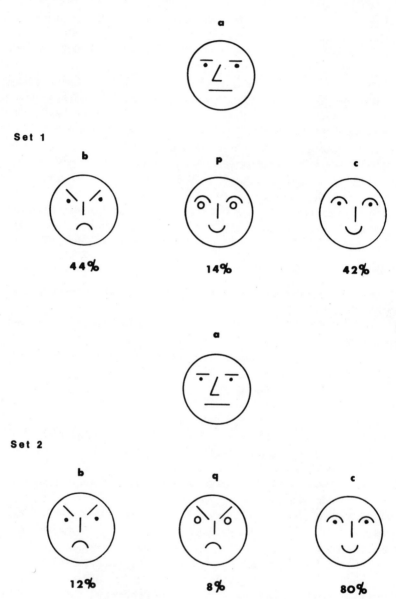

FIG. 9.2.   Schematic faces used to test Tversky's Diagnosticity hypothesis. (After Tversky, A., Features of similarity, *Psychological Revies,* 1977, p. 341.)

Center for the Study of Reading at the University of Illinois has provided evidence for what they call "instantiation" of particular meanings of the polysemous topics (M_1's) of sentences—and these "instantiations" are clearly cases where certain features of the commentaries ($-(m) \rightarrow$ and M_2's) move "leftward" into the topics (M_1's). Anderson and Ortony (1975) found that, given either *the container held the apples* or *the container held the cola*, and then being given both *basket* and *bottle* as probes (among many others on a list for other test sentences with entirely different content), *basket* was a better probe for the former sentence and *bottle* a better one for the latter—i.e., the "instantiations" of the feature code-strip for the general topic, *container*, were the differentially modifying "leftward" fusions from *apples* (solid) vs. *cola* (fluid) in original comprehending of the sentences.

A study by Anderson, Pichert, et al. (1976) demonstrated, for a wide variety of sentence types with polysemous topics, that giving the predicted "instantiations" *as cue words* yielded significantly *better* recalls of the remainder of the sentences than the general topic words actually presented originally. Thus, given *the fish attacked the swimmer*, the word *shark* was a better cue than *fish;* given *the man planned the house*, the word *architect* was a better cue than *man*. That such within-sentence semantic interactions appear at an early age is suggested in a study by Anderson, Stevens, et al. (1977).

METAPHOR

Semantic and syntactic rules are made to be broken. When a Black youngster, accused of a felony, exclaims "Ah ain't nevah done nothin' to nobody nohow!", he is guilty of a quintuple negative at the very least—but his claim to honorable character is being vividly made. However, if rules are to be broken, then there must also be rules for breaking rules. "When I use a word," Humpty Dumpty said, in a rather scornful tone, "it means just what I choose it to mean, neither more nor less." "The question is," said Alice, "whether you *can* make words mean so many different things." "The question is," said Humpty Dumpty, "which is to be master, that's all." There are grains of both truth and untruth here—being master of one's words is not synonymous with being entirely arbitrary in one's use of them—and, as we shall see, metaphors can vary from the tellingly *apposite*, through the tamely *acceptable*, to the ridiculously *anomalous*.

Metaphorical use of language falls naturally into two sub-types. There are *within-constituent* semantic interactions *in phrasing*—witness Winston Churchill's coinage of the phrase *the iron curtain*, which certainly provided an apt characterization of the Cold War situation at that time. There are *between-constituent* semantic interactions *in sentencing*—my favorite example here is a TV beer advertisement, in which, after dropping bottles of the brew from skyscrapers, running them over with steam rollers, and flinging them against brick walls (with nary a scratch to the glass bottle), the assertion is brightly made that *this beer has indestructible flavor!* Our main concern, of course, will be with the cognitive congruence rules operating to determine the location of metaphorical attempts along the appositeness—acceptableness—anomalousness dimension.

In Phrasing

The smallest unit of potential metaphorical usage would seem to be single-word NPs and VPs. The names of many commercial products provide examples. Just poking around my wife's kitchen cupboard, I find these: *Meritene* (a "protein-vitamin-mineral supplement") and *Rose-milk* (skin care cream), both $^+$E; *Ajax* (a cleanser that "bleaches out the toughest food stains"), obviously $^+$P; and *Off!* ("keeps bugs away"), rather $^+$A. Our frequent exhortations to inanimate entities provide VP examples—*Wake up!* (to the "grumbling" coffee pot in the morning), *give!* (to a "recalcitrant" slot machine) and *charge!* (to one's "idling" car as the light turns to green).

"Live" vs. "Dead" Metaphors. According to Brown (1958), "the metaphor in a word lives when the word brings to mind more than a single reference and the several references are seen to have something in common." Using *the foot of the mountain* as an example, he points out that, in the fresh use of this phrase, the minus coding on Top/Bottomness (to coin a feature name!) of *foot* can fuse with *mountain* (my Rule 2) to yield the apposite bottom-of-mountain "live" metaphoric meaning. Of course, *the foot of the mountain* is no longer a "live" metaphor, but rather one long "dead." However, closer to "live" would be *they camped on the shoulder of the mountain* and even more so *he planted his flag on the mountain's head.* Note that the same vertical polarity is used in many other (again, mostly "dead") phrasal metaphors, e.g., *he stands at the head/foot of his class,* but again fresh "live" ones can be generated, e.g., *he's chipper at the head of each day but gets droopy at its foot* (acceptable, even though "temporality" is substituted for "verticality"—as in the *head* vs. *foot* of the *parade*?).

Affect vs. Denotation Based Metaphors. While *the foot of the mountain* is primarily denotation-based, *the foot of the class* clearly involves affect (Evaluation). In metaphoric usage many superficially denotative terms actually convey affective feeling-tones: *A warm person* is typically differentiated from *a cold person* in terms of social Evaluation (E), not skin temperature; *a hard guy* differs from *a soft guy* in terms of social Potency (P), not the resiliency of the body— and Brown (1958, p. 152) most appropriately observes that "if Disney were to give *a boulder* a voice it would be *bass* rather than *treble*"; *a quick mind* differs from *a slow mind* in terms of mental Activity (A), in contrast, say to *a quick trip* vs. *a slow trip* where the difference is denotatively $\pm$Temporal Extent.

The affective/denotative difference can also be demonstrated by differential modifying of the same nominals—thus compare affectively apposite *black traitor, white hope, sweet joy* and *bitter misery* vs. anomalous (but usable in a mind-boggling fashion!) *white traitor, black hope, sour joy* and *sweet misery* with denotatively apposite *disloyal traitor, steady hope, wild joy* and *prolonged misery* vs. anomalous (but again, possible) *loyal traitor, abrupt hope, tame joy*, and *momentary misery*. In a cross-language (Chinese, Mongolian, Yucatan Mayan, and Zulu) study of metaphorical extensions of color terms, Sandra Derrig (1978) finds that shared (by two or more of the unrelated languages) metaphorical uses may be either affective or denotative—thus for BLACK more affective *evil* and *gloomy* and more denotative *ignorant* and *secret*, for WHITE affective *innocent* and *free* and denotative *empty, faded,* and *bare,* and for RED affective *angry* and (sexually) *hot* and denotative *ripe*.

The language of international relations (to say nothing of national politics) is loaded with metaphorical phrases. Although many are stultifying—the phrase *underdeveloped countries* is an insult to people whose written histories often go back much further than our own—the dynamics of metaphor also encourage the creation of potentially effective phrases; here one could speak of *unevenly developed countries,* implying that some may even be *overdeveloped* in certain respects. Another revolutionary phrase I would recommend is *benevolent subversion:* When forced into such affectively anomalous confrontation, the words bring into mind obscure but significant features of each—the potential selfishness of *benevolence* and the potential altruism of *subversion*. The phrase *mutual nuclear deterrence* has a stable, reassuring feel to it—almost like being in a medieval suite of armor; but given its foundations on the shifting psychological sands of mutual fear and distrust, nothing could be much less stable or reassuring—and it is refreshing to note that one well-known strategist dubbed it *the delicate balance of terror!*

In Sentencing

In this final section I will detail the fine semantic interactions in *polysemy* and in *metaphor*—separately, because the types of meaning-shifts are quite different: Polysemy involves selection among alternative *existing senses* of potentially ambiguous topics (M_1's in APG_0) via interactive fusions from commentaries (M_2's); metaphor involves creation of *novel senses* for topics via the same interactive fusions, in which certain old features may be strengthened or weakened and other new features may be added. Finally, following a brief review of some relevant empirical evidence already available, I will suggest a type of research that might serve to distinguish among the somewhat competitive theories of metaphor that are suggested by Tversky (1977), Ortony (this volume) and Osgood (this chapter).

Sketch of Philosophical Background.   It is interesting that etymologically *metaphor* derives from the Greek *meta* (trans) + *pherein* (to carry), i.e., literally "to carry across" or *transfer*—which, of course, is precisely what my $M_1 \leftarrow M_2$ fusive interactions of semantic features presume. Rather unfortunately, I think, this *transfer* notion has subtly shifted in philosophical treatments to one of *comparison* between the "tenor" (topic) and the "vehicle" (commentary), with the "ground" being that which the two have in common and the "tension" being that on which the two differ (cf. I. A. Richards, 1936). I say "unfortunately" because the term "comparison" implies a deliberate, conscious mental process rather than an automatic interaction among constituent meanings of which one is usually unaware. However, as Andrew Ortony notes in a paper appropriately titled "Why Metaphors Are Necessary and Not Just Nice" (1975), whether we call the process "transfer" or "comparison," metaphor is necessary if we are to provide a reasonably faithful portrayal of continuously variable states with a language composed of discrete symbols. Ortony, Reynolds and Arter (1978, pp. 920–925) contrast in some detail the two major traditional theories of metaphor, the earlier Comparison Theory and the more recent Interaction Theory—the latter being closer to that proposed here.

Resolution of Polysemic Ambiguity.   The semantic interactions that resolve polysemic ambiguities may be either within-constituent or between-constituent. Taking some examples from Michael Reddy (1973), the adjectives $ROCK_1$ (derived from the noun *rock,* referring to hard, granitelike substances) and $ROCK_2$ (derived from the verb *to rock* as a rhythmic motion): In *he works in a rock quarry* vs. *he works in a rock band* there is no ambiguity, since the *within*-constituent fusion of the features of *quarry* vs. *band* with *rock* yield appropriately different total meanings. In *they are rock idols,* however, the referent status of *they* is ambiguous—but *between*-constituent interaction easily disambiguates (e.g., *those musicians . . .* vs. *those monuments . . . are rock idols*), and more remote antecedent context can serve the same function (e.g., *I always come to hear these guys perform* vs. *We found these things in our archeological excavations. They are rock idols.*). Or witness the multiple idiomatic uses of the simple word *hand:* In the ordinary usages of *lend me a hand, deal me a hand, I got it second hand,* and *he rules with an iron hand* there are no confusions, due to either within- or between-constituent semantic interactions; but note the "mind-boggling" effects of mixing the contexts, as in *lend me a second hand, deal me an iron hand,* or *he rules with a second hand!*

Particularly interesting are what Reddy—in his paper presented at the University of Illinois Conference on Metaphor and Thought (1977)—has called "conduit metaphors," in which the senses of simple verbs like *have* and *give* are shifted polysemously from Concrete to Abstract. In *I have an apple* and *he gave me an apple* the senses of the stative HAVING and the active GIVING are Concrete, but in *I have an idea* and *he gave me an idea* the senses are obviously Abstract (there is no physical possession or transfer). Reddy's paper provided multitudes of examples—such as *none of Mary's feelings CAME THROUGH to me, try to PACK more thought INTO fewer words*, and *the sentence WAS FILLED WITH emotion*—and he suggests that such verb forms are *dead metaphors* that serve as a "conduit," allowing people to communicate their mental and emotional states via language. Just imagine—immediately after having said "I'm just *buying* time"—the "mind-boggling-ness" of being politely asked "How much are you *paying* for it?" (an abrupt shift from Abstract to Concrete *buying*)!

Creation and Comprehension of Metaphors.   Ortony (1979b, p. 22) says that "no adequate theory of metaphor can ignore the difference between metaphor and simile." He notes that, traditionally, the distinction has been made in terms of distinguishing between *implicit comparison* (metaphor) and *explicit comparison* (simile). While it is true that when a wife creates the metaphor, *my husband is a teddy bear,* no comparison is directly expressed, as it is when she creates the simile, *my husband is like a teddy bear.* Although such explicit comparison does "invite" the intellectual exercise of *qualifying* the relation with "in some respects"—and perhaps looking for these respects—I would suggest that the *psychological* (cognitive) difference between metahpors and similes is primarily one of *intensity of coding of the commentary* (my M_2) *on exactly the same semantic features*. To say *my husband IS a teddy bear* is certainly a stronger "commitment" by the speaker than to say *my husband IS LIKE a teddy bear* (which is a kind of waffling), and hence in APG_0 the polarization of the features of "cuddly," "cute," "playful" meanings will be greater for the former than the latter. In any case, I will concentrate on metaphor.

As was the case for *within*-constituent metaphors in phrasing, *between*-constituent metaphors in sentencing must *optimally* break semantic rules if they are to be effective, let alone comprehensible. In the literal use of English one cannot say *the thunder shouted* or even *the panther shouted*—only humans can *shout*—yet, speaking poetically, one might well say *the thunder shouted down the mountainside.* However I, at least, could not say *the breeze shouted down the mountainside*—without making it a gale! Note that while *thunder* and *shout* share enough features (e.g., affective Potency, denotative Loudness) to "override" the opposition on Humanness—the fusion, indeed, serving to "humanize" the thunder—*breeze* and *shout* do not. Similarly, to say *the daisies smiled at me* is just fine (note even the "facelike-ness" of flowers), but to say *the pebbles smiled at me* is not (at least, without some prior context).

The APG_0 rules for semantic feature interaction (presented earlier) generate explicit predictions for potential metaphors and similes. Rule (1): when a feature has *the same sign* (non-zero) in topic and commentary, (a) equal intensity of coding yields *no change* in topic meaning, (b) greater intensity in comment *increases* polarization in topic, and (c) lesser intensity in comment *reduces* polarization in topic. Rule (2): when a feature is *signed* (either + or −) in the commentary but *unsigned* (O) in the topic, the topic assumes *the same intensity and polarity* on that feature as the commentary. Rule (3): when topic and commentary have *opposed signs* (polarities) on a feature, (a) unequal codings yield *reductions* in intensity toward zero coding in the topic, (b) non-polar equal codings (e.g., +2 vs. −2) yield *cancellation* of that feature (i.e., zero coding) in the topic, and (c) polar equal codings (+3 vs. −3) yield the sense of *anomaly*. I emphasize again that these effects on meaning are *not* deliberate conscious acts by the comprehender, but rather are automatic feature interactions of which one is usually quite unaware.

Table 9.2, titled simply *JOHN and MARY*, offers several sets of sentence types which will serve to illustrate the assumed functioning of these rules—the use of *John* and *Mary* as contrastive topics (one Male, the other Female, and

TABLE 9.2

	JOHN	and	MARY
I	− John / is / a member of the human species − John / is / a male		− Mary / is / a member of the human species − Mary / is / a female
II	+ John / is / a mature male + John / is / clever (generous, tall, etc.)		+ Mary / is / a mature female + Mary / is / clever (thoughtful, short, etc.)
III	+ John / is / handsome ! John / is / pretty		! Mary / is / handsome + Mary / is / pretty
IV	(+) John / is / a teddy bear (!) John / is / a kitten (+) John / is / a bulldozer (!) John / is / a sewing machine (?) John / is / a radio		(!) Mary / is / a teddy bear (+) Mary / is / a kitten (!) Mary / is / a bulldozer (+) Mary / is / a sewing machine (?) Mary / is / a radio
V	(0) John / is / a paper-clip (0) John / is / a formula (0) John / is / an idea		(0) Mary / is / a paper-clip (0) Mary / is / a formula (0) Mary / is / an idea
VI	(+) John / growled at / the salesman (?) John / purred at / the cop + John / laughed at / the clown		(?) Mary / growled at / the salesman (+) Mary / purred at / the cop + Mary / laughed at / the clown
VII	+ John / will make someone / a nice husband (+) John / will make someone / a nice wife (0) John / will make someone / a nice cousin + John / will make someone / a nice parent		(+) Mary / will make someone / a nice husband + Mary / will make someone / a nice wife (0) Mary / will make someone / a nice cousin + Mary / will make someone / a nice parent

both mature, as we are informed on line 3) serving to minimally code them on ±SEX and +Maturity. Sentences that are *literally* informative, uninformative (redundant) or anomalous are marked +, −, or ! respectively; sentences that are potentially *metaphorical* are marked (+) if they are apposite (that is, informative via metaphor), (?) if they are *acceptable* but clearly not apposite, (O) if they are simply "mind-boggling-ly" empty, and (!) if they are *anomalous* (that is, incongruously misinformative). In what follows, we will see how the postulated rules of semantic feature interaction and fusion (here, *across* constituents) would predict the expected effects upon listeners—as checked by the intuitions of my readers, of course!

The first set of sentences (I) are simply redundantly uninformative, − , since in ordinary English the personal names *John* and *Mary* are already coded for Humanness and Sex—i.e., these features of the commentary are already *entailed* in the coding of the topic (just as in sentences like *birds can be robins, storks or even penguins, but not bats*). On the other hand, those in II are clearly *informative* (literally), since new features from the commentaries are transferred to the topics where they were coded zero—thus the +Mature, +Cleverness, etc. features are added to the meanings of *John* and *Mary* (via Rule 2). In contrast, note that in Set III, while *John is handsome* and *Mary is pretty* are similarly informative via fusion, *Mary is handsome* and *John is pretty* are literally *anomalous*, because *handsome* and *pretty* are coded +Sex and −Sex—thus in opposition (Rule 3) on the Sex features for *Mary* and *John* respectively.

We come now to the potentially metaphorical sentences in Set IV. The commentary *is a teddy bear* is clearly *congruent* with the Maleness of *John* (presumably because of the *teddy*)—and hence the Cuddliness, Playfulness etc. feature-sets can be informatively fused with the meaning of *John,* overriding the opposition on Maturity; this same Maleness, along with the Immaturity, are equally clearly *incongruent* for *Mary* as a topic, and hence the anomalousness (indicated by (!)) of *Mary is a teddy bear.* Exactly the reverse of course, applies to *John is a kitten* (!) vs. *Mary is a kitten* (+). A similar comparative analysis holds for *John is a bulldozer:* Both topic and commentary are coded Masculine, this allowing the Potency, Determination and Ruthlessness (?) of *bulldozer* to transfer to *John,* overriding the single opposition on Humanness. For *Mary is a bulldozer,* the oppositions on Sex as well as Potency (?), added to that on Humanness, render the whole anomalous. The analyses of *John is a sewing machine* vs. *Mary is a sewing machine* would be the same—on the assumption that the "feminism" of *sewing machine* not only fits *Mary* but makes a busy little demon out of her! Either *John* or *Mary* might be *acceptable* as topics for ... *is a radio* (making them loudmouthed, gossipy bores??), but the sentences surely are not *apposite* metaphors—hence the (?) rating.

As they stand without any context, the sentences in Set V are (to me, at least) "mind-boggling-ly" empty (0) when the features of the commentaries (*paperclips, formulas,* and *ideas*) are fused with those of the topics *John* and *Mary*—

the more complex fused feature-sets for the topics (M_1's) now being uninterpretably meaningless as wholes. But note that if a prior context *is* given, or even the M_2's expanded, an apposite metaphor can be generated: Thus, for *paper-clip,* either prior sentences about *John* or *Mary* "holding the family together" or an expanded commentary . . . *is a family paper-clip;* for *formula,* prior talk about either *John* or *Mary* providing exactly the "solution" for the other's family problems; for *idea,* expanding the sentence to . . . *is an idea for the job*—except that it would seem to become more "literal" than "metaphoric."

All of the sentence types so far have involved the simple verb *is* as the relation ($-(M) \rightarrow$). However, as noted earlier, relations can be much more complex semantically (the embedded [M] here) and, of course, the relation is also part of the commentary. Set VI illustrate the potential metaphorical functions of relations (VPs), and again the topics, *John* or *Mary,* undergo an interaction-based meaning change. While *John growled at the salesman* would be a literal statement as far as the *salesman* (M_2) is concerned, *growled at* ($-(M) \rightarrow$) contains features that, when fused with *John*, make him at least momentarily rather *mean* and *nasty,* and since *growing* is Dog-like, and hence more Masculine, this fusion is not blocked by opposition on the Sex feature (hence the ($+$) coding). On the other hand, when *Mary* is the topic we must code the sentence (?) because of opposition on Sex. Conversely, since *purring* is clearly Cat-like, and hence more Feminine, *Mary purred at the cop* is coded ($+$) but *John purred at the cop* is coded (?). Both of these potentially metaphoric relations via VPs contrast with *laughed at,* where (at least in the total commentary of my example) *John/Mary laughed at the clown* may have some effect on the meaning of clown, but certainly not on the topics *Mary* or *John.*

My last Set VII is included simply to make it clear that metaphoric interactions between topics and commentaries (here, the M_2's) are by no means limited to the simple verb *to be* (*is, are,* etc.) relations. Note that while *John will make someone a nice husband* and *Mary will make someone a nice wife* are entirely acceptable *literal* assertions, if we *reverse* these ONPs (M_2's) we get *metaphoric* assertions that forcefully modify the "images" of both *John* and *Mary* and are in no way "mind-boggling." To say *Mary will make someone a nice husband* not only reduces her Sex coding toward zero, but actually makes her somewhat Masculine (one imagines this *Mary* to be rather big, strong and domineering); to say *John will make someone a nice wife,* similarly, makes him somewhat Feminine (one imagining this *John* to be rather *small, weak* and *submissive*). This, of course, implies that the ordinary coding on Sex is not maximally polar but only moderately (e.g., not a ± 3 but more like a ± 1.5). Only if this were the case could the polarity be reversed in sentences like these. The last two examples indicate, first, that *John/Mary will make someone a nice cousin* (with *cousin* neutral on Sex and much else) has no such effects, and is in fact quite "*empty*" (0), and, second, that *John/Mary will make someone a nice parent* is merely *literally informative,* $+$, and in no way metaphorical.

There is one very interesting thing that appears when *informative literal* sentences are compared with *informative metaphorical* sentences—and I, at least, have seen nothing about it in the literature. This is the fact that, whereas negation of literals serves to cancel (or even reverse) the features embodied in the commentary, negation of potential metaphors apparently serves only to shift them into literal sentences—i.e., *cancels their metaphoric potential.* Negating the sentences I have coded simply + (literally informative)—e.g., *John is not clever, Mary is not pretty, John did not laugh at the clown,* and *Mary will not make someone a nice parent*—clearly cancels the meanings of the commentaries as applied to *John* or to *Mary,* and even seems to reverse the codings in some (like *John is not clever* implying that he's pretty stupid!). On the other hand, negating the relations I have coded (+) (metaphorically informative)—e.g., *John is not a teddy bear, Mary is not a kitten, John did not growl at the salesman,* and *Mary did not purr at the cop*—seem more like literal denials (albeit rather obvious ones) and certainly do not reverse the meanings. And as to negation of my last sentential examples—*Mary will not make anyone a nice husband* and *John will not make anyone a nice wife*—they are absolutely "mind-boggling," and about all one could say to them (and that after a pause for trying to comprehend) would be "of *course,* not"!

Some Relevant Research with Children and Adults. Ortony, Reynolds and Arter (1978) provide a critical review of much of the literature here, of which only a few particularly relevant studies will be noted. Gardner (1974) reports an experiment explicitly relating synesthesia to metaphor in children tested in three groups with mean ages of 3.5, 7.0, and 11.5 years. Given sets of stimulus-word pairs, the children were asked to say how the pairs should be related (cf., Karwoski, Odbert & Osgood, 1942)—a test item being, e.g., *blue-red:* Which color is *cold* and which is *warm?*" Errors (in terms of adult synesthetic tendencies) were shown to decrease with age, with 11-year-olds performing much like adults. Gentner (1977) compared children 4-5½ years in age with college sophomores on a task in which various parts of the human body (e.g., *nose, head, feet*) were to be located on pictures of objects (e.g., *mountain, car, tree*)—thus, "if the mountain in this picture had a nose, where would it be?"— and the children proved to be as good at this task as the adults.

Winner, Rosentiel and Gardner (1976) postulated three levels of development in comprehending metaphors like *the prison guard was a hard rock:* A "magical" level (that the guard was turned into a rock); a "metonymic" level (that the guard worked in a prison with rock walls), and a "primitive metaphoric" level (that the guard was physically—*not* psychologically, at this stage—hard and tough). Whereas children 6 through 8 gave predominantly "primitive metaphoric" interpretations (and even the youngest gave more "metonymic" than "magical"), "genuine metaphoric" interpretations were dominant for children 10 to 14 years of age. Although Ortony (1980) suggests that a "world-knowledge deficit hypothesis'' would explain an inability to understand metaphors by young children in terms of their having insufficient knowledge about the topic and, especially, the vehicle to permit them to figure out the ground of the metaphor, or possibly even to perceive the "tension," their inability could also be explained simply in terms of *insufficient elaboration* of the semantic features of words and phrases—which, of course, may well be saying a similar thing, but it suggests a finer level of analysis. The Graphic Differential developed by French (see her 1977 paper) for use with aphasics and with young children might be a useful research tool here.

In a particularly relevant adult study, Verbrugge and McCarrell (1977) proposed that metaphors are comprehended only when the *unexpressed* ground between the topic and the vehicle is inferred. For example, *billboards are warts on the landscape* will be comprehended only if the ground—here, something like "ugly protrusions on a surface" (i.e., the affective and denotative features transferred from commentary to topic in APG_0 terms)—is inferred. They then predict that *expressed* grounds will also be effective as prompts *for recall* of the metaphorical sentences. Their results showed that, although topics and vehicles were the best prompts, *relevant* grounds worked nearly as well, with *irrelevant* grounds (drawn from other metaphors with the same topics, here *billboards are yellow pages on the landscape*) being significantly less effective as prompts. Again, whether "inference" of the unexpressed grounds is a deliberate mental process of which comprehenders are aware, *or* is simply the awareness of a particular "fresh" meaning of the topic due to automatic semantic feature transfers, remains a basic theoretical issue.

Most recently Harris (1979) reports a series of three experiments in which *memory* was compared for "live" metaphors vs. "dead" metaphors vs. nonmetaphors (e.g., *The maple tree branches / flirted with* vs. *nudged* vs. *touched / the telephone wires*). Although there were no differences between the three types of sentences in recall, there was a significant trend for recall errors that were meaning preserving to be *less metaphorical* than the input sentences (e.g., that *flirted with* as input in the above example is much more likely to shift in recall to *touched* or *rubbed against* than is *touched* as input to shift to *flirted with* or *caressed*) (see Harris, this volume). This would seem to imply that metaphoric effects are ephemeral (perhaps even limited to interactions while the information is still in the OPERATOR) and that it is not here a Feminimized *maple tree* that is sent to the MEMORY or, in an earlier example, a Femininized *John*, resulting from the metaphor *John will make someone a nice wife* that goes to MEM.

This is surely something to conjure with! Since there is no question but that commentary information in *literal* assertions fuses with topics and goes to MEM (e.g., the meaning of *Tom* for a bystander, who saw Tom's hand in the till, hearing the arresting officer say *Tom is a thief*), there is no reason in APG_0 that such faithful transfers to MEM for the topics of metaphors would be blocked. The resolution, I think, lies in *differentiation of meanings for the same referents* in the topics of processed cognitions stored in the MEMORY: An "ordinary" *maple tree* topic is associated with many commentaries and here an "extraordinary" Femininized *maple tree* topic is associated with the branches *flirting with* metaphoric commentary. Subjects' recalls in the Harris experiment, of course, depended upon *which* topic in MEM was found. Thus also in the MEM of one who has heard *John will make someone a nice wife* there will now be an "extra-ordinary" Femininized *John* along with many "ordinary" *John* topics without this particular meaning.

Proposed Experiment on Metaphor Comprehension.   The general purpose of this experiment would be to see if reasonably precise predictions can be made (and tested) for the shifts in meaning—both affective and denotative—of the *topics* of metaphorical sentences. My friend and colleage at Illinois, Andrew Ortony, has been exceptionally busy with both theory and research on metaphor over the past several years. While the theoretical notions in his earliest paper (1975) seemed reasonably close to mine, his more recent papers, emphasizing "schemata theory" (cf. Ortony, 1980), clearly are not, and the role of "semantic features" is explicitly denied (1979b)—yet terms like "salient components," "salient attributes," and "salient properties" are used liberally.

Tversky's general theory of similarity judgments, "which expresses the similarity between objects (*perceptual or linguistic*) as a linear combination of the measures of their common and distinctive features" (1977, p. 327) seems to be very similar to mine. This seminal "Features of Similarity" paper of Tversky's does not, however, deal directly with metaphor *per se*—and in a sort of coda at the end he says that "the nature of this process is left to be explained." In an equally seminal *Psychological Review* paper (1979a), titled "Beyond Literal Similarity," Ortony accepts Tversky's "challenge" and extends the latter's formuli in ways designed to more adequately handle metaphors and similes. I will be inviting Ortony and Tversky to make their own predictions for the shifts of topic meanings in the proposed experimental sentences. The crucial issue, I think, will be the *fineness* of the predictions of meaning shifts for topics.

The reason I emphasize the measurement of shifts in *both* affective and denotative features of meaning is that, in the literature on metaphor, the very significant role of affective (Evaluation, Potency and Activity) features of meaning has been relatively neglected. As the following set of sentences—all with the common topic *an encyclopaedia*—will clearly demonstrate, affective shifts in topic meaning are not only involved, but are, indeed, often the primary metaphorical effect.

1. an encyclopaedia is a dictionary
2. an encyclopaedia is a goldmine
3. an encyclopaedia is a coal mine
4. an encyclopaedia is a junk yard

5. an encyclopaedia is an oil well
6. an encyclopaedia is a vacuum cleaner
7. an encyclopaedia is a chicken coop
8. an encyclopaedia is a professor
9. an encyclopaedia is a secretary

Sentence (1) is essentially literal, emphasizing the *encyclopaedia* as an organized source of information, albeit much more extensive than a *dictionary*. Sentences (2) through (4) show how the affective meaning of a topic can be modulated—from $^+$E (*a goldmine*) through ^{0}E (*a coal mine*) to $^-$E (*a junk yard*)—with little if any shift in denotation (a goldmine, a coal mine and a junk yard all being places where one must dig around to find things).

On the other hand, sentence (5), *an encyclopaedia is an oil well*, seems to be a rather *inapposite* metaphor, given the basic conflict on denotative features representing the "digging out" (*encyclopaedia*) vs. the "gushing forth" (*oil well*) source of information. While the $^-$Animate and $^-$Human *vacuum cleaner* (6) strikes me as rather apposite ("sucking up a mass of information"), the similarly coded (denotatively) *chicken coop* (7) seems entirely "mind-boggling" ("an enclosure filled with cackling fowl)." And, while the $^+$Animate and $^+$Human *professor* (8) seems at least acceptable as a metaphor (after all, most professors *are* sources of information), the similarly coded *secretary* (9) is again rather inapposite (most secretaries are *recipients* of information). Also note that for sentences (6) through (9) the transfers of meaning into the topic are primarily denotative, not affective.

The measuring instrument for the proposed experiment would be a semantic differential (SD), but one designed to tap both generalized affective and more specific denotative features. Among the highest loading *affective* scales for American English speakers are *good-bad, pleasant-unpleasant,* and *valuable-worthless* for E, *strong-weak, powerful-powerless* and *big-little* for P, and *active-passive, quick-slow* and *lively-dull* for A. Given the high within-factor intercorrelations among these scales, three of each is sufficient. Scales to tap the more specific *denotative* features would have to be selected with the specific topics and commentaries in mind, of course.[5] For the *encyclopaedia* sentence-set above, the following scales can be suggested: *abstract-concrete* (encyclopaedias vs. all the commentaries), *organized-disorganized* (gold mines vs. junk yards), *animate-inanimate* (secretaries vs. vacuum cleaners), *giving-receiving* (oilwells vs. junk yards), *mental-physical* (professors vs. chicken coops), *deep-shallow* (coal mines vs. vacuum cleaners), *simple-complex* (dictionaries vs. encyclopaedias) and *feminine-masculine* (secretaries vs. professors). Other sentence-sets would be devised—metaphors (*billboards are placards/warts/yellow*

---

[5]Techniques for mathematical separation of denotative and affective factors have been developed; see particularly Tzeng (1975) and Tzeng and May (1975).

pages/cartoons) and similes ('*sermons are like lectures/advertisements/sleeping pills/symphonies*).

One group of subjects (control) would rate both topics and commentaries as *isolated* words or phrases against the appropriate SDs; the other group (experimental) would rate *only the topics* (one from each sentence-set), and in the *context* of a metaphor or simile (e.g., *AN ENCYCLOPAEDIA is a goldmine; SERMONS are like sleeping pills*). Using the three rules of semantic interaction and fusion presented earlier, the control group ratings of commentaries would be used to quantitatively *predict* the meaning shifts of topics (e.g., the meaning of *warts* increasing the affectively negative E of *billboards* and adding a denotative Prominence feature). These *predicted* topic meanings would be compared with the *actual* topic meanings in the metaphor contexts, as indicated by their ratings on the same SD forms by the experimental groups.

Although shifts in the meanings of *commentaries* could be predicted and measured, no such shifts would actually be expected. There is a very significant characteristic of *reversible metaphors* that has not been sufficiently highlighted in the literature—namely, that it is the meanings of the *topics* that are shifted, not those of the commentaries (i.e., the transfer is always "leftward" from comment to topic). Compare *butchers are surgeons* (where *butchers* acquire affective $^+$E and denotative $^+$Skill) with *surgeons are butchers* (where surgeons become clearly $^-$E and very $^-$Skill). But note that there is no intuitively detectable shift in *commentary* meaning in either case. Whereas *billboards are warts on the countryside* conveys $^-$E and $^+$Prominence to the *billboards* with no apparent effect upon the meaning of *warts*, the reversal to *warts are billboards on the face* adds denotative $^+$Magnitude and $^+$Communication (advertising one's ugliness!) to the already $^-$E of the *warts* on the face, again with no felt shift in the meaning of the commentary (*billboards*). It might be noted that in the *encyclopaedia* sentence-set (with the possible exception of *a professor is an encyclopaedia*) all reversals produce "mind-boggling" sentences—such as *a goldmine is an encyclopaedia* (!) or *a vacuum cleaner is an encyclopaedia* (!). This seems to be the case for many (perhaps most) metaphor and simile reversals. Again borrowing an example from Ortony (this volume), witness the effect of reversing the apt simile *cigarettes are like time bombs* (+) into *time bombs are like cigarettes* (!).

It may well be that Ortony's predictions here would not be too much different than mine. One can see what looks like a return/swing in his "Beyond Literal Similarity" (1979a) paper—suggesting extensions of Tversky's (1977) semantic feature analysis to incorporate nonliteral (metaphorical) similarity—back toward his 1975 notions. Introducing the recent paper, he states that "the principal source of metaphoricity is the difference in the relative *salience of matching attributes* . . . (*and that*) another variable that affects metaphoricity . . . is *attribute inequality* . . . (*which*) enhances the metaphorical effects of *salience imbalance*" (italics mine).

Now, if one simply substitutes "features" for "attributes," "same-sign" for "matching," "opposed-sign" for "inequality," and "intensity (polarization) differences" for "salience imbalance," then it would seem that we are saying essentially the same things. The basic "translations" between Ortony (1975, p. 48) and APG_0 interpretations of metaphoric transfers still (in Ortony, this volume) appear to be that (1) the potentially transferable set of features (attributes) are those on which the codings are different for topic and comment, which, (2) minus those features on which there is "tension" (the opposed-sign features in APG_0), yields (3) the "ground" common to both that is the basis for the metaphorical shift in meaning. Since Tversky has yet to apply his theory to metaphor per se, we'll just have to see what his predictions would be for the proposed experiment.

REFERENCES

Abelson, R. P., & Rosenberg, M. J. Symbolic psycho-logic: A model of attitudinal cognition. *Behavioral Science,* 1958, *3,* 1-13.

Anderson, R. C., & Ortony, A. On putting apples into bottles: A problem of polysemy. *Cognitive Psychology,* 1975, *7,* 167-180.

Anderson, R. C., Pichert, J. W., Goetz, E. T., Schallert, D. L., Stevens, K. C., & Trollip, S. R. Instantiation of general terms. *Journal of Verbal Learning and Verbal Behavior,* 1976, *15,* 667-679.

Anderson, R. C., Stevens, K. C., Shifrin, Z., & Osborn, J. H. *Instantiation of word meanings in children.* (Technical Report No. 46). Center for the Study of Reading, 1977.

Asch, S. On the use of metaphor in the description of persons. In H. Werner (Ed.), *On expressive language.* Worcester, Mass.: Clark University Press, 1955.

Boucher, J., & Osgood, C. E. The Pollyanna hypothesis. *Journal of Verbal Learning and Verbal Behavior,* 1969, *8,* 1-8.

Brown, R. *Words and things.* Glencoe, Ill.: Free Press, 1958.

Brown, R., Leiter, R. A., & Hildum, D. C. Metaphors from music criticism. *Journal of Abnormal and Social Psychology,* 1957, *54,* 347-352.

Cüceloğlu, D. M. Perception of facial expressions in three cultures. *Ergonomics,* 1970, *13,* 93-100.

Derrig, S. Metaphor in the color lexicon. In D. Farkas, W. Jacobson, & K. Todrys (Eds.), *Papers from the Parasession on the Lexicon,* 1978.

Ertel, S. *Psychophonetik: Untersuchungen über lautsymbolik und motivatien.* Göttingen: Verlag für Psychologie, 1969.

French, P. L. Nonverbal measurement of affect: The graphic differential. *Journal of Psycholinguistic Research,* 1977, *6,* 337-347.

Gardner, H. Metaphors and modalities: How children project polar adjectives onto diverse domains. *Child Development,* 1974, *45,* 84-91.

Gentner, D. On the development of metaphoric processing. *Child Development,* 1977, *48,* 1034-1039.

Gitin, S. R. A dimensional analysis of manual expression. *Journal of Personality and Social Psychology,* 1970, *15,* 271-277.

Greenberg, J. H. Some universals of grammar with particular reference to the order of meaningful elements. In J. H. Greenberg (Ed.), *Universals of language.* Chapter 5. Cambridge, Mass.: M.I.T. Press, 1963.

Harris, R. J. Memory for metaphors. *Journal of Psycholinguistic Research*, 1979, *8*, 61–71.

Hastorf, A., Osgood, C. E., & Ono, H. The semantics of facial expressions and the prediction of the meanings of stereoscopically fused facial expressions. *Scandinavian Journal of Psychology*, 1966, *7*, 179–188.

Hoosain, R. The processing of negative or incongruent perceptual and combined perceptual/linguistic stimuli. *British Journal of Psychology*, 1977, *68*, 245–252.

Kaden, S., Wapner, S., & Werner, H. Studies in physiogonomic perception, II: Effect of directional dynamics of pictured objects and of words on the position of the apparent horizon. *Journal of Psychology*, 1955, *39*, 61–67.

Karowski, T. F., & Odbert, H. S. Color-music. *Psychological Monographs*, 1938, *50*(2), (Whole number 222).

Karwoski, T. F., Odbert, H. S., & Osgood, C. E. Studies in synesthetic thinking: II. The rôle of form in visual responses to music. *Journal of General Psychology*, 1942, *26*, 199–222.

Miron, M. S. A cross-linguistic investigation of phonetic symbolism. *Journal of Abnormal and Social Psychology*, 1961, *62*, 623–630.

Odbert, H. S., Karwoski, T. F., & Eckerson, A. B. Studies in synesthetic thinking: I. Musical and verbal association of color and mood. *Journal of General Psychology*, 1942, *26*, 153–173.

Ono, H., Hastorf, A. H., & Osgood, C. E. Binocular rivalry as a function of incongruity in meaning. *Scandinavian Journal of Psychology*, 1966, *7*, 225–233.

Ortony, A. Why metaphors are necessary and not just nice. *Educational Theory*, 1975, *25*, 45–53.

Ortony, A. Beyond literal similarity. *Psychological Review*, 1979, *86*, 161–180. (a)

Ortony, A. The role of similarity in similes and metaphors. In A. Ortony (Ed.), *Metaphor and thought*. Cambridge University Press, 1979. (b)

Ortony, A. Metaphor. In R. Spiro, B. Bruce, & W. Brewer (Eds.), *Theoretical issues in reading comprehension*. Lawrence Erlbaum Associates, 1980.

Ortony, A., Reynolds, R. E., & Arter, J. A. Metaphor: Theoretical and empirical research. *Psychological Bulletin*, 1978, *85*, 919–943.

Osgood, C. E. The cross-cultural generality of visual-verbal synesthetic tendencies. *Behavioral Science*, 1960, *5*, 146–169.

Osgood, C. E. Dimensionality of the semantic space for communication via facial expression. *Scandinavian Journal of Psychology*, 1966, *7*, 1–30.

Osgood, C. E. On the whys and wherefores of E, P and A. *Journal of Personality and Social Psychology*, 1969, *12*, 194–199.

Osgood, C. E. Interpersonal verbs and interpersonal behavior. In J. L. Cowan (Ed.), *Studies in thought and language*. Tucson, Ariz.: University of Arizona Press, 1970.

Osgood, C. E. From Yang and Yin to *and* or *but* in cross-cultural perspective. *International Journal of Psychology*, 1979, *14*, 1–35. (a)

Osgood, C. E. *Lectures on language performance*. New York: Springer-Verlag, 1979. (b)

Osgood, C. E. Things and words. In M. R. Key (Ed.), *Verbal and nonverbal communication*. The Hague: Mouton, 1979. (c)

Osgood, C. E., & Hoosain, R. Salience of the word as a unit in the perception of language. *Perception and Psychophysics*, 1974, *15*, 168–192.

Osgood, C. E., May, W. H., & Miron, M. S. *Cross-cultural universals of affective meaning*. Urbana, Ill.: University of Illinois Press, 1975.

Osgood, C. E., & Richards, M. M. From Yang and Yin to *and* or *but*. *Language*, 1973, *39*, 380–412.

Osgood, C. E., Suci, G. J., & Tannenbaum, P. H. *The measurement of meaning*. Urbana, Ill.: University of Illinois Press, 1957.

Pečjak, V. Verbal synesthesiae of colors, emotions and days of the week. *Journal of Verbal Learning and Verbal Behavior*, 1970, *9*, 623–626.

Reddy, M. J. Formal referential models of poetic structure. *Proceedings of the Ninth Regional meeting of the Chicago Linguistic Society*, July 1973.

Reddy, M. J. *The conduit metaphor—a case of frame conflict in our language about language.* Paper presented at the Conference on Metaphor and Thought, University of Illinois, September 26–29, 1977.

Richards, I. A. *The philosophy of rhetoric.* London: Oxford University Press, 1936.

Scheinkopf, S. *A comparative study of the affective judgments made by anomic aphascs and normals on a nonverbal task.* Unpublished doctoral dissertation, Boston University, 1970.

Stagner, R., & Osgood, C. E. Impact of war on a nationalistic frame of reference: I. Changes in general approval and qualitative patterning of certan stereotypes. *Journal of Social Psychology*, 1946, *24*, 187–215.

Tversky, A. Features of similarity. *Psychological Review*, 1977, *84*, 327–352.

Tzeng, O. C. S. Differentiation of affective and denotative meaning systems and their influence in personality ratings. *Journal of Personality and Social Psychology*, 1975, *32*, 978–988.

Tzeng, O. C. S., & May, W. H. More than E, P and A in semantic differential scales: an answer to questions raised by S. T. M. Lane. *International Journal of Psychology*, 1975, *10*, 101–117.

Verbrugge, R. R., & McCarrell, N. S. Metaphoric comprehension: Studies in reminding and resembling. *Cognitive Psychology*, 1977, *9*, 494–533.

Winner, E., Rosenstiel, A. K., & Gardner, H. The development of metaphoric understanding. *Developmental Psychology*, 1976, *12*, 289–297.

10

Measurement of Figurative Language: Semantic Feature Models of Comprehension and Appreciation

Robert G. Malgady
New York University

Michael G. Johnson
University of Tennessee

Historically, the study of figurative language in linguistics, philosophy, literary criticism, rhetoric, and psychology can be traced to several fundamental ideas expressed in Aristotle's *Poetics* and Plato's *Dialogues* (Hawkes, 1972). It is not our intention in this chapter to review the ontogeny of scientific thought on the subject of metaphor and related forms of figurative language. Rather, we discuss current psychological accounts of figurative language comprehension, based on the classical Aristotelian notion that a "good" metaphor is sustained by drawing attention to an obscure resemblance between ostensibly disparate concepts, and the contemporary idea that word meaning (Jenkins, 1977) is not contextually invariant (i.e., that apprehension of meaning is largely a function of cues provided by linguistic and extralinguistic context attending sentence perception).

In this chapter, our approach to the study of these notions about figurative language comprehension is quantitatively oriented; that is, we deal with attempts to describe or measure language behavior in such a way that certain mathematical axioms of the measurement scale are satisfied. In addition, we will explore some predictions offered by mathematical "models" of human cognition in this chapter, in an effort to see if these formal representations of the cognitive processes underlying comprehension and appreciation of figurative language can help us in understanding these phenomena.

For a variety of reasons, most quantitative models of metaphor have involved one or another version of a feature or componential approach, and these are the models we will emphasize. One reason for this preponderance of feature models, perhaps, is the ubiquity and usefulness of such models in linguistic theory (Steinberg & Jakobovits, 1971) and cognitive psychology (Neisser, 1967). A stronger reason is probably the special usefulness of such models in dealing with meaning similarity (Johnson, 1970; Tversky, 1977—since similarity in meaning between tenor and vehicle is often invoked in explanations of metaphor (e.g., Johnson & Malgady, 1979; Ortony, 1977; Tversky, 1977; Verbrugge, 1977). Although feature models of metaphor have been criticized on a variety of grounds (see expecially Harwood & Vergrugge, 1977; Pollio, Barlow, Fine & Pollio, 1977; Verbrugge, 1977; Verbrugge & McCarrell, 1977), it is possible to argue that as *models* they have provided as strong an approach to predicting metaphoric comprehension for subject populations as any other. (We do, however, recognize that there are certain limitations inherent in feature models for predicting the comprehension of individual metaphors by individual subjects, and suggest that many arguments against feature models are based on these intrinsic limiations—see Johnson & Malgady, this volume, for a discussion of this point.)

We will begin this chapter with more descriptive (less strongly predictive) studies relating similarity, features, and metaphor comprehension, and move toward more quantitatively formal approaches.

COMPREHENDING THE SIMILARITY OF DISSIMILARS

The ubiquity of hypotheses concerning psychological similarity in studies of perception, concept formation, memory, sentence processing, and learning attests to its importance as a central organizing principle in psychological theory (e.g., Tversky, 1977; Verbrugge, 1977). Understanding the cognitive processes involved in comprehension of semantic relationships among linguistic forms has been of particular interest to psycholinguists, dating at least as far back as Osgood, Suci, and Tannenbaum's (1957) pioneering efforts. For the most part, studies of psychological similarity in language have rather surprisingly neglected figurative relationships. Reasons for disinterest in metaphoric speech are speculative, but probably stem from the literary feeling that figures of speech are stylistic ornaments or simply rhetorical devices for embellishing the commonplace in discourse, especially in poetry (Hawkes, 1972). By and large, psycholinguists have failed to acknowledge metaphor as a common aspect of everyday language usage, tending instead to dismiss the phenomenon as a qualitatively distinct linguistic form, or a mere curiosity of human discourse. On the other hand, we believe, along with a growing cadre of psycholinguists interested in metaphoric speech, that the development of theories of semantics cannot be complete without an ultimate account of the role of metaphoric processes in comprehension.

In an effort to relate metaphor to another aspect of language (in this case, association) utilizing a cognitive-feature model (Johnson, 1970), an early study of metaphor interpretation was undertaken by Johnson, Malgady, and Anderson (1974; see also, Johnson & Malgady, 1979) using 28 metaphors and similes compiled from a variety of literary sources (prose and poetry), ranging from Shakespeare to McKuen. Some examples of these literary figures of speech, with the key nominal comparisons (loosely, topic and vehicle) italicized, are shown in Table 10.1.

Correlational studies conducted with these figures of speech supported the claim that both rated and ranked similarity between the tenor and vehicle play an important part in literary metaphor comprehension and appreciation. Generally speaking, college students found metaphors composed of highly similar terms (e.g., *The* snow *this morning was like* confetti, *picked up by the wind.*) easier to interpret and rated them as "better" figures of speech relative to their more obscure counterparts (e.g., *Your* smile *was a warm* wall.). Students' judgments of tenor-vehicle similarity, in turn, were predictable from the number of semantic features (i.e., characteristic properties listed by a norm group) shared by the two terms in a metaphor. The important result here was that topic-vehicle similarity seems to play an important part in metaphor comprehension; and that similarity, in turn, seems to translate into shared properties or features.

In an experimental follow-up study of propositional sentences of the form "A is B," Malgady (1977a) found that tenor-vehicle similarity and the truth value of the proposition asserted in a sentence accurately distinguished literal, figurative, and anomalous sentences. Not surprisingly, sentences judged by college students as literal in meaning (e.g., *Dew is water.*) consisted of terms rated as highly similar in meaning, that were judged also to form a logically true proposition. By comparison, sentences that were judged anomalous, or decidedly impoverished in meaning (e.g., *Dew is a horseradish.*), were rated as containing very dissimilar terms that formed a false proposition. The most significant result of this experiment, however, was that sentences that aroused a figurative or metaphoric sense in the students (e.g., *Dew is a veil.*) compare two concepts that share some resemblance but when juxtaposed form a logically false proposition.

These descriptive studies tend to support the notion that comprehension of a figure of speech involves the perception of similarity. Metaphoric sentences are those in which the tenor and vehicle share a resemblance, much like literal

TABLE 10.1
Examples of Literary Metaphors and Similes Collected by
Johnson et al. (1974)

The *snow* this morning was like white *confetti* picked up by the wind.
Your *smile* was a warm *wall.*
Life is a *tale* told by an idiot.
The *sunshine* on my path was to me as a *friend.*
The *blossoms* in the sweet May wind were falling like *snow.*
The pale *dew* lies like a *veil* on my head.
Now time throws off his *cloak* again of ermined *frost.*
Her *cheeks* were like the *dawn* of day.
The *sun* is a movable *target.*
And the *fever* called *living* is conquered—at last.

sentences. Unlike literal sentences, however, the resemblance is insufficient to create a basis for a "true" proposition at a literal level of understanding. By stretching the truth somewhat, metaphor seems to serve as a linguistic device enabling new or unusual information to be provided about the subject of a communication. It is in this sense that metaphor, and in general figurative usage, is part of the flexibility and creativity inherent in semantic interpretation (Jenkins, 1977; Johnson, 1975).

It should be noted that the notion of "truth value" as used here, should really be thought of as truth value *in context*. A phrase such as *The well was dry* might be judged literally true in a context dealing with oil drilling, but not literally true (and metaphorical) when used to describe someone having trouble writing a term paper. All such judgments take place in context; the presentation of a metaphorical proposition in isolation (as in the above experiment) is not context-free, but, instead, represents only *one* of the many contexts in which the proposition could occur.

Despite the correlational nature of this research, the earlier study provides initial support for the hypothesis that one appreciates a good metaphor at least in part because of the similarity created between two ordinarily dissimilar ideas. Elaborating on this notion, Malgady (1975) demonstrated that judgments of the "figurativeness" of sentences are nonlinearly related to judgments of tenor-vehicle similarity when a broad range of propositions are sampled from a potential anomaly-metaphor-tautology continuum. That is, sentences judged to be "figurative" (e.g., *Robes are justice.*), as opposed to "literal" (e.g., *Robes are garments.*) or "nonsense" (e.g., *Robes are trucks.*), occupy the middle range of the similarity continuum. As similarity increases or decreases (away from this middle range) "figurative" judgments decrease. The most typically metaphoric propositions seem to be those in which the topic and vehicle terms share a moderate degree of similarity, yet are not so transparent as to be trite, nor so remote as to stretch our imagination too far into the realm of impossibility.

What we have here, then, are a series of demonstrations relating judgments of (and about) metaphor to the idea of topic-vehicle similarity, and (very indirectly) the possibility of a featural basis for similarity. In the next, and succeeding, sections we will begin a more formal quantitative exploration of these ideas.

PSYCHOLOGICAL SCALING OF METAPHOR

Accounting for subjective judgments of differences between any pair of metaphoric sentences with respect to a unidimensional attribute (e.g., similarity of the topic to vehicle, or appreciation of figure "goodness") can be expressed as a problem in psychological scaling. Figure 10.1 illustrates a hypothetical scale of figure "goodness," for example, with the arrow denoting an increasing scale toward the right. The metaphors *Love is a season* and *Mountains are kings* are

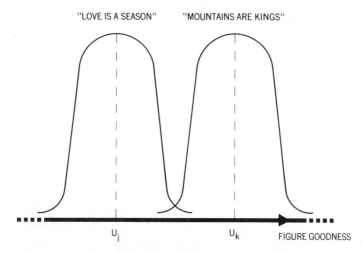

FIG. 10.1.   Hypothetical scale of "figure goodness" illustrating discriminal processes associated with two metaphors, and their characteristic scale values.

characterized on a scale by a distribution of possible values, and an average scale value (μ_j, μ_k) located by the broken vertical line.

The scale distribution of individual subjects' judgments is assumed normal, and portrays a "discriminal process" (Torgerson, 1958) associated with each metaphor, reflecting the relative probability of a given scale value. As Fig. 10.1 suggests, metaphor k is usually preferred to metaphor j.

Thurstone's Law of Comparative Judgment can be used to provide a model for psychological judgments of discriminations among metaphors (see, for example, Coombs, Dawes, & Tversky, 1970; Torgerson, 1958):

$$\mu_k - \mu_j = \zeta_{kj}(\sigma_j^2 + \sigma_k^2 - 2\rho_{jk}\sigma_j\sigma_k)^{\frac{1}{2}}, \tag{1}$$

where ($\mu_k - \mu_j$) is the psychological distance between metaphors j and k on the unidimensional scale; ζ_{kj} is the normal deviate transform of the probability that k is judged as a better figurative comparison than j; and the σ's and ρ_{jk} refer to the standard deviations of and correlations between discriminal processes associated with j and k.

Unfortunately, since in the general case of scaling n metaphors there are more unknown parameters than there are observable equations, the complete form of the Law of Comparative Judgment (Equation [1]) is unsolvable empirically. Therefore, one conventional solution is to assume that the term within the radical in Equation (1) is constant for all possible pairs of stimuli (metaphors). Thus, utilizing this common convention and setting this constant arbitrarily equal to unity, Equation (1) reduces to:

$$\mu_k - \mu_j = \zeta_{kj}, \tag{2}$$

which is solvable empirically as Thurstone's Case V of the Law of Comparative Judgment (Torgerson, 1958).

Measurement of metaphors j and k on a unidimensional interval scale of figure goodness (or, alternately, tenor-vehicle similarity) is possible if it can be shown that preference judgments satisfy the axioms of transitivity and consistency. In a set of n metaphors, $\mu_k > \mu_j$ and $\mu_j > \mu_i$ implies $\mu_k > \mu_i$ for all i, j, and k within the set. A significance test that the consistency of this order relation exceeds chance is provided by Mosteller (1951).

Using the model of paired comparisons in Equation (2), Malgady and Johnson (1976; Malgady, 1976) conducted psychological scaling studies for the purpose of (1) accounting for subjectively perceived differences in figurative meaning of metaphors by development of fundamental scales of tenor-vehicle similarity and figure goodness; (2) investigating the relationship between tenor-vehicle similarity and figure goodness scales; and (3) testing several hypotheses, using the scaling model, arising from a semantic feature model of figurative language comprehension.

An experiment carried out by Malgady (1976) confirmed the relationship between psychological scales derived from similarity and goodness judgments, and provided support for a semantic feature interpretation of metaphor processing. A set of 54 metaphors were constructed for the tenor "Moon," in which the number of semantic features shared by the tenor and vehicle was varied experimentally. Results of the experiment indicated that judgments of similarity and goodness were enhanced by an increase in semantic features shared by the tenor and vehicle, which were (1) explicitly cued by adjectives (e.g., *The moon is a round white pearl* > *The moon is a round pearl*) and (2) implicit in the tenor-vehicle relationship (e.g., *The moon is a pearl* > *The moon is a platter*).

Subsequently, Malgady and Johnson (1976) investigated a semantic feature interpretation of the effects of different sentence contexts on metaphor interpretation. Based on Johnson's (1970) cognitive feature model, which equates interword similarity with the size of the overlap or intersection of feature sets associated with each word, we predicted that contexts that increase the number of semantic features shared by the tenor and vehicle should enhance their metaphoric comparison (via increased similarity), and therefore create "better" figures of speech. One postulate of Johnson's (1970) model is the the addition of an adjective modifier to a noun will increase the strength or salience of the features shared by the adjective and noun in the feature set associated with the meaning of the adjective-noun compound. According to this model, the meaning of an adjective-noun, or noun-noun combination (as in a simple metaphor) is the overlap or intersection of the feature sets of the individual words. If one constructs a simple "Noun A is noun B" metaphor, and adds a modifier to each noun (yielding "Modifier X-noun A is modifier Y-noun B"), the meaning of the metaphor will be the overlap between the feature set associated with the modifier X-noun A compound and that associated with the modifier Y-noun B compound.

If the modifiers (X and Y) both share features with (are appropriate to) both nouns (A and B) the resulting compound—in set theoretic notation, $(X \cap A) \cap (Y \cap B)$—will have a relatively large overlap, be high in "similarity" (by definition, according to the model), and produce a "good" metaphor (based on our previous findings relating similarity and goodness). In order to test this hypothesis experimentally we constructed differend types of adjective-noun relationships, which seemed likely to create variations in the meaning of the nouns compared as tenor and vehicle in literary metaphors (see Table 10.1).

Five metaphoric versions of each of 12 comparisons among nouns were generated by the following algorithm. Simple metaphors of the form "Noun A is noun B" were embedded in adjective contexts that emphasized semantic features shared by both nouns (e.g., *High mountains are mighty Kings*), distinctive features of the tenor and vehicle separately (e.g., *Smoky mountains are noble kings*), or features unrelated to the two nouns (e.g., *Fragile mountains are striped kings*). These adjectives were determined by norms provided by a group of college students. A description of the five versions of each metaphor and some examples of each are illustrated in Table 10.2.

In the first part of the experiment, 56 college students made paired comparisons among the five versions of each metaphor with respect to their goodness as figures of speech. In the second part of the study, an independent group of 56 students judged the similarity of the concepts compared in the metaphors (e.g., "old schoolhouses—poor beggars" versus "ragged schoolhouses—red beggars") without their sentence metaphoric context. Metaphors were scaled accord-

TABLE 10.2
Description of Modification Conditions in the Malgady and Johnson
(1976) Experiment

Modification Condition	Examples
1. Tenor and vehicle modified by adjectives cuing features shared by both nouns	Old schoolhouses are poor beggars. High mountains are mighty kings. Soft hair is shiny silk.
2. Tenor and vehicle modified by adjectives cuing distinctive features of each noun	Red schoolhouses are ragged beggars. Smoky mountains are noble kings. Long hair is elegant silk.
3. Tenor and vehicle modified by adjectives cuing distinctive features of opposing nouns	Ragged schoolhouses are red beggars. Noble mountains are smoky kings. Elegant hair is long silk.
4. Tenor and vehicle modified by adjectives cuing features unrelated to either noun	Curly schoolhouses are sour beggars. Fragile mountains are striped kings. Distant hair is fatal silk.
5. Tenor and vehicle unmodified	Schoolhouses are beggars. Mountains are kings. Hair is silk.

ing to Equation (2) to establish interval scales of tenor-vehicle similarity and figure goodness across the various modification contexts in Table 10.2.

Results of this study indicated that internally consistent (transitive) measurement of the two psychological attributes was possible; moreover, the scaled positions of the five modified versions of the metaphors confirmed the prediction of Johnson's (1970) cognitive feature model. Adjectives that emphasized features shared by both nouns in a metaphor created the most similar concepts and the "best" metaphoric comparisons of tenor and vehicle. Modification by adjectives unrelated to the tenor and vehicle impaired similarity and goodness judgments relative to unmodified metaphors, presumably because irrelevant information about the comparisons was not integrated in the feature overlap defining the meaning of the metaphor. These so-called metaphors seemed to border on what most might regard as anomaly (e.g., *Gay towers are brave necks.*); nevertheless, some persistent students were able to imagine rather creative interpretations of these metaphors. This is consistent with the finding (Hoffman, 1977; Johnson, 1975; Pollio & Burns, 1977) that people *can* interpret anything.

Emphasis of distinctive features of the tenor and vehicle ([2] in Table 10.2) tended to create more similar concepts and better metaphors than when opposing features of the nouns were emphasized (3). Thus, in a more general sense than Johnson (1970) originally proposed, the juxtaposition of an adjective and a noun serves to cue, or make more salient, certain semantic features representing the meaning of the unmodified noun. In a metaphoric context, adjectives (and, certainly other aspects of sentence context) constrain the possible meanings of the tenor and vehicle by reorganizing the nouns' semantic feature representations in cognition. In short, semantic feature models must also explain how distinctive features of the tenor and vehicle, as well as common features, are processed in metaphor comprehension.

The influence of perceived similarity on appreciation judgments was attenuated in this study by the degree to which the tenor and vehicle were judged as similar in the absence of a metaphoric context (similarity judgments were made in the absence of sentence context). The correlation between similarity and goodness scales dropped from .87 to .42 when nonmetaphoric similarity estimates were controlled statistically. Goodness-of-fit of Equation (2) to the subjective judgments suggested that appreciating a metaphoric comparison is probably a unidimensional process when the basis for a metaphoric comparison is remote. On the other hand, a unidimensional model was somewhat less representative of appreciation judgments for less esoteric metaphors. Taken together, the attenuated similarity-goodness correlation and the discrepancy in fitting Equation (2) to the empirical data suggest that factors other than tenor-vehicle similarity (e.g., imagery, pleasantness) may influence comprehension of rather obvious metaphoric comparisons, whereas individuals focus primarily on detecting similarity when the metaphor is less intuitive.

The studies summarized in this section seem to show that metaphor goodness and similarity judgments are scaleable, that these scales are correlated with each other, and that experimental manipulation of metaphor similarity produces corresponding changes in goodness judgments. They also show that these results are consistent with a cognitive feature model of similarity. We now turn to an examination of predictions made by a more recent and more detailed theory of similarity based on features, and the implications of this model for understanding metaphor. This model is unique in that it can deal with the problem of metaphor asymmetry (i.e., "A is B" is not the same as "B is A"), which has been a thorn in the side of feature models of metaphor (Harwood & Verbrugge, 1977; Verbrugge & McCarrell, 1977).

ASYMMETRIES IN UNDERSTANDING AND JUDGING METAPHORS IN CONTEXT

A Contrast Model of Similarity Judgment

Amos Tversky (1977) recently proposed a linear contrast model of similarity judgment, which is based on a cognitive feature-matching process similar in some respects to Johnson's (1970), but considerably more detailed. This portion of the chapter summarizes Tversky's (1977) theoretical position, and extends his model to prediction of (1) asymmetry in comprehension of metaphors, and (2) effects of a variety of sentence contexts upon comprehension and appreciation of similes. Readers interested in a complete development of the mathematical assumptions underlying the contrast model are referred to the original source.

Symbolically, let some metaphor ($\triangle$) be represented by the tenor and vehicle (a, b), so $\triangle = \{a,b\}$. Further, let A and B represent the feature sets (semantic characteristics) that define the tenor and vehicle, respectively. According to Tversky's (1977) contrast model, similarity (S) between the tenor and vehicle is expressed as a weighted linear function of the salience (f) of their common and distinctive features:

$$S(a,b) = \theta f(A \cap B) - \alpha f(A - B) - \beta f(B - A), \qquad (3)$$

where $f(A \cap B)$, $f(A - B)$, and $f(B - A)$ are measures of the salience or information value of features shared by a and b, unique to a, and unique to b, respectively; $\psi = (\theta, \alpha, \beta)$ is defined as a set of contrast parameters or weights, such that $(\theta, \alpha, \beta) \geq 0$; and it is assumed that f and S are interval scales of feature salience and similarity.

Figure 2a illustrates the definition of common and distinctive features in Tversky's (1977) theory using Venn diagrams. Figure 2b also illustrates that an open feature set is assumed to characterize a and b, and by implication any partitioning of a and b. Thus, we introduce the additional assumptions that (1) semantic features may be more or less representative of word meaning, depending on the context in which the word is uttered; (2) meaning cannot be defined by an exhaustive list of semantic features since the set is open-ended; and (3) by studying meaning with respect to a normative reference, we generalize (albeit not without error) to ipsative reference. Thus, we acknowledge that the "momentary" or situational meaning of a word is a function of the linguistic and extralinguistic context, as well as individual differences (e.g., memory, knowl-

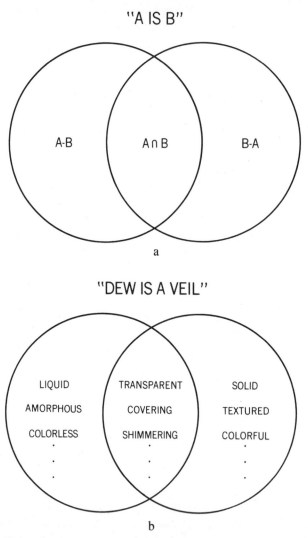

FIG. 10.2.   (a) Venn Diagram illustration of common and distinctive feature sets for the symbolic metaphor "A is B."   (b) Venn Diagram illustration of the partition of open feature sets for the metaphoric example *Dew is a veil.*

edge of the lexicon), in which it occurs in a speech act (see Johnson & Malgady, this volume).

In Tversky's (1977) application of the contrast model to psychological similarity judgments, average feature salience was computed from properties or attributes of stimuli listed by a norm group of college students, and an interval level of measurement was assumed. In the present application of the contrast model to semantic judgments about metaphors and similes, we represented feature salience in terms of the average information value or psychological uncertainty of the tenor and of the vehicle, also based on the responses of a norm group (see Garner, 1962; Johnson, 1970; Johnson et al. 1974; Malgady & Johnson, 1976). The amount of informational uncertainty in feature set A, for example, is a function of the n semantic features defining the meaning of a in a normative reference. Accordingly, the number of "bits" of informational uncertainty (U) in $A = \{a_1, a_2, \ldots, a_n\}$ is defined by Garner (1962) as:

$$U(A) = - \sum_{i=1}^{n} p(a_i)\log_2 p(a_i), \tag{4}$$

where $p(a_i)$ denotes the probability in the normative population of the ith feature in A, or the relative frequency of a property listed by a group of individuals. When the meaning of a is defined by the semantic feature set A (a list of n semantic properties), a normalized measure of feature salience is:

$$f(A) = \frac{-U(A)}{\log_2 n}. \tag{5}$$

In the extremes, $f(A) = 1$ if $p(a_i) = p(a_j)$ for all i and j in A; and $f(A) = 0$ if $A = \{a_1\}$, since $U(A) = 0$. In other words, a summary measure of feature salience is influenced by the number and probability of semantic features in a normative sample, recognizing, of course, that salience varies across individuals. Salience increases as the number of defining features increase, and as their probabilities approach a rectangular distribution.

Asymmetry in Similarity Judgments and Recall

Perhaps one of the most interesting examples of language "flexibility" is achieved when metaphors are reversed. Often, a metaphor is perfectly sensible stated in one direction (e.g., *The man is a wolf.*), but its converse is nonsensical (e.g., *The wolf is a man.*). Other times, meanings can be reversed, as in the case of *The lion is a lamb,* which stresses the docile nature of a seemingly ferocious beast, versus *The lamb is a lion,* which depicts the aggressive nature of a usually tame creature.

Tversky (1977) was able to show that such asymmetry in judging the similarities between pairs of countries, geometric figures, letters, and signals was predictable from his contrast model. On a directional task, such as metaphor interpretation, Tversky (1977) hypothesized that there is a tendency to focus attention on the subject of a comparison (i.e., the tenor), thereby weighting its features more than the referent's (i.e., the vehicle's). Since the number of features common to a and b is constant regardless of their order in this model, asymmetry in judging the similarity of a to b or b to a is a function of *distinctive* features. Asymmetry is defined formally as $S(a,b) \neq S(b,a)$ if $\alpha \neq \beta$ and $f(A) \neq f(B)$. Tversky's (1977) "focusing" hypothesis predicts, therefore, when $\alpha > \beta$, $S(a,b) > S(b,a)$ if $f(A) < f(B)$. In other words, if the vehicle is more salient than the tenor, focusing on the tenor suggests that tenor to vehicle similarity will exceed vehicle to tenor similarity, because fewer distinctive features are emphasized in the former order (see Equation [3]). For example, subjects will judge Poland to be more similar to the U.S.S.R. than the U.S.S.R. to Poland (Tversky, 1977), because of the higher salience of the U.S.S.R.

The first experiment we conducted attempted to assess the suitability of the contrast model (and simultaneously its concomitant assumptions) for predicting asymmetry of tenor-vehicle similarity judgments on a metaphor interpretation task, and also free recall of the metaphors and their reversals. Based on Equation (3), Tversky's model predicts that tenor-vehicle similarity and free recall of metaphors should be greater when the vehicle is more salient than the tenor. To test this hypothesis, we collected a set of 12 noun pairs (from literary metaphors) differing in salience, as defined by the application of Equation (5) to semantic properties of the nouns listed by a norm group of college students. We asked these subjects to simply list as many adjectival properties as possible for each of the 24 nouns, resulting in open-ended sets or distributions of properties. The informational uncertainty measure (U) (Garner, 1962) was then calculated for each of these distributions. Since U is sensitive to the total number of responses in the distribution (which varied, since they were open-ended), these values were normalized by dividing by the maximum possible U, or $\log_2 N$. The two nouns in each pair were classified as either high or low in salience, as is shown in Table 10.3. (Before going on, the reader might try these high/low salience pairs as metaphors in both directions.) Nouns in the low salience classification ranged in value from .122 to .361 (mean = .266), while high salience nouns ranged from .423 to .581 (mean = .509). Two metaphors were constructed from each noun pair by reversing the order of the two terms in sentences of the form "A is B." In one presentation order (low → high salience), the 12 noun pairs were arranged such that the highly salient noun appeared as the vehicle and the less salient noun appeared as the tenor. In the second presentation order (high → low salience), the syntactic position of the two nouns was reversed.

One group of 20 college students was presented the entire set of 12 pairs of metaphors and, after interpreting the metaphors, made directional judgments of the similarity of the tenor to the vehicle. Students decided in which order the

TABLE 10.3
Noun Pairs in Asymmetry Experiment

Low Salience	High Salience
Frost	Cloak
Love	Season
Living	Fever
Memories	Garments
Holidays	Signposts
Moons	Kites
Smiles	Walls
Mountains	Kings
Snow	Confetti
Neck	Tower
Voices	Waves
Rain	Tears

similarity of the "first term to the second term" was maximum for each pair of metaphors. Metaphors were presented in a different random sequence to each student, and the sequence of the two presentation orders was counterbalanced.

In the memory study, two independent groups of 12 college students studied a list of 12 metaphors consisting of different noun pairs, half with each presentation order. Three filler metaphors were included at the beginning and end of each list to control primacy and recency effects. Each student studied a different list of metaphors for five seconds per metaphor, and a two-minute interval separated the acquisition and recall phases of the experiment. In the recall phase, students wrote down as many of the metaphors in the study lists as they could remember.

Tenor-vehicle similarity judgments were made via paired comparisons, and similarity was measured by the proportion of students choosing one metaphor in a pair over its counterpart. Recall was measured as the proportion of subjects correctly recalling the nouns in a metaphor. Individual responses were scored as "2," if both nouns were recalled in correct syntactic order, as "1," if only one noun was recalled in its study position, or "0" otherwise.

Results of the study are summarized in Table 10.4, which indicates mean similarity and recall of the metaphors as a function of the two presentation orders. Table 10.4 also shows the goodness-of-fit of values predicted by the model $(f(B) - f(A))$ to the magnitude of asymmetries in similarity judgments and free recall. Statistical analyses indicated a highly significant correlation between predicted and obtained values in both cases ($p < .001$), with substantially greater values indicated when the tenor was least salient—as predicted by Tversky's model.

Tversky's focusing and asymmetry hypotheses were confirmed as the low → high presentation order was preferred nearly 70% of the time in similarity judgments, and about half of the variance in asymmetry was predictable from the

TABLE 10.4
Mean Asymmetry of Similarity Judgments and Free
Recall, and Goodness-of-fit of Contrast Model to the Data

| | Tenor $\rightarrow$ Vehicle Salience | | |
Variable	Low $\rightarrow$ High	High $\rightarrow$ Low	Fit (r)
Similarity	.69	.31	.68***
Recall	.39	.24	.84***

***$p < .001$

contrast model. Recall was also superior in the low $\rightarrow$ high order of presentation as predicted by the focusing hypothesis, and almost three-fourths of the variance in asymmetry was accounted for by the model. Another interesting outcome of the study was that the majority of students (about 73%) also reported that the metaphors were easier to comprehend when the tenor was less salient than the vehicle, supporting Johnson and Malgady's (1979) finding of a strong relationship between metaphor similarity and interpretability.

Parameter Estimation and Judging Metaphors in Context

Our second experiment was designed to investigate the suitability of Tversky's (1977) linear contrast model for predicting contextual effects on judgments of tenor-vehicle similarity and "figurativeness" of similes. Another purpose of the experiment was to compare several versions of the focusing hypothesis (parameter estimates of ψ) for processing semantic information in similes.

Six noun pairs, compiled from the same source as the first experiment, were used to construct similes of the form "A is like B." The more salient noun always appeared as the vehicle in these similes. Each of the six similes was then embedded in each of six different contextual conditions, as is described in Table 10.5 along with some illustrative examples. Table 10.5 denotes the effects of adjectives (*Adj*) and verbs (*V*) as increasing the salience of either common, tenor-distinctive, or vehicle-distinctive features. Adjectives and verbs were so designated on the basis of their relationship to the tenor and vehicle as suggested by consensus of a norm group. For example, in the first instance (see Table 10.5), the adjective "flowing" cues features shared by both "blood" and "rain," hence its effect is denoted symbolically as $Adj(A \cap B)$. In the third instance, by comparison, the adjective "red" cues a distinctive feature of "blood," which is unrelated to the vehicle "rain," hence the denotation Adj (A − B). The numerical scheme used to represent the various contextual versions of each simile is also shown in Table 10.5. Of course, any test of the contrast model is simultaneously a test of this particular set of assumptions about sentence context.

Two groups of 25 college students compared the six versions of each simile with respect to a single attribute. One group judged tenor-vehicle similarity without specific instructions to employ a directional strategy, whereas the second group judged the degree of "figurativeness" of the similes. "Figurativeness" was defined for subjects by contrasting a highly figurative example (Malgady, 1976) with examples of literal and anomalous propositions. No explicit definition of figurativeness was given, other than that implicit in the contrast. Similes were presented in a different random order to each student.

Similes were scaled according to Equation (2) to develop interval level scales of tenor-vehicle similarity and figurativeness. Results of the Mosteller (1951) test confirmed that students were significantly transitive and consistent in their judgments, thus supporting the assumptions of unidimensionality and interval measurement scales.

Four different focusing hypotheses were formulated, as is described in Table 10.6. Model I assumes that only common features are processed in understanding similes, and distinctive features are de-emphasized (cf. Johnson, 1970; Johnson et al., 1974; Restle, 1961). Model II is a version of the focusing hypothesis that assumes that individuals focus on common features, but distinctive features are equally weighted (as on a nondirectional task). Model III assumes focusing on common features, and that distinctive features of the tenor dominate distinctive features of the vehicle (cf. Tversky, 1977). Finally, no assumptions were made

TABLE 10.5
Description of Context Experiment

Contextual Conditions	Effect on Feature Salience			
Adjective Verb	$f(A \cap B)$	$f(A-B)$	$f(B-A)$	Examples
1. Adj $(A \cap B)$ $V(A \cap B)$	2	0	0	Flowing blood pours like rain. White snow falls like confetti.
2. Adj $(A \cap B)$ Copula	1	0	0	Flowing blood is like rain. White snow is like confetti.
3. Adj $(A-B)$ $V(A \cap B)$	1	1	0	Red blood pours like rain. Soft snow falls like confetti.
4. Adj $(A-B)$ Copula	0	1	0	Red blood is like rain. Soft snow is like confetti.
5. Adj $(B-A)$ $V(A \cap B)$	1	0	1	Blood pours like cloudy rain. Snow falls like paper confetti.
6. Adj $(B-A)$ Copula	0	0	1	Blood is like cloudy rain. Snow is like paper confetti.

Note: The syntactic position of adjectives in (1) and (2) was counterbalanced. The scheme assumes that adjectives and verbs emphasize semantic features equally.

TABLE 10.6
Linear Contrast Models, Parameter Estimates, and Goodness-of-Fit
to Similarity and Figurativeness Judgments

Model	Parameter Description	$\psi = (\theta \quad \alpha \quad \beta)$ $\psi' = (\theta' \quad \alpha' \quad \beta')$		Goodness-of-fit	
				r_s	r_f
I.	$\theta = 1 \quad \alpha = \beta = 0$	$\psi\ = (1 \quad 0 \quad 0)$		.575**	.466
		$\psi' = (1 \quad 0 \quad 0)$			
II.	$\theta > (\alpha,\beta); (\theta, \alpha, \beta) > 0$	$\psi\ = (2 \quad 1 \quad 1)$		.564**	.433
		$\psi' = (.82 \quad .41 \quad .41)$			
III.	$\theta > \alpha > \beta \quad (\theta, \alpha, \beta) > 0$	$\psi\ = (3 \quad 2 \quad 1)$		.611**	.480*
		$\psi' = (.80 \quad .53 \quad .27)$			
IV.	Least-squares Estimates	$\psi_s\ = (.57 \quad .21 \quad .19)$		.622**	—
		$\psi'_s = (.90 \quad .33 \quad .29)$			
		$\psi_f\ = (.46 \quad .17 \quad .22)$		—	.599**
		$\psi'_f = (.86 \quad .32 \quad .41)$			

Note: ψ' is the normalized set of parameter estimates (unit length); the subscripts (s) and (f) denote similarity and figurativeness; $*p < .05$ and $**p < .01$.

about order relations among Model IV parameters, which were estimated empirically contingent on a least-squares criterion.

The numerical parameters of the four versions of ψ are presented in Table 10.6; however, models were reparameterized for meaningful comparisons among models such that ψ' was scaled to unit length. Goodness-of-fit of each model to the similarity and figurativeness judgments was evaluated by correlating similarity and figurativeness scale values calculated from experimental data with corresponding values predicted by the models.

Results of the goodness-of-fit tests suggests that although all four models predict tenor-vehicle similarity judgments significantly, Models I and II are inadequate representations of figure appreciation judgments (see Table 10.6). The fact that Model II offers the poorest fit to either similarity or figurativeness scales supports the directional nature of the judgment tasks. Least-squares parameter estimates provided a substantially better fit to figurativeness judgments relative to the three alternate models, and fit the similarity data about as well as Model III (Tversky's hypothesis), and somewhat better than Model I, which does not provide an account of distinctive features.

Comparison of normalized parameter estimates (ψ') shows that for similarity judgments, the order relation $\theta' > \alpha' > \beta'$ is consistent in the least-squares and Model III solutions, the primary distinction being that the $(\alpha' - \beta')$ difference is slightly exaggerated in Model III. Comparison of figurativeness order relations among parameters suggests quite a different outcome, as least-squares estimates were ordered $\theta' > \beta' > \alpha'$. This order relation implies that in processing the figurativeness dimension, individuals lend greater attention to the distinctive features of the *vehicle,* contrary to Tversky's (1977) expectation. A recent unpublished study by Harwood and Verbrugge (1977) reports a similar finding from a similarity judgment experiment, leading them to question Tversky's (1977) assertion that the first term is the focus of a directional judgment task.

Results of these two experiments concerning similarity judgments in metaphoric contexts corroborated Tversky's (1977) findings; but application of the contrast model to appreciation judgments requires clarification. Focusing on the tenor was not confirmed for figure appreciation judgments, but this does not necessarily impugn the contrast model, merely the generalizability of Tversky's (1977) particular account of a focusing hypothesis. In fact, this finding may be further evidence that some incompatibility of distinctive feature sets is essential to the recognition of figurative meaning (cf. Malgady, 1977a).

SOME CONCLUDING REMARKS

The psychological research discussed in this chapter provides a strong argument in favor of the classical proposal that (judgments of) similarity between tenor and vehicle, whether created by a novel metaphoric juxtaposition or simply dredged up from pre-existing meanings, is closely related to the understanding of metaphoric meaning. Experimental research also presents a case for the conclusion that metaphors are successful, in the sense that one understands and appreciates their purpose, to the extent that the semantic relationship drawn between remote concepts is neither too bizarre nor overly mundane.

The paired comparison model in Equation (2) provides a useful and theoretically meaningful measure of unidimensional attributes of metaphoric meaning. Nevertheless, as we implied earlier, it might also be fruitful to compare undimensional and multidimensional measurement models. In a recent developmental study of metaphor interpretation and appreciation, Malgady (1977b) concluded that as adolescents acquire the cognitive sophistication of formal operations, the transitivity of metaphoric judgments based on a unidimensional model was less consistent compared to semantic judgments of less sophisticated children. Further, Malgady (1977b) argued that formal operational children approach the paired comparison task essentially as an implied proportion problem. Thus, one determines whether metaphor "A is B" is a better figurative comparisons that metaphor "C is D" by creating the symbolic proportion (A : B :: C : D), and solving the problem in terms of similarity of component terms. This interpretation of the paired comparison task bears a resemblance to the growing interest in representing adult understanding of metaphor as a four-term analogy problem (e.g., Honeck, Voegtle, & Sowry, in press; Harwood & Verbrugge, 1977).

The Aristotelian perspective, that interpretation of a metaphoric utterance is possible because of some sort of semantic "transfer" of meaning from vehicle to tenor, is especially popular among modern day theorists embracing a semantic feature approach to language comprehension. Smith, Shoben, and Rips (1974), for example, proposed that the features of the vehicle in a metaphor are transferred to the tenor; and although semantic transfer risks contradiction of a literal level of understanding, a metaphorical reading of the tenor is construed as transfer features (i.e., certain vehicle-distinctive features) are increased in definingness. Similarly, Weinreich's (1966) formal account of metaphor in linguistic theory includes a discussion of transfer features, which are instrumental in the process of construing a nonliteral meaning. Malgady (1975) also proposed a feature-synthesis model of metaphor interpretation, wherein features of the tenor and vehicle are integrated into a single feature set, some elements of which differ in information value or definitiveness.

The semantic feature approach is often contrasted with associative network models of language comprehension, which depict meaning by interconnecting paths of semantic relationships in a semantic "space." One outstanding problem of network models, such as those proposed by Collins and Quillian (1972) and Norman and Rummelhart (1975), is the difficulty they encounter in explaining asymmetries in semantic relationships. These types of models are particular suited to a metric distance interpretation of psychological similarity—perceived similarity is an inverse function of the Euclidean distance between concepts in an n-dimensionally organized semantic space. Tversky (1977) provides a convincing argument for the untenability of the assumptions of a metric distance function for semantic judgments; most notably, the assumption of symmetry of similarity judgments is difficult to verify empirically.

Tversky's (1977) contrast model defined in Equation (3) is an attractive theory of metaphor comprehension for a number of reasons: (1) its conceptual simplicity; (2) adaptability to a wide variety of psychological phenomena; (3) relatively few strong assumptions; and (4) flexibility of order relations on the parameters of the model. The ultimate test of the model is the extent that it predicts behavior better than competing models, however.

Despite the fact that virtually all semantic feature approaches described in this chapter share a concern with semantic properties common to both concepts compared in a metaphor, the various models assign different roles to distinctive features of the tenor and vehicle. Some models assume a focus on the tenor (e.g., Malgady, 1975; Tversky, 1977), some argue that distinctive features of the vehicle are more salient (e.g., Harwood & Verbrugge, 1977; Smith et al., 1974), while others discount distinctive features entirely (e.g., Johnson, 1970; Johnson et al., 1974). One reason for inconsistencies across experiments and theoretical models is that some metaphors may serve different purposes, depending on whether common, tenor-distinctive, or vehicle-distinctive features are emphasized. Unfortunately, it is difficult to reconcile a functional account of metaphor interpretation without recourse to such "fuzzy" considerations as the speaker's intention in uttering a metaphor, or conversely, the listener's inference.

Ortony (1977) has suggested that one type of metaphor activates a recognition of existing similarities between concepts, while a second type leads to the discovery of novel similarities. In the former case, meaning is apprehended through feature selection, and in the latter case through feature rejection. Still, other types of metaphors seem to accentuate contrasting features of the tenor and vehicle (e.g., *The lion is a lamb.*), which leads to oxymoron in the extreme case (e.g., *the thundering silence . . .*). Arguing in the linguistic tradition from examples such as these, one can conjure up metaphors that are explicable in some theories, but not others (and vice versa). Nevertheless, a major attraction of Tversky's (1977) theory is that the general model defines a family of contrast equations, suited to a variety of types of metaphors and behavioral tasks, where the contrast parameters are not contextually or situationally invariant.

REFERENCES

Collins, A. M., & Quillian, M. R. How to make a language user. In E. Tulving & W. Donaldson (Eds.), *The organization of memory.* New York: Academic Press, 1972.

Coombs, C. H., Dawes, R. M., & Tversky, A. *Mathematical psychology.* Englewood Cliffs, N.J.: Prentice-Hall, 1970.

Garner, W. R. *Uncertainty and structure as psychological concepts.* New York: Wiley, 1962.

Harwood, D. L., & Verbrugge, R. R. *Metaphor and the asymmetry of similarity.* Paper presented at the meeting of the American Psychological Association. San Francisco, August, 1977.

Hawkes, T. *Metaphor.* London: Methuen, 1972.

Hoffman, R. R. *Conceptual base hypotheses and the problem of anomalous sentences.* Paper presented at the annual meetings of the American Psychological Association, San Francisco, California, August, 1977.

Honeck, R. P., Voegtle, K., & Sowry, B. M. Figurative understanding of pictures and sentences. *Journal of Psycholinguistic Research,* in press.

Jenkins, J. J. *Context conditions meaning.* Invited paper presented at the annual meetings of the Midwestern Psychological Association, Chicago, Illinois, May, 1977.

Johnson, M. G. A cognitive-feature model of compound free associations. *Psychological Review,* 1970, 77, 282–293.

Johnson, M. G. Some psychological implications of language flexibility. *Behaviorism,* 1975, 3, 87–95.

Johnson, M. G., & Malgady, R. G. Some cognitive aspects of figurative language: Association and metaphor. *Journal of Psycholinguistic Research,* 1979, 8, 249–266.

Johnson, M. G., Malgady, R. G., & Anderson, S. *Some cognitive aspects of metaphor interpretation.* Paper presented at the meeting of the Psychonomic Society, Boston, November, 1974.

Malgady, R. G. *A feature synthesis model of metaphor processing.* Unpublished doctoral dissertation. University of Tennessee, 1975.

Malgady, R. G. Category size, feature comparison, and comprehension of figurative propositions. *Perceptual and Motor Skills,* 1976, 42, 811–818.

Malgady, R. G. Discriminant analysis of psychological judgments of literal and figurativeness meaningfulness versus anomaly. *Journal of Psychology,* 1977, 95, 217–221. (a)

Malgady, R. G. Children's interpretation and appreciation of similes. *Child Development,* 1977, 48, 1734–1738. (b)

Malgady, R. G., & Johnson, M. G. Modifiers in metaphors: Effects of constituent phrase similarity on the interpretation of figurative sentences. *Journal of Psycholinguistic Research,* 1976, *5,* 43–52.

Mosteller, F. Remarks on the method of paired comparisons. III. A test of significance for paired comparisons when equal standard deviations and equal correlations are assumed. *Psychometrika,* 1951, *16,* 207–218.

Neisser, U. *Cognitive Psychology.* New York: Appleton-Century, 1967.

Norman, D. A., & Rummelhart. D. E. *Explorations in cognition.* San Francisco: Freeman, 1975.

Ortony, A. *Reply to Paivio.* Conference on metaphor and thought, Urbana-Champaign, September, 1977.

Osgood, C. E., Suci, G. J., & Tannenbaum, P. H. *The measurement of meaning.* Urbana: The University of Illinois Press, 1957.

Pollio, H. R., Barlow, J. M., Fine, H. J., & Pollio, M. R. *Psychology and the poetics of growth.* Hillsdale, N. J.: Lawrence Erlbaum Associates, 1977.

Pollio, H. R., & Burns, B. C. The anomaly of anomaly. *Journal of Psycholinguistic Research,* 1977, *6,* 247–260.

Restle, F. *Psychology of judgment and choice.* New York: Wiley, 1961.

Smith, E. E., Shoben, E. J., & Rips, L. Structure and process in semantic memory: A feature comparison model for semantic decisions. *Psychological Review,* 1974, *81,* 214–241.

Steinberg, D. & Jakobovits, L. *Semantics.* New York: Prentice-Hall, 1971.

Torgerson, W. S. *Theory and methods of scaling.* New York: Wiley, 1958.

Tversky, A. Features of similarity. *Psychological Review,* 1977, *84,* 327–352.

Verbrugge, R. Resemblances in language and perception. In R. E. Shaw & J. D. Bransford (Eds.), *Perceiving, acting, and knowing: Toward an ecological psychology.* Hillsdale, N.J.: Lawrence Erlbaum Associates, 1977.

Verbrugge, R., & McCarrell, N. Metaphoric comprehension: Studies in reminding and resembling. *Cognitive Psychology,* 1977, *9,* 494–533.

Weinreich, U. Explorations in semantic theory. In T. Sebeok (Ed.), *Current trends in linguistics, Vol. 3: Theoretical Foundations.* The Hague: Mouton, 1966.

11 Toward a Perceptual Theory of Metaphoric Comprehension

Michael G. Johnson
The University of Tennessee

Robert G. Malgady
New York University

INTRODUCTION

There are a good many reasons why psychologists are becoming increasingly interested in metaphor—an interest that has generated a large number of articles, books, and even conferences, in the past few years. Among these various concerns there are two that seem especially important. These are, first, the notion that metaphor is not so much a deviant (though interesting) oddity as it is a prototype or paradigm for language-related cognitive activity in general; and, second, the idea that metaphor provides one of the most intriguing avenues for exploring an oft-hypothesized connection between language and perception. Although these conjectures are by no means universally accepted, a prima facie case can be made for both of them, and they form the central motifs around which the investigations reported in this chapter are organized.

The impression that metaphor is somehow special, deviant, anomalous, or different from normal language forms is a pervasive one and is strongly reinforced in two ways. First, and perhaps most important in recent times, have been the difficulties encountered by language theorists in fitting metaphoric language into the mainstream of formal grammars or machine models of language processing. The linguistic tradition since Katz and Fodor (1963) has been to treat metaphor as a deviant phenomenon to be either ignored or incorporated into linguistic theory via "special" rules (e.g., Bickerton, 1969; Weinreich, 1966). The second, more pervasive but perhaps less explicit, influence has been the traditional association of metaphor with special language-based art forms such as poetry and drama.

Although the metaphor-as-special tradition is a seductive one, and especially so to those interested in formal representation of language, there seems to be a growing realization that psychological and linguistic theory ought to *accomodate* to the fact of metaphor, rather than insist on the *assimilation* of metaphor to current state-of-the-art formalizations. One source for this attitude has been the realization that metaphor is not a low-frequency phenomenon in ordinary discourse, but is a dominant component in the language that everyone uses (Johnson, 1975a; Pollio, Barlow, Fine & Pollio, 1977). There is evidence that metaphoric language is utilized early in the development of language in children (e.g., Gardner, Kircher, Winner, & Perkins, 1975) and that, if anything, metaphoric usage actually declines in frequency as language development advances (Pollio et al., 1977). Given the frequency of metaphor production (estimated at approximately five metaphors per one hundred words of ordinary discourse as an average, Johnson, 1975a) and its early appearance in development, it seems most reasonable to assign metaphor a prominent place in any consideration of the nature of human language.

Another factor that must be taken into account before considering metaphor to be a phenomenon distinct from so-called literal discourse is the difficulty most people encounter when they attempt to define or even detect metaphors. Max Black (1977) opened the proceedings at a recent conference by noting in his keynote address that many of the examples used by investigators of metaphor are questionable as general representatives of the phenomenon and that we ought to identify and argue from clear cases or "touchstones." During the remainder of the conference, one of the chief sources of debate among the participants involved the question of the representativeness or appropriateness of the examples selected by the various speakers. It became clear that there was by no means unanimous agreement over the domain referred to by the term "metaphor."

A similar example can be found in analyzing one of the difficulties encountered by a colleague, Howard Pollio (1978), in setting up his research program in metaphor and figurative language. Since one of his concerns was to examine the frequency and distribution of figurative language in various samples of natural discourse, it was necessary to establish some consistency in identifying and scoring metaphors and other figures in the samples in which he was interested. It is significant, we think, that reliability in the detection of figurative language could be attained only after a rather elaborate training program. He also found that actual scoring sessions had to be kept fairly short (20 minutes or so), because it was difficult to hold consistent criteria for longer periods. These findings, combined with the ease and naturalness with which people habitually deal with metaphors (Johnson, 1975a), make it clear that the application of metaphor as a *separate* category of language use requires a metacognitive act of some sort and is habitually accomplished only by psychologists, philosophers, linguists, and others who are interested in metaphor!

There has also been a good deal of interest lately in the relationship between language and perception (e.g., Miller & Johnson-Laird, 1976; Neisser, 1976), kindled most recently by demonstrations that make it clear that language operates via the knowledge systems (broadly defined) of language users (e.g., Bransford & Franks, 1971; Bransford & Johnson, 1973; Bransford & McCarrell, 1974)—knowledge that is usually seen as originating in the perceptual experience of individuals. This has lead naturally to an interest in the *content* of human cognition ("knowledge"), and the emergence of theories relating language and perceptually based knowledge (e.g., Miller & Johnson-Laird, 1976; Neisser, 1976).

The psychological study of metaphor fits quite appropriately into this current of interest in language and perception. One reason for this is the natural connection between metaphor and imagery. Aristotle, in the *Poetics,* emphasized the role of "vision" in artistic writing and emphasized "command of metaphor" as the foundation of poetic genius (Butcher, 1951). He makes the relationship between metaphor and vision explicit when he states that a command of metaphor requires "an eye for resemblances" (Butcher, 1951, p. 87). (It should be noted that "eye for" can also be translated as "perception of," see Hawkes, 1972). In many cases, the term "imagery" is used as a synonym for figurative language in creative writing. It has been observed that simple noun conjunction, which is the prototypical paradigm for metaphor formation, tends to produce almost universal reports of (visual) imagery experiences in experimental subjects (Johnson, 1970; Johnson & Malgady, 1979). Paivio (1977) has recently emphasized the role of imagery in metaphor comprehension, arguing, in the context of his dual coding hypothesis, that this accounts for both the phenomenal richness of metaphor and the efficiency (with respect to processing flexibility and storage and retrieval considerations) of metaphor as a communication device.

A second, even more compelling, reason for uniting language and perception through metaphor is the existence of a growing number of studies suggesting that language processes are not modality specific. While such demonstrations are not all specific to metaphor (see, for example, Bransford & McCarrell, 1974; Franks, 1974; Pylyshyn, 1973), many of the most convincing arguments come from investigations of figurative language. Honeck and his co-investigators (e.g., Honeck, Riechmann, & Hoffman, 1975; Honeck, Sowry, & Voegtle, 1978) have examined continuities between the comprehension of verbal metaphors (especially proverbs) and pictorial representations, and have been led to postulate a hypothetical "conceptual base"—a modality nonspecific abstract representational system that underlies the comprehension of both verbal and perceptual information. In another interesting series of investigations Verbrugge (Verbrugge, 1975, 1977; Verbrugge & McCarrell, 1977) has examined the effectiveness of various cross-modal prompts in the recall of verbal metaphors, and concludes that metaphoric comprehension is not modality specific. Verbrugge argues that this supports a theory of *direct* metaphoric perception, along the lines suggested by Gibson (1966, 1977). We shall examine this notion more fully in the next section of this chapter. Some of our own work (Johnson, 1977—to be summarized later) also points in a similar direction.

If we assume, as it now seems reasonable to do, that metaphor represents a general characteristic of language—that is, an intrinsic part of the nature or definition of human communication—and that its properties extend even further into human perception, then we may optimistically suppose that an understanding of metaphoric comprehension will go a long way toward facilitating an understanding of human cognition. This suggestion is not original (see, for example, Miller, 1977; Paivio, 1977; Verbrugge, 1977), and it is foolish to suggest that such an understanding has been achieved, but it does remain a worthwhile goal. Before we turn to our outline of a perceptual approach to language, we would like to examine two approaches to understanding metaphor, in an effort to clarify an issue that is true of psychological research in general.

Two Views of Metaphor Research

In the psychological literature on metaphor, two kinds of theoretical traditions seem to predominate (see, for example, Ortony, Reynolds & Arter, 1978; Pollio, et al., 1977). One of these traditions emphasizes the characteristics of the metaphoric stimulus and the process by which these characteristics are transformed into metaphor comprehension. Theories of this kind often involve a featural representation of metaphor characteristics (e.g., Johnson & Malgady, 1979; Malgady & Johnson, 1976, and this volume; Ortony, 1977; Smith, Shoben & Rips, 1974; Tversky, 1977) although this is not necessarily the case (e.g., Honeck, Riechmann & Hoffman, 1975; Paivio, 1977; Tourangeau & Sternberg, 1978; Verbrugge, 1977). The other kind of theory emphasizes the creative aspects of metaphor interpretation and production, and the role that metaphor plays in productive thinking (e.g., Pollio, et al., 1977; Verbrugge, 1978). Adherents of these two ways of understanding the psychological aspects of metaphor often (usually) see them as somehow mutually exclusive and incompatible, and cite different kinds of evidence in support of their respective positions. It is our contention that this incompatibility is not always necessary, but, instead, often represents a confusion of the aims and viewpoints of these positions.

The conceptual error that is commonly committed is this: We persist in taking our measures of aggregate data (data collected from *populations* of subjects) and pushing these measures—which may range from geometric means to aggregated lists of responses—back into the heads of our individual subjects. This practice has been justified traditionally by the discovery (Thumb & Marbe, 1901), which has been canonized as a "law," that the frequency of occurrence of a response in a word association distribution predicts the order in which associates are generated in individual subjects' repeated associations. It is likely that the reliance of psychological research on statistical prediction, as opposed to simulation or parameter estimation, has contributed to this way of thinking (Meehl, 1967).

Whatever the merits of the justification, there are certain dangers inherent in confusing characteristics of an individual and the characteristics of the subject group to which the individual belongs. This conclusion can perhaps be defended in the following way. In the last several years we (Johnson & Malgady, 1979; Malgady & Johnson, 1976) have enjoyed a moderate degree of success in predicting various aspects of metaphor comprehension (primarily ease of interpretation and judged "goodness") from a variety of measures related to the characteristics of the topic and vehicle terms in the metaphors we have studied. Using multiple regression techniques, we can predict, in some cases, these metaphor comprehension aspects at about a .80 correlational level. (These data will be summarized more fully in the next section.) The problem comes when you attempt to look at the *content* of the interpretations provided by individual subjects, and the *variability* of the goodness judgments provided by subjects. It is frustrating to realize that even though you can find a great deal of regularity in the way in which *populations* of subjects deal with populations of metaphors, we can say much less about how an *individual* subject will interpret an individual metaphor. When you examine the individual responses that subjects give when they are presented with a word to associate to, or a metaphor or painting to interpret, you find that they usually make sense, even though they show considerable diversity in their content.

This can be illustrated by the following example. One of the authors (Johnson, 1978) recently gave a group of 75 subjects a series of 20 randomly generated metaphors, which the subjects were to explicate by completing a sentence in the following form:

People are doors, . . . (subject's response).

The 75 subjects gave 27 *different* completion responses for this metaphor, some of which are listed in Table 11.1.

Where do these interpretations come from? What we see here are interpretatons *suggested* by the stimuli, but it seems as though stimuli can suggest a great many things. What a metaphor suggests to an individual seems to be somewhat dependent upon that individual, and not something we can predict entirely from an a priori knowledge of the stimulus—except, of course, on a probabilistic basis.

We are left, then, with the conclusion that there are two possible sources of the content of metaphoric interpretations, namely, the material to be interpreted and the individual doing the interpreting. We also have, as we have seen, an analogous controversy between those who believe that metaphor comprehension can be explained through an examination and understanding of the nature of the metaphoric *stimulus,* and those who believe that it can only be explained via an examination and understanding of the creative process within individuals.

What we would like to argue here is that both positions are correct—that they do not represent mutually exclusive alternatives, but complementary perspectives on the same phenomenon. Each position has its strengths and limitations, and these are built into the points of view that each position is forced to take. The

TABLE 11.1
Examples of Responses to a Metaphor Completion
Task

People are doors, _____.
    they can be either open or closed
    they open into something else
    you have to go through them to get what you want
    behind them are many secrets
    they move back and forth without ever going anywhere
    they are square
    they are rigid
    they squeak unless oiled
    you go through many of them in your life
    you need a key to open them
    you find them most often in houses
    they work best when they are in good condition

---

problem comes when one side fails to realize the perspective of the other. In order to make this point as clearly as possible, and to make explicit the source of limitations on each point of view described above, we would like to outline a theory of comprehension applicable to both of these positions, and which is also consistent with our two earlier arguments: that metaphor is a central characteristic of language rather than a special case; and that there may be found, in the study of metaphor, answers to some old questions (Pastore, 1971) concerning the relationship between language and perception.

A Sketch of a Perceptual Theory of Metaphor

Before we begin, we wish to emphasize that portions of our position are not necessarily original, and that we derive many of our ideas from a variety of sources. Notable among these are the perceptual theories of Garner (1970, 1974) and Gibson (1966, 1977), the cognitive theory briefly outlined by Neisser (1976), and the perceptual approach to metaphor advocated by Verbrugge (1975, 1977). The contributions of these (and other) sources will become apparent as we proceed.

    Several years ago, Garner and his colleagues (Garner, 1966, 1970; Garner & Clement, 1963; Handel & Garner, 1966) did a series of studies involving the perception of five-element dot patterns arranged in a 3×3 (nine-cell) matrix. The most important finding in these studies is that such dot patterns vary in "goodness" (as judged by their subjects), and that such variations in goodness judgments are correlated with the number of different alternative patterns that can be generated when patterns are rotated (through successive 90 degree arcs) or reflected in a mirror-image fashion. Some patterns (such as a simple cross or "X") do not change, or yield different patterns, when such rotation and reflection transformations are applied. These are the patterns which rank highest in judged goodness. Other patterns yield two, four, or eight *different* patterns when the rotation and reflection transofrmations are applied. The eight-alternative patterns rank lowest in judged goodness. Garner contends (Garner, 1970) that these results are related to the concept of stimulus redundancy. According to this interpretation, a subject perceives not only the dot pattern itself, but also the subset of the set of all possible dot patterns to which it belongs. The smaller the subset (now defined in terms of alternative stimuli or patterns generated by rotation and refection transformations) the more redundant the stimulus is. This redundancy is related to judged goodness: Good patterns have few alternatives (Garner, 1970).

The inverse relation between pattern goodness and the size of the sub-set of alternative organizations is a remarkably robust and ubiquitous one, holding not only for visual patterns but auditory patterns as well (Garner, 1970; Garner & Gottwald, 1968; Royer and Garner, 1966). The results of several other experimental probes also seem to be predictable from these pattern characteristics. For example, the variability (across subjects) and latency of verbal descriptions of dot patterns is lower for good patterns than poor ones (Clement, 1964). If subjects are asked to draw dot pattern associates, the variability (again, across subjects) of associative responses is lower for good patterns than for poor ones. In addition, there is a unidirectional effect in these associations. Subjects tend to give a "better" pattern as an associative response than the original stimulus (Handel & Garner, 1966).

It seems to us both reasonable and useful to postulate a connection between Garner's notion of redundancy (i.e., as alternative organizations) and the broader term ambiguity—remembering, of course, that this is our interpretation and not Garner's. Ambiguity is one concept that seems to be relevant to several psychological domains. Stimuli of all sorts, from inkblots and reversible figures to words and sentences, can all be described in terms of their potential ambiguity. The *more redundant* (the fewer the number of alternative organizations, or the smaller the subset of transformationally related stimuli) the *less ambiguous* a stimulus is, and vice versa. To speak very loosely, a diagonally crossing pattern of dots is simply and unambiguously an "X," whereas a less symmetrical pattern is less constrained with respect to its various interpretive possibilities. This viewpoint, by the way, is very similar to Olson's (1970) analysis of meaning.

In order to apply this point of view to language, and especially to metaphor, it is necessary to make some theoretical assumptions about what happens when one encounters a language segment—that is, a word, a phrase, a metaphor, a sentence, etc. Neisser (1976) has suggested that words (at least the acoustic or visual representations of words) are embedded in the perceptual schemata (Neisser's term) associated with the experiential (perceptual) situations in which the words have been encountered. Without invoking all of the theoretical constructs of Neisser's position, which is not well worked out with respect to language in any case, his argument seems to be that when one hears (or sees) a word, the perceptual schemata in which that word is embedded are aroused in much the same way that they may be aroused (in the absence of immediate perceptual stimuli) in imagining or remembering. The word produces a quasi-perceptual experience, in the sense that it shares certain characteristics (not explicitly defined) of direct perception of the physical environment. When multiple words are encountered (as in a sentence or metaphor), the perceptual experience is of the same type, but involves the simultaneous coordination of several schemata.

Our conceptualization (see also Johnson, 1977) is essentially similar, at least at this superficial level. When an individual encounters a word, a metaphor, or some other message unit, the process of interpreting and comprehending that unit involves experiencing an essentially perceptual *context*, which is appropriate to the unit (i.e., in which it is interpretable or "makes sense"). There are two issues this conceptualization immediately raises: (1) what is the nature of this perceptual experience; and (2) why invoke the term "perceptual context," which clearly uses "context" in a nontraditional sense?

We prefer to remain somewhat neutral with respect to what an individual actually experiences when he or she encounters a word or metaphor. While there is strong presumption that some sort of imagery (especially visual) is usually or at least frequently involved (Johnson, 1970; Paivio, 1977), we do not wish to imply that this is necessarily the case. We will simply maintain that the experience is "perceptionlike." Our use of the term *context* is motivated by the experiences that subjects report, and the characteristic behaviors, that they engage in when they are asked to interpret words, metaphors, and other language bits—especially when they are presented in isolation. Our subjects typically respond by describing a context in which the metaphor or word would be a reasonable (even though perhaps a bit "poetic") thing to say. This also corresponds with the behavior of Pollio and Burns' (1977) subjects when they were asked to interpret anomalous sentences, and with Hoffman's recent (Hoffman, 1977) response to Jenkins' (1977) challenge to explain how *Roses are blooming in my garden* can mean the same as *Bombs are falling on New York*. To put it in a slightly different way, it may be that metaphor comprehension *is* the invention of a context or circumstances in which the metaphor might conceivably have been produced. (We offer this as a reasonable suggestion, realizing the dangers that lie in wait for anyone brave enough to assert what meaning *is*.) This interpretive strategy may, then, be dictated by the nature of the comprehension process involved when the subjects are presented with to-be-interpreted verbal items. These contexts need not be static representational landscapes; in fact, they may be thought of as dynamic in two senses. First, instead of being unitary, contexts may consist of a family of experiences that flit in and out of consciousness during interpretation—that is, a set of changing contexts. Second, the contexts themselves may involve movement or action.

Assuming that we can postulate a perceptionlike basis for comprehending language units, we might ask how we can relate this construct to the notion of stimulus ambiguity that we derived from Garner's redundancy concept. In order to do this, we must invoke a Gibson-like (*not* strictly Gibsonian) concept of "affordance" (Gibson, 1977) and a caveat concerning the specification of one's point of view with respect to the perceiving subject.

Although the work of James J. Gibson has inspired some strong theoretical efforts recently (see, for example, Shaw & Bransford, 1977), it is not always clear which ideas are part of Gibson's own position and which emanate from a less well defined "Gibsonian perspective" or way of asking questions—this is especially true when the concepts are applied in an abstract or symbolic realm, which includes metaphor (see Verbrugge, 1975, 1977). For this reason, we wish to make clear that our use of the term affordance is inspired by Gibson (1977), but not necessarily identical with his use of the term. Gibson defines the "affordance of anything as a specific combination of the properties of its substance and its surfaces taken with reference to an animal" (Gibson, 1977, p. 67). Gibsonian affordances include such things as climb-up-ableness, sit-on-ableness, graspableness, etc. A tree, for example, can afford all of these things, and more (Bransford & McCarrell, 1974), depending upon the interest and needs of a perceiving individual.

Although the perceptionlike correlates of language do not have substances or surfaces in the physical sense, they do afford things in a way analogous to the affordances of the physical environment. The context experienced by an individual hearing a word or metaphor can be thought of as having properties that *afford*—what these properties and affordances will be depend entirely on what that individual experiences upon hearing the word or metaphor.

It may be useful to clarify one point here. To say that a perceptual experience (in the sense we are using the term here) or a perceptual object (to use Gibson's sense) *has properties that afford* is not the same as saying that the experience (or object) *consists of a set or bundle of properties*. This is a subtle point, and a confusing one perhaps, but it seems worth the effort to make it. The use of *features* in psychological theories has been so widespread that we are accustomed to thinking of them as if they were things that actually exist somewhere—in the stimulus or in the head. It is not our intention to equate properties with the objects or experiences of perceiving—i.e., to make them the primitives or building blocks of our position. We wish, instead, to think of them as categories of description of objects or meanings. Trees, for example, can be *described* in terms of various properties but such description is not necessarily the same as our perception of a tree. It is perhaps most accurate to say that properties, as catagories of description, are symptoms of perceiving rather than the foundations for perceiving. To put it another way, properties are convenient (and useful) fictions in precisely the same way that Bohr's model of the atom represented a convenient (and useful) fiction in physics.

From the *point of view of the perceiver-hearer*, what will be experienced when a word or metaphor is encountered will depend on all sorts of things: previous experience with the words encountered in the metaphor and the world in general; the immediate linguistic and nonlinguistic context; the current concerns (Klinger, 1977) of the individual (what the individual spends a lot of time thinking about—work, sex, the weather, a bereavement, metaphor, etc.); in short, almost any factor that can enter the flow of consciousness (see Jenkins, 1974).

From the *point of view of an outside observer or speaker* (the point of view that experimental psychologists must necessarily adopt), it is not possible to know precisely what the perceiver-hearer will experience. This simple point does not mean that we must give up the study of metaphor (or meaning), but it does mean that there may be some inherent limits on the completeness of our understanding of metaphoric comprehension—on the level of precision of our analyses. It is possible, from the outside observer's point of view, to make some judgments about the set of possibilities (properties or affordances) that an individual *might* experience. (This is similar to Gibson's insistence on thinking of affordances "with reference to an animal." Substances, surfaces, and associated properties may exist, but whether they afford anything or are attended to depends on the individual perceiving organism.)

If we now define the ambiguity (redundancy or alternative organizations) of a word or metaphor in terms of the characteristics of the (open-ended) total set of possible perceptual contexts a set of individuals might experience—which are in turn describable in terms of associated properties and affordances—we can begin to think of the relevance of this connection to a theory of metaphoric comprehension, and perhaps more generally to other aspects of symbolic comprehension.

If any particular context experienced by an individual can be described in terms of its properties and (potential) affordances, then the combined contexts for a population of subjects can yield a *set* or *distribution* of *possible* properties from which the experienced contexts of the individuals in the population can be drawn. In other words, a metaphor (or word, etc.), from the point of view of an outside observer, is associated with a set of meaning possibilities out of which the comprehension of the metaphor by any given individual can be derived.

A set of properties (meaning possibilities) of this sort can be described with respect to two distributional parameters. These are (1) the number of different properties from which an interpretation might be derived, and (2) the relative salience (or likelihood) of these properties. Metaphors can be thought of as differing in their ranges of potential meaning, or varying in the number of different contexts that might potentially be experienced when the metaphor is encountered. Metaphors can also be thought of in terms of the commonality of the contexts they produce. Some metaphors will strongly suggest certain highly salient properties that will be incorporated in the experienced contexts of most subjects.

It is our suggestion that these two parameters have different influences on the potential ambiguity of a metaphor (or word). Other things being equal, the larger the set of potential properties, the more interpretive or meaning possibilities there are—and therefore the greater the potential ambiguity. Other things being equal, again, the more dominant or salient certain of the potential properties are the more they will constrain the actually realized interpretations (or contexts in the sense discussed earlier)—and therefore the lower the potential ambiguity. If the possible property sets are open-ended (as they must be thought to be)—that is, not limited to any particular number of properties—then these two parameters can vary independently. This will become clearer in the next section when we discuss some examples.

It is extremely important to realize that ambiguity, in the sense we are using the term here, is a third-person concept. That is, ambiguity is always defined from the point of view of the outside observer, and not from the point of view of the perceiver. A metaphor or word that is ambiguous from the outside observer's point of view is not ambiguous from the point of view of the individual who is experiencing a perceptual context—although the perceiver may be (or become) aware of a variety of meaning possibilities upon reflection or over time. It does not appear that Garner (1970) thinks of his stimulus redundancy construct as a third-person concept, although it is quite common for experimental psychologists to move back and forth between the two points of view.

The most important aspect of this way of thinking about words and metaphors is this: Language segments do not have meanings per se, but are instead associated with a set of meaning possibilities that might or might not be realized in any given individual. This means that it is reasonable to explore the relationship between the characteristics of potential property distributions and metaphor comprehension, but we cannot, utilizing group data, be precise about what a metaphor means to a given individual. The flavor of this approach is essentially similar to what Verbrugge has in mind when he talks about "the perception of invariants at the invitation of metaphor" (Verbrugge, 1975).

We will now turn to a brief examination of the usefulness of this approach in three different, but related, domains: The comprehension of single words, the comprehension of metaphor, and the comprehension of surrealist art.

SOME REPRESENTATIVE STUDIES OF COMPREHENSION

The Comprehension of Single Words

There are two reasons for including data from research on single nouns in a chapter ostensibly devoted to metaphoric comprehension. First, it allows us to operationalize some of the concepts in our perceptual approach to comprehension, and to indirectly replicate some of the experiments reported by Garner

(1966, 1970). This has the virtue of strengthening our hypothetical connection between Garner's perceptual constructs and language comprehension. Secondly, if it can be shown that the same basic concepts apply to both single word and metaphor comprehension, it can provide additional evidence for the non-special status of metaphor in cognition.

The first thing that is needed to employ our perceptual approach in experimentation is a way of assessing the characteristics of the sets of possible properties associated with words. Some earlier work by one of the authors provides a convenient way to do this, even though this work (Johnson, 1970, 1971) was undertaken with a different model in mind. Johnson (1971) began by presenting 250 undergraduates with 72 randomly selected nouns. These subjects were asked to attend to what they experienced when they read each noun, and then to list as many properties of the noun as they could that were related to what they thought of when they read the noun. The subjects were told to think of the properties in terms of "adjectival modifiers" that could be used to qualify the particular sense of the noun that they experienced. If the noun was "tree," for example, they could (and did) report such things as GREEN tree, TALL tree, DEAD tree, CLIMBING tree, PINE tree, BARE tree, GNARLED tree, and MENACING tree. The 250 subjects produced, under these instructions, a surprisingly large number of adjectival properties for each noun—ranging from a low of 31 *different* properties (for the noun "matter"), to a high of 137 (for the noun "tree"). The subjects averaged 4.3 properties per noun each.

As we have already indicated, adjectival properties collected in this manner should not be thought of as *the* properties of the subjects' perceptual experiences with the nouns; they can be, however, considered symptomatic of these experiences. As a first approximation, the distributional characteristics of these sets of verbal properties can be considered to be representative of the characteristics of the set of underlying possible perceptual properties.

Because subjects were not restricted in the number of verbal properties they could provide for each of the nouns, the verbal property sets were open-ended in the same way as the hypothesized perceptual sets—that is, the "number of properties" and "property salience" parameters could vary independently. (The correlation between these two parameters was .13.) For purposes of quantifying these parameters for the verbal property distributions, the number of possible properties was calculated by simply counting the number of different adjective "types" for each noun, and property salience was defined as the percentage of total adjectives (tokens) provided by the subjects which were instances of the five most frequently occurring adjective responses. In the case of "tree," for example, 47% of the total responses were accounted for by GREEN, TALL, BIG, BEAUTIFUL, AND LIVING—even though there were 137 different adjectives given. Values on this parameter ranged from a low of 16% (for the noun "mind") to a high of 61% (for the noun "sun").

Although it makes little sense to rate nouns with respect to Garner's "goodness'' (Is a *story* better than *matter*?), it is possible to design analogs of the Clement (1964) and Handel and Garner (1966) experiments using the adjectival property distributions as definitions of noun redundancy (ambiguity, in our terms). Johnson (1971) had 200 subjects provide free association responses to the 72 nouns (providing data for a replication of Handel & Garner, 1966) and another 50 subjects write definitions for the same nouns (providing data analogous to that used by Clement, 1964, in his study relating verbal descriptions to stimulus redundancy). In addition, 30 pairs of subjects were instructed to communicate the nouns to each other, using one-word cues and following the format of the popular ''Password'' game.

These tasks yielded three values for each of the 72 nouns: (1) a measure of the variability/commonality of the 200 response association distributions (calculated by using the univariate uncertainty measure, U, after Garner, 1962); (2) a measure of the variability in definitions for the nouns (obtained by calculating the same uncertainty measure as above on content analyzed and categorized distributions of definitions); and (3) a measure of communication ease for each of the nouns, defined as the inverse of the average number of cues required before the target noun was correctly guessed. Correlations between these three measures and the two property distribution parameters are shown in Table 11.2.

An examination of these data reveals several things. First, the two parameters of the property distributions do seem to exert their influences in opposite directions, as we suggested earlier that they should. High property salience (which is hypothesized to reduce ambiguity) constrains the variability of both the word association and the definition distributions, and makes it easier to guess a word in a password game. A large number of properties (which should increase ambiguity) is related to high variability in both distributions, and to difficulty in password guessing. Secondly, these results are completely in line with the Handel and Garner (1966) and Clement (1964) findings in the perception of dot patterns—although comparisons are difficult, since Garner's (1970) redundancy concept does not involve two parameters working in opposite directions. Third,

TABLE 11.2
Relations between Property Salience and Number of Properties
and Measures from Three Tasks Involving Single Nouns

	Property Distribution Measures	
Task Measures	*Property Salience*	*Number of Properties*
Associative Uncertainty	−.61*	.37**
Definition Uncertainty	−.63*	.41*
Communication Ease	.69*	−.57*

*$p < .01$ (N = 72)
**$p < .05$ (N = 72)

the two property parameters seem to account for a large proportion of the variance in these data—although this may be partly due to task similarity.

These results indicate that our perceptual theory of comprehension is at least consistent with our findings with respect to single noun comprehension, and that some interesting principles from the perceptual domain are perhaps relevant to language as well. We will now proceed to a consideration of metaphoric comprehension in these terms.

The Comprehension of Metaphor

In several recent studies (Johnson, 1975b; Johnson & Malgady, 1979; Malgady & Johnson, 1976, 1977, this volume; Malgady, 1975, 1976, 1977), a consistent pattern of results has emerged, no matter what form of metaphorical stimulus has been employed (i.e., literary metaphors, artificially constructed metaphors, or even randomly generated metaphors). We have found that two aspects of metaphor comprehension—judged goodness and difficulty of interpretation—can be predicted from a knowledge of the relationship between the two key words (topic and vehicle) in metaphorical propositions. These predictors are the judged similarity between the topic and vehicle and two parameters (salience and total number, again) of the common property or attribute distributions generated by subjects for the topic and vehicle and compounds in the metaphors. "Goodness," as we use the term, is not necessarily the same as artistic or literary merit. Our subjects were allowed to define the term for themselves (as were Garner's), and our subjects were not trained in literary criticism. The goodness judgment made by these subjects represent the relatively naive intuitions of normal undergraduates, and are probably more closely related to "goodness" in the Gestalt sense, than they are to the criteria likely to be employed by literary experts (Johnson & Malgady, 1979). The typical pattern of results is illustrated in Table 11.3. These particular results come from 28 literary metaphors taken from a variety of poetry and prose sources (Johnson & Malgady, 1979). Looking at these results, it can be seen that good metaphors are likely to be those that are easily interpretable, those in which the topic and vehicle terms are judged to be "similar," and those in which the topic and vehicle terms share a large number of common properties, and have a number of salient (high frequency) common properties. The common property sets were collected and analyzed in much the same way as they were in the single-word case discussed in the previous section. Subjects (50 in all) were shown each of the 28 tenor-vehicle compounds (e.g., Mountains-Kings, Snow-Confetti) from the literary metaphors, and were asked to list as many properties as they could think of that related to the two terms. The resulting distributions were open-ended in size, since subjects were free to list as many properties as they wished. Common property *salience* was calculated using the "percentage of total responses accounted for by the five most frequently occurring" convention described in the previous section, and *number* of com-

TABLE 11.3
Correlations between Metaphor Comprehension Measures and Interword
Relationship Measures for 28 Literary Metaphors[a]

Measure	Interpretation Difficulty	Interword Similarity	Common Property Salience	Number of Common Properties
Rated Goodness	−.59*	.56*	.47*	.40**
Interpretation Difficulty		−.79*	−.57*	−.40**
Interword Similarity			.69*	.43**
Common Property Salience				.61*

[a] Adapted from Johnson & Malgady, 1979.
*$p < .01$ (N = 28)
**$p < .05$ (N = 28)

mon properties was calculated by simply counting the number of different responses.

While these results were originally interpreted in the context of a more traditional cognitive-feature approach (Johnson, 1970; see Malgady & Johnson, this volume), they are completely consistent with the perceptual approach that we are proposing here. What we are, in effect, doing is redefining the notion "feature," and suggesting a different underlying basis for the feature model we have been using previously.

It will be useful, at this point, to summarize our perceptual account of metaphoric comprehension: When an individual encounters a metaphor, the interpretation and comprehension of that metaphor involves experiencing an essentially perceptual context—a context appropriate to the metaphor (i.e., in which it makes sense). The properties people list when you ask them to tell you what the topic and vehicle have in common (the source for the property distribution parameters in Table 11.3) are essentially lists of characteristics of the contexts triggered by the metaphor. To the extent that it is reasonable to think of the perceptual contexts experienced "at the invitation of metaphor" (Verbrugge, 1975) as having properties (in the sense discussed above), these property listings may be thought of as descriptions of properties.

We are now in a position to compare the relationship between "goodness" and "redundancy" as they relate to dot patterns with the relationship between "goodness" and "ambiguity" with respect to metaphor. Given that metaphors generate contexts that can be described in terms of their characteristics, how can we relate this to metaphor goodness and interpretability? In order to do this, we offer the following account:

Metaphors that are easy to interpret generate contexts that have a large number of characteristics (i.e., are informationally rich with respect to possible properties), when the contexts of a large number of individuals are combined—from the outside observer's point of view, in other words. Easily interpretable metaphors also tend to suggest some interpretive possibilities quickly and easily (have some high salient properties, again from a third-person perspective). We already suggested, when we defined our use of term ambiguity (earlier), that a "good" dot pattern is unambiguous and therefore easy to interpret. If we say that a good metaphor is an easily interpretable one (which is empirically correct, see Table 11.3), we are making much the same kind of statement. The problem is that this seems to be consistent with only one ambiguity parameter—common property salience—since the number of common properties parameter ought to work in the opposite direction. This can be resolved in two ways: (1) In metaphors, unlike single words, the two property distribution parameters co-vary (see Table 11.3). Metaphors having a large number of common properties also tend to have some properties of high salience. In addition, (2) the concept "goodness" is a complex one, and we now turn to a more analytic definition of this concept.

Johnson and Malgady (1979) hypothesized that "goodness" ought to be curvilinear with respect to judged tenor-vehicle similarity over a range of stimuli (from tautology to anomaly), even though this relationship was linear for their literary metaphors. Malgady (1975) showed this to be the case, and suggested a decomposition of the concept "goodness" into "truth value" and "figurativeness." In order to explore this notion further, Johnson(1975b) had 60 subjects scale (using ranking procedures) 36 randomly generated metaphors for "goodness," "truth value," and "figurativeness." These scale values were then compared to the two property set parameters we have already discussed: common property salience and number of common properties. The metaphors in this study were created by randomly combining the 72 words used in the single word studies (reported earlier) into two-word "A is/are B" metaphors (e.g., *People are doors, A mind is a table*).

The results of this study are shown in Table 11.4. It can be seen that figurativeness is unrelated to property salience, but moderately highly correlated with the number of properties ($r = .59$). Figurativeness, then, is a function of the size of the set of possible properties, or, if you will, the number of possibilities for interpretation (i.e., richness) that the metaphor offers. Truth value, on the other hand, is moderately highly related to property salience ($r = .62$) but only barely significantly related to the number of common properties ($r = .31$). *A mountain is matter* is an example of a random metaphor high in property salience, but low in number of properties. It is rated true, but not figurative or particularly good. *A mind is a flower* is, on the other hand, high in number of properties and moderate with respect to property salience, and is rated both figurative and good, but not particularly true. A third example, *Hair is a ship,* is low in both property parameters and is rated neither true nor figurative nor good. It would seem that truth value is related to the probability that certain of the possible properties will be part of the perceptual contexts experienced by individuals when they encounter a metaphor. Goodness falls part-way between figurativeness and truth

TABLE 11.4
Correlations between Property Salience and Number of Common
Properties and Three Judgment Tasks Involving Randomly Generated
Metaphors

| Judgment Tasks | Property Distribution Measures | |
	Property Salience	Number of Common Properties
Ranked Figurativeness	.07	.59*
Ranked Truth-Value	.62*	.31**
Ranked Goodness	.43*	.51*

$*p < .01$ (N = 36)
$**p < .05$ (N = 36)

value, and is related to both property distribution parameters. Goodness, for metaphors, seems to be a mixture of truth value and figurativeness—it probably corresponds more closely to "goodness" in the Gestalt sense, than to the aesthetic judgments of sensitive interpreters. Aesthetic goodness is probably more closely related to figurativeness, in this case.

In summary, our results with respect to metaphoric comprehension are consistent with our perceptual theory and are, in the main, similar to Garner's (1970) findings with respect to dot pattern stimuli. We turn now to a consideration of the comprehension of the paintings of a surrealist artist (Magritte), which seems to have some of the characteristics of both metaphor and ordinary visual perception.

The Comprehension of Complex Pictures

It seems reasonable to suggest, given the fact that our approach to comprehension originates in perception, that the application of this model to picture interpretation is relatively straightforward. It can be argued that the primary difference lies in the fact that in the case of picture comprehension the "perceptual context" is directly given—that is, it consists of the picture itself (Gibson, 1971). It is true, of course, that pictures do not allow for alternative contexts across individuals in the same way that words or metaphors do. In the case of pictures, alternative contexts must come from different subsets of the perceptual information afforded by the picture. Direct pictorial contexts do vary in the amount of information that they contain (which may be related in a straightforward fashion to the number of verbal properties that make up possible property distributions for a number of subjects—via the notion of *potential* interpretive possibilities), and the ease with which this information can be integrated into an interpretation—the salience or usability of the information, in other words. This means that it ought to be possible to make a meaningful comparison between the comprehension of metaphors and the comprehension of paintings in the context of the approach that we have been developing. In order to do this, Johnson (1977) carried out an investigation of the comprehension of the paintings of the surrealist Belgian artist Rene Magritte.

Magritte had several characteristics as an artist that make his work uniquely suited for looking at comparisons between linguistic and visual processes in figurative language. Chief among these, for our present purposes, is the manner in which Magritte chose to achieve his surrealist effects. His usual method was to take familiar objects or elements and conjoin them in unusual ways. For example, in one of his paintings, La Dureé poignardeé ("Time Transfixed," 1939, The Art Institute of Chicago), Magritte depicted an ordinary fireplace, with a clock and two candlesticks on the mantle, and a mirror on the wall over the mantle. The unusual element in this context is the presence of a steam locomotive coming straight out of the rear wall of the fireplace, sending the smoke from its stack up the flue. In another painting, Le Fils de l'homme ("The Son of Man," 1964, private collection, Yorktown, New York), Magritte shows us a front-on view of a man dressed in a black bowler hat, and a black raincoat (a familiar figure in Magritte's work). Superimposed over (and obscuring) the face of the man is a green apple—another frequent element in his paintings. He wished to modify conceptions of reality by manipulating the elements of reality. This aspect of Magritte makes his paintings interesting analogs for verbal metaphors—which typically involve unusual *combinations* of otherwise familiar words. There is some indication that Magritte thought of his own work in this way (Gablik, 1976).

In order to examine the possible relation between picture comprehension and metaphor comprehension, Johnson (1977) devised a series of comparitive judgment tasks, using the paintings as stimuli, which corresponded to the metaphor goodness, interpretability and common property tasks used in the Johnson and Malgady (1979) study. The purpose was to see if the same pattern of results relating these variables would hold for both metaphors and paintings. Johnson took 30 paintings from a standard collection (Larkin, 1972), and randomly divided them into three sets of 10. Twenty-four University of Minnesota undergraduates then ranked all three sets on three judgment dimensions: (1) *Preference*, which corresponds to metaphor goodness; (2) *Visual Complexity*, which corresponds to number of common properties (possible informational units) collected for the metaphors; and (3) *Interpretation Difficulty*, which corresponds to the same measure in the metaphor study. These rankings were then correlated (across 10 pictures) for each of the three picture sets. These results are shown in Table 11.5.

A comparison of these correlations with those shown in Table 11.3 indicates that the patterns are similar. When the correlations in Table 11.5 are averaged across the three picture sets (using the r to z transformation method), all of these correlations are highly significant. We can conclude that, for these tasks at least,

TABLE 11.5
Correlations between Averaged Ranks on Three Picture
Judgment Tasks for Three Sets of Magritte Paintings[a]

Measure	Interpretation Difficulty	Complexity
Picture Set I (N = 10)		
Preference	−.56	.84
Interpretation Difficulty		−.62
Picture Set II (N = 10)		
Preference	−.79	.83
Interpretation Difficulty		−.49
Picture Set III (N = 10)		
Preference	−.43	.42
Interpretation Difficulty		−.77

[a] Each averaged rank based upon 24 judgments.

whatever is going on in metaphor comprehension may also take place in the comprehension of Magritte.

SOME CONCLUDING REMARKS

We have tried to argue in this chapter that there are several areas within the domain of human cognition that can be tied together through a perceptual analysis of comprehension. The fact that it is possible to examine the comprehension of simple visual stimuli (dot patterns), complex and "symbolic" visual stimuli (Magritte paintings), simple verbal stimuli (nouns), and complex (natural literary) metaphors, *and* find a common picture emerging is significant in itself. At a time when there is at least some concern over the speciousness of experimental findings (Jenkins, 1974, 1977; Johnson, 1975a; Newell, 1973) it is comforting to know that there is at least the possibility of a general principle linking a variety of phenomena in several experimental contexts. The fact that metaphor "sits at the center" of this explanatory network strengthens the hypothetical suggestion that the study of metaphor is significant because it is generally representative of comprehension—that is, a central rather than peripheral phenomenon.

One of the themes implicit in this chapter is an attempt to answer the question, "What makes a metaphor work?" That is, what makes some metaphors more satisfying and/or comprehensible than others? In the context of the theory and data presented here, we can begin to offer a tentative answer, from the *third person point of view*, to this rather difficult question—a question that dominates the stylistics and rhetoric literature dealing with metaphor. At a general level, the answer seems to be this: A metaphor will be comprehensible (easy to interpret) to the extent that a relationship can be easily perceived between the topic and vehicle terms in the metaphor. This characteristic of metaphor comprehension seems to be most clearly related to the property salience parameter in our data. A metaphor will be satisfying (good) if it is both comprehensible and "rich"—that is, offers a number of interpretive possibilities. At the data-level, a good metaphor will have both high property salience, and a large number of common properties. It is worth noting that this interpretation is most consistent with the classic *interactive* view of metaphor (Ortony, *et al.*, 1978) which puts a premium not only upon the perception of resemblance between topic and vehicle, but also emphasizes the richness or suggestion of new possibilities as an important part of metaphor. The alternative comparative view (which emphasizes only resemblance or shared features) is consistent with the comprehensibility or interpretability aspect of what makes a metaphor work, but does not deal with the issue of aesthetic satisfaction.

With respect to the theoretical assumptions we put forward in this chapter, we wish to make two points. First of all, we wish to emphasize that our theory is necessarily sketchy and incomplete at this point, and is intended to be used heuristically rather than deductively. Although the discussant at a recent symposium on metaphor argued that it is time to end mere demonstrations and get on with hypothesis testing research in the area of metaphor, we feel that this conclusion is unwarranted on three grounds: (1) As we have previously stated, there is no general agreement concerning the domain of the phenomenon; (2) there are some strong indictments of the efficacy of this approach in general (e.g., Harre & Secord, 1973; Neisser, 1976; Newell, 1973); and (3) there is at least some evidence that the failure of experimental psychology to evolve into a cumulative science of "hard prediction" may be due to an inherent flexibility and context sensitivity in whatever processes underlie human cognition (Jenkins, 1974; 1977; Johnson, 1975a).

One of the advantages of the approach we are advocating here is that it represents an alternative to feature models (e.g., Johnson, 1970; Johnson & Malgady, 1979; Malgady & Johnson, 1976, this volume; Tversky, 1977), without necessarily being incompatible with them. This is accomplished by distinguishing between the experiencing of metaphor in the perceiver, and the examination of metaphor comprehension from an outside observer's point ov view. Most investigations based on feature models (our own previous work included) involve the collection of data from a *population* of individuals (e.g., similarity ratings, common properties or attributes), and then the results of this group effort are conceptually pushed back into the heads of individual experimental participants. This sort of sleight-of-hand maneuver has a long and glorious history in psychology, but it leads, we feel, to a serious error in thinking about intraindividual processes. Feature models are really third-person models, or at least should be thought of in that way.

Many of the more cogent arguments against a feature-analysis approach (e.g., Harwood & Verbrugge, 1977; Verbrugge & McCarrell, 1977) are based implicitly on this difference in perspective. By thinking of the features associated with a metaphor as something that exists in individual heads, one is hard-put to explain the fact that metaphor seemingly involves a creative/constructive process within individuals (Verbrugge, 1975; 1977; Verbrugge & McCarrell, 1977), and that metaphor comprehension is sensitive to nuances of individual variation (Pollio, 1977). The opposite problem has been that metaphor interpretations do not come out of nothing, which seems on the surface to be the only alternative if meaning does not reside somehow "in" the metaphor. This problem is resolved by thinking about metaphors as having an a priori set of meaning *possibilities* (possible properties, or feature if one prefers) out of which individual comprehension experiences (perceptual contexts) are derived. Creativity and context sensitivity are both involved in determining which possibilities will be realized.

One can proceed from *either* the first-person (perceiver's) or third-person (observer's) perspective in metaphor research. Neither approach is inherently better or more virtuous than the other. The danger lies in utilizing the methods appropriate to one approach, and then attempting to explain the outcomes in terms appropriate to the other. The third-person perspective is useful if we wish to discover some general characteristics of metaphor comprehension as they relate to populations, but it will not lead to an understanding of individual metaphor interpretation (except, of course, in aggregate terms). To mirror one of Gibson's (1977) points, it is possible to specify the perceptual information potentially available in a stimulus (verbal or otherwise) but it is not possible to specify whether that information will be picked up or utilized. In order to know what an individual will experience in a metaphor, you need to know a good deal about the individual as well as about the metaphor. The more we know about both the better our predictions will be.

ACKNOWLEDGMENTS

This chapter was prepared while the first author was on leave from the University of Tennessee, and in residence at the Center for Research in Human Learning, The University of Minnesota. This work was supported in part by a Faculty Development Award from the University of Tennessee, and a Postdoctoral Fellowship from the Center for Research in Human Learning.

REFERENCES

Bickerton, D. Prolegomena to a linguistic theory of metaphor. *Foundations of Language*, 1969, *4*, 34–52.

Black, M. Keynote address. Interdisciplinary Conference on Metaphor and Thought. University of Illinois, Champaign-Urbana, 1977.

Bransford, J. D., & Franks, J. J. The abstraction of linguistic ideas. *Cognitive Psychology,* 1971, *2,* 331–350.

Bransford, J. D., & Johnson, M. K. Consideration of some problems of comprehension. In W. Chase (Ed.), *Visual information processing.* New York: Academic Press, 1973.

Bransford, J. D., & McCarrell, N. S. A sketch of a cognitive approach to comprehension. In W. Weimer & D. Palerma (Eds.), *Cognition and the symbolic processes.* Hillsdale, N.J.: Lawrence Erlbaum Associates, 1974.

Butcher, S. H. *Aristotle's theory of poetry and fine art.* New York: Dover, 1951

Clement, D. E. Uncertainty and latency of verbal naming responses as correlates of pattern goodness. *Journal of Verbal Learning and Verbal Behavior,* 1964, *3,* 150–157.

Franks, J. J. Toward understanding understanding. In W. Weimer & D. Palerma (Eds.), *Cognition and the symbolic processes.* Hillsdale, N.J.: Lawrence Erlbaum Associates, 1974.

Gablik, S. *Magritte.* Boston: New York Graphic Society, 1976.

Gardner, H., Kircher, M., Winner, E., & Perkins, D. Children's metaphoric productions and preferences. *Journal of Child Language,* 1975, *2,* 125–141.

Garner, W. R. *Uncertainty and structure as psychological concepts.* New York: Wiley, 1962.

Garner, W. R. To perceive is to know. *American Psychologist,* 1966, *21,* 11–19.

Garner, W. R. Good patterns have few alternatives. *American Scientist,* 1970, *58,* 34–52.

Garner, W. R. *The processing of information and structure.* Hillsdale, N.J.: Lawrence Erlbaum Associates, 1974.

Garner, W. R., & Clement, D. E. Goodness of pattern and pattern uncertainty. *Journal of Verbal Learning and Verbal Behavior,* 1963, *2,* 446–452.

Garner, W. R., & Gottwald, R. L. The perception and learning of temporal patterns. *Quarterly Journal of Experimental Psychology,* 1968, *20,* 97–109.

Gibson, J. J. *The senses considered as perceptual systems.* Boston: Houghton Mifflin, 1966.

Gibson, J. J. The information available in pictures. *Leonardo,* 1971, *4,* 27–35.

Gibson, J. J. The theory of affordances. In R. Shaw & J. Bransford (Eds.), *Perceiving, acting and knowing.* Hillsdale, N.J.: Lawrence Erlbaum Associates, 1977.

Handel, S., & Garner, W. R. The structure of visual pattern associates and pattern goodness. *Perception and Psychophysics,* 1966, *1,* 33–38.

Harre, H., & Secord, P. F. *The explanation of social behavior.* Totowa, N.J.: LIttlefield, Adams, 1973.

Harwood, D. L., & Verbrugge, R. R. *Metaphor and the asymmetry of similarity.* Paper presented at the annual meetings of the American Psychological Association, San Francisco, California, August, 1977.

Hawkes, T. *Metaphor.* London: Methuen, 1972.

Hoffman, R. R. *Conceptual base hypotheses and the problem of anomalous sentences.* Paper presented at the annual meetings of the American Psychological Association, San Francisco, California, August, 1977.

Honeck, R. P., Riechmann, P., & Hoffman, R. R. Semantic memory for metaphor. *Memory and Cognition,* 1975, *3,* 409–415.

Honeck, R. P., Sowry, R., & Voegtle, K. Proverbial understanding in a pictorial context. *Child Development,* 1978, *49,* 327–331.

Jenkins, J. J. Remember that old theory of metaphor? Well, forget it! *American Psychologist,* 1974, *29,* 785–795.

Jenkins, J. J. *Context conditions meaning.* Invited paper presented at the annual meetings of the Midwestern Psychological Association, Chicago, Illinois, May, 1977.

Johnson, M. G. A cognitive-feature model of compound free associations. *Psychological Review,* 1970, *77,* 282–293.

Johnson, M. G. *Word meaning, attributes and inferred sets.* Paper presented at the annual meetings of the Psychonomic Society, St. Louis, Missouri, November, 1971.

Johnson, M. G. Some psychological implications of language flexibility. *Behaviorism,* 1975, *3,* 87–95. (a)

Johnson, M. G. *Some psycholinguistic implications of feature structures.* Paper presented at the semi-annual meetings of the Southeastern Conference on Linguistics, Nashville, Tennessee, March, 1975. (b)

Johnson, M. G. *The abstraction of meaning from complex pictures.* Paper presented at the annual meetings of the Psychonomic Society, Washington, D. C., November, 1977.

Johnson, M. G. *Similarities in the comprehension of metaphors and paintings.* Paper presented at the annual meetings of the American Psychological Association, Toronto, Canada, August, 1978.

Johnson, M. G., & Malgady, R. G. Some cognitive aspects of figurative language: Association and metaphor. *Journal of Psycholinguistic Research,* 1979, *8,* 249–265.

Katz, J. J., & Fodor, J. A. The structure of a semantic theory. *Language,* 1963, *39,* 170–210.

Klinger, E. *Meaning and void: Inner experience and the incentives in people's lives.* Minneapolis: University of Minnesota Press, 1977.

Larkin, D. (Ed.), *Magritte.* New York: Ballentine, 1972.

Malgady, R. G. *A feature synthesis model of metaphor processing.* Unpublished doctoral dissertation, University of Tennessee, 1975.

Malgady, R. G. Category size, feature comparison, and comprehension of figurative propositions. *Perceptual and Motor Skills,* 1976, *42,* 811–818.

Malgady, R. G. Discriminant analysis of psychological judgments of literal and figurative meaningfulness versus anomaly. *Journal of Psychology,* 1977, *95,* 217–221.

Malgady, R. G., & Johnson, M. G. Modifiers in metaphors: Effects of constituent phrase similarity on the interpretation of figurative sentences. *Journal of Psycholinguistic Research,* 1976, *5,* 43–52.

Malgady, R. G., & Johnson, M. G. Recognition memory for literal, figurative, and anomalous sentences. *Bulletin of the Psychonomic Society,* 1977, *9,* 214–216.

Meehl, P. E. Theory-testing in psychology and physics: A methodological paradox. *Philosophy of Science,* 1967, *34,* 103–115.

Miller, G. A. *Images and models, similes and metaphors.* Paper presented at the Interdisciplinary Conference on Metaphor and Thought. University of Illinois, Champaign-Urbana, September, 1977.

Miller, G. A., & Johnson-Laird, P. N. *Language and perception.* Cambridge, Mass.: Harvard University Press, 1976.

Neisser, U. *Cognition and reality.* San Francisco: Freeman, 1976.

Newell, A. You can't play twenty questions with nature and win. In W. Chase (Ed.), *Visual information processing.* New York: Academic Press, 1973.

Olson, D. R. Language and thought: Aspects of a cognitive theory of semantics. *Psychological Review,* 1970, *77,* 257–273.

Ortony, A. *Some psycholinguistic aspects of metaphor.* Paper presented at the annual convention of the American Psychological Association, symposium on Recent Psycholinguistic Research with Metaphors, San Francisco, California, August, 1977.

Ortony, A., Reynolds, R. E., & Arter, J. A. Metaphor: Theoretical and empirical research. *Psychological Bulletin,* 1978, *85,* 919–943.

Paivio, A. *Psychological processes in the comprehension of metaphor.* Paper presented at the Interdisciplinary Conference on Metaphor and Thought, University of Illinois, Champaign-Urbana, September, 1977.

Pastore, N. *Selective history of theories of visual perception: 1650–1950.* New York: Oxford University Press, 1971.

Pollio, H. R. *Metaphoric style: Personal cognition and figurative language.* Paper presented at the annual meetings of the American Psychological Association, San Francisco, California, August, 1977.

Pollio, H. R. Personal Communication, 1978.

Pollio, H. R., Barlow, J. M., Fine, H. J., & Pollio, M. R. *Psychology and the poetics of growth.* Hillsdale, N.J.: Lawrence Erlbaum Associates, 1977.

Pollio, H. R., & Burns, B. C. The anomaly of anomaly. *Journal of Psycholinguistic Research,* 1977, *6,* 247–260.

Pylyshyn, Z. What the mind's eye tells the mind's brain: A critique of mental imagery. *Psychological Bulletin,* 1973, *80,* 1–24.

Royer, F. L., & Garner, W. R. Response uncertainty and perceptual difficulty of auditory temporal patterns. *Perception and Psychophysics,* 1966, *1,* 41–47.

Shaw, R., & Bransford, J. (Eds.). *Perceiving, acting and knowing.* Hillsdale, N.J.: Lawrence Erlbaum Associates, 1977.

Smith, E. E., Shoben, E. J., & Rips, L. Structure and process in semantic memory: A feature comparison model for semantic decisions. *Psychological Review,* 1974, *81,* 214–241.

Thumb, A., & Marbe, K. *Experimentalle Untersuchunger uber die psychologischen Gundlagen der sprachlichen Analogiebildung.* Leipzig: W. Engleman, 1901.

Tourangeau, R., & Sternberg, R. J. *Understanding and appreciating metaphors.* NR150–412 ONR technical Report #11. New Haven: Department of Psychology, Yale University, 1978.

Tversky, A. Features of similarity. *Psychological Review,* 1977, *84,* 327–352.

Verbrugge, R. R. *Perceiving invariants at the invitation of metaphor.* Paper presented at the annual meetings of the American Psychological Association, Chicago, Illinois, August, 1975.

Verbrugge, R. R. Resemblances in language and perception. In R. Shaw & J. Bransford (Eds.), *Perceiving, acting and knowing.* Hillsdale, N.J.: Lawrence Erlbaum Associates, 1977.

Verbrugge, R. R. *Metaphor and the recognition of identities.* Paper presented at the annual meetings of the American Psychological Association, Toronto, Canada, August, 1978.

Verbrugge, R. R., & McCarrell, N. S. Metaphoric comprehension: Studies in reminding and resembling. *Cognitive Psychology,* 1977, *9,* 494–533.

Weinrich, U. Explorations in semantic theory. In T. Sebeok (Ed.), *Current trends in linguistics,* Vol. 3, *Theoretical foundations.* The Hague: Mouton, 1966.

12 Topic-Vehicle Relations in Metaphor: The Issue of Asymmetry

Kathleen Connor

Nathan Kogan
Graduate Faculty, New School for Social Research

Imagine, for a moment, an old man, bent and tired, and a barren, gnarled tree. How are they alike? Try to think of a sentence that expresses this similarity. Now visualize the skyline of a large city lit up at night. How could this scene be likened to a glamorous woman dressed in black and wearing many sparkling jewels?

Most likely, your attempts to express these relationships in words will result in what is called figurative language, for these kinds of comparisons are the raw materials from which metaphors and similes are formed. In each case, the two elements are drawn from different domains, yet share an underlying similarity or "ground" for comparison.

These examples are drawn from items in the Metaphoric Triads Task (MTT). For several years, we have been using this task to study various aspects of metaphoric thinking. Much previous research involving the MTT has addressed developmental and individual-difference issues (Kogan, 1980; Kogan, Connor, Gross, & Fava, 1980). Here, however, an initial set of findings directed toward a different problem will be presented. Our interest in understanding the nature of the cognitive activity involved in comprehending and producing metaphors has led us to examine the relationships between the main elements of a metaphor—the topic and the vehicle. Before discussing this research, however, the MTT will be described in more detail, and the considerations that led to the present approach will be outlined.

THE METAPHORIC TRIADS TASK

The present approach rests on the assumption that metaphor is a cognitive rather than strictly linguistic phenomenon. By this, we mean that there are certain perceptual and conceptual processes involved in metaphoric thinking that are common to a variety of forms of expression (e.g., metaphor, simile, personification, proverb). We do not deny that specific forms may also pose unique cognitive demands; indeed, other researchers have provided evidence to support this claim (e.g., Verbrugge, this volume; Winner & Engel, 1979). Rather, we have simply chosen to direct our attention toward that part of the process common to a variety of figurative forms; that is, the ability to make conceptual links between objects or events from disparate domains. This ability is one that has been consistently overlooked in both individual difference and developmental studies of cognition. Research on divergent thinking, for example, has explored individual differences in the breadth of similarity classes. However, the emphasis on the fluency and statistical uniqueness of an individual's productions has precluded much consideration of the quality or content of responses to divergent-thinking tasks. It is here that a link to metaphor might become apparent.

Other related work reinforces the view that metaphor can operate through sensory or other media as well as through words. Synesthetic and physiognomic phenomena have previously received attention as nonverbal forms of metaphor (e.g., Gardner, 1974; Werner & Kaplan, 1963). Johnson and Malgady (this volume) have suggested that the interpretation of some works of art may parallel the interpretation of verbal metaphors, while Verbrugge (1975) reported some success in using musical passages as prompts for recall of metaphoric sentences. These examples testify to the frequency with which metaphoric relations are expressed in nonverbal media. In keeping with a long tradition in Gestalt psychology (Arnheim, 1949; Asch, 1952; Köhler, 1937), as well as recent writings by Verbrugge (1977) and Johnson and Malgady (this volume), we would further like to suggest that apprehension of figurative relations may normally occur in nonlinguistic media and only later be expressed through verbal forms. Clearly, if this is the case, it becomes important to study these perceptual bases of metaphor and their relation to verbal processes.

The foregoing considerations guided the development of the Metaphoric Triads Task (MTT). Items in the MTT are triads of chromatic pictures. Two of these are metaphorically related and the third shares a nonmetaphoric relation with each of the other two. The latter may be based on function, category membership, or thematic appropriateness. For instance, the triad containing the old man and the gnarled tree includes a third picture of a wooden rocking chair; the woman and the city skyline referred to earlier are accompanied by a third picture of an elegant city street during the day. In its final form, the MTT is comprised of 29 such triads. As the examples suggest, the the nature of the metaphoric relationship varies from triad to triad. Some are more configural, others are more conceptual. For still other items, such as one including a foggy street corner and the veiled face of a woman, the relationship involves both configural and conceptual aspects.

In the standard administration of the MTT, the subject is presented with a triad of pictures and is asked to choose the two that "go together" best and to explain the basis for the pairing. He or she also has the opportunity to form other possible pairings and to explain their bases as well. The interest, of course, is in whether the subject recognizes the metaphoric pairing and explains it clearly. Two points are assigned to each triad where this occurs, while a score of zero is given when the subject fails to make the critical pairing in a particular triad or when the pairing is made for nonmetaphoric reasons (e.g., pairing the old man with the candle because "he could use it to see better"). When the subject's explanation indicates an understanding of the metaphor, yet is not sufficiently explicit or complete to receive full credit, one point is given. Inter-rater agreement has ranged well above 90%, indicating that the scoring system is highly reliable.

Kogan et al. (1980) reported various studies exploring the psychometric properties of the task. Examination of Cronbach's (1951) coefficient alpha within several samples suggested that the MTT demonstrates a reasonable level of internal consistency, with coefficients generally ranging from the mid 70's to the mid 80's. Correlations between alternate forms were also high, with the Pearson coefficient ranging from .55 to .80 over short periods of time, and from .40 to .62 when several months intervened. While mean difficulty levels of individual items varied considerably, the rank ordering of these means remained fairly constant across diverse samples. The MTT has been administered to subjects varying widely in age, yielding steadily improving performance from about 7 years of age to adulthood. However, a ceiling effect was not observed, for many adults fell far short of a perfect score. No consistent sex differences have appeared on the MTT.

Several studies reported in Kogan et al. (1980) offer evidence for both convergent and discriminant validity. For samples of children, teacher ratings of aesthetic sensitivity, quality scores on divergent thinking tasks and performance on the Remote Associates Test (Mednick, 1962) have all yielded significant positive correlations with the MTT. In a sample of college students, quality scores on divergent thinking tasks, category breadth, and physiognomic sensitivity proved to be related to MTT performance. These relations made good theoretical sense since metaphoric sensitivity is often viewed as being closely related to creativity, and involves the ability to make connections across category boundaries. On the other hand, teacher ratings of children on other positive qualities, such as resourcefulness and sense of humor, did not correlate with scores on the triads. Relations with various measures of IQ and academic achievement were also examined as a test of discriminant validity. No consistent pattern of correlations was found, suggesting that general intellective ability cannot account for most of the individual variation in MTT scores.

A series of training studies were conducted to determine whether mean levels of performance observed for various age groups represented maximal performance. We further expected these investigations to tell us something about the processes underlying MTT performance. Initial experiments demonstrated that simply encouraging children to consider all possible pairings among the three members of a triad facilitated performance. Performance was further improved when children were provided with brief explanations of both metaphoric and nonmetaphoric pairings for a few items. A third training study (Kogan & Connor, 1979) grew out of our interest in understanding the way these visual stimuli were apprehended by the children. In order to succeed on the MTT, children must perceive and attend to certain expressive qualities in the critical pictures. Indeed, as we implied earlier, such perceptual activities may well be important to metaphoric thinking in any situation. With these considerations in mind, an experiment was designed to facilitate performance by helping subjects "see" the appropriate qualities in the stimuli. This was accomplished through a verbal labeling procedure.

After initial pretesting, 100 fourth and fifth graders were randomly divided into three groups. One group was asked to provide short captions or labels for each of the three pictures in a triad before making pairs, while another group of children saw labels provided by the experimenter. The third group constituted a control condition, where children simply followed the standard pairing procedure. An analysis of covariance on metaphor scores during the training session, using pretest scores as the covariate, revealed a significant training effect. Inspection of the means indicated that those children who saw labels provided by the experimenter improved dramatically while the children who provided their own labels and the children in the control group improved only slightly. Our initial speculation about the importance of the way in which children encode the stimuli received further support from an examination of change scores for individual items. When one or both members of the critical pair were complex or ambiguous enough to permit multiple encodings, the item benefited from the experimenter's labels. Those items where both pictures were simple and unambiguous showed little improvement.

The relatively clear picture that emerged from these results was somewhat complicated by a further analysis. If our labels served to bring certain qualities to the attention of the children in the experimenter-label group, then children in the own-label condition whose labels indicated that they too were attending to the relevant characteristics would be expected to perform better than children whose labels suggested attention to irrelevant information. Accordingly, we scored the children's own labels and tested the relationship between the quality of the labels for a given item and success on that item using Fisher's exact test. Surprisingly, there was a significant relationship for only one item. This outcome suggests that these children were not treating their own labels as seriously as the experimenter-label group treated ours. Although the present results do not provide enough information to draw conclusive inferences about the reasons for this difference, they point to a possible distinction between the "seeing" and the "attaching significance to" aspects of forming a concept about visual information. Alternatively, perhaps children need the kind of extra encouragement provided by a directive examiner before they will put useful information to work in performing a task—in this case, identifying the metaphorical pair. Clearly, we have only begun to understand the process underlying metaphor recognition, but it seems likely that further examination of the relationship between visual and verbal processes can make important contributions to this problem.

DIRECTIONALITY IN METAPHOR

Like other related tasks (Gardner, 1974; Honeck, Sowry, & Voegtle, 1978; Werner & Kaplan, 1963), the MTT employs an equivalence format in which subjects are asked to pair two items on the basis of an underlying similarity. Yet metaphor often involves a directional comparison, with each of the elements playing a distinct role in creating the metaphoric relation. These two roles have been labeled in a variety of ways; we shall follow Verbrugge (1974) and use the terms topic and vehicle. The relationship between the topic and the vehicle has been the subject of extensive conceptual analysis in psychology as well as other disciplines (e.g., Black, 1962; Malgady, 1975; Ortony, Reynolds, & Arter, 1978; Pollio, Barlow, Fine, & Pollio, 1977; Verbrugge, 1977; Wheelwright, 1962). Since these issues have been thoroughly treated in other sources, we will not attempt to review them here. We would, however, like to point out that despite substantial disagreements as to the mechanisms involved, there seems to be some consensus regarding the major function of the two elements—the vehicle acts to structure the nature of the concept formed about the topic. Even those theorists who suggest that both the topic and the vehicle are modified in the process of creating a metaphor would seem to admit that the modification is asymmetrical. Richards expresses it well; he says that the vehicle controls "the mode in which the topic forms" (1936, p. 122).

Is this distinction a psychologically meaningful one, with implications for the cognitive processing of metaphor, or merely an analytic tool useful in describing different parts of a metaphoric expression? Some evidence that this type of asymmetry does have real significance for metaphor processing has been provided by Verbrugge and McCarrell (1977), who have studied metaphor comprehension in a series of memory prompting studies. Their stimulus materials consisted of a number of verbal similes as well as sentences stating the ground relation expressed by each of these. In one experiment, they presented respondents with anomalous sentences containing either the topic or the vehicle of their original similes. They then used the ground statements of the original similes as prompts for recall of the anomalous sentences. It was found that the grounds were more effective in prompting recall of sentences containing the original vehicle than of sentences containing the original topic. In another experiment, Verbrugge and McCarrell provided their respondents with incomplete sentences based on the ground statements of their metaphors. The sentences were of the form "_____ is (ground)." Respondents were asked to provide at least three possible subjects for each sentence. An analysis of responses revealed that the original vehicle was a more common response than the original topic. Both of these experiments suggest that the metaphoric vehicle is more closely related to the ground of a metaphor than is the topic.

More recently, Verbrugge (this volume) has studied the effect of reversing topic-vehicle structure. Subjects were asked to read either metaphor or simile statements and to record any thoughts or images that passed through their minds in response to these statements. All of the sentences were based on metaphorically related pairs of concepts. Some subjects saw sentences of the form "A is B" (or "A is like B"); others saw the same statements with topic-vehicle order reversed. Part of the analysis was directed toward determining whether the focus of subjects' responses was A or B. Direction of the original statement clearly affected this measure. The term (A or B) appearing first in the statement was more often the domain to be transformed in the subjects' thoughts and images. This effect was stronger for subjects who viewed the sentences in the particular A-B order previously designated as preferred by an independent group of subjects.

Taken together, these three studies clearly suggest that topics and vehicles play functionally distinct roles in metaphor. Verbrugge's (this volume) work also supports the view that these roles are dependent, in part, on the intrinsic characteristics of the concepts joined in the metaphor. He reports that subjects' biases favoring one direction over another were stronger for certain items than for others, and suggests that this is related to the content of the items themselves.

Formal support for the notion that intrinsic characteristics of concepts can influence the relationships in which they participate comes from research in nonmetaphoric similarity. Rosch (1975) demonstrated that asymmetries occur in tasks tapping preferences in direction for hedged equivalence statements ("A _____ is essentially _____.") and in the psychological distance perceived between a referent and a comparison, when one member of the pair compared was more prototypical of the category to which both belonged. When neither of the two stimuli was especially prototypical, these asymmetries were less likely to occur.

Tversky's (1977) review of relevant literature suggests that asymmetry of the foregoing type is typical of similarity relations, rather than a chance occurrence deriving from response biases or other incidental factors. He has formulated an elegant feature-comparison model of similarity in which the similarity between two objects can be represented by a weighted linear combination. The feature sets representing the common and the distinctive features of the two objects compared are designated by scale values reflecting the overall salience of each feature set. The scale values or measures are the terms that compose the linear comparison. These terms are weighted to reflect certain task characteristics such as whether the subject is required to make a directional or nondirectional comparison (i.e., "How similar are A and B?" versus "How similar is A to B?"). The model predicts that a similarity relationship is symmetrical whenever the objects are equal in their overall salience *or* when the task itself is nondirectional (which would be the case, for instance, in the standard administration of the MTT). When the two objects differ in salience, and the task instructions permit a directional response, the model predicts that perceived similarity would be greater when the object with greater salience serves as a referent or standard, and the less salient object is the subject of the comparison. Because perceived similarity is greater under these circumstances, subjects would be expected to express preferences for statements of this form. Tversky and Gati (1978) cite several studies providing empirical support for this model. Tversky (1977) proposes that metaphor might be profitably treated as an instance of an asymmetrical similarity relation. The implication, of course, is that both metaphoric and nonmetaphoric similarity will conform to the same mathematical model.

Rosch's theory of prototypes and Tversky's feature-comparison model represent two ways of thinking about differences in internal conceptual structure that might account for asymmetrical relationships between concepts. Thus far, attempts to identify similar intrinsic topic-vehicle properties in metaphor have been of the feature model type. Indeed, the Tversky approach bears some resemblance to the model of metaphor comprehension proposed by Malgady (1975). A central aspect of Malgady's feature-synthesis approach is his use of Garner's (1962) "uncertainty" construct. Uncertainty refers to the information value of a stimulus, and is a function of both the number of features in the stimulus and the commonality structure of these features. Malgady suggests that metaphor processing should be impeded if the vehicle is relatively more "uncertain" than the topic. This, of course, leads to the prediction that subjects will express a preference for the sentence order in which the more uncertain term serves as topic and the term with lower uncertainty as the vehicle.

More recently, there have been direct attempts to test the applicability of the Tversky model to metaphoric stimuli. Harwood and Verbrugge (1977) reversed both the order of presentation of topic-vehicle pairs and the order of judgment statements, and modified stimulus context by comparing two-term and four-term analogies. Although they did not find an effect of judgment order, as the Tversky model would have predicted, their results did show significant asymmetries in similarity as a function of order of presentation. Further, there was a strong main effect of stimulus, indicating that items were differentially affected by these kinds of reversals. The authors suggest that a more homogeneous pool of items might yield stronger effects of judgment and presentation orders. Malgady and Johnson (this volume) have also tested the applicability of the Tversky model to metaphor. Since this research is presented elsewhere in this volume, we will not describe it here. While these authors were able to identify order-dependent asymmetries in their data, the asymmetries were not of precisely the form specified by the Tversky model. While neither of the above studies has provided unequivocal support for the Tversky model, they do present further evidence that at least some metaphors are asymmetrical—they "work" better in one direction than in the other. Better defining the nature of this asymmetry may prove to be an important key to understanding metaphoric thinking.

One serious problem confronting those who wish to test predictions derived from feature models in a realistic stimulus context is the difficulty of operationally defining "features." Both Tversky (1977) and Malgady and Johnson (this volume) acknowledge that any such test of a model is at the same time a test of this operationalization. Nonconfirmation of the model may be interpreted as casting doubt on the particular measure chosen to represent the features of an object. The difficulties caused by this problem are among the reasons that we have chosen to pursue a more qualitative approach to asymmetry in metaphor. A further consideration stems from our interest in nonverbal metaphor, where the type of semantic-feature analysis used by Malgady and Johnson becomes difficult to apply.

We shall approach the problem of asymmetry by identifying pools of stimulus items that clearly show and do not show this property. These two pools of items can be examined to identify distinctive qualities within each. As Verbrugge (this volume) has noted, these qualities may well be related to the content of the individual items. Kogan (1980) and Kogan, et al. (1980) have offered some speculation as to the nature of asymmetries that might occur in MTT items. A hierarchy is proposed, composed of human, animals, plants and physical objects or events. When members of a comparison pair belong to different levels in this hierarchy, the member at the higher level is more likely to function as the subject or topic of this comparison, and the member at the lower level as the referent or vehicle. In contrast to such comparison between terms from different levels, it should follow that comparison between terms from the same level in the hierarchy would be symmetrical.

There are several reasons why this might be the case. First, the topic of a metaphor is the element of greater interest, the idea upon which attention is focused. It is not unreasonable to think that for many individuals, the human is generally more interesting than the nonhuman. Further, the purpose of a metaphor is to convey something about the topic through the vehicle. This suggests another possible characteristic of a topic; it may be more complex or more ambiguous than the vehicle to which it is compared. The vehicle, in turn, would have a simpler structure, with the metaphoric quality more pronounced or salient. It seems plausible that the continuum from object to person reflects an increasing degree of ambiguity. Persons and animals have more aspects, partake of more relationships, belong to more contexts, than plants and objects. If topics, then, emerge from the higher end of this hierarchy and vehicles from the lower end, it would then be possible for the vehicle to restructure perception of the topic so as to make its quality salient. Although we have taken a different approach to the problem of asymmetry, it is apparent that our expectations are not inconsistent with much of the previously described research and theory (Johnson & Malgady, this volume; Malgady, 1975; Malgady & Johnson, this volume).

The proposed hierarchy is not intended to suggest a rigid framework for topic-vehicle relations. Major exceptions are the attribution of human qualities to animals and to objects. These are so important that special terms have been coined to designate them—anthropomorphism and personification, respectively. Note further that context will influence what constitutes the topic and the vehicle of a particular relationship. The setting in which a metaphor is created may affect the structure of that metaphor. For the natural scientist or the nature-loving poet, for example, animals, plants or objects may well be the focus of attention. They may sometimes be illumunated by comparison to the human domain. Cultural differences represent another type of contextual effect. Conceivably, natural events in less technologically sophisticated societies could be viewed as more ambiguous or complex than the more familiar domain of personal relations. Despite these obvious exceptions, it is our view that the proposed hierarchy may serve as a heuristic device to help us organize our initial analysis of topic-vehicle relations.

AN EMPIRICAL EXAMINATION OF METAPHORIC ASYMMETRY

Statement of the Problem

The remainder of the chapter describes a study investigating metaphorical asymmetry in MTT items. These items are particularly well adapted to this problem, for the elements in the relationship are presented separately rather than as part of an already formed linguistic unit. Thus, subjects can "tell" us what constitutes the topic or the vehicle of a particular metaphoric relation. In the absence of other contextual constraints, these judgments will very likely be based on characteristics of the concepts that subjects form in response to our stimuli. If a large proportion of subjects agree in their judgment of a given item, this would constitute evidence that topic-vehicle structure is partially dependent on the nature of the concepts formed. Further, as indicated earlier, once particular MTT items have been identified as symmetrical or asymmetrical, inferences can be drawn about content-based reasons for the symmetries and asymmetries. Homogeneous item pools will also permit us to confirm and extend previously discussed findings regarding differences between topic and vehicle. These approaches should go a long way toward illuminating the nature of metaphoric thinking.

In planning the present study, we considered two alternative procedures: a preference task, where the subject chooses between two sentences with different topic-vehicle structures, and a production task, where the subject is presented with two metaphorically related terms and asked to write a metaphor or simile based on them. Our decision to use the latter procedure was strongly influenced by the evidence of substantial individual differences in ability to recognize metaphoric relationships in MTT items. Although we planned to minimize individual differences in the present study through modifications in the instructions and use of examples, we did not expect each subject to comprehend each metaphoric relation. By requiring subjects to compose a sentence based on the metaphoric components, information is provided not only about topic-vehicle structure, but also about subjects' perceptions of the ground of the relationship between the two. One can then discard sentences based on nonmetaphoric grounds prior to the examination of topic-vehicle structure.[1]

Although the present task format is based on the production of metaphoric relations, we do not claim to be modeling the production of metaphors in the real world. In the latter context, the topic is often immediately available and the metaphor-producer attempts to find a fitting vehicle. Nevertheless, we would expect that choice to be determined by the kinds of conceptual properties under study in the present investigation.

Stimulus Materials

A pool of 40 items was employed. Twenty were selected from the standard 29-item pictorial form of the MTT. Of the remaining nine items, seven were translated into verbal equivalents; a short verbal phrase was formulated to describe each of the critical pictures. Recognition of the metaphoric linkage in the remaining two MTT triads (a sleeping woman's face and a house with drawn shades; a worn-out woman and a barren landscape) has proven to be very difficult even in adult samples. Since success of the present experiment depended upon subjects' ability to recognize the metaphoric relationship in each case, these two items were dropped. One of them—the sleeping woman and the house—was used as a sample item. Thirteen additional verbal items were constructed. A number of these were based on verbal metaphors and similes used by other researchers (Billow, 1975; Winner, Rosenstiel, & Gardner, 1976; Verbrugge, 1974). Since there are no data on the reliability and validity of these items, we cannot be sure that they are comparable to standard triads of the MTT. Nevertheless, we considered it worthwhile to include these verbal items as an initial examination of visual-verbal comparability. The type of data to be collected will permit an examination of the two types of items in respect to their intercorrelations as well as their similarities and differences in patterns of asymmetry. The 20 pictorial and 20 verbal items are shown in Tables 12.1 and 12.2, respectively.

---

[1]It should be noted that most research on metaphoric asymmetry is based on the assumption of virtually complete comprehension of the metaphoric statements employed. As metaphors become more subtle, this assumption obviously becomes more tenuous.

A sample of 6 pictorial items is presented in the Appendix to this chapter. Note that these are shown in black and white, whereas actual MTT items are chromatic.

Subjects

One hundred and thirty six students (94 females and 42 males) enrolled in four sections of a psychology course in a parochial high school in New York City took part in this study.[2] The sex ratio across the four sections varied from 23% to 37% male. The large majority of the subjects were seniors ranging from 16 to 18 years of age. (Four of the subjects were 16-year-old juniors.) Subjects participated in the experiment in intact classes, each class assigned to a different condition (Groups I, II, III, and IV).

Procedure

In order to create a task of reasonable length, both in terms of available time and students' attention span, stimuli were randomly divided into two sets of 20 items, 10 verbal and 10 pictorial in each set. Metaphors with similar "themes" were approximately evenly divided between the two sets. One member of each pair was arbitrarily designated as "A" and the other as "B."

Subjects were told that the purpose of the research was to find out how people recognize and talk about similarities, especially metaphorical similarities. The experimental session began with brief definitions of metaphor and simile, accompanied by examples of each. The subjects were told they would be viewing pairs of slides containing either pictures or phrases. Each time a pair was shown, they would be asked to write a metaphor or simile based on a comparison between the two. They were told that their sentences would probably look something like this:

"_____ is like _____ because . . . ."

A poster with this format sentence was placed at the front of the room where it could be viewed during the experimental session.[3]

---

[2]The disproportionately large number of females reflects a sex difference in the propensity of students in this school to enroll in a psychology course, rather than any differential willingness to participate in the present study. One of the four sections represented an "Honors" class (Group II). However, enrollment in that class was at least partly a matter of self-selection. The teacher indicated that there were a number of students in the other three sections who would have been eligible to enroll in the Honors class. In any case, there is no reason to expect an interaction between scholastic achievement and preference for a particular topic-vehicle structure.

[3]One might raise the question that ease of explication of the ground of the simile might bias decisions about topic-vehicle order. Pilot data has indicated that the content of ground statements for a particular item does not appear to be related to the choice of A or B as topic or vehicle. Conceivably, the brevity of these ground statements contributed to this outcome.

Subjects were urged not to be unduly influenced by the left-right sequence of the stimulus presentation when composing their sentences. The experimenter pointed out that a change in the direction of a comparison sometimes can change its meaning; she encouraged subjects to think about both possible directions, choosing the one most preferred. Subjects appeared to have little difficulty understanding the instructions; virtually no questions were asked in any of the four groups. The time allowed for each group seemed ample, with most subjects finishing before time was called.

Two pairs of stimuli were shown as examples, one pictorial and one verbal, and appropriate metaphoric sentences were read to subjects. The use of response booklets containing 20 blank pages permitted subjects to record one sentence per page. Slides of stimulus pairs were projected on two screens at the front of the classroom. Each pair was presented for 90 seconds. Groups I and II viewed the first twenty items, while groups III and IV saw items 21–40. Recall that each of these item sets contained an equal number of pictorial and verbal items and was reasonably balanced for thematic content. In Groups I and III, the number of the pair arbitrarily designated as ''A'' appeared on the left screen, and the ''B'' member on the right. For Groups II and IV, this left-right order was reversed.

Results

Sentences generated by subjects in the various conditions were first evaluated to determine whether these were based on the metaphoric relation underlying each stimulus pair. Virtually all of the sentences included enough information about the basis of the comparison to be evaluated in terms of the criteria employed in scoring standard MTT protocols. Sentences meeting the criteria for one or two points in the standard scoring procedure were retained; the others were considered unscorable for the purposes of the present study. Those few sentences where no ground was expressed (e.g., *The top is like a ballerina*) were also eliminated. Finally, those sentences whose structure was nondirectional were excluded (e.g., *The top and the ballerina are alike because both twirl*). These unscorable responses (approximately 20% of the total) were not included in further analyses of the data. For the remaining scorable responses, we determined whether stimulus A or stimulus B was used as the topic of the metaphor or simile. The percentage of subjects choosing stimulus A as a topic for a given pair then became the dependent variable used in subsequent analyses.

In the first stage of data analysis, the effects of sex and the left-right order of item presentation were examined. A two-factor repeated-measures ANOVA was performed on each item set, with individual items constituting the unit of analysis, and sex and order the repeated measures. Since the dependent variable is expressed in percentage form, an arc-sine transformation was applied before the ANOVAs were carried out (Winer, 1971). The outcomes of the two analyses were similar. The effect of left-right stimulus presentation order was significant for both sets of items (first set: $F(1,19) = 8.34$, $p < .01$; second set: $F(1,19) = 74.34$, $p < .001$). Sex and sex $\times$ order interactions did not achieve significance in either analysis.

As might be expected, the left-right effect ensued from a higher proportion of subjects choosing A as topic in the condition where it appeared on the left; this was observed in 35 of the 40 items. This kind of left-right effect could potentially assume one of two forms. In one of these, the majority of subjects in the AB group might choose "A" as topic for a given item, while the majority in the BA group might prefer "B." Alternatively, "A" might be chosen as topic in both groups, with the effect attenuated in the BA group. The latter outcome, of course, would provide stronger support for the asymmetry hypothesis. We examined the 35 items for which "A" was preferred as topic by a larger percentage of subjects in the AB group than in the BA group, and found that the left-right effect took the form of attenuation rather than reversal for 17 of these items. This outcome indicates that many items do demonstrate considerable intersubject agreement on topic-vehicle structure across BA and AB conditions despite the significant left-right effect. Nevertheless, this order effect posed something of a problem for the remaining analyses.

Is there better-than-chance agreement among subjects as to which stimulus (A or B) constitutes the topic of the metaphor? To answer this, we need a single proportion for each item reflecting the judgments of all subjects viewing that item. This proportion can then be evaluated against a .5 baseline representing equiprobable choice of the A or B stimulus as topic. However, responses in this experiment were clearly somewhat biased in favor of the stimulus appearing on the left. Further, there were different numbers of scorable responses for the AB and BA groups for each item. Hence, combining these two conditions into a single percentage would bias the expected value of the null hypothesis in the direction of the stimulus on the left for the larger group. For this reason, we eliminated responses for each item randomly so that the number of subjects in the AB and the BA conditions would be equal. In this way, the expected value of the null hypothesis is restored to .5.

Table 12.1 shows for pictorial items the equalized proportions of choice of A as topic for AB and BA conditions combined. Comparable data for verbal items are presented in Table 12.2. In addition to the raw proportions, Tables 12.1 and 12.2 also offer converted proportions; for those items where the majority of the subjects chose B as topic, we have simply taken the complement of the original proportion. This permits a ranking of items by level of intersubject agreement.

Large sample sizes permitted the use of the normal approximation to the binomial distribution for evaluating the deviation of each proportion from the expected value of .5. The small number of scorable responses for item #11 necessitated the use of exact binomial probabilities. The probability values are listed in the last column of Tables 12.1 and 12.2. It is evident that the number of significant proportions is well in excess of chance expectancy. Nineteen of 40

TABLE 12.1
Levels of Asymmetry in Topic-Vehicle Preference for Pictorial Items

Groups	Items		% of Subjects Choosing A as topic (x)	Converted % (1-x) for x < .5	N	1-tail p
	A	B				
I & II	17. explosion	man in a rage	.053	.947	38	.000
	13. ancient tree	a grandfather	.205	.795	44	.000
	16. woman with long hair	hanging plant	.680	.680	50	.008
	1. spinning top	dancing ballerina	.357	.643	56	.023
	14. veiled woman	foggy street corner	.632	.632	38	.072
	5. rooster crowing	farmer showing muscles	.381	.619	42	.082
	3. broken down house	moldy swiss cheese	.577	.577	52	.166
	11. cracks in ice near skating boy	boy with beehive	.400	.600	10	.377
	9. car wheel	traffic circle	.525	.525	40	.436
	8. baby	rose bud	.520	.520	50	.444
III & IV	38. thunderstorm	angry man	.214	.786	56	.000
	22. sunflower	tall thin woman	.229	.771	48	.000
	30. city lit up at night	woman with jewels	.259	.741	54	.000
	28. wilted plant	hot tired runner	.397	.603	58	.075
	37. "droopy" house	drowsy person	.391	.609	46	.092
	25. winding river	snake	.419	.581	62	.127
	24. fish on hook	plane on fire	.464	.536	56	.174
	36. melting snowman	waves running into a sandcastle	.558	.558	52	.245
	40. old woman sick in bed	wilted flowers	.524	.524	42	.440
	34. sad woman	weeping willow	.483	.517	58	.448

TABLE 12.2

Levels of Asymmetry in Topic-Vehicle Preference for Verbal Items

Groups	Items A	B	% of Subjects choosing A as topic (x)	Converted % (1-x) for x < .5	N	1-tail p
I & II	18. teeth	pearls	.813	.813	48	.000
	2. an unfriendly guard	a boulder	.740	.740	50	.001
	10. a man pushing through a crowd	a bulldozer	.740	.740	50	.001
	12. an avalanche	heavy suitcases on a baggage chute	.261	.739	46	.001
	6. a strand of beads	a freight train	.262	.738	42	.002
	7. a deep snowfall	a thick blanket	.711	.711	38	.007
	15. a ship in stormy seas	a man lost in the desert	.326	.674	46	.013
	19. a giraffe	the Empire State Building	.558	.558	52	.245
	20. a blind man walking alone	a boat at sea on a foggy night	.477	.523	44	.326
	4. a flock of geese	marching soldiers	.480	.520	50	.444
III & IV	21. a boxer	a charging bull	.721	.721	68	.000
	26. a violin	a canary	.310	.690	58	.006
	32. a broken bottle	a bum on the street	.359	.641	64	.017
	23. a child skipping	a white rabbit	.638	.638	58	.025
	33. a pond	a mirror	.636	.636	66	.018
	31. messy hair	a mound of spaghetti	.576	.576	66	.133
	27. flies caught in a spider web	a net full of fish	.429	.571	56	.174
	39. the trunk of a tall tree	a straw in a can of soda	.432	.568	44	.227
	35. an old man in a wheelchair	a lit candle almost burnt down	.537	.537	54	.341
	29. cancer	crabgrass	.467	.533	60	.349

items yielded p-values significant at better than the .05 level; three additional items met the asymmetry criterion at the .10 level. Note, finally, that the separate sets of items (Groups I and II vs. Groups III and IV) generated approximately equivalent distributions of p-values. This is particularly reassuring given that random assignment to treatments was not feasible.

Since we were still concerned about the effects of left-right order on the results of the asymmetry analysis, we performed a further analysis on the significantly asymmetrical items. For these items, all of the raw proportions for the AB and BA groups were evaluated separately. We reasoned that if a particular item retained its significant level of asymmetry in the more unfavorable of the two conditions, i.e., when the "topic" appeared on the right, then the degree of asymmetry must indeed be very strong. As Table 12.3 shows, this was the case for 9 of the 19 items (11 of 19 if a relaxed p-value of .10 is employed). Note further that only 3 of the 19 items (#1, #32, and #33) failed to show consistent asymmetry across the AB-BA conditions.

TABLE 12.3
Consistency of Asymmetry (Choosing A as Topic) for Significantly
Asymmetrical Items

Groups	Items			AB			BA		
	Pictorial			%	N	1-tail p	%	N	1-tail p
	A		B						
I & II	1. top		ballerina	.500	28	.500	.207	29	.001
	13. old tree	**	grandfather	.227	22	.004	.250	28	.007
	16. woman		hanging plant	.800	25	.003	.538	26	.421
	17. explosion	**	angry man	.136	22	.000	.000	19	.000
III & IV	22. sunflower	*	woman	.300	30	.051	.125	24	.000
	30. city at night	**	woman	.323	31	.036	.185	27	.002
	38. thunderstorm	*	angry man	.364	33	.082	.071	28	.000
	Verbal								
I & II	2. guard	**	boulder	.720	25	.021	.800	30	.001
	6. beads		train	.381	21	.192	.148	27	.001
	7. snowfall	**	blanket	.737	19	.033	.760	25	.008
	10. man	**	bulldozer	.680	25	.027	.828	29	.001
	12. avalanche	**	suitcases	.304	23	.023	.222	27	.003
	15. ship		man	.435	23	.337	.214	28	.003
	18. teeth	**	pearls	.833	24	.001	.759	29	.005
III & IV	21. boxer	**	bull	.771	35	.001	.676	34	.026
	23. child		rabbit	.687	32	.026	.586	29	.230
	26. violin		canary	.471	34	.430	.172	29	.001
	32. bottle		bum	.500	32	.500	.219	32	.001
	33. pond		mirror	.806	36	.001	.455	33	.363

*p < .10 for both AB and BA; **p < .05 for both AB and BA

Consider now, the difference between the outcomes for pictorial and verbal items reported in Tables 12.1 and 12.2, respectively. With .05 as the accepted significance level, 7 pictorial and 12 verbal items were distinguished by asymmetry. This difference is less than substantial, however, for the contrast becomes 11 pictorial vs. 12 verbal items at the .10 level. Thus, it is apparent that the pictorial-verbal contrast had a negligible impact upon the extent of metaphoric asymmetry observed in the present study. The comparability of the two item types with respect to direction of asymmetry will be discussed in a later section of this chapter.

Consider next the correlation between the two item types in respect to recognition of the metaphoric relation. The number of sentences reaching this criterion for both visual and verbal items was noted. Correlations between pictorial and verbal items were .53 and .66 for the first and second sets of items, respectively. Although these correlations were of moderate magnitude, both were highly significant ($p < .005$). It must be emphasized that instructions and task format were designed to reduce the impact of individual differences on outcomes. This, along with the lenient scoring criteria used here, limited the extent of variance in the scores and hence, probably attenuated the correlations. The restriction of range is reflected in the mean levels of performance for the two types of items. The means for pictorial metaphors were 8.28 (Set I) and 8.84 (Set II) out of 10 items. The comparable means for verbal items were 9.57 (Set I) and 9.34 (Set II), again out of 10. It is interesting to note that in each item set the verbal items appeared to be somewhat easier. Whether this is a function of the medium of presentation or individual item content is unclear from the present data. In either case, the data clearly support the view that comparable cognitive processes distinguish metaphoric operations in the pictorial and verbal media.

Discussion

The results as a whole indicate that particular visual and verbal pairings generated asymmetrical metaphors in the productions of our subjects. Approximately half of the stimulus pairs met the criterion of significant asymmetry. However, the analyses of variance demonstrated that left-right order of stimulus presentation contributed significantly to subjects' decisions about sentence structure, despite efforts to dissuade them from relying on order as a cue. Apparently, the habit of working from left to right is a well-learned and powerful one. Clearly it was not potent enough to obscure the phenomenon under study, for we would not then have observed so many significant asymmetries. Yet, the left-right effect was strong enough to complicate the process of interpretation. Only 9 of the 19 significant pairs maintained significant levels of consensus in the more unfavorable of the two presentation situations—that is, where the "topic" stimulus appeared on the right. These seem to be strong cases of asymmetry, since the effect overrides life-long scanning habits. On the other hand, the other 10 metaphors appear to be weak instances of asymmetry, for the effect was attenuated when extraneous influences were introduced.

The results further suggest that asymmetry characterizes items cast in both pictorial and verbal forms. Indeed, the number of items of each type manifesting significant asymmetry was approximately equal. Such outcomes are at least mildly surprising, for one might have expected the left-right order effect to be more prominent with words rather than with pictures. Yet, there was no indication that the left-to-right reading habit interfered more with asymmetry in the verbal than in the pictorial domain. Caution must be exercised in interpreting these outcomes, however, for there is no guarantee whatever that the pictorial and verbal item sets are equally representative of an hypothetical universe of metaphor content. Further research devoted to this issue should clearly make use of pictorial and verbal items matched for content. If extent of asymmetry is not influenced by this kind of contrast, we would be able to state quite confidently that the phenomenon under study manifests strong pictorial-verbal generality.

METAPHORIC CONTENT AND DIRECTIONALITY

Let us now take a close look at both kinds of items—those that demonstrated asymmetry and those that did not—to see whether they have distinctive properties. We had previously offered some speculation about the nature of the asymmetries likely to appear in MTT items. When comparisons are drawn between human and nonhuman stimuli, we proposed that subjects might frequently assign the human to the role of topic. The results provided support for this, although by no means without exception. All of the asymmetrical pictorial items—significant or nearly significant—involved comparisons between humans, on the one hand, and objects, plants, or physical events, on the other (see Table 12.1). Among the verbal items, a number of person-animal and person-thing comparisons were significantly asymmetrical. In all of these cases, the person served as "topic." However, among the verbal items, several object-object comparisons also proved to be asymmetrical (see Table 12.2). The most strongly asymmetrical verbal item, the comparison between teeth and pearls (#18), is an ambiguous case. The topic, "teeth," carries the implication of human reference. Yet it does not refer to a person in the same sense as the guard in the guard-boulder comparison or as the boxer in the boxer-bull metaphor. In addition, in both the pictorial and verbal item sets, some of the clearly symmetrical items were also human-nonhuman comparisons. Before considering these symmetrical items, however, we shall examine the unexpectedly asymmetrical items more closely.

The proposed hierarchy rests on the notion that a metaphor involves a comparison between a more ambiguous or multifaceted topic and a less ambiguous vehicle, the latter serving as a guide for the interpretation of the topic. Our definition of ambiguity is consistent with that offered by Johnson and Malgady (this volume)—"the larger the set of potential properties the more interpretive or meaning possibilities there are—and therefore the greater the potential ambiguity." Examination of the five significantly asymmetrical object-object comparisons supports this reasoning. Consider the avalanche-suitcase comparison (#12) as an example. Here, the topic stimulus "heavy suitcases on a baggage chute" does not necessarily call to mind the movement of the suicases down the chute. They could be visualized as stationary and could call to mind a number of different aspects of traveling (e.g., traveling one's self, meeting someone, preparing to leave, arriving at a destination, lost luggage). There seems to be a great deal of room for idiosyncrasy in conceptualizing the content of the above expression. By contrast, it is hard to imagine that the phrase "an avalanche" would not evoke an image of the forceful, falling motion of snow and rocks. Similar reasoning could be employed to account for each of the other significant object-object comparisons. We must stress that this is post-hoc interpretation, and we offer it primarily for its heuristic value.

Consider next those human-nonhuman comparisons that were not statistically significant (lack of consensus respecting direction). One of these cases, the geese-soldier comparison (#4), bears a similarity to the teeth-pearls item discussed earlier. While soldiers are indeed human, the underlying ground of the metaphor pertains to the structure or formation of a group of soldiers, an aspect that does not really tap their "humanness." The woman-willow item (#34) is an unusual case. Given that the tree's name—"weeping willow"—is already a form of personification imparting human activity to the tree, it is hardly surprising that some subjects based their responses on this already present metaphor. Perhaps we should in fact be surprised that only about half the subjects chose to do this; possibly, we can interpret this as indirect testimony to the strength of the tendency to focus on people as the topics of metaphors. The blind man and the ship (#20) present a somewhat similar instance. The real ground of this metaphor is blindness, clearly a human quality. (The ship may be viewed as blindly groping its way through fog.) Although perhaps not as strong as the woman-willow comparison, this item again seems to be an invitation to personification. Yet here again, subjects were about evenly divided in their choice of direction.

We are left with three symmetrical person-thing or person-plant comparisons. Interestingly, they are all age related metaphors: the old man and the candle (#35), the old woman and the flowers (#40), and the baby and the bud (#8). There is an additional age-related metaphor in the item set that was strongly asymmetrical—the old man and the tree (#13). How can we explain the difference between this last item and the other three? All four concern aging— changes over time. The old tree suggests a gradual change over an extended period. This view of change seems a distinctively human one. Accordingly, the ancient gnarled tree is an especially apt vehicle for the old man as topic, and the resultant asymmetry is consistent with the hierarchy proposed earlier. For the other three items, in contrast, many subjects were clearly "pulled" by the imminent transitions of a candle about to be extinguished, a budding rose about to blossom forth, and flowers on the verge of death. For these subjects, transition in the nonhuman domain appeared to be sufficiently important and dramatic to warrant using human stimuli as a referent or vehicle to shed further light upon such nonhuman events. These preferences did not characterize all of our subjects; many continued to be guided by the proposed hierarchy. The resultant outcome, of course, was a decided lack of consensus regarding the topic-vehicle structure of the three items at issue.

Unlike the three items just discussed, many items expected to be symmetrical involved comparisons between persons or objects in analogous situations—the snowman and the sandcastle (#36), for instance. In the case of these particular items, the ground seems to be equally well related to each member of the pair, though manifested somewhat differently in each. A snowman about to melt and a sandcastle on the verge of destruction by waves are in essentially the same predicament. Similarly, in item #27, a fly caught in a spider web and fish caught in a net face similar consequences.

The two items just discussed are cases of "pure" symmetry in the sense that the comparative terms appear to be interchangeable as topic and vehicle. In contrast, the symmetrical items described earlier (e.g., the old man and the candle) clearly involve comparisons that cut across the hypothesized hierarchy, suggesting that the choice of topic and vehicle may not be arbitrary. In this connection, Henle (1958) has offered a theoretical analysis of "inversion" metaphors (i.e., those in which topic-vehicle reversals yield different metaphors). In brief, that author has postulated two levels of similarity in metaphor. He suggests that metaphor involves a transfer or shift of qualities from the vehicle to the topic. He further proposes two levels of relationship between the elements of a metaphor. The antecedent relation reflects a prior similarity at least partly iconic in character that makes possible the substitution of one element for the other. When a metaphor is formed based upon this prior level, an induced similarity is created through a transfer of cognitive content and affect from vehicle to topic. In inversion metaphors, this transfer can move in either of two possible directions. However, the two ensuing metaphors have somewhat different grounds; this difference is primarily in resultant feeling tone. Some of our symmetrical metaphors may well have this property of working both ways. In other words, lack of consensus about topic or vehicle status may not imply an arbitrary decision on the subject's part. Rather, different subjects may be responding to different metaphors. It is interesting to note that Henle's example of inversion metaphor compares "old age" and "evening." This example seems very similar in nature to our own symmetrical aging metaphors. Again, these are post hoc explanations in need of independent verification. We shall later discuss ways of possibly accomplishing this.

IMPLICATIONS FOR FUTURE RESEARCH

As the foregoing discussion indicates, the present research might best be characterized as hypothesis-generating rather than hypothesis-testing. Our results clearly indicate that certain metaphorically related concept pairs strongly imply directional comparisons while others do not. Further, it is evident that the content of the concepts compared is a key factor in determing the "natural" direction of a comparison. These findings raise a number of interesting questions, and the identification of item pools homogeneous with respect to symmetry-asymmetry should facilitate investigations in this area. It should prove possible to extend the findings of other studies linking the topic-vehicle distinction to asymmetries in other aspects of psychological processing. For instance, the Verbrugge and McCarrell (1977) study described earlier provides evidence that the vehicle of a metaphor may be the element more closely associated with the metaphoric ground, the better example of the quality or characteristic conveyed by the metaphor. If this is the case, then we should be able to demonstrate that subjects recognize the relationship between the two critical members of MTT triads more readily when the vehicle is presented first. The vehicle might then serve as a clue to the ground. If only asymmetrical items have "natural" topics and vehicles, the facilitating effect of the vehicle-first presentation order should appear only for these items.

It should also be possible to determine whether asymmetries in perceived similarity are linked to the asymmetrical decisions about direction identified in the present study. We can ask subjects to rate the similarity of the critical stimulus pairs as other investigators have done (Harwood & Verbrugge, 1977; Malgady & Johnson, this volume). Some subjects would be asked to compare A to B, while others would make the opposite judgments. Here again we would expect asymmetrical judgments to occur only for those items that proved to be asymmetrical in the present study. Should these kinds of functional asymmetries prove to be consistently linked to preference for a particular directional comparison, it would further increase our confidence that these preferences reflect an important aspect of metaphoric thinking.

Identifying such functional asymmetries in MTT items would serve an additional purpose. We have suggested that in some cases our symmetrical stimulus pairs may be "inversion" metaphors. In these cases, both directional comparisons support a metaphor, although the quality of that metaphor may be somewhat different in the two directions. A test of this hypothesis would require a method of differentiating between these inversion metaphors and truly symmetric relations. The completion of the experiments described above would make such a test possible. If we are able to demonstrate that items that were asymmetrical in the present paradigm also reflect consistent asymmetries in, for example, similarity ratings, then a group of subjects could be asked to perform both tasks.

For inversion metaphors we would predict that subjects who chose to cast the comparison in the "A is like B" form perceive greater similarity when presented with this comparison than when presented with "B is like A." For subjects whose sentences were formed in the opposite direction, the relative magnitude of the similarity judgments should be reversed. Where metaphoric pairs are genuinely symmetrical, this consistency should not be observed, for choice of direction would be purely arbitrary. In the case of these symmetrical pairs, similarity judgments should not change with a shift in direction.

This raises an important question in regard to the nature of any symmetrical pairs we might be able to identify. Is is possible that these purely symmetrical pairings are not genuinely metaphoric relationships in the first place? Perhaps such pairings reflect nonmetaphoric concept attainment, suggesting that the symmetry-asymmetry contrast may have implications for the operational definition of metaphor. We acknowledge, of course, the speculative element in the foregoing line of reasoning.

Completion of the research outlined here should take us further along the way toward a thorough understanding of the processes responsible for symmetrical and asymmetrical topic-vehicle relations in metaphoric comprehension and production. One can be sure, however, that further issues will be raised by the research described, and it is possible to foresee what some of these might be. Thus far, we have had little to say about the quality of metaphors. Yet, there is little doubt that some metaphors will be judged trite, others will be found incomprehensible, and still others will be deemed particularly appropriate in conveying an intended similarity. Malgady (1975) was the first to examine the relation between symmetry-asymmetry and metaphor quality. This is clearly a problem that deserves further research attention.

A second issue concerns the developmental course of symmetry-asymmetry in metaphoric comparisons. Can extensive asymmetric similarities be detected at a relatively early age (children as young as 6 years of age can respond to the MTT), or are such similarities largely confined to adolescents and adults? There is a dearth of information relevant to this question at the present time.

Finally, there is the matter of individual differences. As research in the present area proceeds, it may eventually prove feasible to examine the extent of individual consistency in preference for asymmetric topic-vehicle relations. Some persons may be more inclined than others to interpret metaphors asymmetrically. Conceivably, such a tendency might be associated with a heightened metaphoric sensitivity. The availability of the MTT as a measure of the latter should facilitate research directed to these individual-difference issues.

There is obviously more to metaphor than the matter of its symmetry or asymmetry. At the same time, topic-vehicle structure lies at the very core of the metaphor construct, and the more we learn about the factors contributing to the symmetry or asymmetry of that structure, the greater will be our understanding of the cognitive and psycholinguistic bases of metaphoric operations. We have described some of these contributing factors in the present chapter and have pointed the way toward further research in the area. There is much more to be learned about symmetry-asymmetry, but the paths toward acquiring this knowledge are clear for those who wish to follow them.

ACKNOWLEDGMENTS

We would like to acknowledge the cooperation of the Office of Catholic Education of the Diocese of Brooklyn. We are particularly grateful to Hugh Kirwan, John Corcoran and the students and staff of Christ the King Regional High School for their participation in the present study. The present chapter has profited from the thoughtful comments of the editors, Richard Honeck and Robert Hoffman, on an earlier draft. Of course, they do not bear any responsibility for whatever shortcomings remain. Celia Fisher, Keith Nelson, and Judith Feldman also made helpful comments on earlier versions of this paper, for which we are grateful. Finally, we are indebted to Robert Leahy for the use of his equipment, to Lisa Rosenberg for typing the manuscript, and to the Graduate Faculty, New School for Social Research, for financial support.

REFERENCES

Arnheim, R. The Gestalt theory of expression. *Psychological Review,* 1949, *56,* 156–171.

Asch, S. E. *Social psychology.* Englewood Cliffs, N.J.: Prentice-Hall, 1952.

Billow, R. M. A cognitive developmental study of metaphor comprehension. *Developmental Psychology,* 1975, *11,* 415–423.

Black, M. *Models and metaphors.* Ithaca, NY: Cornell Univeristy Press, 1962.

Cronbach, L. J. Coefficient alpha and the internal structure of tests. *Psychometrika,* 1951, *16,* 297–334.

Gardner, H. Metaphors and modalities: How children project polar adjectives onto diverse domains. *Child Development,* 1974, *45,* 84–91.

Garner, W. R. *Uncertainty and structure as psychological concepts.* New York: Wiley, 1962.

Harwood, D. L., & Verbrugge, R. R. *Metaphor and the asymmetry of similarity.* Paper presented at the 85th Meeting of the American Psychological Association, San Francisco, August, 1977.

Henle, P. Metaphor. In P. Henle (Ed.), *Language, thought and culture.* Ann Arbor: University of Michigan Press, 1958.

Honeck, R. P., Sowry, B. M., & Voegtle, K. Proverbial understanding in a pictorial context. *Child Development,* 1978, *49,* 327–331.

Kogan, N. A cognitive style approach to metaphoric thinking. In R. E. Snow, P. A. Federico, & W. E. Montague (Eds.), *Aptitude, learning, and instruction: Cognitive process analyses.* Hillsdale, N.J.: Lawrence Erlbaum Associates, 1980.

Kogan, N., & Connor, K. *The role of verbal processes in children's comprehension of visual metaphor.* Paper presented at the Biennial Meeting of the Society for Research in Child Development, San Francisco, March, 1979.

Kogan, N., Connor, K., Gross, A., & Fava, D. Understanding visual metaphor: Developmental and individual differences. *Monographs of the Society for Research in Child Development,* 1980, in press.

Köhler, W. Psychological remarks on some questions of anthropology. *American Journal of Psychology*, 1937, *50*, 271–288.

Malgady, R. G. *A feature synthesis model of metaphor processing*. Unpublished doctoral dissertation, University of Tennessee, 1975.

Mednick, S. A. The associative basis of the creative process. *Psychological Review*, 1962, *69*, 220–232.

Ortony, A., Reynolds, R. E., & Arter, J. A. Metaphor: Theoretical and empirical research. *Psychological Bulletin*, 1978, *85*, 919–943.

Pollio, H. R., Barlow, J. M., Fine, H. J., & Pollio, M. R. *Psychology and the poetics of growth: Figurative language in psychology, psychotherapy, and education*. Hillsdale, N.J.: Lawrence Erlbaum Associates, 1977.

Richards, I. A. *The philosophy of rhetoric*. New York: Oxford University Press, 1936.

Rosch, E. Cognitive reference points. *Cognitive Psychology*, 1975, *7*, 532–547.

Tversky, A. Features of similarity. *Psychological Review*, 1977, *84*, 327–352.

Tversky, A., & Gati, I. Studies of similarity. In E. Rosch & B. Lloyd (Eds.), *Cognition and categorization*. Hillsdale, N.J.: Lawrence Erlbaum Associates, 1978.

Verbrugge, R. R. *The comprehension of analogy*. Unpublished doctoral dissertation, University of Minnesota, 1974.

Verbrugge, R. R. *Perceiving invariants at the invitation of metaphor*. Paper presented at the 83rd Meeting of the American Psychological Association, Chicago, August, 1975.

Verbrugge, R. R. Resemblances in language and perception. In R. Shaw & J. Bransford (Eds.), *Perceiving, acting, and knowing: Toward an ecological psychology*. Hillsdale, N.J.: Lawrence Erlbaum Associates, 1977.

Verbrugge, R. R., & McCarrell, N. S. Metaphoric comprehension: Studies in reminding and resembling. *Cognitive Psychology*, 1977, *9*, 494–533.

Werner, H., & Kaplan, B. *Symbol formation*. New York: Wiley, 1963.

Wheelwright, P. *Metaphor and reality*. Bloomington, IN: Indiana University Press, 1962.

Winer, B. J. *Statistical principles in experimental design*. New York: McGraw-Hill, 1971.

Winner, E., & Engel, M. *The pragmatics of metaphor comprehension*. Paper presented at the Biennial Meeting of the Society for Research in Child Development, San Francisco, March, 1979.

Winner, E., Rosenstiel, A. K., & Gardner, H. The development of metaphoric understanding. *Developmental Psychology*, 1976, *12*, 289–297.

APPENDIX:
SAMPLE PICTORIAL ITEMS

A   B

#8

#13

#16

A   B

#17

#24

#30

IV DEVELOPMENTAL ASPECTS

13 The Developmental Structure of Figurative Competence

Marilyn R. Pollio

James D. Pickens
Maryville College

As recently as 1974, it could be said that very little research had been done in the specific area of figurative language development. Needless to say, this is not the case today, since many new studies have been reported. Despite this, it seems reasonable to wonder why there was so little research prior to 1974. The major reasons probably have to do with the conception of the nature of metaphor as well as with the difficulties involved in measuring this aspect of language. In adults, metaphor was often considered as ornament, while in children it was considered simply as mistake not commensurate with "true" metaphoric expression. When something is seen as either ornament or error, there is little need to study its development. Although adult use of metaphor and the place of metaphor in linguistic theory is no longer at issue, the concept of child metaphor as mistake still is (Ortony, Reynolds, & Arter, 1978).

Basically, the argument seems to be that children use metaphor inadvertently; that is, they say something (which "sounds" metaphoric) because they are unaware of the linguistic constraints inherent in the word(s), or because they have an inadequate vocabulary. Occasionally a child may use metaphor unintentionally when merely "playing" with language. If, for example, a child says "My truck died," when his toy truck rolls over and ceases to move in a forward direction, he could be unaware of the marking "animate" for the word *died* and be making a semantic error. He could also not know all of the lexical items and/or be incapable of using the syntax necessary for saying, "My truck has rolled over and is no longer moving in a forward direction," thereby making another, if different, mistake. Finally, he might just be "joking" by saying his truck died and thus not understand the figurative significance of his utterance.

This problem of children's metaphoric usage can best be discussed in terms of a distinction between formal and functional views of metaphor. A formal view holds that metaphor is a deliberate, purposeful deviation from the literal based upon a deep understanding and knowledge of all of the characteristics of the literal meaning as well as all of the ramifications of metaphoric usage. Formalists tend to view child language as "incomplete" or "underdeveloped" adult language and would consider "My truck died" as error and not as metaphor.

A functional view would address itself to the purpose or function of the usage for the speaker. It holds that if the use of the figure serves a definite purpose at either a reflected or an unreflected level, then it was a valid figure. For this view, there are many functions of figurative language: as additional vocabulary, as intellectual history, as heuristic, as mask, as ornament (Pollio, Barlow, Fine, & Pollio, 1977), and as verbal shorthand (Pollio, 1971). The child who said "My truck died" may have used the figure simply as additional vocabulary or as verbal shorthand. He may very well have been unaware of the "animate" marking of *died*. On the other hand, he may have noted similar properties among dead things that are nonfunctioning, i.e., his truck and an animal. In any case, his utterance was functionally figurative. No one would question the fact that an adult who said "My car died right in the middle of the street" was speaking metaphorically. The functional viewpoint, therefore, would inquire into the purposes of the metaphoric use and would accept as figurative utterances that did indeed communicate meaningfully.

In addition to these problems of conceptualization, there were also questions of measurement. When figurative language is studied, is it necessary to consider all of the categories described by rhetoricians? Should there be a distinction made between frozen or clichéd figures that are established lexical items and novel or original figures? Which type of language behavior, e.g., production, comprehension, explanation, and/or preference should be studied? What type(s) of tasks—open-ended, multiple-choice, etc.—should be used? In the 1970's many researchers answered these questions by studying all types of metaphors in all four categories of language behavior and by developing tasks, procedures, and definitions appropriate to their own conception of figurative language and the figurative process. In short, investigators did what they wanted to do, or what they knew best how to do, and the field flourished, even if a bit chaotically.

REVIEW OF RECENT LITERATURE

Production and Preference

Examining, in turn, the four areas of metaphoric language behavior studied since 1974, one can determine that much has been learned. In a series of studies in the area of production, Pollio and Pollio (1974; Pollio, 1973) examined figurative usage on three different tasks in third through sixth graders from schools varying in socioeconomic level. They found that each task elicited differential developmental trends in each of the different settings. On an open-ended comparisons task, where children were asked to make as many comparisons as they could to three different pairs of words (e.g., clock and child), children produced more novel than frozen figures. In the highest socioeconomic school, both categories of figurative usage increased significantly over grades; while in the middle to upper-middle socioeconomic schools, novel production decreased with grade. Children in the lower socioeconomic schools seemed to have a difficult time completing the task and results for them were quite variable.

On an open-ended sentences task, where children were required to write as many different sentences as they could to five different double-function words (e.g., sweet, hard, etc.) children produced more frozen than novel figures and total figures increased significantly over grades. On the third task, which asked children to write a composition on one of five different imaginative topics, children produced more frozen than novel figures. In the middle to upper socioeconomic schools, total figurative usage decreased significantly over grades, while in the lower socioeconomic schools usage was variable although, in general, it increased over grades.

On the basis of these results, it was concluded that children can and do use figurative language as early as Grade 3, but developmental trends are differentially affected by demands of the tasks and school settings. On a non-school-related task, i.e., not usually graded (sentences task), children show a regular increase with grade in figurative production. On a school-related task (compositions), children produce fewer total figures of speech (and novel figures in particular) at each successive grade, particularly in middle to upper class schools. This finding was interpreted to mean that where a letter grade might be given children would not risk the use of deviant language and "rock the boat" (Pollio & Pollio, 1974).

In order to carry this research further and study figurative production in older children, Schonberg (1974) evaluated the figurative content of written work produced by high school seniors. Using an objective composition and comparisons task (similar to those used in Pollio & Pollio, 1974) and a subjective composition and comparisons task (e.g., *Who Am I?,* as a composition topic), Schonberg found that adolescents produce more figurative language than younger children. She also found that subjective tasks produced more figurative output than did objective tasks. These results, in conjunction with the Pollio and Pollio (1974) and Pollio (1973) studies, indicate that figurative production is present (and may perhaps decrease) in elementary school children and increases again sometime during the high school years.

An issue pertaining to this pattern of results involves whether production rates are a function of development per se or the demands of the classroom. Three pieces of evidence support the latter: (a) This pattern is more pronounced for composition data than comparisons or multiple sentences; (b) compositions are more closely related to classroom activities; and (c) the pattern is less pronounced in lower socioeconomic schools where academic pressures are assumed to be less significant.

In a different study of figurative production, Gardner, Kircher, Winner, and Perkins (1975) investigated children's metaphoric productions and preferences. Children were of five different age levels (3-4, 7, 11, 14, and 19). They were asked to produce an ending, and also to choose one of four provided endings to incomplete stories containing simile stems (e.g., *His voice was as quiet as . . .* (a) *the quietest sound we've heard;* (b) *a mouse sitting in a room;* (c) *dawn in a ghost town;* (d) *a family going on a trip).* Answers (and choices) were coded into one of four sets: literal, conventional, appropriate, and inappropriate. Results of the production task showed that preschoolers produced an absolutely higher number of figures than any other group. These results also revealed that the majority of productions at all ages were coded as conventional and that the oldest group produced more appropriate endings than any other group. In terms of choice, preschoolers showed no dominant preference for ending type; seven-year-olds preferred literal responses; eleven-year-olds conventional responses; and 14- and 19-year-olds conventional and appropriate responses.

In a study of spontaneous figurative production, Billow (1977b) analyzed metaphoric utterances produced by young children (ages 2.7 to 8.0) engaged in free play. Results revealed that figurative verbalizations appeared with high frequency in early childhood and, in fact, peaked in three-year-olds. In addition, Billow found that figurative usage was frequent until children were 6 years old and decreased thereafter. Again, these results suggest a decreasing trend in production from preschool to elementary school.

In a study concerned with both production and explication of metaphor, Arlin (1977) used several Piagetian tasks (e.g., class inclusion, conservation, and combinatorial and proportional reasoning) to determine cognitive level. She also asked both children and adults to produce a word for one deleted in a metaphor and to explain the meaning of the metaphor with the correct word supplied. Arlin used three metaphor types: representational (a word used to describe new experiences, e.g., stretched), similarity (figures comparing two or more disparate objects on the basis of a shared attribute, e.g., my shadow is like a piece of the night), and proportional (figures that compare four or more elements indirectly in a communication, e.g., one lonely chunk of the night grows legs and follows me to school). Arlin concluded that pre-operational children produced and comprehended representational metaphors; children who were clearly in concrete operations produced and comprehended similarity metaphors as well as representational metaphors; and formal operational subjects produced and comprehended proportional metaphors as well as representational and similarity metaphors.

Taken together, these results support a functional view of metaphoric production in that children as young as 3 can and do produce figures of speech both spontaneously and when requested to do so and, in fact, can produce more figures of speech than older children in similar contexts doing similar tasks (Billow, 1977b; Gardner et al., 1975). Spontaneous production seems to decrease during the elementary school years (Billow, 1977b; Gardner et al., 1975; Pollio, 1973; Pollio & Pollio, 1974), and to increase in adolescence (Schonberg, 1974). In tasks requiring metaphoric response (i.e., preference, comparisons, and sentences), the same pattern does not hold (Gardner et al., 1975; Pollio, 1973; Pollio & Pollio, 1974). In addition, there seems to be a differential ability to produce (and comprehend or explicate) different types of metaphor according to developmental level (Arlin, 1977).

Comprehension and Explication

What does it mean to say a child can comprehend figurative language? Obviously, it means that a child understands the meaning of a figurative utterance and can demonstrate this understanding to someone else. The problem, however, comes in operationalizing our understanding of understanding. For some investigators, understanding has been defined in terms of paraphrase; for others it has meant explaining a metaphor. For still others, it has meant a multiple-choice test, with appropriate paraphrases of the metaphor provided as alternatives. Methodologically, both paraphrase and explanation require something more than simple comprehension; they require the ability to abstract and either rephrase or talk about the utterance. Obviously, the more complex the process required, the older the child must be to perform it successfully. In some studies it may not be that the child does not *understand* the metaphor, but that he simply hasn't the ability to demonstrate that understanding in the specific manner required. In this regard, Honeck, Sowry, and Voetgle (1978) noted a similar problem in studies of proverb understanding. How then should we assess comprehension? Organizing these procedures from simple to complex, the task that demonstrates comprehension of figurative language most directly would seem to be a multiple-choice test where the child is required only to recognize—and then choose—the proper paraphrase of a figure of speech. Next, in order of difficulty, would be paraphrase, where the child would rephrase the figure using his or her own language. Finally, explication would require the child to abstract and discuss the relationships inherent in the figure, a much more demanding task.

There have been few studies that utilize a simple multiple-choice test with right and wrong alternatives. Pollio and Pollio (1979) constructed such a test using as items figures of speech derived from the protocols of the children involved in earlier research (Pollio, 1973; Pollio & Pollio, 1974). They determined developmental trends in comprehension using children in Grades 4 through 8. Results showed that comprehension increased regularly with grade and that novel figures were more difficult to understand than frozen or clichéd figures. Correlations between comprehension of frozen and novel figures were high, unlike correlations between frozen and novel figures produced spontaneously in compositions. This finding, combined with differential results found in studies of different aspects of figurative development using different tasks, led Pollio and Pollio to stress the need for studying all aspects of figurative development in the same children in order to obtain a complete picture of figurative competence.

In a study designed to explore the developmental course of both comprehension and explication, Winner, Rosenstiel, and Gardner (1976) required their subjects (age levels 6, 7, 8, 10, 12, and 14) to explain the meaning of a short metaphoric sentence, e.g., *The prison guard was a hard rock;* to choose among four possible meanings for the same sentence; and to paraphrase their choice.

Results for the multiple-choice task showed differences among ages for each type of response, with metaphoric responses chosen more by older children. Results for the explication task were quite similar: Only children beyond age 8 tended toward metaphoric explication. Winner, Rosenstiel, and Gardner claim that these data suggest a sequence of steps that children go through on their way to true metaphoric comprehension.

The remaining studies concerned with metaphoric comprehension seem more properly to deal with metaphoric explication. The classic in the field is, of course, Asch and Nerlove's (1960) evaluation of the development of double-function terms. In this study, subjects ages 3 through 12 were questioned about figurative possibilities for words such as *hard, sweet,* etc. They found that mastery of these terms followed a regular developmental course, with children first comprehending the physical-object meaning, then the psychological meaning, and finally the nature of the relationship between the two.

Billow (1975) was interested in studying cognitive development and metaphoric comprehension. In the first part of his experiment, he presented 50 boys (ages 5 through 14) with similarity metaphors (e.g., *Hair is spaghetti*) and tested comprehension by asking for explanations of the figures. He then determined cognitive developmental level by a standard Piagetian task. He found that children as young as 5 were able to solve similarity metaphors and that past 7 years of age intuitive solutions declined. On the basis of these results, he suggested that concrete operational mechanisms are *not* necessary for many types of metaphoric comprehension, whereas Piagetian theory (Inhelder & Piaget, 1969) suggests the attainment of at least concrete operational thought as a precondition to metaphoric comprehension.

In the second part of his experiment, Billow presented proportional metaphors (e.g., *Ideas echo in my mind*) and a combinatorial reasoning task to older children (ages 9 to 14). He found that the better the performance on the combinatorial task, the more proportional metaphors solved, suggesting a relationship between attainment of formal operational thinking and comprehension of proportional metaphors.

To clarify cognitive developmental level and metaphoric comprehension in terms of both paraphrase and explication, Cometa and Eson (1978) had children perform several Piagetian tasks (e.g., conservation, intersectional matrices, and combination of chemicals). The children were then divided into four groups: pre-operational, concrete operational, intersectional (those concerete level children who could perform successfully the intersectional matrices task), and formal operational. They reasoned that the ability to paraphrase metaphor developed prior to the ability to explicate it and that the latter ability arose only after complete development of intersection (toward the end of the concrete operational stage). Cometa and Eson then presented children with a series of metaphors (e.g., *When the wind blew, the leaves began to dance*) and asked them to paraphrase the metaphors. If the paraphrase was acceptable in adult terms, Cometa and Eson asked the children to explain them. Results showed that the ability to paraphrase occurred in children demonstrating concrete operational thinking, while the ability to explicate occurred in children showing fully developed intersectional class structures.

The comprehension and explication studies reviewed reveal that comprehension and explication abilities develop in an incremental way with recognition of correct paraphrases of figurative expressions occurring first (Pollio & Pollio, 1979), followed by paraphrase (Cometa & Eson, 1978), and finally by explication of the paraphrase (Asch & Nerlove, 1960; Billow, 1975; Winner, et al., 1976; and Cometa & Eson, 1978). Children also offer different types of explications as they progress towards adult explication, with 6 and 7-year-olds offering thematic explanations and 8-year-olds offering concrete ones (Winner, et al., 1976). The ability to explicate in a manner acceptable to adults seems to increase after the age of 8 (Winner, et al., 1976) or at approximately 9 through 11, with the attainment of intersectional class structure (Cometa & Eson, 1978). In addition, different types of metaphors are understood at different ages (and stages) with representational metaphors comprehended first, perhaps in the pre-operational stage (Arlin, 1977); similarity metaphors next, in the late pre-operational or early concrete operational stages; and proportional metaphors last, in formal operations (Arlin, 1977; Billow, 1975). How frequently a metaphor appears in general usage also seems to have an effect on comprehension, with more common (or frozen) easier to comprehend and less common (or novel) more difficult to comprehend at all ages studied (Cometa & Eson, 1978; Pollio & Pollio, 1979).

THE RESEARCH PROGRAM

In most of the studies completed to date, different researchers have used different methodologies with different groups of children and have found different, yet somewhat parallel, results. Development has been viewed according to the task and cognitive process tested, and extensions to other processes have been assumed rather than empirically tested. One study (Pickens & Pollio, 1979), using adults as subjects, examined the patterns of relationships among three aspects of figurative diction: production, preference, and comprehension. Pickens and Pollio found that although the distinction between frozen and novel diction was a meaningful one, different task requirements influenced the patterns of relationships found. They concluded that "figurative language competence may not be a unitary process but one that is strongly affected by specific task and situational constraints." If this conclusion is correct, it becomes necessary to view the different figurative competencies both developmentally and in relation to one another within the same children. The present study represents one attempt to do this.

The Children and the Tasks

The Children.   The children studied in the present analysis were selected from public school students in a suburban-rural school district. Task materials were administered to students in the third, fifth, sixth, seventh, ninth, and eleventh grades at three schools: an elementary school, a middle school, and a high school. These grades characteristically include children who range in age from 8 to 17. Particular note should be taken of the fact that children in the fifth *and* sixth *and* seventh grades were included. The reason for this was because children shift from concrete operational to formal operational thinking sometime during these grades and it was hoped that some pattern of differences in metaphoric competence would appear in data collected from this specific set of children.

From those children completing all of the written tasks, 30 subjects, 15 male and 15 female, were randomly selected in each of the six grades, producing a total of 180 children. Two constraints modified the random sampling: inclusion of an equal number of male and female subjects in each grade and deletion of all children who had been retained in a grade and were a year or more older than normal for that grade.

The Production Task.   Measures of spontaneous metaphoric production were obtained from a composition task similar to those used by Pollio (1973), Pollio and Pollio (1974), Schonberg (1974), and Pickens and Pollio (1979). Each subject was given the opportunity to choose one of three fanciful topics and to write a story of at least a page in length. Where possible, topics crossed schools and grade levels, although some were varied to allow for differing interests and reading abilities. Each topic also included a set of questions designed to provide a common starting point for subjects, as well as hints on how to proceed with the story. Topics and accompanying questions were written to permit, if not encourage, fanciful thinking and metaphoric prose. Examples of topics and motivating questions are as follows:

Elementary School (Grades 3 and 5) and *Middle School* (Grades 6 and 7)

You have just found out that the new kid in your class is really from the moon. Write a story telling what his life on the moon was like. (Tell what it looks like, smells like, feels like. What do moon-people do? What do moon-people think about the earth?)

Middle School (Grades 6 and 7) and *High School* (Grades 9 and 11)

What would you do if everything metal on the earth disappeared? (Think of all the metal things there are and all the ways in which metal is used. What would happen? What would you do?)

The Preference Task.   Children were also questioned concerning preferences for figurative usage. This was accomplished through the presentation of a written version of a task developed by Gardner and Winner (Gardner, et al., 1975). The task, which will be referred to as the Gardner–Winner Test, involves a set of 18 vignettes, each ending in an incomplete simile. Subjects were instructed to choose which of four endings was preferred as a completion for each simile stem. Each set of alternatives contained four types of endings: (1) a novel, metaphorically appropriate, ending; (2) a frozen or conventional ending; (3) a literal ending; and (4) a metaphorically inappropriate ending. (See page 314 for an example.)

The Comprehension Task.   The ability of a subject to comprehend the metaphorical productions of others was measured by a multiple-choice test (Pollio & Pollio, 1979). This test, which will be referred to as the Pollio Test, consists of 20 items. The stem of each item contains a metaphoric target phrase set apart from the rest by underlining. The choices for each item were constructed to represent four types of interpretation, three of which result in incorrect conclusions. The subjects were instructed to choose the alternative that ''*best* tells what the person who wrote it *wanted* to say.''

Half of the items on the Pollio Test contain frozen metaphors, while the other half contain novel metaphors. This test, therefore, allows for the separate assessment of frozen and novel figurative comprehension.

An example of a Pollio Test item with a frozen target phrase is:

I went into the kitchen and *ate up a storm.*

(a)   I ate a lot.
(b)   I drank some white lightening from the refrigerator.
(c)   I ate so much it rained.
(d)   I like to eat when it's raining.

An example of a novel target phrase is:

Then all of a sudden, the trees disappeared *like melting ice cream*.

(a)   The trees lost their shape and disappeared slowly.
(b)   Trees look a lot like ice cream cones.
(c)   It was very hot, and the trees started melting.
(d)   The trees melted and dripped down the trunk.

The Explication Task.   The fourth probe was designed to determine whether subjects could paraphrase and/or explain metaphoric phrases. To this end, an oral presentation of the Pollio Test was used. Each subject was individually interviewed and asked to tell ''in his own words'' what a specific phrase (the target) in the sentence(s) read to him meant. Partial responses, unclear responses, and long pauses were followed by cue questions from the interviewer in an attempt to get complete, clear responses to each metaphor.

The subject's own responses to the Pollio Test (written form) were repeated to him if they were incorrect in order to give him an opportunity to explain why he made that choice. These sessions were tape recorded and later transcribed for evaluation.

Administration and Scoring

Administration.   The production, preference, and comprehension materials were administered as group tests. Proctors for these sessions were eight undergraduate students in an educational psychology course who were familiarized with group test administration techniques. Specific instructions for the administration of each test, including sentences to be said verbatim, were constructed for each grade level. Proctors were familiarized with these instructions and memorized specific directions prior to going into the classrooms.

For the elementary school (Grades 3 and 5) and middle school (Grades 6 and 7) entire classes received all of the written materials. In order to control reading ability as a determiner of score for third grade subjects, composition choices, as well as the entire Pollio and Gardner–Winner Tests were read aloud to the class. Proctors were instructed to help children in all grades with any difficult words encountered. In the high school (Grades 9 and 11) all materials were administered to English classes.

The order of task presentation was the same for all subjects; only the number of sessions differed. Tests were administered in the following order: Composition, Pollio Test, Gardner–Winner Test. In the elementary grades three separate sessions were used to complete the administration. Middle school and high school grades required only two sessions, with the Pollio Test and the

Gardner-Winner Test presented in the second session. All sessions took place during the fall semester, primarily in November.

The explication task was administered only to those students selected as subjects. An individual interview was held with each subject. Most of the interviews were conducted by one of the authors. A small proportion (9%) were conducted by a volunteer research associate, an adult female with teaching experience who had been familiarized with the procedure and had heard several tapes of interviews.

Scoring.   Each probe was evaluated in the manner most appropriate to its structure and content. For the Pollio Test, two scores were computed for each subject: number correct-Frozen, number correct-Novel. For the Gardner-Winner Test, four scores were computed: number of appropriate, conventional, literal, and inappropriate choices.

The compositions were examined for metaphoric content. The procedures for determining the presence of figures of speech are presented fully in a training manual prepared by Barlow, Kerlin, and Pollio (1971). Briefly, this procedure involves the independent reading and rating of each composition by a team of three judges. Independent ratings, as well as judgments of frozen or novel, are compared in a group session and the incidence of metaphoric usage, as well as reliability data, recorded.

Two of the raters for this study were the authors, both of whom had previous experience using the Barlow et al. method. The third rater was a senior psychology major who was trained in the system. Before rating the compositions, the rating team evaluated a number of compositions from students who were not sampled. This procedure allowed the team to establish rapport and insured that the newest member became fully competent before actually generating data. The rate of agreement was 90%, which is within the range of acceptability and compares favorably with similar ratings reported by other researchers (Pollio, et al., 1977, Chapter 3).

Two measures are generated for each composition: number of frozen figures and number of novel figures. To control for differing lengths of compositions within and between grades, raw scores were converted by dividing each by the number of words in the composition and multiplying by 100. For this reason, the measures for compositions which are analyzed below are: number of frozen figures per 100 words and number of novel figures per 100 words.

The explication task also required a special rating system. From typed transcripts of interviews, judgments were made concerning the level of explication of each metaphor. These judgments were made following a procedure similar to that used in rating compositions, i.e., each rater independently read and rated each transcript. The raters then met and compared judgments. In the vast majority of cases (88%) ratings were identical; for cases of disagreement the raters re-read the explication in question and arrived at agreement. The rating scale used for the explications was:

0 — no response, incorrect paraphrase, repetition of the metaphor
1 — paraphrase without further explication
2 — paraphrase plus explication induced by cueing
3 — paraphrase ánd spontaneous explication.

Since the explication task was based on the Pollio Test, ratings were combined into two measures: the mean rating for frozen target explications and the mean rating for novel target explications.

DEVELOPMENTAL RESULTS

Given the specific tasks used in the present study, it seems reasonable to analyze separately developmental trends for each aspect of metaphoric competence, i.e., production, preference, comprehension, and explication. Also, certain questions must be addressed *within* each aspect: (1) How does each aspect develop, i.e., do children in different grades produce, comprehend, etc. greater or fewer figures of speech? (2) Is there a difference developmentally between novel and frozen figurative diction? (3) How do present results relate to findings obtained from other studies using the same or similar tasks? With these questions in mind, let us begin with the production task.

Production

A preliminary step in the analysis of the compositions was an examination of the number of words produced within and between grades. As expected, the mean number of words produced for Grade 3 (105.80) was significantly lower than the means obtained for all other grades ($p < .01$). Only one other between grades comparison was significant: Grade 11 ($\bar{X} = 179.53$) was lower than Grade 9 ($\bar{X} = 224.47$, $p < .02$). Since all metaphoric production scores were converted to rate per 100 words scores, and since the mean for Grade 3 was above 100 words, cross-grade comparisons could be made.

The mean rates per 100 words of both novel and frozen figurative usage were computed for each grade and are shown in Fig. 13.1. As can be seen, there was a strikingly higher rate of production for frozen than for novel figures. This difference is most dramatic for the high school subjects (Grades 9 and 11). A fixed effect repeated measures analysis of variance computed over these data revealed a highly significant difference [$F(1,174) = 207.93$, $MS_e = 1.19$, $p < .001$] between the number of novel and frozen figures produced across all grades studied. Frozen production decreased from Grades 3 through 6 and then in-

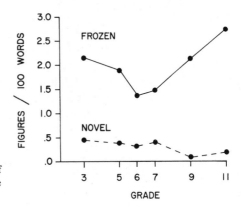

FIG. 13.1. Rate per 100 words of text of novel and frozen figurative production for grades 3 through 11

creased sharply from Grades 7 through 11. Novel production, on the other hand, decreased slowly, but steadily, from Grade 3 through Grade 11. As is obvious from Fig. 13.1, there was a significant grade effect [$F(5,174) = 2.89$, $MS_e = 1.09$, $p < .02$], and a significant grade by frozen-novel interaction [$F(5,174) = 4.38$, $MS_e = 1.19$, $p < .001$].

It is somewhat difficult to compare these results with other studies using a composition production task since other studies: (a) used a smaller range of grades, and (b) used schools having different demographic properties. It needs to be reiterated that differing socioeconomic schools do produce widely different production patterns (see Pollio, et al., 1977, Chap. 7). Nonetheless, it is still illuminating to compare bits and pieces of the present study, as appropriate, with earlier studies. For example, the differences obtained between frozen and novel production were quite in keeping with earlier studies using children (Pollio & Pollio, 1974; Pollio, 1973), adolescents (Schonberg, 1974), and even college age adults (Pickens & Pollio, 1979). All of these studies agree in finding that people of all ages use more frozen than novel figures. In comparing figurative production across grades, it is interesting to note that trends found in the Pollio and Pollio (1974) study to a large extent are also replicated here. That is, novel figurative usage declined somewhat consistently across grades, while frozen figurative usage declined from Grades 3 through 6 and (in this study) rose from Grades 7 through 11.

These results are unusual in terms of development in that a language function first declines over a period of years and then increases. One possible explanation involves children's perception of language. Younger school children may experience language as either ordinary or strange. Looking at data obtained from the younger children in this light, it is possible to assume that both types of figures (novel and frozen) are perceived in somewhat the same way; they are strange and/or unusual ways of saying something that could possibly be said in a more ordinary way and, therefore, be more acceptable in a school situation.

Although the absolute level of frozen production was much higher than novel production, this could be explained by the fact that frozen figures are more familiar to children and, as ordinary lexical items, are used more often. Another explanation for this might involve the procedures used to identify and categorize instances of metaphoric language. Adult judges read and rated all compositions and what may be frozen for an adult may be somewhat novel for a child. Nonetheless, total figurative production declined through Grade 6. Indeed, a written production task seems progressively to inhibit figurative usage at least through the middle school years, and the "don't rock the boat" philosophy described by Pollio and Pollio (1974) seems to operate. Clearly, written production gathered in a school situation is quite prone to social, school, and task constraints.

Results obtained from older children, on the other hand, show a progressive differentiation between frozen and novel figures so that production of frozen figures increases, while novel production continues to decrease. What appears to have happened is that frozen figures have become familiar phrases, have acquired dependable meanings, and, therefore, have become more acceptable. Usage increases as the "strangeness" of frozen figures decreases. This does not mean that older children are more willing to risk on a school-related task, just that there is less risk involved. Indeed, the stricture against "strange" language still exists as evidenced in the continued decline in novel usage. High school students are even less inclined to "rock the boat," but using frozen figures no longer imperils the vessel.

Preference

On the preference test, unlike the other tasks used, categories of response are interdependent. That is, since each of the 18 items on the test can be responded to in only one of four ways, the ratios of appropriate to conventional to literal to inappropriate responses are codetermined. If all four categories were to be included in an analysis of variance, or later in correlational analyses, this codetermination would result in an inaccurate picture of the data. For this reason, only the appropriate (novel) and conventional (frozen) categories were introduced as variables and treated statistically.

Means were computed for the Gardner–Winner test results and are presented graphically in Fig. 13.2. As can be seen, the patterns of preference across grade level for appropriate and conventional figures are similar in that an increase in grade level was generally accompanied by an increase in both categories of figurative preference. Remembering the forced-choice nature of this task, it is obvious that if preference for both conventional and appropriate figures increased over grade, then preference for literal and/or inappropriate responses decreased. In the present data, preference for inappropriate responses was low and remained low

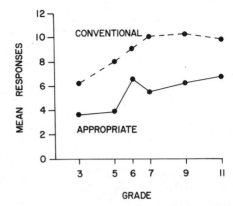

FIG. 13.2.   Mean number of appropriate and conventional responses, Gardner-Winner Test, for grades 3 through 11

across all grades, while preference for literal responses decreased as preferences for both novel and frozen metaphoric responses increased.

A repeated measures analysis of variance computed over the data presented in Fig. 13.2 indicated what is obvious from inspection of the figure: There is a significant grade effect $[F(5,174) = 18.09, MS_e = 6.45, p < .001]$ with preference for figurative endings increasing as grade and age increase. Inspection of Fig. 13.2 also suggests a difference between preference for conventional and appropriate figures, with conventional figures being preferred over appropriate ones at all levels. The effect due to response type was significant $[F(1,174) = 72.82, MS_e = 14.71, p < .001]$. In addition, there was no interaction of grade with figurative category $[F(5,174) = 0.78, MS_e = 14.71, p = .56]$.

The present results are essentially parallel to earlier ones reported by Gardner, et al. (1975). There was an increase in preference for appropriate and conventional endings with conventional figures more preferred at all ages except for the oldest group (age 19) where appropriate endings were preferred. Since this group was two to three years older than the oldest group used in the present study (ages 16 and 17), it may be that further changes occur between Grade 11 and college. Results obtained for the same test used with college age subjects (Pickens & Pollio, 1979), however, do not support such an interpretation. Pickens and Pollio found that their subjects preferred conventional over appropriate figures as did older subjects in the present study.

The process in operation here appears to be similar to that operating in the production task, i.e., a combination of task demands and children's perception of acceptable language. On any task, whether presented in a school situation or in a laboratory, subjects try to supply what appears to them to be the "right" answer or the answer the examiner/experimenter desires. For children in all grades, the inappropriate alternative was perceived as just that—inappropriate—and, therefore, clearly wrong and unwanted. For younger children, the literal alternative may appear to be the response most desired by the examiner and, thus, there was little risk involved in choosing an obvious, literal response. As children grow older, the literal response is perceived as increasingly more obvious (and perhaps trivial) and therefore not the preferred response. Children then decreasingly choose a literal alternative.

Conventional endings fit the simile stems, are increasingly more familiar in meaning, and, therefore, are increasingly chosen as "right" or what is desired by the examiners. Appropriate endings chosen ($\bar{X} = 6.53$) surpass literal endings ($\bar{X} = 2.03$) at Grade 6, but are still considerably lower than conventional endings ($\bar{X} = 9.0$). This difference between conventional and appropriate endings chosen continues through Grade 11. Appropriate endings, therefore, are probably thought of as "possibly right," but not quite as "right" (and therefore less desirable) as conventional endings. Most children again play it safe, do not risk, and pick conventional endings more frequently. Within this context, it is difficult to know whether children are responding more strongly to the materials or to the demand properties of the situation. It seems likely that on this task, as on the composition task, demands inherent in the task itself may determine results to a great degree.

Task demand properties also have differential effects within different modes of presentation. In Gardner et al.'s experiment, all materials were presented orally to individual subjects by individual experimenters. Their oldest group was probably equally as sensitive to this experimental situation as to the task itself. This may account for the difference in results obtained for this group when compared to results obtained by Pickens and Pollio who presented written materials to their subjects in a more anonymous group setting.

In summary then, results found for the preference portion of the present study largely parallel earlier results and indicate: (a) an increase in preference for both conventional and appropriate figures as age increases; and (b) a preference for conventional over appropriate figures that appears stable as age increases.

Comprehension

Means for correct choices for both frozen and novel items on the Pollio Test are presented graphically in Fig. 13.3. As can be seen, there is a progressive improvement in comprehension for both frozen and novel figures over grades. The curve for the frozen items shows a steady increase from third to seventh grade and a less pronounced increase thereafter. The corresponding curve for novel items shows a sharp increase between third and fifth grades and then a more gradual one. Gradual increases after Grade 7 occurring in both curves may be due to somewhat of a "ceiling effect" as originally noted by Pollio and Pollio (1979). The original items for this test were derived from figures produced by children in Grades 3 through 6 and may, therefore, be somewhat easy for the older subjects in this study.

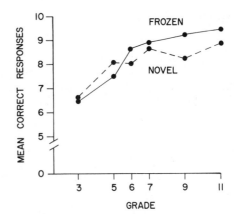

FIG. 13.3. Correct responses, Pollio Test, frozen and novel, for grades 3 through 11.

An analysis of variance revealed a significant grade effect [$F(5,174) = 17.32$, $MS_e = 3.29$, $p < .001$], with, as can be seen in Fig. 13.3, figurative comprehension increasing over grades. In addition, there was a significant difference between frozen and novel figures [$F(1,174) = 7.12$, $MS_e = 1.04$, $p < .005$], with frozen figures understood more easily than novel figures, and, as is obvious from the figure, a significant interaction [$F(5,174) = 4.40$, $MS_e = 1.04$, $p < .001$].

Both the increase in figurative comprehension and the difference between frozen and novel comprehension strongly parallel results found by Pollio and Pollio (1979). The major difference between the studies is that Pollio and Pollio found that frozen figures were more easily understood at all grade levels whereas present results indicate that novel comprehension was greater for Grades 3 and 5. Pickens and Pollio (1979), using college age students, also found frozen comprehension greater than novel.

Results obtained from this task lend support to the familiarity thesis presented earlier. For the younger children, Grades 3 and 5, novel figures are understood at least as well, if not better, than frozen ones. This suggests that novel and frozen figures are all somewhat unusual to young children and, therefore, are functionally equivalent. Starting in the sixth grade and progressing through the eleventh grade, however, children are increasingly able to choose the proper paraphrase for frozen items, which, in all likelihood, are familiar to them. Figurative meanings, therefore, are becoming more and more firmly established and easier to select from among alternatives, and for this reason, comprehension increases.

In summary then, results found for the comprehension portion of the present study agree for the most part with earlier results and indicate: (a) an increase in the comprehension of both frozen and novel figures as grade increases; and (b) an ability to comprehend frozen figures more easily than novel ones, at least from Grade 6 onwards.

Explication

The metric for the explication test was a scale ranging from 0 to 3. Mean performance on this task is presented graphically in Fig. 13.4. As can be seen, there is a general increase in the ability of children to explain both frozen and novel figures as grade increases. The only exception to this trend occurs with ninth grade subjects, for whom there seems to be a slight drop. A repeated measures analysis of variance indicated a significant grade effect [$F(5,173) = 16.33$, $MS_e = .196$, $p < .001$]. The analysis also indicated a significant difference between explications supplied for frozen and novel target items [$F(1,173) = 99.09$, $MS_e = .048$, $p < .001$] with novel items eliciting a higher score than frozen items for all grades. In addition, there was a slight interaction [$F(5,173) = 2.26$, $MS_e = .048$, $p < .05$].

Since this was the first time this particular test was used, it is not possible to compare results directly with earlier studies. It is fairly obvious, however, that most studies dealing with comprehension in terms of paraphrase and/or explanation have found that the quality and quantity of figurative explication does improve as children age (Arlin, 1977; Asch & Nerlove, 1960; Billow, 1975; Cometa & Eson, 1978; Winner et al., 1976). The present results, therefore, parallel earlier results in that the ability to explain both novel and frozen figures of speech clearly improves as children grow older. The present data also indicate that for these materials it was generally easier to explain novel figures than frozen ones.

These results are in keeping with our prior discussion. Children may understand (are able to choose as correct alternatives) and prefer frozen figures, but they are better able to explain novel figurative language. This is best understood by considering the nature of novel figures. By definition, novel figures are unusual, strange, and by their very strangeness call attention to themselves. A reader/listener cannot help but notice a novel figure and will try to determine just what the writer/speaker meant by the unusual juxtaposition of words. A person who hears/reads a novel figure, therefore, will be forced to think about the figure and the relationships within it.

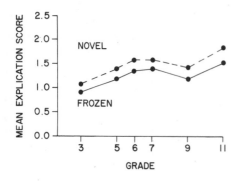

FIG. 13.4.   Mean explication scores, frozen and novel, for grades 3 through 11

Frozen metaphors, on the other hand, are more familiar and may suffer from a phenomenon not unlike functional fixity. This means that frozen figures are "frozen"—they absorb a particular meaning so completely that they are not seen as figurative. Their meanings become fixed. When this happens the constituent elements of the original metaphor may lose their unique identities and merge into a single item. At this point it may be extremely difficult to parse the frozen item and adequately explicate the metaphor.

What happened on the explication task is that children, when presented with a novel metaphor, felt compelled to explain the figure fully. Many children continued talking until they were sure they had adequately explained the figure and that the interviewer had understood them. Prompts and cues for further explication were less needed for novel targets, leading to higher scores since in terms of the scoring procedure a fully adequate spontaneous answer received a higher value.

Frozen targets elicited short, concise statements of meaning. Children did not feel it was necessary to explain further. Prompts and cue questions were needed to obtain more than an adequate paraphrase, thereby yielding lower scores. Indeed, qualitative examination of explication transcripts by the experimenters suggests that many children found explaining frozen figures almost impossible. Although older children were better able to perform the task, it required many prompts for them to do so adequately. Explication, therefore, is more easily accomplished if the figure is unusual or novel.

CORRELATIONAL AND FACTOR ANALYTIC RESULTS

In addition to a concern for developmental trends occurring across grades within each of the four aspects of figurative competence studied, there was also an interest in the interrelationships among these aspects within and across grade levels. Specifically, the following questions were addressed: (1) Is there a definite pattern of interrelationships among the various tasks? (2) If such a pattern exists, is it consistent across all grade levels? (3) Is there a general factor underlying figurative competence at all ages or are there several factors that change as children age?

As a first step, correlations were computed across the eight variables (novel and frozen for each of the four tasks) for each of the six grades. Table 13.1 presents these data for Grades 3, 5, and 6, while Table 13.2 presents comparable data for Grades 7, 9, and 11. The first and most significant point of note is the sheer number of significant correlations (both positive and negative) in Table 13.1 as compared to Table 13.2. Of the 28 correlations possible in each of the matrices composing Table 13.1, there are ten significant correlations in Grade 3, ten in Grade 5, and nine in Grade 6. This is in contrast to five significant correlations in Grade 7, six in Grade 9, and five in Grade 11 (see Table 13.2). Of

TABLE 13.1
Intercorrelations Among the Four Tasks: Grades 3, 5, and 6

Grade 3

Task	1. Composition		2. Pollio Test		3. Gardner–Winner		4. Explication	
	F/100	N/100	Frozen	Novel	Appr.	Conv.	Frozen	Novel
1. Composition								
F/100	—	.12	−.25	−.15	−.19	−.06	−.26	−.28
N/100		—	.15	−.05	.06	.06	−.06	.12
2. Pollio Test								
Frozen			—	.63**	.41*	.12	.39*	.32*
Novel				—	.37*	.04	.64**	.59**
3. Gardner–Winner								
Appr.					—	.18	.51**	.46**
Conv.						—	.28	.13
4. Explication								
Frozen							—	.71**
Novel								—

Grade 5

1. *Composition*								
F/100	—	-.36*	.31*	.28	-.14	.12	-.15	-.11
N/100		—	-.39*	-.45**	.15	.03	-.26	.06
2. *Pollio Test*								
Frozen			—	.65**	.06	.15	.44**	.35*
Novel				—	.02	-.22	.45**	.45**
3. *Gardner–Winner*								
Appr.					—	.17	.16	.30
Conv.						—	-.05	-.08
4. *Explication*								
Frozen							—	.72**
Novel								—

Grade 6

1. *Composition*								
F/100	—	-.19	.21	-.05	.19	.13	-.04	.08
N/100		—	-.02	.14	.19	-.06	.28	.37*
2. *Pollio Test*								
Frozen			—	.54**	.18	.39*	.39*	.29
Novel				—	.32*	.16	.24	.43**
3. *Gardner–Winner*								
Appr.					—	-.50**	.26	.31*
Conv.						—	.04	.03
4. *Explication*								
Frozen							—	.64**
Novel								—

*p < .05
**p < .01

TABLE 13.2
Intercorrelations Among the Four Tasks: Grades 7, 9, and 11

Grade 7

Task	1. Composition		2. Pollio Test		3. Gardner–Winner		4. Explication	
	F/100	*N/100*	*Frozen*	*Novel*	*Appr.*	*Conv.*	*Frozen*	*Novel*
1. Composition								
F/100	—	-.31*	.08	-.18	.30	-.14	.13	-.07
N/100		—	-.27	-.31*	.07	-.09	.13	.27
2. Pollio Test								
Frozen			—	.46**	.05	.17	-.17	-.24
Novel				—	-.04	.26	.15	.21
3. Gardner–Winner								
Appropriate					—	-.71**	-.00	.14
Conventional						—	.01	-.17
4. Explication								
Frozen							—	.61**
Novel								—

Grade 9

	1. F/100	N/100	2. Frozen	Novel	3. Appropriate	Conventional	4. Frozen	Novel
1. Composition								
F/100	—							
N/100	-.24	—						
2. Pollio Test								
Frozen	.20	.10	—					
Novel	-.09	.17	-.01	—				
3. Gardner–Winner								
Appropriate	-.16	-.07	.11	.31*	—			
Conventional	-.06	.17	-.02	-.04	-.71**	—		
4. Explication								
Frozen	-.14	.02	.09	.13	.37*	-.45**	—	
Novel	-.06	-.07	-.14	.00	.14	-.31*	.48**	—

Grade 11

	1. F/100	N/100	2. Frozen	Novel	3. Appropriate	Conventional	4. Frozen	Novel
1. Composition								
F/100	—							
N/100	.33*	—						
2. Pollio Test								
Frozen	-.02	.23	—					
Novel	-.14	.30	.40*	—				
3. Gardner–Winner								
Appropriate	.39*	.15	-.20	.10	—			
Conventional	-.19	-.03	.10	-.04	-.62**	—		
4. Explication								
Frozen	.07	.06	.04	.08	.00	.12	—	
Novel	.04	.19	.01	.22	.01	.14	.49**	—

$*p < .05$
$**p < .01$

even more importance in Table 13.2 is the fact that the vast majority of significant correlations occur within the same task. In contrast, there were more significant cross-task correlations in Grades 3, 5, and 6. This indicates that for the younger subjects performance on different tasks was more closely related.

Before continuing, it should be noted that tests for homogeneity of variance were performed. These tests revealed homogeneity for all tasks except for the Pollio Test, which can be explained by recalling that the mean number correct for both novel and frozen items approached an asymptote at about Grade 7, so that variances for each grade level progressively decreased. On the basis of these tests it was felt that the correlations were not likely to be spurious due to a violation of homogeneity assumptions underlying correlational analyses.

To examine further the trends revealed in the correlation matrices, a principal components factor analysis was performed for each grade separately and for two sets of data combining Grades 3, 5, and 6 and Grades 7, 9, and 11. The resultant factors were rotated orthogonally (varimax) to achieve simple solution. As might be expected from examination of the individual correlation matrices, analyses for each of the lower grades were quite similar, as were analyses for the upper grades. Since the patterns obtained were virtually the same and a greater number of subjects give more power to the analyses, only data for combined groups will be considered. Results of these analyses are presented in Tables 13.3 and 13.4. Immediately apparent from inspection of these tables is that the analysis for the lower grades resulted in a three factor solution (accounting for 66% of the variance), while the analysis for the upper grades resulted in a four factor solution (accounting for 75%).

TABLE 13.3
Factor Analytic Results for Grades 3, 5, and 6 Combined

Variable	Factor I	Factor II	Factor III
1. *Composition*			
Frozen	−.307	−.367	.178
Novel	−.132	.879	.125
2. *Pollio Test*			
Frozen	.715	−.111	.369
Novel	.800	−.276	.079
3. *Gardner–Winner*			
Appropriate (N)	.574	.313	−.179
Conventional (F)	.128	.035	.929
4. *Explication*			
Frozen	.839	.042	.086
Novel	.835	.235	.053
Percent Variance	39	14	13

TABLE 13.4
Factor Analytic Results for Grades 7, 9, and 11 Combined

Variable	Factor I	Factor II	Factor III	Factor IV
1. *Composition*				
Frozen	.208	.225	−.084	.827
Novel	.308	.125	−.160	−.561
2. *Pollio Test*				
Frozen	−.069	−.053	.744	.351
Novel	−.213	.052	.834	−.221
3. *Gardner–Winner*				
Appropriate (N)	.073	.907	.105	.087
Conventional (F)	−.020	−.902	.101	.003
4. *Explication*				
Frozen	.874	.015	.099	.065
Novel	.880	.070	.041	−.094
Percent Variance	25	20	17	13

Of more importance than the number of factors is the composition of the factors at each level. The first factor for the lower grades is defined by high positive loadings for the following variables: Pollio Test (frozen and novel), Gardner–Winner Test (appropriate), and Explications (frozen and novel), (five of the eight variables). This factor, which accounts for 39% of the variance in the model, can best be described as a general factor of figurative competence. The remaining two factors, which together account for 12% less variance than the first factor alone, were defined by only one variable each, Productions (novel) and Gardner–Winner, (conventional).

In contrast, the four factor solution for the upper grades is clearly differentiated by task. That is, Factor I is defined by the two explication variables, Factor II by a contrast between the two Gardner–Winner variables, Factor III by the two Pollio variables, and Factor IV by a contrast between Production task variables.

Of equal importance is the percent of variance accounted for by each of the four factors. As can be seen from Table 13.4, the first factor accounts for only 25% of the variance, while the remaining three factors account for 20, 17, and 13%, respectively. In contrast to results obtained for the younger children, the pattern of variance accounted for in this analysis is more equally distributed among the four factors, suggesting a more highly differentiated structure of figurative competence for older children. Thus, there seems to be a definite difference between younger and older children in the relationships obtaining among the four aspects of figurative diction. For the earlier grades, the major relationship is one involving those of the four probes, suggesting a general figurative factor. For the later grades, however, this pattern changes and figurative competence can be sharply delineated into four task specific factors, with very little interaction among factors.

FIGURATIVE COMPETENCE AND DEVELOPMENTAL THEORY

The major purposes of the present study were to view four aspects of figurative competence developmentally and to determine the relationships among these aspects and tasks that may measure them. Since the metrics used for each of the probes differed considerably, care is needed in making cross-task comparisons. Nonetheless, it is obvious that children demonstrate some level of figurative competence on all four measures as early as Grade 3, and that these competencies, in general, increase with age except in the area of production.

The developmental pattern that emerged from these data reveals that for three of the developmental probes unanticipated changes occurred at or just before the sixth grade. For example, frozen usage reached its low point in Grade 6 and increased steadily thereafter. Comprehension showed a cross-over between novel and frozen figures at Grade 6, which was maintained through Grade 11. Finally, there was a sharp rise in preference for appropriate figures at Grade 6. Something clearly seems to be happening, figuratively speaking, when children reach sixth grade.

A similar conclusion emerges from an examination of correlational and factor analytic results. As may be remembered, the pattern of correlations was different in Grades 3, 5, and 6 from that in Grades 7, 9, and 11. In the lower grades, the correlational data indicated that the probes were strongly interrelated. Children who do well on one task will, in all likelihood, do well on the others. In the upper grades, however, the inter-relationship among probes appeared to be negligible; children who do well on one task may or may not do well on others. Results obtained from principal component analyses showed a fairly large general factor of figurative competence for Grades 3, 5, and 6; and four task-specific factors each accounting for quite similar amounts of variance in Grades 7, 9, and 11. Obviously, children in the upper grades deal with these tasks in quite different ways than children in the lower grades.

Changes in factor patterns over age involving cognitive activities are not new to developmental research and were noted as early as 1936 by Asch. In his study, a total of 161 children took a battery of eight tests (4 verbal, 3 numerical, and parts of the Army Beta) at the ages of 9 and 12. Correlations and factor analyses revealed a large "general ability" factor at each age and a significant decrease in the amount of variance accounted for by this general ability factor at age 12. Asch concluded that "mental traits change and undergo reorganization as the individual develops" and that these "factors or organization probably become systematized and established under the influence of training and maturation" (Asch, 1936).

Anastasi (1949, 1958), in reviewing studies concerned with trait organization, concluded that in spite of conflicting results, a hypothesis based on differentiation (i.e., from general to specific factors), appeared to be the most promising one in accounting for changes in organization or structure for different aged children. Such conflicting results can perhaps be attributed to differences in educational levels and backgrounds of groups used in the various studies.

Considerations raised by both Asch and Anastasi seem to have implications within the present context. There does appear to be differentiation in the structure of metaphoric competence from earlier to later grades. This structure changes from a somewhat global, general ability capable of handling most aspects of figurative diction (and the tasks that measure them) to a set of highly differentiated competencies involving each task as a separate, essentially unrelated, entity. This change occurs somewhere around Grades 6 and 7.

When the data of a developmental study suggest that development proceeds from general to specific, the theoretical approach that springs naturally to mind is that of Werner (1948, 1957). Here, the most relevant feature would be Werner's orthogenetic principle, which assumes "that whenever development occurs it proceeds from a state of relative globality and lack of differentiation to a state of increasing differentiation, articulation, and hierarchic integration" (Werner, 1957, p. 126). In this study, factor analytic results clearly indicate the differentiation of an initially global factor of figurative competence into a series of more highly differentiated task components. Unfortunately, present results do not offer any support for the second part of Werner's principle, and it seems reasonable to wonder when and if further development might indicate a restructuring of figurative competence into a more articulated, hierarchic structure.

At this point, data involving college age respondents reported by Pickens and Pollio (1979) seem relevant. In their study, three of the four probes used here were presented to college age subjects. Results of their analysis of the following four task probes—compositions (novel and frozen), Pollio Test (novel and frozen), Gardner–Winner Preference (appropriate and conventional), and Gardner–Winner Production—revealed a consistent three factor solution: The first factor was primarily one of novel diction (accounting for about 38% of the variance); the second, a task specific factor—comprehension (27%); and the third, frozen diction (16%). These factors make sense in terms of present results and can be interpreted to fulfill the "hierarchic integration" portion of Werner's orthogenetic principle. That is, the adult pattern represents a reasonable integration of organizational processes begun earlier.

Consider again results for the production and comprehension tasks. Younger children responded to the tests as if both frozen and novel figures were functionally equivalent, i.e., were "strange" language. On the production task, starting in seventh grade, and on the comprehension task, sixth grade, children begin differentiating between frozen and novel and come to consider frozen diction as less strange. At this point, novel diction, as representing all of figurative language, seems to begin.

Thus, it all comes down to a question of progressive definition and redefinition of the *functional* meaning of figurative language. Results of the Billow (1977b) and Gardner et al. (1975) studies seem to suggest that young children (ages 3-7) seem to divide language into two categories—strange and ordinary—and use strange (i.e., metaphoric) language quite frequently. Younger school age children seem to have, as present results indicate, an overall figurative factor, with small separate factors for novel and frozen diction. In adolescence, this general factor differentiates into specific task factors, which partially reintegrate and become more highly and hierarchially organized in college age students. Although no data are available for the mature adult, it seems reasonable to suppose that novel diction may become synonymous with all of figurative diction; witness the difficulty raters have in selecting frozen usage as metaphoric (Pollio, et al., 1977, p. 72) and the difficulty even metaphor researchers have in acknowledging frozen diction as figurative.

The qualitative change that occurs in these data between ages 11 and 12 suggests a Piagetian interpretation in terms of a shift from concrete to formal operational thinking. This conclusion is further supported by results obtained by Cometa and Eson (1978). The Piagetian view of metaphor and the metaphoric process, however, needs to be re-examined. For Piaget, "true" metaphor implies formal operational thinking, thus placing him in the company of those who have been characterized as holding a "formal" view. From this perspective, the utterance "My truck died," when produced by a young child would be glossed as unintentional mistake and/or confusion of image with object since the logical operations for metaphoric transformations are not present in preoperational children (Piaget, 1962). From a functional view, this position appears to be more concerned with theoretical niceties than with empirical data. The sentence "My truck died" is certainly metaphoric.

Finally, methodological issues must be considered. In studying the development of figurative language, and perhaps language in general, multiple probes which explore different aspects of the domain in question must be used. In the case of figurative language, for example, the use of a single probe would not have permitted the discovery of figurative differentiation so evident in the present study. Similarly, as many have noted, the use of explanation as the unique probe of interest obscured the fact that children were able to deal with figurative language well before age levels suggested by studies using tasks of explanation alone. Although further examples could be cited, the general methodological point seems quite clear: Multidimensional domains require multidimensional probes, and, in this, figurative language is no exception.

ACKNOWLEDGMENTS

The authors wish to acknowledge the invaluable assistance of the following good people: Howard Pollio, for comments and suggestions; Sherry P. Bonham, for editorial and interviewing assistance; Julie Clements, for rating; and Dee Ambrister, Martha Anderson, Mitch Garland, Steve Harrison, Sue Lanan, Pam McCroskey, Gary Spears, Anne Van Pelt, Susan Williams, and Nancy Winslow for gathering and assembling data. Thanks are also due to the Knox County School System and, in particular, to Dr. Anne Roney, Dr. Alvin Scott, Dr. Sandra Quillin, Mr. Billy K. Nicely, and the teachers and children of Bonny Kate, Doyle Middle, and Doyle High School.

REFERENCES

Anastasi, A. *Differential Psychology* (3rd ed.). New York: Macmillan, 1958.

Anastasi, A., & Foley, J. P., Jr. *Differential Psychology*, Revised Edition, New York: Macmillan, 1949.

Arlin, P. K. *The function of Piagetian operational levels in the preference and production of metaphors*. Paper presented to the Society for Research in Child Development, New Orleans, 1977.

Asch, S. E. A study of change in mental organization. *Archives of Psychology*, No. 195, 1936.

Asch, S. E., & Nerlove, H. The development of double-function terms in children. In B. Kaplan & S. Wapner (Eds.), *Perspectives in psychological theory*. New York: International Universities Press, 1960.

Barlow, J. M., Kerlin, J. R., & Pollio, H. R. *Training manual for identifying figurative language*. (Technical Report No. 1). Metaphor Research Group, University of Tennessee, Knoxville, 1971.

Billow, R. M. A cognitive developmental study of metaphor comprehension. *Developmental Psychology*, 1975, *11*, 415–423.

Billow, R. M. Metaphor: A review of the psychological literature. *Psychological Bulletin*, 1977, *84*, 81–92. (a)

Billow, R. M. *Spontaneous metaphor in children*. Unpublished manuscript, 1977. (b)

Cometa, M. S., & Eson, M. E. Logical operations and metaphor interpretation: A Piagetian model. *Child Development*, 1978, *49*, 649–659.

Gardner, H., Kircher, M., Winner, E., & Perkins, D. Children's metaphoric productions and preferences. *Journal of Child Language*, 1975, *2*, 125–141.

Gardner, H., & Winner, E. Development of metaphoric competence: Implications for humanistic disciplines. *Critical Inquiry*, Vol. 5, No. 1, 1978, 123–141.

Honeck, R., Sowry, B. M., & Voegtle, K. Proverbial understanding in a pictorial context. *Child Development*, 1978, *49*, 327–331.

Inhelder, B., & Piaget, J. *The early growth of logic in the child*. New York: Norton, 1969.

Ortony, A., Reynolds, R., & Arter, J. Metaphor: theoretical and empirical research. *Psychological Bulletin*, 1978, *5*, 919–943.

Piaget, J. *Play, dreams and imitation in childhood*. New York: Norton, 1962.

Pickens, J. D., & Pollio, H. R. Patterns of figurative language competence in adult speakers. *Psychological Research*, 1979, *40*, 299–313.

Pollio, H. R., Barlow, J. M., Fine, H. J., & Pollio, M. R. *Psychology and the poetics of growth: Figurative language in psychology, psychotherapy and education*. Hillsdale, N.J.: Lawrence Erlbaum Associates, 1977.

Pollio, M. R. *Figurative language in the elementary school*. Unpublished Masters Thesis, The University of Tennessee, 1971.

Pollio, M. R. *The development and augmentation of figurative language.* Unpublished Doctoral Dissertation, The University of Tennessee, 1973.

Pollio, M. R., & Pollio, H. R. Development of figurative language in school children. *Journal of Psycholinguistic Research,* 1974, *3,* 185–201.

Pollio, M. R., & Pollio, H. R. A test of metaphoric comprehension and some preliminary developmental data. *Journal of Child Language,* 1979, *6,* 111–120.

Schonberg, R. B. *Adolescent thought and figurative language.* Unpublished doctoral dissertation, University of Tennessee, 1974.

Werner, H. *Comparative Psychology of Mental Development* (Rev. Ed.), New York: Follett, 1948.

Werner, H. The concept of development from a comparative and organismic point of view. In D. Harris (Ed.), *The concept of development.* Minneapolis: University of Minnesota Press, 1957.

Winner, E., Rosenstiel, A. K., & Gardner, H. The development of metaphoric understanding. *Developmental Psychology,* 1976, *12,* 289–297.

14 The Ontogenesis of Metaphor

Ellen Winner

Margaret McCarthy

Howard Gardner
Harvard Project Zero
Boston College
Boston Veterans Administration Hospital

INTRODUCTION: A DEBATE OVER ORIGINS

As long as metaphor was consigned to the domain of literature and philosophy, questions about the origins of figurative language could be safely ignored by the psychological community. But now that metaphor has become less of an intruder, now that it has promise of membership "in good standing" within the establishment of empirical investigation, an examination of its ontogenesis has become inevitable. Like many searches for ancestors, however, this one has proved to be more complicated than originally suspected; moreover, even the very legitimacy of this quest has been called into question.

In developmental studies, it is standard to search for rudimentary manifestations of an ability and then to observe their continued growth and differentiation. The case of metaphor may not, however, present the standard pattern of improvement with age. Two sharply contrasting accounts of the nature of this skill seem, on the surface, to have equal plausibility. Moreover, each of these perspectives has been defended with some eloquence and conviction, thus challenging researchers to more closely inspect the data pertinent to these competing accounts.

When a resemblance is noted between things that are usually seen as very different from each other, an act of metaphorical perception has occurred. Metaphor has been viewed as one of our most elementary ways of knowing the world (Arnheim, 1974; Cassirer, 1957), a mode that comes naturally to the young child. Early language has been viewed as richly metaphoric, reflecting this primitive but fundamentally human way of perceiving the world. Researchers of this ''early-metaphor'' persuasion have stressed the early emerging capacity to effect metaphoric matches (Gardner, 1974), to map modalities onto one another (Bond & Stevens, 1969; Gentner, 1977), and to construct striking figures of speech (Billow, 1977; Gardner, Kircher, Winner, & Perkins, 1975; Pollio, Barlow, Fine & Pollio, 1977; Winner, 1979). Moreover, they call attention to an apparent decline in the proclivity to produce metaphors—a finding that has sometimes led to a ringing endorsement of the genius of early child language and a critique of a society bent on undermining spontaneous creation (Chukovsky, 1968).

Starkly arrayed against this ''early metaphor'' position is a rival view that considers metaphor as one of the highest and most developed achievements of human beings. Rejecting the notion of the young child as poet, those sympathetic to this tradition view the creation of figures of speech as a late-emerging capacity, one dependent upon prior mastery of considerable intellectual ground (cf. Elkind, 1969; Gombrich, 1961; Inhelder & Piaget, 1958). According to this view, apparent figures of speech by young children are more accurately seen as overextensions (Clark, 1973) or reflections of the child's preconceptual system (Piaget, 1962). The implication of such a position is that metaphor is not possible until one has a rich understanding of language, a clearly defined notion of categorical boundaries, and an awareness of the rules for crossing these boundaries.

The dispute over the status of metaphor within the child's developing linguistic and conceptual capacities remains unresolved. Indeed, virtually no systematic information exists on children's early potentially metaphoric behaviors: Little is known about the natural course of metaphoric skill in the child, equally little about the circumstances under which metaphor may be elicited in clinical or experimental settings. (For a review, see Gardner, Winner, Bechhofer, & Wolf, 1978.) Until such data have been collected and considered, the argument described above will continue to rage.

TWO EMPIRICAL APPROACHES TO THE EMERGENCE OF EARLY METAPHOR

Unraveling the enigma of the ontogenesis of metaphor proves to be a challenging task. The problems are terminological, methodological, and inferential. One needs to have ways of securing metaphors from children and then assessing their significance, for the child no less than for the observer. Although no single-pronged investigation can provide an unambiguous answer to the issues raised above, it is possible to gain some insight into the problem by adopting both observational and experimental methods and bringing their respective findings to bear on one another.

One needs, first of all, a working definition of metaphor. While recognizing that linguistic metaphor depends upon nonlinguistic mental processes, we restrict ourselves here to metaphor as it manifests itself in language. By metaphor we refer to those cases in which a word (or phrase) is transported from its customary context to a novel domain, and in which such a transfer is deemed appropriate (rather than anomalous) by the community. Consider a case in which a streak of skywriting is called "a scar in the sky." Here, "scar," a term usually restricted to marks left by incisions on the skin, is applied to a very different domain. The link uniting the two elements (the *topic*, skywriting and the *vehicle*, "scar") is the *ground* of the metaphor (Richards, 1936)—in this case a linear mark that defaces an otherwise unblemished surface.

While this definition is suitable for most linguistic purposes, it harbors a central psychological difficulty: It is quite possible to create a striking figure of speech by applying a word to a novel domain with neither prior intention nor subsequent recognition. And it is for precisely this reason that investigators who favor an "overextension" interpretation of children's early speech dismiss most candidate metaphors. Establishing an individual's intention to produce a metaphor proves a most difficult, yet necessary undertaking. As indication of prior intention rather than mistake, we have required evidence that the child knows the literal name of the "misnamed" referent, e.g., the child who called the skywriting a "scar" must know the word "skywriting" in order to be credited with metaphor. Of course, this criterion is not, in principle, necessary. The child may not know "skywriting" but may know that "scar" is not used literally. (Indeed, in the history of language, metaphors are often born of necessity: A word is needed to fill a lexical gap and a metaphor is consciously invented where no prior literal reference exists.) However, because of the subjectivity involved in determining whether a child believes a name to be nonliteral, we have required evidence that the conventional name is known.

Given our interest in charting the beginnings of metaphor, we began by examining the emergence of metaphor in its natural surroundings—in the spontaneous speech and play of the young child. Only through such an open-ended exploration is it possible to determine the contexts in which metaphors spontaneously emerge and the frequency with which they arise. Yet, on its own, spontaneous behavior is extremely difficult to evaluate. One is uncertain about the extent to which the child's behavior is simply a repetition of something heard in the same situation at an earlier time. One is unclear about the child's knowledge of the words in question—and it is hardly possible to intervene in the midst of play to secure a definition or to administer the relevant classification tasks.

Following tradition in developmental research, we used evidence from spontaneous speech to suggest hypotheses about metaphoric development that could then be systematically tested. Suppose, for instance, that in spontaneous speech metaphors first emerge in the course of actions upon objects. It is possible to determine, in an experiment, whether this is simply an indication of how the child *prefers* to make metaphors, or whether this is the only way in which they can be constructed. Similarly, suppose a certain kind of object or experience seems to elicit a disproportionate amount of metaphor in spontaneous play. Through presentation of a controlled set of objects to be renamed, one can determine whether such a finding represents a general trend or is idiosyncratic to a particular child.

Through this pairing of observational and experimental methods, we were able to confront a number of basic questions about metaphor. For example, what kinds of experiences elicit metaphoric speech? Does such language first take the form of renaming concrete objects? And if so, to what extent does the fact that an object has a specifically defined function encourage or militate against the production of metaphor? That is, are children more likely to produce metaphoric names for objects with well-defined functions and salient names (e.g., a cup) or for objects with less strictly defined functions and names, such as wooden blocks or shapes cut out of paper? An answer to this question provides a measure of the degree to which children are capable of overriding familiar names and functions and, by inference, an assessment of the extent to which they are aware of the "tension" involved in such overriding.

STUDY I: THE EMERGENCE OF METAPHOR
IN SPONTANEOUS SPEECH

To obtain information concerning the initial instances of metaphor in a child's language, we examined the protocols of one of the subjects, Adam, studied by Roger Brown (1973) in his pioneering examination of early language. Adam's speech (as well as that of his mother and the experimenter) was recorded at regular intervals between the age of 27–58 months. Because the transcripts contained notes on the contexts in which utterances were made, we were able to use these records to determine whether, and in what form, instances of metaphoric language occurred in the early language of one child.

The most crucial phase of this investigation entailed the establishment of criteria by which metaphoric and literal utterances could be distinguished from one another. A set of definitions was devised according to which it proved possible to distinguish reliably between overextension (where the meaning of a word was *mistakenly* generalized); anomalies (where no ground for the nonliteral name was apparent to the adult judges); misclassifications (where the child mistakenly believed the object named to be something that it was not); and genuine metaphors (where the child deliberately used language in a nonliteral but appropriate manner). (See Table 14.1 for the definitions used and examples of candidate figures.)

The metaphors that survived our criteria of acceptability were classified in several ways. First, metaphors were defined as either "Action Metaphors"

TABLE 14.1
Classification of Types of Nonliteral Utterances Found in Early
Spontaneous Speech

Type of Utterance	Example	Criteria Used to Classify
Metaphors	piece of string is called "my tail," immediately after is called "string" [2;11]	literal name for renamed object is in child's lexicon
	holds horn like eggbeater, makes turning motions with hand, says "mixer" [2;5]	renaming accompanied by parallel transformation of object through symbolic play
	2 irons facing each other are called, in turn, the "boy" and the "mommy" who are talking to each other [3;1]	sheer probability (given age of child and familiarity of renamed object) that child knows literal name
	"This (the letter J) looks like a cane" [3;4]	utterances expressed in form of simile (is like)
Overextensions	toy snake and tail of monkey were called "wiggle-worm" [3;4 and 3;5]	word incorrectly extended to set of similar referents
	cowcatcher in front of train was called "sweep-broom" [2;3]	no evidence that literal name is known
Misclassifications	telescope was called "pipe" [2;10]	object unfamiliar and likely to be confused with similar but familiar object
	picture of monkey eating a banana was called monkey eating a "crayon"	object unclearly represented in picture
Anomalies	label on briefcase was called "spaghetti" [2;3]	no apparent ground for name given

(themselves subdivided into Pretend-Action and Nonpretend Action) and "Nonaction Metaphors" (see Table 14.2). Second, the type of object renamed was identified. And third, the grounds underlying each metaphor were determined (see Table 14.3). Two judges achieved 93% reliability for the classification of type of utterance and 91% for the classification of grounds. In all cases of disagreement, the particular utterance was reviewed until consensus was reached.

Finally, for the purposes of a developmental analysis, the transcripts were divided into three age categories: 27–35 months, 36–47 months, and 48–58.5 months (henceforth year 2, 3, and 4, respectively). The number of each kind of metaphor produced at each age was tallied.

During the 112 hours of testing, Adam produced 185 figures of speech that met our criteria for metaphor. One hundred and sixty-two of these utterances were names given to physical objects (and hence nouns); 15 were names applied to actions (thus, nouns plus verbs); and 3 were names given to properties of

TABLE 14.2
Classification of Metaphors Found in Early Spontaneous Speech

Type of Metaphor	Example	Definition
Pretend action	Hangs ball on string from chin: "Look, my beard." [3;4]	Noncharacteristic action performed on object in order to suggest a new, pretend identity. Object renamed accordingly.
Non-pretend action	Puts paper cover back on crayon after it has slipped off: "I am putting on your clothes, crayon" [3;3]	Object handled in characteristic, non-pretend manner. Similarity is perceived between normal function of one object and normal function of another object. Object renamed accordingly.
Nonaction	Looks at red balloon attached to green tube for blowing it up: "Dat's de apple on de tree." [4;9]	Renaming elicited by perception of similarity between the properties of two objects, with no action involved in the metaphoric transfer.

objects (thus, adjectives). Clearly, then, it was in the course of renaming physical objects that most of Adam's early metaphors arose.

Significant differences were found in the incidence of the three forms of metaphor across the three age periods ($\chi^2 = 52.7$, $df = 4$, $p < .001$). As can be seen in Fig. 14.1, pretend action metaphors decreased in absolute number from 62% at year 2 to 10% at year 4. In striking contrast, nonaction metaphors increased in absolute number, rising from 25% at year 2 to 76% at year 4. The incidence of non-pretend actions, the least common kind of renaming, remained stable over age. It seems, then, that while metaphors arise initially in the course

TABLE 14.3
Classification of Grounds Found in Spontaneous Metaphors

Type of Ground	Example
contour	pencil = "big needle" [2;7]
spatial configuration	one alphabet letter on top of another one = "Adam sleeping on Daddy" [3;3]
color	hair = "dark woods" [3;10] (Also grounded in texture)
size	small balloon = "tiny little baby" [2;10]
sound	dropping small blocks on floor so that they clattered = "Listen, dirty dishes [2;5]
motion	a spinning top = "It wobbles in like a snake" [4;10]
texture	cracker crumbs = "a load of dirt" [4;10]
function	microphone cord, as child crawls under it = "tunnel" [2;7]
affect	isolated marble = "lonesome" [4;7]

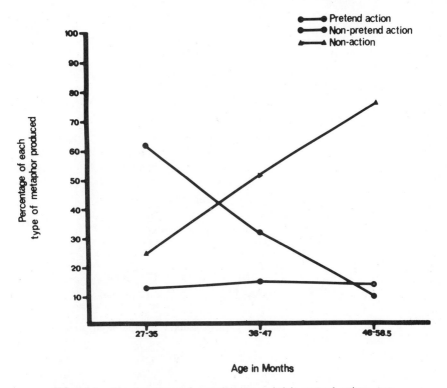

FIG. 14.1. The percentage of metaphors grounded in pretend actions, non-pretend actions, and nonaction modes produced by Adam during successive periods of time.

of symbolic play, metaphors based on perceptual resemblance come increasingly to the fore in the latter pre-school years.

A tally of the grounds on which metaphors were based permits inferences about the kinds of similarities salient to the young child. Pretend action metaphors proved equally likely, at all ages, to be based on solely functional grounds, or on functional grounds buttressed by perceptual ones. Nonaction metaphors, however, always took into account the physical dimensions of the object. In fact, these metaphors were elicited by the same kinds of physical properties as those that give rise to overextensions and misclassifications (Bowerman, 1976; Clark, 1973)—that is, primarily by the overall shape of an object. Only rarely were early metaphors based on multiple perceptual grounds; rather, an isolated physical feature characteristically served to ground the metaphor.

We expected that the earliest metaphors would be renamings of objects with rather loosely defined functions (e.g., a wooden block), since the renaming of such objects requires less overriding than the renaming of objects with conventionally defined functions (e.g., a comb). Surprisingly, however, it was the objects for which well defined functions and names had to be overridden that proved more susceptible to metaphoric renaming.

Finally, the study provided data on the relative frequency of metaphors, as opposed to overextensions, misclassifications, and anomalies. Again, somewhat to our surprise, overextensions and misclassifications (21% of utterances) proved much less frequent than metaphors (79% of utterances). Instances of anomaly were fairly infrequent at year 2 and almost nonexistent thereafter. It appears that metaphoric utterances have reliably been found in the language of one child as early as age 2, and that these figures exhibit a number of regular features related to the kinds of objects selected, the grounds exploited, and the situations in which such renamings typically occur. Moreover, a recent investigation has confirmed this pattern of early metaphor production in two other preschool children (cf. Winner, McCarthy, Kleinman, & Gardner, 1979).

STUDY II: AN EXPERIMENTAL INVESTIGATION OF METAPHORIC RENAMING IN EARLY CHILDHOOD

While our study of spontaneous metaphor production lends initial plausibility to the thesis that metaphoric production emerges at a young age, it is attended by one central difficulty. As already noted, distinguishing genuine metaphor from overextension requires an assessment of the intention of the child. Whether or not an utterance sounds metaphoric to adult ears, the utterance clearly is metaphoric only if the child intended to use the word(s) nonliterally. Where such intention is lacking, we have not a metaphor but a mistake in the guise of a metaphor. In order to establish such intention, we had no choice but to make inferences from Adam's prior linguistic output. Thus, when he called a yellow pencil "corn," we allowed ourselves to count this as a metaphor because we had evidence that he had previously called the pencil by its literal name. However, the possibility that he had *forgotten* its literal name at the time of the utterance, or believed both names to be *equally* appropriate, cannot be ruled out in such an "after-the-fact" study.

These weaknesses can be overcome, however, by means of an experimental intervention in which children are given a metaphoric renaming task. Immediately after a metaphoric name for an object has been produced, the experimenter can simply ask the child the "real" name for the object. In addition to thus providing stronger evidence of "boundary-crossing," such an experiment allows a more rigorous test of the conclusions that emerged from our initial study. Therefore, in our follow-up study we sought confirmation of the initial importance of action in the construction of metaphors; the ease of renaming objects whose strictly defined functions and names must be overridden; and the tendency to produce single-grounded metaphors based primarily on shape or function. Finally, we probed children's ability to make judgments about the relative appropriateness of metaphors fashioned by another person.

In order to elicit metaphors from young children, we devised a turn-taking game in which both child and experimenter, each using a puppet, provided pretend names for a series of objects differing along a variety of dimensions. Of course, renaming individual concrete objects is only a rudimentary kind of metaphoric skill. But in view of the youthfulness and reticence of our subjects, and the difficulty of engaging them in an experimental task, we had to design a game that was extremely simple in its demands and yet also one that captured something of the essence of metaphor. The ability to offer a nonliteral, but motivated name for a simple physical object was judged a feasible index of metaphoric skill. Children were also asked to have their puppets decide whether pretend names offered by the experimenter's puppet were acceptable or "silly" (anomalous). Forty-five preschoolers, 15 at each of three age groups (3:0–3:7, mean age 3:4; 3:10–4:6, mean age 4:1; and 4:10–5:6, mean age 5:0) constituted the main sample. In addition, twelve 8-year-olds, twelve 10-year-olds, and 8 adults were included.

Each child participated in five counterbalanced conditions. In three conditions, the child was asked to provide a pretend name for a series of objects. If a child offered a literal name for an object, the experimenter probed in the following manner. The first literal response offered in each condition was explicitly probed: "That's what it really is, right? Can you think of a pretend name?" Thereafter, the child was reminded of the pretend nature of the task: "You're pretending it's an X?" and was allowed to try once more. Otherwise, only one response was elicited for each item; if subjects spontaneously offered two responses they were asked to choose between them. Conditions varied in the kind and amount of action involved in the renaming task. In the Child Enactive Condition, children were allowed to manipulate the objects prior to providing a new name. In the Perceptual Renaming Condition, no manipulation of the objects was allowed—children were required to simply look at the object held by the experimenter and give it a pretend name. In the Experimenter Enactive Condition, the child was not permitted to act on the object, but was allowed to watch the experimenter manipulate the objects in such a way as to suggest a pretend identity. For example, the experimenter "hopped" a small green block across the table, in a motion suggestive of a frog. The child was then asked to invent a pretend name for the object. (This condition was the least metaphoric of the three since one can conceivably succeed by attending only to the experimenter's gesture and ignoring the object used. However, this condition was included as a baseline in order to determine whether children who failed on the other conditions could succeed in making a leap when the transformation was strongly suggested by the experimenter's gesture.)

The two remaining conditions were designed to tap the child's judgment skills. In the Perceptual Multiple Choice Condition, children were asked to look at, but not touch, a series of objects. For each object (e.g., a cone shaped block) subjects heard three possible names from which they were required to select the "best" pretend name. The three choices were literal (a block), anomalous (a fire engine), and metaphoric (a rocketship). In the Perceptual Correction Condition, children were given the choice of accepting or rejecting pretend names offered by the experimenter's "silly puppet." Eleven of the names offered were anomalous, three were metaphoric. Children were also asked to improve on any names that they rejected as "silly."

Before receiving any of the five conditions, each child participated in a practice session in which the experimenter's puppet metaphorically renamed three stimuli and offered three other stimuli to the child's puppet for renaming. Thereafter, each condition was preceded by a modeling of the task.

The stimuli consisted of five sets of objects. Each set consisted of six objects with conventional functions and salient names (e.g., a crayon), and eight objects with more flexible functions and less salient names (two painted blocks, two unpainted blocks, two unfamiliar gadgets, and two small square-shaped pieces of colored construction paper). (The two pieces of construction paper were not used in the two enactive conditions as they were introduced to determine whether perceptually grounded, nonaction metaphors were ever based solely upon color.) Each child received a different set of objects in each condition, but the objects were rotated systematically among conditions to avoid any potential biases arising from differences in the relative ease of renaming particular objects.

Conservative scoring systems were devised in order to distinguish metaphors from nonmetaphors, to classify nonmetaphors, and to characterize metaphors in terms of the grounds employed (see Tables 14.4 and 14.5). Two judges achieved 84–97% reliability for each of these scoring procedures on 84% of the data. The quality of the metaphors produced in the Child Enactive and Perceptual Renaming conditions was also analyzed. For this analysis, a subset of 575 metaphors was given to five independent adult judges, blind to the age of the subject. Each judge was asked to select between 30–40% of the metaphors as particularly apt.

A variety of analyses were performed on the data. To begin with, a 4 way (Age × Sex × Condition × Object) analysis of variance was performed on the sheer number of metaphors produced in the three renaming conditions. A main effect of Age was found, $F(5,65) = 30.07$, $p < .001$; and Newman-Keuls post hoc tests revealed (at $p < .01$) that 3-year-olds produced significantly fewer metaphors than older children; and 4-year-olds produced fewer than all older groups except 5 year olds. A main effect for Condition was also found, $F(2,130) = 48.08$, $p < .001$; and Newman-Keuls post hoc tests revealed (at $p < .01$) that the Experimenter Enactive Condition elicited more metaphors than the other two. No difference was found between the Child Enactive and Perceptual Renaming Conditions. This pattern of results suggests that, while observing another's action facilitates metaphoric renaming, the opportunity to manipulate the object oneself is no more helpful than merely looking at the object (see Table 14.6).

TABLE 14.4
Percentage of Nonmetaphors Produced in the Renaming Study

	Age					
	3	4	5	8	10	Adult
Total number of nonmetaphors	348	174	131	47	28	14
Kinds of nonmetaphors produced	*Distribution of nonmetaphors produced*					
Anomalous: e.g., a clothespin is called a coconut; there is no apparent ground	47	37	37	31	21	43
Literal: e.g., a pen as a pencil (what is it really?) a pencil; a pen as a pen; overextensions are scored as literal	31	11	11	3	—	—
Embellished Literal: e.g., string is called "a big big string for eating"; an element of pretense is added to the literal identity	6	16	22	5	14	29
Associative: e.g., a pen as a pencil (what is it really?) a pen	8	29	24	46	54	14
Vehicle Associative: e.g., a block shaped like a bowling pin is called a bowling ball	1	1	1	—	—	7
Literal Affordability: e.g., an unfamiliar gadget used to cut potatoes is called a playdo cutter; no metaphoric leap is involved; the unfamiliar object "literally affords" the suggested identity	4	6	5	5	11	7
No response	3	—	—	—	—	—

While there were significant main effects for Age and Condition, their interaction ($p < .001$) was equally important. The Experimenter Enactive Condition was relatively easy for all ages, whereas performance on the other conditions was relatively low for 3-year-olds and improved with age. The Experimenter Enactive Condition yielded 70% more metaphors than the other conditions for 3-year-olds but only 25% more for 4-year-olds and 20% more for 5-year-olds. Thus, the youngest children benefit most from the modeling of metaphor-inducing action.

A main effect of Object was also found, $F(1,65) = 69.94$, $p < .001$. As expected, objects with loosely defined functions elicited more metaphors than ones with well defined functions. However, the factors of Condition and Object type interacted. Object type made no difference in the Experimenter Enactive Condition, but objects with ill-defined functions facilitated performance in the other two renaming conditions. Age and Object type also interacted. Object type proved a crucial variable for 3-year-olds, from whom the more abstract objects elicited 38% more metaphors (means = 3.98 vs. 2.82). However, such objects elicited only 18% more from 4-year-olds (means = 5.12 vs. 4.28), 27% more from 5-year-olds (means = 5.54 vs. 4.44), and made little, if any, difference for

TABLE 14.5
Percentage of Types of Grounds Employed in Metaphoric Renaming

	Age					
Ground	3	4	5	8	10	Adult
shape: e.g., a flat round block as a pancake	74	76	77	79	83	85
minimal shape: e.g., a tall cylindrical block as a person	13	15	14	14	11	9
color: e.g., an orange block as a carrot (vehicle is characteristically the color or the topic)	8	11	9	12	14	16
color-adjectival: e.g., a red piece of paper as a red rug	1	2	4	2	3	3
material: e.g., aluminum gadget as a toaster	4	7	4	6	4	5
other: auditory, tactile, configuration, metaphoric affordability	4	4	4	4	2	3
Experimenter Enactive Condition only:						
motion: e.g., a block hopped is called a frog	91	93	95	96	100	97

Note. Since multiple grounded metaphors were produced, columns can total more than 100%.

the older subjects. Finally, performance on the two judgment conditions was unaffected by Object type. Evidently, the familiarity of an object can be a hindrance to the initiation of the metaphoric leap, but not to its recognition and appreciation.

Because the two tests of "metaphoric judgment" use immobile objects, the results on these conditions were compared with the Perceptual Renaming Condition in order to determine the relative difficulty of production vs. appreciation of appropriate metaphors. A three way analysis-of-variance (Age × Sex × Condition) was performed on the raw number of metaphors produced, chosen, or correctly judged. With chance level performance factored out, significant effects of both Age ($p < .001$) and Age × Condition ($p < .003$) were found. Newman-Keuls post hoc tests revealed the following differences: For 3-year-olds, the Multiple Choice Condition was the most difficult of the three ($p < .01$); however, performance on Multiple Choice rose sharply with age, and by age 5 (and at all older ages), subjects performed as well on Multiple Choice as on Perceptual Renaming and Correction. At age 4, Perceptual Renaming proved easier than Correction ($p < .05$), but no difference was found between Multiple Choice and either of the other two conditions (see Table 14.6). It should be noted that, within the Correction Condition, accepting metaphoric names proved easier than rejecting inappropriate names for both 3- and 4-year-olds ($p < .01$).

Thus, no significant differences between these three conditions were found after age 4 when age groups were taken individually. However, subjects were then collapsed into two groups: younger (3-, 4-, and 5-year-olds) and older (8-

and 10-year-olds and adults) and a chi-square test was carried out on the number of older subjects who performed at a higher level on Perceptual Renaming than on each judgment condition taken separately. This test revealed an interaction of Age and Condition ($p < .001$): For preschoolers, production was easier than both Multiple Choice and Correction. For the older group, the reverse pattern was found: Production proved more difficult than both judgment conditions. It is possible that the egocentrism of young children hinders them from judging metaphors constructed from another person's point of view. Alternatively, the greater information processing load of the judgment conditions, or their metalinguistic nature, may have been responsible for this finding.

Several additional analyses were performed. Across ages, the grounds of the metaphors produced, the quality of the metaphors, and the kinds of nonmetaphors offered were compared. An unexpected result was found in the analysis of the grounds employed in the renaming conditions and in the renaming aspects of the Correction Condition. Although, as predicted, shape appeared most frequently as a ground for subjects of all ages, there was actually very little difference in the profile of grounds across ages (see Table 14.5). Although there was a trend, with age, toward more frequent use of color and material grounds, this difference proved quite small even between the oldest and youngest subjects. And, although there was also an age-related increase in the number of double and triple grounded metaphors, this increase was again quite slight (see Table 14.7). The fact that individuals of all ages seem to exploit the same kinds of grounds in the same kinds of ways (and to avoid other conceivable grounds) is powerful evidence in favor of the assertion that metaphoric procedures work similarly in populations of diverse ages, at least when metaphors consist of renaming single objects. Moreover, the similar pattern in types of grounds across conditions legitimizes comparisons that involve the Experimenter Enactive Condition and suggests the important role played by action and gesture in the earliest phases of metaphoric development.

TABLE 14.6
Performance on the Five Conditions

	Percentage of Correct Judgments Made[a]		Percentage of Renamings Scored as Metaphoric		
Age	Perceptual Correction	Perceptual Multiple Choice	Perceptual Renaming	Child Enactive	Experimenter Enactive
3	24	15	43	48	78
4	40	61	74	72	91
5	56	81	78	79	97
8	78	98	88	90	98
10	96	94	92	92	98
Adults	96	100	97	95	98

[a] Chance level performance was factored out.

TABLE 14.7
Percentage of Single, Double, and Triple Grounded Metaphors
Produced in the Renaming Study

*Perceptual Renaming, Child Enactive Renaming, and Perceptual
Correction (production)*

	Age					
Complexity	3	4	5	8	10	Adult
single grounded	87	80	82	82	76	76
double grounded	13	20	18	18	24	24
triple grounded	—	—	—	—	1	1

Experimenter Enactive Renaming (motion is a possible ground)

	Age					
Complexity	3	4	5	8	10	Adult
single grounded	27	18	16	12	11	8
double grounded	62	65	74	69	74	78
triple grounded	11	17	10	19	15	14

As for the quality of metaphors produced, those metaphors judged to be superior by adult judges were more frequently produced by the grade school subjects than by preschoolers, and more frequently produced by adults than by grade school children. The mean percentage of preschool metaphors chosen was 25%, compared to 37% of the grade school children's metaphors and 50% of the adults' metaphors. Although the increased frequency with age of superior metaphors is not surprising, it is noteworthy that as many as one quarter of the metaphors produced by preschoolers were judged to be apt and appealing. Examples of apt preschool metaphors include a dishwashing tool with strips of orange sponge attached to a plastic handle that was called a windmill (3 years), a tree with fall leaves (4 years), and a palm tree (5 years).

Even stronger evidence that preschoolers possess substantial metaphoric capacity is the finding that the least adequate metaphors (so judged because they were based on only minimal resemblance or because they failed to take account of a major part of the stimulus) declined only slightly with age. Fourteen percent of the metaphors uttered by 3-year-olds and 8% of the metaphors produced by adults fell into this category.

Finally, an examination of the kinds of nonmetaphors produced revealed that 3-year-olds, when they failed to invent a metaphor, offered either literal names or names bearing no apparent relation to the stimulus. Four- and 5-year-olds, on the other hand, rarely produced simple literal responses, but rather embellished the literal appellation with a touch of the pretend (e.g., a flower was called "a flower with bees on it"). Only 11% of the metaphors produced by 4- and 5-year-olds were literal responses, compared to 30% by the 3-year-olds; in contrast, the embellished literal responses increased over the three preschool ages from 6% through 16% to 22%. The number of nonmetaphoric responses among grade school children and adults was negligible (cf. Table 14.4).

Summing up the results of this study, preschool subjects emerge once again as surprisingly competent on a measure of metaphoric ability. Whether the measures used here are the only—or even the best—way of assessing the origins of metaphor is of course debatable. Yet their potential for tapping the subjects' ability to cross domains, coupled with their ease of administration to preschoolers, makes them a useful point of departure for such explorations. While there is clearly improvement with age on certain dimensions, the consistent finding is that 4- and 5-year-old subjects can readily handle the task, make few inappropriate choices, and offer relatively few anomalous utterances. Equally important, the way in which they approach the task, the kinds of grounds they use, and the types of inappropriate answers that they offer are not remote from those produced by older subjects. And, in quality of metaphor, even the 3-year-olds demonstrate considerable mettle. To be sure, 3-year-olds are aided by action and by objects with ill-defined functions. However, it seems fair to conclude that children as young as 3 are able to produce metaphoric names for objects given only the opportunity to observe: Such production is made possible by the apparently early emerging capacity for metaphorical perception based upon the overall *shapes* of things in the world.

COMPARING THE TWO STUDIES:
POINTS OF AGREEMENT AND CONFLICT

Taken together, our two studies present a relatively consistent picture of early metaphor. Both document the ability of preschool children to produce acceptable and even striking metaphoric renamings. Generally speaking, the metaphors produced are new names for physical objects, and the grounds seized upon are those of shape, color, and less frequently, texture or size. Overextensions and anomalies are not common but understandably occur less frequently in the course of spontaneous expression than in the laboratory situation in which a pretend name is required for each object presented. Certainly this set of findings calls into question the claim that all early unconventional reference is evidence of underdeveloped lexical knowledge (e.g., Bowerman, 1976; Clark, 1973) or immature concepts (Piaget, 1962).

Some contradictions also emerge. First of all, the two studies suggest conflicting conclusions about the grounds of early metaphors. Adam's earliest metaphors arose in the course of symbolic play and only gradually came to be based solely on perceptual features; however, in the experimental investigation, performance was not enhanced by the opportunity to manipulate the object. This difference seems more apparent than real, however. To begin with, Adam's speech was taped from a younger age than that of the youngest group in the experimental task. Thus, he may have produced metaphors on a basis no longer as relevant for the subjects in the experimental study. More critically, however, the results from Adam do not prove that he is incapable of metaphors based solely upon a perceptual ground, but only that he tends (and perhaps prefers) to produce metaphors while engaged in the action of symbolic play. It is quite possible that he could from the first have produced metaphors on either basis. Moreover, examination of Adam's data fails to indicate a genuine stage-sequence in the shift from action to nonaction metaphors. Rather, both types are present from the first, with only a shift in degree over the course of three years.

Another apparent contradiction concerns the kind of object that elicited the most metaphors. While Adam produced more metaphors for objects with defined functions, the objects without such functions proved most readily renamed in the experimental study. The latter finding seems quite reasonable, in view of the fact that there is less to be overridden in renaming an object with no strictly defined function. Why Adam did not show the same trend is not known, but it is likely that he had many more opportunities to rename objects with conventionally defined functions. Moreover, much of his early renaming was accompanied by the gestural transformations of symbolic play, and it has been suggested by a further study of spontaneously produced metaphor that children become less willing to override distinctive appearances and well-known functions as they become less enactive in their metaphor use (Winner, McCarthy, Kleinman, & Gardner, 1979). Furthermore, less "busy," more regular geometrical forms such as wooden blocks may hold less interest for the child at play and thereby less frequently elicit metaphoric renamings.

A final difference worth mentioning is the greater number of inappropriate metaphors produced in the experimental task. A décalage seems at work here, with the anomalous utterances sometimes found among the 3-year-olds in the experimental task as possible vestiges of behaviors exhibited by younger children in spontaneous conversation. What appears to militate against anomalies in spontaneous speech is the fact that children are generally naming objects of their own choice and doing so in a rich play context; even nonmetaphoric renamings are often rendered sensible through the gestural and narrative context provided by the child at play. In contrast, when children are required to produce a name in an artificial situation, where little if any contextual support is provided, they may be more prone to produce a name that is anomalous at least to adult ears. The various strategies used by preschool children in an effort to "figure out" the metaphoric game (e.g., the strategy of simply providing any name as long as it was not literal) are also artifacts of an experimental situation, one with little counterpart in the real world of Adam's spontaneous play.

CONCLUSIONS

To demonstrate categorically that children possess the capacity to produce metaphor at a young age may be an impossible assignment. Final proof requires not only an impeccable definition and operationalization of metaphor but also knowledge of the speaker's intention and unambiguous evidence of the child's goals. Such demanding criteria may overwhelm the experimenter's meager tools. Perhaps the most that one can hope for is a marshalling of lines of converging evidence which, taken together, point the way toward a verdict of either "probably so" or "not likely" to the riddle of early metaphor.

The central line of evidence relevant to such an investigation is the status of the speaker's lexical knowledge. If a child calls a river a "snake," it is important to determine whether the name "river" was available to him or whether he had no other word with which to label the object. If "snake" was chosen in favor of "river," and if "snake" had not been regularly extended to other curvilinear forms, support is gained for viewing the name as a metaphor. Of course, the possibility that the child may simply have two literal names for river cannot be ruled out. However, to insist that all unconventional namings are simply literal overgeneralizations risks offering an impoverished and misleading representation of what the child knows.

Persuasive lines of support in favor of the metaphor hypothesis must begin with an acknowledgement that the child possesses the essential nonlinguistic capacities requisite for metaphor. This requires, at a minimum, the ability to perceive similarity, and second, the ability to conceive of one object or event as if it were another. We know from many lines of investigation that both of these criteria are met by 2- and 3-year-olds. The perception of similarity is a capacity that must be present at birth since it is necessary for even the most rudimentary learnings. And, in symbolic play, the child regularly demonstrates the ability to see one object as if it were another. Indeed, both Adam and the subjects in the experimental study presented considerable evidence that they could distinguish "real" from "pretend," that they were engaged in pretense or play when they offered a metaphoric renaming, and that they could revert back to the "real name" when asked to do so. Moreover, examination of the kinds of errors made and grounds exploited gives little comfort to those who would argue that the metaphoric practices of preschool children are based upon a fundamentally different set of mental processes than those exhibited by older children.

Having established the plausibility of the view that the child of 4 or 5 is capable of genuine metaphoric creation, we can outline a tentative model of the steps through which children pass in the evolution of this capacity. Building upon the results of the present investigations and other studies (Asch & Nerlove, 1960; Billow, 1975, 1977; Gardner, 1974; Gardner, Winner, Bechhofer, & Wolf, 1978; Pollio, Barlow, Fine, & Pollio, 1977), we suggest a number of sequential steps:

1. Action Based Metaphors.   Growing out of symbolic play, the first metaphors produced by 2- and 3-year-olds are elicited by virtue of resemblances perceived among ordinary objects in the child's environment. These resemblances do not at first inhere solely in the objects themselves but are constructed out of the pretend actions of symbolic play. While these metaphors may exploit perceptual properties, their critical feature is that a relevant transformation has occurred on both the verbal and the gestural plane. In fact, the verbalization often strikes the observer as epiphenomenal to the transformation effected through gesture.

2.   Perceptually Based Metaphors.   In spontaneous speech, the rudimentary metaphors growing out of symbolic play decline sharply with development, giving rise to metaphors based on an appraisal of the properties of the object beheld without the support of action. Such nonaction metaphors are readily elicited in the renaming games of our experimental study. At three, children are still helped by seeing a new identity suggested by the experimenter's action on an object and can more readily rename objects for which little overriding is required (e.g., blocks). By the age of four or five, however, the need for an action is much less compelling and the advantage gained by such objects proves increasingly marginal.

3.   A Possible Decline in Metaphoric Production.   Two earlier studies have suggested a decline in the amount of spontaneous metaphor produced by school age children (Billow, 1977; Gardner, Kircher, Winner, & Perkins, 1975). This decline has been attributed to a general literalism at this time of life, one brought about by the lesser need to exploit the innovative resources of language (given a larger vocabulary), and increased motivation to follow rules and conform to one's peers. Such literalism need not surprise us, as it has parallels in the domain of children's drawings, which become increasingly realistic (and decreasingly striking) after the preschool years (Gardner & Wolf, 1979).

While uncovering various dips and rises in the incidence of early renaming behaviors, however, this study gives little support to the notion of a dramatic decline in metaphoric production under experimental conditions. The absence of evidence for a literal stage suggests that adhering to the literal reference of words may be a motivational rather than a competence problem: When given explicit instructions and encouragement to follow the rules and produce a good "pretend name," children of all ages fare well. Lack of evidence for a literal stage in the experimental task may also reflect the greater ease of renaming objects in the child's immediate presence (as opposed to completing similes with no visual cues, as in the Gardner, Kircher, Winner, & Perkins, 1975, study); or it may reflect the differing criteria used by various investigators in establishing word usages as metaphorical. Certainly the issue of the literal stage—its existence, its nature, its necessity—invites further investigation, and it is to this question that some of our current work is directed.

Given the little that is known about the literal stage, speculations about later metaphor are risky. We do know that the ability to appreciate metaphors based on abstract, nonperceptual links rises sharply after the early school years and that, given some incentive, most adults have the potential to produce metaphors. But we must also remember that the making of fresh metaphors is not a common pursuit in our society, and perhaps not in any society. Thus, the search for a *universal* theory of metaphoric production may prove, by definition, elusive.

Our search for the origins of metaphor has produced considerable support for the view that metaphoric capacity is an early-emerging and generative human capacity. Efforts to withhold from the competence of the young child the common garden-variety of metaphor we have been investigating seem unfounded. At the same time, it is only reasonable to catalogue the various aspects of metaphor that one fails to encounter among younger populations. In our studies with Adam and his peers, we found few signs of metaphors constructed upon psychological or expressive grounds; no inclination to make metaphors about abstract issues removed in space or time; and little extension of a metaphoric theme across time. Rather, these early metaphors are simply renamings of familiar objects, in their immediate presence, based largely on physical properties and functional affordances (Verbrugge & McCarrell, 1977), and for the most part, on isolated properties of objects, rather than on a converging set of dimensions. In all of these ways, then, the metaphors of the young child differ from those of the adolescent or the poet, and, at least in these respects, those individuals favorable to the "metaphor as crowning achievement" point of view may gain comfort.

In the final analysis, whether metaphor is a primary ability or a late achievement depends on the criteria and definitions one chooses. There is no single point at which metaphor begins (or ends); and any insistence on evidence for full-blown metaphoric competence effectively cripples a search for roots. We can, in any case, gain considerable insight into the ontogenesis of this capacity through a careful description of the production of metaphors under various conditions, through a consideration of which features they do (and do not) possess, and, eventually, through an analysis of the circumstances that cause those metaphors to take the forms that they do. Our own expectation is that, as we come to know the realm of metaphor better, we will find that it is indeed ancestrally a part of all of us and all that we know—there is no need to admit it to the club for it has been there all along.

ACKNOWLEDGMENTS

The research reported in this chapter was supported by grants from the National Science Foundation (BNS-77-13099) and the National Institute of Education (G-78-0031). We are grateful to the following people for their help in the conduct of this research: Rain Miller and Sheila Hoadley, directors of the Gerry Street Preschool; Barbara Beatty, director of the Lesley-Ellis Preschool; Myra Bennett, director of Harvard Yard Child Care Center; Diane Driscoll, director of Garden Nursery School; Mary Murphy, Principal, Dallin School; and the many teachers who offered assistance during the testing phase of this research. We also thank Drs. Roger Brown and Jill deVilliers for valuable suggestions in the formulation and interpretation of this research.

REFERENCES

Arnheim, R. *Art and visual perception: A psychology of the creative eye . . . the new version.* Berkeley: University of California Press, 1974.

Asch, S., & Nerlove, H. The development of double-function terms in children: An exploratory investigation. In B. Kaplan & S. Wapner (Eds.), *Perspectives in psychological theory: Essays in honor of Heinz Werner.* New York: International Universities Press, 1960.

Billow, R. A cognitive developmental study of metaphor comprehension. *Developmental Psychology,* 1975, *11,* 415–423.

Billow, R. *Spontaneous metaphor in children.* Unpublished paper, Adelphi University, 1977.

Bond, B., & Stevens, S. S. Cross-modal matching of brightness to loudness by five-year-olds. *Perception and Psychophysics,* 1969, *6,* 337–339.

Bowerman, M. The acquisition of word meaning: An investigation of some current conflict. In N. Waterson & C. Snow (Eds.), *Proceedings of the Third International Child Language Symposium.* New York: Wiley, 1976.

Brown, R. *A first language: The early stages.* Cambridge, Mass.: Harvard University Press, 1973.

Cassirer, E. *The philosophy of symbolic forms.* New Haven: Yale University Press, 1957.

Chukovsky, K. *From two to five.* Berkeley: University of California Press, 1968.

Clark, E. V. What's in a word? On the child's acquisition of semantics in his first language. In T. E. Moore (Ed.), *Cognitive development and the acquisition of language.* New York: Academic Press, 1973.

Elkind, D. Piagetian and psychometric conceptions of intelligence. *Harvard Educational Review,* 1969, *39,* 319–337.

Gardner, H. Metaphors and modalities: How children project polar adjectives onto diverse domains. *Child Development,* 1974, *45,* 84–91.

Gardner, H., Kircher, M., Winner, E., & Perkins, D. Children's metaphoric productions and preferences. *Journal of Child Language,* 1975, *2,* 125–141.

Gardner, H., Winner, E., Bechhofer, R., & Wolf, D. The development of figurative language. In K. Nelson (Ed.) *Children's language Vol. 1* New York: Gardner Press, 1978.

Gardner, H., & Wolf, D. First drawings: Notes on the relationships between perception and production in the visual arts. In D. Fisher & C. Nodine (Eds.), *Perception and pictorial representation.* New York: Praeger, 1979.

Gentner, D. Children's performances on a spatial analogies task. *Child Development,* 1977, *48,* 1034–1039.

Gombrich, E. H. Meditations on a hobby horse. In L. L. Whyte (Ed.) *Aspects of form.* Bloomington, Ind. Midland Books. 1961.

Inhelder, B., & Piaget, J. *The growth of logical thinking from childhood to adolescence.* New York: Basic Books, 1958.

Piaget, J. *Play, dreams, and imitation.* New York: Norton, 1962.

Pollio, H. R., Barlow, J., Fine, H. J., & Pollio, M. *The poetics of growth: Figurative language in psychotherapy and education.* Hillsdale, N.J.: Erlbaum Associates, 1977.

Richards, I. A. *The philosophy of rhetoric.* London: Oxford University Press, 1936.

Verbrugge, R., & McCarrell, N. Metaphoric comprehension: Studies in reminding and resembling. *Cognitive Psychology,* 1977, *9,* 494–533.

Winner, E. New names for old things: The emergence of metaphoric language. *Journal of Child Language,* 1979, *6,* 469–491.

Winner, E., McCarthy, M., Kleinman, S., & Gardner, H. First metaphors. *New Directions for Child Development,* 1979, *3,* 29–41.

V PROBLEM SOLVING

15 Metaphoric Competence and Complex Human Problem Solving

Howard R. Pollio

Michael K. Smith
The University of Tennessee

INTRODUCTION

In an article entitled "A Study of Poetic Talent" published in 1928, Dorritt Stumberg made use of a series of tasks designed to discriminate between a group of individuals having poetic talent and a second group of individuals showing little or no poetic talent. Although there were no differences in measured IQ between her two groups, Stumberg did find that the poet's group, not surprisingly, had more facility with rhyming, imagery, and memory for poetic material. As she put it, however, "the most striking and significant... differences between the two groups (occurred) with respect to figures of speech. The ability to see a likeness in two otherwise dissimilar things (as well as) the tendency to use phrases involving such an apprehension are especially characteristic of the poetically talented group." Stumberg then went on to note that figurative ability was "the mark of genius in any field" and the question of figurative language was "certainly provocative of further research."

Fifty years later a number of psychologists have begun to pursue Stumberg's suggestion. Within the context of more contemporary work, research in figurative language has come to be organized around two major questions: (1) How can figurative competence be understood in terms of current semantic theories such that we can both relate and disentangle metaphor from anomaly and vice versa; and (2) how does figurative ability relate to more general cognitive activities such as are involved in various forms of problem solving? Both questions would seem to run counter to one of the more frequently asserted opinions concerning figurative usage: Namely, that such usage is simply a pretty way of saying something that could be said more directly and more economically in ordinary, literal language.

METAPHOR, ANOMALY AND THE PEOPLE WHO LOVE (HATE) THEM

One general question that must be addressed by any theory of metaphor concerns the borderline between metaphor and anomaly; that is, between sense and non-sense. In the psycholinguistic literature, most research dealing with anomaly seems to fall into two categories: one deriving from George Miller's early work on sentence perception and a second deriving from Danny Steinberg's somewhat later work on the categorization of logical sentence types.

Almost all of the early work by Miller (Miller & Isard, 1963; Marks & Miller, 1964) found poorer performance on tasks involving anomalous sentences when compared to more standard ones. These results revealed that anomalous sentences were perceived, recalled, and recognized considerably more poorly than their nonanomalous counterparts. Miller and his group usually explained these findings in terms of some type of organizational hypothesis in which they argued that meaningful sentences were easier to chunk than anomalous ones, which in turn made them easier to store, which in turn made them easier to recall, and so on.

Within this context, Pollio and Burns (1977) were not satisfied that anomalous sentences were necessarily nonsensical. Consider two sentences defined as anomalous by earlier investigations: (1) *The popular latin mare worked tempers,* and (2) *The odorless child inspired a chocolate audience.* In neither case would a native speaker of English seem to have too much difficulty in providing a meaningful interpretation for these sentences if allowed the liberty of poetic diction.

To determine, more generally, if anomalous sentences could be interpreted if and when subjects were given "poetic license," Pollio and Burns asked college students to paraphrase sentences constructed on the basis of a random word-selection procedure similar to that used in other studies of anomaly. The subjects were also asked to learn these sentences as response terms in a paired-associates task. Results of a series of experiments were quite clear in showing the usual difference between anomalous and natural sentences when subjects were first asked to learn and, only secondly, to interpret these sentences. When, however, subjects were first asked to interpret sentences and then to learn them, differences in ease of learning disappeared: Anomalous sentences were now just as easy to learn as more natural ones. For both procedures Pollio and Burns found that between 75 and 90% of the subjects tested were able to provide meaningful interpretations for the specific anomalous sentences used. Based on these findings, Pollio and Burns argued that the sharp (logical) division between anomaly and metaphor was untenable and that subjects were quite able to interpret supposedly nonsensical sentences.

In this experiment subjects were explicitly asked to provide interpretations for anomalous sentences. If, however, the subject were given a choice between dealing with an anomalous sentence as either nonsensical or metaphoric, would all subjects necessarily react in the same way? Theoretically, this raises the possibility that some individuals might see only anomaly while others might be particularly alive to metaphoric options. To evaluate this possibility in a somewhat less demanding task than that used by Pollio and Burns, Pollio and Smith (1979) investigated preference for metaphoric coding within the sentence categorization task originally designed by Steinberg (1970a, 1970b, 1975).

In much of this work, a featural approach to sentence meaning was followed. For example, a sentence such as *The man is a husband* is meaningful because the latter part of it, *husband* (+ animate, + human, + adult, + male, + married), provides a new component, 'married,' to the subject of the sentence, *man* (+ animate, + human, + adult, + male). On the basis of a similar analysis, a sentence such as *The husband is a man* is redundant because the word *man* supplies no new information concerning the subject of the sentence, *husband*. A sentence such as *The man is a woman* is contradictory since both nouns share a number of common features but conflict on a single *lower-level* feature, i.e., ± male. Finally, a sentence such as *The man is a sheep* was defined as anomalous because of a conflict on a major feature, i.e., ± human.

Using these sentences as a guide, Steinberg asked college-age subjects to categorize examples of the four different sentence types described above, i.e., synthetic, analytic, contradictory, and anomalous, and found that they were able to do this task easily and well. Steinberg also found that subject codings depended upon (and revealed) the featural structure of the particular set of sentences used.

So far so good: The real problem only appears, however, when the question of metaphor is at issue. If we start by considering a (logically) anomalous sentence such as *The man is a sheep,* it is possible to wonder if all adult speakers would treat it as anomalous given the option of treating it metaphorically. To explore this possibility Pollio and Smith (1979) added a fifth, or metaphoric, option to the Steinberg task. For their experiment all other materials and procedures were similar to those used by Steinberg. Results of this experiment were quite clear in showing that subjects coded 11% of all sentences, and over 20% of logically anomalous sentences, as metaphoric. In addition, Pollio and Smith found significant differences in the number of sentences "correctly" coded into each of the major categories, with logically anomalous sentences showing the sharpest decline across the two experiments. By introducing a metaphoric option, the logical coding of all four sentence categories seemed to have suffered a clear decline in codability.

Within the context of this experiment, it was also possible to determine if all subjects were equally likely to turn anomaly into metaphor. An examination of the distribution of the number of metaphoric categorizations produced by each individual revealed that subjects could be divided into three separate subgroupings, with one group hardly ever using the category of metaphor (only 1 or fewer times out of a possible 156 opportunities), with a second using this category quite frequently (29 or more times), and with a third producing responses that spread erratically between these two extremes. These data suggested that it was possible to partition subjects on the basis of their tendency to see metaphoric possibilities for logically anomalous sentences.

If subjects differ so obviously on as isolated a task as the Steinberg sentence categorization test, might we not expect a similar pattern of individual differences for other, more complicated, tasks? In fact, might we not reasonably expect that subjects who display a willingness to use figurative expression would also perform differently on other logical and/or creative tasks? These general questions suggest that it might prove instructive to examine the relationship of complex human problem solving to figurative ability. Operationally, this comes down to a question of selecting tasks designed to tap both of these domains and of then evaluating individual performances on these, and other, tasks.

One specific way to do this might be to select individuals on the basis of their performance on the Steinberg Task. Although this, in fact, was the way the present series of studies began (see Pollio, 1977) a different, more general, strategy would be to gather a large number of verbal tasks, figurative and otherwise, and then select individuals on the basis of their performance on these tasks. This strategy has the added advantage of allowing an examination of not only the factorial composition of tasks comprising the selection battery, but also the degree of correlation between different measures of figurative usage. In all of this, we should never lose sight of our overall purpose: to examine the pattern of relationships existing between complex problem solving and figurative competence. Indeed, this concern forms an appropriate theoretical and empirical background against which to view the following set of studies.

VERBAL PROBLEM SOLVING AND FIGURATIVE COMPETENCE

To investigate the relationship of verbal problem solving to metaphoric competence, a series of tasks was needed that not only would assess logical thinking and creativity as traditionally defined, but that would also measure different aspects of what we have come to call "figurative competence," i.e., the ability of an individual to understand and use figurative language as well as his or her ability to paraphrase and/or explain it. Our first concern thus became one of finding appropriate task materials. Fortunately, logical reasoning tasks such as those involving analogies and syllogisms abound in the experimental literature. In addition, where existing tasks proved inappropriate, new problems of this type were easy to construct. Similarly, it was also possible to select from among a wide variety of creative problem-solving tests. Here we chose to use the multiple-uses subtest of the battery developed and evaluated by Torrance (1974).

Unfortunately, tests of figurative ability are not so easy to come by; in fact, there is very little in the way of standardized (or even archival) material on which to draw in order to study figurative competence. Researchers concerned with memory for metaphor (Honeck, Riechmann, & Hoffman, 1975; Harris, 1976), for example, have often made use of proverbs or Shakespearean metaphors. Other researchers, particularly those working with children (Gardner, 1974), have had to construct their own evaluation procedures. Such procedures have examined metaphor production in response to specific questions (Gardner, 1974; Pollio & Pollio, 1974) as well as in terms of compositions written in the classroom (Pollio & Pollio, 1974). The only multiple-choice test of metaphoric comprehension presently available was constructed from figures of speech occurring in compositions written by children and young adults (Pollio & Pollio, 1979). Perhaps the most complete set of figurative tasks is provided in the article by Stumberg (1928) referred to earlier. Included among these are tests for simile- and symbol-production as well as a word association task designed to assess not only associative fluency but associative figurativeness as well.

Although many of these tasks have not been standardized in terms of usual psychometric criteria, they do provide a set of procedures for assessing figurative competence and of then relating such competence to other tasks of logical and/or creative ability. The test procedures described in the following sections were chosen with these objectives in mind. Some represent rather standard laboratory tests of logical and/or creative problem solving; others represent procedures designed specifically to assess one or another aspect of figurative competence. In general, our overall strategy was to look for patterns of interrelationship among the various tasks in order to enable us to come to some conclusion(s) concerning the structure of figurative competence as well as to determine its relationship to complex cognitive tasks of a more general problem-solving nature.

THE TEST BATTERY

1. *Analogies:* The analogies task used in the present context consisted of two general categories: (a) simple analogies composed of part-whole or opposite relationships, and (b) random analogies containing three terms (selected at random) for which each subject had to supply a fourth term and then give an explanation as to why his or her particular completion made sense.

Nearly all subjects correctly completed the simple analogy problems. Solutions to the more difficult analogy problems were not so easily accomplished nor so easily scored. For this reason, random analogy solutions were evaluated in terms of a 4-point scale (0–3), with higher scores representing more imaginative and/or reasonable completions. For example, for the analogy, "Picture : Crime :: Pillow : _____," several people wrote that there was no relationship (score = 0). Some simply supplied an answer such as "Feathers" with the justification that "there are always pictures at crimes and there are always feathers in pillows" (score = 1). Some subjects solved these analogies on the basis of similar functions or common attributes; i.e., one person supplied the term "Sleep" with the explanation that "a picture remains after a crime, while a pillow remains after sleep" (score = 2). To receive a score of 3, the analogy had to be solved on the basis of common functions or common attributes but with a more elaborate (and clearly reasoned) explanation. For example, in response to the "Picture:Crime" analogy, one subject produced the response of "Bed" with the explanation that "you can look at a picture to solve a crime just as you can look at your pillow to see if anyone has been in your bed."

2.   *Associations I:*   For this task, the subject was read a noun and asked to think of as many adjectives as possible that modified that noun within a 1-minute time period. The 4 measures derived from these data were: (1) fluency, the total number of responses produced; (2) originality, a weighted score derived from the uniqueness of each response compared to the frequency distribution of responses produced by the complete group of subjects; (3) literal, the total number of responses judged to be literal; and (4) figurative, the total number of responses judged to be figurative. These latter two measures were scored on the basis of judgments made by a team of three raters according to techniques developed by Pollio, Barlow, Fine and Pollio (Chapter 3; 1977). For the stimulus *Butterfly,* typical (literal) examples were "attractive," "bright," "gold," etc. Figurative examples included "drunk," "easy-going," "innocent," "lonely," etc.

3.   *Associations II:*   Here, subjects were asked to produce as many noun responses to adjective stimulus words as they could in a 1-minute period. The same 4 dependent measures—frequency, originality, literal, and figurative— were used for Associations II as for Associations I. For the stimulus word *Blue,* typical literal responses were "airplane," "boat," "house," etc. Figurative answers included responses such as "attitude," "depression," "music," etc. Both association tasks were derived from Stumberg (1928).

4.   *Creative Composition:*   Here, subjects were asked to write a short composition on the topic of "What animal are you like and why are you like this animal?" Scoring was done in terms of the number of words produced as well as in terms of the number of descriptive comparisons the person made between himself and the animal selected. For example, one subject wrote:

I feel as though I'm like a groundhog. Groundhogs lie in the sun and eat, <u>just being</u>
        1   ·   2
<u>lazy much like I am</u>. They <u>are active</u> in something that interests them; but not

everything. A groundhog will fight³ to keep what is his and protect its own. And a groundhog has some fame⁴ come February as I also get some, but he is not always in the limelight.

For this composition, 4 major comparisons were made between the subject and the groundhog.

5. *Gardner Metaphor Preference Test:* This test contains 18 incomplete simile stems. (*The weather was as warm as* _____) to which the subjects were asked to select one ending from the four provided. Each ending exemplified one of the following types of relationships described by Gardner, Kirchner, Winner and Perkins (1975):

(a) A literal (or nonmetaphorical) ending that repeats the adjective in the story ("the warmest day in spring").

(b) A conventional (or frozen figurative) ending that is appropriate but not original ("toast in the early morning").

(c) An appropriate (novel) ending in which the adjective is "transported" to a realm where it is not ordinarily applied and where, in the present case, it is appropriate ("the smile of a friend you haven't seen for years").

(d) An inappropriate ending in which the adjective is "transported" to a realm where it is not ordinarily applied and where it is appropriate ("a shoestring lying in the middle of the floor").

All endings chosen were coded into their appropriate category. Because the various endings are negatively related (i.e., choosing an appropriate metaphoric ending precludes choosing any of the remaining 3 categories) each subject's score was simply the number of novel (appropriate) metaphoric endings chosen. For this reason, individual subject values could vary between 0 and 18.

6. *Logical Syllogisms:* To measure a subject's ability to reason deductively from a given premise, a set of 12 verbal syllogisms, selected from earlier work by Lefford (1946), was used. These syllogisms were constructed on the basis of both emotional and nonemotional premises in order to determine how well an individual reasoned aside from his or her emotional response to the context of an argument. For both types of syllogisms, the dependent variable used was simply the number of syllogisms correctly solved out of a total of 6 for each type.

7. *Oxymorons:* In this task, each subject was asked to produce one response to an oxymoron, such as *delicate armor*. All answers were rated on a 0–3 scale of originality similar to that used for the Analogies Task. For the stimulus *delicate armor* frequent responses were "skin," "a knight's armor," or "clothes." More original responses were "negligee," "civilization," "makeup," and "emotions."

8. *Metaphoric Comprehension:*   The Pollio and Pollio test of metaphoric comprehension (1979) was used to evaluate a subject's understanding of both novel and frozen figures of speech. In this task, subjects were asked to read a sentence and then select an appropriate paraphrase from among the 4 multiple-choice alternatives provided. Items involve both novel and frozen figurative exemplars selected from compositions written initially by elementary and high school students. Original test items were selected on the basis of an item analysis carried out over choices made by 149 children in grades 4 through 8.

Two sample test items, one frozen and one novel, taken from this test are as follows:

(1)   I went into the kitchen and *ate up a storm.*
   * (a) I ate a lot.
      (b) I drank some white lightning from the refrigerator.
      (c) I ate so much it rained.
      (d) I like to eat when it's raining.

(2)   I saw a coffin and was scared. I walked slowly toward it. I was amazed my *feet were brave enough to take me there.*
      (a) My feet have a mind of their own.
      (b) My new sneakers made me feel I could do anything.
   * (c) I did not think I would have the courage to do it.
      (d) Somehow I was pulled to the coffin against my will.

The dependent variables used in the present set of analyses were the number of correct alternatives chosen for both novel and frozen items.

9. *Similes:*   Here, each subject was given an incomplete poetic line and asked to finish it with as many comparisons as he or she could think of in 2 minutes. For the item, *The other was a softer voice, as soft as* _____, typical (frozen) figurative responses were: "a baby's bottom," "a pillow," and "snow." Novel figurative answers were: "silent air," "melted chocolate," a "distant echo." For this task, 4 different dependent measures were scored: (1) fluency, the total number produced; (2) originality, a statistical measure of uncommonness; (3) number-frozen, a rated evaluation of the total number of cliched responses; and (4) number-novel, a rated evaluation of the total number of novel figurative completions produced.

10. *Symbols:*   For the Symbols Task, subjects were given an abstract concept and asked to produce as many symbols as they could think of (in a 2-minute period) appropriate to that concept. Again, 4 different dependent measures were derived from answers given in response to this task: fluency, originality, number-novel, and number-frozen. (A score of literal was not used since, by the very nature of the task, subjects were asked to produce figurative responses.)

One example of a novel response to the concept *Courage* was "A candle in the wind."

A specific examination of answers given in responses to this task suggested that subjects often provided examples rather than symbols. For *Courage,* typical responses were "Battling your dog for your newspapers," "A football player," or "People with a terminal illness." None of these responses seem particularly innovative and for this reason were scored as frozen and then made part of a given subject's score.

11. *Torrance Task:* The Torrance Test provides a number of different tasks designed to assess potential creative ability. For our purposes, one subtest—The Unusual Uses Test—was selected. This task required the subject to find as many novel and interesting uses for a particular item as possible. The dependent measures specified by Torrance and used in the present set of analyses were as follows: (1) fluency, total number of responses produced; (2) flexibility, total number of different categories used, with each response assigned to a particular category from Torrance's standardized scoring scheme; and (3) originality, a 0, 1 or 2 value for each response as scored in Torrance (1974).

The total battery of tests presented to subjects thus consisted of 11 different tasks. To keep track of these tasks, Table 15.1 presents a complete listing of all tests as well as specific examples. In addition, each of the dependent measures derived from each test is also described, thereby making Table 15.1 a good summary of what it was subjects were asked to do in the present set of experiments.

FACTOR ANALYTIC RESULTS

Given this battery of tasks, a number of specific empirical questions can be raised. For present purposes, four seem of primary importance:

(1) Would meaningful subgroupings (i.e., factors) appear across the complete set of tasks used in the present experiment? That is, would it be possible to recover the structure of verbal problem solving implicit in the present battery?

(2) Would an index of problem-solving skill derived from the present analysis allow for the prediction of individual performance on other tasks of creative imagination and/or logical reasoning?

(3) What relationship would the various tasks of figurative competence have to one another as well as to the major, factor-defining, tasks uncovered by the present analysis?

(4) What general implications would present results have for theories of figurative language?

TABLE 15.1
Tasks Used in the Present Set of Studies

Task	(N)	Example of Task	Dependent Measures
1. Analogies	14	(a) Good : Bad : : Happiness :___ (b) Dog : Airplane : : Sun :___	1. Rating of Good- ness
2. Association I (1 min/per)	5	I am going to read a list of nouns to you. After each noun is read, you are to write as many adjectives as you can that apply to that noun (e.g., Mountain or Dream)	1. Originality 2. Fluency 3. Number Literal 4. Number Figura- tive
3. Association II (1 min/per)	5	I am going to read you a list of adjectives and after each adjective, I want you to think of as many nouns as you can which that adjective might modify (e.g., Smooth or Deep)	1. Originality 2. Fluency 3. Number Literal 4. Number Figura- tive
4. Composition	1	Topic: What animal are you like and why are you like this animal?	1. Number Words 2. Number of Descriptions
5. Gardner et al. Preference Test*	18	Question: The weather was as warm as _____. Novel preference: the smile of a friend you haven't seen for a year.	1. Number Novel Figures Preferred
6. Logical Syllogisms: Nonemotional	6	All philosophers are human, and all human beings are fallible; therefore philosophers are fallible, too.	1. Number Correct
Emotional	6	Man, faced between choosing between life and death, is ennobled by the experience. War is a situation in which man must make this supreme choice. War, therefore, is an experience ennobling man to the most exalted degree.	2. Number Correct
Total	12		3. Total Correct**
7. Oxymoron	5	*Delicate armor* describes _____. *Frozen haste* describes _____.	1. Rating of Good- ness
8. Pollio Test Metaphoric Comprehension*	10 10	Frozen: I was so excited, I *couldn't stand it.* Novel: When all of a sudden, the trees disappeared *like melting ice cream.*	1. Number Correct* 2. Number Correct*

(*Continued*)

TABLE 15.1 (*Cont.*)

Task	(N)	Example of Task	Dependent Measures
9. Similes (2 min/per)	4	With the stars aswirl behind them like _____.	1. Fluency 2. Originality 3. Number Frozen* 4. Number Novel*
10. Symbols (2 min/per)	5	I am going to read a list of things to you and you are to suggest the symbols that may stand for them. For example, sadness may be symbolized by a rainy day. Find all the symbols or metaphors you can for each word that I read (e.g., Life, Failure, Courage)	1. Fluency 2. Originality 3. Number Frozen* 4. Number Novel*
11. Torrance Test	1	Most people throw their empty cardboard boxes away, but they have thousands of interesting and unusual uses. In the spaces below list as many of these interesting and unusual uses as you can think of.	1. Fluency 2. Flexibility 3. Originality

*Only used in the second set of factor analyses.
**Only used in the first factor analysis.

The Original Study.   To answer these questions, two different and independent groups of subjects were asked to complete some, or all, of the tasks described in Table 15.1. Since results produced by our first group of 74 subjects have been presented elsewhere (Pollio, 1977), all that need be done here is to summarize them. Basically, this first group was tested on a battery of 10 different tasks (Associations I and II, Similes, Symbols, Torrance Multiple Uses Test, Analogies, Oxymoron, Composition, Syllogisms, and the Steinberg sentence categorization task). Since most of these tasks yield 2 or more different scores, the initial study concerned a total of 27 different dependent variables.

To determine the factorial structure of these 27 variables, correlations were computed between all possible pairs of measures producing a matrix of 351 intercorrelations. An examination of this matrix revealed that 204 or 58% of these correlations were significant at equal to, or better than, the 5% level of significance. Meaningful subgroupings were determined on the basis of a principal components factor analysis employing orthogonal rotation to simple structure. Before deciding on this specific analysis, a number of preliminary analyses were run without specifying any a priori number of factors. Almost all of these analyses produced 9 factor solutions accounting for 100% of the variance, with the first 5 factors accounting for well over 80%. In addition, Factors 6, 7, 8 and 9 usually only involved loadings for individual test variables.

For these reasons, the data were "forced" into a 5-factor solution producing the following factor patterns (factor loadings in parentheses):

Factor I: Associations I-fluency (.78) and literal (.78); Associations II-fluency (.90) and literal (.88); Similes-fluency (.46); and Symbols-fluency (.47). For obvious reasons, the first factor was called Verbal Fluency.

Factor II: Torrance-fluency (.88), flexibility (.86), and originality (.74); and Analogies (.36). Somewhat less obviously, the second factor was initially called Flexibility of Verbal Comparisons.

Factor III: Associations I-originality (.70) and figurative (.56); Associations II-originality (.61) and figurative (.48); Similes-originality (.38); and Symbols-originality (.33). The third factor was called Innovative Figurative Use.

Factor IV: Syllogisms-total (.86), emotional (.44) and nonemotional (.68); Steinberg sentence categorizations percent-correct Synthetic (.46) and percent-correct, contradictory (.40). Factor IV was called Logical Reasoning.

Factor IVa: Steinberg-analytic (.35), anomaly (.76) and metaphoric ($-$.48). Largely because Factor IVa involved only a further specification of the Steinberg Task, it was not considered as a unique factor and was disregarded in future analyses of data produced by this first group of subjects.

The Replication Study. Since our first factor analysis was clear in defining a meaningful space of 4 factors, it seemed important to replicate this result before any degree of confidence could be placed in its generality. For this reason, a new group of 70 subjects was asked to complete the same battery of tests with two exceptions: (1) the Steinberg Test was deleted, and (2) two additional, more strictly figurative, tasks were added even though they were not used in the initial study.

One of the more important findings of this second study concerns the pattern of results produced by a factor analysis done over tasks directly comparable to those used in the initial study. Table 15.2 presents the results of this second analysis where it can be seen that each of the 4 major factors was defined by sets of tests similar to those in the first study. Factor I, accounting for about 50% of the variance, was defined most strongly by tests of fluency: Associations II-fluency (and literal), Associations I-fluency (and literal), and less strongly by fluency values for Symbols and Similes. Factor II (21% of the variance) was defined by Torrance variables again indicating that these three measures formed a consistent grouping across both analyses. Factor III (11%) was defined by the Syllogisms Test, while Factor IV (10%)—the figurative factor—was defined by high positive loadings for Associations I-original, Associations I-figurative, and Associations II-figurative. This factor also revealed reasonably high loadings for both composition measures: number of words and number of comparisons. As in the first analysis, Factor V (8%) was defined by high positive loadings for only

TABLE 15.2
Factor Analytic Results for Replication Study

Dependent Variable	Factor I	Factor II	Factor III	Factor IV	Factor V
Analogies	.15	−.02	.07	.18	.11
Association I-Fluency	.87	.18	−.17	.25	.02
Association I-Originality	.42	.18	−.24	.58	.02
Association I-Literal	.89	.19	−.13	.10	−.04
Association I-Figurative	.02	.07	−.16	.57	.21
Association II-Fluency	.95	.17	.03	.10	.09
Association II-Originality	.58	.15	−.11	.26	−.24
Association II-Literal	.92	.20	.02	−.10	.08
Association II-Figurative	.18	−.06	.03	.52	.04
Composition-Length	.07	.03	.17	.48	−.08
Composition-Description	−.03	.05	.16	.38	−.06
Logical Syllogisms-Total	.00	−.19	.81	.15	.51
Logical Syllogisms-Emotional	−.05	−.22	.87	.17	−.11
Logical Syllogisms-Nonemotional	.07	−.03	.14	.03	.84
Oxymoron	.05	.01	−.06	.01	−.03
Similies-Fluency	.33	.23	.24	.07	.10
Similies-Originality	.22	.19	.06	−.03	−.02
Symbols-Fluency	.54	.12	−.03	.29	.32
Symbols-Originality	−.02	.06	−.01	.11	.09
Torrance-Fluency	.29	.89	−.03	.02	−.03
Torrance-Flexibility	.23	.83	−.20	.14	.04
Torrance-Originality	.23	.79	−.25	.11	−.02
Percent Variance	50	21	11	10	8

one test (Syllogisms-nonemotional) and seems best construed as a further specification of Factor III.

Factor Structure for Major Study. The most important differences between the replication study and the major study to be reported concerned the use of an additional pair of dependent variables for both the Symbols and Similes Tests as well as the use of the Pollio and Gardner Tests. In the present case, responses to the Symbols and Similes Tests were scored not only for fluency and originality but for novel and frozen usage as well. Taking these new measures into account, as well as those produced by the Pollio and Gardner Tests, a third factor analysis was done involving the now-expanded set of 28 dependent variables. Of the 378 correlations possible among these measures, 129 (34%) were significant at $p < .05$.

Results of a principal components analysis, rotated to simple structure on the basis of a Varimax procedure and constrained to a five factor solution, produced the pattern of relationships presented in Table 15.3. As can be seen, the first factor seems best described as an (associative) fluency factor defined by high loadings for Associations I- and Associations II-fluency and literal as well as by Symbols-fluency. In addition there were reasonably high loadings for Associations I- and II-originality and Symbols-frozen. These variables all seem to reflect how fluent the person is in a number of different verbal tasks and suggest Associative Fluency as an appropriate description for this factor. Literal and

TABLE 15.3
Factor Structure for Major Task Variables

Dependent Variable	Factor I	Factor II	Factor III	Factor IV	Factor V
Analogies	.08	.11	—.06	.27	.17
Association I-Fluency	.86	.08	.20	.17	.21
Association I-Originality	.48	−.06	.24	−.02	.58
Association I-Literal	.87	.13	.20	.13	.07
Association I-Figurative	.04	−.13	.13	.15	.52
Association II-Fluency	.90	.19	.13	.23	.08
Association II-Originality	.67	−.06	.16	−.17	.25
Association II-Literal	.88	.14	.19	.21	−.15
Association II-Figurative	.15	.14	−.13	.15	.60
Composition-Length	.06	.04	−.04	.10	.44
Composition-Descriptions	−.01	.03	.00	.04	.32
Gardner Preference	−.06	−.06	.04	.21	.19
Logical Syllogisms-Emotional	−.11	.18	−.38	.00	.12
Logical Syllogisms-Nonemotional	−.03	−.02	.03	.54	.01
Oxymoron	.02	.22	.04	−.01	.04
Pollio-Novel	.08	.32	−.29	.24	.06
Pollio-Frozen	.01	.20	−.14	.41	.11
Similes-Fluency	.16	.94	.14	.21	.11
Similes-Originality	.19	.03	.16	.13	−.01
Similes-Novel	.17	.12	.15	.22	.27
Similes-Frozen	.13	.89	.08	.13	.00
Symbols-Fluency	.46	.03	.16	.76	.20
Symbols-Originality	.01	−.28	.13	.10	.10
Symbols-Novel	.21	−.14	.03	.43	.17
Symbols-Frozen	.45	.11	.17	.63	.17
Torrance-Fluency	.28	.19	.85	−.05	.05
Torrance-Originality	.23	.11	.83	.04	.14
Torrance-Flexibility	.25	.05	.80	.01	.11
Percent Variance	50	18	14	10	8

frozen measures owe their inclusions in Factor I to high correlations with their respective fluency scores.

One further point to be noted about Factor I concerns loadings for 3 of the 4 Symbols variables. As can be seen, Symbols-fluency and frozen loaded not only on Factor I but also on Factor IV. Similarly, Symbols-novel produced loadings (although of a lower magnitude) on both factors. These results suggest (for reasons to be explained more fully in connection with Factor IV) that the Symbols task is perhaps best construed as a special type of vocabulary test having more to do with Factor I than Factor IV. A careful examination of answers given in response to this test also supported this conclusion. By and large, such responses fell into one of three different categories consisting primarily of examples, synonyms, or paraphrases of the stimulus concept. Only infrequently did subjects produce a clearly figurative image. On this basis it does not seem wrong to see a vocabulary-like skill as underlying successful performance on the Symbols task, at least as responded to by subjects in the present study.

Factor II was most highly defined by loadings on Similes-fluency and Similes-frozen, variables indicating a capacity to produce a large number of frozen figures of speech. In addition, there were reasonably large positive loadings for Pollio-novel and to a lesser degree for the Oxymoron Task. Factor II seems to concern a great diversity of figurative variables and seems best described as a Sensitivity to Poetic Diction factor.

Factor III is clearly recognizable from earlier analyses in which it was appropriately called the Torrance Factor. The major variables defining this factor all concern the Torrance Test, a finding characteristic of both earlier analyses as well. Across all three-factor analyses, the ability to produce a great many different and varying responses to the Torrance Test has resolutely stood alone; in no single analysis did it intercorrelate (to any appreciable degree) with any of the other tasks included in the battery.

Factor IV involves a number of different tasks, yielding high loadings for Symbols-fluency and Symbols-frozen and moderately high loadings for Symbols-novel, Pollio-frozen and Syllogisms-nonemotional. At first glance, these tests seem to form a coherent factor with the exception of Syllogisms. A more careful analysis, however, reveals that all three measures derived from the Symbols Test loaded not only on Factor IV but on Factor I as well. Similarly, the Pollio Test (frozen) also produced loadings on an additional factor (Factor II). An examination of the cross-factor pattern for Syllogisms, however, revealed that it alone, of all the variables loading on Factor IV, had no additional loading on any other factor suggesting that Factor IV may be most uniquely defined by the Syllogisms Test.

This conclusion might be a bit suspect if not for results of an earlier factor analysis (Pollio, 1977) in which Symbols-fluency was found to load only on a Verbal Fluency Factor and not on any other. A careful comparison of the correlation matrices giving rise to both factor analyses indicated that only in the present case did all of the dependent variables involving the Symbols task produce significant correlations with one another as well as with Syllogisms. A reexamination of our earlier matrix revealed no such pattern of intercorrelations, decreasing any confidence we might have in defining Factor IV in terms of the Symbols rather than the Syllogisms task.

Factor V also seemed a bit heterogeneous, showing strong loadings for the following set of six measures: Association I-figurative and Association I-original, Association II-figurative, Composition-length and Composition-number of descriptions, and Similes-novel. In almost all cases, these variables represent different aspects of novel and/or original figurative usage, primarily as these occur in relatively open-ended production tasks. For this reason, Factor V was seen to provide a further measure of novel figurative response and for this reason was called Innovative Figurative Usage.

Taken in toto, these results suggest both a theoretical analysis of creative problem-solving as well as one of the structure of individual abilities required. For the case of individual abilities the scenario is a simple one and might well run as follows: Any individual who is skillful in verbal problem solving ought be able to produce a wide variety of relevant possibilities in a given problem setting (Factor I); ought be able to suggest alternative ways of using a particular set of materials (Factor III); ought be able to understand verbal metaphors and other figures of speech that might arise from manipulations of the problem (Factor II); and finally, ought be able to produce novel metaphors capable of linking together diverse aspects of the problem at hand (Factor V). Finally, this individual ought also be able, logically, to evaluate both the problem and its proposed solutions (Factor IV).

For the case of more general problem-solving theory, present results suggest that solving a problem depends upon an integrated blending of three different sets of process operations: (1) analytic thinking including both inductive and deductive reasoning; (2) ideational fluency including both the number and diversity of ideas produced; and (3) metaphoric competence including the ability to produce and understand figurative comparisons. Within the present battery, analytic reasoning was operationalized solely in terms of the syllogisms task; within an earlier study (Pollio, 1977) it was also operationalized in terms of the Steinberg sentence categorization task. Ideational fluency and flexibility were represented by both association tasks as well as by the Unusual Uses subtest of the Torrance. Finally, metaphoric competence was defined in terms of the various tests of figurative ability as well as in terms of figurative scorings for as many of the remaining tasks as possible.

Contemporary research in complex human problem solving has been particularly concerned with describing the component process operations comprising analytic thinking; here we need think only of the chronometric descriptions offered by Sternberg (1979). Processes involved in ideational fluency and flexibility have also been fairly well studied and conceptualized both by Torrance (1974) and Guilford (1967). The one domain in which process descriptions are lacking concerns that of metaphoric comparison. Although earlier analyses tried to describe such activities in associationistic (Mednick, 1962) or in more impressionistic perceptual terms (Gordon, 1961) no one, as yet, has been able to offer a highly articulated theory of combinatorial activity such as might be exemplified in various aspects of metaphoric competence.

A more major lack in contemporary theorizing, however, would seem to concern the overall integration of these three sets of component processes within an individual problem solver. Here, many anecdotal and case-study reports (see Gordon, 1961; Koestler, 1964) have attempted to describe the interaction of such processes in a single individual. Within more experimental analyses, however, the person as a total problem-solving system has been strangely absent. Although results of the present study do not explicitly provide such an integration, they do mean to suggest that people, and not processes, solve problems. Only if future work is begun with this understanding firmly in mind will we be able to develop a theoretical description approaching the complexity of human problem solving as it occurs in naturally significant task contexts.

INITIAL STEPS TOWARD PREDICTING INDIVIDUAL DIFFERENCES IN PROBLEM SOLVING

The factors isolated on the basis of the present analysis represent a wide diversity of individual abilities related to the domain of verbal problem solving. Given this collection of factors, and our analysis of their potential role in problem solving, it seemed reasonable to wonder if we could predict individual performance in terms of the sub-abilities circumscribed by the five factors defined by the present analysis.

In order to test this prediction experimentally, a skill in verbal problem solving index, Svp, was first calculated for each of the 70 subjects participating in the second, or major, study according to the following formula:

Svp = (z-scores for) Association II-fluency + Similes-fluency +
     Torrance-flexibility + Syllogisms(nonemotional)-correct +
     Association II-figurative.

Note this score represents a linear combination of 5 z-scores and, for this reason, is distributed normally with mean = 0 and variance = 5σ (S.D. = 2.23). Following the calculation of individual Svp scores, a distribution of such scores was established and individuals in the upper ($N = 16$) and lower ($N = 17$) quartiles selected to represent high and low levels of problem-solving skill, respectively. For the high group the z-score cutoff was greater than or equal to +2.00; for the low group, $z \leq -2.00$. Both groups thus include individuals scoring approximately one standard deviation above or below the mean.

Under this type of selection procedure, the prediction is quite straightforward: Those individuals having high scores should do well across the board on all tasks comprising the battery. Some individuals may, of course, have higher values on any one or two of the particular variables entering into the total score; only those individuals who are high on the composite index, however, should turn out to be among the best problem solvers in the present group of subjects.

Data relevant to this prediction are presented in Table 15.4 where it can be seen that high Svp individuals did indeed significantly outperform low Svp

TABLE 15.4
Breakdown of Tasks for High Svp ($z \geq 2.0$)
And Low Svp ($z \leq =2.0$) Groups

Dependent Variable	High Svp (z) (n = 16)	Low Svp (z) (n = 17)	Diff.
Analogies	.11	−.35	.46
Association I-Fluency	.95	−.77	1.72**
Association I-Originality	.67	−.52	1.19**
Association I-Literal	.94	−.67	1.61**
Association I-Figurative	.21	−.59	.80**
Association II-Fluency	1.07	−.77	1.84**
Association II-Originality	.58	−.43	1.01**
Association II-Literal	.89	−.61	1.50**
Association II-Figurative	.66	−.60	1.26**
Composition-Length	.21	−.17	.38
Composition-Description	.03	−.27	.30
Gardner Preference	.01	−.25	.26
Logical Syllogisms-Total	.33	−.29	.62*
Logical Syllogisms-Emotional	−.09	.15	−.24
Logical Syllogisms-Nonemotional	.65	−.66	1.31*
Oxymoron	−.12	−.26	.14
Pollio-Total	.34	−.40	.74*
Pollio-Novel	.29	−.16	.45
Pollio-Frozen	.27	−.48	.75*
Similes-Fluency	.91	−.75	1.66**
Similes-Originality	.34	.00	.34
Similes-Novel	.43	−.34	.77**
Similes-Frozen	.82	−.69	1.51**
Symbols-Fluency	.87	−.56	1.43**
Symbols-Originality	.16	.07	.09
Symbols-Novel	.35	−.39	.74**
Symbols-Frozen	.49	−.20	.69*
Torrance-Fluency	.72	−.59	1.31**
Torrance-Originality	.55	−.66	1.21**
Torrance-Flexibility	.67	−.90	1.57**

$*p < .05$
$**p < .01$

individuals on 21 of 30 different dependent variables used in the present battery. The significance of these differences was evaluated on the basis of t-tests computed between the high and low groups. Perhaps more important is the fact that many of these variables were not among the factor-defining tasks used to produce Svp scores in the first place. Of the 9 nonsignificant variables, 8 were in the predicted direction (high Svp > low Svp) while only 1 was not.

It should be noted that one of the predictor variables, Associations II-fluency, not only loaded quite highly on Factor I (a factor accounting for 50% of the variance) but that it also intercorrelated with other tasks contained in the present battery. As such, this variable alone might be expected to produce significant high vs. low differences on many of the remaining variables independent of the other 4 components of the Svp index. An examination of the degree to which this occurred revealed that Associations II-fluency was able to predict significant high vs. low differences in 15 cases. This is to be compared to 21 cases predicted on the basis of the total Svp score. While it is impossible to say with any degree of confidence that 6 additional variables do (or do not) mean a great deal given the very real constraints of the present prediction situation, it is important to note that each of the 15 variables predicted by Associations II-fluency was also predicted by Svp. The 6 additional variables predicted by Svp included two logical reasoning tasks, both measures of figurative comprehension (the Pollio Test), as well as both figurative variables for Associations I and II. This set of 6 variables would seem to include those logical and figurative tasks most distinct from a pure fluency ability thereby suggesting that to define a skillful problem solver is not just to define a fluent person; rather, such a person must also be able to reason logically as well as to use and comprehend figurative language.

For this reason, present results may be taken to suggest that it would be wise to continue using the total Svp score as a major predictive index in future work. Although not all of the variables contained in Svp may be essential in all contexts, they do seem to represent minimal skills necessary to predict complex verbal problem solving. Whether this combination of skills will also predict the performance of future groups of subjects in different contexts with different problems is yet to be determined; results produced by two independent analyses do lend some support for an optimistic outcome.

IMPLICATIONS FOR A THEORY OF METAPHOR

While one major purpose of the present analysis was to examine the relationship of figurative competence to complex human problem solving, a second purpose was to determine the specific relationship of various measures of figurative competence to one another as well as to each of the major components of the Svp index. Operationally, this comes down to a question of examining the pattern of intercorrelations obtaining between pairs of figurative measures as well as between each of these measures and the major factor-defining tasks. In this analysis, we were simply following a lead provided by Pickens and Pollio (1979) and Pollio and Pollio (1979) who found that presumably equivalent measures of figurative competence did not always yield equivalent results.

Tables 15.5A and B provide the complete set of relevant correlations for our second group of 70 subjects. Perhaps the most obvious, and most significant, aspect to Table 15.5A is the lack of inter-test correlations for almost all of the figurative tasks used. Two of the three significant values reported in Table 15.5A involve correlations between novel and frozen scores for the same test while the one remaining (and unique) cross-figurative test correlation concerns frozen comprehension on the Pollio Test and frozen production on the Symbols Test. The pattern in evidence in Table 15.5B reveals that neither the Analogies Test nor the number of comparisons produced in the creative composition intercorrelated with any of the major factor-defining tests. This pattern complements results reported in Table 15.5A, where these scores also failed to correlate with any of the remaining figurative task variables. A similar pattern (with the exception of a .25 correlation between Gardner Preference and Associations II-figurative and a .30 correlation between Similes-fluency and Oxymoron) also applied to the Gardner and Oxymoron tests. For 4 of the 8 figurative tasks used in the present study, there were only slight correlations between the task in question and the major factor-defining variables.

The remaining 4 tasks did produce a few significant intercorrelations both within subsections of the same test as well as with factor tasks. Of these, Associations II-fluency and figurative and Similes-fluency produced the greatest number of significant correlations. Perhaps the most theoretically meaningful correlations concerned the Pollio Comprehension Test in so far as it, among all the tests used, was a multiple-choice rather than a production task.

Taken in conjunction with the total pattern of findings uncovered in the present study, these results suggest a number of implications for any would-be analysis of figurative language. These implications are, perhaps, best expressed in terms of the following series of maxims:

1. *To know is not to use.* The lack of correlation between different measures of figurative competence presents yet another instance of a classic problem in psychological research. Although no one knows for sure what to do when different measures of presumably the same process do not intercorrelate, we must be especially concerned about this state of affairs in a newly emerging area of research such as figurative language so as not to reach partial or even completely erroneous conclusions. In this regard, a number of metaphor watchers (Gardner, 1974; Honeck, Sowry & Voegtle, 1978; Pickens & Pollio, 1979) have pointed out that an exclusive use of one procedure can hide certain important aspects of figurative competence. In the case of figurative development, for example, earlier work obscured the fact that figurative production, preference, and even paraphrase could be observed in children well before age levels that had been established using only a child's ability to explain figures of speech as the unique experimental operation of interest.

TABLE 15.5
Intercorrelations Among the Various Test Probes and Between These Probes and the Major Factor-Defining Variables

	Analogies	Composition-Descriptions	Gardner Preference	Oxymoron	Pollio-Novel	Pollio-Frozen	Symbols-Novel	Symbols-Frozen
A. Figurative Probes								
Analogies	—	-.08	.15	.10	.20	.18	.23	.24
Composition-Descriptions		—	-.03	-.08	-.05	.08	.04	.14
Gardner Preference			—	-.15	-.07	.15	.07	.03
Oxymoron				—	-.03	-.11	.00	.10
Pollio-Novel					—	.36*	-.02	.15
Pollio-Frozen						—	.05	.29*
Symbols-Novel							—	.26*
Symbols-Frozen								—
B. Factor-Defining Variables								
Association II-Fluency	.13	.02	.06	-.02	.17	.14	.30*	.57*
Association II-Figurative	.16	.10	.25*	-.01	.30*	.29*	.18	.21
Torrance-Flexibility	.04	.05	.09	-.07	-.17	.02	.06	.29*
Logical Syllogisms-Nonemotional	.10	-.02	.20	-.07	.19	.21	.39*	.21
Similes-Fluency	.12	.09	.01	.30*	.30*	.17	.06	.34*

*p < .05

Although it is possible to consider a lack of cross-task correlation as a purely methodological problem, it seems clear that it must also have theoretical import as well. Here two significant and quite general questions are at issue: (1) What is the relationship of experimental procedures to theoretical principles? and (2) Is it reasonable to assume that all of the various ways in which human speakers/hearers deal with figures of speech (i.e., produce, understand, explain, prefer, etc.) depend upon identical or even similar cognitive processes?

In terms of the first question, Dashiell (1935) long ago noted that even within the well-worked area of learning it was possible to discern the role of different experimental reference situations (e.g., classical conditioning) in the development of specific theories of learning (e.g., Hull). In the case of figurative language it seems reasonable to propose that derived-process theories of the type described by Clark and Clark (1977) and almost everybody else (Bickerton, 1969; Sternberg, Tourangeau, & Nigro, 1979; etc.) grow out of a special concern for (and with) the explanation task as their primary reference procedure. Similarly, nontransformational (i.e., direct process) models of the type described initially by Kohler (1929) and later by Werner and Kaplan (1963) seem to be based on an immediate perceptual grasp of the equivalence between items compared figuratively.

The lack of correlation between different experimental procedures is not a theoretically neutral issue. Perhaps the reason transformational theories of the type proposed by Clark and Clark as well as perceptual theories of the type proposed by Kohler yield reasonable explanations and/or predictions is that there is more than one type of figurative activity; i.e., figurative competence in the adult does not necessarily reflect the operation of a unitary cognitive process. Without belaboring the point, it does not seem wrong to suggest that transformational theories are more properly related to metaphoric explanation and that perceptual theories are more appropriate to the perception of figurative equivalence. Even if these are not exactly the correct matchings, it is important to leave open the question of whether or not figurative competence is (or is not) a unitary process.

2. *Metaphor is not analogy; analogy is not metaphor.*   One of the more enduring explanations as to how metaphor works assumes a transfer of meaning between two or more initially disparate items. Aristotle long ago noted that such items can be related to one another taxonomically or as a logical consequence of analogical reasoning. Approaches of this genre usually assume that an understanding of two or more terms in a single metaphor is the result of an *indirect* process in which the person must first find some Term D that relates to some Term C in the same way that Term B relates to Term A. For example, Brown (1966) described the metaphoric process in terms of an analogic transfer between proportions. His analyses of the phrase, "his brilliance dimmed the sun," went as follows:

A : B:: Cause 1 : Effect 1

X : Y :: Cause 2 : Effect 2

The subject's superior intelligence (A) overpowers the intelligence of others (B) as Cause 1 is related to Effect 1. Similarly, some luminous brilliance (X) overpowers the brilliance of the sun (Y) in just the same way as Cause 2 relates to Effect 2. Analogical reasoning leads us to the conclusion that A is Y, and on this basis we come to appreciate the meaning and significance of the original metaphor.

A recent and more quantitative version of this approach has been pursued by Sternberg (1977) and associates (Sternberg, Tourangeau & Nigro, 1979; Tourangeau & Sternberg, 1978) and is based on an earlier analysis initially devised by Rumelhart and Abrahamson (1973). In their original paper, Rumelhart and Abrahamson were concerned with problems of the following type:

Pig : Sheep :: Goat : _____

(a) monkey
(b) lion

The mechanism by which such analogies were thought to be solved consisted of a two-stage process: one that recognized the relationship between A and B (as in the formula A:B::C:X) and a second, which directed the search for some X such that the A to B and C to X relationships would be analogically equivalent. The second (or C:X) process was assumed to operate over semantic elements having relatively fixed locations in some multidimensional space such as that described for animal names by Henley (1969). Given this approach an initial vector was first constructed between the A and B terms. A second vector was then computed in terms of some location (i.e., word or concept) capable of completing the analogy within constraints imposed by the A:B vector.

This line of analysis has been extended by Sternberg to the case of metaphor. As an example, consider the following two-choice problem:

Bees in a hive are a Roman mob _____

(a) in the streets
(b) in the coliseum

To solve this problem the subject must encode the terms of the metaphor, infer a relation between *bees* and *hive,* map the relation between *bees* and a *Roman mob,* and then apply the inferred relation from a *Roman mob* to one of the two choices; presumably *in the coliseum* because a coliseum encloses a multitude in about the same way as a hive encloses bees. To understand a condensed metaphor such as *Bees are a Roman mob* the subject simply has to supply the missing concepts, "in a hive" and "in the coliseum."

Sternberg's analysis lays claim to some pretty fair historical ancestry in suggesting analogy as the major process underlying metaphoric use and/or understanding. It was for similar historical and theoretical reasons that the Analogies Task was included in the present battery of tests. The ability to solve analogies should, on the basis of almost everyone's analysis, relate to other metaphoric activities. As results presented in Tables 15.2, 15.3 and 15.5B revealed, however, the ability to solve analogies did not correlate significantly with any other metaphoric task including such obvious relatives as oxymoron and/or frozen metaphoric comprehension. As such, present results should diminish, if not rule out entirely, the idea that analogical reasoning is the basic process underlying a subject's ability to deal with other tasks of metaphoric competence.

A second problem to any analogically-based analysis of figurative language must be that such analyses constrain the number of metaphoric comparisons to a single, uniquely correct, possibility. Consider again the metaphor, *Bees are a Roman mob*. To understand this phrase figuratively suggests not only a transfer of attributes between *bees* and a *Roman mob* but a new conception of bees *as a* Roman mob and vice versa. Under this conception we may see both *bees* and a *Roman mob* as swarming over an enemy (Wasps or Barbarians), as adoring their emperor (the Queen or Caesar), or as in any one of a number of other additional senses not yet circumscribed (or even thought of) by prior analyses of the figure.

Examples such as this could be multiplied many times over. The major point, however, is that a strict use of analogy as *the* model for metaphor may serve to impoverish metaphoric diction rather than enrich it. To describe metaphor in terms of the transfer of a single analogical attribute (or even a set of attributes) severely diminishes the possibilities and pleasures offered by metaphor. Although under some circumstances analogy may be considered a special case of metaphor, present data argue against considering it as a general model for all adult figurative activity.

Despite this conclusion, there may be a more subtle issue here than meets the correlational eye: To find that the number of analogies solved did not relate to other tasks of metaphoric capacity need not necessarily rule out analogy as an underlying process in metaphoric comprehension. There may be a huge difference between solving a specific set of analogy problems and the theoretical mechanism proposed as underlying the solution of these problems. While it is always possible to invoke this type of post hoc explanation, such a strategy seems a bit strained in any situation in which the major operational procedure fails to co-vary with as many as seven other theoretically related tasks. In the end, it all comes down to a question of whether analogy is a good metaphor for metaphor; the present data suggest it is not. Until some clear and compelling reasons can be offered to explain the lack of correlation reported, it seems more parsimonious to assume that metaphor is not analogy and that analogy is not metaphor.

3.   *One person's folly is another's figure.*   One fact clearly emerging from the present set of analyses must be that not everyone has the same tendency to understand and/or use figurative expression. In the earlier Pollio and Smith (1979) categorization experiment, for example, one group of subjects preferred

to use metaphoric diction while another group chose to disregard it. Data produced in the present study by subjects attempting to solve the various problems set them also revealed that high Svp individuals had significantly better capacity to understand and use novel and frozen figures than their low Svp counterparts. Taken together, these findings suggest that individual differences must be included in any general theory of metaphor.

Neither this conclusion, not the data on which it is based, should be all that surprising; rather, human beings when asked to do almost any task reveal individual differences in how they go about doing that task. In the case of metaphor the important implication should not be that individual differences occur—they should—but that they must be taken into account theoretically. At the most obvious level, these findings suggest that one person's folly is another's figure and that metaphoric sentences are only meaningfully metaphoric within the context of some specific listener and/or speaker. While it has been fashionable to describe metaphor in terms of a reorganization in the meaning of words and phrases comprising a figurative utterance, present results suggest that such reorganization depends as much on the individual as on semantic interactions occurring within the particular sentence. The person and the context are never irrelevant for what is meant nor, for that matter, for what is understood or thought.

Does this line of argument suggest that psychologists ought come to deal only in individual case studies of figurative language, or can something of a more general nature be said about the metaphoric process? As in the case of our first maxim, "To understand is not to use," the issue of disentangling idiographic and nomothetic description has been a venerable one for psychological theory. For the case of figurative language the question would seem best addressed in terms of an answer to the following question: Are differences obtaining between individuals a question of quality or quantity?

Standing on the side of quality would seem to be poets, writers and literary critics; standing on the side of quantity would seem to be psychologists, linguists and a philosopher or two. The artist tends to see "true" metaphoric competence as indicative of a unique style of dealing with one's world and one's language. For this reason only a special person, with special sensitivity, might be expected to do it meaningfully and well. This line of argument was implicit in Stumberg's (1928) analysis of poetic talent. A similar notion pervades many poet's first-person descriptions of what they say it is they do. For Wallace Stevens (see Sheehan, 1966), the poet's job is to discover resemblances between real and imagined objects, for James Dickey (1967) the poet's job is to seek iconic threads by, and through, which to render a unique perception of reality; while for Paul Valery (1961), the poet's job is to change "the walking of prose to the dancing of poetry." The poet's task is thus seen as one of expressing a unique view of reality through a unique use of language.

Psychologists are decidedly uncomfortable with each and every individual standing so resolutely aloof from the rest. Instead we prefer to think in quantitative terms where differences between people are to be understood in terms of "more or less" than in terms of "different." The only psychological analysis of individual differences in figurative competence—that provided by Tourangeau and Sternberg (1978)—begins by considering the problem of how experts and novices deal with metaphor. For this model, differences between the expert and the novice are phrased in terms of different locations on dimensions such as novelty, comprehension, etc., with the location of a figure on any such dimension depending on the background of the person doing the task. The novice and the literary sophisticate differ in their handling of metaphor in, at least, the following ways: For the novice, comprehension is hard and finding novelty easy; for the sophisticate, comprehension is easy but finding novelty difficult. Consequently, the critic will often prefer more "obscure" metaphors than the novice and, in this way, past experience in dealing with metaphor determines how easily a figure will (or will not) be understood. Not only does past experience determine what will be judged a good figure, it may even determine if a particular word or phrase will be considered as figurative in the first place.

The most important theoretical issue emerging from any consideration of individual difference in figurative competence must be this: Are processes involved in metaphoric competence different for different individuals or can we simply talk about quantitative differences in the same process(es) that only "look different" if and when they are sufficiently extreme? A diplomatic resolution to this issue would be to render unto Quality what is Quality's and unto Quantity what is Quantity's. What this means is that it is probably wise to accept qualitative differences among individuals and then look for quantitative gradations within different categories. In this, we are simply noting that there are both good and bad poets just as there are both good and bad engineers or, more relevantly for experimental psychologists, both poetic and nonpoetic undergraduates.

As in the case of Maxims 1 and 2, the question of individual differences is not without theoretical import. For one, it raises the (awkward) theoretical possibility that different individuals may use different processes in dealing with figurative language. It also forces us to take the specific person into account before making any statement concerning what will, or will not, be seen as figurative. For the domain of figurative language, the speaking person is never an irrelevant fact to be explained away in the service of some abstract concept; rather, the speaking person must always be at the very center of our concerns as to how it is that human beings produce, understand, explain, or even prefer poetic diction.

REFERENCES

Bickerton, D. Prolegomena to a linguistic theory of metaphor. *Foundations of Language,* 1969, *5,* 34–52.

Brown, S. J. M. *The world of imagery: Metaphor and kindred imagery* (2nd Ed.). New York: Harcourt Brace Jovanovich, 1966.

Clark, H. H., & Clark, E. V. *Psychology and language*. New York: Harcourt Brace Jovanovich, 1977.

Dashiell, J. F. A survey and synthesis of learning theories. *Psychological Bulletin*, 1935, *32*, 261–275.

Dickey, J. *Metaphor as pure adventure*. Lecture delivered at the Library of Congress, December 4, 1967.

Gardner, H. Metaphors and modalities: How children project polar adjectives onto diverse domains. *Child Development*, 1974, *45*, 84–91.

Gardner, H., Kirchner, M., Winner, E., & Perkins, D. Children's metaphoric productions and preferences. *Journal of Child Language*, 1975, *2*, 125–141.

Gordon, W. J. J. *Synectics*. New York: Harper and Row, 1961.

Guilford, J. P. *The nature of human intelligence*. New York: McGraw-Hill, 1967.

Harris, R. J. Comprehension of metaphors: A test of the two-stage processing model. *Bulletin of the Psychonomic Society*, 1976, *5*, 191–202.

Henley, N. M. A psychological study of the semantics of animal terms. *Journal of Verbal Learning and Verbal Behavior*, 1969, *8*, 176–184.

Honeck, R. P., Riechmann, P., & Hoffman, R. Semantic memory for metaphor: The conceptual base hypothesis. *Memory and Cognition*, 1975, *3*, 409–415.

Honeck, R., Sowry, B., & Voegtle, K. Proverbial understanding in a pictorial context. *Child Development*, 1978, *49*, 327–331.

Koestler, A. *The act of creation*. New York: Macmillan, 1964.

Kohler, W. *Gestalt psychology*. New York: Liveright, 1929.

Lefford, A. The influence of emotional subject matter on logical reasoning. *Journal of General Psychology*, 1946, *34*, 127–151.

Marks, L. E., & Miller, G. A. The role of semantic and syntactic constraints in the memorization of English sentences. *Journal of Verbal Learning and Verbal Behavior*, 1964, *3*, 1–5.

Mednick, S. A. The associative basis of the creative process. *Psychological Review*, 1962, *69*, 220–232.

Miller, G. A., & Isard, S. Some perceptual consequences of linguistic rules. *Journal of Verbal Learning and Behavior*, 1963, *2*, 217–228.

Pickens, J. D., & Pollio, H. R. Patterns of figurative use in adult speakers. *Psychological Research*, 1979, *40*, 299–313.

Pollio, H. R. *Personal cognition and metaphoric style*. Paper presented at American Psychological Association, San Francisco, August, 1977.

Pollio, H. R., Barlow, J. M., Fine, H. J., & Pollio, M. R. *Psychology and the poetics of growth: Figurative language in psychology, psychotherapy, and education*. Hillsdale, N.J.: Lawrence Erlbaum Associates, 1977.

Pollio, H. R., & Burns, B. C. The anomaly of anomaly. *Journal of Psycholinguistic Research*, 1977, *6*, 247–260.

Pollio, H. R., & Smith, M. K. Sense and nonsense in thinking about anomaly and metaphor. *Bulletin of the Psychonomic Society*, 1979, *13*, 323–326.

Pollio, M. R., & Pollio, H. R. The development of figurative language in school children. *Journal of Psycholinguistic Research*, 1974, 138–143.

Pollio, M. R., & Pollio, H. R. The comprehension of figurative language in children. *Journal of Child Language*, 1979, *6*, 111–120.

Rumelhart, D. E., & Abrahamson, A. A. A model for analogical reasoning. *Cognitive Psychology*, 1973, *5*, 1–28.

Sheehan, D. Wallace Stevens' theory of metaphor. *Papers on Language and Literature*, 1966, *2*, 57–66.

Steinberg, D. D. Analyticity, amphigory and semantic interpretation of sentences. *Journal of Verbal Learning and Verbal Behavior*, 1970, *9*, 37–51. (a)

Steinberg, D. D. Negation, analyticity, amphigory and the semantic interpretation of sentences. *Journal of Experimental Psychology,* 1970, *84,* 417–423. (b)

Steinberg, D. D. Semantic universals in sentence processing and interpretation: A study of Chinese, Finnish, Japanese and Slovenian speakers. *Journal of Psycholinguistic Research,* 1975, *4,* 169–193.

Sternberg, R. J. *Intelligence, information processing, and analogical reasoning.* Hillsdale, N.J.: Lawrence Erlbaum Associates, 1977.

Sternberg, R. J. The nature of mental abilities. *American Psychologist,* 1979, *34,* 214–230.

Sternberg, R. J., Tourangeau, R., & Nigro, G. *Metaphor, induction, and social policy: The convergence of macroscopic and microscopic views.* In A. Ortony (Ed.), *Metaphor and thought.* Cambridge, England: Cambridge University Press, 1979.

Stumberg, D. A study of poetic talent. *Journal of Experimental Psychology,* 1928, *20,* 219–234.

Torrance, E. P. *Torrance tests of creative thinking.* Lexington, Mass.: Ginn & Co., 1974.

Tourangeau, R., & Sternberg, R. J. *Understandings and appreciating metaphors.* NR 150–412 ONR Technical Report #11. New Haven: Department of Psychology, Yale University, 1978.

Valery, P. *The art of poetry.* New York: Vintage Books, 1961.

Werner, H., & Kaplan, B. *Symbol formation.* New York: Wiley, 1963.

16 Metaphor in Science

Robert R. Hoffman
University of Minnesota

INTRODUCTION

To some scientists and philosophers, metaphorical theories are preposterous: "That theory's for the birds—it's just a metaphor." And yet, a point is often reached in scientific theorizing where scientists are stuck with little *but* fantasies, hunches, free associations "couched in figures of speech, metaphors, etc. We may begin as a poet talks rather than as a scientist is supposed to talk." Here, Abraham Maslow (1969, p. 129) describes some root mental machinations of scientists. Maslow, Kuhn (1965), and others throughout the history of science have described the roles of psychological factors in the scientific enterprise. But how do scientists who are steeped in metaphor tell when they are on the right track? More specifically, how can a metaphor have scientific utility? How can it mislead?

This chapter begins with summaries of the views of some philosophers and scientists—pro and con—about the status and use of metaphors in scientific theories. Following this is an examination of some specific scientific metaphors, their character and foibles, which leads here to an attempt at a description of the place of a metaphor in a theory. The discussion involves some ideas about how to assess metaphorical theories. Much of the literature on this topic is from the philosophy of science, a discipline populated by an inordinate number of physicists. This chapter uses example metaphors from many sciences, especially psychology (*The mind is a computer*), but it also relies on some well-worn examples from physics (*An atom is a solar system*).

ATTITUDES ABOUT METAPHOR IN THE PHILOSOPHY
OF SCIENCE

Attitudes Con

Some in philosophy of science and in the philosophy of psychology feel that metaphor is no good when used in a theory (e.g., Carnap, 1959; Hemple, 1965; Turbayne, 1962). They rule out metaphor as legitimate in science as a consequence of the positivistic attitude: Scientific explanation, it is claimed, consists of the use of logical generalization, laws, and literal deductive relations between the theory language (of concepts or constructs) and the observation language (or behavioral language) of operational definitions (Bergmann, 1940; Bergmann & Spence, 1941). By this view, a metaphorical theory is at best a possibly heuristic I.O.U. At worst it is an irreal fungus doomed eternally to a prescientific twilight zone. Any good, rigorous theory should be literal and precise (Boyd, 1979; Pylyshyn, 1979; Royce, 1978; Ryle, 1949). Bergmann (1940, p. 422) gave this specific critique of the Lewinian (introspectionistic) "field" theories of the 1940s: "what is the predictive value of the suggestive metaphor, 'psychological environment'? Is it not the business of science to ascertain which *objective* factors in the past and present state of the organism and its environment account for the difference in response?" Psychologists MacCorquodale and Meehl (1957) also prefer literal theories—those with intervening stimulus and response variables—to theories with anthropomorphic or metaphorical hypothetical constructs. The literal properties involved in hypothetical constructs are said to be the properties that matter for the theory anyway: metaphors are so much excess baggage or "surplus meaning." The *Zeitgeist* from about 1920 to about 1955 involved a somewhat compulsive semantics. Theories were said to rely on the formal logic of postulates, propositions, and curve-fitting, and not on the content of the propositions (Carnap, 1937; McGuigan, 1953; Woodrow, 1942). Theories were supposed to avoid all the vulgarities, ambiguities, mentalisms, and vaguenesses of ordinary language (George, 1953; Kantor, 1941; Kattsoff, 1939; Maatsch & Behan, 1953; Rokeach & Bartley, 1958; Rozeboom, 1956; Spiker & McCandless, 1954). The meaning of theoretical terms was to be given only by operational definitions—this was what was supposed to make theories testable (Bridgman, 1927; Kantor, 1938; Stevens, 1935). Rapoport (1935) admonished theorists to tolerate metaphor with an attitude of "linguistic hygienics"—one should be constantly on guard against metaphors. As Max Black put it (1962), some philosophers of science proclaimed, "Thou shalt not commit metaphor!" Black's own philosophy is more liberal. But even then he tells scientists to use many metaphors, if any are used at all, so that our favorite metaphors do not lead us astray!

It is one thing to be sensitive to the metaphoricalness of a theory—as a possible pratfall or tool—and quite another thing to reject a theory because it is a metaphor.

Attitudes Pro

In contrast to the logical positivists' campaign for a theory devoid of metaphor and ambiguity, some in philosophy have attributed to metaphor an important role in scientific theorizing (e.g., Hornsburgh, 1958). Indeed, it has been the expressed goal of some in philosophy to show how the psychological aspects of metaphor use (e.g., word-meaning change, cultural effects, context effects, novelty) make the logical positivistic approach untenable. On the basis of the psychological aspects, Beardsley (1962), McCloskey (1964), Mooij (1975), and Nemetz (1958) asserted that the "logic" of metaphor is beyond the grasp of any exclusively philosophical analysis. To cite one specific argument, Berggren (1963) pointed out that *any* scientific explanation, though ostensively a logical deduction, can nonetheless rely on metaphor, since metaphors may creep into the premises of the deduction from somewhere else in the theory!

To summarize, some in philosophy of science maintain that scientific explanation should be a purely logical-rational affair. Hence, to them, ordinary language, including metaphor, is a bad vehicle for stating theories. Others assert that since metaphors are used in science and in ordinary language, and since the "logic" of metaphor is not obviously rational, then the search for a purely logical-rational basis for science may be misguided.[1]

SCIENTISTS' ATTITUDES ABOUT THEIR METAPHORS

Attitudes Con

Some scientists are critical of the use of metaphor in theories. Here's a sampling. Some physicists objected to the use of metaphor in their discipline—Mach, Sir Oliver Lodge, and, in particular, Rene Duhem (1906) (see Gregory, 1931). To linguist Noam Chomsky (1965, Chapter 1), at least one theory, the associationist-habit view, in *only* a metaphor and is misleading for what it disguises. Psychologist Weimer (1973) prefers a nonmetaphorical description of the evolutionary survival value of knowledge over a teleological description that is said to be "at best" a metaphor—as if metaphoricalness were somehow to blame. Other social scientists claim that metaphor has *only* pedagogic value. It is

---

[1]The doctrines involved in operationism and logical positivism also had critics who did not focus on metaphor per se, but on the notion that theories need concepts from ordinary language in general. Some expressed the need in philosophy for "nonstrict" or tacit modes of inference or judgment (Hall, 1942; Polanyi, 1968; Scriven, 1962). Some expressed the need for meaningful ways of relating operational definitions (Bentley, 1937; Bills, 1938; Israel & Goldstein, 1944; Maze, 1954; Suppe, 1973). Some pointed out the failure of operationists to obtain the precision they claimed they could obtain (Chomsky, 1959; Polanyi, 1958). Physicist Bridgman (1936) was himself convinced to alter his initial operationistic philosophy (1927; see Lambley, 1970). The history of operationism and logical positivism from the perspective of psychology is reviewed in Leahey (1977), Meissner (1960), Rozeboom (1956), and Stevens (1939).

said that metaphor serves as a shorthand mnemonic device for remembering or explaining ideas, and not as a valid medium for creating or inference-making (Deese, 1972; Green, 1979; R. Miller, 1976). In Arbib's (1972) treatise on the "computer model of the mind," he is explicit about the metaphor involved and hopes that it will be refined and its false importations will be discarded—so that the metaphorical aspects can be ignored (p. 11). In a paper on issues involved with psychological theories of memory representations, Palmer (1978) argues that the important aspect of representations is the preservation of information as in information theory metrics. In this way, he seems to rule out metaphor and other semantic aspects of cognitive theories.

On the main, however, most scientists seem to have a favorable attitude toward the use of metaphor. This may be related to the simple fact that metaphors abound in science.

Attitudes Pro

First, consider physics. James Clerk Maxwell and William Thomson (Lord Kelvin) explicitly acknowledged their metaphors—the "lines of force" notion of magnetism, the concept of a "dance of molecules," and the idea that heat is a "fluid." To Maxwell, the creative scientific mind does not seek some sort of thermodynamic equilibrium or quiescence, the mind is a "tree shooting out branches which adapt themselves to new aspects of the sky toward which they climb." The progress of science cannot be predicted or anticipated by logic (Maxwell, 1890, p. 226). Maxwell encouraged the use of diverse forms of thought, including imagery, mathematics, drawings, models, and metaphors. He was quite explicit on this—metaphors are not only "legitimate products of science, but capable of generating science in turn" (1890, p. 227).[2] Another fascinating theorist was Michael Faraday—at almost every turn he relied on metaphor. For electrical conduction to occur, he reasoned, either the particles must touch and have volume, or the particles might be pointlike centers of force with "atmospheres" of energy. The latter case suggests that matter is

---

[2]"I never sailed through a plate of meerschaum on a molecule, so that I do not know whether the passage is like the Forth & Clyde canal or like the Caledonian canal but I should not expect to have many long reaches, but rather plenty of locks and sluices so that it would not be very much like a tube but more like a cullender" (From a letter to William Thomson dated August 25, 1879). Maxwell, though fatally ill, kept on playing/thinking. He signed his name,

$$\frac{1}{\frac{dp}{dt}}$$

Maxwell's mathematics *were* mind-boggling. But his papers and lectures relied also on poems from Milton, on drawings, and on illustrative images and metaphors—to *generate* as well as explain the math. It may seem ironic that physics is touted as the most precise and mature science and yet physicists themselves are usually very playful and flexible in their creativity.

everywhere continuous—leading Faraday to the notions of a "field" theory, and an "elastic" fluid. Faraday, who used little in the way of math, thirsted for metaphors and images, such as the use of iron filings to show the magnetic "lines of force." Philosopher Mary Hesse (1962) found that she could use metaphors as a means of analyzing the history of physics, including a demonstration of trends in attitudes about the use of metaphors and models.

In a broader psychological context of science, general problem-solving, many treatments of problem-solving strategies describe the use of metaphor in the creation of solutions (e.g., Gordon, 1961; Schon, 1979). A favorite example is the invention of the plastic twist-top that turns to open and close for dispensing sticky substances like glue. Its action makes it self-cleaning. The metaphor used in the generation of this device was that of a horse's rectum.

The utility of metaphor has been recognized by rhetoricians and linguists who have analyzed discourse and communication (Culler, 1975; Stelzer, 1965). Discourse can be described in terms of the military metaphor of attack and defense. The philosophical world view called Mechanism was instantiated in Hume's metaphor of speech as a set of tools and Herbert Spencer's metaphor of speech as a set of symbols arranged in a machinelike manner, still current notions. By Reddy's (1979) estimation, well over half of the terms used to describe communication are metaphors. *Words* are said to contain and transfer thoughts, ideas, meanings, or feelings. Thus, the listener's task is to extract the meaning from the words. Meanings can come across or pour out. They can be captured, loaded, forced, pregnant, hollow, empty, buried, exposed, lost, and so on. Indeed, language seems to prefer metaphors for facilitating communication about communication (theories are maps!).

Nemetz (1958) went one step further. His claim was that theories of metaphor must also be metaphorical. Consider Plato's metaphor of the "fabric of discourse," or "woven ideas." The modern manifestation of this is the "tension" theory of metaphor: A metaphor is deviant or anomalous and recognition of the anomaly induces a tension that needs to be resolved through the process of interpretation or assimilation (Beardsley, 1962; Osborn & Ehninger, 1962; Perrine, 1971). Metaphor has also been likened to a filter or selection of characteristics (Black, 1962; Hesse, 1966; Richards, 1936), an idea that shows up as the semantic feature transfer view of metaphor meaning. According to rules, features are transferred or transformed.

Psychology also makes much use of metaphor. *This couch reeks of verbosity* is an item from the Harvard Anal Disposition Scale (Couch & Keniston, 1960). Psychodynamically oriented writers have, since Freud (1905), considered nonliteral meanings to be special—not only in terms of the insights metaphors give into the patient's deepest thoughts and motivations, but also as a medium for theorizing. The ego is a helmsman, libidinal drives are energy, striving is a flow, and attitudes are a river bed (Nash, 1962). As a part of the theory of psychoanalysis, since metaphor is a basic mechanism for the expression of subliminal drives, so too is it a means of analyzing the drives. Jung's elaborate system of "archetypes" is a set of metaphors tailored to unpack culturally rich symbols and allusions. The archetypes are meaningful themes that describe the unconscious as it is manifested in tribal lore, sculpture, religious myths, fairy tales, and neuroses. Two such archetypical symbols are the *Mother*—spirit mother, earth mother, sympathy, fate, passion, depth, receptivity; and the *Trickster*—representative of saint, fool, divine, animal, innocence, childishness (see Jung, 1969).

One can wonder with Edie (1963), Roediger (1978), Paivio (1974), and Snell (1960) if there is *any* literal term for thoughts, memories, and mental images (see also Turbayne's analysis of the picture or camera metaphor for vision, 1962). Cognitive terms cluster into themes: Greek metaphors for seeing—theory, idea, intuition, reflect, focus, introspect, outlook, perspective, recognize; Latin metaphors (somewhat more obscure) from agriculture—recollect, comprehend, observe; and both Latin and Greek metaphors for sex—intercourse, conception, impression. From these possibly illicit parents spring modern memory metaphors. A mind is closed, open, narrow, a switchboard, a wax tablet, a garbage can, a tuning fork, a lock and key, and of course it is "filled" with vivid picture-images that "firmly tie" the memories together. Such metaphors indicate the attitudes and philosophies adopted by entire language cultures. They are to Breal (1887) a museum of language and to Edie (1963) an etymological storehouse of previous ponderings. In effect, we cannot avoid either our history or our metaphors.

Metaphor, it seems, can be and perhaps must be brought to bear on whatever problem scientists may be grappling with.

THE STATE OF THE ART IN PHILOSOPHICAL CRITICISM

Granting for now that metaphors do play a helpful role, *how* do they work? The few ideas presented by those who have done some analysis on this point can be boiled down to two notions: (1) Metaphor can often result in new descriptions or in choices between theories (Boyd, 1979; Chapanis, 1961; Hesse, 1966; Rapoport, 1953), and (2) metaphor works in a theory like analogy works, but metaphor is analogy that is fancied-up by inference-making and resemblance-finding (Nagel, 1961; Nemetz, 1958). Most of the seminal works, like those of Black and Hesse on philosophy, focused on the problems of how to identify metaphors and of whether metaphors can be given literal paraphrases. Their noble goal was to get philosophers of science to admit metaphor as a legitimate description of aspects of science by showing how metaphor is important and by attempting some definitions. This, however, is not enough. If metaphor allows for special insights, then it does something a literal theory could not or might not do. If metaphor is so rich and communicative, then we might see all operational definitions and careful descriptions give way to layers of gooey metaphors. The *Journal of Experimental Psychology* might read more like Joyce than Spence. In actuality, metaphors do not run quite so rampant. Even so, no specific criteria for assessing a metaphorical theory have been offered. Nor has any explicit attempt been made to represent the place of a metaphor within a theory. What if metaphoricalness itself *can* be used to make some rational decisions about the theory? Can we establish decision criteria for throwing out or keeping a metaphorical theory based on the circumstances in which a metaphor will have scientific utility? Such criteria would tell us what to look for in a metaphor and what to look out for. Furthermore, how can we *know* if a decision criterion is a good one? That is, how can it be known that a decision to throw out a metaphor, on the basis of metaphoricalness, was a sound decision?

The next section is a step toward answering these questions—a skeletal (but hopefully adequate) account of what metaphor can do that's bad for science and what it can do that's good. From this I go into a more formal (but sufficiently skeletal) description of how a metaphor might fit in with the network of predications and postulates that constitutes a theory.

METAPHOR AND TRUTH, HIDE AND SEEK

It is sometimes claimed that a scientific metaphor, being nonliteral, will always hide the truth. Usually when this argument is made, the metaphor ends up being used to *disclose* that which it supposedly hides. To say, *Metaphors can hide,* is to be a victim of the very defense one is trying to overcome. As the following examples show, metaphor can *seem* to hide truth in different ways, some more remediable than others.

Metaphor, Mass, Math, and Myth

Sometimes metaphors seem to hide the truth, not because of metaphoricalness but because of the use of metaphor in flabby theorizing. One can speak in physics of elementary particles "feeling" a force without really committing a sin. The domains of particles and (human) feelings are too disparate for this metaphorical language to imply (to a physicist) a teleological or cause-effect relation. In biology one can speak of cells "feeling" the effects of toxins. This is not a scientific metaphor in that it is not strictly an attempt at explaining a concept in biological theory or methodology. The term "feel" has no obvious counterpart in biological theories of cell behavior (excepting observable reactions like movement). "Feel" is a descriptive short-hand. Since cells and people are similar domains, at least more similar than people and particles, the statement *The cells feel the toxin* can suggest certain cause-effect or teleological relations—it may hide the truth. The metaphor may give a false sense of understanding; important questions may go unasked. The classification that the metaphor implies may thus keep the experimenter (or student) from making distinctions that should be made. That is, the theory might need or require a number of concepts where the metaphor suggests only one . . . unless, of course, the experimenter recognizes the metaphor and *uses* it to get at what is "hidden."

An example of faulting a metaphor when it's really the theorizing that is to blame is Hinde's (1955) critique of Tinbergen's theory of instinct mechanisms. The ambiguous word "drive" is used by Tinbergen to refer to the biological causes of behavior, to the mechanism that connects the biological processes to behavior, and to the state of the organism when so motivated. A drive is sometimes said to flow and be discharged, sometimes it is called a fire that can be put out, sometimes drives are said to be fed or satisfied, sometimes drives are said to be generalized or thwarted. Certainly Tinbergen makes fast and easy use of a rich set of metaphors. To Hinde, this results in an ethological theory that is a cause-effect nightmare. The principles in the theory are confused; the theory has many implicit postulates of entities and dispositions; and the theory makes some claims that are false (i.e., that there is no role of feedback, that there is no role of consciousness). But the metaphors do not hide the truth—Hinde *used* the metaphors to disclose the implicit assumptions! It is Tinbergen's depth of theorizing that was insufficient.

It is claimed that another way in which metaphors hide the truth is by being pervasive and going unrecognized. In this way, metaphors are sometimes said to acquire the status of "myth" (Berggren, 1963; Hoffman, 1979). There are alleged instances of scientists "confusing" their metaphorical mechanical models with the theories that the models instantiate (Hempel, 1965, pp. 433–435). Physicist William Thomson is often cited as an example: "If I can make a mechanical model I can understand it" (1884, pp. 131–132). Far from being an unreasoned confusion, this was deliberate on his part, a matter of his philosophy of science. It may be improper to use the value-laden term, "myth," to label viewpoints that rely on metaphors and models in the construction of theories.

Metaphor can mess us up (simply enough) by suggesting an entity or property that is wrong. So much the worse for the theorist if the property or entity is somehow regarded as special. A good example of this is the physicists' penchant for using odd terms to talk about particles. The most elementary particles, called quarks, come in many varieties. Some have "color," some have "charm," some are "strange." Quarks seem inextricably bound together as if "tied by a string" or "contained in a bag," or so some theories of quarks describe it. One begins to wonder if leptons can sin and if baryons can die. Let me focus on the property called "spin." At the level of description in physical theory "particles" are not masses. They do not spin. But then, why use the word "spin" and where did its use arise? Spin *is* a property word used to describe the angular momentum of particles. Spin does not refer to motion as in a spinning top. Nothing actually rotates, or speeds up or slows down, for that matter. The property is fundamental to the particle—change the spin and the particle has changed. Beams of particles can be magnetized, accelerated, collimated, and otherwise separated out into bunches of pure types. Observations show that some particles break up into two photons. One is labeled a "spin-up" photon, the other is labeled a "spin-down" photon. Otherwise, they are alike in the math. If it seems confusing, that's because it is. An elementary particle in quantum mechanics is not even a particle in the sense of being a spatially extended body. In this case, metaphorical language persists despite its falseness.

Metaphor and Verisimilitude

If pressed, scientists generally admit, Realist Hat in hand, that theories are not THE TRUTH, that theories are functional or "instrumentalist" fictions.[3] It's not that the theory is WRONG. If it is, then some other theory should be doing the predicting. It's that theories are not entirely true. Metaphor certainly qualifies. But it is debatable on logical and philosophical grounds whether any theory can be TRUE (see Carnap, 1945; Nagel, 1961). For present purposes, the best we might say in order to get the discussion off the ground is that any theory (verbal, mathematical, metaphorical) is to some degree "truthlike" or has some verisimilitude (Popper, 1959).[4] A falsified theory should not necessarily be abandoned, whether or not it contains metaphor. Theories without metaphor can need some simplifying auxiliary postulates ("all other things being equal . . ."), short-hand mathematical theorizing, temporary hypotheses, entities that are not "real," incompletenesses, phenomena or properties that are not "directly sensible," and the like. So it may be unwise to reject a theory (only) because aspects of its metaphoricalness may seemingly detract from its truthlikeness. Even what appear prima facie to be absurd metaphors may be useful. For instance, to suggest that concrete blocks are springs seems absurd. Yet, the behavior of concrete blocks subjected to brief stresses can be approximated by a mathematical instantiation of a spring model (see Feld, McNair, & Wilk, 1979).

Metaphor Could Rhyme with Popper

We might inquire as to what a good metaphor *should* do for its theory; what we might want it to do. At least, we would like it to do what *any* positively Popperian postulate should: generate falsifiers. A theoretical postulate, metaphor or not, should lead to demonstrations of how the theory needs modification of its assumptions or other "ad hocery." The phenomena in the universe of discourse

---

[3]For a description of the various versions of the philosophies of instrumentalism and realism in metatheoretics, with an eye toward the role of psychological factors (i.e., reference, perception, intelligibility), see G. Maxwell, 1970.

[4]The concept of verisimilitude or degree of truth-likeness is problematic in philosophy (see D. Miller, 1976; Popper, 1976; Tichy, 1976), yet it continues to be a very useful concept.

can then be reexamined to see if they behave as the theory says they ought. Deviation from the predictions may show how to fancy-up the theory. As Hornsburgh (1958) stated, it should be possible to show how the metaphor is wrong in important respects. Indeed, it should be possible to show how the metaphor is wrong in *exactly* those respects that the scientist relies on to make the metaphor useful! In other words, a metaphor should show how to produce *strong* falsifiers of the theory: what the *experimenter* regards as strong predictions that would kill the theory if not borne out. In fact, an interesting dividend from metaphorical theories is that they make obvious some of the ways in which they are false. An example is the hydraulic pipes and fluids metaphor for the nervous system or for motivation and drives.

> Lorenz postulates for each instinctive act, a particular 'reaction specific energy' which he pictures as accumulating in a reservoir with a spring-valve at its base. In an appropriate situation, the spring-valve is released partly by the hydrostatic pressure of the reservoir's contents and partly by the action of the external stimulus, which is pictured as a weight on a scale pan pulling against the spring (Hinde, 1955, pp. 321-322).

The metaphor does account for facts, for instance the reduction of response strength following a reaction—the reservoir has been drained and a stronger stimulus is needed to evoke the response again. But this is, perhaps deservedly so, the whipping-post of scientific metaphors. It shouts, "I'm a metaphor!" The question is not one of whether we can bring about observations that constitute falsifiers of the theory, but a question of when we should choose to use the obvious falsehoods in a criticism or refutation of the theory. Based on myriad factors of preference, we can choose to disbelieve the metaphor at any point.

The general rule some scientists and philosophers seem to follow, today as in the past, is this: If you don't like a theory (or theorist) and if the theory is metaphorical or contains metaphor, you can usually get away with criticising the theory by saying, "It's only a metaphor." Often, however, this is a matter of attitudes and may have little or nothing to do with metaphoricalness. Ironically, the falsifiability of metaphors is why those who dislike metaphors may have been able to serve a helpful role—by focusing our attention on falsification. However, they would see metaphor as negative and scientific progress as degenerative. Metaphor can also be regarded as possibly constructive. Since any theory may be falsifiable and may have some verisimilitude, rejection of a theory or hypothesis *because* it is a metaphor may actually be based on a philosophical commitment to certain literal logical theories and unfortunately may not regard the creative role of metaphor at all.

Putting Metaphors "On Hold"

In order to be falsifiable or confirmable, a statement in a theory must at least be interpretable in terms of observations or empirical consequences. Other criteria have been proposed, for example, that the empirical consequences also should not be entailed by other principles in the theory alone. However, the logic of falisification is debatable (see Ayer, 1959, versus Carnap, 1956, versus Hesse, 1962). The point here is that it is the fate of scientific metaphors to be modified as the theories change in light of evidence. The way the scientific community often treats metaphors is to "put them on hold"—to regard them as falsified but to use them creatively until such a time as when they might be thrown out altogether. This seems ironic, for many writers in the philosophy of science are careful to warn, often in an admonishing tone, that metaphors should not be too figurative, that is, misleading (e.g., Black, 1962, p. 225; Hinde, 1955). But scientists are not all suckers, they can be quite well aware of the differences between concepts given by the theories and concepts suggested by metaphors. The metaphors and theories are not "confused" but *used* to explore nature and to lead to modifications of principles.

The holographic model of memory may be taken as a good example of this, since debates about it have been well documented (see Arbib, 1972, Chapter 6; Pribram, 1971, Chapter 8). A mathematical instantiation of the holographic hypothesis makes predictions of associations on the basis of interference patterns and reference beams, but the "predictions" of associations ("ghost images") are due largely to the power of the transformations allowed by the mathematics, and not to any model. The mathematics is Fourier analysis and wave mechanics. Any spatially localizable difference between two energies can be expressed as a wave or wave interference effect by changing the resolution or grain of the equations. In fact, the holographic hypothesis has infinite power—it "predicts" (allows for) too much.

One reason why the holographic hypothesis has been troubled by debate is because, it may be said, it is a multileveled or mixed metaphor. Mixing of metaphors occurs in science when a metaphor that is used to explain a theoretical concept refers in its vehicle term to a domain that has its own special explanatory physical theory *and metaphor*. The holographic hypothesis needs constraints based on psychological principles. Pribram (1971) tries to incorporate the holographic hypothesis into an information processing view. This serves the purpose of injecting psychological principles into the hypothesis, but it does so by making the metaphor mixed: The possible combinations of processing-holographing models in the eclecticism are legion. Philosopher Pepper (1942) anticipated the possibility of such eclectic metaphors. He said they would be confusing.

The notion that memories or associations act like holograms may be a powerful notion. We know that memories act like holograms in that no individuated memory seems to be "stored" in an individualizable neural locus—this is the phenomenon that led to the postulation of the holographic hypothesis in the first place. But this may be as far as the holographic hypothesis *can* go—it also does not work at another level—the level of its optical reference. A student once asked Pribram, "But doesn't the laser process destroy brain cells?" (quoted in Arbib, 1972, p. 186). To use the hypothesis and satisfy the equations of wave mechanics one must regard the nervous system as a neural lattice, associative net, or other form of coherent medium. The angle of incidence is equal to the angle of reflection. So what? Yet, at some time in the future a brain or conscious analog may indeed be found for the hypothesis, for example in neuromagnetic waves or electromagnetic graded potentials or something. It has been suggested that those areas of the brain that have layers of interconnected neurons may be regarded as if they generate "waves"—that is, graded electromagnetic potentials (Lashley, Chow, & Semmes, 1951; Pribram, 1971, Chapter 8).

Arbib says that we can use the hypothesis *now* by not taking it "too literally." What he means is that we form a new version of the hypothesis: Memory is conceived of as a dynamic analysis of psychologically relevant perceptual features, with recall conceived of as a reconstructive process based on feedback. Indeed, here Arbib has nearly eliminated the metaphor altogether! Pribram also is clear on the limitations of the hypothesis (1971, pp. 63–66), and he too comes close to modifying the metaphor out of existence. "The essence of the holographic concept is that images are reconstructed when representations in the form of distributed information systems are properly engaged" (p. 152). As J. C. Maxwell pointed out (1890, p. 301), as the incompletenesses of a metaphor are disclosed, the metaphor can be modified, perhaps to the point of generating a literal lypothesis.

Metaphor and Verification

In contrast to the requirement of falsifiability and the attendant possibility of modification of theories and metaphors, we might also require metaphors to be verifiable. Ideally, metaphors should be verifiable in many ways. Just as aesthetically rich metaphors can be given a variety of distinct interpretations, we should be able to check out our scientific metaphors in a number of ways. The best case, the scenario in which scientists have the most to gain, is the case in which we know a little about the topic of the metaphor (the to-be-explained entities in the theory) and a lot about the vehicle term. A good example comes from the kinetic theory of gasses, which relied historically on the metaphor that likened the particles of a gas to billiard balls that bounced off one another, thereby generating heat and pressure. On the basis of assumptions of perfectly elastic pointlike particles and a correspondence of temperature and kinetic energy one can derive statements about gas diffusion rates and expansion rates and one can derive the "ideal gas" laws—which real gases do not follow under all conditions. Dutch physicist Van der Waals pursued the metaphor to refine the theory. "Real" particles, he reasoned, do take up some volume. At the lower temperatures their volume becomes considerable with respect to the paths taken by the particles' motions. Hence, there are deviations from the ideal laws. As a part of the bargain, from Van der Waals's equations one can also derive statements about viscosity. Thus, in redefining the theoretical concept, a metaphor can have an effect on the entire network of principles and concepts in the theory: It can add order and harmony.

THE MANY FORMS OF SCIENTIFIC METAPHOR

The Rhetoric of Scientific Metaphors

There is more than one way to involve a metaphor in a theory. Particular rhetorical forms of figures of speech can be identified with the roles served by metaphor: Metonymy involves attribute-whole and cause-effect relations: *Particles are billiard balls*. Synecdoche involves exchanges of elements within a classification system: *A person is a communications channel*. Oxymoron involves paradox and contradiction: *Particles are waves*. Perhaps a rhetorical analysis could be used by scientists to help generate metaphors tailor-made to the scientific task at hand!

In a *metaphor theme* (Black, 1962), the universe of discourse of the theory is compared *en masse* to some other domain. The mind/brain as a computer is an example of a metaphor theme. As Black saw it, and as philosopher Stephen Pepper foresaw it (1942), metaphor themes can be central to a world view or paradigm, almost a part of metaphysics (*Everything is water*). Pepper showed how metaphor themes are the basis of philosophical "world hypotheses" such as Mechanism, Atomism, and Organicism. Perhaps the existence of this global form of scientific metaphor is why some were led to equate metaphoring with mythologizing. A metaphor theme, at least when expressed as a sentence, will obviously be too terse for use as an actual full-blown scientific theory. It is the more specific properties perceived by the experimenter that lead to the creation of hypotheses or principles. That is, a metaphor theme provides a bunch of related little metaphors, in which a concept or phenomenon in the theory is used as the topic in a metaphor. *Thoughts and brains work like computers work* is perhaps the most salient of psychological metaphor themes. It is *not* a way of making a vague generalization, but a way of introducing specifications or constraints on the definitions of theoretical concepts (e.g., *Short-term memory is a push-down stack*). The vagueness is only apparent and occurs as an epiphenomenon of the search for explanations rather than because of the use of metaphor. Uhr (1966, pp. 366-367) wondered what was meant by the plethora of terms that were being taken from the language of information processing and applied to the description of human memory and pattern recognition, terms such as trace, reconstruction, transformation, operation, mapping, and the like. But compare this criticism, that is, that the computer model is in one way or another vague (cf. Dresher & Hornstein, 1976; Dreyfus, 1972; Moor, 1978), to recent treatments of the complexities in the philosophy of artificial intelligence (Haugeland, 1978; Hunt, 1971; L. Miller, 1978; Pylyshyn, 1978). Here are some of the specific issues: (1)

How do types of computer memory correspond with types of human memory? Do computers represent information and meaning in ways like people do? (2) How do the types of computer message analysis (parsing routines) correspond with how people parse messages? (3) How can computers show intention or will? (4) How would computer subroutines correspond with brain structures? Can psychological functions be "carved up" spatially as they are in computers? (5) Should a human capability be programmed by "brute forcing" information into memory or should the capability be represented by strategies and programs that modify themselves? Psychologists have also benefited from the metaphor. The information processing language is precise and powerful. Distinctions such as between encoding, storage, and retrieval have for some time been used to extend cognitive-learning theory and to lead to new experiments (cf. Anderson & Bower, 1972). In short, there is as much detail derivable from the metaphor theme as the analyst cares to look for.

Indeed, this can be taken a step further. It may be possible to analyze and classify information processing models, mental representations, and even syntactical or propositional representations according to their manner of metaphorical expression of time, process and structure.

Image, Metaphor, Model, and Theory

Galleons of scholars describe an important role of mental imagery in scientific metaphors (Asch, 1958; Deese, 1972; Kuhn, 1979; McCloskey, 1964; Paivio, 1979; Steenburgh, 1965; Vico, 1948; and others). They describe metaphors as namings based on a salient image or powerful perceptual resemblance that can somehow take precedence over a theory that may be more abstract or elaborate. Thus, metaphor may be inevitable and necessary to science, and cognitively prior to scientific description, because of psychological factors in learning, inference-making, symbol-formation, and explanation (Hester, 1967; Langer, 1957; Pollio, Barlow, Fine, & Pollio, 1977; Ortony, 1975; Schon, 1963). Einstein's images of riding a beam of light and other *Gedanken* experiments, as they were later called, were essential to and psychologically prior to the mathematical laws that so influenced physics. In fact, Einstein himself created a flow diagram representing the process of creative thought, including places for imagery and intuition (see Greenberg, 1979). An examination of the vehicle terms used in scientific metaphors supports the claim that images are important. It seems as if anything concrete goes—pinwheels, elevators, pumps, apples, paper bags, pianos, garbage cans, bullets, funnels, maps, puzzles, snakes, playing cards, etc. (see Dreistadt, 1968). Available analyses of scientists' thinking, the questionnaire studies by Roe (1951) and Walkup (1965), show that scientists often report using mental imagery.

It should come as little surprise then, that metaphor is implicated in theorizing by what J. C. Maxwell called "physical analogy" and by what others called material analogy, picture theories, isomorphic theories, analogistic theories, scale models, analog models, substantive analogy, or analogistic models.[5] Black (1962, Chapter 13) and Kaplan (1965, Chapter 7) clarified the various meanings and uses of the term *model*. According to the semantics of the word, a model instantiates some of the structure of the theoretical entities in a real substantive thing. The theory *describes* the structure in a symbolic representation. A model, thus, can be distinguished from the theory and hypotheses it instantiates and from the metaphor used to express the theory in terms of, or by reference to, the model. In the model, the universe of discourse of the theory is instantiated by a physical thing with visualizable parts and relations that somehow correspond with the theoretical entities and their relations. For example, the computer metaphor theme involves a theory (linguistic descriptions in information processing terms of the theoretical principles that govern the workings of cognition), the model (actual computer mechanisms and their hardware and software instantiations of the principles) and the metaphor theme itself.

The distinction between theory, metaphor, and model is a good working scheme, yet it does get fuzzy since people can conceive of a model, not only by an act of perception of a thing, but also by an intentional mental act of representation in imagery (cf. Black, 1962, pp. 220, 222). That is, some models can be mental and yet model-like. Engineering wizard Nikola Tesla could design, construct, and test machines all in the medium of mental imagery: "As a child he often confused his visions and the real world. Later his ability made it possible for him to imagine a motor, for instance, and then mentally to build the motor from scratch, run it, and then inspect it for wear" (Spurgeon, 1977, p. 65). Tesla's idea for alternating current circuitry came as a vision when he recited some lines from *Faust:*

> The glow retreats, done is the day of toil;
> It yonder hastes, new fields of life exploring;
> Ah that no wing can lift me from the soil,
> Upon its track to follow, follow soaring.

"As I spoke the last words, plunged in thought and marveling at the power of the poet, the idea came like a lightning flash. In an instant I saw it all." His image involved solutions to the problem of constructing a workable electric motor and a working AC system—the whole thing was designed mentally before being written down and patented (Spurgeon, p. 65).

But not all models can be imagined by all people.

---

[5]Black, 1962; Brodbeck, 1968; Gregory, 1953; Hanson, 1970; Hemple, 1965; Hesse, 1966; Hutten, 1954; Lachman, 1960; Nagel, 1961; Simon & Newell, 1956; Turbayne, 1962. They all meant pretty much the same thing by the terms they used—a model as defined here.

There are men who, when any relation or law, however complex, is put before them in a symbolic form, can grasp its full meaning as a relation among abstract quantities. Such men sometimes treat with indifference the further statement that quantities actually exist in nature which fulfill the relations. The mental image of the concrete reality seems rather to distract them than to assist their contemplations. . . . Others, again, are not content unless they can project their whole physical energies into the scene which they conjur up (Maxwell, 1890, pp. 218–220).

Some models can be imagined and yet will retain some important functional characteristics of the stuff being modeled. Few could imagine a full working computer model, say for playing chess, yet most people could imagine a schematic flow diagram of a chess-playing program. My preference, since not all of us have the right-brained intellectual capacity of Tesla, is to regard the mental representation (conceptual, mental speech, or mental imagery) as metaphorical. The explicit sentence metaphor is called the *metaphor,* the actual thing is referred to as the *model,* and the theory and hypotheses that the model and image and metaphor instantiate are called the *theory.* With Hutten (1954) I think these distinctions are prudent. Certainly they are preferable to the compound ambiguities:

1. Equating models and theories or models and metaphors (Brodbeck, 1968), which has the effect of allowing one to say that theories can model other theories and laws can model other laws.
2. Defining models as being symbolic (mathematical or linguistic), which means that no thing could be a model (Duhem, 1906, Part 1, Chapter 4; Turner, 1967).
3. Calling any formal representation, mathematization, quantified hypothesis, or conceptualization a model (Bjork, 1973; Bunge, 1967; Hesse, 1953).

The distinction between model, metaphor, and theory is best seen in physics, where the theories themselves are distinct by virtue of being mathematical, the models are quite tangible, and the metaphors quite explicit. In James Clerk Maxwell's words, the key to the metaphor and model is "a collection of imaginary properties which may be explored for establishing certain theories in pure mathematics in a way more intelligible to many minds and more applicable to physical problems than that in which algebraic symbols alone are used" (Maxwell, 1890, p. 160).

Some recent psychologists who consider the cognitive-semantic status of scientific metaphors have tried to relate them to "mental schemas" (Brown, Collins, & Harris, 1979; Collins & Gentner, 1978; Gentner, 1978; Rumelhart, 1979). Though a valid enough psychological notion, this must not be taken to suggest that models can be of abstract content. Such is usually not the case for scientific models and metaphors. Indeed, Campbell (1920, 1953), Hesse (1966), Hanson (1970), and J. C. Maxwell (1890, pp. 155–156) claim that *by definition* theories in physics rely for their interpretation and intelligibility on concrete imageable referents and representations, models possibly referred to in the form of a metaphor.

The distinction between model, image, theory, and metaphor indicates another way in which some accusations that metaphors "hide truth" may themselves be misguided. To illustrate this I'll explain a widely cited scientific metaphor, the orbit metaphor for atomic structure. First, consider why this metaphor is used so much as an example—because the idea was very insightful and because the metaphor led to a concrete expression of a conceptual paradox, the wave-particle duality.

In the years 1913–1925 the quantum hypothesis was hot news. Physicist Niehls Bohr began his search for a structural explanation of the behavior of atoms with Ernest Rutherford's metaphor—Bohr called it the *Atommodell*. The electron, a lesser mass, could be likened to a planet orbiting a sun, the larger mass. Using the Rutherford metaphor to set the stage for a mechanistic description of atoms, Bohr was free to borrow equations from astronomy. He did. He took Hamilton's astronomical principle of orbital angles and made it work for atoms:

> If we apply the usual laws of mechanics, then we obtain directly [an equation] from Hamilton's Principle that holds for all systems in which the frequency of the wave is a constant. . . . Let us consider an electron that revolves around a positively charged nucleus with an infinite mass. In the stationary condition of the system, the movement of the electron, without any other field, will be an ellipse with the nucleus in the focus.[6]

This seems to be straight-forward Keplerian astronomy. Bohr derived a specific principle, itself actually a terse mathematical expression. The motion of the electron about the nucleus (a difference between two energies) is restricted to integral multiples of Planck's constant. This constant relates packets or quanta of energy to wavelength. This was Bohr's insight. An electron orbit path exactly "fits" a wave, each atom has its own spectral fingerprint. One can imagine a sine-wave, as Louis deBroglie did, in undulation on a path such that an orbit of

---

[6]The German reads: "*Gebrauchen wir die gewhönlichen Gesetze der Mechanik, so erhalten wir unmittelbar aus den Hamiltonischen Prinzip . . . [an equation] . . . dass für jedes System, in dem die Frequenz der Schwingung konstant ist . . .*" (Bohr, 1914, p. 125), and, "*Betrachten wir ein Elektron, das um einen positiven Kern von unendlich grosser Masse kreist. In den stationären Zuständen des Systems wird die Bewegung des Elektrons ohne irgend ein Feld eine Ellipse mit dem Kern im Fokus sein*" (Bohr, 1914, p. 519). These passages are from Bohr's important early papers on atomic structure, reprinted in Bohr, 1921.

the wave exactly evens out to a multiple of the frequency: Higher frequency, more energy, "wider orbital path."[7]

The solar system orbit metaphor for atoms does without the algebraic assistance of Planck's constant. The Bohr principle cannot do without the math, it *is* math. It is in this sense that it is said a metaphor or model is crude, that it hides truth (Chapanis, 1961). But is it right to say that either the solar system model or metaphor for atom structure hides truth? No. It is the job of the theory to express all the detailed math. Why fault the metaphor for hiding what it was not intended to express, for lacking details it never hid? Witness Bohr's own words: "When it comes to atoms, language can be used only as in poetry. The poet, too, is not so concerned with describing facts as with creating images" (quoted by Bronowski, 1973, p. 340).

The Role of Metaphor in Scientific Discovery

Metaphor helps in the scientific enterprise in educational or pedagogic ways—to explain a principle or theory. Metaphor can be used to learn a theory, to teach a theory, to remember a theory. It can be used to describe methods, too. My favorite is the gene experiment where enzymes are used to break up a DNA strand so that the pieces can be examined. This has been called a "shotgun blast design." Metaphor, in sum, can provide a satisfying explanation of a method, theory, or phenomenon: "So *that's* what you mean!"

Philosophers regard the pedagogical aspects to be important for the cognitive status of theories, and therefore important for science itself. If a metaphor or model explains the unfamiliar in terms of the familiar, then it can do so for the theorist as well as the student (Hanson, 1970; Nagel, 1961; Pylyshyn, 1979). Indeed, it can be argued that the metaphors that really led to scientific advancement are those that evoke a deep sense of insight in scientists and students— "Aha!"—metaphors like Kekule's snake image for the benzene ring. Kekule's conception of atoms wriggling and turning like a snake biting its tail suggested to him that molecules may be so shaped, rather than being only chains of atoms. This metaphor solved many problems in chemistry.[8]

---

[7]The trick for Bohr was to show why the electron did not decay continuously toward the nucleus, emitting continuous radiation as it fell. Bohr argued for stable, limited orbits or energy states. Electrons "jumped" from one "shell" to another. From the modern perspective, this seems to have led Bohr away from a strictly Keplerian ("classical") mechanics—the orbit atom of the 1910's became an "onion atom" in the 1920's. But the orbit atom was not ad hoc. It explained a lot, in detail, and it predicted x-ray spectra, the possibility and characteristics of synthetic elements, and it explained the properties of elements as given in the periodic table. It did leave unexplained how, in Ernest Rutherford's terms, "an electron knows beforehand where to stop." Louis deBroglie's notion of standing matter-waves got at this.

[8]Feynman (1965) is an excellent source of examples of explanation that rely on playful, creative, pedagogic metaphors.

It is possible for a metaphor to be intended as purely illustrative. For example, Reichenbach (1951, p. 182) moralized Heisenberg's uncertainty principle (also actually a terse mathematical expression): "In our intercourse with electrons we cannot don civilian clothes; when we watch them we always disrupt traffic." But having a pedagogical intention does not preclude scientific utility (cf. Black, 1962, p. 237). In other words, metaphors do not play the role of pedagogic but otherwise sterile crutches (Chapanis, 1961, p. 120). They can be sources of creativity, and they can be deliberately used in learning situations (Collins & Gentner, 1978; Gentner, 1978).

Within science, metaphor plays many creative roles. Simply by virtue of the fact that scientists can recognize them, metaphor can add both structure and a healthy playful spirit to the inquiry. In the language of experimental design, metaphor can suggest new predictions, new demonstrations, and new experiments both of the hypothesis test and converging operation sort. A metaphor can suggest new theoretical entities or concepts, or reinterpretations of old ones. A metaphor can suggest new structural interrelations or similarities between the theoretical entities, that is, new categories of entities or properties. Not all of the concepts in a theory are translatable into observables, only some are. The metaphor may suggest new functional relations, possibly of a specified mathematical form. The relations will suggest correspondences between concepts, principles, or dispositions in the theory and certain observations. For example, Bohr's quantization of electrons meant that an electron "jump" should show up as spectral lines of radiated energy.

In comparison to a rival theory or hypothesis, a metaphor may show how a literal description may be wrong; the metaphor may be better. A good example of a metaphor outdoing a literal theory is given by Hesse (1962). Paul Dirac elegantly interpreted the equations of quantum mechanics (a bunch of vectors) in terms of a metaphor of holes (vector spaces) and jumps in state. This led him to postulate the existence of positrons, but the literal equations would not so directly have identified the negative energy states involved for these particles. Another good example of a metaphor winning out is Mendeleev's adherence to the concept of a periodic table—a name derived from a metaphor likening the properties of the elements to acoustic (periodic) harmonics. Mendeleev used cards identifying the elements, and he tacked the cards up so that they fell into "suits" according to their properties. The concept of a periodic table ran into snags since it assigned some elements the "wrong" properties (i.e., atomic weights). The discovery of isotopes cleared the classification problem up, and Mendeleev's concept was vindicated.

MAKING A METAPHOR

Hanson (1958) and Simon (1973), and others, proposed that the "logic" of scientific discovery is a psychological affair, a matter of heuristics and efficiency, and not a philosophical affair of deductions, inductions, and prediction. Some in the philosophy of science who realized this, like Popper (1959, pp. 31–32), argued that the topic of scientific discovery was therefore irrelevant to the philosophical-logical analysis of theories. The psychologist who follows Simon's lead need not necessarily view scientific discovery and theorizing as *irreducibly* intuitive, irrational, or even mystical. The creative process in scientific problem-solving *can* be described (metaphor seems to be one important way of describing it), and the description may indeed have implications for the philosophy of science. For instance, as James Deese (1972, Chapter 2) pointed out, different theories in different disciplines will have different domains to explain, and since human theorists may understand the domains in different ways, the theories may differ in form, as well as content, and they may have to be assessed by different kinds of metatheoretic criteria. A theory of personality may be written as words and will have to make intuitive sense to psychologists. A theory in physics may make intuitive sense to physicists, but will have to be written at least in part with mathematics. A metaphor may be necessary for one domain of theory and yet metaphor may not be needed for another domain.

Suppose there is a phenomenon or concept or theoretical entity for which the scientist seeks an understanding. The Concept, as I'll label it, is to appear as the Topic in a metaphor. The Concept may begin with some properties or affordances that are literally and explicitly dictated by the principles, measures, and entities already in the theory.[9] The Concept may also start off with some properties from the ordinary language if the Concept happens to involve a term in the ordinary language (e.g., atom, ego, mind). The Concept will be used in a metaphor with some Vehicle. The Vehicle will also begin with some literal properties due possibly to the use of the Vehicle term in ordinary language (e.g., solar system, helmsman, computer) or possibly due to the reference the Vehicle term makes to some substantive theory from a domain other than that of the Topic (e.g., Keplerian mechanics, information processing terminology). As a consequence of the metaphor, the properties of the Vehicle may be regarded as being distinguishable into at *least* two subsets. Certain properties of the Vehicle can be regarded as literally applicable to the Topic, some as figuratively applicable to the Topic. If the Vehicle refers to a domain with its own substantive theory, laws that describe the Vehicle may be applied to the Topic Concept.

Property Correspondence and Property Similarity

For a metaphor to work some of its implications must fit with the rest of the theory of which the Topic Concept is a part. That is, some of the properties

---

[9]Here, I dance around the psycholinguistic issue of "features." Feature systems in semantics are really a special kind of metaphor for representing the distinctions we draw. As such, there's nothing necessarily wrong with them. Serious philosophical and psychological problems arise when features are granted ontological status, that is, when it is assumed that features represent something that is really "out there," or really "in there," as the case may be.

suggested by the Vehicle must correspond with properties of the Topic as dictated by the theory. If none of the properties correspond, the metaphor might never have been conceived. To illustrate, suppose we "turn a metaphor on its head" and try to explain solar systems by saying that they are like atoms. With a little "ad hocery" the Bohr equations *can* be used to make predictions of the orbits of the planets. This is a great exercise in number-crunching, but little more, for the metaphor, *Solar systems are atoms*, fails because it refers to an inadequate model. The set of literal properties of atoms does not seem to contain properties that clearly correspond with those of solar systems as dictated by the astrophysical equations of gravity and acceleration.[10]

Some overlap of the Topic and the Vehicle is inevitable because anything can be seen as similar to anything. But overlap is not enough for a metaphor to have value. It may reflect only the hunch-seeking stage where metaphoring and theorizing can be more like a remote associates test. Jones' theory says that cancer cells act like springs in response to traumas. Both certain cancers and certain springs follow exponential laws. So what?

The utility of a metaphor shows up when it suggests ("new") properties in the Vehicle that were not attributed to the Topic on the basis of the theory and that could not be attributed to the Topic on the basis of the theory alone. Some of the literal properties of the Vehicle may not be applicable to the Topic and may even trivialize the theory. An atom (Topic) cannot be said to have a diameter of billions of miles (literally true of the solar system), but it can be said to have a limit to its diameter, and the Bohr equations could be used to set bounds on an atom's "diameter." In other words, a property of the Vehicle may seem irrelevant or trivial or absurd when applied to the Topic Concept in the theory—the property will *not* correspond with a property that is given by the theory (Hesse [1966] called this the "negative" part of the analogy!). However, a derivative or related property might be relevant! A once-literal property of the Vehicle is conceived and the experimenter realizes that *something like* that property may be applicable to the Topic. The experimenter can try and find ways of coordinating the "new" property of the Vehicle with some heretofore undescribed property of the Topic as yet not directly attributed to the Topic by the theory. Thus, the metaphor entails modification of the theory by redefining the Topic. But the redefinition occurs in a certain way . . . the use of metaphor in science can be, must be, described as complex mapping operations, not a single mapping based on property correspondence, that is, overlap of Topic and Vehicle domains. The similarity of Topic and Vehicle depends not only on the perception of property correspondence but also on the perception (creative discovery) of property similarity.

---

[10]For scientific metaphors, the Topic is based not only on the meanings of the term from ordinary language, but also on the theory. The Vehicle may also tap into a theory (e.g., Bohr's metaphor, *Atoms are solar systems*, tapped into principles from Keplerian astronomy). Thus, scientific metaphors may not be symmetrical (see Connor & Kogan, this volume). There may be little reason to suppose why scientific metaphors might or should be symmetrical.

The Metaphoring Process

Metaphoring cannot be regarded as a static aspect of theorizing. One cannot be certain a priori about all the properties in the Vehicle that will make for a useful metaphor as long as one cannot know how or where to separate the Vehicle into literal and figurative properties, in other words, as long as the Topic is open for further conceptualization. Thus, perhaps one cannot know how to decide correctly about a theory only on the basis of metaphoricalness. For example, aether theory involved a hypothetical medium for the transmission of energy, a metaphor. But aether theorists could not have known it was a blind alley until its implications were pursued. One cannot be certain that all the relevant properties of the Vehicle have been found. To presume so would be to adopt a static view of the science process. Kaplan (1965) said it less formally: "There is no limit to the metaphors by which we can effectively convey what we know. . . . It would be rash indeed to attempt a priori to set limits on the fruitfulness of models" (pp. 287, 292). To perpetuate a sharp literal-figurative distinction is, in effect, to rule out the utility of metaphors. Metaphors must be pursued or intuited away: There can be no rational basis for a decision until the metaphor has been explored. To have a metaphor means to have hope.

Psychological Hypotheses About Metaphor Comprehension

How does this analysis compare with available views about how metaphors are understood? Numerous scholars have speculated about metaphor comprehension. To make sense of the various positions I consider here some general viewpoints and only a few specific theorists. In the general tradition of rhetoric and the notion of "poetic compression" are those who claim that it may be impossible to give a complete literal paraphrase of some metaphors, or that it may be impossible to fully specify the rules for comprehending metaphors (Black, 1962; Campbell, 1975; Ortony, 1975; Henle, 1958). The distinction between theory, model, and metaphor suggests that as far as the theory is concerned, the model is an interpretation. It is not *the* interpretation. But whether or not a metaphor can be given a (verbal) literal paraphrase need not keep us from analyzing and using our scientific metaphors. The moral is that the meaning of metaphors is open— there may always be something new to learn.

In the Aristotelian tradition are those who consider metaphor to be a statement of resemblance, simile, analogy, or comparison in which the topic and vehicle are somehow regarded as having shared features (Fraser, 1979; Nemetz, 1958). Property correspondence is an important aspect of the use of metaphor in science. But a theory is not metaphorical just because it may point out correspondences of features, nor does the content of scientific metaphors consist only of statements of shared features. The present analysis fits more with the tradition following Richards (1936). The words of a metaphor are said to "interact" and to be comprehended together to allow the creative discovery of a new meaning

(Berggren, 1962; Ortony, 1979). In the present analysis this is called the perception of property similarity.

There are more detailed theories in psychology that are processing views. In general, they assert that the literal meaning of a metaphor is always comprehended first, resulting in an anomalous reading. The literal meaning and structure are then used to "compute" or derive the intended figurative meaning. This notion, or subtle variations of it, is common to many scholars (e.g., Clark & Clark, 1977; Cohen, 1979; Kuhn, 1979; Searle, 1979; Smith, Rips, & Shoben, 1974). On some thought, this view actually suggests entire classes of possible process-representation hypotheses that can be used to make predictions about, say, the time it takes people to comprehend metaphors as opposed to literal statements. In Kintsch's (1974) version, any sentence that contains a contradiction of semantic features (oxymoron) is a potential metaphor. Its figurative meaning is derived by special transformation and analogy rules. One could postulate that metaphorical meaning relies on the filtering out of usual word meanings and the discovery of unusual ones. If meanings are scanned in parallel, one would not necessarily expect it to take longer to comprehend metaphorical meaning. On the other hand, even with a parallel search process, if the metaphorical word meanings are stored low down in a push-down stack then it might take longer to comprehend metaphors even if there is not a special metaphor comprehension process.

Metaphoring in science is often a very long and drawn-out process. Metaphor themes have long lives because of thematic inclusiveness, but even a specific metaphor can take years to unravel. In science one can latch upon a metaphor or intuitively appealing vision (e.g., waves) and ride the vision for years, for generations, trying to unpack its implications (e.g., Bohr equations, wave-particle dualities, etc.). Psychological processing hypotheses about the *creation* of metaphors (the scenario of interest in the case of scientific discovery and use) are nearly nonexistent, excepting the accounts by psychodynamic and motivational theorists. But on a fundamental level, the process of metaphoring in science does not seem to be one of an exclusively sequential series of operations based on the recognition of anomaly. Scientists do sometimes try and make sense out of anomalous *phenomena*. Metaphors do not begin anomalous, but meaningful—concepts are being compared. It is only after the analysis, perhaps when it all is put down in linguistic form (i.e., after the original insight) that what come to be labeled as the "unacceptable" or "anomalous" aspects of a metaphor can possibly be singled out to have their sway over the useful aspects.

BACK TO PHILOSOPHY

Finally, a return to consider the sources in philosophy in light of the present analysis. There is an important complication in the sparring match over the use of metaphors in science, a complication yet to be brought explicitly into the ring (cf. Black, 1962, p. 236). One can be either for or against the use of metaphor in *theorizing* without necessarily being either for or against the use of metaphor in *theories*. Those philosophers of an operationist persuasion who see metaphor as a linguistic curse might want to eliminate metaphor altogether. On the other hand, those who advocate the use of metaphor often rely on examples that seem to involve metaphor in theorizing. On close inspection of some scientific metaphors, however, the metaphors do seem to be, at least in part, actually ''in'' the theory.

It would be possible to rewrite the Bohr atom theory (1921), eliminating all the words and leaving only the math. Some philosophers would say that what is left *is* the theory. That may be, but only to a person who knows how the math is to be interpreted. Is the issue whether to include in the theory the metaphorical parts of the interpretation of the math? The metaphorical parts helped Bohr generate the math—they were a part of Bohr's theorizing. But, it turns out, in Bohr's theory metaphorical expressions occur in the derivations of the math and in the sentences that exposit theory. For some equations and derivations, as well as sentences, some parts seem to properly be called astronomy and some parts seem to be atomic physics. (See Footnote 6.) For scientific metaphors, as exemplified in this chapter, the metaphor is important in theorizing *and* it can be a part of the theory. Psychologically, comprehension and *theorizing* are all we really have, anyway. There are no theories—if theories are to be conceived of as written ''carriers'' of meaning with an existence independent of a cognizing theorist. Written ''theories,'' like words, are stimulus symbols that have to be the objects of someone's mental acts to be labeled as ''theories.'' When a metaphor is used as part of a written exposition of a theory, it reflects the fact that the Vehicle was used in theorizing to define or redefine (at least) the Concept (Topic) in the theory. The metaphor Vehicle interacts with the theory. So some of the metaphor, at least, is a ''part'' of the theory. To J. C. Maxwell, a scientific metaphor is a ''golden mean''—it stands halfway between the physical analogy or model and the theory and mathematization. It is generative of both, and a part of both.

Assuming that a metaphor or part of a metaphor can be included in a theory, operationists might want to chop up the metaphor, to eliminate the figurative Vehicle from the theory while including the redefined Topic Concept. That is, they would try by some logical means to make the sets of literal and figurative properties separate. All the meaning of the Topic Concept would be regarded as coming from the properties given by the theory plus whatever notions came into the theory from the metaphor before the metaphor was thrown out. This disjunction, interestingly, would occur as a logical consequence of writing the ''Ramsey sentence'' of the theory (see Braithwaite, 1953, p. 58). Simply, each occurrence of the concept that is used metaphorically would be replaced by an abstract symbol that would denote a list of the properties of the concept dictated by the theory. In the grandest spirit of operationalism-positivism, this would indeed "demetaphor" the theory and eliminate surplus meaning, but it also eliminates any further utility the metaphor might have had.

The present analysis supports a claim made by Popper, by Carnap, and by G. Maxwell (1970) that there can be no strict inductive justification (a priori) for belief in scientific (here, metaphoric) principles. Hesse argued somewhat similarly that the postulation of new entities for a pre-existing theory must involve metaphorical extensions since a strictly deductive or rational method cannot make such postulations without recourse to further thought and experiment. One may not be able to see which characteristics of a model can be exploited and which are irrelevant. Hutten (1954) and Lachman (1960) argued that models may be evaluated a priori, that is, by rational rather than by empirical means, according to their scope and precision. Yet, they too maintained that there can be no sufficient rational grounds for determining how *well* a model will work out. As Berggren (1963) put it, "By the interaction of formal theory with experimentally determined fact both are transformed yet preserved . . . neither scientific nor poetic metaphors can reveal except by creating, precisely because they partially create what in fact they reveal" (p. 462). In terms of the present analysis, there is no deductive means for deciding exactly which metaphor to introduce (or throw out), or for deciding which correspondence rules to use to fit the redefined terms back into the theory. The moral? Don't reject any metaphor offhand because of metaphoricalness.

Although an exploration of the meaning and implications of metaphor is necessary to determine whether the metaphor will pay off, science does not act this way. Metaphors get rejected for some fundamental reasons involving the theorist's motivations, the *Zeitgeist*, etc.

I believe that this exercise has been fruitful, partially for the listing out of the uses and misuses of metaphor in science. It was not clear before, nor is it crystal clear afterwards, how different types of scientific metaphors fit in with scientific progress. The situation is complex; many specific questions can be asked. In what cases, if any, will a metaphor serve a necessary scientific function? How must the nature of a metaphor fit in with how people understand the domain of a theory? I have described the mixed scientific metaphor, the scientific metaphor theme, and the scientific metaphor that redefines a concept from a theory. How can these, and possibly other forms of scientific metaphors, be reliably distinguished? Would a knowledge of the rhetorical forms of metaphors assist people in problem-solving situations? How can cognitive psychologists describe more aspects of metaphoring, such as the unconscious emotive mental work that results in insight and the creation of new meanings? It is now pretty much old hat in philosophy of science to recognize the role of psychological factors in the scientific enterprise. Beyond this, this chapter suggests that more specific rapprochment between the disciplines would be useful—to examine the more specific types of cognition and to turn ideas such as those presented here into principles that working scientists and educators might make use of. I hope, at least, to have encouraged debate on all this.

Perhaps a rhetorician would have claimed at the outset that the comprehension of meaning must come before the discovery of merit. Both poetry and science can be means of validating what we apprehend. But it seems to be a long way from actual poems to actual theories and there are few explicit bridges between them.

ACKNOWLEDGMENT

Preparation of the chapter was supported by grant 1T32-HD07151 from the National Institute for Child Health and Human Development to the Center for Research in Human Learning. I would like to thank my friends, Dr. Walter Carnahan of the Department of Physics, Indiana State University, Mark Dorfmueller of the Kettering Laboratory of the University of Cincinnati, and David Tukey of the Center for Research in Human Learning. Our discussions were very fruitful of new ideas and of clarifications of old ones. I would also like to thank those at the Center and at the Department of Psychology of the University of Minnesota who provided some fantastic feedback on earlier incarnations of this chapter: Liam Bannon, Joseph Blount, Maddy Brouwer-Janse, David Finkelman, Leah Larkey, James Nead, and Dr. Ruth Pitt. None of these people deserves any blame for the outrageous things I say here; they all receive my thanks for our many stimulating debates. I would also like to acknowledge a debt to Paul E. Meehl, whose lectures on the philosophy of science were extremely influential. Address all correspondence to: Robert R. Hoffman, 205 Elliott Hall, 75 East River Road, Minneapolis, Minnesota 55455.

REFERENCES

Anderson, J. R., & Bower, G. H. *Human associative memory*. Hillsdale, N. J.: Lawrence Erlbaum Associates, 1972.

Arbib, M. A. *The metaphorical brain*. New York: Wiley, 1972.

Asch, S. The metaphor: A psychological inquiry. In R. Taguiri & L. Petrullo (Eds.), *Person perception and interpersonal behavior*. Stanford, Calif.: Stanford University Press, 1958.

Ayer, A. J. (Ed.) *Logical positivism*. New York: Free Press, 1959.

Beardsley, M. C. The metaphorical twist. *Philosophy and Phenomenological Research*, 1962, *22*, 293–307.

Bentley, M. The nature and uses of experiment in psychology. *American Journal of Psychology*, 1937, *50*, 452–469.

Berggren, D. The use and abuse of metaphor I. *Review of Metaphysics*, 1962, *16*, 237–258.

Berggren, D. The use and abuse of metaphor II. *Review of Metaphysics*, 1963, *16*, 450–472.

Bergmann, G. The subject matter of psychology. *Philosophy of Science*, 1940, *7*, 415–433.

Bergmann, G., & Spence, K. W. Operationism and theory in psychology. *Psychological Review*, 1941, *48*, 1–14.

Bills, A. Changing views of psychology as a science. *Psychological Review*, 1938, *45*, 377–394.

Bjork, R. A. Why mathematical models? *American Psychologist*, 1973, *28*, 426–433.

Black, M. *Models and metaphors*. Ithaca, N. Y.: Cornell University Press, 1962.

Bohr, N. Über den Einfluss elektrischer und magnetischer Felder auf Spektrallinen. *Philosophical Magazine*, 1914, *27*, 506–524.

Bohr, N. *Abhandlungen uber Atombau aus den Jahren 1913–1916*. Braunschweig, Germany: Druck and Verlag, 1921.

Boyd, R. The role of metaphor in conceptual change. In A. Ortony (Ed.) *Metaphor and thought*. Cambridge, England: Cambridge University Press, 1979.

Braithwaite, R. B. *Scientific explanation*. Cambridge, England: Cambridge University Press, 1953.

Breal, M. *Semantics: Studies in the science of meaning*. New York: Dover, 1969. Originally published 1887. See Chapters 6 & 11.

Bridgman, R. *The logic of modern physics*. New York: Macmillan, 1927.

Bridgman, R. *The nature of physical theory*. Princeton, N. J.: Princeton University Press, 1936.

Brodbeck. A. Models, meaning and theories. In M. Brodbeck (Ed.), *Readings in the philosophy of the social sciences*. New York: Macmillan, 1968.

Bronowski, J. *The ascent of man*. Boston, Mass.: Little, Brown, 1973.

Brown, J. S., Collins, A., & Harris, G. Artificial intelligence and learning strategies. In H. F. O'Neil (Ed.), *Innovations in instructional systems development*. New York: Academic Press, 1979.

Bunge, M. *Scientific research II: The search for truth*. New York: Springer-Verlag, 1967.

Cambell, N. R. *Physics: The elements*. Cambridge, England: Cambridge University Press, 1920.

Cambell, N. R. The structure of theories. In H. Feigl & M. Brodbeck (Eds.), *Readings in the philosophy of science*. New York: Appleton-Century-Crofts, 1953.

Campbell, P. N. Metaphor and linguistic theory. *Quarterly Journal of Speech*, 1975, *61*, 1–12.

Carnap, R. Testability and meaning. *Philosophy of Science*, 1937, *4*, 1–40.

Carnap, R. On inductive logic. *Philosophy of Science*, 1945, *12*, 72–97.

Carnap, R. The methodological character of theoretical terms. In H. Feigl & M. Scriven (Eds.), *Minnesota studies in the philosophy of science, Volume 1*. Minneapolis: University of Minnesota Press, 1956.

Carnap, R. Psychology in physical language. In A. J. Ayer (Ed.), *Logical positivism*. New York: Free Press, 1959.

Chapanis, A. Men, machines and models. *American Psychologist*, 1961, *16*, 113–131.

Chomsky, N. Review of B. F. Skinner's *Verbal behavior*. *Language*, 1959, *35*, 26–58.

Chomsky, N. *Aspects of the theory of syntax*. Cambridge, Mass.: The M.I.T. Press, 1965.

Clark, H. H., & Clark, E. V. *Psychology and language*. New York: Harcourt Brace Jovanovich, 1977.

Cohen, T. Reply to Sadock. In A. Ortony (Ed.), *Metaphor and thought*. Cambridge, England: Cambridge University Press, 1979.

Collins, A., & Gentner, D. *The role of analogical models in learning scientific topics*. Cambridge, Mass.: Bolt, Beranek and Newman Report, Proposal Number P78–ISD-64, 1978.

Couch, A., & Keniston, K. Yeasayers and naysayers: Agreeing response set as a personality variable. *Journal of Abnormal and Social Psychology*, 1960, *60*, 151–174.

Culler, J. *Structuralist poetics*. Ithaca, N. Y.: Cornell University Press, 1975, Chapter 5.

Deese, J. *Psychology as science and art*. New York: Harcourt Brace Jovanovich, 1972.

Dreistadt, R. An analysis of the use of analogies and metaphors in science. *The Journal of Psychology*, 1968, *68*, 97–116.

Dresher, B. E., & Hornstein, N. On some supposed contributions of artificial intelligence to the scientific study of language. *Cognition*, 1976, *4*, 321–398.

Dreyfus, H. *What computers can't do*. New York: Harper and Row, 1972.

Duhem, P. *The aim and structure of physical theory*. Originally published 1906, Translated by P. P. Weiner. Princeton, N. J.: Princeton University Press, 1954.

Edie, J. M. Expression and metaphor. *Philosophy and Phenomenological Research*, 1963, *23*, 538–561.

Feld, M. S., McNair, R. E., & Wilk, S. R. The physics of karate. *Scientific American*, 1979, *240* (4), 150–158.

Feynman, R. *The character of physical law*. Cambridge, Mass.: The M.I.T. Press, 1965.

Fraser, B. Reply to Paivio. In A. Ortony (Ed.), *Metaphor and thought*. Cambridge, England: Cambridge University Press, 1979.

Freud, S. *Psychopathology of everyday life*. London: Liveright, 1905.

Gentner, D. *The role of analogical models in learning scientific topics*. Cambridge, Mass.: Bolt Beranek and Newman Report, 1978.

George, F. H. Logical constructs and psychological theory. *Psychological Review*, 1953, *60*, 1-6.

Gordon, W. J. *Synectics*. New York: Harper, 1961.

Green, T. F. Metaphor and learning: A response. In A. Ortony (Ed.), *Metaphor and thought*. Cambridge, England: Cambridge University Press, 1979.

Greenberg, J. Einstein: The gourmet of creativity. *Science News*, 1979, *115*, 216-217.

Gregory, J. C. *A short history of atomism*. London: A. & C. Black, 1931.

Gregory, R. L. On physical model explanations in psychology. *British Journal for the Philosophy of Science*, 1953, *4*, 192-197.

Hall, E. W. Some dangers of the use of symbolic logic in psychology. *Psychological Review*, 1942, *49*, 142-169.

Hanson, N. R. *Patterns of discovery*. Cambridge, England: Cambridge University Press, 1958.

Hanson, N. R. A picture theory of theory meaning. In R. G. Colodny (Ed.), *The nature and function of scientific theories*. Pittsburgh: University of Pennsylvania Press, 1970.

Haugeland, J. The nature and plausibility of cognitivism. *The Behavioral and Brain Sciences*, 1978, *2*, 215-260.

Hemple, C. G. *Aspects of scientific explanation*. New York: Free Press, 1965.

Henle, P. Metaphor. In P. Henle (Ed.), *Language, thought and culture*. Ann Arbor: University of Michigan Press, 1958.

Hesse, M. B. Models in physics. *British Journal for the Philosophy of Science*, 1953, *4*, 198-214.

Hesse, M. B. *Forces and fields*. Westport, Conn.: Greenwood Press, 1962.

Hesse, M. B. *Models and analogies in science*. Notre Dame, Ind.: University of Notre Dame Press, 1966.

Hester, M. B. *The meaning of poetic metaphor*. The Hague: Mouton, 1967.

Hinde, R. A. Ethological models and the concept of drive. *British Journal for the Philosophy of Science*, 1955, *6*, 321-331.

Hoffman, R. R. On metaphors, myths and mind. *The Psychological Record*, 1979, *29*, 175-178.

Hornsburgh, H. J. H. Philosophers against metaphor. *Philosophical Quarterly*, 1958, *8*, 231-245.

Hunt, E. B. What kind of computer is man? *Cognitive Psychology*, 1971, *2*, 57-98.

Hutten, E. H. The role of models in physics. *British Journal for the Philosophy of Science*, 1954, *4*, 284-301.

Israel, H., & Goldstein, B. Operationism in psychology. *Psychological Review*, 1944, *51*, 177-188.

Jung, C. G. *Four archetypes*. From *Collected works, Volume 9*, Part 1. Princeton, N. J.: Princeton University Press, 1969.

Kantor, J. R. The operational principle in the physical and psychological sciences. *Psychological Record*, 1938, *2*, 3-32.

Kantor, J. R. Current trends in psychological theory. *Psychological Bulletin*, 1941, *38*, 29-65.

Kaplan, A. *The conduct of inquiry*. San Francisco, Calif.: Chandler, 1965.

Kattsoff, L. O. Philosophy, psychology and postulational technique. *Psychological Review*, 1939, *46*, 62-74.

Kintsch. W. *The representation of meaning in memory*. Hillsdale, N. J.: Lawrence Erlbaum Associates, 1974.

Kuhn, T. *The structure of scientific revolutions*. Chicago: University of Chicago Press, 1965.

Kuhn, T. Metaphor and conceptual change: A reply to Boyd. In A. Ortony (Ed.), *Metaphor and thought*. Cambridge, England: Cambridge University Press, 1979.

Lachman, R. The model in theory construction. *Psychological Review*, 1960, *67*, 113-129.

Lambley, P. Psychology and epistemology: Operationism revisited. *The Psychological Record,* 1970, *20,* 229-234.

Langer, S. *Philosophy in a new key.* Cambridge, Mass.: Harvard University Press, 1957.

Lashley, K. S., Chow, K. L., & Semmes, J. An examination of the electrical field theory of cerebral integration. *Psychological Review,* 1951, *58,* 123-136.

Leahey, T. H. *The myth of operationism.* Paper presented at the annual convention of the American Psychological Association, San Francisco, Calif., September, 1977.

Maatsch, J. L., & Behan, R. A. A more rigorous theoretical language. *Psychological Review,* 1953, *60,* 189-196.

MacCorquodale, K., & Meehl. P. E. On a distinction between hypothetical constructs and intervening variables. *Psychological Review,* 1957, *55,* 95-107.

Maslow, A. *The psychology of science.* Chicago, Ill.: The Henry Regnery Company, 1969.

Maxwell, G. Theories, perception and structural realism. In R. G. Colodny (Ed.), *The nature and function of scientific theories.* Pittsburgh: University of Pennsylvania Press, 1970.

Maxwell, J. C. Address to the mathematical and physical sections of the British Association. *British Association Report,* 1870, *11.* Reprinted in W. D. Niven (Ed.), *The scientific papers of J. C. Maxwell, II.* Cambridge, England: Cambridge University Press, 1890.

Maxwell, J. C. Letter to William Thomson dated August 25, 1879. In J. Larmor (Ed.) *Origins of Clerk Maxwell's electric ideas.* Cambridge, England: Cambridge University Press, 1937.

Maze, J. R. Do intervening variables intervene? *Psychological Review,* 1954, *61,* 226-234.

McCloskey, M. A. Metaphors. *Mind,* 1964, *73,* 215-233.

McGuigan, F. J. Formalization of psychological theory. *Psychological Review,* 1953, *60,* 377-382.

Meissner, W. W. Intervening constructs—dimensions of controversy. *Psychological Review,* 1960, *67,* 51-72.

Miller, D. Verisimilitude redeflated. *British Journal for the Philosophy of Science,* 1976, *27,* 363-402.

Miller, L. Has artificial intelligence contributed to an understanding of the human mind?: A critique of arguments for and against. *Cognitive Science,* 1978, *2,* 111-127.

Miller, R. M. The dubious case for metaphors in educational writing. *Educational Theory,* 1976, *26,* 174-181.

Mooij, J. J. A. Tenor, vehicle and reference. *Poetics,* 1975, *4,* 257-272.

Moor, J. H. Three myths of computer science. *British Journal for the Philosophy of Science,* 1978, *29,* 213-222.

Nagel, E. *The structure of science.* New York: Harcourt, Brace and World, 1961.

Nash, H. Freud and metaphor. *Archives of General Psychiatry,* 1962, *7,* 51-55.

Nemetz, A. Metaphor: The Daedalus of discourse. *Thought,* 1958, *33,* 417-442.

Ortony, A. Why metaphors are necessary and not just nice. *Educational Theory,* 1975, *25,* 45-53.

Ortony, A. The role of similarities and similes in metaphors. In A. Ortony (Ed.), *Metaphor and thought.* Cambridge, England: Cambridge University Press, 1979.

Osborn, M. M., & Ehninger, D. The metaphor in public address. *Speech Monographs,* 1962, *29,* 223-234.

Paivio, A. *Images, propositions and knowledge.* Paper presented at the conference, Images, Perception, and Knowledge, University of Western Ontario, London, Ontario, May, 1974.

Paivio, A. Psychological processes in the comprehension of metaphor. In A. Ortony (Ed.), *Metaphor and thought.* Cambridge, England: Cambridge University Press, 1979.

Palmer, S. E. Fundamental aspects of cognitive representation. In E. Rosch & B. Lloyd (Eds.), *Cognition and categorization.* Hillsdale, N. J.: Lawrence Erlbaum Associates, 1978.

Pepper, S. C. *World hypotheses.* Berkeley: University of California Press, 1942.

Perrine, L. Four forms of metaphor. *College English,* 1971, *33,* 125-138.

Polanyi, M. *Personal knowledge: Towards a post-critical philosophy.* London: Routledge & Kegan-Paul, 1958.

Polanyi, M. Logic and psychology. *American Psychologist,* 1968, *23,* 27-43.

Pollio, H. R., Barlow, J. M., Fine, H. J., & Pollio, M. R. *Psychology and the poetics of growth.* Hillsdale, N. J.: Lawrence Erlbaum Associates, 1977.

Popper, K. *The logic of scientific discovery.* London: Hutchinson, 1959.

Popper, K. A note on verisimilitude. *British Journal for the Philosophy of Science,* 1976, *27,* 147-164.

Pribram, K. H. *Languages of the brain.* Englewood Cliffs, N. J.: Prentice-Hall, 1971.

Pylyshyn, Z. Computational models and empirical constraints. *The Behavioral and Brain Sciences,* 1978, *1,* 93-127.

Pylyshyn, Z. Metaphorical imprecision and the "top-down" research strategy. In A. Ortony (Ed.) *Metaphor and thought.* Cambridge, England: Cambridge University Press, 1979.

Rapoport, A. *Operational philosophy.* New York: Harper and Brothers, 1953, Chapter 17.

Reddy, M. The conduit metaphor: A case of frame conflict in our language about language. In A. Ortony (Ed.), *Metaphor and thought.* Cambridge, England: Cambridge University Press, 1979.

Reichenbach. H. *The rise of scientific philosophy.* Berkeley: University of California Press, 1951.

Richards, I. A. *The philosophy of rhetoric.* London: Oxford University Press, 1936.

Roe, A. A. A study of imagery in research scientists. *Journal of Personality,* 1951, *19,* 459-470.

Roediger, H. L. *Memory metaphors.* Paper presented at the annual convention of the Psychonomic Society, San Antonio, Texas, November, 1978.

Rokeach, M., & Bartley, S. H. Some pitfalls in psychological theorizing. *American Psychologist,* 1958, *13,* 283-284.

Royce, J. R. How can we best advance the construction of theory in psychology? *Canadian Psychological Review,* 1978, *19,* 259-276.

Rozeboom, W. W. Mediation variables in scientific theory. *Psychological Review,* 1956, *63,* 249-264.

Rumelhart, D. E. Metaphor and linguistic theory: A reply to Sadock. In A. Ortony (Ed.), *Metaphor and thought.* Cambridge, England: Cambridge University Press, 1979.

Ryle, G. *The concept of mind.* New York: Barnes and Noble, 1949, Chapter 9.

Schon, D. A. *Displacement of concepts.* London: Tavistock, 1963.

Schon, D. A. Generative metaphors: A perspective on problem-setting in social policy. In A. Ortony (Ed.), *Metaphor and thought.* Cambridge, England: Cambridge University Press, 1979.

Scriven, M. Explanations, predictions and laws. In H. Feigl & G. Maxwell (Eds.), *Minnesota studies in the philosophy of science, Volume III.* Minneapolis: University of Minnesota Press, 1962.

Searle, J. R. Metaphor. In A. Ortony (Ed.), *Metaphor and thought.* Cambridge, England: Cambridge University Press, 1979.

Simon, H. A. Does scientific discovery have a logic? *Philosophy of Science,* 1973, *40,* 471-480.

Simon, H. A., & Newell, A. The uses and limitations of models. In L. D. White (Ed.), *The state of the social sciences.* Chicago: University of Illinois Press, 1956.

Smith, E. E., Rips, L. J., & Shoben, E. J. Semantic memory and psychological semantics. In G. Bower (Ed.), *The psychology of learning and motivation, Volume 8.* New York: Academic Press, 1974.

Snell, B. *The discovery of mind.* Translated by J. Rosenmeyer. New York: Harper and Row, 1960.

Spiker, C. C., & McCandless, B. R. The concept of intelligence and the philosophy of science. *Psychological Review,* 1954, *61,* 255-266.

Spurgeon, B. Tesla. *Coevolution Quarterly,* Winter, 1977, Issue No. 16, 64-76.

Steenburgh, E. W. Metaphor. *Journal of Philosophy,* 1965, *62,* 678-688.

Stelzer, H. Analysis by metaphor. *Quarterly Journal of Speech,* 1965, *51,* 52-61.

Stevens, S. S. The operational definition of psychological concepts. *Psychological Review,* 1935, *42,* 517-527.

Stevens, S. S. Psychology and the science of science. *Psychological Bulletin,* 1939, *36,* 221-263.

Suppe, F. Theories, their formulation and operational imperative. *Synthese,* 1973, *25,* 129–164.

Thomson, W. *Notes of lectures on molecular dynamics and the wave theory of light.* Baltimore, Md.: The Johns Hopkins University Press, 1884.

Tichy, P. Verisimilitude redefined. *British Journal for the Philosophy of Science,* 1976, *27,* 25–42.

Turbayne, C. M. *The myth of metaphor.* New Haven, Conn.: Yale University Press, 1962.

Turner, M. B. *Philosophy and the science of behavior.* New York: Appleton-Century-Crofts, 1967.

Uhr, L. Pattern recognition. In L. Uhr (Ed.) *Pattern recognition.* New York: Wiley, 1966.

Vico, G. *The new science.* Translated by T. Berginard & M. H. Fisch. Ithaca, N. Y.: Cornell University Press, 1948.

Walkup, L. E. Creativity in science through visualization. *Perceptual and Motor Skills,* 1965, *21,* 35–41.

Weimer, W. B. Psycholinguistics and Plato's paradoxes of the *Meno. American Psychologist,* 1973, *28,* 15–33.

Woodrow, H. The problem of general quantitative laws in psychology. *Psychological Bulletin,* 1942, *39,* 1–27.

Author Index

Italics denote pages with bibliographic information.

Subject Index